DATE DUE

~~AP 2 98~~		
~~DE 18 98~~		
~~DE 19 00~~		
~~MY 17 05~~		

DEMCO 38-296

THE FINANCIAL SERVICES REVOLUTION

To my Mom and Dad—with love and thanks for all you've done and still do.

CONTENTS

ABOUT THE EDITOR

Clifford E. Kirsch is chief counsel, Variable Products, at The Prudential Insurance Company of America. Prior to that he was first vice president and associate general counsel at Paine Webber's asset management subsidiary. From 1985 to 1994, he was on the staff of the U.S. Securities and Exchange Commission, Division of Investment Management, in Washington, D.C. At the SEC he held several positions including assistant director and was a recipient of the Manuel F. Cohen Younger Lawyer Award.

Cliff Kirsch has written on various topics relating to mutual funds and the securities activities of insurance companies and banks. He teaches at the University of Pennsylvania Law School and Cardoza School of Law, and he previously taught at Georgetown University Law Center.

Mr. Kirsch serves as chair for two annual American Law Institute/American Bar Association Course offerings—Investment Management Regulation and Investment Adviser Regulation. He is also the author of *Investment Adviser Regulation: A Step-by-Step Guide to Compliance and the Law* (P.L.I. 1996).

CONTRIBUTORS

Diane E. Ambler

Diane Ambler is a partner in the Washington, DC office of Mayer, Brown & Platt. For the past 14 years, Ms. Ambler has specialized in representing financial institutions in the development, distribution and maintenance of investment company, mutual fund, and fixed and variable insurance products.

Ms. Ambler is a frequent speaker and author on securities laws issues in this area. Among other things, she is a member of a blue-ribbon task force appointed to write a *Mutual Fund Board of Directors Guidebook,* expected to be published this year. As co-chair of the American Bar Association's Subcommittee on Investment Companies and Investment Advisers, Ms. Ambler works with industry members to respond and comment on all Commission rulemakings. She is currently an adjunct professor at Georgetown University School of Law, LLM program.

George J. Benston

George J. Benston is the John H. Harland professor of finance, accounting, and economics at the Goizueta Business School and professor of economics in the College of Emory University, Atlanta, GA. He also serves as area coordinator of finance, and previously served as associate dean for Research and Faculty Development and area coordinator of accounting. He is a member of the Shadow Financial Regulatory Committee. Benston's Ph.D. is from the University of Chicago (finance and economics), M.B.A. from New York University (accounting) and B.A. from Queens College (liberal arts and accounting), and he is a CPA (North Carolina).

He has published 126 books, monographs, and articles in reference and academic journals and books: 31 in accounting, 76 in finance, 6 in urban studies, and 13 in economics, and his most recent book is *The Separation of Commercial and Investment Banking: The Glass-Steagal Act Revisited and Reconsidered* (Oxford University Press, 1990).

Martha L. Cochran

Martha L. Cochran is a partner at Arnold & Porter, Washington, DC, where she counsels clients on legislative and oversight matters before the U.S. Senate and the House of Representatives and represents clients on banking and securities law issues. She previously served as chief counsel and staff director of the Subcommittee on Securities of the U.S. Senate Committee on Banking, Housing and Urban Affairs, was Senator Christopher Dodd's legislative director and senior domestic policy adviser, and served as senior finance counsel to the Subcommittee on Telecommunications, Consumer Protection and Finance, U.S. House of Representatives. She also served as an attorney and special counsel in the Division of Enforcement, Securities and Exchange Commission.

Christopher L. Culp

Christopher L. Culp is an independent financial risk management consultant in Chicago, Illinois, and is Senior Fellow in Financial Regulation with the Competitive Enterprise Institute in Washington, DC. His risk management consulting clients have included swap dealers, financial exchanges, commercial and investment banks, pension funds and other institutional investors, insurance companies, accounting firms, and industry trade association. He has held positions previously in the Supervision and Regulation Department at the Federal Reserve Bank of Chicago, at G.T. Management (Asia) Ltd., and at TradeLink LLC. Culp has been published widely on issues in corporation finance, risk management, derivatives, and financial regulation, and he lectures often on these topics. He holds a B.A. in economics form The Johns Hopkins University and is completing his Ph.D. in corporation finance at the Graduate School of Business of The University of Chicago.

Jane W. D'Arista

Jane D'Arista is lecturer on Law and Economics for the graduate program in International Banking Law Studies at Boston University School of Law, and a research associate of the Economic Policy Institute in Washington, DC.

From 1983 through 1986, she was chief finance economist for the Subcommittee on Telecommunications and Finance, House Energy and Commerce Committee, and before that served for five years as an international analyst for the Congressional Budget Office and 12 years as a member of the staff of the House Banking Committee.

Her publications include studies of U.S. "Monetary Policy" (1972), "The Operations of U.S. Banks Abroad and Foreign Banks in the United States" (1976), "Debt Problems of Developing Countries" (1979 and 1984), "International Capital Flows" (1984), "Financial Restructuring in the United States" (1986), "Deposit Insurance Reform" (1991), and "The Parallel Banking System" (1993). Some of these studies have been revised and included in *The Evolution of U.S. Finance* (1994), a two-volume work published by M.E. Sharpe, Inc., in the Columbia University Seminars series.

Michael J. Downer

Michael J. Downer is a senior vice president of the fund business management group of Capital Research and Management Company (investment adviser to The American Funds Group, the fourth largest group of mutual funds in the U.S.). Mike joined the Capital Group companies in 1980. He is a frequent speaker at industry conferences on topics relating to fund regulation,

Chairman of the Compliance Committee and member of several other committees of the Investment Company Institute (the mutual fund industry's primary trade association) and Chairman of the California '40 Acts Committee. He graduated from Southwestern University School of Law in 1981 (J.D.) where he was a member of the law review and won the school's American Bar Association sponsored client counseling competition and UCLA in 1977 (B.A. history—honors program).

Susan C. Ervin

Susan C. Ervin is chief counsel and deputy director of the Division of Trading and Markets, Commodity Futures Trading Commission, with responsibilities for regulation of commodity brokers, futures exchanges and clearing organizations, review of new derivative products, and development and interpretation of rules governing commodity professionals. Previously, Ms. Ervin was assistant general counsel of the Commodity Futures Trading Commission and a corporate and securities litigator in private law practice in New York City. Ms. Ervin has also been an adjunct professor at both the Georgetown University Law Center and the George Washington University School of Business and Public Management. She is a frequent speaker and author on financial services regulation, particularly derivative products, money management, and bankruptcy issues. Ms. Ervin is an honors graduate of Mount Holyoke College and Rutgers Law School.

Michael Frankel

Michael Frankel is a corporate attorney with Skadden, Arps, Slate, Meagher & Flom in New York specializing in corporate finance and mergers and acquisitions. He has also worked at the Chicago Mercantile Exchange as Manager of International Strategy. Mr. Frankel received his BA, MA, MBA and JD from the University of Chicago and has published work on financial markets, bankruptcy law, and economics and international trade including "The Emerging Fixed Cramdown Rate Regime: A Market-Driven Argument for Effective Fixed Rates in Bankruptcy Cramdown", University of Chicago Roundtable, Vol. 2, No. 2, and "Futures and Options Markets: Their New Role in Eastern Europe", *Journal of Banking and Finance,* Vol. 17, No. 5.

Tamar Frankel

Professor Tamar Frankel teaches at Boston University School of Law. She authored a two-volume treatise, *Securitization* (1991), and a four-volume treatise, *The Regulation of Money Managers* (1978, 1980), both published by Little, Brown & Co. Her scholarship covers the laws of trust, fiduciaries, banking, insurance, mutual funds, pension funds, and the securities markets. Professor Frankel was a visiting scholar at the Securities and Exchange Commission, Washington, DC, a Guest Scholar at the Brookings Institution, Washington DC, and a visiting professor at the Harvard Law School, Harvard Business School, and University of

California Law School at Berkeley. She served as consultant to Bankers Trust Company, New York, and was a member of the Advisory Committee, American Law Institute, Restatement of Trusts (Third).

David F. Freeman, Jr.

David F. Freeman, Jr. is a partner with Arnold & Porter in Washington, DC. Mr. Freeman represents financial institutions and securities firms. Mr. Freeman graduated from the University of Virginia School of Law in 1987, where he was an editor of the *Virginia Law Review*, and received an MBA from the University of Virginia's Darden Graduate Business School.

Mark Greenstein

Mark Greenstein held a variety of positions at the Department of Labor's Pension and Welfare Benefits Administration, including acting chief, Division of Fiduciary Interpretations. Since leaving the Department he has practiced at Rosenman & Colin LLP. He frequently speaks concerning the application of the Employee Retirement Income Security Act of 1974, and is the chair of the Prohibited Transactions Sub-Committee, American Bar Association, Section of Taxation.

Robert W. Helm

Robert W. Helm is a partner with Dechert Price & Rhoads, resident in its Washington, DC office. He represents investment companies, investment advisers, insurance companies, broker-dealers, and other financial institutions in regulatory and general corporate matters, including international securities and investment fund matters. He graduated from Stanford University (A.B., with distinction, 1979), and Stanford Law School (J.D., 1982). He was a Fulbright-Hays Direct Exchange Fellow to Italy in 1982–83. From 1982 to 1984 he was a researcher affiliated with the European University Institute in Florence, Italy. Mr. Helm has lectured on securities law topics in the United States and in Europe, and during 1990 spent several months as a visiting lawyer with a Luxembourg law firm. His publications include "European Investment Funds", which appeared in the *Review of Securities & Commodities Regulation* in 1989; "Investment Funds in Luxembourg", which appeared in the *Journal of International Banking Law* in 1990; "Offering Shares of Non–U.S. Investment Funds in the United States: A U.S. Securities and Tax Law Perspective," which appeared in the *Journal of International Banking Law* in 1992; "Self-Directed Employee Benefit Plans and Private Investment Companies: Unraveling *PanAgora*," which appeared in *The Investment Lawyer* in March, 1995; "The U.S. Market for U.K. Investment Trust Companies," which appeared in the *Journal of International Banking Law* in October, 1995; and "Offshore Investment Funds," which will appear in *The Financial Services Revolution* in 1996. Mr. Helm is a member of securities and commodities law committees of the American Bar Association, the District of Columbia Bar Association, and the International Bar Association, and a member of the Managed Futures Association. Mr. Helm is a member of the State Bar of California and the District of Columbia Bar.

Howell E. Jackson

Howell E. Jackson is a professor at Harvard Law School, where he teaches courses on the Regulation of Financial Institutions, Securities Regulation, Pension Law, and the Federal Budget Process. Prior to joining the Harvard Law School faculty in 1989, Professor Jackson practiced law with the Washington, DC, firms of Caplin & Drysdale Chartered and Arnold & Porter. He previously served as a law clerk to Honorable Jon O. Newman of the United States Court of Appeals for the Second Circuit and Associate Justice Thurgood Marshall of the United States Supreme Court. Professor Jackson received his J.D. *magna cum laude* from Harvard Law School in 1982 and also earned an M.B.A. degree from the Harvard Business School. He received his bachelor's degree from Brown University *magna cum laude* in 1976, where he majored in the Economic Development of Modern China. Prior to entering graduate school, he served as an escort officer for the National Council for U.S.-China Trade and associate editor of the *China Business Review.*

George G. Kaufman

Before teaching at Loyola University, Professor Kaufman was a research fellow, economist and research officer at the Federal Reserve Bank of Chicago from 1959 to 1970, and has been a consultant to the Bank since 1981. From 1970 to 1980, he was the John B. Rogers Professor of Banking and Finance, and Director of the Center for Capital Market Research in the College of Business Administration at the University of Oregon. He has been a visiting professor at the University of Southern California (1970), Stanford University (1975–76), and the University of California at Berkeley (1979), and a visiting scholar at the Federal Reserve Bank of San Francisco (1976) and the Office of the Comptroller of the Currency (1978). Professor Kaufman also served as Deputy to the Assistant Secretary for Economic Policy of the U.S. Treasury in 1976. He has taught at Loyola since 1981. Professor Kaufman received his B.A. from Oberlin College (1954), M.A. from the University of Michigan (1955), and Ph.D. in economics from the University of Iowa (1962).

John M. Kimpel

John M. Kimpel is vice president and pension counsel for Fidelity Investments, where the group he leads is responsible for all legal issues relating to the management of retirement plan assets. Prior to joining Fidelity in 1986, he was a partner at Gaston Snow & Ely Bartlett in Boston, where he was in charge of the law firm's ERISA group. Mr. Kimpel is chairman of the Investment Company Institute Pension Committee, a member of the

Profit Sharing/401(k) Council of American Legal and Legislative Committee, and a member of the Massachusetts Continuing Legal Education Curriculum Committee. Mr. Kimpel received a B.A. from Denison University and a J.D. from the University of Chicago.

Robert F. Klein

Until April 1996, Mr. Klein was chief counsel to the Division of Enforcement of the Commodity Futures Trading Commission, where he participated in developing enforcement actions and regulatory initiatives concerning off-exchange derivative transactions. Mr. Klein is a 1980 graduate of Duke Law School, and has worked in private practice in Washington, DC. He now practices law in Austin, Texas.

Lawrence J. Latto

Lawrence J. Latto was graduated from Columbia Law School in 1948 where he was editor in chief of the *Columbia Law Review*. Since then he has been continuously associated with Shea & Gardner in Washington, DC. He is now the senior actively practicing partner in the firm. He has served as member and chairman of the DC Court of Appeals Board on Professional Responsibility and as trustee and chairman of the Center for Law and Social Policy, a Washington, DC based public interest law firm. He is a life member of the American Law Institute. A significant part of his practice has involved the regulation of variable contracts issued by life insurance companies.

Martin E. Lybecker

Martin E. Lybecker is a partner in the Washington, DC Office of Ropes & Gray, and co-chair of the firm's Financial Services Practice Group. Mr. Lybecker received his B.B.A. (Accounting) and J.D. degrees from the University of Washington in 1967 and 1970, respectively; Mr. Lybecker also received an LL.M. (Taxation) degree from New York University in 1971, and an LL.M. degree from the University of Pennsylvania in 1973 where he was a Graduate Fellow of the Center for the Study of Financial Institutions and the Securities Markets. Mr. Lybecker served as associate director of the SEC's Division of Investment Management from 1978 to 1981; previously, he had been an attorney, Office of Chief Counsel, in that Division (1972–1975). Mr. Lybecker has also been a law teacher at Georgetown University, State University of New York at Buffalo, Duke University, and the University of North Carolina. Mr. Lybecker is chair of the Committee on Developments in Investment Services, chair of the Subcommittee on Bank Holding Company Activities, and a member of the Subcommittees on Bank Securities, Investment Company and Investment Advisers, and Fiduciary Law of the ABA Business Law Section. Mr. Lybecker is an active speaker on various matters of current interest to investment companies, investment advisers, depository institutions, insurance companies, venture capital companies, and business development companies.

Nell Minow

Nell Minow is managing principal of Lens, Inc., a "relationship investor." Lens works with institutional investors to enhance the value of focus companies, through use of shareholder ownership rights. She has lectured and published widely on issues of corporate governance, government regulation, communications, and management, and contributed chapters for treatises on shareholder meetings, institutional investors, and proxy regulation.

James A. Overdahl

James A. Overdahl is a senior financial economist in the Risk Analysis Division at the Office of the Comptroller of the Currency in Washington, DC. He serves as a staff consultant on issues involving trading risk at federally charted multinational banks. He has also worked as a staff economist at the Commodity Futures Trading Commission and the Securities and Exchange Commission in Washington, DC. He has taught MBA finance courses at the University of Texas at Dallas, Virginia Tech, George Mason University, and Georgetown University. He has also served as a risk management consultant to several leading financial firms. He holds a Ph.D. in economics from Iowa State University and a B.A. degree from St. Olaf college.

Tom Schlesinger

Tom Schlesinger is director of the Southern Finance Project, an independent research center that monitors financial markets and policy issues. Founded in 1986, the Virginia-based center has worked with policymakers, journalists, labor unions and civic organizations around the United States.

William A. Schmidt

William A. Schmidt, a partner in the Washington, DC office of Paul, Hastings, Janofsky & Walker, practices extensively in legal areas relating to the investment activities of employee benefit plans. Mr. Schmidt received his B.A. and J.D. degrees from the University of Virginia, and his LL.M. in Taxation from the Georgetown University Law Center. He is an Adjunct Professor of Law at Georgetown University Law Center and speaks and writes frequently on employee benefit issues.

Joel Seligman

Joel Seligman is the dean and Samuel M. Fegtly professor of law at The University of Arizona College of Law. A 1974 graduate of Harvard University School of Law, Seligman taught earlier at the University of Michigan (1986–1995), George Washington University (1983–1986), and Northeastern University (1977–1983) law schools. He is coauthor with Louis Loss of an 11 volume treatise on securities regulation and author of seven other books including *The Transformation of Wall Street: A History of the Securities and Exchange Commission and Modern Corporate Finance* (Rev. ed. 1995 Northeastern University Press).

Karol K. Sparks

Karol K. Sparks is a partner in the Indianapolis-based law firm of Krieg, DeVault, Alexander & Capehart, currently practicing out of Western New York. Her practice concentration relates to mergers, acquisitions, and corporate activities of financial institutions, with special emphasis on the impact of mergers on competition and on the design and implementation of programs for the distribution of annuities, life insurance and mutual funds. Mrs. Sparks attended Sweet Briar College, holds a B.A. degree from Butler University and a J.D. degree from Indiana University School of Law. She is a member of the New York, Indiana, and California Bars.

As an active member of the Banking Law Committee of the Business Section of the American Bar Association, Mrs. Sparks currently serves as its vice-chair. She formerly chaired the Subcommittee on Bank Holding Companies from 1988 through 1994.

Mrs. Sparks is the author of numerous articles on bank acquisitions and activities and is a frequent lecturer on issues relating to the regulation of financial institutions.

Mark D. Young

Mark D. Young has been a Washington, DC-based partner in the law firm of Kirkland & Ellis since 1984 where he plays a leading role in the firm's Derivatives and Financial Services Group. Mr. Young is a 1977 graduate of the Georgetown University Law Center. He received his undergraduate degree, *magna cum laude,* from Tufts University in 1974. Prior to joining Kirkland & Ellis in 1982, Mr. Young served as assistant general counsel to the Commodity Futures Trading Commission. Since 1991, Mr. Young has been an Adjunct Professor at the Georgetown University Law Center where he teaches a graduate level course in derivatives as part of the Securities Regulation curriculum.

INTRODUCTION

Clifford E. Kirsch*

Signs in the storefronts of the financial services marketplace are changing. Where they once touted "safety," "income," "guarantees," and "saving accounts," they now herald "investment," "growth," "risk," and "managed money." The last 20 years have witnessed a financial services revolution.

Workers who at one time were promised a set pension are today responsible for investing their own retirement money. Money management, once the prerogative of only the very wealthy, is now increasingly available to middle-class households through their participation in mutual funds and other investment vehicles. Middle schools and high schools, where the personal finance curriculum was once limited to balancing a checkbook, now offer students courses in how to read the financial pages. More now than ever before, individuals are no longer just savers, they are investors.

Accompanying this transformation of individuals' financial behavior have been dynamic changes in the role of banks, insurance companies, and mutual funds in the financial services industry. These institutions have broken out of the pigeonholes they once inhabited—banks as places to make deposits, insurance companies as places to shift mortality risk, and mutual funds as places to pool investments.

Today, people make "deposits" daily into money market mutual funds, while banks and insurance companies offer a variety of investment products. Of course, to simply say that a bank or an insurance company offers investment products does not do justice to the full impact of the financial revolution. Banks today actively advertise advisory services and mutual funds, a far cry from the days when banks promoted savings accounts by offering free toasters. Insurance companies have expanded their product base to include policies such as variable annuities and variable life insurance, which offer consumers an investment return based on an assortment of investment choices in contrast to traditional policies, which offer a fixed investment return. Insurance companies have also become big players in money management by creating advisory and brokerage subsidiaries and by establishing their own mutual funds, making them hardly recognizable from the days when they provided primarily burial insurance and widows' stipends.

*I would like to thank Lorna MacLeod for her helpful suggestions during the course of my work on this book and Thomas Loftus and Professor Howell Jackson for their comments on this introduction.

As insurance companies and banks restructure, mutual funds continue to assert themselves as a significant participant in the financial services industry. Beginning in the 1980s and continuing today, mutual funds have attracted middle-class households as an easy and effective way to participate in a soaring stock market. Today, thousands of mutual funds with countless strategies and objectives stand ready to provide the public with investment management.

New distribution channels for mutual funds appear regularly. Whereas mutual funds used to be sold only by brokerage firms or by the funds directly, in recent years increasing sales have taken place through banks, 401(k) pension plans, and independent financial planners.

Not surprisingly, mutual funds have attracted a great deal of attention from policy makers. Some would like to see funds used as an instrument for promoting social good. For example, the argument has been made that mutual funds (in particular, money market funds) should be subject to the Community Reinvestment Act, as banks are. Also, some contend that mutual funds, similar to many pension plans, should play an active role as shareholders in the companies they own. Others, including the mutual fund industry, respond that funds are properly viewed as passive vehicles that simply pool investor money. (Interestingly, a new book about the history of Fidelity Investments and the mutual fund industry declares that although mutual funds seek to portray themselves as passive investors, they are in fact "boardroom bullies.")

A third phenomenon, along with the changes in both the financial institution landscape and the financial behavior of individuals, is a dramatic change in the nature of financial instruments. Years ago, financial products were neatly divided into stocks and bonds and easily categorized along a risk spectrum. Today exotic financial products are being created. In contrast to vintage stocks and bonds, these products, which are typically repackaged or derived from conventional securities, are not easily classified according to risk.

Most notable among the new financial products are derivatives, which derive their value from an underlying instrument. In their safest use, derivatives give purchasers financial protection against adverse moves in areas such as interest rates or foreign currencies. At their riskiest, derivatives are used in an attempt to amplify returns.

Huge losses attributed to derivative investments by mutual funds and public corporations, among others, have attracted regulatory and press scrutiny. While many assert the virtues of derivatives, others claim that the potential institutional losses threatened by derivatives could endanger the financial system.

Another new instrument, asset-backed securities, allows banks and other institutions to transform illiquid financial assets such as residential mortgages, automobile loans, and credit card receivables into securities. To a large extent, mutual funds, which are steady purchasers of asset-backed securities, are responsible for the vibrant market in these instruments.

It seems there is no limit on the types of financial products that can be created. A recent episode of *60 Minutes* told the story of a company that is in the business of buying life insurance policies from people who are terminally ill and reselling the policies to investors.

DEVELOPMENTS IN THE LAW

The financial services revolution has prompted the need to rethink financial services regulation. Many jurisdictional issues once thought resolved are being raised again: When is a financial instrument a security subject to federal securities regulation or a commodity subject to the Commodity Exchange Act? What is the proper role of state securities regulation vis-à-vis federal securities regulation? Should banks be able to underwrite and sell securities? Should banks be able to underwrite and sell insurance products? Should institutional investors be accorded the same level of protection under the financial services laws as individuals?

Another set of questions has been raised regarding the nature of the relationship between consumers and their investment intermediaries. These questions primarily have arisen in the context of large losses due to complicated derivative products that were invested in a risky manner, provoking claims that the intermediary acted inappropriately with respect to the level of risk involved.

In dealing with such claims it must be determined whether the level of risk the client knowingly assumed was inappropriate and if so, whether the intermediary should be held at fault. The resolution to these claims hinges on whether the intermediary is acting in a fiduciary capacity and, if so, on what the bounds of this fiduciary duty ought to be.

Financial services law is being challenged to define when a fiduciary relationship is established. This question has been raised in the context of various situations such as whether a broker is a fiduciary when it has a long-standing relationship with a client through an investment program that involves complicated financial instruments. Similarly, the level of information that employers and others may provide to employees about their 401(k) plans without becoming a fiduciary is at issue.

Issues surrounding the bounds of the fiduciary duty of an investment intermediary present perhaps one of the most dynamic areas in financial services law. It has been said that the concept of fiduciary duty is reinvented each generation, and it appears that the financial revolution has caused the need for another evaluation.

Some argue that the fiduciary duty of an investment intermediary extends to permitting a client to assume only that level of risk that is appropriate and that a fiduciary should forgo implementing an investment program in which a client undertakes an unreasonable amount of risk. Others contend, and the law appears to be headed in this direction, that an adviser needs to assure only that clients understand the level of risk that they are assuming. A related issue is whether it is sufficient for intermediaries to simply disclose the risk to clients or whether they must expressly indicate levels of risk they deem inappropriate.

In addition to questions concerning jurisdictional issues and the nature of the relationship between an investor and intermediary, the revolution has challenged a fundamental precept on which financial services regulation is founded: that banks, insurance companies, and mutual funds should be categorized and regulated according to their activities with respect to deposit taking, mortality risk assumption, and investment. A rethinking of these regulations must be predicated on understanding the changing roles of banks, insurance companies, and mutual funds, as well as some of the newer financial instruments being introduced into the financial marketplace.

This book seeks to help us to understand many of the important changes that have taken place in the last two decades. In so doing, it is intended to bridge the interests of policy makers, practitioners, and academics and serve a useful role in laying a new foundation for financial services law. In structuring this book, I invited experts with various perspectives to contribute. To that end, I am pleased to include submissions from practitioners, academics, as well as officials from regulatory agencies.

THE STRUCTURE OF THIS BOOK

This book is divided into eight parts. Part I examines the evolution of bank and insurance company activities.

Professors George J. Benston and George G. Kaufman provide a survey of bank securities activities including a review of the history of commercial bank securities activity since the Civil War and an analysis of the riskiness of commercial bank securities activity. Lawrence J. Latto examines the regulatory structure that applies to equity-based insurance products, which combine elements of securities with insurance. Diane E. Ambler discusses the regulatory and judicial developments that have allowed banks to become sellers of securities and insurance products, and she also explores issues relating to bank underwriting of these products. Finally, Karol K. Sparks looks at the tension between bank regulators and insurance regulators over issues concerning the authority of banks to sell insurance and the manner in which they may do so.

Part II focuses on derivatives. Christopher L. Culp and James A. Overdahl present an overview of derivatives including an explanation of how these products work and why they are used. Mark D. Young discusses an increasingly important jurisdictional question: What type of derivative activity should be covered by the Commodity Exchange Act? Robert F. Klein focuses on the issue of whether off-exchange derivative transactions should be subject to antifraud provisions of federal law.

In Part III, Professor Tamar Frankel demystifies securitization, explaining the process by which illiquid loans are converted into securities. She also discusses future prospects for this financing vehicle.

Part IV examines the policy issues related to the growing popularity of the defined contribution pension plan and in particular, the "401(k) plan", a market in which banks, insurance companies, and mutual funds vigorously compete. William A. Schmidt discusses the reasons for the popularity of the 401(k) plan and identifies significant policy issues arising from this development. John M. Kimpel focuses on the regulatory framework governing communications to participants concerning their investment options. Finally, Mark A. Greenstein reviews recent initiatives of the Department of Labor related to defined contribution plans.

In Part V Nell Minow discusses the role of mutual funds in corporate governance and contrasts that role with the role of banks and insurance companies.

Part VI focuses on issues relating to the mutual fund industry. Michael J. Downer looks at issues raised by the growing use by mutual funds of computer networks and other types of electronic media as a means to reach investors. Martin E. Lybecker discusses money market fund investments in derivatives in light of SEC regulations requiring money market funds to invest only in top-quality securities with low volatility and a short maturity. Finally, Michael E. S. Frankel discusses issues related to effectively disclosing risk to mutual fund investors, particularly with respect to derivatives investments.

Part VII looks at pooled investment management vehicles designed for the wealthy and non–U.S. investors. Susan C. Ervin focuses on issues related to hedge funds, which are sold to wealthy individuals and institutions and avoid much of the regulatory scheme imposed on mutual funds, although they are structurally similar to them. Robert W. Helm looks at offshore investment funds, which are pooled vehicles that are established by U.S. advisers for non–U.S. resident investors.

The final section, Part VIII, examines issues related to the regulatory framework applying to mutual funds, banks, and insurance companies. Professor Tamar Frankel examines whether a self-regulatory organization, similar to that which exists for brokerage firms, should be established for mutual funds and advisers. Dean Joel Seligman discusses the overlapping jurisdictions among federal or federal and state regulatory agencies that apply to financial services regulation. Jane D'Arista and Tom Schlesinger examine the changes in the U.S. financial markets caused by the growth and the expanded role of mutual funds and suggest certain changes to financial services regulation. Martha L. Cochran and David F. Freeman, Jr., discuss functional regulation, a structure where financial activity is regulated by the same regulator regardless of the type of financial institution conducting the activity. Professor Howell E. Jackson concludes our discussion by contrasting the various regulatory methods used to regulate risk in the financial services industry.

BANK AND INSURANCE COMPANY INVESTMENT PRODUCTS

1

COMMERCIAL BANKING AND SECURITIES ACTIVITIES

A Survey of the Risks and Returns

George J. Benston, *Emory University*
George G. Kaufman, *Loyola University Chicago**

The ability of commercial banks in the United States to engage in securities activities, either directly or indirectly through affiliates of parent holding companies, has been restricted through much of U.S. history. But the boundaries of the restrictions have varied both through time and according to regulatory jurisdiction. Restrictions were imposed for a variety of reasons, including fear of potential conflicts of interest, fear that commercial banks would have excessive economic power, concerns about unfair competition favoring commercial banks relative to others, assumed adverse effects on bank safety and soundness, a desire to protect nonbank securities dealers, and misperceptions about the extent to which these fears and concerns are, indeed, valid. This paper reviews only the respect to issues of commercial bank safety and soundness. We focus on the possible effects of different types and amounts of private (nongovernment) securities activities by

*This paper was funded with a grant from the American Bankers Association and originally published by the ABA Securities Association. The analysis and conclusions are those of the authors's alone. It is published here in somewhat modified form with the permission of the American Bankers Association.

commercial banks or commercial bank holding companies on their risks and returns. Our study of the evidence leads us to conclude that moderate increases in private securities activities have not increased either the riskiness or the failure rate of commercial banks in the past, nor do they promise to do so in the future. Our discussion covers the following areas:

1. The nature of bank risk.
2. The history of commercial bank involvement in securities activities in the United States since the Civil War.
3. The riskiness of commercial bank securities activities in different time periods and regulatory regimes.
4. The riskiness of commercial banks and investment banks, both separately and in different possible combinations.

THE NATURE OF BANK RISKS

Financial risk may be defined as the probability (uncertainty) of realizing a return (outcome) on an investment that is lower than the investor expected at the time the investment was made. As losses net of gains must be charged against an institution's capital (net worth), sufficiently large losses can drive it into economic insolvency. Thus, excessively risky activities relative to an institution's capital-to-asset ratio can have an adverse impact on its safety and soundness. Because most deposits at most banks are insured by the FDIC, the safety and soundness of banks are a public policy concern.

The risk that a bank might fail depends on the riskiness of all of its activities and on the amount of its capital account. The greater the value of a bank's capital, the greater the risk it can assume without endangering its solvency. Similarly, the riskier its activities, the more capital it must have to protect its safety and soundness.

The riskiness of a bank's activities depends both on the riskiness of all of the individual activities conducted in its asset, liability, and off-balance sheet portfolios and on the interaction or covariance of the returns on these activities through time. That is, the riskiness of the overall bank cannot be determined by simply summing the risks of its individual activities. Such a sum will overstate the riskiness of all the activities combined. Some activities are likely to generate losses at the same time others generate gains; thus, the gains and losses offset each other, at least partially.

Indeed, even if the returns on all activities always move in the same direction at the same time (all generating losses or gains in the same period) but are not perfectly correlated, the combined risk of loss will be relatively smaller than the risk of the sum of the individual activities. That is, banks can reduce their risks by diversifying their activities.

However, banks would never want to eliminate all risks; they could do so only at the expense of lower returns. Rather, well-managed banks seek to control their risk exposures through risk management. Risk management involves selecting individual activities with known risk and return profiles and combining them through diversification so as to obtain the highest overall net income gains possible while exposing the bank to an aggregate risk exposure that is consistent with the bank's capital position. The greater the amount of capital, the greater the acceptable risk exposure.

Indeed, the acceptance of risk is a basic attribute of banking. Borrowers who are well known generally can bypass banks and obtain funds directly from investors. Borrowers from banks, on the other hand, often are not known to investors generally. These borrowers also often want to be able to obtain funds on demand and in varying amounts. Depositors place their funds with banks in large measure because they can withdraw those funds at almost any time. Banks can deal effectively with the cash flow requirements of loans and deposits by offering both products, because cash inflows and outflows tend to offset each other. Banks also have a comparative advantage over many other lenders in estimating the risk that borrowers may not repay their loans as promised, in monitoring their performance, and in dealing with them should they default on their obligations.

In addition, and in part because banks have developed expertise in estimating and processing risks, banks offer risk management as a product to their customers. This product involves offering purchases and sales of government securities, foreign exchange, and futures, options and other derivatives, as well as loan structuring.

The risks that banks generally assume are as follows:

Credit risk.
Interest rate (price or market) risk.
Liquidity risk.
Foreign exchange risk.
Operations risk.

Regulatory risk.

Legal risk.

Black box (ignorance) risk.

All banks may not wish to assume all of these risks. Individual banks can choose both the types and degrees of risks they are willing to take on.

Although the return on an investment is relatively easy and straightforward to measure, risk is more difficult to quantify and to measure. Because economic risk is defined as the probability of realizing a return that is different from what is expected, risk is generally approximated by some measure of the volatility of returns. The greater the volatility, the greater is the likelihood of realizing a lower-than-expected return and the greater is the risk of the activity. Statistically, volatility is typically measured by the standard deviation, variance, or some variation of these measures.

Before we analyze the risk to banks of securities underwriting and trading and the extent to which these risks affect the overall risk incurred by commercial banks, we review the history of U.S. banks' involvement in securities activities. This brief review is important because some observers have asserted that commercial banks were barred from securities activities because these activities were particularly risky and were responsible for a significant portion of bank failures, especially during the 1930s Great Depression. As this review shows, these assertions are unfounded.

THE HISTORY OF COMMERCIAL BANK INVOLVEMENT IN SECURITIES ACTIVITIES

The activities in which commercial banks may engage are enumerated either in their charters or in legislation. If not explicitly stated or widely perceived to be implicitly permitted, banks may not engage in the activity. Because banks may be chartered either by their home states or by the federal government and are subject to legislative restrictions from these different jurisdictions, the permissible powers can differ greatly among otherwise similar banks.

Before enactment of the National Bank Act of 1863, banks were only chartered by the states (with the exception of the First and the Second Bank of the United States). Most states permitted their banks to underwrite and deal in all or almost all types of securities. In a review of the history of commercial bank involvement in securities activities in the United States, Carter Golembe concluded that commercial banking and investment banking have been closely intertwined from the time banks first appeared on this continent. In part, this appears to have been due to the absence of other highly developed, specialized financial institutions designed to provide long-term credit to business. As a result, Golembe (1976, p. 31) concluded that between 1800 and 1840 "commercial banks were also the leading investment banking institutions, and may even have dwarfed all other institutions and individuals combined in the volume of securities underwritten and distributed." Similarly, in his study of the history of investment banking in the United States, Vincent Carosso (1970, p. 2) noted that "[t]he investment banking function was also performed by incorporated commercial banks...By the mid-1830s chartered banks in several states were successfully bidding for new issues and reselling them in smaller lots either to subcontractors or directly to investors."

Although after the Civil War the states permitted their banks to continue these activities almost without constraints, the newly chartered national banks were restricted. Early Comptrollers of the Currency tended to interpret the incidental powers clause of the National Bank Act as permitting national banks to deal only in those securities that they could own for their own accounts, that is, primarily U.S. federal, state, and local government securities. Through time, particularly to keep national banks on a level and competitive playing field with state banks, successive comptrollers broadened their interpretations of the act to include corporate bonds, but not equities. Apparently because of the restrictions, as well as to avoid the comptrollers' interpretation of the act as limiting national banks to a single office, in the early 1900s some large national banks shifted their securities activities to state chartered "affiliates" that were owned by the same shareholders. These affiliates could open offices anywhere and could engage in activities that were prohibited to national banks, including investing in equity securities, extending mortgage loans, and providing trust services.

To make the securities powers of national banks clearer and more explicit and to reduce the banks' reliance on affiliates, which were supervised and examined by state banking agencies and whose operations had been called into question by the congressional Pujo Committee money trust investigation in 1912 (among others), the comptroller recommended legislation that would codify existing practice (Kaufman and Mote,

1992, p. 372). Congress responded by enacting the McFadden Act of 1927 (better known for granting national banks limited branching powers), which made explicit the authority of national banks to underwrite and deal in "investment securities" and authorized the comptroller to define such securities within the limitations of the National Banking Act. Both the Senate and House reports accompanying the Act noted that "this is a business that is regularly carried on by state banks and trust companies and has been engaged in by national banks for a number of years . . . The effect of this provision, therefore, is primarily regulative."[1]

Relying on the language of the incidental powers clause in the National Bank Act, the comptroller initially limited the definition of investment securities to "marketable debt securities." But, in short order both national and state banks or their affiliates were permitted to engage in almost all available securities activities, and many of the larger institutions took advantage of these powers. The involvement of commercial banks in securities activities expanded rapidly and, by the end of the decade, commercial banks, trust companies, and their affiliates underwrote more than 60 percent of all new bond issues, up from only 37 percent three years earlier.

Between 1929 and 1933 the United States experienced the worst economic and financial depression in its history. The number of commercial banks declined by some 9,000 from more than 24,000 to nearly 14,000, mostly by failure. The failures were caused primarily by sharp increases in loan defaults, as both businesses and households experienced sharp declines in income and wealth. Some legislators, journalists, and others claimed that commercial banks had gotten themselves into additional trouble by engaging in securities activities or investing in securities, which they viewed as inherently riskier than other bank activities and assets. As we later show, research does not support this claim. Indeed, banks that engaged in securities activities had lower failure rates than otherwise similar banks.

The separation of commercial and investment banking had been a pet proposal of Senator Carter Glass for many years. Glass firmly believed in the real bills doctrine of commercial bank management, which held that because most bank deposits were short term, banks should restrict their lending to short-term credits. He held hearings in 1931 that were designed to show that banks' involvement with securities underwriting was responsible for much of the financial problems being experienced by banks and the country as a whole (Benston, 1990, pp. 23–29). Nevertheless, Glass was unsuccessful in getting legislation enacted that would separate commercial and investment banking. Senate hearings on Stock Exchange Practices in early 1933 (commonly called the Pecora Hearings) gave rise to what appeared to be evidence that commercial banks' stock and bond underwritings had been conducted unethically and even fraudulently. In that part of the hearings that dealt with banks' securities operations, National City Bank, its securities affiliate, National City Company, and their president, Charles Mitchell, were strongly criticized. Largely as a result, restrictions on bank involvement in securities activities were included in the omnibus Banking (Glass-Steagall) Act of 1933,[2] which also restricted a wide variety of other bank activities that were alleged to have contributed to the bank failures, including lending on securities collateral to purchase securities, interest payments on demand and time deposits, and the entry of new banks. The act also established federal deposit insurance.

Just as the separation of commercial and investment banking was not a new idea, none of these proposals was new. Most had been introduced in Congress on numerous occasions, but had failed to gain the necessary support to be enacted on their own merits. In the rush to enact a legislative package to respond to public pressure and deal with the banking crisis of early 1933, the Roosevelt administration and individual members of Congress participated in a round of "horse-trading" in which they agreed to accept other parties' favorite proposals if the latter accepted theirs.

However, the "separation of commercial and investment banking" mandated by the Banking Act of 1933 was neither as complete nor as ironclad as frequently pictured. Commercial banks could continue to underwrite and deal in Treasury securities, which were both the largest type of security outstanding at the time and had the greatest trading volume, and in general obligation bonds of state and local governments, which were the dominant type of municipal security at the time. These exceptions were permitted to assure that the securities of these governmental units would be underwritten efficiently and competitively. In addition, important parts of the relevant sections of the Glass-Steagall Act dealing with securities—primarily Sections 16 and 20—were vaguely worded and open to differing interpretations. But, neither the banks nor their regulators acted aggressively or imaginatively to expand the range of permissible securities activities past those few unambiguously permitted, primarily because the economic depression and its immediate aftermath sharply depressed the demand for new securities to finance new private investment to nearly zero. Indeed, although securities brokerage activities were specifically permitted, banks did not pursue them agressively until the early 1980s.

As investment banking became more profitable again in the 1970s and demand for the traditional commercial banking activities of taking in deposits and making loans continued to decline in relation to other financial services, banks increased their permitted securities activities and intensified their efforts to expand their permissible range of securities activities. They found both the regulatory agencies, first the Comptroller of the Currency and then the Board of Governors of the Federal Reserve System, and the courts sympathetic. These bodies, particularly the Board of Governors, reinterpreted many of the ambiguous sections of the acts so as to expand the range of permissible securities activities.

As a result, by the mid-1990s, large commercial banks could again engage in almost all the securities activities that they could before Glass-Steagall, although not necessarily in the most efficient, convenient, or cheapest way.[3] Many new activities could only be undertaken in separate affiliates of the parent holding company (commonly referred to as Section 20 subsidiaries after the section of the Glass-Steagall Act that prohibits these activities in the bank itself), could only be conducted up to a maximum amount per bank tied to the revenues from bank permissible securities activities (e.g., revenues from underwriting and trading primarily U.S. government securities), and subject to stringent fire-wall restrictions that could interfere with potential economies of scope. These restrictions made it costly for all banks to engage in the new activities, but particularly costly for all but the very largest banks that were already engaged heavily in government securities activities. Table 1 shows a list of currently permissible securities activities of bank holding companies and the year in which each was explicitly permitted. Some of these activities are permissible for commercial banks and others only through Section 20 subsidiaries of the bank holding company.

Nevertheless some bank holding companies (BHCs) now play major roles in the securities markets. For example, in 1994 J.P. Morgan and Citicorp both ranked among the top 15 underwriters of all new domestic securities sold in the United States. In some segments of the securities markets commercial banks were even more important. Three BHCs ranked among the top 15 underwriters of both investment-grade and junk bonds, and four among the top 15 underwriters of asset-backed

T A B L E   1

Securities Activities of U.S. Domestic Commercial Bank Holding Companies (as of January 1994)

Permissible	*Year Started*[a]
Underwriting, distributing, and dealing	Always
U.S. Treasury securities	Always
U.S. federal agency securities	Various years
Commercial paper[c]	1987
Mortgage and other asset-backed securities	
Collateral originated by other banks[c]	1987
Collateral originated by issuing bank	1989
Municipal securities	
General obligation	Nearly always
Some revenue bonds	1968
All revenue bonds[c]	1987
Corporate bonds[c]	1989
Corporate equity[c]	1990
Financial and previous metal futures brokerage and dealing	1983[b]
Private placement (agency capacity)	Always
Sponsor closed-end funds	1974
Underwrite deposits with returns tied partially to stock market performance	1987
Offshore dealing in Eurodollar securities	Always
Mergers and acquisitions	Always
Trust investments	
Individual accounts	Nearly always
IRA commingled accounts	1982
Automatic investment service	1974
Dividend investment service	Always
Financial advising and managing	
Closed-end funds	1974
Mutual funds	1974
Restricted	Always
Brokerage	
Limited customer	Always
Public retail	1982
Securities swapping	Always
Research advice to investors	
Separate from brokerage	1983
Combined with brokerage	
Institutional	1986
Retail	1987
Nonpermissible	
Mutual funds sponsorship and underwriting	

[a] After the Civil War. Different dates may apply to national and state banks and among state banks. With some exceptions, the earliest date is shown. Regulatory rulings frequently concluded that a specific activity was permissible before the date of ruling. If the activity was halted by enactment of the Glass-Steagall Act, the date of renewed activity is given.

[b] Restricted to futures contracts for which banks may hold the underlying security or that are settled only in cash.

[c] Can only be conducted in Section 20 subsidiaries.

Source: George G. Kaufman, *The U.S. Financial System*, 6th ed. (Englewood Cliffs, N.J.: Prentice Hall, 1995), p. 395.

securities. Seven of the largest 15 over-the-counter (OTC) swap dealers in the United States in 1992 were BHCs; the largest five of these were all BHCs. Moreover, eight BHCs accounted for 56 percent of worldwide interest-rate and foreign-currency swap contracts (which are nearly all swap contracts).

Commercial banks are also major managers and brokers of mutual funds and are important securities brokers. In 1993, commercial banks managed one-quarter of the dollar assets of all mutual funds, including 40 percent of the assets of all money market funds. In 1992, more than one-third of the total nonbank assets of commercial bank holding companies were invested in securities brokerage and underwriting affiliates.

Some large money center commercial bank holding companies also are major players in overseas securities markets. The Federal Reserve's Regulation K lists activities that the Board of Governors believes are permissible because they are "usual in connection with the transaction of banking or other financial operations abroad." These activities include underwriting long-term debt for U.S. banking organizations and managing a mutual fund if the shares are not sold to U.S. residents. U.S. banking firms with important overseas securities activities include Bank of Boston Corp., Bank of New York Co., BankAmerica Corp., Bankers Trust NY Corp., Chase Manhattan Corp., Chemical Banking Corp., Citicorp., JP Morgan & Co., Mellon BC, NationsBank Corp., and Republic NY Corp.

EVALUATION OF THE RISKINESS OF SECURITIES ACTIVITIES

In theory, security activities can increase, decrease, or not change the risk exposure of commercial banks or bank holding companies. The potential impact can be measured in two basic ways: (1) by changes in the volatility (or other risk measure) of banks' total earnings due to the addition of securities activities; and (2) by changes in the failure rate of banks engaging in these activities.

Changes in Volatility and Return

A number of studies seek to measure the impact on bank risk if banks were permitted to engage in additional securities activities, either through hypothetical acquisitions of existing investment banking firms or through *de novo* expansion of the same activities as undertaken by existing securities dealers. Basically, these studies estimate the change in measures of volatility (as a proxy for risk) and return that would occur if banks generally would hypothetically acquire different percentages of investment banking activities, or if specific large banks were to acquire specific investment banking firms.

As noted above, the change in risk assumed by a commercial bank that undertakes securities underwriting and trading should not be measured by the sum of the risk of its previous and its new activities. Most of the studies estimate the total risk by calculating the covariance of returns from banking and other activities that might be combined with banking. Some studies also estimate the additional revenue earned by summing the revenues from the activities. However, these studies do not calculate the additional revenue that might be obtained from offering customers a wider range of products and the savings in costs that might be achieved from conducting these activities in a single organization (economies of scope). Hence, the findings of these studies should be considered as lower bounds on the benefits from and upper bounds on the costs of recombining commercial and investment banking.

The studies suffer from some important additional shortcomings that limit the value of their findings for determining if commercial banks engaging in securities activities would increase or decrease the risk that they might fail. The studies that use accounting data have limited value, primarily because banks tend to use accounting alternatives to smooth income, which reduces the variability of returns, while investment houses mark all investments to market, which increases variability.

Several of the papers that use market returns on the shares of commercial banks and securities companies do not include measures of capital available to absorb losses. Hence, they provide useful information only if the correlation of returns implies smaller risk. Other studies relate risk to capital by calculating a "Z" score, which measures the probability that a reduction in return might exceed a firm's capital.[4]

All the studies suffer from an additional serious shortcoming. They fail to account for the fact that both commercial banks and investment banks hold, underwrite, and trade U.S. government and municipal general obligation bonds. It is unlikely that, after combining, the merged institution would hold and trade the sum of its predecessors' securities. After all, there is nothing to prevent commercial banks now from expanding to any volume of these securities. Consequently, the studies tend to overstate the risk exposure of the new entity.

Table 2 presents a summary of 11 studies (presented in 10 papers) that consider the combination of commercial banking and investment banking or securities firms. The studies cover a variety of years, and the results appear to be sensitive to the period examined. Six studies find a reduction in risk; three of these also consider the effect on returns

T A B L E   2

Risk Reduction Implications of Studies of Combinations of Commercial Banks with Companies Involved in Securities Activities

Study	Period	Risk Measure	Affect on Risk: R = reduced I = increased N = no change
Heggestad (1975)	1953–67	Correlation of accounting returns	R: correlation coefficient is negative
Eisemann (1976)	1962–68	Market returns relative to risk (variance of returns)	R: significant improvement of returns relative to risks
Johnson and Meister (1974)	1954–69	Market returns relative to risk (variance of returns)	R: significant improvement of returns relative to risks
Stover (1982)	1959–68	Correlation of accounting earnings	N: but the value of the bank increases
Litan (1987)	1962–82	Market returns relative to risk (variance of returns)	R: significant improvement of returns relative to risks
Brewer, Fortier, and Pavel (1982)	1980, 1982, 1986	Standard deviation of market returns	I: effect on returns not reported
Eisenbeis and Wall (1984)	1970–80	Coefficients of determination (return ÷ risk)	R: returns are negatively correlated with banks' returns
Boyd and Graham (1988)	1971–84	Risk of failure (Z score)	N: slightly greater risk of bankruptcy
Saunders and Walter (1994)	1984–88	Interest rate risk; standard deviation of market returns and returns	R: with respect to interest rate risk I: with respect to standard deviation of market returns; returns also are reduced
Boyd, Graham, and Hewitt (1993)	1971–87	Risk of failure, returns	I: risk of failure greater and returns are greater

and find that returns are higher. Two studies find no reduction in risk; one of these finds that the value of the bank increases. The remaining three find an increase in risk; one of these does not report the effect on returns, one reports a decrease in returns, and one higher returns but a greater risk of bankruptcy as measured by the Z score.

Thus, the published studies that attempt to estimate the effect on risk and the probability of failure of banks engaging in securities activities are of limited value for policy purposes, both conceptually and because they report conflicting results. Nevertheless, we can conclude that the measured effect on risk of permitting commercial banks to engage in securities activities appears to be small.

Changes in the Failure Rate of Banks Engaging in Securities Activities

Throughout history, few if any U.S. commercial banks have failed because of their involvement in securities activities either before or after Glass-Steagall. J.F.T. O'Connor, Comptroller of the Currency from 1933 to 1938, catalogued the reasons for the failure of all 2,955 national banks that failed from 1865 through 1936, including the depression years 1929 to 1933 (O'Connor, 1938, p. 90). Securities activities were not a sufficiently frequent reason to be classified separately among the top seven categories of the reasons listed for these failures.

Nevertheless, it was strongly asserted at the time that banks' involvement in securities underwriting and trading was an important cause of the great number of bank failures experienced during the Great Depression. No evidence was presented in support of this belief.[5] Eugene White (1986) later studied the issue. He compared the survival of national banks with securities operations in 1929 with the survival of other national banks. He found (ibid., p. 40): "While 26.3 percent of all national banks failed in this period [most in 1931], only 6.5 percent [4 banks] of the 62 banks which had affiliates in 1929 and 7.6 percent [11 banks] of the 145 banks which conducted large operations through their bond departments closed their doors." Further, an examination of these 15 failed national banks with securities operations indicates that their failures were due not to securities operations, but to loan losses and other factors (Benston, 1989). The largest of these failed banks was the First National Bank of Detroit. Its securities affiliate's assets were only 10.7 percent of its total assets. Indeed, the Senate

Stock Exchange Practices Hearings in 1934 that concentrated on Detroit banking do not mention the bank's securities activities. The next two largest failed banks had total assets of $37.1 million and $7.8 million. Thus, almost all of the 15 failed national banks with securities operations were small. Even if these banks had failed because of their securities activities, they could not have been responsible for any but a trivial part of the banking crisis that characterized the period.

White also compared statistically the national banks with securities activities that failed in 1931 with nonfailed national banks of similar sizes from similar locales. He concluded that "the presence of a securities affiliate and whatever characteristics were associated with it tended to reduce the likelihood of failure." (White, 1986, p. 42.) In addition, he found that banks' securities activities were either not related to their financial problems or mitigated the severity of those problems. The banks' securities affiliates were neither undercapitalized nor dependent on borrowed funds. Thus, he concludes (ibid., p. 50): "National banks' liquidity does not appear to have been weakened by the presence of an affiliated securities business."

Nor is there evidence supporting the contention that securities purchased by smaller banks from banks that dealt in securities was a cause of the smaller banks' failures. The issue was first raised as part of the Glass Subcommittee Hearings (1931). The U.S. Treasury Department's "Issues Paper" (1975, p. 81) states (incorrectly) that the Subcommittee "found that a major cause of bank failures of commercial banks in the early 1930s had been the extensive investment of bank assets in long-term securities, many of which were acquired from security affiliates." In fact, the subcommittee did not attempt to discover the source of funding of the banks' securities. Although many witnesses were asked what they believed were the causes of the large number of bank failures, none identified banks' investments in securities as a cause. The bankers and regulators who answered this question identified demographic changes, overbanking, fraud and mismanagement, and poor farming as causes.[6]

There is also evidence on the relationship of securities activities and bank failures since the enactment of Glass-Steagall in 1933. As noted, commercial banks could participate and have participated in underwriting and dealing in Treasury securities. Some 10 of the 40 or so security dealers designated by the Federal Reserve Bank of New York as primary Treasury securities dealers and eligible for trading with the Fed's Open Market Desk were typically domestic commercial banks. (Another 15 or so were owned by foreign banks.) A list of current primary Treasury securities dealers is presented in Table 3. Only one of the banks that has been a primary Treasury securities dealer has failed since the end of World War II—the Continental Illinois National Bank in 1984—and securities operations played no role in that failure. Nor have any of the 11 major commercial banks that engage importantly in securities operations overseas, other than the Continental, failed.

Since 1987, under Section 20 of the Banking Act of 1933 (the Glass-Steagall Act) separately capitalized affiliates if commercial bank holding companies have been permitted, upon approval by the Fed, to deal in a progressively broader range of municipal and private securities activities. The number and identity of these Section 20 subsidiaries as of July 11, 1995, is shown by year in Table 4. No bank affiliated with a Section 20 sub has failed.

Six papers, one of which deals with two separate time periods, have examined the effect on the risk incurred by bank holding companies of their engaging in permissible securities activities. Table 5 summarizes these seven studies (two in one paper and two by the same authors). Three of the studies find a significant reduction in risk, two find an increase, and two find little effect. Indeed, the two studies by the same authors come to conflicting conclusions. Thus, as with the statistical studies reviewed earlier, the findings of these studies are sensitive both to the specifications of the models and the sample periods tested. On net, the studies provide weak evidence that securities activities reduce overall bank holding company risk. More strongly, these studies, as well as the earlier ones of hypothetical combinations of banks with securities firms, indicate neither a major increase nor a major decrease in risk exposure.

To summarize, studies that attempt to simulate the effect of combining commercial banks with investment banks and securities firms are inconclusive and of limited value due to inherent statistical problems and results that vary depending on the time period studied. Evidence from the pre–Glass-Steagall years indicates that commercial banks' involvement in securities activities has been associated with lower rates of failure. Indeed, almost no banks that underwrote or traded securities failed during the Great Depression. The post–Glass-Steagall years also reveal little risk of banks' involvement in securities, to the extent permitted by law. Banks that underwrote and dealt with securities in

T A B L E   3

Primary Securities Dealers (as of September 1995)

Firm	Section 20 Sub	Foreign
B A Securities, Inc.	X	
Barclays de Zoete Wedd Securities, Inc.	X	British
Bear Stearns, & Co., Inc.		
B T Securities Corporation	X	
Chase Securities Inc.	X	
Chemical Securities Inc.	X	
Citicorp Securities, Inc.	X	
CS First Boston Corporation		Swiss
Daiwa Securities America Inc.		Japanese
Dean Witter Reynolds Inc.		
Deutsche Bank Securities Corporation	X	German
Dillon, Read, & Co. Inc.		40% Dutch
Donaldson, Lufkin & Jenrette Securities Corporation		
Eastbridge Capital Inc.		Japanese
First Chicago Capitad Markets, Inc.	X	
Fuji Securities Inc.		Japanese
Goldman, Sachs & Co.		
Greenwich Capital Markets, Inc.	X	Japanese
HSBC Securities, Inc.		Hong Kong
Aubrey G. Lanston & Co., Inc.		Japanese
Lehman Government Securities, Inc.		
Merrill Lynch Government Securities Inc.		
J.P. Morgan Securities Inc.	X	
Morgan Stanley & Co. Incorporated		
Nationsbanc Capital Markets, Inc.	X	
Nesbitt Burns Securities Inc.		Canadian
The Nikko Securities Co. International, Inc.		Japanese
Nomura Securities International, Inc.		Japanese
Paine Webber Incorporated		
Prudential Securities Incorporated		
Salomon Brothers Inc.		
Sanwa Securities (USA) Co., L.P.	X	Japanese
Smith Barney Inc.		
SBC Capital Markets Inc.	X	Swiss
UBS Securities Inc.		Swiss
Yamaichi International (America), Inc.		Japanese
Zions First National Bank		

Source: Board of Governors of the Federal Reserve System

TABLE 4

Bank Holding Companies with Section 20 Subsidiaries (as of July 11, 1995) by Federal Reserve District

Atlanta District	*New York District (continued)*
Bank South Corp.	Deutsche Bank AG
Barnett Banks, Inc.	Long-Term Credit Bank of Japan, Ltd.
SouthTrust Corp.	J.P. Morgan & Co., Inc.
SunTrust	The Royal Bank of Canada
Synovus Financial Corp;	Republic New York Corp.
TB&C Bancshares, Inc.	Swiss Bank
	The Toronto-Dominion Bank
Boston District	
Fleet/Norstar Financial Group, Inc.	*Philadelphia District*
	CoreStates Financial Corp.
	Dauphin Deposit Corp.
Chicago District	*Richmond District*
Amsterdam-Rotterdam Bank N.V.	First Union Corp.
First of America Bank Corp.	NationsBank Corp.
The Bank of Montreal	
First Chicago Corp.	
Cleveland District	*San Francisco District*
Banc One Corp.	BankAmerica Corp.
Huntington Bancshares Inc.	Dai-Ichi Kangyo Bank, Ltd.
Mellon Bank Corp.	Sanwa Bank, Ltd.
National City Corp.	
PNC Financial Corp.	
Minneapolis District	*St. Louis District*
Norwest Corp.	Liberty National Bancorp, Inc.
New York District	Total: 25 Domestic 12 Foreign
The Bank of Nova Scotia	
Bankers Trust New York Corp.	
Barclays Bank PLC	
Canadian Imperial Bank of Commerce	
The Chase Manhattan Corp.	
Chemical Banking Corp.	
Citicorp	

Source: American Bankers Association

foreign markets have not experienced financial distress as a result. Banks that importantly underwrote and traded domestically in permitted securities also have not suffered financial problems, with the

TABLE 5

Risk Reduction Implications of Studies of Bank Holding Companies Engaged in Permissible Securities Activities

Study	Period	Risk Measure	Affect on Risk: R = reduced I = increased N = no change
Boyd and Graham (1986)	1971–77	Risk of failure	I: risk higher
	1978–83	Risk of failure	R: weak reduction
Wall (1987)	1976–84	Standard deviation of market returns, returns, and risk of failure	N: little effect on risk
Kwast (1989)	1976–87	Risk of failure	R: but diversification gains are small and sensitive to time period analyzed
Brewer (1989)	1976–86	Standard deviation of market returns	R: bank holding companies with more nonbank securities activities have lower risk
Demsetz and Strahan (1955a)	1991–93	Firm-specific and systematic risk	I: same as above, but Section 20 subs have positive and significant correlation with risk
Demsetz and Strahan (1955b)	1987–93	Firm-specific and systematic risk	R: greater securities trading activities have negative, but statistically insignificant overall risk

exception of Continental Illinois, which got into difficulty as a result of its traditional banking operations, not its securities activities. Studies of bank holding companies' permitted securities operations indicate that securities activities generally helped these institutions reduce risk through more effective diversification. Thus, it appears that securities activities, to the extent presently permitted, have tended to be risk reducing, on the whole.

The remaining concern, to which we now turn, is the risk that might be incurred by commercial banks were they permitted to conduct securities activities without the restraint of Glass-Steagall.

Prospects for Increased Risk Were the Glass-Steagall Act Repealed

If the securities provisions of the Glass-Steagall Act were repealed and there were no limitation on the securities activities in which commercial banks or bank holding companies could engage, three risks need to be considered: underwriting, holding securities for trade, and increased brokerage. All these activities are subject to operations risk; the costs of the activity might exceed the earnings (on a present value basis). This risk is no different from the risks ordinarily taken now by commercial banks and all enterprises. There is no reason to expect these risks to affect seriously the safety and soundness of banks, except, perhaps, for a few pathological instances that authorities can deal with as they now deal with similar excesses and incompetencies in presently permissible activities. Consequently, we dismiss operating risk as a matter for additional concern.

Underwriting Risk

Securities underwriting is riskless when the issue is underwritten on a "best efforts" basis. In these situations, the underwriter contracts to market the issue and is not liable if the amount obtained is less than the amount expected. When underwriters purchase and then sell the issue, they may incur risk. However, even in these situations, there is almost no risk when underwriters obtain firm or close-to-firm offers from their clients for the entire issue before they contract to purchase it, as they frequently do. The risk, then, is limited to underwriting securities that are not presold.

Ian Giddy (1985) studied the extent to which securities underwriters have taken losses on unsold securities. He examined all SEC-registered common stock issues of $5 million or more offered from 1976 through 1983, 2,540 issues in all. He found that underwriters typically held shares for no longer than a day, and took almost no losses as a result of decreases in the price of the shares. He then measured what the net profit to underwriters (spread plus holding gain or less holding loss) would have been if they had held the issue either 1, 5, or 10 days after issue. Table 6 shows the average (mean) net profit per

TABLE 6

Profits and Losses Experienced by Equity Security Underwriters of 2,540 Issues, 1976–1983, Had the Issues Been Held for 1, 5, or 10 Days after Issue

| | Millions of Dollars | | | |
Period	Net Profit	Standard Deviation	Range	Percentage of Issue that Yield Losses
1st day after issue	1.3	(1.8)	− 10.4 to 25.6	3.4%
5th day after issue	1.1	(2.0)	− 18.7 to 25.6	11.1
10th day after issue	1.1	(2.1)	− 13.8 to 25.6	12.2

Source: Giddy (1985), Table 6.4

issue, standard deviation (in parentheses), range, and percentage of issues that resulted in losses. Very few underwritings resulted in losses, even if the underwriter held the issue for as long as 10 days, which they rarely do. The underwriters' average profits per issue would be slightly lower if it were held longer than one day ($1.1 instead of $1.3 million), and the percentage of issues that yield losses would be higher (11.1 percent or 12.2 percent instead of 3.4 percent).

Dealing (Trading) Risk

Securities held for trade could pose additional risk to the extent that the market values of the securities might decline. These potential costs are offset by gains in these values. Both stock and bond prices are volatile and dealers at times have experienced large losses on net. But, the addition of private securities to those in which commercial banks now can trade is unlikely to increase risk significantly. Banks already can assume as much interest rate risk as they wish through dealing and investing in government securities and collateralized mortgage obligations. The new component of market risk introduced by dealing in corporate securities is credit risk—and banks have considerable experience in dealing with this risk in their corporate lending operations.

Furthermore, it is not clear whether equity securities would pose more risk to banks than do the other assets in which they now can invest. Although there have been times, such as October 1987, when stock prices declined precipitously, there also have been times when interest rates have increased substantially, such as in 1979, 1981, and 1994, resulting in considerable losses on assets in which banks may now invest. There also have been times when the prices of these assets have not moved in concert and have moved in opposite directions. Hence, as we discuss above, banks dealing in and holding equity securities could reduce the total risk that they face. It is doubtful if the risk would increase.

Brokerage Risk
Securities brokerage activity at banks (which now is permitted) is likely to increase were commercial banks permitted to underwrite and sell securities without limit. However, this activity involves no price risk.

Overall Effect on Total Risk
In addition to the reasoning and evidence that leads us to conclude that commercial banks' involvement in securities underwriting, dealing, and brokerage is unlikely on average to increase the risks assumed, we should point out that banks now are permitted to accept the maximum amount of risk in their permissible activities that they find consistent with the interests of their shareholders. They can make riskier loans, specialize in loans that are affected similarly by economic events (e.g., farm, energy, and foreign loans), invest in long-term government securities that are funded with shorter term liabilities, and invest in or sell options, futures, and other derivative products. They also can invest in real estate by constructing buildings that are larger than operational requirements, and (if underwriting and dealing in private securities were risky) many commercial banks can underwrite securities overseas. As we discuss above, banks' propensity to take risks is a function of the returns expected from risk taking and their capital (which would have to absorb losses from risk taking). Unrestrained securities underwriting and dealing, therefore, would not enhance commercial banks' opportunities for risk taking over what they presently can do.

However, securities activities would provide commercial banks with opportunities to diversify their operations and assets more effectively. They also would have greater opportunities to increase their net income, both from additional revenues and from lower costs as a result of economies of scope and scale economies from expanded securities activities. Consequently, their safety and soundness would be enhanced.

It is possible, of course, that some banks might use a particular activity to increase risk proportionately more than return and increase the bank's probability of failure. In such situations it is far more efficient to require that bank to hold capital sufficient to absorb any potential losses, as is mandated by the prompt corrective action and least-cost resolution provisions of FDICIA, than to prohibit the activity. Such prohibitions would prevent all banks (and their customers) from obtaining the benefits from that activity.

E N D N O T E S

1. U.S. Senate, 1926, p. 7.

2. See Benston (1996) for a more complete analysis of the reasons underlying passage of the Glass-Steagall Act's separation of commercial and investment banking.

3. A detailed review of the reentry of commercial banks into securities activities appears in Kaufman and Mote (1990).

4. $Z = (-C/A - Er) \div \sigma$, where C = capital, A = assets, Er = expected return, and σ = the standard deviation of return, all for a specific enterprise.

5. The Bank of United States, a large New York City bank with 59 affiliates, which failed in 1930, was mentioned often as a prime example of banks' abuse of securities affiliates. However, none of these affiliates underwrote or dealt in securities, with the exception of one that was engaged in purchases of the bank's own stock.

6. See Benston (1990, pp. 37–38) for quotations from the witnesses.

REFERENCES

Benston, George J. "Why Did Congress Pass New Financial Service Laws in the 1930s? an Alternative Opinion." *Economic Review* (Federal Reserve Bank of Atlanta), 67 (April 1982), pp. 7–10.

Benston, George J. *The Separation of Commercial and Investment Banking: The Glass-Steagall Act Revisited and Reconsidered.* New York: Oxford University Press, 1990.

Benston, George J. "The Origins of and Justification for the Glass–Steagall Act," in *Financial Systems Design: Universal Banking Considered*, eds. Anthony Saunders and Ingo Walter. Burr Ridge: Irwin Professional Publishing 1996.

Boyd, J.H., S.L. Graham, and **R. Hewitt.** "Bank Holding Company Mergers with Non-Bank Financial Firms: Effects on the Risk of Failure." *Journal of Banking and Finance* 17, 1993, pp. 43–63.

Boyd, John H., and **Stanley L. Graham.** "The Profitability and Risk Effects of Allowing Bank Holding Companies to Merge with Other Financial Firms: A Simulation Study." *Quarterly Review* (Federal Reserve Bank of Minneapolis), Spring 1988, pp. 3–20.

Boyd, John H., and **Stanley L. Graham.** "Risk Regulation and Bank Holding Company Expansion into Nonbanking." *Federal Reserve Bank of Minneapolis Quarterly Review* 10 (Spring, 1986), pp. 2–17.

Brewer, Elijah III. "The Risk of Existing Nonbank Activities." *Proceedings: Conference on Bank Structure and Competition*, Federal Reserve Bank of Chicago, 1989, pp. 401–423.

Brewer, Elijah III, Diana Fortier, and **Christine Pavel.** "Bank Risk from Nonbank Activities." *Economic Perspectives* (Federal Reserve Bank of Chicago), July/August 1988, pp. 14–26.

Carosso, Vincent P. *Investment Banking in America: A History.* Cambridge, MA: Harvard University Press, 1970.

Demsetz, Rebecca S., and **Philip E. Strahan.** "Diversification, Size, and Risk at Bank Holding Companies." Working Paper, Federal Reserve Bank of New York, May 1995.

Demsetz, Rebecca S., and **Philip E. Strahan.** "Historical Patterns and Recent Changes in the Relationship between Bank Holding Company Size and Risk." *Economic Policy Review* (Federal Reserve Bank of New York) 1 (July 1995), pp. 13–26.

Eisemann, Peter C. "Diversification and Congeneric Banking Holding Companies." *Journal of Bank Research.* 12 (Summer 1976), pp. 68–77.

Eisenbeis, Robert A., and **Wall, Larry D.** "Bank Holding Companies and Diversification." in *Proceedings of a Conference on Bank Structure and Competition.* Chicago: Federal Reserve Bank of Chicago, 1984, pp. 340–367.

Federal Reserve Committee. *225 Bank Suspensions: Case Histories from Examiners' Reports.* Material prepared for the information of the Federal Reserve System by the Federal Reserve Committee on Branch, Group, and Chain Banking, 1933.

Glass Subcommittee Hearings. *Operation of the National and Federal Reserve Banking Systems.* Hearings before a Subcommittee of the Committee on Banking and Currency, United States Senate, 71st Congress, 3rd Session, Parts 1 through 6 and VII, 1931.

Golembe, Carter. "Commercial Banks and Investment Banking," in Golembe Associates: Washington DC, paper prepared for the American Bankers Association, November 29, 1976, p. 31.

Heggestad, Arnold. "Riskiness of Investments in Nonbank Activities by Bank Holding Companies." *Journal of Economics and Business* 27 (Spring 1975), pp. 219–223.

Johnson, Rodney D., and **David R. Meinster.** "Bank Holding Companies: Diversification Opportunities in Nonbank Activities." *Eastern Economic Journal* 1 (October 1974), pp. 316–323.

Kaufman, George G., and **Larry R. Mote.** "Glass-Steagall: Repeal by Regulatory and Judicial Reinterpretation." *Banking Law Journal* 107 (September-October 1990), pp. 388–421.

Kaufman, George G., and **Larry R. Mote.** "Commercial Bank Securities Activities: What Really Happened in 1902." *Journal of Money, Credit, and Banking* 24 (August 1992), pp. 370–374.

Kwast, Myron L. "The Impact of Underwriting and Dealing on Bank Returns and Risk." *Journal of Banking and Finance* 13 (March 1989), pp. 101–125.

Litan, Robert E. *What Should Banks Do?* Washington, D.C.: The Brookings Institution, 1987.

O'Conner, J.F.T. *The Banking Crisis and Recovery Under the Roosevelt Administration.* Chicago: Callaghan and Co., 1938.

Saunders, Anthony, and **Ingo Walter.** *Universal Banking In The United States.* New York: Oxford University Press, 1994.

Stover, Roger D. "A Reexamination of Bank Holding Company Acquisitions." *Journal of Bank Research* 12 (Summer 1982), pp. 101–108.

U.S. Department of the Treasury. "Public Policy Aspects of Bank Securities Activities: An Issue Paper," in *Securities Activities of Commercial Banks.* Hearings before the Subcommittee on Securities of the Committee on Banking, Housing and Urban Affairs, United States Senate, 94th Congress, 1st Session, 1975 pp. 22–87.

U.S. Senate, 69th Cong., 1st sess. *The National Bank Act* (report 473). Washington DC, March 25, 1926.

Wall, Larry D. "Has Bank Holding Companies' Diversification Affected Their Risk of Failure?" *Journal of Economics and Business* 39 (1987), pp. 313–326.

White, Eugene N. "Before the Glass-Steagall Act: An Analysis of the Investment Banking Activities of National Banks." *Explorations in Economic History* 23 (1986), pp. 33–55.

2

FEDERAL REGULATION OF THE CONTRACTS ISSUED BY LIFE INSURANCE COMPANIES

Lawrence J. Latto, *Shea & Gardner*

Long years ago, when the business of life insurance was much simpler than it is today, the general understanding was that this business—in contrast with virtually every other business except the production and display of baseball games—was not regulated at all by the federal government, only by the 50 state governments. Although this is not quite what the McCarran-Ferguson Act (Ch.20, 59 Stat 33 [1945], 15 USC §§ 1011–1015 [1988]) says,[1] Congress has not, in fact, enacted any laws regulating the conduct of the insurance business, leaving the many state laws to occupy the field. The Internal Revenue Code, of course, has always been a significant source of federal regulation over insurance companies, not only through the provisions imposing taxes and determining how taxable income is to be calculated, but also, as discussed below, through the statutory provisions and regulations relating to qualified and other tax-advantaged employee benefit plans. But the actual conduct of the business itself has been, and still is, subject almost entirely to the often conflicting regulation of 50 states, conflicting despite efforts to foster uniformity through the numerous model laws and regulations adopted by the National Association of Insurance Commissioners (NAIC). The nature and extent of that state regulation is outside the scope of this chapter. Our goal here is to examine the growth of federal regulation of the business, where it stands today, and where, so far as we can dimly perceive, it is likely to go in the next 5 to 10 years.[2]

Another limitation upon the scope of this chapter is made necessary by the way in which the business—at least, of the largest companies—has expanded into the provision of financial services generally. For example, a recent restructuring of The Prudential Insurance Company of America created seven groups: individual insurance, money management, securities, health care, private asset management, international insurance, and diversified.[3] At an earlier time the traditional main elements of the business were issuing life insurance policies or contracts and annuity contracts, and, at least for the larger companies, administering "insured" retirement plans. These are the areas to which this chapter will be devoted.[4]

FIXED DOLLAR (NONVARIABLE) LIFE INSURANCE AND ANNUITY CONTRACTS

Until the 1960s, life insurance policies and annuity contracts (from now on both will be referred to as *contracts*, following Securities and Exchange Commission terminology) were all "fixed-dollar." That is, the amounts the insurance companies agreed to pay (often called the "benefits provided under the contract") were always expressed as a stated number of dollars, rather than based upon the value of a number of shares or units. As a result, there were severe restrictions upon what percentages of the companies' assets could be invested in equities. If life insurance assets were invested so that the company could count on being repaid the full amount of its original investment (if it had correctly appraised the credit risk) plus some interest, the company could keep its promises, which were also couched in specific fixed amounts.[5] The combination of simple, quantitative contractual promises and strict state regulations that had solvency as a primary objective were important factors that led to the decision to exempt this business from the federal securities laws, and to leave it untouched by other federal laws.

Statutory Exemptions from the Securities Laws

Life insurance companies, as well as all other kinds of insurance companies, are excluded from the definition of "investment company" by

Section 3(c)(3) of the Investment Company Act of 1940. They are free, accordingly, from the significant substantive regulation imposed by that Act. Their principal products, also, until the introduction of equity-based products, were long and unqualifiedly regarded as not subject to the disclosure requirements of the Securities Act of 1933 (the "1933 Act").

Fixed-Dollar Life Insurance Contracts

Section 3(a)(8) exempts from registration but not from the application of the antifraud provisions of the 1933 Act, "…any insurance or endowment policy…" In a much-quoted sentence in *Tcherepin* v. *Knight*, 389 U.S. 332, 342 n.30 (1967), however, the Supreme Court asserted that the adoption of this provision was "clearly supererogation" and that life insurance contracts are not securities at all. This conclusion is now universally accepted, and no one has yet urged seriously that term insurance, or "classic," "conventional," or "traditional" fixed-dollar whole life insurance, or universal life insurance contracts, are "securities" under the 1933, 1934, or 1940 Acts. A few scattered sentences to the contrary can be found, but, as a practical matter, this very significant part of the life insurance business is still conducted today outside the reach of the federal securities laws, including the antifraud provisions.[6]

Group and Individual Fixed-Dollar Annuity Contracts

Section 3(a)(8) also exempts any "…annuity contract or optional annuity contract issued by a corporation subject to the supervision of the insurance commissioner, bank commissioner, or any agency or officer performing like functions, of any state or territory of the United States or the District of Columbia." For the most part, these contracts are also regarded as falling outside the definition of *security* so that their sale is not subject to the antifraud provisions.[7] In contrast to fixed-dollar life insurance contracts, a stronger case can be made that annuity contracts are, indeed, "securities" and, therefore, only exempted from registration. However, except for certain fixed-dollar annuity contracts with provisions that differ significantly enough from the provisions of annuity contracts sold in 1933 to cause them to no longer fall within § 3(a)(8) (these contracts are discussed below), traditional fixed-dollar annuity contracts, like traditional life insurance contracts, are widely regarded as not being securities at all. As a practical matter, since so much time has passed without any decision to the contrary, it is now politically and legally correct to join in this conclusion.

The Fixed-Dollar Funding and Administration of Pension Plans

For many decades the funding and administration of pension plans has been, and still is, an important part of the business of many life insurance companies, certainly the larger ones. The vehicle for this purpose has most often been the group annuity contract. Accordingly, the arrangements and legal relationships under which this part of the business has been conducted were also generally deemed to arise out of or be created by a contract that falls within § 3(a)(8). As these contracts evolved in connection with the funding of defined-benefit plans, a wide variety of forms blossomed, many of which are so intricately written as to make them not easily accessible and, in some cases, close to incomprehensible to any other than experienced readers. Moreover, the insurance company's contractual obligations are often not crisply and precisely stated, appearing to leave to the unfettered discretion of the insurance company the determination of just what amounts will be credited to the contract. The result is that the legal relationships that these documents create are often difficult to describe with precision and clarity.

This problem has led to some important and incorrect decisions. See, for example, *John Hancock Life Insurance Co.* v. *Harris Trust*, 114 S.Ct. 517 (1993) (which interprets ERISA rather than the securities laws, but reflects a less-than-perfect understanding of the documents and arrangements before the Court), and *Peoria Union Stock Yards* v. *Penn Mutual Life Insurance Co.*, 698 F.2d 320 (7th Cir. 1983) (which interprets both ERISA and the securities laws, and also reflects an imperfect understanding of the contracts). However, this part of the business still has generally been conducted without being subjected to the federal securities laws.[8] The equity funding of pension and other retirement plans by life insurance companies using separate accounts is quite another matter, and we will discuss it below.

Fixed-Dollar Annuity Contracts Not Exempted by Section 3(a)(8)

The traditional annuity contracts issued when the 1933 Act was adopted generally promised that contract values would grow through crediting relatively low interest rates, leading to resistance in the market place. One of the industry's responses was the development of variable annuity contracts, discussed below. Another response was the development of "interest sensitive" contracts, which promised interest at a safe low rate, but also promised that additional "excess interest" would be credited at rates that were guaranteed only for relatively short periods and frequently changed. After a while, the staff of the Securities and Exchange Commission (the SEC or the commission) began to worry whether the investment features of some of these contracts had so overwhelmed the "insurance" features as to make the § 3(a)(8) exemption inapplicable. The SEC issued interpretive releases providing guidance as to when section 3(a)(8) applied and when it did not, then modified them, then withdrew them. The end result was the adoption of a safe harbor rule, Rule 151. The SEC staff acknowledged that there was still some moderately choppy water outside the safe harbor but still within the shadowy indistinct line that marks the outer limits of § 3(a)(8). A few court decisions may have significantly—and erroneously—reduced the distance between § 3(a)(8) and Rule 151, but the full story remains to be written.[9] The commission staff has insisted, however, with little resistance from the insurance industry, that one form of annuity contract is well outside of § 3(a)(8).

In order to credit the highest possible rates of interest, annuity purchase payments had to be invested in longer term debt securities. As new forms of contracts emerged that imposed smaller penalties upon surrender and as investor sophistication increased, contracts that guaranteed specific rates for longer periods (contrasted with the excess interest contracts that guaranteed the rates for only as long as one year) presented unacceptable disintermediation risks. The solution was to guarantee that higher rates would be credited (based upon matching long-term investments) for those contract owners who kept their contracts in force, while the redemption values would be adjusted upon surrender. This is accomplished by multiplying the unadjusted redemption value by an appropriate factor that takes into account the difference between the promised crediting rate and the interest rate generally available at the time of redemption for fixed income securities with a maturity equal to the time remaining until the end of the agreed-upon original period. Basically, the adjustment changes the redemption value in approximately the same way the market value of a bond with a comparable initial maturity would have changed. If interest rates have fallen, the amount paid upon redemption is correspondingly greater than the current value of the contract.[10]

Because the issuers of these market value adjusted annuity contracts are life insurance companies rather than separate accounts, they are not registered under the 1940 Act. See page 39. Since the contract values do not depend upon the investment results of assets held in a separate account that meets the definition under the 1940 Act and since Section 3(c)(3) excludes insurance companies from the 1940 Act definition of investment company, there is no "company" that must be registered.[11]

The annuity contract, however, must be registered under the 1933 Act. Since there is no specific applicable form, Form S–1 is used for this purpose. The staff has taken a sensible and flexible approach and has permitted the omission of much of the information specific items of the form call for simply because that information would not be meaningful or of any particular interest to prospective purchasers.

The Fixed-Dollar Funding of Retirement Plans

Although many major corporations had adopted funded employee retirement plans prior to World War II, a sharp growth began during and after the end of that war. Two types of funding agency—banks and trust companies and life insurance companies—together held about 98 per cent of the assets of those plans. Life insurance companies refer to these plans as *insured plans* and *noninsured plans*. The lion's share of their assets were held in trust, with banks almost always the trustees, but the amounts held under insured plans were still a considerable part of the whole.

The earliest life insurance contracts were fairly simple, straightforward deferred-annuity contracts. Under these contracts the insurance company undertook to be responsible for payment of the benefits accrued each year for each employee. The low crediting rates under these contracts that prudence dictated were ameliorated somewhat by provisions for experience rating. The actual amounts credited, however, were determined without significant contractual constraints upon the insurance companies, and in time plan sponsors demanded something better. The initial response was the Group Deposit Administration contract, which, until each employee retired, allowed employers to participate more directly in the actual investment experience of the insurance company. Investment year methods for determining the crediting rate were introduced in order to satisfy the continuing demands of employers. However, the contracts generally still left to the insurance company the discretion to determine what the actual crediting rate would be, limited only by vague promises to make the determination in accordance with their "customary practices." Under trusted (noninsured) plans, however, employers were able to enjoy the benefits of superior performance of the investments of the assets dedicated to the payment of pension benefits (as well as accepting the risks of poor performance), not only while employees were still working but also during their retirement years. The life insurance response was the Immediate Participation Guarantee (IPG) contract, which offered the same opportunity. The interest rates credited, however, were still not determined by the investment return of an identified portfolio of plan assets but, rather, by the insurance company, acting in good faith based upon the net return it was able to earn upon the assets of the company held primarily in fixed-rate debt instruments.

Despite these efforts by the life insurance companies to satisfy the demands of the marketplace, many employers still sought to enjoy the even higher returns (and to accept the greater risks) that came with having their plans' assets invested in equities. Bank trustees were able and willing to oblige, and the percentage of plan assets invested in common stocks grew sharply. Insurance companies needed to find an innovative way to compete for this business. Virtually all state laws, however, forbade insurance companies from holding assets in trust or from engaging in a trust business. That prohibition, fortunately, was not inconsistent with amendments to state insurance laws authorizing the establishment of "separate accounts" or with amendments to the Internal Revenue Code providing the freedom from taxation of the income of "segregated asset accounts."[12] With the development of these instruments, insurance companies were prepared to offer the same services and to do essentially the same things as banks and trust companies. Before turning to that development we describe, far more summarily than it deserves, the elaborate administrative action and litigation surrounding the application of ERISA to the "insured" funding of retirement plans.[13]

ERISA Coverage of Insured, Fixed-Dollar Employee Retirement Plan Funding

Prior to 1974 the only extensive federal regulation of employee benefit and profit-sharing plans was set forth in Treasury regulations adopted under the Internal Revenue Code. These regulations stemmed largely from a deceptively simple statutory requirement that retirement plans should not discriminate unfairly against average employees in favor of more highly compensated employees, and they constituted an elaborate exegesis. That is a testimonial to the loophole-finding abilities of lawyers and the loophole-closing abilities of the Internal Revenue Service. That regulation has expanded significantly since 1974, in statutory as well as regulatory form, until today the requirements are infuriatingly complex and accessible only to the cognoscenti.

The Treasury regulations left relatively untouched the need for adequate funding, the lack of standards for fiduciary conduct, and the widespread existence of troublesome self-dealing.[14] Those matters were principal objectives of ERISA. The draftsmen of that act took the funding mechanisms pretty much as they found them. All plan assets had to be held in trust, but that requirement applied only to noninsured plans. For insured plans, employers could still make contributions directly to insurance companies, where they lost their identity by being merged with all the other assets of the insurance company. But by botching the definition of the important concept of *plan assets*, the ERISA drafters created additional problems. Actually, they did not define the term at all. The investment company industry was able to add a provision, section 401(b)(1), stating that the assets of a registered investment company whose shares were held by a plan were not to be deemed assets of the plan. The insurance industry thought it had obtained a similar exception but, as it turned out, it was not as successful.[15]

By 1974 several banks had already established commingled investment trusts that held the assets of many small plans and invested them, even though they continued to hold the assets of the plans of very large companies in "single" dedicated trusts. These commingled trusts were similar to the common trust funds that many banks throughout the country had adopted for the investment of assets other than those of retirement plans. On a smaller scale, life insurance companies were doing the same thing. Their vehicles were pooled and single customer separate accounts that supplemented the traditional fixed-dollar funding described above. The ERISA drafters wanted to include as plan assets the assets held in single trusts and in single customer separate accounts as well as the assets held in commingled investment trusts and pooled separate accounts.[16] They wanted to exclude the assets held by insurance companies under fixed-dollar insured plans because those assets were no longer traceable back to the employers who had contributed them.[17] They ineptly chose the term *guaranteed benefit policy* to describe the contracts under which these plan contributions were made.[18] Insurance company representatives have always been excessively fond of the word *guaranteed* to describe features of their contracts. They failed to appreciate that as these contracts evolved, the guarantees had diminished in force, or so it might appear to an objective and untutored observer. See *John Hancock Mutual Life Insurance Company* v. *Harris Trust and Savings Bank*, 114 S.Ct. 517 (1993). This is not to say that insurance companies administering pension funding contracts such as deposit administration or IPG contracts are not fiduciaries under ERISA. Section 3(21)(A) of ERISA defines the term *fiduciary* to include any person who exercises any discretionary authority or discretionary control respecting management of such plan or who has any discretionary authority or discretionary responsibility in the administration of such plan. The *Harris Trust* court focused on another part of the definition that referred to "control respecting management or disposition of its assets." Putting that part of the definition aside, it would not be difficult to conclude that an insurance company that retains in its contract the right to determine how much interest should be credited annually to the plan's account, thereby determining the amount available for the payment of benefits, is a fiduciary within the meaning of these provisions. The nature and extent of *that* fiduciary duty, however, would be quite different from that of the broader fiduciary duty found to exist by the *Harris Trust* court, although it would still raise perplexing questions about how a single pool of assets could be managed for the "sole" benefit of several different classes of beneficiaries.

The damage done by the decision in *Harris Trust* is bearable, although not comfortable. The Department of Labor at the industry's behest provided one class exemption that exempted certain transactions from the prohibited transaction sections, 406(a) and 407(a) (see Prohibited Transaction Exemption 95–60, 60 F.R. 35925 [July 12, 1995]). Other requests for exemption and interpretive relief are still pending (see, however, DOL Opinion Letter [Feb. 22, 1995] WSB File No. 0453). It might have been better, however, if the ERISA drafters had expressed themselves with greater clarity or if the Supreme Court had been more perceptive and understanding.

THE EQUITY FUNDING CONTRACTS OF LIFE INSURANCE COMPANIES

It is worth dwelling a bit upon the history of the development of equity-based contracts of life insurance companies if only because that history helps to illuminate how, on the one hand, a somewhat illogical regulatory structure came to be erected and, on the other hand, in the non-qualified area, rigid and unwarranted substantive requirements were installed (a conclusion supported by the SEC staff's May 1992 study of the 1940 Act). The story proceeds along two parallel paths: (1) the need of insurance companies to compete more effectively with the other major funding agency of defined benefit retirement plans, and (2) market dissatisfaction with life insurance contracts that credited relatively low and uncompetitive interest rates, leading first to the development of variable annuity and later variable life insurance contracts.

The Application of the Federal Securities Laws to the Equity Funding of Employee Retirement Plans

In the following section we discuss how variable annuity and variable life insurance contracts became subject to the federal securities laws and how those laws have been applied. These developments also had a significant effect on how, and the extent to which, federal securities laws now apply to the separate account funding of employee retirement plans. As pointed out above, when the life insurance industry invented the concept of the separate account, it was seeking only to provide similar services to those that were already being provided by banks and trust companies. At that point, probably over 95 percent of the assets of retirement plans that were invested in common stock and other equities were held in trust, with banks as the trustees. The banking industry—and its lawyers—could not even imagine that their activities in this regard might involve the sale of securities or the creation of investment companies. From their standpoint nothing could be more plain than that a trust or a trustee does not issue "securities" to the trust's beneficiaries. To be sure, commingled investment trusts that pooled and invested the assets of many different plans were already in use and growing rapidly. There was, however, nothing unusual about trusts with multiple beneficiaries. It may be that from today's vantage point a commingled investment trust looks more than a little like a management investment company. To the bankers and bankers' lawyers of 1960, such an idea was unimaginable.

It was not unimaginable, however, for the life insurance companies that wanted to do through their separate accounts exactly what banks were doing through their trusts. The Supreme Court had just held in *SEC* v. *Variable Annuity Life Insurance Company*, 359 U.S. 65 (1959) (*VALIC*), that variable annuity contracts were not within Section 3(a)(8) of the 1933 Act and were securities (or, some purist lawyers insist, included within the contracts, units of interest in the separate account) that had to be registered under that Act. Remember also that the analog to the banks' "Declaration of Trust" was the "Group Variable Annuity Contract," so that it was not entirely foolish to worry whether those contracts, too, might be held to be registerable securities. Soon thereafter, the SEC held and the Court of Appeals agreed that the separate account through which variable annuity contracts were issued was a management investment company, a legal entity distinct from the insurance company that had created it (*Prudential Insurance Company of America* v. *SEC*, 326 F.2d 383 [3rd Cir. 1964)] cert. denied, 377 U.S. 953 [1964]. Thus, both the commission staff and the industry could not avoid thinking about whether the same conclusions might be drawn concerning the separate accounts and contracts employed in connection with pension funding.

The life insurance industry did the expected. It descended upon the SEC, waving the familiar "Level Playing Field" banner. "Why," they asked, "should we have to register, when banks, with nearly identical products do not?" The staff did not have the stomach to satisfy that demand by explaining to the banks that they were really engaged in the business of issuing securities. Instead, it embarked upon a program of granting no-action and interpretive relief that enabled the insurance industry to compete for this business—at least, in part—with the banks.

A fully detailed account of this process is no longer relevant. The commission *might* have drawn a distinction between corporate defined benefit and defined contribution plans. However, the defined contribution plans had not yet experienced the dramatic growth that has taken place in the last two decades, and it did not occur to the staff to make this distinction. The staff did make a number of other distinctions and a number of interpretations, not all of them entirely logical, that have largely survived until today.

Most important, perhaps, was the staff's interpretation of § 3(c)(13) (now § 3(c)(11)) of the 1940 Act. That section, at the time, excluded from the definition of investment company any "pension or profit-sharing plan which meets the conditions of section 165 of the Internal Revenue Code of 1939.[19] The commission concluded that a separate account—whether single customer or pooled—that held assets derived solely from contributions under plans that satisfied the requirements for qualification under section 401 ("qualified plans") fell within this provision.[20] By necessary implication the same was true of the trusts and commingled investment trusts of banks. No distinction was then made (although one often has been made subsequently) between the interests in the "plan" and interests in the trust or separate account that held and invested the assets of the plan.[21] Thus, as early as 1963, pension funding of qualified plans could be provided without the need to worry about compliance with the 1940 Act.

This decision did not apply to the funding of all retirement plans that were accorded favorable tax treatment. One form of retirement plan quite similar to today's 401(k) plan, which could be adopted only by states, state agencies, and charitable foundations, had to comply with section 403(b) of the code rather than section 401 to obtain favorable tax treatment. Any separate account that was used to fund such 403(b) plans, therefore, was not entitled to the exclusion provided by section 3(c)(13) for the only discernable reason that these were section 403(b) plans rather than section 401(a) plans.[22] Strict statutory construction rather than thoughtful analysis was the guiding principle. Similarly, because individual retirement accounts (IRA's) were accorded favorable tax treatment by section 408 of the code and so were not technically qualified, these plans could be funded only by separate accounts that were registered as investment companies and which issued contracts registered under the 1933 Act. In the same category were defined compensation plans because they, too, were not "qualified." Similarly adding assets derived from deferred compensation plans to a separate account that held qualified plan assets would destroy the exclusion of that account from the definition of investment company.

The SEC's willingness to recognize a blanket exemption from the 1940 Act for qualified plans and the two major funding mechanisms was quite different from its reaction with respect to the need for registration under the 1933 Act of the annuity contracts or "interests" in the separate accounts. Although the interests issued to the sponsors of retirement plans by bank trusteed trusts were not required to be registered (because of SEC staff inaction rather than no-action, as well as because of the previously mentioned confidence of banking lawyers that no securities were involved at all) the commission could not bring itself to grant similar sweeping relief with respect to 1933 Act registration of the interests in separate accounts. Instead, it began by slowly doling out permission to fund discrete types of these plans without registration. In 1963 the SEC allowed funding of noncontributory defined benefit plans at the same time as the industry agreed to register securities issued in connection with funding plans of self-employed persons (Keogh or HR10 plans). (See the no-action letter issued to The Prudential Insurance Company in endnote 20.) This process was extended from time to time either by no-action positions or by painfully worked out interpretative rules.

That unsatisfactory minuet ended in 1970 when the commission sponsored and the Congress enacted a major revision of the 1940 Act. The insurance industry was able to add its Christmas tree ornament to the Act, with commission acquiescence if not enthusiastic approval. The industry contribution took the form of a "clarification" of section 3(c)(13) (renumbered by the Act as 3(c)(11)), which added to the exclusion of qualified stock bonus pension or profit-sharing plans an explicit exclusion for commingled trusts maintained by banks and for separate accounts that held only qualified plan assets. This exclusion was accompanied by an amendment to Section 3(a)(2) of the 1933 Act that exempted from registration interests issued by these entities (except for interests issued for the funding of Keogh plans). The committee reports explained that these amendments did no more than codify the existing commission interpretations of the Act. In fact, the statutory exemption from the 1933 Act went somewhat beyond what the commission had theretofore grudgingly allowed in that no reference was made to the type of plan, thereby essentially providing almost the level playing field that the insurers had long sought.[23]

Ten years later a further clarification was made in these sections as part of another major revision of the 1940 Act. Excluded collective trusts and separate accounts were permitted to hold the assets of government plans, and interests in such plans were also exempted from registration under the 1933 Act.[24] The exemption in Section 3(a)(2) of the 1933 Act was also clarified by extending it to all contracts issued by life insurance companies in connection with qualified plan funding, whether or not a separate account was involved. And that is where we are today and likely to be for the remainder of the century.

That is not to say, however, that there has not been opposition and suggestions for further change. Although this opposition has thus far been unsuccessful, it has not entirely dissipated. The last decade has seen a dramatic shift from defined benefit to defined contribution plans. The significant factor in this shift has been the enormous growth of section 401(k) plans—a development that has enabled employers to shift quite a large part of the cost of their retirement plans to their employees. To a much greater extent than defined contribution plans,

Section 401(k) plans are funded by employee contributions. They are also most often "participant-directed," that is, each employee is able to decide in which pooled funds his or her accumulated contributions should be invested. The Investment Company Institute (the ICI), interested in participating in or even in dominating the funding of these plans, saw what it viewed as a playing field that was tilted in favor of banks and insurance companies. The ICI regarded its ability and obligation to deliver prospectuses as a marketing disadvantage rather than as an advantage. Its officers concluded that the 1970 amendments, at least to the extent that they dealt with participant-directed defined contribution plans, either inadvertently provided banks and insurance companies with a greater exemption from registration than was intended or else granted the exemption without adequately understanding the relevant factors and policy considerations.

The ICI embarked upon a vigorous campaign to repeal the 1970 and 1980 amendments, at least to the extent that they applied to section 401(k) and similar defined contribution plans. It elaborated its position in several extensive submissions to the SEC staff that was engaged in the massive 1992 study of the 1940 Act.[25] The insurance industry responded with equally elaborate submissions of its own. The staff report, Protecting Investors: A Half Century of Investment Company Regulation, took a middle course and recommended retention of the 1940 Act exclusions and repeal of the exemptions from the 1933 Act. A number of commissioners agreed with this recommendation and repeatedly urged its adoption in speeches around the country, an activity that occupied much of the time of some of the commissioners. Fortuitously, however, the Department of Labor was concurrently engaged in formulating regulations under section 404(c) of ERISA. A major objective of that section was to expand and improve the disclosure about plan investment options, particularly under those plans in which participants were entitled to direct how their plan assets should be invested. The adoption of these regulations, 29 CFR § 404(c), took some of the vigor out of the Investment Company Institute's drive for repeal. It may, of course, be revived, but at the moment it is quiescent. Indeed, as another chapter in this book indicates, the investment company industry is seeking ways to provide useful disclosure to plan participants that will be more succinct and informative than the statutory prospectuses.[26]

Interestingly, the failure of the ICI to hobble its bank and insurance company competitors with the expense of complying with the 1933 and 1940 Acts has not prevented its mutual fund clients from becoming the major funding agency for 401(k) plans. A recent study by Cerulli Associates reports that mutual funds now hold 37 percent of 401(k) assets, up from 26 percent two years ago, while the insurance industry's share dropped from 34 percent to 30 percent.[27] Moreover, this study may overstate the percentage of funding by insurance company separate accounts with equity portfolios. To a considerable extent section 401(a) participants are risk-averse and prefer, at least in part, a less risky investment than common stocks for their plan assets. As pointed out above, GICs and GIC pools provide, with major insurance company participation, fixed-rate investment options that promise return of principal plus stated interest. Thus, many plans offer several equity options through mutual funds and a fixed-rate option through GICs, and the percentages given above include fixed-income funding. Insurance company statistics concerning IRAs and self-employed or Keogh plans confirm this observation. At the end of 1994, insurance company plans held $63 billion of IRA assets compared with $284 billion held by mutual funds. Keogh plan assets held by insurance companies were $6 billion, compared to $35 billion for mutual funds.[28]

Why did the banks and insurance companies, which dominated for so long the funding and administration of employee benefit plans, lose so much ground to the investment company industry? There must be many reasons but one is surely the failure of the industry to develop and market aggressively a price-competitive equity product for this rapidly burgeoning market, in addition to the unique and highly attractive fixed-dollar product that it did develop. Such a product was well within its capability, utilizing group annuity facilities for investment and administration. Instead the industry relied heavily upon the individual variable annuity, which is more expensive and harder to understand than the better known mutual funds, although it does have some desirable features that mutual funds do not have. It seems likely, as the sophistication of plan sponsors and participants increases, that mutual funds will continue to add to their market share.

Variable Annuities and Variable Life Insurance

We turn now to the second parallel path, the path that led to federal regulation over variable annuities and life insurance (henceforth, *variable contracts*). The SEC and the industry proudly describe this type of regulation as an example of the remarkably successful way in which the it has been able to fit a square peg into a round hole. Nevertheless, the 1992 study of the 1940 Act concluded that, in very significant respects, current regulation is unjustified and excessively intrusive and should be corrected by appropriate legislation. Essentially, the report concluded that although Section 6(c) of the 1940 Act gives the commission extremely broad authority to provide exemptions from all or part of the Act, it does not authorize the commission effectively to repeal some of the most significant provisions of the Act. There are limits, the authors of the study believed, upon what an administrative agency may properly do. Accordingly, they recommended corrective legislation rather than administrative exemptive relief.

Variable Annuities

As stated above, the traditional, fixed-dollar annuity, which promises that a specific interest rate will be credited over a very long period of time, could not prudently guarantee what most investors would regard as a satisfactory interest rate. The industry turned to variable annuities as one way of providing an attractive alternative. This decision was not without opposition but ultimately every state adopted legislation authorizing separate accounts and assigning supervisory regulation to the insurance departments rather than to the state securities commissioners.[29] The industry, of course, believed that since these new products were annuities, they were exempted from registration under the 1933 Act. But the Supreme Court held to the contrary in *SEC* v. *Variable Annuity Life Insurance Company*, 359 U.S. 65 (1959) (*VALIC*), a case that should be of interest to Supreme Court scholars as well as to the industry.

It is reasonably clear from the structure of the opinions that the vote at the conference following argument was five to four in favor of affirming the decision of the lower court that the issuance of variable annuities was not subject to federal securities laws, with the majority made up of Justices Harlan, Frankfurter, Clark, Stewart, and Whittaker. The majority opinion was evidently assigned to Justice Harlan and the dissenting opinion to Justice Douglas, who was joined in his position by the Chief Justice and Justices Black and Brennan. Justice Douglas, who always wrote with breakneck speed, dashed off a typical, terse opinion. Justice Brennan, however, was not satisfied and wrote a lengthy and thoughtfully reasoned separate dissenting opinion, which must have caused Justice Stewart to change his vote. The decision, therefore, went the other way, though still five to four. It is a reasonable guess that Justice Douglas, with a few quick strokes, converted his dissenting opinion into a majority opinion. Justice Harlan did the same, converting his initial opinion for the court into a dissenting opinion.

Justice Douglas's majority opinion contained several quotable sentences, but many of them are simply inaccurate. It states that a variable annuity guarantees "nothing to the annuitant except an interest in a portfolio of common stocks or other equities—an interest that has a ceiling but no floor." In fact, a variable annuity really has no ceiling and, as a practical matter, does have a floor. The opinion concluded, "There is no true underwriting of risks—the only earmark of insurance as it has commonly been conceived of in common understanding and usage." But the opinion had earlier acknowledged that the insurance companies assumed the risk of mortality. In an earlier opinion, *Helvering* v. *LeGierse*, 311 U.S. 531, 539, the Court stated that risk shifting and risk distributing were the "essential" features of life insurance. Justice Douglas's opinion went on to say that the risk was "apparent rather than real," which is also plainly incorrect. Finally, the opinion rested entirely upon its conclusions that to constitute insurance there must be a "guarantee that at least some fraction of the benefits will be payable in fixed amounts." But that is true of every bond issued by a government, a corporation, and a bank, and bonds are assuredly not insurance.

Justice Brennan's concurring opinion is subject to none of these criticisms.[30] His conclusion, perhaps unfairly summarized, was that each new contract had to be carefully analyzed to determine whether it differed in degree or in kind from the contracts being offered in 1933 when the Act was adopted. A difference in degree would represent only a natural evolution that would not destroy the exemption. The variable annuity, his analysis persuasively demonstrated, differed in kind.

The United Benefit Life Insurance Company took Justice Douglas at his word and designed a variable annuity contract that satisfied the conditions that he had stated were essential to the section 3(a)(8) exemption. Although its contract provided for guaranteed, fixed-dollar payments after annuitization rather than variable annuity payments, like *VALIC*'s contract it provided that the assets would be invested in a pool of diversified common stock during the accumulation period. United Benefit added the "floor" that Justice Douglas had thought necessary by guaranteeing that no matter how low the market fell, the amount available for annuitization would never be less than 50 percent of the total purchase payments.

The commission also challenged that contract, and when the challenge reached the Supreme Court, the Court ruled that it was a security that had to be registered (*SEC* v. *United Benefit Life Insurance Company*, 387 U.S. 202 [1967]). Although the Court simplified its problem by declaring that the contract could be severed into two parts—the accumulation phase and the annuity phase—and each could be considered separately, it also gently made it clear that it was Justice Brennan's opinion rather than the majority opinion of Justice Douglas that was the true rationale of the earlier decision (see 387 U.S. at 210). Unfortunately, with the passage of time this learning has been forgotten, and the commission later relied on Justice Douglas's opinion in formulating its Rule 151. More recently, Justice Ginsburg also relied on the Douglas opinion in her opinion in *Harris Trust*. So, too, Douglas's opinion has been the primary basis for the decisions of several courts of appeals, which have woodenly interpreted section 3(a)(8) of the 1933 Act so as to make it virtually coextensive with the safe harbor of Rule 151, (see the cases cited in endnote 9). It is possible that these and other similar decisions would have gone the same way if the courts had applied the Brennan analysis in *SEC* v. *VALIC* rather than the Douglas *ipse dixits*, but that is far from certain.

The decision in *Prudential Insurance Company of America* v. *SEC* (referred to above) that a separate account issuing variable annuities had to register as an investment company under the 1940 Act, raised nice conceptual issues. The separate account had to have its own board of directors (often called something else to reduce confusion) which, presumably, had final authority over the assets of the separate account. Most state laws provided that an insurance company's board of directors had to have ultimate control over all the assets of the company, and under state law the separate account was a division of the company and its assets were owned by the company. These contradictory requirements caused frowns on the brows of insurance company lawyers. Nonetheless, a number of separate accounts were established and the conflict was avoided by pretending it was not there.

A better solution was suggested by a director of the Division of Investment Management, Alan Conwell, and this solution has now been adopted by almost every life insurance company. The assets of the separate account, Mr. Conwell suggested, could be invested entirely in the shares of one or more separate and distinct open-end management investment companies. The separate account could then register as a unit investment trust rather than as a management company. A unit investment trust does not have a board of directors, just a trustee, a requirement that could be waived by exemption under Section 6(c). That approach smoothed the furrowed brows.[31] Mr. Conwell also thought that this two-tier structure would solve another troublesome problem: how to forestall SEC regulation over the insurance features of the contracts, regulation that was not within its expertise and that it did not wish to exercise. As matters developed, however, this objective was not met.

As hinted above, it was not possible for variable annuity issuers to comply with every provision of the Act. Numerous exemptive rules have been issued, literally hundreds of individual exemptive orders have been granted, and scores of no-action letters have been issued to those issuers.[32] These exemptions and no-actions have enabled the contracts to be sold successfully. Sales for the last few years have been in the $50 billion per year range, not a large amount when compared with mutual fund sales but not insignificant, either. However, the commission's rigid and overboard interpretation of two central provisions of the Act has not only greatly increased the work of the staff by requiring the processing of the numerous exemptive orders that had to be granted, but also made necessary a number of somewhat fictional representations by issuers, concerning unreal conditions. The system works but it is rather creaky.

Because variable annuity contracts are treated as periodic payment plans under Section 27 of the Act, the issuers may not charge a sales load in excess of 9 percent per year. This limitation has not been a serious problem. Most variable annuities provide for a sales load that starts at 7 percent or 8 percent that is imposed upon redemption rather than sale, and reduces each year or two until it drops to zero in the 7th to 10th year. Because variable annuity contracts are periodic payment plan certificates and because the issuers are registered as unit investment trusts, the issuers must also comply with Section 26(a)(2)(C) of the Act. In relevant part this section provides:

> SEC. 26. (a) No principal underwriter for or depositor of a registered unit investment trust shall sell, except by surrender to the trustee for redemption, any security of which such trust is the issuer (other than short-term paper), unless the trust indenture, agreement of custodianship, or other instrument pursuant to which such security is issued—

* * *

(2) provides, in substance,

* * *

(C) that no payment to the depositor of or a principal underwriter for such trust, or to any affiliated person or agent of such depositor or underwriter, shall be allowed the trustee or custodian as an expense (except that provision may be made for the payment to any such person of a fee, not exceeding such reasonable amount as the Commission may prescribe as compensation for performing bookkeeping and other administrative services, of a character normally performed by the trustee or custodian itself);

Note that this section does not forbid a trustee from charging a reasonable fee or from making a profit for its services. The section was designed to prevent the proliferation of charges by the trust sponsor and to ensure that those charges were not excessive.

In addition to the disappearing sales load (which, as noted, is zero for contracts that are held for several years), the insurance company's major charge is a "mortality and expense risk" charge. This is always a percentage of net assets, deducted daily at an equivalent rate of from 50 to 140 basis points per year. Many insurers also make a charge for administering the contract usually either an asset-based charge of about 15 basis points, or a per capita charge of about $25 to $30 per year, or both. A few insurers make other, smaller charges.

The commission has interpreted Section 26(a) to mean:

1. The insurance company must represent that all charges for performing administrative services are its actual cost, without profit. Why a profit-making corporation that is in the business of administering contracts, among other things, should be required to perform that function without profit and why the language of Section 26(a)(2) requires such action is not clear. Nonetheless, that is now settled doctrine.

2. No deduction or charge of *any* kind can be made from the assets of a separate account without an exemptive order. That, of course, requires a finding that the exemption is consistent with the purposes and policies of the Act and with the protection of investors. In practical terms this means that the staff can control the amount of these charges.

Indeed, over the last two decades the industry and the commission have engaged in a polite tug-of-war over what charges may appropriately be made. To repeat, the commission does this job, but it doesn't like it and the 1940 Act study recommends that Congress should take this function away. Since that recommendation applies to all variable contracts, we describe it after our discussion of variable life insurance.

Variable Life Insurance

The path toward the erection of the regulatory scheme over variable life insurance has been even more tortuous and rock-strewn than those already discussed. Fortunately, a full description of how we got to where we are is not particularly illuminating and hence not relevant. For present purposes, it is enough to describe the contracts and the nature and extent of the regulation to which they are subject.

Variable life insurance contracts come in two forms, with variations upon each of the themes. Both forms are fairly complex, with the first to arrive on the scene, scheduled premium variable life insurance, more difficult to understand fully than the second, flexible premium or variable universal life insurance. As a result, the prospectuses are lengthy, often turgidly written, and so not as useful to prospective buyers as they might be. Also, they are boring, sometimes excruciatingly so. And it seems unlikely, for reasons discussed below, that despite cyclical commission agendas to simplify prospectuses and make them more user-friendly, including one movement actively underway in early 1996, there will be much improvement in the foreseeable future.

Scheduled premium variable life insurance is, loosely speaking, analogous to whole-life fixed-dollar insurance. A specified premium must be paid when due, or within a grace period, or the contract will lapse. The face amount of insurance is payable on death and the death benefit cannot drop below this amount as long as the contract remains in force. The benefit can go higher, however, since both the cash value and the death benefit vary so as to reflect the investment performance of the assets held in a separate account that support the payment of contract benefits.[33] Paraphrasing Justice Douglas, there is no floor under the cash value—it can go to zero, or even lower—and, like the Dow, there is no ceiling. How the cash value varies is easy to explain. It goes up with each premium payment, down with each withdrawal, up or down by the contract's pro-rata share of each day's investment results, and down by the amounts of daily and monthly charges. How the death benefit varies is easily understood by any competent actuary.

The flexible or universal life contract is by far the one most widely sold today and is much simpler, although that may not be immediately apparent from reading the prospectuses. It is structured around a Contract

Fund to which all net premiums (gross or actual premiums paid less charges) are credited. Investment results are credited daily. Other charges are deducted daily or monthly. The principal charges are sales load (if not deducted from gross premium), administrative charges, a mortality and expense risk charge, and what can be thought of as a monthly term insurance charge generally called the *cost of insurance charge*. There are usually two forms of a flexible contract, a level death benefit form (many insurers call this Option A) and a variable death benefit form (Option B). Under the level benefit form, the contract fund value and the cash surrender value (the contract fund less surrender charges, if any) change daily but the death benefit remains fixed.[34] Under the variable benefit option the death benefit is generally a specified amount that is added to the changing contract fund value. Under either option premiums need not be paid regularly or in any specified amount although most insurers strongly urge that at least a target premium be paid. Payment of insufficient premiums greatly increases the chances of lapse, which occurs if the cash value drops too close to zero. Paying premiums that are too high can have adverse tax consequences.

The drafters or designers of fixed-dollar insurance contracts have always valued fair pricing and the availability of useful additional bells and whistles more than they value simplification and comprehensibility. It is anathema to an actuary that a shareholder of a mutual fund with shares valued at $5 million should pay 1 percent or $50,000 in fees and expenses while a shareholder holding shares worth $5,000 should be charged 1 percent or $50. Both shareholders get one prospectus and one annual report. So life insurance pricing marches to a different understanding of what constitutes equity or nondiscrimination. Also, the contracts have many features: partial withdrawals and loans that affect contract values in ways not instantly understandable, increases and decreases in face amount, a number of "riders" that offer inexpensive additional term insurance, protection against disability, protection against accidental death, and so forth. This culture has been carried over to variable life insurance contracts, and the disclosure requirements of the 1933 Act cannot be simplified by declaring these important features to be nonmaterial.

Tailoring the requirements of the 1940 Act, which itself has many technical provisions specifically drawn to regulate a unique form of enterprise and to make unlawful several abusive practices, that were identified in 1940, was obviously not simple. Elaborately constructed exemptions from a dozen of the Act's provisions were necessary. They are found in two exemptive rules, Rule 6e–2, applicable to scheduled premium contracts, and Rule 6e–3(T), applicable to flexible premium contracts.[35]

These rules grant exemptions from many provisions of the Act but the most controversial are the exemptions from Sections 26 and 27. Section 27 applies to "periodic payment plan certificates" and was drafted with a specific unusual security in mind. Beginning in the 1930s and continuing until the early 1970s, "contractual plans for the acquisition of mutual fund shares" were sold in significant amounts. These were contracts to purchase mutual fund shares on an installment basis. The issuers were registered as unit investment trusts and, as originally enacted, Section 27 authorized the deduction of a 50 percent sales load of the first year's payment, in addition to the sales load on the mutual fund shares. When, as was often the case, later installment payments were not made, the permissible 9 percent load on the aggregate of the planned installment payments was exceeded. A major commission study in 1966 spoke harshly of the issuers of these securities[36] and a major objective of the 1970 amendments, referred to earlier, was to put the scoundrels out of business. The industry fought back, however, and the compromise took the form of the refund and notice provisions that are now included in Section 27.[37]

Section 26 also applied to periodic payment plan certificates and, more directly, to the registered unit trusts that issued the contractual plans. Section 26 limits the trustee's or custodian's fees to those set forth in the trust instrument and actually incurred. It also prohibits the trustee from subcontracting bookkeeping and administrative functions back to the sponsor of the plan unless the payment qualifies as reasonable (see page 47).

Variable life insurance contracts, like variable annuity contracts, fall within the definition of a periodic payment plan certificate. In its petitions for exemption, the industry pointed out that variable contracts were as similar to contractual plans as the moon was to cream cheese and sought extensive exemption from what it asserted were the inapplicable and inappropriate proscriptions of these sections. The commission agreed that the two securities were altogether different but couldn't bring itself to give away the entire store, which is what the commission perceived the industry to be asking. The end result is that the registered investment companies that issue variable life insurance contracts are subject to quantitative restrictions that go beyond those applicable to any other investment company currently offering securities and which, in many respects, are more severe than is justified:

- Sales loads are held to maximums that are too low.
- Mortality and expense risk charges were for many years subject to illogical and unsupportable maximums although there are recent signs that the constraints may be loosening.[37]
- The elaborate services performed in administering these contracts—a major part of the business of the issuers—have to be done under the pressure of a formal representation that they are being performed at actual cost.

These artificial restrictions have not halted the sale of variable life insurance. Life insurance companies have learned to design their contracts so that they satisfy the restrictions and conditions imposed by the exemptive rules. However, the contracts are not as good, not as equitable and, perhaps, not even as cheap as they would be if these restrictions were removed.

To its great credit the SEC staff that prepared the 1992 study of the 1940 Act concluded that the commission should get out of the business of regulating prices. Their report recommended that Sections 26 and 27 be amended so as to be inapplicable to variable contracts and that a new section be added requiring the issuer to represent only that their charges are reasonable in the aggregate. Regrettably, although over three years have passed since the study was published, no action has yet been taken to act upon this recommendation.[39]

In addition to providing an alternative to whole-life or fixed-dollar universal life insurance to people who seek to protect their families against the economic hardship that often follows an early death, variable life insurance is being purchased with other objectives in mind. It is useful in estate planning. Corporations purchase it to fund supplementary benefit plans that do not qualify under Section 401 and to fund other corporate obligations such as medical care or severance payments. This branch of the business is referred to as corporate owned life insurance (COLI). As sales of this kind increase in volume, the level of interest and concern of the tax-writing committees of the Congress grow correspondingly. Legislation is likely soon to be adopted that reduces but does not eliminate entirely the tax advantage of this type of funding.

LIKELY FUTURE DEVELOPMENTS

Looking briefly at the several products and areas discussed in this chapter permits some predictions to be made.

1. Fixed-Dollar Annuity Contracts   Life insurance companies will continue to devise innovative contracts or features that will not fit within the Rule 151 safe harbor and will raise questions about whether they are within Section 3(a)(8). For example, contracts that guarantee a minimum return, say 3 percent, and promise to credit an additional amount tied to a stock index have begun to emerge. The SEC staff is not likely to be aggressive in this area, and whether the contracts will be registered will depend upon how bold or conservative the issuer's lawyers are. The reaction of the courts may also be affected by whether they revive the Brennan analysis in *VALIC*.

2. Insured Benefit Plan Funding   Through inertia the industry is likely to maintain, though not increase, its share of the defined benefit plan market. The grave uncertainties created by the Supreme Court's *Harris Trust* decision may be resolved by administrative or even legislative action, but more likely the industry will learn to live with the uncertainty and hope to do better with the litigation that is certain to emerge.

As the movement from defined-benefit to defined-contribution plans continues, life insurance participation through GICs will probably be maintained. Legal issues may emerge in connection with the use of GICs in the tax-deferred or 403(b) market where the exemption of Section 3(a)(2) is not available.[40]

3. Separate Account Employee Benefit Funding   The ICI effort to repeal Section 3(a)(2) for 401(k) and other defined-contribution plans will probably not bear fruit. The mutual funds are satisfactorily increasing their market share, without repeal, and that is likely to continue. Conceivably, the development of a better product combined with quality servicing will bring some of this business back to the banks and insurance companies. No significant legal issues are likely to be raised.

4. Nonqualified Variable Annuities   The regulatory climate here is stable and not likely to be an important factor. Whether variable annuity sales will continue to stay at the $50 billion annual level where they are today is uncertain. Despite the intense search for increased federal revenue, the tax advantage provided by variable annuities will probably remain. But tax-deferral is advantageous only when an investment is held for at least 10 years or more and it is sharply diminished if the cost differential, when compared with competing taxable products, becomes too high. If experience demonstrates, as it will in many cases, that the advantages have been oversold, there could be an adverse market reaction. Any significant reduction in the capital gains tax rate could eliminate the tax advantage now enjoyed by owners of variable annuity contracts.

5. Variable Life Insurance   Premium receipts, which are probably about 10 percent of variable annuity sales today, will surely show a steady increase, for several reasons. First, and most important, variable life insurance is an excellent product that will almost certainly produce greater benefits for each premium dollar than the fixed-dollar products it will slowly replace. Simply put, it's a better buy. The contracts and prospectuses are still too hard to understand but agent familiarity and improved sales literature will be significant factors.

Second, the regulatory climate is certain to improve. The current House of Representatives has a majority of members who firmly believe that much administrative regulation is unnecessary and unduly burdensome to the business community. Where an agency staff itself has singled out statutory provisions that can be so characterized, it seems inconceivable that the recommendations of the 1940 Act study will not be acted upon. If that occurs, there will be a new round of improved contracts, always a stimulant to increased sales.

Finally, a registration form specifically designed for variable life insurance is likely to be adopted in the next two years. At the suggestion of the SEC's Office of Insurance Products, the American Council of Life Insurance, aided by representatives from many companies who worked long and hard, drafted a proposed Form N–6 that would be used to register variable life insurance contracts instead of the inappropriate Form S–6 that is now used. The commission has repeatedly said that this is a high priority item and has said it again recently. Shortage of personnel and higher priority projects have combined to delay the introduction of the new form. At some point soon, however, this project is likely to move forward. We can hope that this form, when adopted, will lack some of the rigidity that now characterizes Forms N1–A, N–3 and

N–4. Long years ago there was a weak joke that the SEC staff required all disclosure to be divided into two categories, favorable to the offering and unfavorable; and that all the information in the latter category had to be put on the cover page of the prospectus. The current staff is not subject to that not entirely unwarranted charge. Something remains, however, in the insistence upon slavish adherence to the letter of the items in the applicable forms.[41]

A side benefit will be clarification of what may appropriately be shown in variable life illustrations. By far the most instructive and useful sales literature takes the form of individualized illustrations that depict what cash values and death benefits would be under a contract purchased by a person of the same age, sex, and risk category as the prospective purchaser, under any chosen assumption about future investment returns. These are frequently referred to as ledger statements and are available on agents' laptops with increasingly accurate and sophisticated software. With appropriate regulation, these presentations will have something like the uniformity the commission has achieved with respect to mutual fund performance data, without sacrificing the flexibility that enables the prospective purchaser to be given the information and data useful to informed purchases. At present the illustration formats of the many issuers are so different that only the most knowledgeable purchaser can use these illustrations to make intelligent comparisons between competing products. So also efforts to show how actual past investment performance translates into contract values have gone off into many directions. Greater uniformity is desirable. There is some useful work to be done here. One small but important improvement would be to replace the gross return that every illustration now uses—a concept unknown to and unused by anyone else in the investment community as a measure of investment performance and the result of an historical accident.[42] Illustrations should start instead with the total return of the underlying fund, a performance measurement already familiar to and understood by most investors.

In short, variable life insurance in the next decade will become a major product of the industry producing a much larger share of annual gross revenues than it does today, provided it is allowed, by the SEC and the NASD to be given the improved market support that it deserves.

E N D N O T E S

1. "The business of insurance, and every person engaged therein, shall be subject to the laws of the several States which relate to the regulation and taxation of such business...No Act of Congress shall be construed to invalidate, impair or supersede any law enacted by any State for the purpose of regulating the business of insurance...unless such act specifically relates to the business of insurance...." See *Prudential Ins. Co.* v. *Benjamin*, 408 U.S. 408, 429 (1940).

2. Throughout this chapter we will cite significant decisions or administrative actions. We will not make any effort, however, to provide complete documentation, which would both extend the length unduly and severely impair its readability. For those interested in the detail of the changing patterns of regulation and of the issues, The American Law Institute–American Bar Association Committee on Continuing Education (ALI/ABA) has held an annual conference on life insurance products, and the published "faculty" outlines provide a wealth of detail that is often not available through the customary research sources.

3. See *National Underwriter*, Nov. 20, 1995, page 1. Although it is not immediately apparent into which group they fall, Prudential assuredly did not withdraw from what has often been thought of as a separate category called "group life insurance" or from the major function of funding and administering employee retirement plans and programs.

4. Health insurance, which was an early addition to these three elements of the business, involves only to a trivial extent the evaluation of "life contingencies"—the rates at which people live and die—the hallmark of life insurance. A significant source of regulation of life insurance companies is the objective of ensuring that contractual obligations involving life contingencies that are to be carried out many years in the future will, in fact, be kept. Other sources of that regulation are public policies that prohibit making certain promises, that prevent charging excessive prices, and that require fair sales practices and business conduct. Entities other than life insurance companies, which are not comparably regulated, also deal with life contingencies—notably the employers who establish, and the trustees who administer, defined-benefit pension plans (and, therefore, need the help of actuaries).

5. These simplistic statements ignore the far more sophisticated reserving and financial statement requirements introduced in recent years, which are also outside the scope of this chapter. Insurance companies are also required, in addition to establishing reserve liabilities representing their obligations to pay future benefits, to establish asset valuation and interest maintenance reserves (AVR and IMR) designed to mitigate

losses in asset values attributable to changes in equity prices and changes in interest rates. Increased protection against insolvency is also provided by the introduction of the concept of risk-based capital. See the N.A.I.C. Risk-Based Capital for Life and/or Health Insurers Model Act.

6. This is not to say that state regulation has not long been intensely concerned with adequacy of disclosure, possible fraud or misrepresentation, and abusive sales practices. A lengthy and abstruse Model Life Insurance Illustration Law, currently about to be adopted, is a recent product of those concerns.

7. It is interesting, in connection with pending litigation concerning the authority of banks to issue annuity contracts and the taxability of such contracts, that this section is satisfied if the issuer is regulated by a "bank commissioner" or the equivalent. I leave to the others to delve into the legislative history to discover how this phrase chanced to be included in this provision.

8. Jumping the gun slightly, these contracts generally are not subject to federal securities laws not so much because they are not regarded as securities but because the overwhelming majority are issued in connection with employee retirement plans that meet the requirements for qualification under §401(a) of the Internal Revenue Code. Such contracts, through amendments in 1970 and 1980, are exempt from registration by §3(a)(2) of the 1933 Act and their issuers and distributors enjoy exemptions from the other two securities laws.

9. See, for example, *Otto* v. *Variable Annuity Life Insurance Company*, 814 F.2d 1127 (7th Cir. 1986) *cert. den.* 486 U.S. 1026 (1988); *Home Life Ins. Co.* v. *Associates in Adolescent Psychiatry*, 941 F.2d 561 (7th Cir. 1991).

10. The current value is basically the net purchase payment plus all interest credited to the redemption date.

11. For purposes of avoiding unwarranted reserve requirements under state insurance law, something known as a *non-unitized separate account* may be used and state regulations deal explicitly with this product. Although the commission staff had a flurry of interest in whether these special separate accounts might raise problems under the 1940 Act, that appears to have dissipated, and rightly so. See *Equitable Life Assurance Society* (pub. available Dec. 22, 1995) withdrawing *The Travelers T-Mark Annuity* (pub. available May 13, 1933) and *Fortis Benefits Insurance Company* (pub. available June 8, 1993).

12. If the decision to provide equity funding had first been made in the 1980s instead of the early 1960s, the simple solution would have been

the establishment of subsidiary banks or trust companies to conduct this business. In the earlier period, however, the establishment of a subsidiary of this kind by an insurance company, and particularly by a mutual life insurance company, was unaccountably considered unthinkable. It is interesting to speculate about what kind of federal regulation would have occurred had such an approach been taken. The only thing that can be said for certain is that regulation would have been quite different from what it is today.

13. We omit, except for a brief mention in connection with separate account funding, another major product of life insurance companies, the guaranteed investment contract (GIC), together with the separate account GIC. Initially, the GIC was a medium-term group annuity contract issued primarily to defined benefit plan trustees. Its more significant and important use is to provide "benefit sensitive" fixed-interest-rate investment options in defined contribution plans. Most commonly, these provide a stated interest return for a five-year period with restrictions on large scale withdrawals by employers or trustees but permitting withdrawals or transfers by participants. Quite often these options are provided by a small pool of GICs of different insurers.

14. The Treasury regulations included requirements that plan assets be held and managed solely for plan participants and regulations concerning funding and fiduciary conduct, but they had nothing like the significance or effect of the similar requirements enacted by ERISA.

15. Much of the Act was drafted, if not exactly in haste, under conditions not conducive to precision. Multiple congressional committees, each jealous of its jurisdiction and control, held hearings and prepared drafts. The final terms of the Act were hammered out in lengthy conference committee meetings, with the helpful participation of interested and affected companies, always in the wings and sometimes in attendance.

16. This is not as simple as it sounds. Elaborate class exemptions had to be requested, negotiated, and finally adopted in order to validate many ordinary course-of-business transactions.

17. The Department of Labor agreed and soon after the adoption of ERISA issued an interpretive bulletin stating that the receipt of contributions under a fixed-dollar insured plan would not cause the assets of the insurance company to be "plan assets" for purposes of the prohibited transaction provisions. Interpretive Bulletin 75–2, 29 C.F.R. § 2509.75–2(b) (1992).

18. See Section 401(b)(2) of ERISA. In subsection (B), the term is defined to mean a policy "to the extent that such policy provides for benefits, the amount of which is guaranteed by the insurer." An exception to the

exception follows, which is meaningless unless the context is provided. The subsection states that a guaranteed benefit policy excludes the assets held in a separate account except for those assets that are "any surplus in a separate account." Evidently, at least one of the participants in the drafting process was aware that although the assets held in separate accounts were generally to be regarded as plan assets, it was often the case that something less than 100 percent of those assets "belonged to" or were "owned by" the employee retirement plan or plans. Insurance companies could own an undivided percentage of the separate account assets because they had contributed some seed money to get the separate account started or because periodic charges made against the assets of the account might not be withdrawn on a daily basis. As a practical matter, this "exception to the exception" is quite meaningless. Its existence does confirm, however, the drafters' inadequate understanding of how the Act would apply to this kind of funding.

19. The 1939 code was significantly rewritten in 1954 and section 165 became section 401 of the Internal Revenue Code of 1954.

20. *Prudential Insurance Co. of America* (pub. available Oct. 7, 1963).

21. See Release Nos. 33–6188 (Feb. 1, 1980) and 33–6281 (Jan. 15, 1981).

22. At the time these plans could be funded only by annuity contracts, giving insurance companies monopoly. Subsequently, mutual fund funding was authorized.

23. Banks were already excluded from the definition of *broker* and *dealer* in Section 3(a)(4) of the Securities and Exchange Act. The insurance companies doubted that they could obtain a similar exemption from Congress. They settled for a provision, section (3)(a)(12)(A)(iv), declaring interests in excluded separate accounts to be exempted securities. Hence, these could be "sold" by persons who were not registered broker-dealers or registered representatives of such persons. Some of the provisions of the 1934 Act, however, for example Section 10, apply to securities rather than exempted securities. Thus, receipt of plan contributions must be confirmed by any broker who participates in effecting the transaction, a requirement that has largely been ignored.

24. In describing the collective trusts of which banks were trustees, the drafters of these sections inadvertently used the term "trusts maintained by a bank." The commission staff seized upon this language to deny the exclusion of bank-established trusts with portfolios that were managed by unaffiliated advisers. This position, now a settled one, was established in a large number of no-action letters.

25. Those submissions told a very different story about the genesis of the 1970 amendments than that set forth in the text. The ICI asserted that

the proponent of the legislation was the banking rather than the insurance industry. But that was supposition rather than fact.

26. See Chapter 10.

27. *National Underwriter*, Nov. 20, 1995, page 3.

28. American Council of Life Insurance, 1995 Life Insurance Fact Book Update (supplementing the 1994 Fact Book). The statistics from different sources do not always coincide. A 1995 study of 401(k) plans by the Investment Company Institute also shows (p. 7) insurance companies with a 34 percent share at the end of 1993 (down from 40 percent in 1988) and mutual funds with a 26 percent share (up from 14 percent in 1988). The same report (p. 44) states that GICs account for 30 percent of all 401(k) plan assets.

29. The two giant mutual insurance companies—The Prudential and the Metropolitan—had sharply conflicting views about the desirability of introducing variable annuities. The Metropolitan believed that the cobblers should stick to their lasts and offer only products with guaranteed investment returns. The Prudential favored the development of the new product. The two companies were on opposite sides on the many occasions when each state considered legislation that would authorize issuance of the new product. In the end the Prudential prevailed and today, of course, the Metropolitan is a major player in the market.

30. As stated above, there is grist here for scholars of the Court. Justice Brennan has many devoted admirers but opponents criticize him as more interested in the outcome of great constitutional issues and cases involving civil liberties than in close legal analysis. Why, one may wonder, did he take the time and effort to think so hard and well—and to win over an adherent—about this boring technical subject, one in which the Court as a whole could hardly have been much interested? The answer may be, simply, that he was a very good judge who did his job conscientiously.

31. Initially, the sponsoring insurance company advised and managed these underlying funds. In due course a number of prominent mutual fund advisers created funds that sold shares only to separate accounts of many different life insurance companies that were either too small or lacked the expertise to create funds of their own. Soon thereafter some of the larger insurance companies concluded that these funds added customer appeal. Both "captive" and "shared" funds must, for tax reasons, sell shares only to insurance companies or tax-favored retirement plans. See IRC Section 817(h).

32. See Rules 6c–3, 6c–6, 6c–7, 6c–8, 14a–2, 22d–2, 22e–1, and 26a–2.

33. As is the case with variable annuities, the assets are generally allocated to separate accounts, each of which holds shares in an underlying captive or shared mutual fund.

34. Well, almost. If the cash value gets high enough the death benefit, which must be a multiple of the cash value (the multiple decreases with age) in order to satisfy the IRC definition of life insurance in Section 7702, will increase over the guaranteed initial face amount.

35. Rule 6e–2 drew heavily upon an early exemptive order issued to The Equitable Life Assurance Society for which Harry Walker, an Equitable actuary, and Gary O. Cohen, a Washington lawyer, were primarily responsible. Stephen E. Roth, also a Washington lawyer, pulled the laboring oar in drafting the industry petition that led to Rule 6e–3(T).

36. *SEC, Public Policy Implications of Investment Company Growth,* H.R. Rep. No. 2337, 89th Cong., 2nd Sess. (1966).

37. In fact, although it was not clear who won the battle, the commission won the war. The new Section 27 proved too difficult for the issuers of contractual plans to live with, in other words, to market the securities successfully. Sales fell sharply and are insignificant today.

38. These restrictions were the work of a one-person legislature, a Chief of the Office of Insurance Products of the Division of Investment Management. Using average charges of contracts already on the market, he let it be known that hearings would be held on any exemptive applications where the M&E charge for variable annuities exceeded 1.25 percent, were higher than 0.5 percent on scheduled life insurance contracts or 0.90 percent on flexible contracts. This meant, for an issuer anxious to bring a new contract to market, a delay of one or two years. Not one company accepted the challenge.

39. In March 1966 a bill was introduced in the House of Representatives that would carry out these recommendations. Passage remains uncertain, although at the time this was written the prospects that the bill would be adopted were increasing.

40. Through the issuance of a large number of no-action letters, the SEC staff has confirmed that deferred compensation plans adopted by governmental agencies, which meet the requirements of I.R.C. §457, will be regarded as "governmental plans" within the meaning of Section 3(a)(2). That interpretation is likely to hold.

41. A sharp reader may find an inconsistency between this criticism and the praise given to the staff on page 34, *supra.* Oddly enough, both statements are true. Where a contract must be registered on a wholly inappropriate form because there is no other available, the staff has been sensible and flexible in striving for useful disclosure rather than responses to each item. After creating a special form (such as N–1A or N–4), literal and precise compliance with each item on the form has been the general practice.

42. It was Justice Holmes who observed that "[i]t is revolting to have no better reason for a rule of law than that it was laid down in the time of Henry IV. It is still more revolting if the grounds upon which it was laid down have vanished long since, and the rule simply persists from blind imitation of the past." Holmes, *The Path of The Law*, reprinted in *The Common Law and Other Writings* (Legal Classics Library, 1982) p. 187.

3

BANK SALES AND UNDERWRITING OF INVESTMENT PRODUCTS

Diane E. Ambler, *Mayer, Brown & Platt**

Commercial banks have aggressively expanded their traditional role in the financial services community and have revolutionized their profile as distribution channels for mutual fund securities and insurance products. In part, their success can be attributed to their broad retail customer base and customer service expertise. It may also reflect a competitive response to the erosion of commercial banks' traditional depository and lending businesses caused by the popularity of mutual funds and other investment products. Whatever the reason, in today's world of heightened competition for investor dollars, commercial banks now offer retail customers a variety of investment products, such as mutual funds and annuities, as well as investment-related services, such as mutual fund asset allocation programs.

Favorable rulings by bank regulators and courts, as discussed in greater detail below, have enabled banks, bank holding companies and other affiliated nonbank entities (nonbank institutions) to make significant inroads recently into markets traditionally reserved for securities

*The author gratefully acknowledges the assistance of C. Dirk Peterson in the preparation of this chapter.

dealers and insurance companies. With these new markets come new and unfamiliar regulators. As banking institutions adjust their business structures to accommodate sales of mutual funds, annuities, and other investment products, they must bend to complex and often competing regulatory requirements, at both the federal and the state level, that apply to govern these securities and insurance sales activities. At the same time, commercial banks' firm resistance to these regulatory structures is indelibly reshaping the industry as a whole.

This chapter will discuss the primary regulatory and judicial developments that have paved the way for banks and nonbank institutions to have so radically redirected their focus into the securities and insurance markets. The first section of this chapter addresses banks' expanding roles in the distribution of securities and insurance products. The second section addresses the potential for bank underwriting of securities and insurance products.

BANK DISTRIBUTION OF SECURITIES AND INSURANCE PRODUCTS

The role of commercial banks in the distribution of securities and insurance products shatters old notions of traditional banking activities, which served as the backdrop of federal and state regulation for over two generations. Commercial banks' advances into these areas have successfully tested the bases of long-standing restrictions in the banking laws; yet, banks resist the regulation associated with these expanded activities. At the same time, entering the world of nondepository sales activities is causing for commercial banks and nonbank institutions to take stock of their existing marketing and compensation structures in light of the new regulations to which they become subject.

Banking Regulation of Bank Securities Activities

The extent of permissible bank securities activities is regulated, first, by federal and state banking laws. The bank regulatory structure in the United States is a dual system, meaning that depository banking institutions and their affiliates are organized under and primarily supervised by either federal authority, state authority, or both. At the federal level, the National Bank Act and the Bank Holding Company Act of 1956 (BHCA) apply to national banks and bank holding companies respectively.

State-chartered banks are subject to the state banking law in the state where they are chartered. In general, banking laws are designed primarily to ensure the safety and soundness of the financial institution.

Regulators in the bank regulatory system include the Office of the Comptroller of the Currency (OCC), which has oversight of national banks; the Board of Governors of the Federal Reserve System (board), which has oversight of bank holding companies, other nonbank institutions, and state-chartered banks that are members of the Federal Reserve System; the Federal Deposit Insurance Corporation (FDIC), which provides permanent deposit insurance to eligible commercial banks; and the state banking commissioner of the particular state in which a state-chartered bank, whether or not a member of the Federal Reserve System, is chartered.

Federal Banking Law—Background

The principal restrictions against commercial banks engaging in securities activities are derived from four provisions of the Banking Act of 1933, commonly known as the Glass-Steagall Act (Glass-Steagall).[1] Glass-Steagall, adopted along with the Securities Act of 1933 and other reforms responsive to the decline in the financial markets and economic collapse of the Great Depression, is generally regarded as separating the depository functions of commercial banks from the securities activities of investment banks. To this end, Glass-Steagall prevents commercial banks from engaging in securities underwriting activities or acting as principal in securities transactions, practices viewed as compromising a bank's safety and soundness.[2] In addition, Glass-Steagall prohibits affiliations between commercial and investment banks, either through ownership or overlapping management.[3]

Glass-Steagall, however, does not prohibit all banks from engaging in securities activities absolutely.[4] Among other things, national banks are permitted to purchase "investment securities," defined as marketable obligations evidencing indebtedness "in the form of bonds, notes and/or debentures commonly known as investment securities" (but not the shares of stock of any corporation) subject to OCC regulations.[5] In addition, Glass-Steagall does not prohibit national banks generally from acting in an agency capacity when engaged in a securities transaction for a customer.[6]

The BHCA governs the scope of securities activities for bank holding companies and their nonbank subsidiaries and, like Glass-Steagall, is intended to separate the banking functions of bank holding companies from investment-related functions of other entities.[7] In general, bank holding companies are able to perform nonbanking activities if the activity is closely related to banking and the public interest served by the activity outweighs any possible adverse consequences.[8]

The BHCA prohibits any company that owns or controls a bank[9] from acquiring proprietary interests in any organization other than a bank, subject to specified exemptions.[10] One of the most significant of these exemptions, and the one that has authorized the greatest expansion for securities activities of nonbank institutions, is a provision giving the board authority to permit bank holding company ownership of any nonbank institution whose activities are "so closely related to banking or managing or controlling banks as to be a proper incident thereto."[11] The board maintains a "laundry list" of permissible nonbank activities that satisfy these requirements in its Regulation Y,[12] which has significantly grown to encompass broader securities-related activities in recent years.[13]

Over the past decade, the board also has vastly expanded the scope of activities of bank holding company nonbank subsidiaries, known as Section 20 subsidiaries, through broad interpretations, that have largely withstood judicial challenge.[14] The board has also successively loosened so-called firewall limitations on the extent of securities-related activities of Section 20 subsidiaries.[15] The considerations underlying the Board's actions relate to Glass-Steagall's goals of preventing conflicts of interest, unsound banking practices, and unfair competition.

State Banking Law—Background

State-chartered banks can become member banks of the Federal Reserve System (state member banks), in which case they are regulated and examined by the board in addition to the state banking authority, or they can be solely state-chartered banks (state nonmember banks), in which case they are regulated by the FDIC as well as by the state banking authority. State member banks are subject to the securities restrictions of Glass-Steagall in the same manner as national banks and generally are granted powers no greater than those granted to bank holding companies.[16]

State nonmember banks are insured by the FDIC and are primarily regulated by their state banking authority. State nonmember banks may enjoy greater permissiveness than national banks, state member banks, or bank holding companies when it comes to certain securities activities, depending on authority granted under their relevant state law.

Notwithstanding this potential for greater freedom, the relatively recent Federal Deposit Insurance Corporation Improvement Act of 1991[17] now essentially prevents a state nonmember bank from engaging in activities and investments not allowed a national bank. As such, state nonmember banks may only engage as principal in those activities, including securities-related activities, in which a national bank may engage as principal.[18] Certain restrictions also apply to an insured state nonmember bank's establishment or acquisition of a securities subsidiary.[19]

Bank Securities Powers—Overview

Although the provisions of Glass-Steagall (principally Section 20 and Section 16) were originally structured in 1933 to separate commercial banking from investment banking activities, these restrictions have been actively and effectively eroded by regulatory and judicial interpretations over the course of the past 15 years. Based in part on the belief, perhaps, that Glass-Steagall may have unnecessarily duplicated of the protections afforded by the federal securities laws, the banking agencies and the federal courts have expanded the range of securities products and services that commercial banks can provide as agent and broadened permissible affiliations between banks and securities firms engaged in brokerage activities.

Section 20 prohibits a bank's affiliation with any entity that is "engaged principally in the issue, flotation, underwriting, public sale, or distribution...of stocks, bonds, debentures, notes, or other securities."[20] Section 16 prohibits national banks from dealing in or underwriting securities except for the purchase and sale of securities "without recourse, solely upon the order, and for the account of, customers, and in no case for its own account." Thus, a national bank may purchase and sell securities on an agency basis for its customers. The extent to which national banks may provide brokerage services for investment products has been, over time, tested, clarified and expanded.[21]

The authority of national banks to provide brokerage services to the general public was established by a federal district court decision that upheld the OCC's approval, in 1982, of the ownership of discount brokerage firms[22] by national banks.[23] The court observed that Glass-Steagall prohibits national banks only from underwriting securities issues or otherwise acting in the capacity of principal in effecting securities transactions, and does not prohibit a bank from acting as agent for existing and potential customers.[24] Similar authority was approved shortly thereafter for bank holding companies, and it was ultimately affirmed by the Supreme Court.[25]

Armed with the authority to offer brokerage services to a broad customer base, banks naturally entered the mutual fund arena, with its obvious broad appeal to retail investors. Approval of bank mutual fund sales activity began with an OCC interpretive letter issued in 1985, which allowed a national bank to execute mutual fund share orders as agent and provide related administrative, but not advisory, services to customers.[26] In consideration for mutual fund execution and administration services, the bank received customer service and 12b–1 fees.[27] The board followed suit and shortly thereafter authorized similar activities in the context of bank holding companies.[28]

The OCC's 1985 position, which established that banks could broker mutual fund shares, was expanded in 1987 to enable banks to add full-service brokerage and advisory services for customers to its mutual fund agency functions.[29] The board similarly permitted bank holding companies to engage in full-service brokerage activities through nonbank subsidiaries, and ultimately amended Regulation Y to add full-service brokerage to the "laundry list" of permissible nonbank activities.[30] Regulation Y also permits a bank holding company with full-service brokerage authority to provide discretionary investment management services to institutional customers.[31]

Subsequently, the OCC approved a proposal by a national bank to establish a subsidiary that would provide brokerage and advisory services for both proprietary and nonproprietary funds.[32] Similarly, the board permits bank holding company subsidiaries to engage in full-service brokerage activities with respect to proprietary and nonproprietary mutual funds.[33]

Securities Regulation of Bank Securities Activities

To the extent that commercial banks take advantage of their expanded authority to enter the securities marketplace, they subject themselves to regulation under an intricate securities law structure, at both the federal and the state level, that for the past 60 years has developed separately from regulation of traditional bank depository activities.

At the same time that Congress acted to isolate commercial banking from investment banking in Glass-Steagall, it embarked on the creation of a well-ordered structure for the regulation of all aspects of investment banking and other securities activities. It first passed the Securities Act of 1933 (Securities Act)[34] a few weeks before Glass-Steagall, which established disclosure requirements for offering and selling securities to the public. The Securities Act was followed a year later by the Securities Exchange Act of 1934 (the Exchange Act),[35] which created the Securities and Exchange Commission (SEC), established a foundation for the regulation of brokers, dealers, and securities exchanges, and prohibited manipulative and deceptive acts and practices in the sale of securities. Within several years Congress also passed the Investment Company Act of 1940 (Investment Company Act)[36] and the Investment Advisers Act of 1940,[37] which respectively regulate the activities of investment companies, such as mutual funds, and investment advisers.

The SEC is charged with overseeing these federal securities laws. The National Association of Securities Dealers, Inc. (NASD), a self-regulatory organization (SRO) established under the authority of the Exchange Act, provides additional oversight of certain registered broker-dealers. The basic purpose of securities regulation, generally speaking, is the protection of investors and securities markets.

Federal Securities Law—Background

Although many securities-related activities now open to banks functionally fall within the activities regulated by the SEC, the banking industry has strongly opposed regulation as such, relying on bank exclusions from federal securities law regulation enacted when banks were performing their more traditional roles.[38]

The bank exclusions from the federal securities laws are construed narrowly, however, and may well be eliminated in the event of actual repeal of Glass-Steagall. Regardless of whether a bank exclusion may be literally available, many banks have more recently found it to their advantage to engage in securities distribution activities through affiliated nonbank entities registered under the federal securities laws.[39]

Broker-Dealer Regulation   In general, institutions or individuals that are in the business of effecting securities transactions on behalf of another person, as agent, are required to register with the SEC as a broker, unless an exclusion or exemption is available.[40]

Banks that satisfy the Exchange Act bank definition[41] enjoy a broad exclusion from broker-dealer regulation. National banks and state member banks, among others, are covered by the bank exclusion;[42] however, thrifts, credit unions, and federal savings banks are not similarly covered. By the same token, bank holding companies and nonbank institutions, even if affiliated with a national bank or state member bank, are unable to rely on this bank exclusion. Accordingly, any of these nonexcluded nonbank institutions that engage in providing brokerage services must be registered and regulated by the SEC and the NASD as broker-dealers.

Broker-dealer regulation consists of a comprehensive set of rules that, in general terms, subject an entity to the SEC's inspection and examination power,[43] net capital requirements,[44] recordkeeping requirements,[45] customer protection requirements,[46] and trading practice requirements.[47] In addition, broker-dealers that are registered with the SEC are required to become members of an SRO,[48] which, in the case of bank securities activities, would be the NASD. As an SRO, subject to SEC oversight, the NASD subjects its members to a separate set of rules designed generally to promote fairness and just and equitable principles of trade.[49]

Individuals engaged in the sale of securities on behalf of a broker-dealer firm are deemed "associated persons" (e.g., registered representatives) of the broker-dealer firm.[50] Essentially, this means that a broker-dealer is responsible for supervising its registered representatives and ensuring that they comply with the federal securities laws. Associated persons are required to be registered with the NASD,[51] not the SEC, and must satisfy NASD examination requirements.[52]

Investment Adviser Regulation   Institutions or individuals that perform investment advisory functions for customer accounts or for mutual funds generally must register with the SEC under the Advisers Act as an investment adviser.[53] The Advisers Act contains a bank exclusion from investment adviser regulation, much like that under the Exchange Act.[54] As stated above, not all banks can rely on this exclusion, and neither can nonbank institutions, such as nonbank subsidiaries or affiliates.

Accordingly, a bank that provides investment advice to individual or institutional customers or to mutual funds through a nonbank affiliate must register that affiliate with the SEC as an investment adviser. Although investment adviser regulation does not involve nearly the level of regulation as does broker-dealer regulation, the Advisers Act generally deems investment advisers to be fiduciaries of their customers, if the customer has put reliance and trust in the advice that an adviser provides,[55] and therefore must act in the customer's best interests.[56] In addition, investment advisers must maintain certain records,[57] make certain disclosures to clients when acting as principal for its own account and otherwise not engage in fraudulent practices,[58] and comply with compensation and solicitation prohibitions.[59]

Regulation of Asset Allocation Programs   Many financial institutions, including commercial banks, offer investment management services in the form of asset allocation programs that allocate an investor's portfolio among various asset classes to achieve a certain balance between investment risk and potential gains.[60] In any asset allocation program, the provider of the service analyzes a customer's financial goals and selects the optimal mix of investments, including mutual funds, to maximize these goals.

Offering asset allocation programs raises various issues under the federal securities laws. If the program appears to pool customer funds or accounts, it might create a separate investment company, requiring registration under the Investment Company Act, and a separate investment company security, requiring registration under the Securities Act. When the underlying investments offered through the program include mutual fund shares, it may create a "fund of funds."[61]

The SEC has proposed a rule that would address these issues by providing a nonexclusive safe harbor from registration, subject to certain conditions designed to ensure that the advisory programs provide individualized investment advice.[62] Among other things, the proposed rule requires sponsors of programs intending to rely on the rule to file a notice with the SEC and subject themselves to SEC inspection. Thus, under the proposed rule, commercial banks could subject themselves to SEC jurisdiction by virtue of selling mutual funds in a manner that has the potential for creating, in effect, a regulated investment company product.

State Blue-Sky Law—Background

Broker-dealers and investment advisers are also subject to regulation by state securities laws, known as blue-sky laws, that impose their own broker-dealer and investment adviser registration and regulatory requirements. Although many state laws contain bank and even bank holding company exclusions from broker-dealer and investment adviser regulation,[63] others do not.[64] States also require the registration and examination of associated persons of a broker-dealer[65] and of an investment adviser.[66]

Each state statute and regulation is subject to its own interpretation and nuances. Thus, a bank is best advised to examine the laws of each state in which it intends to engage in a securities business.

Regulation of Bank Insurance Activities—Overview

As in the securities context, the permissibility of bank sales of insurance and annuity products is governed by federal and state banking laws and regulations. In addition, state insurance laws and regulatory requirements also govern these sales within a given jurisdiction, typically through the imposition of licensing requirements and sales practice restrictions, and may limit or even prohibit insurance product sales by banking institutions or their affiliates. Moreover, because variable annuities have conventional insurance features as well as fluctuating investment features of securities, they are also regulated under federal and state securities laws.[67] Although the authority of banks to broker securities has become settled to some extent, the authority of banks to distribute insurance products has been the focus of more recent challenges.

Bank Insurance Powers

National banks rely on two provisions of the National Bank Act for authority to engage in the sale of insurance products to customers. The incidental powers clause, Section 24 (Seventh) of the National Bank Act, broadly authorizes banks to exercise "all such incidental powers as shall be necessary to carry on the business of banking."[68] Section 92 of the National Bank Act, the small town exception, more specifically allows national banks to engage in a general insurance business, but only if the bank is located and does business in a town where the population is 5,000 or less.[69] At least one court has interpreted the small town exception to implicitly prohibit insurance activities by banks located in larger communities.[70]

For many years national banks have engaged in certain insurance-related activities as incidental to their traditional deposit-taking business. Obvious examples are national bank sales of credit life insurance, credit health and accident insurance, credit disability insurance, and mortgage life and disability insurance.[71] Other examples include bank sales of involuntary unemployment insurance,[72] vendor's single interest insurance (a form of credit-related property damage insurance),[73] and title insurance.[74] In contrast, national banks can sell traditional life insurance only under the small town exception.[75]

In 1990, the OCC boldly authorized the brokerage subsidiary of a national bank—one not located in a small town—to act as agent in the sale of fixed and variable annuities to bank customers.[76] In granting this authority, the OCC concluded that the brokerage of annuities is incidental to the business of banking, under the incidental powers clause, and that annuities are not "insurance" for purposes of the small town exception but financial instruments that national banks inherently may broker. Concerned that the OCC's conclusion that annuities are not "insurance" would undermine the important tax-deferred treatment accorded annuities,[77] the insurance industry challenged this action. In *Nationsbank* v. *The Variable Annuity Life Insurance Company (VALIC)*[78] the Supreme Court recently upheld the OCC's conclusions.

One of the significant aspects of the Supreme Court's decision in *VALIC* was the deference it accorded the OCC's administrative interpretations. After considering various characteristics of annuities, the Court concluded that the OCC's interpretation of the incidental powers clause, and its conclusion that both fixed and variable annuities are not "insurance" for purposes of the small town exception, were "reasonable."[79]

Also significant are the questions left unanswered by the *VALIC* Court. Because the OCC's opinion was limited to bank activities as agent in the sale of annuities, the Court did not address bank underwriting of annuities. In addition, the Court carefully restricted its finding that annuities are not classified as "insurance" to interpretations of the federal banking law only, thus leaving open whether states continue to have authority to regulate annuities under state insurance law. Not surprisingly, these questions are now the focus of additional court challenges and industry debate, discussed further below, as the business of banking continues to be reshaped and redefined.

The Garn-St Germain Depository Institutions Act of 1982

The Garn-St Germain Depository Institutions Act of 1982 (Garn-St Germain) amended the BHCA to circumscribe strictly the insurance activities of bank holding companies and their nonbank subsidiaries.[80] Garn-St Germain basically precludes, with limited exemptions, a nonbank institution from acting as principal, agent, or broker of insurance on the grounds that insurance activity, for the most part, does not closely relate to banking.[81] As a result of Garn-St Germain, bank holding companies generally are more limited in their ability to offer insurance products than are national banks.

The McCarran-Ferguson Act

Congress enacted the McCarran-Ferguson Act[82] in 1945 in response to a Supreme Court holding that threatened the historic powers of states to regulate the insurance business.[83] The McCarran-Ferguson Act was intended to retain that power for the states, but not absolutely. It provides that "no act of Congress shall be construed to invalidate, impair, or supersede any law enacted by any State for the purpose of regulating the business of insurance...unless such Act specifically relates to the business of insurance."[84] This particular provision of the McCarran-Ferguson Act has come to be known as the reverse preemption doctrine and would restrict federal law preemption only under the limited circumstances in which the federal law is specifically related to the business of insurance.

State Insurance Law

The McCarran-Ferguson Act grants to the states broad authority to regulate the "business of insurance, and every person engaged therein."[85] Under this authority, state insurance laws extensively regulate the licensing, regulation, and compensation of persons attempting to engage in the insurance agency business. Although state laws vary, approximately one-half of the states have antiaffiliation laws or practices in place that may preclude banks or their affiliates from engaging in insurance activities at all, or may prohibit licensing banks or their affiliates as agents to sell annuity or insurance products. Antiaffiliation laws are typically codified in state insurance law but, alternatively, may be part of a state's banking law.

Generally speaking, state insurance laws affecting bank insurance activities have historically been broken down into five broad categories: (1) states that expressly permit bank insurance activities; (2) states that impliedly permit bank insurance activities as incidental to the business of banking; (3) states that are silent on bank insurance activities; (4) states that prohibit bank insurance activities; and (5) states that allow state-chartered banks to engage in the same insurance activities allowed national banks.

The potential limitations created by state antiaffiliation statutes on the post-*VALIC* interpretations of the incidental powers clause and small town exemption of federal banking law are the subject of current judicial challenges. These challenges raise legal questions as to the application of the McCarran-Ferguson Act and what it means for a state to regulate insurance or for federal law to relate specifically to insurance.

As noted above, the recent *VALIC* case did not decide the regulatory status of annuities for purposes of state insurance law. Thus, even in light of *VALIC*, it is unclear how states will regulate the newly expanded authority of banks to engage in annuity sales or if antiaffiliation states will continue to prohibit banks from selling annuity products. It is this ambiguity in the *VALIC* decision that has lead some state insurance commissioners to regulate aggressively the sale of annuities to the point of absolutely prohibiting their sale by national banks.[86] Other states allow banks to sell annuities and have worked to fashion various sales practice rules in connection with their sales. Florida, for example, a state that has historically been relatively hostile to bank insurance activities, has agreed to allow banks to broker annuity products through properly licensed insurance agents.[87] Following this determination, two banks in Florida have announced plans to sell annuities.[88] In addition, the Department of Banking of Pennsylvania recently announced that Pennsylvania chartered banks, bank and trust companies, savings banks, and national banks in Pennsylvania can sell annuities as incidental to their banking business, provided that Pennsylvania-chartered financial institutions develop a program to address advertising, supervision, agent qualifications, and customer disclosure factors, and make available for examination the annuity product and promotional materials used in their sale.[89] The Commissioner of Insurance of Connecticut has authorized banks to sell annuities, as well.[90]

Several states have challenged the right of national banks to engage directly in insurance sales activities and have unsuccessfully tested the relationship between the small town exemption of the National Bank Act and state antiaffiliation statutes.[91] Recently, a unanimous U.S. Supreme Court decision clarified the ability of national banks to sell insurance products from towns having a population of 5,000 or less. The Court had granted *certiorari* to resolve two conflicting federal court decisions that had decided the relationship between Section 92 and conflicting state antiaffiliation statutes.[92] The U.S. Supreme Court, in *Barnett Bank of Marion County, N.A.* v. *Nelson* ("Barnett Bank"),[93] held that Section 92 preempts state antiaffiliation statutes and that such statutes are not preserved by the McCarran-Ferguson Act's reverse preemption doctrine.[94] The Court concluded that Section 92, the federal statutes, was in "irreconcilable conflict" with state antiaffiliation statutes, and thus, under the Supremacy Clause of the U.S. Constitution and a long line of judicial precedent, federal law must reign.

In arriving at this conclusion, the Court analyzed the reverse pre-emption doctrine of the McCarran-Ferguson Act and concluded that Section 92 "specifically relates" to insurance.[95] The Court, however, left room for states to regulate in some form the insurance activities of national banks engaged in insurance sales from small towns. For instance, the Court states that in defining the preemptive scope of the statute it does not necessarily "deprive states of the power to regulate national banks, where (unlike [in the case of antiaffiliation laws]) doing so does not prevent or significantly interfere with the national bank's exercise of its powers." Congress was awaiting the *Barnett Bank* decision before proceeding with further legislative initiatives involving bank insurance powers. As discussed below, recent versions of bank-insurance legislation have been introduced and have created further controversy.

Business Structures

Implementation of these expanded bank securities and insurance powers can be an overwhelming task for commercial banks unaccustomed to regulation in these new areas. In addition to designing a business structure to accommodate mutual fund and insurance activities, commercial banks must also address compensation issues, establish appropriate compliance programs, and otherwise adjust to the new regulatory regimes.

Commercial banks can establish a variety of relationships to offer increased investment products and services to their customers. Banks and bank holding companies can develop discount brokerage or full-service brokerage subsidiaries. They can also enter into contractual networking arrangements with third-party vendors or service providers or establish other types of joint venture arrangements or marketing relationships. Establishing any of these relationships requires a detailed review of complex legal, financial, and business issues, including banking, securities, ERISA, tax, insurance, and other regulatory requirements.

Bank Sales of Mutual Funds

Because mutual fund shares are typically registered as securities under federal and state securities laws, a commercial bank considering alternatives for distributing mutual fund shares must be aware of the compliance issues raised under these laws. Thus, a commercial bank itself could sell mutual fund shares directly to its customers as agent and, if falling within the bank exclusions from broker-dealer and investment adviser regulation,[96] would avoid registration and regulation under federal and state securities laws.

Alternatively, a bank itself could provide investment advisory services to its customers, relying on the bank exclusion from registration, or it could employ an affiliated entity, registered as an investment adviser under federal and state securities laws, to provide advisory services. By the same token, a bank or bank holding company could establish a separate brokerage affiliate for brokering mutual fund shares, which would register as a broker-dealer, although, as a business matter, the level of anticipated securities-related activities would need to be sufficient to warrant the financial and organizational commitment to do so. A separate brokerage subsidiary does provide greater flexibility in the long run for establishing incentive-based compensation arrangements, which may not easily fit within a bank's existing compensation scheme, and for developing new distribution channels outside of the bank branch network. Commonly, where asset allocation services are being compensated, the broker-dealer entity and investment adviser entity are the same.

Banks also may look outside their own organizations and enter into contractual arrangements with third-party financial services providers. These arrangements can take many forms, each with its own advantages and disadvantages, depending on the parties' ultimate economic and marketing goals as well as legal and regulatory requirements and limitations. Typically the bank's major contributions to the relationship are its existing opportunities for customer access and marketplace credibility, for which it generally seeks to acquire market expertise and distribution or related financial services capabilities. Most common among these arrangements are percentage lease and/or dual employee arrangements in which a bank leases space to an unaffiliated registered broker-dealer that may or may not share employees with the bank.[97] In return, the bank may receive commissions from the mutual fund sales as well as rental payments.[98]

Banks willing to commit more substantial resources into development of securities-related businesses have entered into partnerships or joint ventures with financial services organizations. Banking regulators, at least on the federal level, are more closely involved in the development of these relationships to minimize a bank's exposure to economic loss.[99]

Other common arrangements involve banks providing fee-producing services to the issuer of a product that is made available to the bank's customers. Services that are permissible for commercial banks or their affiliates to perform include providing investment advice, shareholder services, transfer agent services, and custodial functions. The nonbank parties to the arrangements typically perform underwriting and distribution functions, which the banks are unable to perform. Separating the underwriting functions from the service functions is a common means by which commercial banks establish structures to receive fees from mutual funds or to establish their own private-label mutual funds.

In another type of arrangement, a commercial bank may refer its customers to a nonbank company's product in exchange for a fee. Alternatively, the bank may sell or rent its customer list.

The parties to any of these business arrangements must comply with the Interagency Statement, developed by banking regulators to govern financial institution activities in nondeposit financial products.[100] Among other things, the Interagency Statement requires that the bank's board of directors adopt and maintain written policies and procedures governing, in detail, the sale of investment products and enter into written agreements, addressing specified areas, with third-party vendors. The Interagency Statement requirements extend beyond traditional concerns of bank regulators—the safety and soundness of the financial institution—to address the classic concerns of the SEC by imposing substantial disclosure obligations and other customer protection standards on the bank and nonbank parties to these arrangements.

Bank Sales of Annuities

Additional basic organizational and structural issues must be addressed whenever banks propose engaging in insurance-related activities. In addition to considerations of the relative roles of the entities involved in any bank distribution activity[101] and the compensation structure, insurance law issues raised in the states involved must be accommodated.

Many state insurance law issues can be avoided by a bank simply contracting with properly licensed insurance agencies to offer insurance products to its customers. Typically, under this structure an insurance agency establishes an office on bank premises and performs supervisory functions. The licensed agents may or may not be bank employees subject to limitations of state antiaffiliation laws or federal law restrictions on partnerships or joint ventures.[102] Common forms of contractual arrangements include lease arrangements, in which the bank receives a fixed lease payment or, where permissible under state law,[103] a percentage of the insurance agency's revenues from its activities on the bank premises;[104] or, where not prohibited by antiaffiliation laws, joint venture relationships with an insurer.

Other common forms of distribution relationships include employing a bank subsidiary that is both registered under the securities laws as a broker-dealer and licensed under the insurance laws as an insurance agency. Another variation avoids securities laws issues for the bank entity by having an insurance company directly supervise and license certain bank employees under state insurance law. Third-party networking arrangements with unaffiliated broker-dealers are also common and may take many forms.[105] In each of these cases, relevant state antiaffiliation laws must be considered.

Other insurance products, such as fixed annuities or other forms of traditional insurance do not require a broker-dealer, but do require an insurance agent. Thus, a bank may simply contract with a properly licensed insurance agent to sell other insurance products, although antiaffiliation statutes may prohibit such an arrangement if the insurance product is something other than a fixed or variable annuity.

Variations in compensation arrangements are as broad and complex as the structure of the relationships among the entities involved. Compensation generally follows from whatever roles the bank intends to assume. The most common forms of compensation derive from fees charged for managing the assets, typically mutual fund advisory fees, fees charged for distributing the product, such as sales load or 12b–1 fees, or fees for asset-allocation or administrative services.

The bank or its affiliates may charge customers directly, as in the case of investment advice provided in an asset allocation program. They also may be compensated by the issuing insurance company distributing the insurance product or by an unaffiliated third-party provider under a networking arrangement. To the extent that the bank or its affiliates provide services to the underlying mutual fund, such as investment advisory, transfer agency, custodial, shareholder servicing, brokerage or administrative services, they may also receive compensation from the fund.[106]

An awareness of the regulatory issues created when compensation is received is critical in establishing these compensation arrangements. Often minor variations in a compensation structure may have a radical impact on the manner in which a given entity is regulated. This is often the case, for example, in asset allocation programs, where broker-dealer functions and investment advisory functions are often intermixed and application of the broker-dealer regulatory structure, on the one hand, or investment advisory regulatory structure, on the other, may depend solely on the nature of the compensation arrangement. The structure of relationships, in turn, will define the manner in which each entity in the compensation chain is regulated.

Appropriate compliance programs are essential because they call for clear delineations of responsibility among the parties. The success of any of these arrangements, then, depends on properly negotiated and carefully drafted contracts with all parties involved.

As with bank involvement in securities-related activities, bank insurance activities also require compliance with the Interagency Statement.[107] In one important requirement, the OCC has stipulated that national banks cannot use terms such as *guaranteed* or *insured* to describe annuity products unless they disclose the identity of the entity providing the guarantee or insurance.[108]

Banking Reform Legislation

For better or for worse, many of the regulatory and judicial interpretations discussed above are, to some extent, filling the void created by Congress's failure after many attempts in recent years to adopt, as part of a roll-back of Glass-Steagall, banking reform legislation responsive to the changing financial services marketplace. Two of the three principal areas addressed in Congress' most recent attempt at banking reform legislation are expanding bank securities powers and permitting bank insurance sales.[109]

The proposed securities reform is relatively noncontroversial. Among other things, it would expand the scope of permissible activities for bank affiliates to include all financial activities, including underwriting corporate debt, equity, and mutual fund shares.[110] Conversely, it would permit securities firms to acquire banks, remove many restrictions on joint ventures between banks and securities firms, and remove bank exclusions from securities law regulation.

The issue of bank insurance sales continues to be hotly contested in the courts and Congress by both the banking and the insurance industries.

Congress has revised various bills concerning the roll-back of Glass-Steagall, which have included provisions regarding the extent of bank insurance powers. Following *Barnett Bank*, a recent version of this roll-back legislation, according to the OCC, contained a permanent moratorium on the OCC's ability to create any new bank insurance powers other than those in existence as of May 15, 1995, a result much sought after by insurance agents.[111]

In addition, it has been argued that the current version of this roll-back legislation retreats from the U.S. Supreme Court's *Barnett Bank* decision in that the legislation would allow states to regulate small town national bank sales of insurance, provided that state law did not discriminate against small town banks. The OCC has raised concerns with the current version of the legislation.[112] It believes that the current version would allow states to enact laws that could on their face apply to all financial institutions, but when applied would discriminate against national banks. For example, according to the OCC's Chief Counsel, a state law could require that any financial institution selling insurance have most of its revenue derived from insurance sales, a requirement that a national bank could not satisfy[113] The General Counsel to the House Banking Committee disagrees with these OCC assertions.[114]

BANK UNDERWRITING OF SECURITIES AND INSURANCE PRODUCTS

Bank Underwriting of Securities

Although commercial banks have wide latitude to engage in securities agency activities, Glass-Steagall severely circumscribes their ability to underwrite securities issuances.[115] Glass-Steagall, however, allows commercial banks to participate in underwriting obligations of the U.S. government and its instrumentalities and obligations of states and their political subdivisions.[116] Otherwise, it generally prohibits widespread bank underwriting activities, primarily to avoid potential conflicts of interest when a bank has an investment stake in a securities issuance. The purposes behind the Glass-Steagall prohibitions against bank underwriting activities were most clearly set forth in the Supreme Court case of *The Investment Company Institute* v. *Camp* (ICI), which involved the sponsorship and operation of a collective investment fund by a national bank.[117]

The *ICI* case continues to serve as a bulwark preventing banks from acting as underwriter for mutual fund shares or variable annuities. As a result, national banks enter into various types of arrangements with broker-dealers whereby the broker-dealer acts as principal underwriter of mutual fund shares or variable annuity contracts, and the bank, in return, provides administrative and other types of services. The bank typically provides these services under a selling agreement with the broker-dealer. They include maintaining mutual fund records, computing net asset value and other performance figures, preparing and filing registration statements with the SEC and various state securities commissions, and providing facilities for mutual fund or variable annuity distribution.[118] As noted earlier, banks may be paid for these services by 12b–1 fees, even though such fees could suggest that the bank acted as an underwriter on the grounds that 12b–1 fees are paid in connection with mutual fund share distribution.

Bank holding companies are not as restricted in their ability to underwrite securities and often engage in underwriting activities through subsidiaries (so-called Section 20 subsidiaries), notwithstanding Glass-Steagall's prohibition against bank affiliations with securities firms.[119] Although bank holding companies have been granted greater powers in the underwriting context, the Federal Reserve governors have not yet approved of a bank holding company or a Section 20 subsidiary underwriting the mutual funds or variable annuities.

Bank Underwriting of Insurance Products

In general, national banks derive their authority to underwrite forms of insurance from the incidental powers clause of the National Bank Act. Although some states have been liberal in authorizing state nonmember banks to engage in insurance agency activities, these same states have not been as liberal in allowing state nonmember banks the power to underwrite general forms of insurance. This restriction may be due, in part, to the Federal Deposit Insurance Act,[120] which basically prevents state-chartered banks from engaging in insurance underwriting activities to the extent of the restrictions on national banks (unless the state-chartered bank had been engaged in the activity prior to November 21, 1991).[121]

In addition, a current version of the Glass-Steagall roll-back legislation could have the effect of restricting bank holding company affiliates from underwriting insurance. A previous version (the so-called "Baker Amendment") would have provided greater authority for bank holding companies to underwrite insurance.[122] The current version would allow a bank holding company affiliate to underwrite insurance only if the underwriting is "in full compliance with [relevant state law], including but not limited to, laws that restrict a bank in [the] state from having an affiliate, agent, or employee in [the state] licensed to provide insurance as principal, agent, or broker." The OCC has argued that this current version of the Baker Amendment could result in states discriminating against bank holding company affiliates by applying special restrictions to them.[123]

Underwriting Retirement CDs

In 1994, the OCC gave the Blackfeet National Bank a no-objection letter concerning the marketing of a hybrid financial product that has become known as a *Retirement CD, CD annuity,* or *Blackfeet CD*.[124] The Retirement CD combines the lifetime payout features of an annuity with the guaranteed interest rates of a certificate of deposit, but it is designed to compete directly with annuities issued by insurance companies. Unlike insurance company annuities, the Retirement CD also qualifies as an FDIC deposit and is protected by deposit insurance, together with the customer's other accounts at the same bank, up to $100,000.[125]

The Blackfeet CD requires a minimum initial deposit of $5,000. The customer has the flexibility to choose its maturity date, as well as the period of time (between one and five years) that its interest rate will remain fixed. Payments during the pay-in phase are credited to a customer's account. Upon maturity, the customer can receive as much as two-thirds of the account in a lump sum, and the remainder will be paid out in monthly payments during the life of the owner.

The Blackfeet CD promotional materials claimed the favorable deferred tax treatment given to annuities under Section 72 of the Internal Revenue Code.[126] On April 6, 1995, the Internal Revenue Service (IRS) released proposed regulations that tax a contract that is otherwise a debt instrument, such as a Retirement CD, as a certificate of deposit unless *all* of the payments under the contract: (1) are made at least annually over life or life expectancy; (2) do not increase at any time during the terms of the contract; and (3) begin within one year of the initial investment in the contract. These regulations would invalidate most forms of the Retirement CD that banks currently issue or are considering unless the instrument has a payout beginning within one year of issue. Because the Retirement CD is designed and priced to be marketed as a long-term CD, these regulations substantially reduce the attractiveness of the Retirement CD in the marketplace. The proposed regulations were intended to apply to contracts issued after April 6, 1995. The IRS held a hearing on them on August 8, 1995, but has not yet published any final regulations.

The IRS action precipitated a response from Congress. Senator Max Baucus of Montana questioned the legality of the action by the IRS. In a letter to Treasury Secretary Robert E. Rubin, Senator Baucus stated that the Retirement CD, which Senator Baucus concluded was basically an annuity contract, should be tax-deferred just like an insurance company annuity.[127] He argued that the effect of the IRS's proposed rule making prevents deferred annuities from receiving deferred tax treatment, unless they are issued by insurance companies. Moreover, he indicated that the IRS, in proposing its recent rules, violated an executive order (Executive Order 12866), requiring consultation with parties that will be burdened by any proposed rule or regulation. He stressed that the Blackfeet National Bank, which serves a vast and impoverished area, would have been burdened and should have been consulted prior to the IRS proposed rules.

In addition to the action taken by the IRS, some insurance regulators in the several states took action against the Blackfeet National Bank, after it began marketing the Retirement CD to force compliance with state insurance licensing requirements.[128] For instance, in Illinois, the Director of Insurance issued an *ex parte* cease-and-desist order to the bank, ordering the bank not to advertise the Retirement CD in Illinois on the grounds that to advertise the Retirement CD would involve offering insurance without a license. The Seventh Circuit recently sided with the Illinois Insurance Commissioner in holding that the Retirement CD would be subject to the state's insurance regulations.[129] The Seventh Circuit concluded that the insurance laws of Illinois "regulated" the business of insurance; the underwriting and sale of the Retirement CD constituted the business of insurance; and the provision of the National Bank Act (12 U.S.C. § 24 (Seventh)) relied upon did not specifically relate to insurance.

The Court distinguished the *VALIC* decision by stating that the *VALIC* holding was limited to the brokering, not the underwriting, of annuities. In addition, the court stated that the *VALIC* holding is limited to the issue of whether a national bank may broker annuities as a matter of federal banking law, and not whether a national bank, in brokering annuities, would be subject to state insurance regulation.

The court also distinguished the case of the Retirement CD from the recent U.S. Supreme Court decision in *Barnett Bank*. The court noted that the small town provision of the National Bank Act (Section 92) did, in fact, specifically relate to the business of insurance, thus allowing national banks to engage in the insurance business from small towns. Conversely, Section 24 (Seventh) does not contain specific provisions relating to the business of insurance.

Accordingly, the Seventh Circuit agreed with the Illinois Insurance Commissioner that the Blackfeet National Bank would need to satisfy the various licensing provisions of the Illinois Insurance Code (*i.e.*, establish an insurance agency subsidiary) before it could offer the Retirement CD to residents of Illinois.

Moreover, Congress raised objections to the OCC and FDIC positions on the Retirement CD and expressed concerns over whether customer protections would be adequately observed if the Retirement CD were offered outside the scope of insurance laws.[130] In its defense the OCC noted that its no-objection position was not an authorization for banks to underwrite annuities.

The maelstrom created by the introduction of the Retirement CD may be greatly reduced due to the IRS proposals, which would effectively deny annuity tax treatment for Retirement CDs.[131] Presently, a bank's ability to market the Retirement CD has not been finally resolved either as a result of judicial decision or congressional or IRS action. If the IRS proposed regulations become final, however, the viability of the Retirement CD as a bank-sponsored product is largely in doubt, and, independent of threatened litigation or possible legislation, banks may abandon it purely for business reasons.

CONCLUSION

About 15 percent of total mutual fund assets are now attributable to bank sales.[132] Banks are also now responsible for 25 to 30 percent of the insurance industry's individual annuity business.[133] This substantial presence was made possible by regulatory and judicial support of banks' movement into these markets. Mutual fund complexes and insurance companies, at first hostile to banks' incursion into their preserves, have contributed to the growth of banks' presence by engaging in joint arrangements that take advantage of the customer convenience of one-stop financial services shopping that banks can offer. This confluence of products and services in the financial services industry shows no signs of abating as developments, such as computer-linked sales and service transactions, facilitate consumer demands for low-cost commodity product distribution and underwriting.

E N D N O T E S

1. These provisions are contained in §§ 16, 20, 21, and 32 of Glass-Steagall, which are codified in 12 USC §§ 24, 377, 378 and 78, respectively. Section 16 applies to national banks; Sections 20 and 32 apply to member banks, including all national banks and any state member banks; Section 21 regulates nonbank institutions.

2. See, 12 USC §§ 24 and 378. See *Securities Industry Association* v. *Board of Governors of the Federal Reserve System*, 468 U.S. 137 (1984) (which discusses the purposes of Glass-Steagall in preventing banks from entering the risk environment of the securities markets and the potential conflicts of interest if a commercial bank also were to underwrite securities).

3. See 12 USC §§ 377 and 78.

4. For example, Sections 16, 20 and 32 do not apply to state nonmember banks, and Section 21 has been interpreted to be similarly limited. See *Investment Company Institute* v. *Federal Deposit Insurance Corporation*, 815 F.2d 1540 (D.C. Cir. 1987), *cert. denied*, 484 U.S. 847 (1988). For an excellent discussion of the history and application of Glass-Steagall, see Horn, "The Legal Barrier Between U.S. Investment and Commercial Banking: Its Origins, Application and Prospects," Chapter 14 in *Current Legal Issues Affecting Central Banks*, ed. Robert C. Effros, International Monetary Fund Washington) (1992).

5. 12 USC § 24 (Seventh). This section also authorizes national banks to purchase, deal in, and underwrite general obligations of the United States and its instrumentalities and general obligations of states and political subdivisions thereof.

6. Ibid. See also, *Investment Company Institute* v. *Camp*, 401 U.S. 617 (1971).

7. Codified in 12 USC §§ 1841–1844, 1845 note, and 1846–1849.

8. See 12 USC § 1843(c)(8) and 12 C.F.R. § 225.25.

9. Section 2(a) of the BHCA so defines a bank holding company. 12 USC § 1841(a).

10. See Section 4(c) of the BHCA. 12 USC § 1843(c). These exemptions include a provision permitting bank holding companies to acquire up to 5 percent of the voting shares of any nonbank entity, subject to the limitation that the bank holding company not obtain controlling influence over the entity's management. See Section 4(c)(6) of the BHCA, codified in 12 USC § 1843(c)(6) and regulations thereunder. Bank holding companies are also permitted to acquire up to 5 percent

ownership in an investment company, subject to certain limitations. Section 4(c)(7) of the BHCA.

11. Section 4(c)(8) of the BHCA. 12 USC § 1843(c)(8).

12. 12 C.F.R. § 225.25. Once an activity appears on the laundry list, bank holding companies need not obtain prior board approval to engage in that activity.

13. The range of bank holding company capital markets activities is fully discussed and analyzed in Michael G. Capatides, *A Guide to the Capital Markets Activities of Banks and Bank Holding Companies*, (New York: Bowne & Co., 1993).

14. Section 20 of Glass-Steagall prohibits a member bank from affiliating with an entity "engaged principally in the issue, flotation, underwriting, public sales or distribution...of stocks, bonds, indentures, notes, or other securities." However, the Board has effectively eroded this limitation by interpreting "engaged principally" quite narrowly and thereby permitting affiliations with entities involved in these activities to a limited extent. See, e.g., *Securities Industry Association* v. *Board of Governors*, 839 F.2d 47 (2d Cir. 1988), *cert. denied*, 486 U.S. 1059 (1988).

15. See, e.g., 73 Fed. Res. Bull 473 (1987); 57 Fed. Reg. 33,507 (1992); 57 Fed. Reg. 33,961 (1992); 59 Fed. Reg. 35,516 (1994).

16. See 12 USC §§ 24 and 377.

17. 12 USC § 1841 *et seq.*

18. 12 USC § 1831a.

19. See 12 CFR § 337.4.

20. Section 20 defines an *affiliate* to include organizations of which a member bank owns or controls a majority of the voting shares or otherwise controls the election of a majority of the members of its governing body; organizations of which control is held by the shareholders of a member bank who own or control a majority of the shares of the bank or control the election of a majority of the bank directors; organizations with interlocking directorships with a member bank; and organizations that own or control a majority of the shares of a member bank or otherwise control the election of a majority of the banks' board members.

21. See also *Investment Company Institute* v. *Camp*, 401 U.S. 617 (1971). For example, banking practitioners have interpreted certain positions of the OCC as permitting, under certain circumstances, a national bank to "broker" securities in a primary distribution. See, e.g., OCC Letter *re* Continental Bank (Jan. 19, 1993).

22. Discount brokerage firms offer execution services of customer orders. They are able to charge low fees because they do not provide research or analytical services to customers.

23. *Securities Industry Association* v. *Comptroller of the Currency*, 577 F.Supp. 252 (D.D.C. 1983)(upholding the OCC's approval of the purchase of Brenner Sneed and Associates, Inc., a registered broker-dealer, by Union Planters National Bank of Memphis and a proposal by Security Pacific National Bank to create a separate account brokerage subsidiary). The securities industry had argued, unsuccessfully, that Glass-Steagall allowed a bank to engage in securities activities only with respect to preexisting bank customers.

24. Ibid. at 256. The court noted that, prior to the passage of Glass-Steagall, banks offered brokerage services to the general public, and that nothing in the legislative history suggested that Congress intended to dramatically change that function. Ibid. at 255. It also read Section 16 in light of the purpose of Section 20 to avoid risks of securities underwriting and not retail securities brokerage. Ibid. at 256.

25. In 1983, after amending Regulation Y to include securities brokerage services to the general public as a permissible nonbanking activity, the Board approved the sale of Charles Schwab & Co. to BankAmerica Corporation, a bank holding company. 69 Fed. Res. Bull. 105 (1983). This acquisition was challenged in *Securities Industry Association* v. *Board of Governors*, 468 U.S. 207 (1983). The Supreme Court unanimously agreed with the board's findings in approving the Charles Schwab acquisition and concluded that providing discount brokerage services is so closely related to banking that it is a proper activity for a bank. Ibid. at 221. Interestingly, the Court concluded that the statutory limitation against a "public sale" did not encompass discount brokerage activities, in contrast to underwriting or distribution activities. Ibid. at 217–218.

26. OCC Interpretive Letter No. 332 (March 8, 1985), reprinted in, [1985–1987 Transfer Binder] Fed. Banking L. Rep. (CCH) para. 85,502. See also, OCC Interpretive Letter No. 363 (May 23, 1986), reprinted in [1985–1987 Transfer Binder] Fed. Banking L. Rep. (CCH) para. 85,533.

27. Fees paid under a 12b–1 plan are governed by a rule adopted by the Securities and Exchange Commission under the Investment Company Act of 1940, 17 CFR §270.12b–1, and are known as 12b–1 fees. Because 12b–1 fees are paid to cover expenses in connection with the distribution of mutual fund shares, an issue was raised and resolved in the negative as to whether the bank, by accepting 12b–1 fees, was

acting as principal by virtue of receiving fees associated with a distribution.

28. See Letter of Board General Counsel to Sovran Financial Corp. (July 27, 1986), reprinted in [1985–87 Transfer Binder] Fed. Banking L. Rep. (CCH) para. 86,620.

29. See OCC Interpretive Letter No. 386 (June 19, 1987), reprinted in [1988–1989 Transfer Binder] Fed. Banking L. Rep. (CCH) para. 85,610. The OCC required certain customer disclosures that the mutual funds were sponsored and distributed by an independent third party and were not bank deposits or insured by the FDIC. The Supreme Court previously held that rendering investment advice is not prohibited by Glass-Steagall. See *Board of Governors* v. *Investment Company Institute*, 450 U.S. 46 (1981).

30. See 12 CFR § 225.25(b)(15). The board also imposed certain disclosure requirements.

31. See note 17.

32. OCC Interpretive Letter No. 403 (Dec. 9, 1987), reprinted in [1988–1989 Transfer Binders] Fed. Banking L. Rep. (CCH) para. 85,627. See also, Decision of the OCC Concerning American National Bank of Austin, Texas (Sept. 6, 1983), reprinted in [1983–1984 Transfer Binder] Fed. Banking L. Rep. (CCH) para. 99,732.

33. 12 CFR § 225.125.

34. 15 USC §§ 77a *et seq.*

35. 15 USC §§ 78a *et seq.*

36. 15 USC §§ 80a–1 *et seq.*

37. 15 USC §§ 80b–1 *et seq.*

38. See, e.g., *American Bankers Association* v. *SEC*, 804 F.2d 739 (D.C. Cir. 1986)(bank trade association lawsuit seeking to invalidate Exchange Act Rule 3b–9 limiting the bank exemption from Exchange Act registration on functional basis).

39. See *Bank Mutual Funds: Sales Practices and Regulatory Issues* (GAO/GGD–95–210)(only 8 percent of banks selling mutual funds do so directly; the other 92 percent use SEC-registered broker-dealers).

40. 15 USC § 78o(a)(1).

41. The definitions of *broker* and *dealer*, in Sections 3(a)(4) and 3(a)(5) of the Exchange Act, respectively, specifically exclude banks. Section 3(a)(6) of the Exchange Act defines banks as "(A) a banking institution organized under the laws of the United States, (B) a member bank of the Federal Reserve System, (C) any other banking institution doing business, a substantial portion of which consists of

receiving deposits or exercising fiduciary power similar to those permitted to national banks upon approval of the OCC and which is supervised and examined by State or Federal authority having supervision over banks, and which is not operated for the purpose of evading the provisions of the Exchange Act, and (D) a receiver, conservator, or other liquidating agent of an institution described above."

42. The antifraud provisions of the federal securities laws, however, apply to any person, including a bank, involved in the purchase or sale of a security. See, e.g., 17 C.F.R. §240.10b–5.

43. See 15 USC §78q(b).

44. See 17 C.F.R. §240.15c3–1.

45. See 17 C.F.R. §§240.17a–1, 17a–2, 17a–3, 17a–4, and 17a–5.

46. See, e.g., 17 C.F.R. §240.15c3–3. In addition to specific rules governing customer protection duties, broker-dealers have a duty to treat their customers fairly and in accordance with standards of the industry. See *In re Duker & Duker*, 6 SEC 386, 388–89 (1939).

47. See, e.g., 17 C.F.R. §240.10b–10 (requiring disclosure of trade information in connection with customer securities transactions).

48. 15 USC §78o(b)(8).

49. See, e.g., NASD Rules of Fair Practice, Art. III, Section 1 *et seq.*, NASD Manual (CCH) para. 2001. The NASD also has specific rules governing the sale of mutual fund shares and variable annuity products. See NASD Rules of Fair Practice Art. III, Section 26, NASD Manual (CCH) para. 2176 (rules governing mutual fund sales); and Section 29, NASD Manual (CCH) para. 2179 (rules governing variable annuity sales).

50. Section 3(a)(18) of the Exchange Act defines the term "person associated with a broker-dealer" as (1) any partner, officer, or branch manager of a broker-dealer; (2) any person directly or indirectly controlling, controlled by, or under common control of a broker-dealer; and (3) any employee of a broker-dealer, except employees whose functions are solely clerical or ministerial.

51. See NASD Schedule to By-Laws, Schedule C, Part III(1)(a), NASD Manual (CCH) para. 1785.

52. See NASD Schedule to By-Laws, Schedule C, Part VII, NASD Manual (CCH) para. 1788. For example, representatives engaged solely in sales of mutual fund shares or variable annuities are required to pass the NASD Series 6 examination. State law typically requires representatives who engage in sales in a particular state also to have passed the NASD Series 63 examination.

53. 15 USC § 80b–3(a). In addition, the mutual funds themselves must be registered under the Investment Company Act of 1940. 15 USC § 80a–8. The shares issued by the mutual fund must be registered under the Securities Act of 1933. 15 USC § 77e. No blanket bank exemptions are available under these two statutes. But see, 15 USC § 77c(a)(2) and 15 USC § 80c–3(c)(11).

54. 15 USC § 80b–2(a)(11).

55. See, e.g., *In re Hughes*, 27 SEC 629 (1948), *aff'd*, 174 F.2d 969 (D.C. Cir. 1949).

56. It is well recognized that an investment adviser has a fiduciary duty to its clients. See *SEC* v. *Capital Gains Research Bureau, Inc.*, 375 U.S. 180, 191–92 (1963). As such, the investment adviser cannot act in a way that would jeopardize its duty to act solely in the best interests of its client. This duty is generally derived from Section 206(1)–(4) of the Advisers Act. 15 USC § 80b–6. To the extent that a conflict between the adviser and the client arises, the adviser would be required to disclose the conflict and obtain written consent from the client before completion of the transaction (before trade date). See, e.g., *In re Piper Capital Management*, Investment Advisers Act Release No. 1435 (Aug. 11, 1994).

57. See 17 C.F.R. § 275.204–2.

58. See 15 USC § 80b–6.

59. See, e.g., 17 C.F.R. §§ 275.206(4)–1 and 275.206(4)–3.

60. Asset allocation techniques are derived from the seminal work produced by Nobel Prize–winning economists Harry Markowitz and William Sharpe in the 1950s and 1960s, termed "modern portfolio theory." The basic elements of modern portfolio theory are diversification and low correlation of investment returns among portfolio assets. *Correlation* refers to the degree of similarity of investment returns experienced by investment alternatives. With low correlation, the expectation is that, while a portion of a diversified asset class does poorly, another portion will do well.

61. This is prohibited, except in limited circumstances, by Section 12(d) of the Investment Company Act. 15 USC § 80c–12(d).

62. Proposed Rule 3a–4, SEC Release No. IC–21260 (July 27, 1995). The proposed rule conditions include, among others, the following requirements: The program's sponsor must obtain and maintain information from each client necessary to manage the client's account individually; the sponsor and portfolio manager must be reasonably available for client consultation; clients must be able to impose reasonable restrictions on the management of the account; each client

must receive quarterly statements of all activity in the account; and the client must retain certain specific indicia of ownership over the account. See also, *United Missouri Bank of Kansas City*, SEC No-Action Letter (Jan. 23, 1995); *Qualivest Capital Management, Inc.*, SEC No-Action Letter (July 30, 1990); and *Scudder Fund Management Service*, SEC No-Action Letter (June 10, 1988).

63. See, e.g., Fla. Stat. § 517.021(6)(b)(2) (excluding from the definition of dealer any bank authorized to do business in Florida, except a nonbank subsidiary of a bank); Fla. Stat. § 517.021(10)(a) (2) & (3) (excluding from the definition of investment adviser any bank authorized to do business in the state and any bank holding company as defined in the Bank Holding Company Act of 1956 authorized to do business in Florida).

64. For example, Texas law takes a very narrow approach and does not exclude banks or any other type of financial institution from its dealer regulations. See generally, Tx. Rev. Civ. Stat., Art. 581–4. See also, Exemption Request, 3 Blue Sky L. Rep. (CCH) para. 55,812W (refusing to grant no-action from dealer regulation for bank allowing dealer, registered under Texas law, to sell securities from bank premises).

65. A majority of states require proof of passing the NASD Series 63 examination for representatives of a broker-dealer.

66. Some states require proof of passing either the NASD Series 65 or Series 66 examination for associates of an investment adviser.

67. See *SEC v. Variable Annuity Life Insurance Co.*, 359 U.S. 65 (1959).

68. 12 USC § 24 (Seventh).

69. 12 USC § 92. The OCC extended the reach of the small town exemption beyond the geographic limits of the small town in which the bank is located by permitting the bank to solicit out-of-town customers. See OCC Interpretive Letter No. 366 (Aug. 18, 1986), reprinted in [1985–1987 Transfer Binder] Fed. Banking L. Rep. (CCH) para. 83,090; and *Independent Insurance Agents of America v. Ludwig*, 997 F.2d 958 (D.C. Cir. 1993). A recent Seventh Circuit decision followed the D.C. Circuit's analysis. See *NBD Bank v. Bennett*, 63 F.3d 629 (7th Cir. 1995).

70. See *Saxon v. Georgia Association of Independent Insurance Agents*, 399 F.2d 1010 (5th Cir. 1968).

71. See 12 CFR § 2.6 and 12 CFR § 2.3(3)(e). The ability of banks to sell forms of credit life insurance was judicially upheld as an incidental power necessary to carry on the business of banking in *Independent*

Bankers Association of America v. *Heimann*, 613 F.2d 1164 (D.C. Cir. 1979).

72. OCC Interpretive Letter No. 283 (March 16, 1984).

73. Ibid.

74. OCC Interpretive Letter No. 368 (July 11, 1986). This position was upheld in *American Land Title Association* v. *Clarke*, 968 F.2d 150 (2d. Cir. 1992).

75. OCC Interpretive Letter No. 241 (March 26, 1982).

76. OCC Interpretive Letter No. 499 (Feb. 12, 1990), reprinted in [1989–1990 Transfer Binder] Fed. Banking L. Rep. (CCH para. 83,090. Banks had previously been given authority to sell variable annuities, based on the incidental powers clause and its grant of securities dealing powers, in OCC Interpretive Letter No. 331 (April 14, 1985), reprinted in [1985–1986 Transfer Binder] Fed. Banking L. Rep. (CCH) para. 85,501.

77. See Section 72 of the Internal Revenue Code of 1986. 26 USC § 72.

78. 115 S.Ct. 810 (1995).

79. The *VALIC* Court also affirmed that the OCC has full discretion to interpret the incidental powers clause to include powers beyond those specifically enumerated in that section, provided that discretion is "kept within reasonable bounds." See note 2.

80. 12 USC § 1843(c)(8).

81. The BHCA sets forth seven exemptions allowing bank holding companies to engage in insurance activities. The exemptions allow bank holding companies to engage in: (1) credit life insurance, credit accident and health insurance and involuntary unemployment insurance; (2) single interest property insurance by finance company subsidiaries; (3) general insurance agency activities in towns of less than 5,000 in population; (4) grandfathered insurance agency activities if the bank holding company engaged in insurance agency activities prior to May 1, 1982; (5) supervisory activities of retail insurance agents; (6) general insurance agency activities of small holding companies (e.g., those with total consolidated assets of $50 million or less); and (7) grandfathered activities if the bank holding company engaged in the insurance activity pursuant to board approval prior to January 1, 1971.

82. 15 USC § 1012.

83. See *United States* v. *South-Eastern Underwriters Association*. 322 U.S. 533 (1944). The Court held that the insurance business was conducted in interstate commerce subject to regulation by Congress pursuant to

the Commerce Clause of the U.S. Constitution. This Supreme Court decision basically overturned an earlier Supreme Court decision to the contrary in *Paul* v. *Virginia*, 75 U.S. (8 Wall) 68 (1868).

84. 15 USC § 1012(b).

85. See 15 USC §§ 1011, 1012(b).

86. Since *VALIC*, the insurance commissioners of Illinois and Mississippi have taken action to prohibit national banks operating in towns of greater than 5,000 from selling annuities. The Illinois Insurance Commissioner has argued that *VALIC* only addressed whether the OCC had the power to authorize bank sales of annuities and not whether states can regulate or ban bank annuity sales.

The positions taken by the Illinois and Mississippi insurance commissioners have led to litigation concerning state authority over bank annuity sales. See *Mississippi Deposit Guarantee Bank* v. *Dale*, *U.S. District Court Southern District of Mississippi*, Civ. Action 95–CV640WN.

87. The Florida Department of Banking and Finance and the Florida Department of Insurance issued proposed regulations that would permit banks to sell annuities. According to the proposal, sales of annuities must be brokered by a licensed insurance agent and accompanied by disclosure that annuities are not insured by the FDIC and are subject to investment risk.

88. Barnett Banks Inc. and First Union Corp. announced plans to sell annuities in Florida. See "Branch Sales of Annuities Starting in Fla.," *American Banker*, Aug. 21, 1995. Florida-chartered banks apparently intend to follow Barnett and First Union in selling annuity products as well.

89. *See* Letter from Richard C. Rishel, Secretary of Banking, Department of Banking of the Commonwealth of Pennsylvania, to Chief Executive Officers of Pennsylvania State-Chartered Banks, Bank and Trust Companies, Savings Banks and National Banks Located in Pennsylvania (April 16, 1996).

90. The Connecticut Commissioner of Insurance (commissioner) authorization arises from a settlement with Shawmut National Corp. concerning a challenge of Connecticut restrictions on bank insurance activities. Shawmut had filed suit against the commissioner seeking a declaratory judgment allowing Shawmut to keep its insurance agency even though a Connecticut statute prohibited an affiliation of insurance agencies with banks. (See *Shawmut Bank Connecticut, N.A.* v. *Googins* (D. Conn. No. 3:94 CV 146 (RVC)). The portion of the suit dealing with annuities was settled on July 26, 1995, and allows Shawmut to

broker annuities products through a licensed insurance agent. The part of the suit that deals with the ability of banks to engage in a general insurance business pursuant to the small town exemption was not part of the settlement of July 26, 1995. This portion of the case is awaiting final resolution of *Barnett Bank* v. *Gallagher*, currently pending in the U.S. Supreme Court. See note 78, and accompanying text above.

91. The OCC has long maintained that federal law preempts state law on this issue. OCC Interpretive Letter No. 475 (March 22, 1989), reprinted in [1989–1990 Transfer Binder] Fed. Banking L. Rep. (CCH) para. 83,012.

92. In *Barnett Bank of Marion County, N.A.* v. *Gallagher*, 43 F.3d 631 (11th Cir. 1995), the Eleventh Circuit addressed a Florida insurance law prohibition against banks engaging in insurance activities. The Eleventh Circuit in that case upheld the district court's decision that Florida's insurance law was *not* preempted by Section 92. Critical to the court's conclusions were its findings under the McCarran-Ferguson Act that the Florida antiaffiliation law was enacted for the purpose of regulating the business of insurance. The Eleventh Circuit concluded that a state insurance law "regulates" the business of insurance within the meaning of McCarran-Ferguson if the law has as its aim to regulate the essential part of the business of insurance, which may be evidenced if the law regulates the relationship between the policy holder and insurer. The Eleventh Circuit further concluded that Section 92 did not specifically relate to the business of insurance. The Eleventh Circuit held that the small town exemption cannot "specifically relate" to insurance because, when Section 92 was enacted in 1916, state insurance regulation was considered to be solely the function of state regulation. Moreover, the Eleventh Circuit concluded that the small town exemption specifically relates to banking, not insurance. The Eleventh Circuit also agreed with the Florida Insurance Commission on a policy basis that the antiaffiliation statute protected potential policyholders from a bank exerting undue influence in tying the provision of loans with the purchase of insurance. The Eleventh Circuit held to this view notwithstanding references to insurance throughout the small town exemption. A Louisiana state court followed this reasoning. *First Advantage Insurance, Inc.* v. *Green*, 654 So.2d 331 (La. 1995).

In *Owensboro National Bank* v. *Stephens*, 44 F.3d 388 (6th Cir. 1994), the Sixth Circuit addressed an antiaffiliation provision of Kentucky banking law. The Sixth Circuit in that case concluded that the antiaffiliation provision dealt with banking powers, not insurance powers, and therefore was not covered by the McCarran-Ferguson Act limits on federal preemption. The court found that the Kentucky statute did not regulate the business of insurance on the basis that excluding an entity from participating in an activity is different form regulating the activity. The Sixth Circuit relied on factors set forth in a U.S. Supreme Court decision, *Union Labor Insurance Co.* v. *Pireno*, 458 U.S. 119 (1982), to determine whether the Kentucky statute regulated the business of insurance. The Court in *Pireno* determined that the business of insurance is made up of many practices, the relevant ones being (1) whether the practice has the effect of transferring or spreading a policyholder's risk; (2) whether the practice is an integral part of the policy relationship between the insurer and insured; and (3) whether the practice is limited to entities within the insurance industry. Hence, federal banking law prevailed. The Sixth Circuit noted that the purpose of the small town exemption was to increase the number of banks serving small towns by providing additional sources of revenue in the form of insurance business. However, because it determined that the Kentucky statute did not "regulate" insurance for purposes of McCarran-Ferguson, it did not decide whether the small town exemption "specifically related" to insurance.

93. 1996 U.S. LEXIS 2161 (March 26, 1996).

94. As a result of the U.S. Supreme Court's decision in *Barnett Bank*, the Court denied *certiorari* to the *Owensboro* case, (1996 U.S. LEXIS 2174 (April 1, 1996)) but granted *certiorari* to the *First Advantage* case and vacated the decision to the Court of Appeals of Louisiana (1996 U.S. LEXIS 2169 (April 1, 1996)) for consideration in light of *Barnett Bank*.

95. In analyzing the term "specifically relates," the Court stated that Section 92 explicitly grants small town national banks permission to "act as the agent for any fire, life, or other insurance company," and to "receive for services so rendered...fees or commissions" subject to OCC regulations. According to the Court, Section 92 focuses directly on industry-specific selling practices and determines the relationship of the insured and the insurer.

96. Not all states have bank-related exemptions similar to the federal securities laws exemptions. See note 64. Also, federal antifraud provisions apply despite reliance on the bank exclusions. See note 42.

97. The SEC staff has attempted to indirectly regulate the structures that banks, otherwise exempt from broker-dealer regulation, must adopt in this context. See Chubb Securities Corp., SEC No-Action Letter (Nov. 23, 1993). Service agreements involving NASD member firms are required to incorporate terms dictated by the *Chubb* letter to ensure

that brokerage services are provided by registered broker-dealers and personnel. See also, *NASD Notice to Members* 94–94 (Dec. 1994). On December 28, 1995, the NASD submitted rules to the SEC concerning the securities activities of NASD member firms on the premises of banks. Basically, these rules are designed to reduce customer confusion in connection with sales of nondeposit investment products on a bank's premises. In addition, these rules would govern compensation arrangements for registered representatives who are also bank employees. Nonregistered bank employees would be prohibited from receiving cash or noncash compensation for referral of customers to representatives who are registered to sell securities. (The prohibition on referral fees departs from *Chubb.*) The SEC has not yet published for public comment these rules proposals in the *Federal Register.* The rule proposals are in File No. SR-NASD–95–63.

98. The OCC has placed certain limitations and conditions on lease arrangements with national banks. See OCC Interpretive Letter No. 274 (Dec. 2, 1983), reprinted in [1983–1984 Transfer Binder] Fed. Banking L. Rep. (CCH) para. 85,512; OCC Interpretive Letter Nos. 406, 407 and 408 (Aug. 4, 1987), reprinted in [1988–1989 Transfer Binder] Fed. Banking L. Rep. (CCH) paras. 85,630; 85,631; and 85,632.

99. For example, the OCC permits these relationships only to the extent the activities are those the bank could engage in itself. The OCC also imposes substantive limitations on the structure of the relationship. The board has taken similar positions. See note 104.

100. The Interagency Statement is a joint statement of the OCC, board, FDIC, and Office of Thrift Supervision and covers bank activities in mutual fund shares and annuities. It does not cover additional life insurance products. See Interagency Statement on Retail Sales of Nondeposit Investment Products (Feb. 15, 1994). See also, *Chubb Securities Corp.*, SEC No-Action Letter (Nov. 24, 1993)(setting forth conditions for financial institutions offering securities to retail customers).

101. Of course, banks cannot distribute these products directly without running afoul of the underwriter limitation of Section 24 (Seventh) of the National Bank Act.

102. See e.g., OCC Interpretive Letter No. 625 (July 1, 1993), reprinted in [1993–1994 Transfer Binder] Fed. Banking L. Rep. (CCH) para. 83,507. As a practical matter, insurance-related partnerships or joint venture relationships for the most part do not involve bank holding companies because of restrictions under Garn-St Germain.

103. Many states prohibit premium splitting with unlicensed entities. Some of these states specifically carve out percentage lease arrangements, which would be permitted subject to certain restrictions.

104. The OCC has authorized national banks to enter into this type of arrangement. OCC Interpretive Letter No. 274 (Dec. 2, 1983).

105. The SEC has granted relief from the broker-dealer registration requirements for insurance agencies and personnel selling variable insurance products, subject to certain conditions, including, among others, that a registered broker-dealer exercise supervision and control over the activities of the sales agents. See *First of America Brokerage Services, Inc.*, SEC No-Action Letter (Sept. 28, 1995).

106. Certain restrictions apply to payments made by a fund to an affiliated bank entity. See Section 23B of the Federal Reserve Act. 12 USC § 371c.

107. See note 102, above.

108. OCC News Release 94–88 (Sept. 19, 1994).

109. See, HR 2520, 104th Cong., 1st Sess. (1995). The third area is regulatory reform, which is intended primarily to rationalize the home mortgage process, eliminate and reconcile certain unnecessary disclosure and reporting requirements, and streamline government regulations regulatory approval issues.

110. Ibid. The bill provides that permissible activities must be "financial in nature" rather than "closely related to banking," repeals Section 20 of Glass-Steagall, and eliminates many of the firewalls the board imposed on Section 20 subsidiaries.

111. *See* Memorandum from Julie L. Williams, Chief Counsel, to Eugene A. Ludwig, Comptroller of the Currency, OCC (April 8, 1996).

112. Id.

113. *See* "OCC: Leach Bill Leave States Opening to Ban Bank Insurance,' *American Banker* (April 11, 1996).

114. *See* Memorandum from Joe Seidel, General Counsel, House Banking Committee, to David Runkel (April 10, 1996).

115. The OCC has not issued an opinion on the ability of national banks to underwrite a securities issuance on a best efforts basis. Basically, in a best efforts underwriting, the underwriter does not take a stake in the shares being distributed, but merely agrees to use its best efforts in distributing the issuer's shares. In this regard, an underwriter acts as agent in the distribution.

116. 12 USC § 24 (Seventh).

117. 401 U.S. 617 (1972). The Court concluded that although national banks had long been able to manage collective investment trusts as a fiduciary, the particular fund in the *ICI* case caused the bank to have a

stake in the investment. As a result, the Court noted, a host of hazards could arise such that customers might lose confidence in the bank or the bank might not act as an impartial lender. For instance, a bank might prop up its investment stake by making imprudent loans either to stabilize the securities activities of the bank or to assist companies in which the bank invests. These activities, along with the potential for losses due to fluctuating securities markets, could lead to a loss of confidence in banks, a result that Glass-Steagall was intended to prevent.

118. See Letter from Frank Maguire, Senior Deputy Comptroller to Michael Bleier, General Counsel, Mellon Bank, N.A. (May 4, 1994); and Mellon Bank Corporation, 79 Fed. Res. Bull. 626 (1993).

119. Section 20 subsidiaries have been instrumental in underwriting asset-backed securities, such as mortgage-backed securities and securities backed by consumer financing arrangements. See, e.g., Citicorp, J.P. Morgan & Co., Inc., and Bankers Trust N.Y. Corp., 73 Fed. Res. Bull. 473 (1987).

120. 12 USC § 1831a. FDIC regulations implementing Federal Deposit Insurance Act can be found in 12 CFR Part 362.

121. See Section 24(b)(1) of the Federal Deposit Insurance Act. 12 USC § 1831a(b)(1).

122. Memorandum from Julie L. Williams, Chief Counsel, OCC, to Eugene A. Ludwig, Comptroller, OCC (April 8, 1996).

123. Id.

124. The OCC's authorization of the Blackfeet National Bank to offer the Retirement CD derived from the express authority for banks to receive deposits, to enter into contracts and to borrow to fund operations. See Letter from William P. Bowden, Jr., Chief Counsel, to Jack Kelly, President and Chief Executive Officer, Blackfeet National Bank (May 12, 1994). The Retirement CD was developed by American Deposit Corp., Inc., which owns the rights to the product and is seeking patent protection. Blackfeet National Bank of Browning, Montana, was the first licensee of the product.

125. See Letter from Douglas H. Jones, Acting General Counsel, FDIC (May 12, 1994). During the accumulation phase, the covered amount would be equal to principal and accrued interest, as with any other type of CD. During the withdrawal phase, the FDIC would only cover the balance at maturity, less any lump sum or monthly payment amounts.

126. This may have been based on an analysis under Section 1275 of the Code, which relates to annuity contracts issued by noninsurance companies. 26 USC § 1275. This section requires that annuity contracts issued by noninsurance companies must depend in whole or in substantial part on the life expectancy of one or more individuals\ in order to receive tax-deferred treatment.

127. See Letter from The Honorable Max Baucus, United States Senate, to The Honorable Robert E. Rubin, Secretary, The Department of the Treasury (Feb. 16, 1996).

128. The Florida Insurance Commissioner ("Commissioner") instituted an administrative proceeding by issuing an Order to Show Cause alleging that the Blackfeet National Bank was unlawfully engaged in the business of insurance in Florida. The Blackfeet National Bank responded by filing suit in Montana federal court seeking, among other things, an injunction against the Commissioner from interfering with the marketing of the Retirement CD. The Montana District Court granted the Blackfeet National Bank a restraining order preventing the Commissioner from pursuing its administrative proceeding. The bank, on the other hand, was prevented from accepting Retirement CD deposits from citizens of Florida. (See Blackfeet National Bank v. Gallagher, D. Mont. No. CV-94-75-CF-PGH).

A challenge also was lodged in New Mexico but, following the VALIC decision, the New Mexico insurance commissioner dropped its challenge.

129. ___, F.3d___, 1996 WL 252869 (7th Cir. 1996).

130. See Letter from Representative John Dingell, Chairman of the House Energy and Commerce Committee (May 25, 1994).

131. The Blackfeet National Bank filed suit against the Treasury Department seeking to set aside the proposed IRS rules and seeking injunctive and declaratory relief on the basis that the proposed IRS regulations are contrary to the plain language of the Code. (*See Blackfeet National Bank* v. *Rubin*, D.D.C. No. 95–0979 PIF). On June 29, 1995, the U.S. District Court for the District of Columbia dismissed the suit as not ripe for adjudication because the IRS regulations are only in the proposal stage. The bank has appealed to the United States Court of Appeals for the District of Columbia.

132. *Fundamentals* (September/October 1995), p. 3.

133. *National Underwriter* (Nov. 27, 1995), p. 9.

4

UNTANGLING BANK REGULATION FROM STATE INSURANCE REGULATION

Karol K. Sparks, *Krieg DeVault Alexander & Capehart*

A *financial services supermarket* offering a selection of stocks; bonds; mutual funds; fixed and variable annuities; whole, term, and variable, life insurance; demand deposit accounts; cash management accounts; certificates of deposit and derivations of them—this is the goal, the obsession of visionaries in the financial services industry and it has been for more than a decade. As the assault on the Glass-Steagall wall[1] escalates and the distinction between the banking industry and securities industry blurs, the vision becomes attainable.

But what of insurance? It is a logical component of the "financial services revolution." However, the question of its availability for sale by banks raises a whole new host of challenges. The crumbling of the Glass-Steagall wall is not dispositive in this regard. In its place, a new barrier of potentially conflicting federal and state laws and regulations exists. Each and every step taken by the banking industry to assault this barrier falls victim to the emotion of the insurance trade groups, who are committed to preserving, through protest, lobbying, and litigation, the turf of their members.

At the heart of this turf battle lurk two issues: the *authority* of banks to sell insurance generally and the *manner* in which banks may sell insurance. Both bank regulatory agencies and insurance regulatory agencies lay claim to these territories. The vision cannot be attained until these regulatory schemes are untangled.

THE AUTHORITY TO SELL

In order for any bank or affiliate to conduct an insurance-related activity or offer for sale an insurance product (including, for this purpose, annuities), it must have the *legal power* to do so. The statutory framework applicable to the charter of each entity embodies the grant of its powers: for national banks, this is the National Bank Act[2] as interpreted by the Comptroller of the Currency (comptroller); for state banks, this is the banking law of its state of charter as interpreted by the respective state banking authority, with oversight by the Federal Deposit Insurance Corporation;[3] and for bank holding companies and their nonbank subsidiaries, it is the Bank Holding Company Act[4] as interpreted by the Board of Governors of the Federal Reserve System. Essentially, the members of the bank family may only engage in activities specifically allowed by these laws or either "incidental"[5] or "closely related"[6] thereto.

Bank Regulatory Authority

Bank Holding Companies   Under current law, it is not "closely related to banking" for a bank holding company or its nonbank subsidiaries to provide insurance as a principal, agent, or broker.[7] Thus, these entities are generally not viable vehicles for insurance operations.

State Banks   As state banks are incorporated under state law, with their powers determined by the respective state legislatures, they may have powers in one state that differ substantially from the powers of banks in another state. In this vein, state banks represent a continuum of insurance powers—some have the express power to sell all general lines of insurance,[8] whereas some are limited to selling specific types of insurance.[9] Many have wild card authority,[10] which aligns their rights to those of national banks.

Until December of 1992, state law exclusively controlled the process of empowering state banks. That changed with passage by Congress of the Federal Deposit Insurance Corporation Improvement Act of 1992, Section 303 of which added a new Section 24 to the Federal

Deposit Insurance Act,[11] limiting activities of state banks and their subsidiaries acting *as principal*; limiting specifically insurance underwriting and equity and preferred stock investments; and leaving unaffected the ability of state banks to act *as agent* in the sale of insurance.

National Banks   The only provision of the National Bank Act expressly permitting national banks to act as agents in the sale of insurance is 12 USC §92 (Section 92), which limits such activity to small towns with a population of 5,000 or less. In 1986, the comptroller expanded his previous construction of Section 92 and determined that national banks operating general insurance agencies from small towns were authorized to sell insurance to customers without geographic limitation.[12] The insurance industry challenged the comptroller's perceived liberal construction of Section 92[13] and the comptroller was eventually upheld by the D.C. Circuit Court in 1993, with the court recognizing that time and technology had opened up a loophole in national bank authority.[14]

In 1985 and 1990, respectively, the comptroller expanded insurance authority by permitting national banks to participate in the brokering of variable annuity contracts and fixed annuity contracts, both under the authority of the incidental powers clause of Section 24 of the National Bank Act[15] (Section 24 (Seventh)). The comptroller reasoned that such products are regarded purely as investment vehicles and are, therefore, in the nature of securities as opposed to insurance.[16] The comptroller's subsequent approval of an operating subsidiary for NationsBank of North Carolina, N.A., to sell both variable and fixed-rate annuities was challenged by Variable Annuity Life Insurance Company (VALIC) in a lawsuit brought in the State of Texas. After months of jurisdictional squabbles, the suit was transferred to the District Court in the Southern District of Texas. On November 22, 1991, the District Court ruled in favor of the comptroller, holding that his opinion constituted a reasonable construction of the law and was, thus, entitled to deference.[17] On appeal, the Fifth Circuit reversed in its now infamous *VALIC* v. *Clarke* decision,[18] concluding that annuities were insurance within the purview of Section 92, and that Section 92 precluded the comptroller from permitting an insurance activity as an incidental power. In February of 1995, the U.S. Supreme Court disagreed in *NationsBank of North Carolina, N.A.* v. *VALIC*, unanimously overturning the Fifth Circuit's decision.[19] In so doing, the court reaffirmed that decisions by an agency charged with interpreting and applying a statute must be accorded substantial deference.

As a result, after 10 years of move and countermove, of litigation and appeals, authority issues regarding national banks are clear: they may sell insurance without geographical limitation from an office in a town of 5,000 or less, and they may sell fixed and variable annuity products. This, however, is not the end of the story.

Insurance Regulatory Overlay

Antiaffiliation Laws   When banks attempt to exercise their hard-won powers, they may yet encounter new challenges in the states. A number of states have effectively "trumped" bank insurance authority by enacting laws, enforced by state insurance commissioners, that prohibit banks, their subsidiaries, affiliates, and even employees from selling insurance. These statutes that attempt to separate the banking industry from the insurance industry are known as *antiaffiliation laws*.[20]

What happens when a bank power clashes with an antiaffiliation law? Bank holding companies and state banks must comply with the prohibitions of the state insurance law because they have no superior claim. However, national banks are federal instrumentalities, imbued with supremacy by virtue of the United States Constitution. Consequently, when an insurance law of any state deprives a national bank of the right to engage in an authorized activity, its force is frequently deemed preempted by the comptroller.[21]

The Supremacy Clause of the United States Constitution is, however, not necessarily dispositive in the context of insurance. Instead, issues of preemption in this context are specifically addressed by federal law in the McCarran-Ferguson Act[22] (McCarran-Ferguson), which may reverse the traditional supremacy of federal laws over state laws in the realm of insurance:

> No Act of Congress shall be construed to invalidate, impair, or supersede any law enacted by any State for the purpose of regulating the business of insurance, or which imposes a fee or tax upon such business, unless such Act specifically relates to the business of insurance...[23]

Thus, under McCarran-Ferguson, a state law is not preempted by federal law if a two-prong test is met:

- The state law was "enacted...*for the purpose of regulating the business of insurance.*"

- The federal law does not *"specifically relate to the business of insurance."*

Recently, the McCarran-Ferguson analysis was applied to several state antiaffiliation laws with differing results at the outset. The first such case arose in the Commonwealth of Kentucky, following the refusal of the Commissioner of Insurance to license national banks under Section 92. A coalition of banks led by Owensboro National Bank sued the Kentucky commissioner. In granting summary judgment in favor of the plaintiff banks, the District Court in *Owensboro Nat. Bank* v. *Stephens* held that national banking law preempted state law.[24] On December 29, 1994, the Sixth Circuit affirmed the lower court's opinion,[25] finding that the Kentucky statute that prohibited bank ownership of insurance agencies was not enacted for the purpose of regulating the business of insurance, but merely to regulate the people who own insurance agencies. The Sixth Circuit thus held that the Kentucky statute failed the first prong of McCarran-Ferguson. The court did not address the second prong of McCarran-Ferguson. The dissenting judge, however, foreshadowed the next two cases and opined that McCarran-Ferguson does, in fact, shield the Kentucky antiaffiliation statute from federal preemption because:

- The state enacted its antiaffiliation statute to regulate the business of insurance.
- Section 92 does *not* specifically relate to the business of insurance, but relates instead to the business of banking.

In a parallel development, the Louisiana antiaffiliation statute came under similar fire. The Louisiana Court of Appeals upheld a trial court ruling that Section 92 does not preempt a state law limiting the sale of insurance products by banks.[26]

Finally, Barnett Bank sued the Florida Insurance Commissioner in federal district court in Florida in 1993 over his cease and desist enforcement order addressed to the insurance agency Barnett Bank had purchased and intended to operate from a branch located and doing business in a town of 5,000 or less. Florida insurance law prohibits licensed bank employees from soliciting the sale of insurance on bank premises. The Florida District Court granted summary judgment in favor of the commissioner, stating that the court could find no reason for preemption.[27] The Eleventh Circuit agreed in *Barnett Bank of Marion County, N.A.* v. *Gallagher* (*Barnett*), finding that McCarran-Ferguson shielded the state law from preemption because:

- It was enacted to regulate the relationship between insurers and policyholders, as verified by its legislative history.
- Section 92 did not regulate insurance.[28]

Petitions for review of all three cases were filed with the United States Supreme Court. The Court granted certiorari originally only to *Barnett*, holding the other petitions pending its decision on *Barnett*, and on March 26, 1996, the Supreme Court rendered another unanimous decision in favor of national banks.[29] It ruled that state antiaffiliation laws are preempted by Section 92. The Supreme Court's holding could have been quite different. It could have been much more narrow or quite broad: at its narrowest, it could have merely invalidated Florida's anti-affiliation law on the basis of a failure to meet the first prong of McCarran-Ferguson; at its broadest, it could have potentially swept away all antiaffiliation laws, even as to section 24 (Seventh), on the basis that all antiaffiliation statutes were not enacted to regulate insurance.

However, in a departure from the lower court cases, the Supreme Court bypassed the first prong of McCarran-Ferguson completely, relying instead on ordinary principles of preemption and the second prong of McCarran-Ferguson. As to ordinary principles of preemption, the Court found clear preemption by the federal law because it prevents or significantly interferes with the ability of a national bank to exercise its powers under Section 92. As to McCarran-Ferguson, the Court held its reverse preemption effect did not apply because Section 92 permits national banks to solicit insurance and receive commissions; consequently, it specifically relates to insurance. Thus, all state antiaffiliation laws fell to Section 92.

But *Barnett* did not answer all of the questions regarding the conflicts between state insurance law and federal banking law. On August 21, 1995, Mississippi became the next forum for a bank-insurance industry showdown when *Deposit Guaranty Nat. Bank* v. *Dale*,[30] (*Deposit Guaranty*) was filed in the U.S. District Court of the Southern District of Mississippi. In this case, the plaintiff national bank sought to sell annuity products without interference from the Mississippi Department of Insurance. Significantly, *Deposit Guaranty* asked the questions left unanswered by *Barnett*:

- Does Section 24 (Seventh) permitting national banks to sell annuity products pre-empt the Mississippi antiaffiliation statute?[31]

- Does such federal law pre-empt all Mississippi insurance law and regulations of the Department of Insurance, including those requiring insurance agencies to be licensed as such?

Thus, *Deposit Guaranty* reaches the ultimate issue: where does preemption by federal banking law begin and end?

Untangling Authority Issues

The comptroller believes that Congress in enacting McCarran-Ferguson did not intend to give the states the authority to preclude otherwise lawful activities of national banks.[32] In fact, the comptroller believes that national banking law monopolizes the field of national bank powers and that issues under Section 24 (Seventh) are not even within the purview of McCarran-Ferguson.[33] As articulated by the comptroller's Chief Counsel, Julie Williams, this "is not simply an abstract question of federal law intersecting the state law. It is about providing services to customers. If banks can provide better service, regulators should let them compete."[34]

Foreseeably, the states also claim that they are protecting the rights of the consumer. In that regard, the states are reportedly concerned that insurance not be sold through institutions that require such coverage in order to conduct other business. As the District Court in the *Barnett* decision noted:

> in order to make a profit on automobile loans or home mortgages, the insurance agents may incur business they might otherwise reject because they would be pressured by the bank to do so in order to consummate the bank's loan transactions. This might lead to the over-insurance of risky business, which could result in the insolvency of the insurer. Additionally,... loan officers could steer customers to the bank's insurance agent for the purpose of suggesting the sale of insurance that is not needed, in order for the bank to make a profit on the insurance policy.[35]

What is the role of the states in insurance regulation?

THE MANNER OF SALE

As indicated above, there is no body of federal insurance law—no regulatory agency has national authority in this regard. Instead, by virtue of McCarran-Ferguson,[36] the business of insurance is regulated exclusively by state law. There are thus 50 state laws and 50 state commissioners overseeing the underwriting and sale of insurance. The states each regulate the manner of insurance sales in terms of who may sell, the educational requirements they require, and sales practices. All 50 states uniformly define annuity products as insurance for these purposes.

Insurance Regulatory Framework

Licensing Requirements   One critical element of state regulation of insurance is the inherent grant of authority to state insurance commissioners to require licensing of insurance agents. Any party who will sell insurance and receive a commission must usually obtain a license. Thus, the sale of insurance, including annuity products, normally requires insurance agency licensing and individual agent licensing under applicable state law. There are many traps for the unwary in the insurance licensing laws of the various states:

+ First, several states do not license corporations.[37]
  Consequently, a bank desiring to sell insurance or annuity
  products in these states must assure itself of its ability
  to receive commissions on sales made by its licensed
  employees. Unfortunately, the states are not consistent
  in this regard, although most permit licensed employees
  to make commission assignments to their employers.

+ Second, a number of states have laws that limit who may
  own agencies. Ohio[38] and Texas[39] only permit ownership
  of insurance agencies by natural persons resident in the
  state. Oklahoma[40] requires ownership by another licensed
  insurance agency, which could not be met by bank holding
  companies.

+ Third, in some states licensing laws include innocuous
  restrictions that tend to have an adverse impact on banks,
  in particular. As an example, some, such as Oklahoma,[41]
  require that the sale of insurance be the sole purpose in the
  articles of incorporation. Others, such as Maryland,[42] require
  that the "principal purpose" of the corporation be the sale of
  insurance. Obviously, these provisions require banks to form
  subsidiaries (other than brokerage subsidiaries) in order to
  obtain licensing.

- Fourth, several states have "controlled business" laws that prohibit a licensed agent from soliciting insurance sales from related parties. Definitions of *controlled business* vary from state to state, but several are onerous. The state law of Ohio,[43] for instance, is sufficiently broad in its definition of controlled business to encompass bank depositors and borrowers, which has an impact on the potential profitability of bank marketing endeavors in that state.

The state licensing laws apply to anyone who sells insurance and/or annuity products—*wherever they sell such products*. Thus, a bank with interstate operations must comply with applicable law in its home state and in each other state of its operations. The vast majority of states license individuals and corporations both resident in or out of the state. Nonresident licenses are typically issued only on a *reciprocal basis*—an agent may enter a foreign state so long as its home state permits equal entry. Most states are reciprocal for individual agents; however, for corporations, some states are reciprocal and others are not. Lack of reciprocity makes movement from one state to another a little like moving around a chess board. In certain instances, states grant reciprocity but limit it to specific activities. Thus, an agent entering a foreign state may engage only in those activities, and be subject only to those limitations, that a resident of that state may conduct or be subject to in the other's home state. For instance, if a foreign state will only permit a nonresident agent to place insurance (instead of soliciting insurance), then the agent's home state will place the same limits on the activities of agents from that foreign state. As a result of reciprocity issues, a bank may be required to form one or more separate subsidiaries or affiliates in order to conduct insurance activities outside of its home state. For instance, insurance agencies organized under the laws of Ohio or Texas will be unable to operate in any other state, because those states do not offer reciprocity. Thus, a bank in those states would need to form a subsidiary in a friendlier state that would permit operations in additional reciprocal states.

Educational Requirements   Virtually all of the states now require individuals who seek insurance agent licensing to attend classes and successfully complete examinations prior to licensing. There are certain limited licenses, for example, a credit insurance license, that generally do not require examinations. The states are typically reciprocal in nonresident licensing and require examinations only in the home state. In addition, virtually all of the states now require continuing education for insurance agents.

Sales Practices   State laws represent a comprehensive framework for establishing rules for the conduct of insurance sales. All of the states forbid premium rebating[44] as the cornerstone of their respective regulation of "unfair and deceptive trade practices."[45] In a litany similar to the securities laws, states prohibit misrepresentations in the sales process, fraudulent acts, coercion and the like. The states have enforcement powers, similar to the banking agencies, including the ability to institute cease and desist proceedings and the ability to levy fines. Obviously, they have the valuable statutory right to suspend or revoke licenses.

Bank Regulatory Overlay

Where does preemption by federal banking laws begin and end? According to historical positions of the comptroller, it may sweep as far as attempts by the states to impose licensing requirements on national banks. In fact, several comptroller interpretive letters have taken the position that insurance licensing interferes with the objectives of the national bank system.[46] In taking that position the comptroller has claimed preemption not only of the licensing of banks, but of the licensing of bank employees as well. In addition, the comptroller has determined that states have no visitation powers over national banks— state officials have no authority to conduct examinations or to inspect or require the production of books or records of national banks, except for the limited purpose of ensuring compliance with applicable state unclaimed property and escheat laws.[47] The Office of the Comptroller, in its opinion, has the exclusive power to enforce any law that is directly related to federal banking powers.

In an attempt to codify this opinion, on March 3, 1995, the comptroller proposed to revise the interpretive rulings that appear in Part 7 of Title 12 of the Code of Federal Regulations.[48] Specifically, the comptroller sought comments on whether the principle of preemption of state licensing laws should be included as an interpretive ruling. No action has been taken on this proposal.

Untangling Licensing Issues

It does not come as a surprise that the comptroller should take the position that states may not require national banks to obtain licenses in general—that is consistent with the history of the national bank system. However, when the license involved is for the sale of insurance, the issues become more complicated than issues surrounding lending or safe deposit licenses because of the reverse preemption effect of McCarran-Ferguson and the stake of 50 insurance commissioners in functional regulation. The commissioners argue that the expertise lies in their departments—state laws ensure that agents are knowledgeable and qualified to sell specific products and that they understand relevant laws and regulations.

Is there a federal banking analogue to the state regulatory scheme? Certainly the comptroller has addressed safety and soundness concerns in the sale of annuity products, as have the other federal banking agencies,[49] but aside from compelling training of agents, has the comptroller stepped up to provide that training? Is the comptroller prepared to examine national banks for violation of unfair trade practices, such as rebating, that exist in the realm of insurance sales, but not in the realm of traditional banking?

The comptroller's battle for preemption clearly evolved from overriding state attempts at sweeping powers prohibitions to overriding state regulation of the manner of sale, where the states arguably have the expertise. In the opinion of Donna Bennett, the Commissioner of Insurance of the State of Indiana:

> It is imperative that all persons who sell insurance to consumers in a state be qualified and subject to the same regulatory and enforcement provisions. Citizens of a state may suffer if they purchase insurance from a person affiliated with a national bank if that person has not undergone the same application and qualification process as an agent not affiliated with a bank. There is no valid reason to extend such exempt status to national banks at the expense of consumers.[50]

Certainly, the comptroller recognizes the massive undertaking it would assume should it disenfranchise states from national bank insurance powers. The comptroller generally admits the valid role of state law in aspects of national bank operations and encourages banks to comply with certain types of consumer protection laws as a matter of sound business practices.[51] Further, the comptroller has indicated that it will not prohibit national banks from voluntarily undergoing examinations by state departments of insurance.

Is this *unofficial* spirit of comptroller concession, in the face of the uncompromising language in *official* pre-emption letters, sufficient? Maybe. Certainly Shawmut Bank found a way to balance both federal and state interests. In settling its litigation against the Connecticut Department of Insurance[52], Shawmut agreed to obtain insurance licensing for its employees to sell annuity products. On its part, the Department of Insurance agreed not to enforce the state antiaffiliation statute[53]. Further, and perhaps most significantly, in January of 1996, representatives of the comptroller invited state insurance commissioners to meet with them in an effort to mutually resolve their respective roles in the regulation of the conduct of national bank insurance sales. A resolution from these parties may serve both industries much more efficiently than decisions from the courts, which tend to be piece-meal, and actions of Congress, which tend to be mere expectation. Finally, following the Supreme Court's decision in *Barnett*, officials of the comptroller adopted a seemingly moderate position, indicating informally that national banks would be expected to comply with all nondiscriminatory state laws. The determination as to what laws, other than antiaffiliation laws, meet that description awaits another day, but the efforts of the comptroller lead to the conclusion that, despite its impressive legal wins, what is ultimately beyond *Barnett* is...compromise.

E N D N O T E S

1. The Glass-Steagall Act is the popular name for essentially four provisions of the Banking Act of 1933, 48 Stat. 184 (1933), which separate the business of banking from the securities business. Section 16 of the Act (12 USC §24 (Seventh)) limits the ability of national banks to underwrite and deal in securities and prohibits national banks from purchasing or selling securities except upon the order and for the account of customers. Section 20 (12 USC §377) prohibits Federal Reserve member bank affiliation with a company engaged principally in underwriting and other securities activities. Section 21 (12 USC §378) prohibits organizations that are engaged in underwriting and other securities activities from simultaneously engaging in the business of receiving deposits. Section 32 (12 USC §78) prohibits officer, director, or employee interlocks between member banks and companies that are primarily engaged in securities activities.

2. 12 USC §1, *et seq.* The powers provisions are found generally in 12 USC §24.

3. 12 USC §1831a provides certain limitations on the powers of state banks.

4. 12 USC §1841 *et seq.*

5. National banks are permitted to exercise powers that are incidental to the business of banking. 12 USC §24 (Seventh). Many states have adopted similar language for state bank powers. *See, e.g.,* New York Banking Law §96(1).

6. Bank holding companies are restricted to conducting only activities that are closely related to banking and a proper incident thereto. 12 USC §1843(c)(8).

7. 12 USC §1843(c)(8).

8. *See, e.g.,* Delaware Code Ann. tit. 5, §761(14); Michigan Stat. Ann. §500.1243; New Jersey Stat. Ann. §3:11–11.5(a)(7), and Virginia Code §38.2–513, 514 and 38.2–1824.

9. *See, e.g.,* Maine RSA tit. 24-A, §1514–A, sub-§2, excepting credit insurance and annuities from the general prohibition on insurance sales; Pennsylvania Stat. Ann. tit. 40, §281, excepting credit insurance and title insurance; New Mexico Stat. Ann. §59A–12–10, excepting sales and credit insurance under the town of 5,000 exception.

10. *See, e.g.,* Kansas Stat. Ann. §9–1715 and Alabama Code §5–5A–18.1.

11. 12 USC §1831a.

12. OCC Letter No. 366 (August 18, 1986), *reprinted in* [1985–1987 Transfer Binder] Fed. Banking L. Rep. (CCH), para. 85,536.

13. *National Ass'n. of Life Underwriters* v. *Clarke*, 736 F. Supp. 1162 (DDC 1990).

14. *Independent Ins. Agents* v. *Ludwig*, 997 F. 2d 958 (D.C. Cir. 1993); *Accord, NBD Bank, N.A.* v. *Bennett*, 67 F.3d 629 (7th Cir. 1995).

15. 12 USC § 24 (Seventh).

16. OCC Letter No. 331 (April 4, 1985), *reprinted in* [1985–1987 Transfer Binder] Fed. Banking L. Rep. (CCH), para. 85,501 (variable annuities); OCC Letter No. 499 (February 12, 1990) *reprinted in* [1989–1990 Transfer Binder] Fed. Banking L. Rep. (CCH), para. 83,090 (fixed annuities).

17. *VALIC* v. *Clarke*, 786 F. Supp. 639 (S.D. Texas 1991).

18. *VALIC* v. *Clarke*, 998 F.2d 1295 (5th Cir. 1993).

19. *NationsBank of North Carolina, N.A.* v. *VALIC*, 115 S. Ct. 810 (1995).

20. There are 22 antiaffiliation jurisdictions: Arizona, Arkansas, Colorado, Connecticut, Florida, Georgia, Illinois, Kentucky, Louisiana, Maine, Massachusetts, Mississippi, Nebraska, Nevada, New Hampshire, New Mexico, New York, Pennsylvania, Rhode Island, Tennessee, Vermont, and West Virginia. Most of these states exempt from their prohibitions sales of credit insurance and sales from small towns. Several have recently amended their antiaffiliation statutes to specifically permit annuity sales.

21. OCC Letter No. 475 (March 22, 1989), *reprinted in* [1989–1990 Transfer Binder] Fed. Banking L. Rep. (CCH), para. 83,012 (Tennessee law); OCC Letter No. 623 (May 10, 1993), *reprinted in* [1993–1994 Transfer Binder] Fed. Banking L. Rep. (CCH), para. 83,505 (Connecticut law).

22. 15 USC §§ 1011–15.

23. 15 USC § 1012(b).

24. *Owensboro Nat. Bank* v. *Stephens*, 803 F. Supp. 24 (E.D. Ky. 1992).

25. *Owensboro Nat. Bank* v. *Stephens*, 44 F. 3d 388 (6th Cir. 1994).

26. *First Advantage Insurance* v. *Green*, 652 So.2d 562 (La. App. 1995).

27. *Barnett Bank of Marion County, N.A.* v. *Gallagher*, 839 F. Supp. 835 (M.D. Fla. 1993).

28. *Barnett Bank of Marion County, N.A.* v. *Gallagher*, 43 F.3d 631 (11th Cir. 1995).

29. *Barnett Bank of Marion County, N.A.* v. *Nelson*, 116 S.Ct 1103 (March 26, 1996).

30. *Deposit Guaranty Nat. Bank* v. *Dale*, Civil Action No. 3:950V640WS (F.D. Miss., filed August 21, 1995).

31. Miss. Code. Ann. §§ 83-17-227 to 83-17-231.

32. OCC Letter No. 623, see note 21.

33. OCC Letter No. 475, fn 2, see note 21; But see, *American Deposit Corp.* v. *Schacht*, ___ F. 3rd___ (7th Cir. 1996) wherein the court determined that McCarran-Ferguson did apply to the sale of retirement C.D.'s by national banks.

34. "In 3 Cases, Top Court Is Asked to Decide on Insurance Issues," *American Banker*, July 13, 1995, p. 3.

35. *Barnett Bank of Marion County, N.A.* v. *Gallagher*, 839 F. Supp. 835 at 842 (M.D. Fla. 1993).

36. 15 USC § 1011.

37. *See, e.g.,* Iowa Code § 522.1; Tenn. Code Ann. § 56.6–133; and Fla. Stat. § 626.112.

38. Ohio Rev. Code Ann. § 3905.18.

39. Texas Ins. Code Ann. art. 21.07, Sec. 2(d).

40. Okla. Stat. tit. 36, § 1424(B)(6).

41. Ibid.

42. Md. Ann. Code art. 48A, § 168(e)(2)(i).

43. Ohio Rev. Code Ann. § 3905.18.

44. Rebating involves returning a portion of the premium to a policyholder, although the language of state statutes oftentimes sweeps quite broadly to encompass providing anything of value as inducement to insurance or in connection therewith. *See, e.g.,* Indiana Code § 27–1–20–30.

45. *See, e.g.,* Kansas Stat. Ann. § 40–2404 (unfair methods of competition or unfair and deceptive acts or practices); Missouri St. § 375.936 (unfair practices and frauds).

46. *See,* OCC Letter No. 623 and Letter No. 475, *see* note 21.

47. 12 C.F.R. § 7.6025(b).

48. Notice of Proposed Rulemaking, 60 *Fed. Reg.* 11,924 (1995).

49. *See* Interagency Statement on Retail Sales of Nondeposit Investment Products (February 14, 1995).

50. Letter from Donna D. Bennett, Commissioner, State of Indiana Department of Insurance, to Eugene Ludwig, Comptroller of the Currency (May 1, 1995) (unpublished).

51. 60 *Fed. Reg.* 11,924 (1995).

52. *Shawmut Bank Connecticut, N.A.* v. *Googins* D.C. Conn., filed Feb. 1, 1994).

53. Conn. Gen. Stat. § 38a–775.

DERIVATIVES

5

AN OVERVIEW OF DERIVATIVES

Their Mechanics, Participants, Scope of Activity, and Benefits

Christopher L. Culp, *Competitive Enterprise Institute*
James A. Overdahl, *Office of the Comptroller of the Currency*[1]

By now the headlines are familiar: "Gibson Greetings Loses $19.7 Million in Derivatives"..."Procter and Gamble Takes $157 Million Hit on Derivatives"..."Metallgesellschaft Derivatives Losses Put at $1.3 Billion"..."Derivatives Losses Bankrupt Barings." By reading such popular press accounts one could easily conclude that derivatives were not only *involved* in these losses, but were *responsible* for them as well. Over the past few years derivatives have become inviting targets for criticism. They have become demonized, the *D* word, the 11-letter "4-letter word." When considering how the financial services industry might look in the future, such characterizations of derivatives might lead to the conclusion that whatever the financial services industry looks like, it will *not* include derivatives.

Such a conclusion would, to say the very least, be premature. Derivatives were around long before their recent arrival on the public media scene.[2] Even without any analysis, the longevity alone of these financial transactions suggests something more than what the headlines imply. The goal of this chapter is to examine what derivatives really are. We accomplish this by answering several fundamental questions: What are derivatives? How do they work? Who uses them? How much are they used? and Why are they used? The answers to these questions paint quite a different picture of derivatives than their recent attention suggests and gives us reason to believe that the evolving financial services industry will be using derivatives for a long time.

WHAT ARE DERIVATIVES?

The first question—"What are derivatives?"—might appear to be the *easiest* of all to answer, but in fact it is probably the most difficult. Economists, accountants, lawyers, and government regulators have all struggled to develop a precise definition. Imprecision in the use of the term, moreover, is more than just a semantic problem. Dangerous misclassifications by the press of "anything that loses money" as a derivatives contract[3] do appear to reduce the demand for these instruments—at least in the short run.

Although several competing definitions exist,[4] we define a derivatives contract as *a zero net supply, bilateral contract that derives most of its value from some underlying asset, reference rate, or index.*[5] This definition contains three distinct characteristics: zero net supply, based on some "underlying," and bilateral.

"Zero net supply" means that for every "purchaser" of a derivatives contract there is a "seller." If we view a purchaser of an asset as having a long position in the asset and a seller as having a short position, we can restate the zero net supply criterion as follows: for every long, there is a corresponding short.

An asset that exists in zero net supply is essentially *created* by the agreement of parties to establish corresponding long and short positions in the market. Prior to the agreement of buyer and seller to exchange the asset in the future, the contract defining the terms of future exchange for that asset *did not exist.* Derivatives, moreover, are not the only type of zero net supply asset. A more familiar example is a bank loan, which is literally *created* by agreement of a lender to temporarily transfer a cash balance to a borrower.

Derivatives contracts must also be based on at least one "underlying." An *underlying* is the asset price, reference rate, or index level from which a derivatives transaction inherits its *principal* source of value. In practice, derivatives cover a diverse spectrum of underlyings, including physical assets, exchange rates, interest rates, commodity prices, equity prices, or indexes. Practically nothing limits the assets, reference rates, or indexes that can serve as the underlying for a derivatives contract.[6] Some derivatives, moreover, can cover more than one underlying.

Finally, derivatives are bilateral contracts. They represent obligations by one party to the other party in the contract, and vice versa. The value of a bilateral contract thus depends not only on the value of its underlying, but also on the performance of the two parties to the contract. The value of a contract in which one party sells a shoe to another party, for example, depends not just on the value of the shoe, but also on the ability and intention of the seller to actually deliver the shoe to the buyer.

Even this seemingly detailed three-part definition of derivatives still has some serious drawbacks. Most of the problem comes from the term *underlying*. Because a bond is just a fungible loan, debt securities could satisfy our definition of a derivatives contract. Such inconvenient classifications that just do not "feel right" are usually dismissed by saying that bonds are not derivatives because they derive their value from something *under the control* of the issuer, the performance of the company.[7] Derivatives, by contrast, are usually linked to variables determined by the market at large, such as broad-index interest rates. Such definitional finessing, however, is not very useful, is totally unscientific and unsystematic, and illustrates the swamp into which one wades when trying to consistently define this term.

That the term *derivatives* is difficult to define, however, should not be a source of concern. In fact, a recurring theme throughout this chapter is that *derivatives are not fundamentally different from other financial instruments*. The difficulty of defining derivatives thus traces to their basic similarity to other instruments of finance. That the term exists at all owes more to a desire by popular commentators to popularize and homogenize finance than to any real economic distinction.[8] For the remainder of this chapter, we thus adhere to the definition we postulated above entirely for concreteness of exposition.

HOW DO DERIVATIVES WORK?

All derivatives are either constructed with or are one of two simple and fundamental financial building blocks: forwards and options.[9] A forward obligates one counterparty to buy and the other to sell an asset or commodity in the future for an agreed-upon price. In return for the payment of a premium, an option contract gives the buyer (or holder of the option) the right, *but not the obligation*, to buy or sell an asset in the future at an agreed-upon price. Smithson refers to these two building blocks as the LEGOS® with which all derivatives contracts are built.[10] Once these building blocks are defined, the cash flows on virtually any derivatives transaction can be viewed as the net cash flows on a portfolio comprised of some combination of these building blocks.

Forward Contracts

Forward Delivery Contracts

The most basic forward contract is a forward delivery contract. A forward delivery contract is a bilateral contract negotiated for the delivery of a physical asset (e.g., oil or gold) at a certain time in the future for a certain price fixed at the inception of the contract. No actual transfer of ownership occurs in the underlying asset when the contract is initiated. Instead, there is simply an agreement to transfer ownership of the underlying asset at some future delivery date. A forward transaction from the perspective of the buyer (seller) is thus actually the establishment of a long (short) position in the underlying commodity.

A simple forward delivery contract might specify the exchange of 100 troy ounces of gold one year in the future for a price agreed upon today, say $400 per ounce. If the discounted expected future price of gold in the future is equal to $400 per ounce today, the forward contract has no value to either party *ex ante* and thus involves no cash payments at inception. If the price of gold rises to $450 per ounce one year from now, the purchaser of this contract makes a profit equal to ($450 minus $400) times 100, or $5,000, due entirely to the increase in the price of gold above its initial discounted expected present value. Suppose instead the price of gold in a year happened to be $350 per ounce. Then the purchaser of the forward contract loses $5,000, and she would prefer to have bought the gold at the lower spot price at the maturity date.

Algebraically, the payoff at maturity on a long forward contract based on one unit of some underlying is

$$S_T - X$$

where X is the delivery price fixed at the contract's inception ($400 per ounce in our example) and S_T is the spot price of the underlying (in this case gold) *at the delivery date*. For the long, every dollar increase in the price of gold above the price at which the contract is negotiated yields a $1 per ounce increase in the contract's maturity value, and every dollar decrease in the price of gold yields a $1 per ounce decrease in the contract's value at maturity. If the price of gold at maturity is exactly $400 per ounce the forward purchaser is no better or worse off than if the contract had not been entered.[11]

The cash flow at maturity date T on a short position in a forward contract on one unit of the underlying asset is

$$X - S_T$$

For the short, every dollar increase in the price of gold above the price at which the contract is negotiated causes a $1 per ounce loss on the contract at maturity. Every dollar decline in the price of gold yields a $1 per ounce increase in the contract's value at maturity. If the price of gold at maturity is exactly $400 per ounce the forward seller is no better or worse off than if the contract had not been entered.

Combining the payoffs to the long and short on the forward contract also confirms that the transaction is zero net supply. Because $(S_T - X) + (X - S_T)$ equals zero exactly, the creation of the forward contract by the agreement of the long and short has left the supply of the underlying asset unchanged and, all else equal, has not affected any other market participants except the two that engaged in the forward transaction.

Cash-Settled Forward Contracts

Forward contracts on foreign exchange and physical commodities are commonly observed, and both involve *physical* settlement at maturity. A contract to purchase Japanese yen for Swiss francs three months hence, for example, involves a physical transfer of francs from the buyer to the seller, in return for which the buyer receives yen from the seller at the negotiated exchange rate. Many forward contracts, however, are "cash settled" rather than physically settled. At the maturity of such contracts, the long receives (makes) a cash payment if the spot price on the underlying prevailing at the maturity date of the contract is above (below) the prearranged fixed purchase price.

An especially popular cash-settled forward contract is the "forward rate agreement," or FRA. A FRA is just a cash-settled forward contract based on the London Interbank Offered Rate (LIBOR), or the rate on large-dollar, interbank term Eurodeposits. In a typical FRA, Firm Wells may agree to pay one year hence to Firm La Salle the then-prevailing three-month LIBOR based on an assumed principal value of $1 million, *less* a fixed interest rate of, say, 6 percent of the $1 million principal amount. If three-month LIBOR one year hence turns out to be above 6 percent, Firm La Salle receives a net cash payment from Firm Wells. Firm La Salle thus gains at the expense of Firm Wells. If three-month LIBOR is below 6 percent in a year, the opposite is true. Because the principal amount used to calculate the net cash flow is not actually exchanged, it is referred to as *notional*.

Futures Contracts

Forward contracts are important not only because they play an important role as financial instruments in their own right but also because many other financial instruments embodying complex features can be decomposed into various combinations of long and short forward positions. Derivatives are thus forward-based if the contract can be decomposed into a forward contract or a portfolio of forward contracts.

Perhaps the most common forward-based derivatives contract is a futures contract, or a forward contract that is traded on an organized financial exchange such as the Chicago Mercantile Exchange (CME). Customized derivatives like forwards are often called *privately negotiated derivatives*, whereas the more standardized derivatives transactions negotiated on an organized exchange are referred to, not surprisingly, as *exchange-traded derivatives.*

Like forwards, futures can be based on a variety of underlyings and can be settled either physically or with cash. A popular cash-settled futures contract is the CME's Eurodollar futures contract, which has a value at expiration based on the difference between 100 and the then-prevailing three-month LIBOR. Eurodollar futures are currently listed with quarterly expiration dates and up to 10 years to maturity. The 10-year contract, for example, has an underlying of the three-month LIBOR prevailing 10 years hence.

Although exchange trading is the principal economic distinction between futures and forwards, that implies a lot.[12] A necessary condition for exchange trading, for example, is at least some degree of standardization in contract terms, such as the amount of the underlying on which the contract is based. In turn, standardization facilitates *offsetting*, the process by which a long (short) position on an organized exchange may be neutralized or reversed when a trader takes a short (long) position in the same contract. Standardization and the ability to offset exchange-traded contracts usually results in relatively deeper liquidity for exchange-traded contract markets than in customized, off-exchange contracting.[13]

Another feature typically associated with futures is the daily recognition of gains and losses. At least daily, futures exchanges mark the value of all futures accounts to current market-determined futures prices. Any gains in value from the previous "mark to market" period can be withdrawn by the winners, and those gains are financed by the losses of the losers over that period. The zero net supply feature of derivatives ensures that total gains will exactly offset total losses on any given day. We will return to some of the other features of exchange trading under "The Importance of Credit Risk" below.

With few exceptions, most futures transactions in the United States occur through the "open outcry" trading process, in which traders literally cry out their bids to go long and offers to go short in a physical trading pit. This process helps ensure that all traders in a pit have access to the same information about the best available prices.

One exception to open outcry trading in the United States is electronic trading.[14] GLOBEX™, for example, is an electronic trading system maintained by several futures exchanges. Like open outcry, however, GLOBEX™ still ensures that bids and offers are posted publicly on an electronic screen. Although the traders do not shout, they are still presumed to have access to the best available prices.

When prices are negotiated in a public trading environment in contrast to the opaque environment of privately negotiated derivatives, trading is said to be *transparent*. Transparency in futures trading is more than just a competitive feature of trading provided by exchanges, however. Regulation also forces some degree of transparency by requiring most futures transactions to be negotiated in the transparent environment of the exchange.[15] Federal regulations generally prohibit pre-arranged trades, for example, or private agreements between buyers and sellers outside of exchange hours and off the exchange.

One important exception to the prohibition on off-exchange futures trading in the United States pertains to exchange for physicals (EFP) transactions. An EFP enables certain types of futures transactions to be privately negotiated. If two traders have previously established positions in futures to offset or hedge an actual physical or financial commitment, those traders may engage in an EFP in conjunction with a spot market transaction to offset simultaneously their cash and futures positions off exchange. Suppose, for example, Trader Huron is long crude oil futures to hedge an underlying forward sale of crude oil and Trader Superior is short crude futures and long the underlying oil. If Trader Superior buys the crude in the spot market from Trader Huron, *both* parties' underlying obligations are simultaneously eliminated. Traders Huron and Superior may then engage in an EFP to offset their respective futures positions at a price to which they agree privately. The EFP and its price are then reported to the relevant futures exchange, which processes the transaction as if it were a normal futures trade. This EFP process has become a common way for swap dealers and other traders to establish and liquidate market positions.[16]

Swap Contracts

Another popular forward-based derivative is the swap contract. Swaps are privately negotiated agreements between two parties to exchange or swap cash flows or assets at specified times in the future according to some specified payment formula. Interest rate swaps and currency swaps are the most widely used, although swaps can in principle be based on any underlying asset, reference rate, or index.

Although swaps are commonly pilloried by the popular press as highly complicated products of "rocket science" rather than economics, the basic building blocks underlying a swap are no different than those underlying forward delivery contracts, futures contracts, and many other assets. The cash flows on a simple swap contract, in fact, can always be decomposed into the cash flows on a portfolio of forward contracts. Equivalently, a forward contract is just a one-period swap with a single settlement date (a date on which a cash flow occurs).

An interest rate swap obligates the counterparties to exchange interest payments periodically for a specified period of time. In the most common form of interest rate swap, called the "plain vanilla" fixed-for-floating swap, one payment is based on a floating rate of interest that resets periodically (e.g., three-month LIBOR) and the other on a rate fixed at the inception of the contract. The actual amounts exchanged are calculated based on a notional principal amount. Like FRAs, the notional principal of interest rate swaps is not exchanged. Interest rate swaps can also involve multiple underlyings. A basis or "diff" swap, for example, has periodic settlements based on the difference between two *floating* reference rates, such as LIBOR and some constant maturity Treasury rate.

Currency swaps are similar to interest rate swaps in that one party makes a series of fixed or floating-rate payments to its counterparty in exchange for a series of fixed or floating receipts. In a currency swap, though, the payments and receipts are in different currencies, and the principal amounts of each currency *are* exchanged at the beginning of the swap and returned at its conclusion. The principal of a currency swap is, therefore, *not* notional.

To illustrate how the cash flows on a swap can be viewed as the cash flows on a portfolio of forward contracts, consider the following example. Suppose Firm La Salle enters into an interest rate swap with Firm Wells with a notional principal value of $10 million. La Salle may agree to pay a fixed 6 percent of the notional amount underlying the contract to Firm Wells semiannually for one year, in exchange for which Firm Wells will pay La Salle an amount equal to the six-month LIBOR percentage of the notional amount on the same dates. Firm La Salle thus has "swapped" a 6 percent fixed interest payment for the floating six-month LIBOR.

Now suppose that instead of entering into the interest rate swap, Firm La Salle had entered into a six-month FRA with a notional principal of $10 million that entitled it to receive the six-month LIBOR prevailing six months hence in exchange for paying 6 percent fixed. If Firm La Salle also entered a second FRA maturing in 12 months obligating it to exchange 6 percent fixed interest for the six-month LIBOR prevailing *12 months hence*, the *net* cash flows on the portfolio of two FRAs would be exactly the same as the net cash flows on the single interest rate swap.

In addition to plain vanilla interest rate swaps, many other "flavors" of swaps can be found, most of which are distinguished by differences in the key underlying economic terms of the swap. Even in fixed-for-floating interest rate swaps, numerous terms of the swap contract can be customized, including:

* The notional amount.
* Whether or not the notional amount is subject to an amortization schedule, and if so what that schedule is.
* Who pays and who receives fixed-rate payments.
* The currency in which the interest and/or principal payments are to be made.
* The holiday convention governing payments schedules.

- The length of time the swap will be in effect (i.e., the swap's "tenor").
- The level of the fixed rate.
- The index to which the floating rate resets (e.g., six-month LIBOR).
- The spread (if any) to be added to the floating-rate index, reflecting considerations such as credit risk.
- The frequency of cash flows.
- The day-count convention for each payment stream.
- The frequency and timing of the floating-rate reset.
- Any terms affecting the credit risk of the settlements.

The Importance of Credit Risk

Two elements of credit risk are of potential concern to participants in forward-based derivatives: the probability of counterparty default, and the credit exposure (i.e., how much the company will lose if the counterparty does default). Another distinction between exchange-traded and privately negotiated derivatives is the means by which such credit risk is mitigated.

Credit Risk Reduction in Futures   Credit risk in futures is addressed by exchanges in several ways. First, after a futures trade is negotiated between a long and a short, the clearinghouse of the exchange on which the transaction occurred intersperses itself as the counterparty to *both* transactions. If Buyer Culp and Seller Overdahl consummate a transaction at a particular price, for example, the trade immediately becomes *two* legally enforceable contracts: a contract obligating Culp to buy from the clearinghouse at the negotiated price, and a contract obligating Overdahl to sell to the clearinghouse at the negotiated price. Individual traders thus never have to engage in credit risk evaluation *of other traders. All* futures traders face the same credit risk–the risk of a clearinghouse default.[17]

Second, clearinghouses engage in the multilateral netting of cash flows. *Bilateral netting* is the process by which the gross cash flows of all contracts between two parties (e.g., a trader and the clearinghouse) are netted to a single cash flow. Suppose at the end of a mark to market period Trader Erie owes $100 to the clearinghouse on one trading account, owes $25 to the clearinghouse on a second trading account, and is due $200 from the clearinghouse on a third account. Without bilateral netting, three gross cash flows occur. The trader bears credit risk from the clearinghouse on the $200 she is owed, and the clearinghouse bears credit risk from the trader for a total of the $125 it is owed. If Trader Erie and the clearinghouse bilaterally net their cash flows, the three gross cash flows are reduced to a *single* net cash flow of $75 by the clearinghouse to the trader (i.e., $200 less $100 less $25). The clearinghouse thus faces *no* credit risk, and Trader Erie's credit exposure to the clearinghouse is reduced by $125. Multilateral netting occurs when a futures clearinghouse bilaterally nets its obligations with all futures traders *and then* nets again all the gains and losses *across* traders, thereby further reducing the total cash flow credit exposure of the clearinghouse.

Third, the distribution of daily profits and losses to futures traders ensures that the length of any relevant credit exposure is never longer than the time between mark to market times.

Fourth, futures clearinghouses typically specify stringent capital requirements for their members, as well as conservative loss-sharing rules should a clearinghouse default occur.

Finally, exchanges require all traders to post margin or performance bonds with the exchange before trading, and the level of such initial deposits is generally set at a level perceived high enough to cover any loss that might reasonably occur before the next marking to market.[18]

These features of futures markets work in concert to limit *both* the credit exposure of futures *and* the probability of a clearinghouse default.

Credit Risk Reduction in Swaps   For privately negotiated derivatives, credit exposure and the probability of default are often managed separately. Part of the reason for this is that swaps and other privately negotiated derivatives can be very credit-sensitive instruments due to the often long-dated tenors of the transactions. Whereas daily marking to market limits the credit exposure on futures to the time between mark to markets, the credit exposure on a 10 year swap lasts 10 years.

To manage the credit *exposure* on a given transaction, companies typically set limits on their exposure to any one counterparty and try to ensure adequate capital is on hand to absorb a default if it occurs. To ensure that counterparty credit limits are not exceeded, participants must continually monitor the market value of their positions with each counterparty.[19] In addition, cash flows on notional swaps negotiated with a single counterparty for the same product (e.g., interest rates) are virtually always bilaterally netted. Cross-product bilateral netting is also becoming more common as a means of reducing aggregate counterparty credit exposure.

The terms of the swap contract can also be used to reduce the credit exposure of the transaction. Swap participants often use standard-form contracts called *master agreements* to minimize risks such as the potential for ill-specified contract terms to inhibit netting if one of the parties goes bankrupt. Credit enhancements are also often required in swaps to reduce the exposure of the transactions. Collateral, for example, may be demanded by one or both swap counterparties at the inception of the transaction and/or after an adverse credit event, such as counterparty downgrade by a rating agency. Alternatively, some financial institutions act as credit support providers by guaranteeing all or part of the performance on a transaction in which they are not directly involved, thereby creating a third-party credit support.

Beyond just reducing credit exposures, some institutions mitigate credit risk by attempting to reduce the probability of a default. The simplest and most widely employed way to manage such default risk is to establish a cutoff level for credit quality below which the company will not do business. Many users of swaps, for example, only deal with AAA-rated counterparties. Firms that do not themselves have a AAA credit rating, in addition, often set up separately capitalized affiliates with adequate capital and risk management systems to receive a AAA rating, thereby facilitating their ability to engage in swaps and other credit-sensitive derivatives.

Options

Options are the other component of the derivatives LEGOS®. An option is a contract giving its holder the *right* but not the obligation to purchase or sell an asset on or before some date in the future. A *call option* gives its holder the right to buy an asset, and a *put option* gives its holder the right to sell. When a call or put option is sold, the seller (or "writer") must honor the purchaser's right to buy or sell if the purchaser exercises that right. In exchange for agreeing to honor such exercises when they occur, option writers collect premiums from the option purchasers. The use of the term *premium* is not accidental. Whereas forwards give their purchasers unlimited upside and unlimited liability, purchased options are limited-liability assets and thus can act as a form of price insurance for their holders.[20]

Explicit Options

Options are often negotiated as explicit financial contracts both on exchange and privately. Such explicit options are generally either European- or American-style. A European option is an option that allows its holder to buy or sell only on the option's specified expiration date. An American option, by contrast, enables its holder to buy or sell an asset *at any time on or before the option's expiration date.* Options have a variety of assets, reference rates, or indexes underlying them, including foreign exchange, securities, interest rate indexes (e.g., LIBOR), and commodities.

The value of an option at any given time can be characterized by the relation between the strike price and the current market price of the underlying. For a call option, if the price of the underlying exceeds the strike price, it is said to be *in-the-money.* If the price of the underlying equals the exercise price the call is *at-the money.* For the residual case in which the market price of the underlying is below the strike price, the call is *out-of the money.* The definitions for put options are symmetric.

Option prices can be decomposed into two components: *intrinsic value* and *time value.* Intrinsic value refers to the amount, if any, by which the option is in-the-money. If the underlying price is $114 and the strike price of the call option is $112, for example, the intrinsic value is $2. Time value is whatever value the option has in addition to its intrinsic value and reflects the possibility that currently unforeseen changes in the value of the underlying may occur during the option's remaining life to increase the payoff at expiration. All else being equal, the greater the time to expiration, the more valuable the option to its purchaser.

The value at expiration of a call option per share of the underlying stock is summarized in the following expression:

$$c = \text{Max}[0,(S_T - X)]$$

In other words, the value of the call option at expiration depends on the terminal stock price. If at expiration the terminal stock price is higher than the exercise price, the payoff to the option owner is S_T minus X, and the payoff (expense) to the writer of the call is the reverse—X minus S_T. The seller thus loses, and the buyer gains. The converse is true if S_T is below X. The payoff at expiration for the call buyer and the call seller are pictured in panels (a) and (b) of *Figure 1.*

FIGURE   1

The Valuation at Expiration of European-Style Call and Put Options

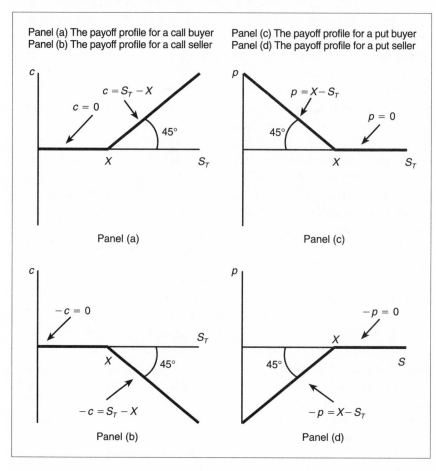

Panel (a) The payoff profile for a call buyer
Panel (b) The payoff profile for a call seller

Panel (c) The payoff profile for a put buyer
Panel (d) The payoff profile for a put seller

$c = S_T - X$

$c = 0$

45°

X S_T

Panel (a)

$p = X - S_T$

$p = 0$

45°

X S_T

Panel (c)

$-c = 0$

S_T

X 45°

$-c = S_T - X$

Panel (b)

$-p = 0$

X

45° S

$-p = X - S_T$

Panel (d)

Notice from Figure 1 that the owner of the option has *limited liability* on the contract. At the option's expiration date, if the price of stock is below the strike price, the option will be out-of-the-money and will not be exercised. The option purchaser, however, loses nothing due to the decline in the price of stock, *unlike* the owner of the forward contract who loses dollar-for-dollar at expiration for a given price decline. If the price of stock has risen above the strike price, the option holder, like the owner of a forward contract, gains dollar-for-dollar from the price rise. This right to participate in price appreciations while limiting loss potential, of course, is not free, and the premium paid for the option by its purchaser reflects this limited liability.

The call writer, by contrast, faces potentially *unlimited* liability in the event of a price increase. If the stock price at expiration finishes below the strike price, the buyer of the option does not exercise it, and the writer happily collects the premium income paid by the option purchaser. If the stock price finishes above the strike price, the buyer does exercise her right to purchase at the strike price, however, and the writer must honor that commitment. Just as the purchaser must pay to eliminate downside risk, the premium collected by an option writer must compensate her for surrendering upside potential and bearing the downside risk of the position.

The valuation of a put at expiration is symmetric with the call. Mathematically, the value of a put option to its purchaser at expiration thus can be expressed as

$$p = \text{Max}[0,(X - S_T)]$$

which is depicted in panel (c) of Figure 1. Panel (d) depicts the reverse, or the value at expiration of the put to its writer. The put option is worthless (i.e., p equals zero) when the price of the stock at expiration is greater than the exercise price because the stock can be sold in the market for more than the exercise price, and conversely if the stock price is below the exercise price.

"Option-Based" Derivatives
Beyond being bought and sold as separate instruments, options are also the basis for numerous other financial contracts. Just as forward-based derivatives can be viewed as bundles of forward contracts, option-based derivatives are combinations of options sold as single products. Two types of option-based derivatives are commonly observed: portfolios of options sold as single financial contracts and compound options.

Portfolios of Options   Perhaps the most common example of an option portfolio sold as a single product is a *cap*. A borrower can buy a LIBOR cap, for example, and pay the lesser of the fixed strike rate in the cap and the prevailing LIBOR at specified intervals. Suppose the rate on a loan is reset every three months to the three-month LIBOR and a borrower purchases a cap with a strike rate of 10 percent. If the rate of interest on the loan goes above 10 percent, the seller of the cap (i.e., the lender) pays the difference to the buyer. Because the higher borrowing costs are offset exactly by the gains on the cap, the *net* effect for the borrower is a borrowing rate capped at 10 percent.

Because loans generally involve multiple interest payments, a portfolio of interest rate call options with maturities corresponding to interest payment dates is required to cap the interest payment on the whole loan. Each of these LIBOR call options is called a *caplet*, and a portfolio of caplets sold as a *single* financial contract is a cap.

A floor guarantees that its buyer (i.e., the lender) receives the greater of the floor rate and the prevailing interest rate. If the rate on a loan contract is reset every three months to three-month LIBOR and the lender wants to guarantee a minimum payment of 5 percent on the loan, she can purchase a floor, or a portfolio of interest rate put options with strike rates of 5 percent and settlement dates corresponding to interest payments on the loan. Each option in the floor is called a *floorlet*.

Caps are also often used in conjunction with floors to create *collars*. The combination of a purchased cap and a written floor results in a collar for a borrower. A borrower, for example, may purchase a cap at 12 percent and sell a floor at 8 percent, thereby allowing the company to borrow at a floating rate that does not fall below 8 percent or rise above 12 percent. Purchasing a collar is sometimes viewed as a way for a borrower to reduce the cost of a cap by accepting the obligation to make payments to the floor buyer if rates fall below the floor rate. (Recall that the borrower *pays* premium for the purchased cap and *collects* premium for the written floor.) A lender also can purchase a collar by purchasing a floor and selling a cap. Like the collared borrower, the collared lender views a collar as a way of reducing the gross cost of purchasing a floor.

Compound Options   Option-based derivatives also include *compound options*, or options whose underlyings are other options. A caption, for example, gives its holder the right to buy a cap with a given strike rate at a specific price on or before a given date. The caption contract specifies not only the cap rate and the maturity for the underlying cap but also the premium that will be paid for the cap itself if the caption is exercised (i.e., the strike price for the caption) and the tenor of the caption. Other compound options include floortions (options on a floor) and collartions (options on a collar).

Combination Derivatives

Forward and forward-based derivatives are often bundled together with explicit or embedded options or option-based derivatives to form combination derivatives. As a simple example, consider a putable swap in which one or both counterparties to a simple interest rate swap may terminate the swap early for a specified cash value if the underlying interest rate moves more than a specified amount. A fixed-rate payor, for example, may be allowed to terminate her pay fixed/receive floating swap if the underlying floating rate falls more than 200 basis points below the fixed swap rate. The cash flows on such a putable swap to the fixed-rate payor are the same as the cash flows on a portfolio comprised of a plain vanilla swap and a floor.

What at first may seem like simple forward-based contracts are also often combination derivatives due to the presence of embedded options, some of which may not be immediately obvious. Consider, for example, a forward contract requiring one party to sell 5,000 bushels of wheat to the forward purchaser in 90 days at a fixed price. Suppose also that the contract allows the seller to deliver *either* No. 2 Dark Northern Spring wheat *or* No. 1 Northern Spring wheat, one of which is likely to be cheaper than the other 90 days hence. The seller possesses a valuable option (written implicitly by the forward purchaser) to sell the cheaper of the two wheat grades.[21] Such cheapest-to-deliver options are commonly embedded in commodity and some financial futures contracts.[22]

Other popular combination derivatives include the following:

- A *forward-start swap*, or a swap contract whose terms are negotiated in advance of the period in which settlements occur—a forward contract with a swap as its underlying.

- A *swaption,* or an option on a swap.

- A *fraption,* or an option on a FRA.

- A *futures option*, or an option on a futures contract.

- An *index amortizing swap*, or a swap whose notional principal value amortizes over time according to some schedule, often indexed to some reference rate like LIBOR. Although viewed as a single product, many index amortizing swaps simply are combinations of caps or floors coupled with plain vanilla interest rate swaps.

The process by which new financial contracts are built from the elemental forward and option building blocks is often referred to as *financial engineering*.[23]

Synthetics

Sometimes combining the elemental derivatives building blocks replicates *another building block* instead of a new financial instrument. When the net cash flows of two building blocks held in the same portfolio are equivalent to the cash flows on some other building block, the position is called a *synthetic* and the portfolio of original building blocks is said to be *synthetically equivalent* to the resulting building block whose cash flows are replicated.

To take a specific example, suppose two European options—a short call and a long put—are entered at the same strike price. If the asset underlying the options is physical, the following relation must hold to preclude arbitrage opportunities:

$$c - p = S_t - Xe^{-r(T-t)}$$

where c is the price of a European call, p is the price of a European put, S_t is the price of the underlying commodity today (which is assumed to pay no dividends), X is the strike price of the call and put, r is the interest rate, T is the expiration date of the options, and e is the exponential function. We have assumed costless transacting for simplicity. This relation is called *put-call parity*.[24] The relation says that borrowing the present value of the option strike price, purchasing a put, and selling a call are synthetically equivalent to selling the underlying asset short. Lending the present value of the option strike price, purchasing a call, and selling a put are synthetically equivalent to purchasing the underlying asset. If the asset underlying the option is a contract on which no initial cash flow occurs (e.g., a forward contract), borrowing is not required to establish the underlying contract and the put-call parity can be rewritten as

$$c - p = e^{-r(T-t)}(F - X)$$

where F is the fixed price of the subsequent purchase or sale of the underlying.

Structured Notes

Given the definition of derivatives we set forth earlier, a *structured note* can be defined as a debt security whose cash flows can be decomposed into the cash flows on a traditional, straight debt security (e.g., a level-coupon or zero-coupon bond) and a derivatives contract.[25] For that reason, structured notes are also sometimes called *derivative securities*[26] or *hybrid debt*.

Structured notes can contain embedded forward-based or option-based derivatives. Perhaps the simplest type of forward-based structured note is a floating rate note (FRN), or a note whose coupon payments are indexed to a floating interest rate such as LIBOR. The cash flows on a FRN can be decomposed into the cash flows on a straight fixed-rate, level-coupon bond and a fixed-for-floating interest rate swap whose notional principal is the same as the face value of the bond and whose settlement dates correspond to the bond's coupon dates.[27]

A simple option-based structured note is an equity-linked medium term note (MTN). The Stock Index Growth Notes (SIGNs) issued by the Republic of Austria several years ago, for example, were five-year MTNs that paid no coupons and returned a principal value to investors at maturity equal to the face value of the note or the percentage increase in the S&P 500 index of stocks. If the S&P 500 declined in value over the life of the note, investors received only the face value of the note. If the S&P 500 rose, however, investors received for every $10 face value of the bond the percentage increase in the S&P 500 over the life of the note *plus* the face value of the note. The cash flows on the SIGNs thus were equivalent to the cash flows on a portfolio of a zero-coupon bond and a long, at-the-money call option on the S&P 500.[28]

WHO ARE THE PARTICIPANTS IN DERIVATIVES ACTIVITY?

The broadest way to categorize derivatives activity is to distinguish between those transactions privately negotiated in an opaque, off-exchange environment and those conducted on organized financial exchanges. A description of the different participants involved in these contracting activities follows.

Privately Negotiated Derivatives

Privately negotiated derivatives involve two types of participants: dealers and end users. Dealers act as agents for a variety of end user principals in privately negotiated derivatives transactions, generally standing ready to accept both sides of a transaction (e.g., long *or* short) depending on which is demanded at the time. These dealers generally run close to a "matched book," in which the cash flows on numerous transactions on both sides of a market net to a relatively small risk exposure on one side of the market. When exact matching is not feasible, dealers typically lay off the residual risk of their dealing portfolio by using other derivatives. Interest rate swap dealers, for example, rely heavily on CME Eurodollar futures to manage the residual risks of an interest rate swap dealing portfolio.

Because dealers act as financial intermediaries in privately negotiated derivatives, they typically must have a relatively strong credit standing, large relative capitalization, good access to information about a variety of end users, and relatively low costs of managing the residual risks of an unmatched portfolio of customer transactions. Firms already active as financial intermediaries are natural candidates for being dealers. Most dealers, in fact, are commercial banks, investment banks, and other financial enterprises such as insurance company affiliates. (See Table 6 and the discussion later in the text.)

End users of privately negotiated derivatives are institutions that engage in derivatives transactions as principals, or for a purpose other than generating fee income such as risk management. End users do not usually take both sides of a contract but instead enter into derivatives *either* as a long *or* a short to obtain or modify a particular risk exposure. Some of the reasons for principals to engage in derivatives are discussed later in "Why Are Derivatives Used?"

End users of derivatives include commercial banks, investment banks, thrifts, insurance companies, manufacturing and other nonfinancial corporations, institutional funds (e.g., pension and mutual funds), and government-sponsored enterprises (e.g., Federal Home Loan Banks). Dealers, moreover, may use derivatives in an end-user capacity when they have their own demand for principal derivatives exposure. Bank dealers, for example, often have a portfolio of privately negotiated interest rate derivatives separate from their dealing portfolio in order to manage the interest rate risk they incur in traditional banking (i.e., borrowing at short maturities and lending at longer ones).

Exchange-Traded Derivatives

Because the primary distinction between exchange-traded and privately negotiated derivatives is exchange trading, the role of organized exchanges as participants in the former is of central importance. In fact, the role of all other participants in exchange-traded derivatives can usually be explained in terms of their relationship with an exchange.

Organized Exchanges

There are two primary types of organized financial exchanges in the United States—securities exchanges and futures exchanges. The distinctions between them are entirely due to regulation. The Commodity Exchange Act requires that futures contracts and options on futures contracts trade only on designated contract markets, futures exchanges like the Chicago Board of Trade (CBOT) and the CME. Securities exchanges, such as the Chicago Board Options Exchange, Philadelphia Stock Exchange, and American Stock Exchange, list for trading products such as options on individual stocks, options on cash equity indexes, and options on foreign currency. The Commodity Futures Trading Commission (CFTC) regulates futures exchanges, and the Securities and Exchange Commission (SEC) regulates securities exchanges.

Organized exchanges are often used as examples of unfettered free enterprise and perfect competition. Yet, transactions in these markets are actually highly regulated. In addition to the regulation of trading by the CFTC or SEC, organized exchanges also rely heavily on their own rules to create fair and competitive markets. Exchanges specify the rules of trading, the terms of exchange-listed contracts, the conditions of exchange membership, and the technology employed for order entry and trade execution. The exchanges invest heavily in developing and maintaining their reputations by policing their markets to deter inappropriate behavior. Exchanges have the power to conduct disciplinary hearings and may fine, suspend, or expel members who harm the integrity of the market by behaving inappropriately.

Futures Exchange Participants

Participation in trading on futures exchanges is limited to exchange members. To become an exchange member, a firm or individual must purchase a seat on an exchange from a current seat holder.[29] The market for exchange seats tends to be quite competitive, and many firms hold more than one membership at any time.

Memberships come in two types: those that grant owners access to trading pits, and those that grant owners access to the clearinghouse. Most memberships of the first type are defined for specific products or groups of products. A full membership on the CBOT, for example, entitles the seat holder to trade all CBOT futures and futures options, whereas other smaller CBOT memberships restrict trading to particular types of products. Benefits of holding such product-based memberships include direct access to the trading floor and reduced fees.

Memberships that grant their owners access to the clearinghouse are called *clearing memberships* and are structured differently depending on the particular exchange. A clearing member provides capital to back the clearinghouse in return for reduced clearing fees. Clearing members also face strict capital requirements and are subject to loss-sharing liability rules should a clearinghouse default occur.

Product-based and clearinghouse-based memberships, moreover, are often rolled into one. On the CME, for example, firms cannot purchase clearing memberships alone. Instead, traders must apply to the clearinghouse for designation as a clearing member, and such members must not only meet clearinghouse capital adequacy requirements but also must already own at least two *each* of the three types of *product-based* CME memberships: CME full memberships, entitling holders to trade all products; International Monetary Market (IMM) memberships, entitling holders to trade financial futures and options only; and Index and Options Market (IOM) memberships, entitling owners to trade all index futures and futures options.

Futures exchange members and clearing members may trade for their own accounts, for the account of another member, or for the account of an outside customer. Because all trading occurs in the pits, a trader may act as a principal to one transaction and an agent to another. Futures exchange participants who are primarily in business to act as agents, executing or clearing transactions for *nonmember* customers, are called futures commission merchants.

Securities Exchange Participants

As with futures exchanges, direct participation in the price negotiation process on securities exchanges is limited to members. Unlike futures exchanges, however, securities exchanges often have a specific classification of membership called *market maker*. One or several market makers on a securities exchange are obliged by exchange rules to buy *or* sell the listed contract at any time for a fair price, given demand for transactions by other members. Market makers can benefit from this privilege by earning profits on the bid-ask spread, but they in turn are generally expected to sell into a rising market and buy in a declining one. Capital requirements on market makers thus are generally high.

All nonmember customer trades on securities exchanges go through a broker/dealer agent with an exchange membership, who in turn executes its trades on behalf of the customer through a market maker.

HOW WIDELY USED ARE DERIVATIVES?

Measurement Issues

Measuring the size and growth of derivatives activity, especially for privately negotiated derivatives, is difficult. For exchange-traded derivatives, volume and open interest are the standard proxies for the size and growth of these financial contracts. *Volume* is a measure of contracts traded, and *open interest* measures the number of contracts outstanding. But even these seemingly straightforward measures are subject to definitional nuances, with some exchanges complicating the task by adding their own twists to the way these aggregates are measured.

Quantifying privately negotiated derivatives activity is even more problematic, largely because disclosure and reporting are not required on a widespread basis. Most aggregate data is thus dependent on voluntary participation in surveys. Data on prices for privately negotiated derivatives transactions, moreover, are virtually nonexistent because by their nature such transactions are customized and bilateral. Data are reported on the more standard, plain vanilla varieties of interest rate and currency swaps, but the absence of standard conventions for products such as equity and commodity swaps makes quotation and data access nearly impossible.

Data routinely are reported that provide some information on privately negotiated derivatives activity. Three popular measures are notional principal amounts, replacement costs, and volume. Notional principal is simply the total principal amount outstanding on privately negotiated derivatives of a particular variety. Recall, however, that although some products such as currency swaps have principal that actually is exchanged, many products such as interest rate swaps do not—hence, the term *notional*. The notional amount underlying a swap reveals *nothing* about the capital actually at risk in that transaction. If one party to a swap agrees to pay 5 percent of a $100 million notional amount while the other party pays LIBOR as a percentage of $100 million, using $100 million as a measure of the value of the swap is of little practical relevance. In most cases, the cash flows actually exchanged are at least an order of magnitude smaller than the notional principal amount. And that is *before* considering the risk-reducing effects of any bilateral netting and/or credit enhancements.

An alternative sometimes used for reporting the extent of a firm's derivatives activity is replacement cost, or the current mark-to-market value of its swap contracts. The replacement cost of a particular transaction is simply the discounted present value of expected future net cash flows, or the cost of replacing the swap at current market prices. Replacement cost thus measures capital at risk on the same order of magnitude as bilaterally netted settlement payments.

Finally, volume is a useful measure of activity in privately negotiated derivatives. For the same reason that price data are scant, volume data are equally difficult to aggregate for opaque, customized privately negotiated derivatives. Some information is available on new swap contracts negotiated, however, which serves as the closest available analogue to the volume data reported for exchange-traded derivatives.

Sources of Information and Data

Derivatives activity can be tracked on a regular or semiregular basis through several sources. Exchange-traded derivatives data are maintained and distributed primarily by the exchanges themselves. Aggregate market data are also compiled by the Futures Industry Association (FIA), the FIA's Futures Industry Institute, and price reporters such as Knight Ridder.

For privately negotiated derivatives activity, perhaps the most regular and reliable source of cross-sectional information is contained in quarterly surveys conducted for the International Swaps and Derivatives Association (ISDA) by Arthur Andersen. As with virtually all data on privately negotiated derivatives relating to aggregate activity, the ISDA/Andersen surveys are entirely dependent on firms' voluntary responses to surveys—neither full participation nor full disclosure is ensured. Surveys on commodity and equity derivatives, for example, historically have had lower response rates than surveys on rate and currency swap activity.

In addition to the ISDA/Andersen surveys, several publications collect and report data on privately negotiated derivatives. *Swaps Monitor* newsletter, for example, publishes an annual report of privately negotiated derivatives activity based largely on information contained in SEC filings and additional, voluntary disclosures. Sporadic surveys of derivatives activity are also conducted by other accounting firms (e.g., Price Waterhouse) and private organizations (e.g., The Group of Thirty).

Finally, mandatory regulatory disclosures provide some limited information on derivatives activity. Aggregate notional positions are required, for example, in reports filed by banking institutions with banking regulators such as call reports (RC-L) and bank holding company reports (Y-9).

Recent Size and Growth in Derivatives Activity

Exchange-Traded Derivatives

For exchange-traded derivatives including futures and options on futures, Table 1 provides the breakdown of 1994 annual volume by product type. The table shows that interest rate products (e.g., Treasury Bond and Eurodollar futures) are by far the most popular form of exchange-traded derivatives contract, constituting nearly 50 percent of U.S. trading volume. The table also shows that exchange-traded derivatives can be characterized as contracts with financial rather than physical underlyings.

TABLE 1

1994 Total Exchange-Traded Annual Volume, U.S. Futures and Futures Options

Type of Underlying	Number of Contracts Traded
Interest rates	314,727,875
Equity indexes	145,405,519
Agricultural commodities	69,560,443
Energy products	57,142,180
Foreign exchange	49,491,268
Precious metals	18,708,782
Nonprecious metals	2,922,133
Other	514,067
TOTAL	658,472,267

Source: Futures Industry Association

Table 2 shows that the total number of contracts traded on U.S. exchanges, which were once virtually unchallenged in the international arena, has now fallen behind foreign exchanges. Table 3 shows the top 10 global futures contracts in 1994 by volume, again confirming the popularity of interest rate products. Finally, Table 4 presents the 10 most active global exchanges (by 1994 volume).

TABLE 2

Total Exchange-Traded Futures and Futures Options by Region

	Millions of Contracts Traded		Change	
	1993	**1994**	**Percent**	**Contracts (millions)**
United States	521.7	658.5	26.2	136.8
Abroad	538.3	776.8	44.3	238.5
TOTAL	1,060.0	1,435.3	35.4	375.3

Source: Futures Industry Association

TABLE 3

Top Ten Global Futures Contracts (by 1994 volume)

Rank	Product	Exchange	Contracts (millions)
1	3-mo. Eurodollars	CME	104.8
2	U.S. Treasury Bonds	CBOT	100.0
3	French Notional Bond	MATIF (France)	50.2
4	U.S. dollar	BM&F (Brazil)	39.2
5	3-mo. Euroyen	TIFFE (Japan)	37.4
6	German Bund	LIFFE (London)	37.3
7	3-mo. EuroDmark	LIFFE	29.3
8	Interest rate	BM&F	28.5
9	IBEX 35	MEFF (Spain)	27.0
10	Light, sweet crude oil	NYMEX (U.S.)	26.8

Source: Futures Industry Association

T A B L E   4

Top Ten Global Futures and Options Exchanges (by 1994 volume)

Rank	Exchange	Contracts (millions)
1	Chicago Board of Trade (CBOT)	219.5
2	Chicago Mercantile Exchange (CME)	205.2
3	London International Financial Futures Exchange (LIFFE)	148.7
4	Chicago Board Options Exchange (CBOE)	115.0
5	BM&F (Brazil)	103.0
6	MATIF (France)	93.4
7	New York Mercantile Exchange	78.7
8	DTB (Germany)	49.3
9	London Metals Exchange	47.7
10	TIFFE (Japan)	38.0

Source: Futures Industry Association

Privately Negotiated Derivatives

Table 5 shows several different estimates of privately negotiated derivatives activity by product type. Depending on the source and products included, the notional amounts reported for derivatives activity vary widely. All sources, however, agree that interest rate and currency derivatives represent the largest segment of privately negotiated derivatives activity, whereas equity and commodity derivatives have a smaller showing.

Table 6 shows a breakdown of total derivatives by dealer. Dealers are ranked according to the notional value of their total positions. In general, swap dealers are dominated by U.S. commercial banks and overseas banks, which is not surprising in light of our previous discussion of the expected characteristics of a competitive dealer.

Table 7 gives a slightly different perspective of privately negotiated derivatives activity. That table gives the net replacement cost for all derivatives positions of 125 dealers surveyed as of June 30, 1994. As the difference in the average and median replacement cost indicates, the largest exposures are concentrated among a few dealers. Even then, the numbers in Table 7 give a much better perspective on capital at risk in privately negotiated derivatives. They are much smaller than the notional amounts shown in Tables 5 and 6.

T A B L E   5

Notional Amounts ($ billions) of Privately Negotiated Derivatives Outstanding

Source (# reporting)	Year	Total	Interest Rate	Currency	Equity & Commodity	Other
Swaps monitor (50 Dealers)	1992	$25,985	$10,844	$9,757	$874	$4,510
Swaps monitor (1,139 Firms)	1992	$15,541	$5,115	$5,675	n/a	$3,661
Federal Reserve (n/a)	1991	$7,446	$3,836	$3,472	$138	$0
Federal Reserve (n/a)	1992	$8,789	$4,892	$3,783	$114	$0
GAO (875 Firms)	1991	$24,708	$10,752	$9,537	$678	$3,741

Source: General Accounting Office, *Financial Derivatives: Actions Needed to Protect the Financial System*, Report GGD–94–133 (May 1994)

T A B L E   6

Top 10 Global Dealers in Privately Negotiated Derivatives, 1993

Rank	Firm	Notional Outstanding ($ millions)
1	Chemical Bank	$2,479,271
2	Citicorp	$1,975,190
3	Bankers Trust	$1,903,784
4	Societe Generale	$1,824,483
5	J.P. Morgan	$1,651,063
6	Union Bank of Switzerland	$1,559,469
7	Mitsubishi Bank	$1,559,280
8	Swiss Bank	$1,477,400
9	Hongkong Shanghai Bank Corp. Holdings	$1,233,989
10	Paribas	$1,136,509

Source: *The World's Major Derivatives Dealers*, Swaps Monitor Publications, Inc. (1994)

T A B L E   7

1994 Dealer Replacement Costs for Privately Negotiated Derivatives

Total Replacement Cost of All Derivatives	Number of Responding Dealers
Less than $10 million	16
$10 million – $300 million	21
$300 million – $2 billion	28
Over $2 billion	28
No response	32
Total number of firms surveyed	125
Average replacement cost	$6 billion
Median replacement cost	$0.5 billion

Source: *Derivatives: Practices and Principles Follow-Up Surveys of Industry Practice* (Washington, DC: The Group of Thirty, December 1994)

Finally, Table 8 shows the volume and open interest of privately negotiated derivatives negotiated by the 125 surveyed dealers for the *first half* of 1994 (between January 1 and June 30). In comparing these figures to the corresponding aggregates in exchange-traded derivatives, it is important to keep in mind that the average *size* of transactions tends to be much larger for privately negotiated derivatives than for exchange-traded contracts.

WHY ARE DERIVATIVES USED?

One question frequently asked about derivatives is whether these fancy instruments have any redeeming social value. "Isn't this all a big game of 'hide the ball?' Isn't risk just being shuffled from one investor to another without anything of value being created?"[30] Thus far, we have explored only what derivatives are, who uses them, and by how much. In this section we will see *why* they are so popular.

Companies that demand derivatives transactions as principals are called *end users*. Because of the economic similarities between exchange-traded and privately negotiated derivatives, most of the potential benefits to such end user participants do not depend on the type of instrument chosen. This does not does not imply, of course, that end users are indifferent between exchange-traded and privately negotiated derivatives. A

T A B L E   8

Number of New Derivatives Privately Negotiated and Outstanding at 125 Dealers

Contract Type	New Transactions, 1/1/94–6/30/94	Contracts Outstanding, 6/30/94
Interest Rate	439,250	1,036,750
Currency	1,595,125	805,250
Equity	1,069,000	259,875
Commodity	28,375	28,375
Multiasset	1,625	3,500
TOTAL	3,133,375	2,133,750

Source: *Derivatives: Practices and Principles Follow-Up Surveys of Industry Practice* (Washington, DC: The Group of Thirty, December 1994)

firm desiring a highly customized contract might choose privately nego- tiated derivatives, whereas a firm wishing to avoid costly analyses of counterparty credit risk might opt for exchange-traded transactions. Such considerations do not usually affect the underlying source of demand for the derivatives, however.

   The suppliers of derivatives differ depending on the type of trans- action at issue, and we turn to these types of market participants first.

Benefits to "Suppliers" of Derivatives

By providing a set of trading rules and listing contracts for trading, organized exchanges are suppliers of exchange-traded derivatives con- tracts. The supply of *transactions* in those contracts—the supply of liquidity—is furnished by exchange *participants*, but the contracts them- selves are supplied by exchanges. In contrast, swap dealers are suppli- ers of privately negotiated derivatives *and* the liquidity underlying such contracts. Not surprisingly, the benefits to the two types of suppliers are different.

Benefits to Privately Negotiated Derivatives Dealers
There are several obvious benefits to dealing in privately negotiated derivatives. First, fee income is generated whenever a dealer acts as an agent rather than a principal in a transaction. Matching trades allows dealers to make profits by essentially fulfilling a brokerage capacity and

earning bid-offer spreads. Dealers also sometimes earn transaction fees from structuring complex products. In these cases, derivatives dealers are benefiting not so much from their supply of the derivatives contracts but from their supply of liquidity—dealers effectively earn profits by standing ready to help end users repackage cash flows using derivatives.

Second, dealers can benefit from positive clientele effects. Good reputations and competitive pricing over time will result in repeat business that benefits dealers. Establishing an ongoing dealing relationship with an end user may allow the dealer the opportunity to offer complementary services. A dealer bank may be able to offer the end user *combined* derivatives dealing and commercial banking services at a lower marginal cost than if the two services were sold separately. Although the size of the economies of scope (i.e., cost complemenarities across product lines) in banking are subject to dispute, the success of existing financial intermediaries (e.g., banks and investment banks) as derivatives dealers attests to their presence.

Finally, even if economies of scope are not present, privately negotiated derivatives dealers can derive revenues from add-on services, such as risk management consulting services, which are provided as a related extension to the dealing function.

Benefits to Organized Exchanges

Whereas dealers earn much of their profits from supplying transactions services, exchanges benefit from supplying derivatives by earning a return for financial innovation. Designing and listing futures and options contracts is costly, and many listed contracts are ultimately delisted due to lack of demand. Several benefits accrue to exchanges, however, when new contracts are designed and successfully listed. Principally, the exchange earns fee income from transactions in the listed contracts. The fees paid by clearing members to execute transactions under the exchange's clearinghouse guarantee also generate fee income for the exchange.[31] In turn, larger fees and more successful futures contracts increase the demand for access to an exchange's pits, hence raising the value of the exchange by increasing membership prices.

Exchanges also have property rights in the information produced from transparent futures trading. Because futures markets are relatively liquid, new information about an asset generally enters a market *first* in the futures market for that asset, making futures prices very valuable for price discovery and resource allocation. By charging fees to companies that report futures prices on a real-time basis (e.g., Reuters), an exchange thus can reap some benefit from listing the contract.[32]

Benefits to End Users[33]

End users of exchange-traded and privately negotiated derivatives include commercial and investment banks, thrifts, financial corporations (e.g., insurance and finance companies), nonfinancial corporations (e.g., airlines and manufacturing firms), institutional investors (e.g., pension funds), and specialized trading firms. Corporations use derivatives in a variety of ways, some of which are explained below.

First, corporations benefit from derivatives through lower funding costs. A U.S. corporation, for example, might borrow 75 million deutsche marks in German capital markets, then use a currency swap to convert the deutsche mark currency exposure to U.S. dollars. The final result could be a lower cost of funds in U.S. dollars than if the firm had sought direct financing in U.S. capital markets. Though an apparent arbitrage opportunity, international differences in taxation, regulation, and controls on capital often make these types of transactions *persistently* advantageous for some firms.

Second, derivatives allow firms to diversify their funding sources. A firm might raise capital in one market and then swap its cash flows into the currency of another market in order to diversify its creditor base. Corporations also can diversify the currency exposure of their liabilities in this manner. In today's global capital market, currency and interest rate swaps give firms the ability to borrow in the cheapest capital market, domestic or foreign, without regard either to the currency in which the debt is denominated or the nature of the interest payment.

Third, derivatives allow corporate institutional investors, such as pension plans, to enhance asset yields. In cases where securities trade poorly because of some undesirable feature, derivatives can be used to neutralize that feature by creating a synthetic instrument with a higher yield than a traditional instrument of the same credit quality. Asset swaps, for example, are swaps that allow firms to swap illiquid securities for similar cash flows with the same probability of default but greater liquidity.

Fourth, derivatives allow firms to expand their primary lines of business or diversify into new product and service lines. A trucking company in the primary business of supplying transportation services to a regional market might choose to expand nationally only if it can ensure that it has access to diesel fuel over time. The trucking company may choose to offset some of its price risks by using derivatives, such as entering a commodity swap to receive deliveries of diesel fuel over time at fixed prices or make (or receive) cash payments based on a floating price of diesel fuel relative to the fixed price. In this sense, the company makes its decision to expand jointly with its decision to hedge its fuel costs using the commodity swap.

Fifth, corporations may use derivatives to manage the risks of *anticipated* expansions or business investments. A corporation that has trouble borrowing for research and development, for example, may hedge various risk exposures by using derivatives to ensure that enough cash is available to exploit future profitable investment opportunities. By reducing the variance of the firms's net cash flows, hedging can sometimes help ensure that the company has sufficient cash to make positive net present value investments.

Sixth, derivatives provide an efficient method for all types of corporations to better manage the exposures to interest rate and currency risk that result from existing primary business lines. Interest rate swaps, for example, help banks of all sizes to manage better the asset/liability mismatches inherent in funding long-term assets, such as mortgages, with short-term liabilities that reprice more frequently, such as certificates of deposit. Currency forwards, options, and swaps help importers, exporters, and multinational corporations better to manage the foreign exchange risk inherent in their ordinary business operations.

Seventh, many institutions engage in derivatives transactions not to manage risks but rather to increase their profits, thus making derivatives a part of a firm's primary line of business. Small regional banks offering equity-linked certificates of deposit, for example, generally hedge the equity price risk and thereby seek only to generate fee income. Firms may also enter into derivatives to exploit perceived profit opportunities resulting from better information. When a firm has a view on the direction or volatility of asset prices or interest rates, it may use derivatives to exploit that view while still reducing its overall capital at risk.

Finally, derivatives provide a low-cost and effective means for both corporations and institutional investors to respond quickly and cheaply to new information and manage their portfolios of assets and liabilities more efficiently as a result. A fully invested equity fund, for example, can reduce its market exposure quickly and cheaply by using futures on stock indexes instead of selling off that part of its cash equity assets that comprises the index. Corporate borrowers can also effectively manage their liability structure—fixed to floating debt ratio and currency composition—by using interest rate and currency swaps and futures. Derivative instruments can be substantially less costly to trade than the underlying instrument itself. Without access to derivative instruments, altering risk exposure in response to new information, for example, would be much more costly to accomplish.

Not all corporations find the various potential benefits of derivatives equally appealing. A firm using derivatives to reduce the expected costs of financial distress, for example, would be unlikely also to find the inventory management use of derivatives appealing. The latter use of derivatives, although beneficial to many firms, does not necessarily reduce the volatility of a firm's value or of its cash flows, both of which may be important for a financially distressed firm. In any event, a significant number of firms and organizations find that at least one of the above benefits applies to them.

Benefits for the Economy

The innovation and growth in derivatives activity also has yielded substantial benefits to the U.S. economy. By facilitating the access of U.S. corporations to international capital markets and enabling these organizations to lower their cost of funds and diversify their funding sources, derivatives have improved the competitive position of U.S. firms in an increasingly competitive, global economy. U.S. firms have also gained access to new and more effective tools to manage their exposures to interest rates, foreign exchange rates, and commodity prices. Derivatives thus have reduced the likelihood of financial distress due to volatile prices and interest rates.

By providing investors and issuers with a wider array of tools for managing risks and raising capital, moreover, derivatives improve the allocation of credit and the sharing of risk in the economy. That lowers the cost of capital formation and stimulates economic growth.

Finally, because world markets for trade and finance have become increasingly integrated and accessible, derivatives strengthen important linkages between markets, increase market liquidity, and improve market pricing efficiency.

CONCLUSIONS

This overview has explored several aspects of derivatives: what they are, how they work, who uses them, by how much, and why. Although often portrayed otherwise, we have shown that legitimate economic answers exist for all these questions. No one knows for sure what financial services will look like in the next millennium. A safe bet, however, is that derivatives will continue to play a large and constructive part of the financial services revolution.

ENDNOTES

1. We are grateful to Barb Kavanagh, Robert Mackay, and Tom Miller for their comments on earlier drafts. We also thank Cory Anger for her research assistance. The views expressed herein are those of the authors only and do not necessarily reflect the views of the Office of the Comptroller of the Currency or its staff.

2. For an historical overview, *see* Christopher L. Culp, *A Primer on Derivatives: Their Mechanics, Uses, Risks, and Regulation* (Washington, DC: Competitive Enterprise Institute, 1995), and Chicago Board of Trade, *Commodity Trading Manual* (Chicago: Board of Trade of the City of Chicago, 1989).

3. See, e.g., Kathy McNamara-Meis, "Defining Derivatives" and "Financial Frankensteins," *Forbes MediaCritic* (Fall 1995), and Christopher L. Culp, "Derivatives: A Lessons from *60 Minutes*," *MediaNomics* 3, no. 3 (April 1995).

4. See especially Global Derivatives Study Group, *Derivatives: Practices and Principles* (Washington, DC: The Group of Thirty, July 1993).

5. Christopher L. Culp, Dean Furbush, and Barbara T. Kavanagh, "Structured Debt and Corporate Risk Management," *Journal of Applied Corporate Finance* 7(3) (Fall 1994), and Culp, op. cit.

6. Regulation sometimes serves as such a limit. U.S. law prohibits, for example, many derivatives contracts based on individual shares of common stock.

7. Financial economists, in fact, argue that common stock and corporate bonds *are* a type of derivatives contract. Stock can be viewed as a "call option" on the underlying value of a firm, and debt can be viewed as a "put option" with the same underlying.

8. An unfortunate result of the attempt to pigeonhole "derivatives" as a single class of financial product is the desire by some government agencies and legislators to regulate them as such.

9. Charles W. Smithson, "A LEGO® Approach to Financial Engineering," *Midland Corporate Finance Journal* 4 (1987).

10. Ibid.

11. That a terminal price equal to the fixed price set at the contract's inception leaves both the long and short no better or worse off than if they had not entered the transaction is true by definition. The fixed price for future delivery is set precisely to ensure that both parties *expect* no gain or loss on the contract *ex ante*. If the realized price is equal to the expected price, no gain or loss results *ex post*, as well.

12. The *legal* distinctions between futures and forwards are much more complex and are not discussed here.

13. Liquidity can be viewed most usefully as the "supply of immediacy," or the degree to which companies can get immediate transaction execution when they demand it. See Sanford J. Grossman and Merton H. Miller, "Liquidity and Market Structure," *Journal of Finance* 43, no. 3 (July 1988).

14. Electronic trading and other forms of trading than open outcry also characterize numerous foreign futures exchanges.

15. For an historical overview and legal analysis of these regulations, see Christopher L. Culp, "Regulatory Uncertainty and the Economics of Derivatives Regulation," *The Financier* 2, 5 (December 1995).

16. The EFP process is controversial with most exchanges, however, because the exchange clearinghouse guarantees the transaction without being able to collect a fee for providing such coverage.

17. The clearinghouse guarantee extends only to members of the clearinghouse. A futures trader using a broker as an intermediary must consider the creditworthiness of the broker in addition to the creditworthiness of the clearinghouse.

18. Losses at each mark to market period are actually deducted from these margin deposits, and gains are added to margin accounts. If a single account falls below a certain threshold level called the *maintenance margin* after a mark to market cash flow debit occurs, the trader must deposit additional funds to bring that margin account back up to its initial level. For a more detailed discussion, see Culp, op. cit.

19. For a discussion of some issues in measuring credit risk, see Christopher L. Culp and Robert J. Mackay, "Managing Derivatives Risk: A Strategic Guide," in *1995 Handbook of Business Strategy* (New York: Faulkner & Gray, 1995).

20. See Clifford W. Smith, Jr., and Charles W. Smithson, "Financial Engineering: An Overview," in *The Handbook of Financial Engineering* eds. Clifford W. Smith, Jr., and Charles W. Smithson (New York: Harper Business, 1990).

21. Such an option is usually called an *exchange option*, or an option to exchange one asset for another. The forward contract is valued *assuming* the underlying is one type of wheat, and the value of the cheapest-to-deliver option is then the value of an option to exchange that type of wheat for the other deliverable grade.

22. For a discussion of the cheapest-to-deliver option embedded in long-term government bond futures traded on the Chicago Board of Trade,

see Galen D. Burghardt and Terrence M. Belton, *The Treasury Bond Basis* (Chicago: Probus, 1994).

23. See, for example, Smith and Smithson, *op. cit.*

24. See Hans R. Stoll, "The Relationship Between Put and Call Option Prices," *Journal of Finance* 24 (1969).

25. Structured securities can also involve the combination of equity securities with derivatives. For a survey of some of these, see Jack Clark Francis, William W. Toy, and J. Gregg Whittaker, eds., *The Handbook of Equity Derivatives* (Chicago: Irwin Professional Publishing, 1995).

26. See, for example, Global Derivatives Study Group, op. cit.

27. See Christopher L. Culp and Robert J. Mackay, "Structured Notes: Mechanics, Benefits, and Risks," in *Derivatives Risks and Responsibilities* eds. Robert A. Klein and Jess Lederman (Chicago: Irwin Professional Publishing, 1995).

28. See Culp and Mackay, "Structured Notes," *op. cit.*

29. Exchanges occasionally increase the number of seats, thereby allowing memberships to be purchased directly from the exchange. In general, however, the supply of most exchanges' memberships is close to constant.

30. As early as Adam Smith's *Wealth of Nations*, innovative financial activities were pilloried because they involved too much mental acumen and not enough sweat. For a historical perspective, see Christopher L. Culp and Fred L. Smith, Jr., "Speculators: Adam Smith Revisited," *The Freeman* 39 (10) (October 1989).

31. See Franklin Allen and Douglas Gale, "Incomplete Markets and Incentives to Set Up an Options Exchange," *Geneva Papers on Risk and Insurance Theory* 15(1) (March 1990), and Dennis W. Carlton, "Futures Markets: Their Purpose, Their History, Their Growth, Their Successes and Failures," *Journal of Futures Markets* 4(3) (1984).

32. J. Harold Mulherin, Jeffry M. Netter, and James A. Overdahl, "Prices Are Property: The Organization of Financial Exchanges from a Transaction Cost Perspective," *Journal of Law and Economics* 34 (1991).

33. This section draws heavily from Christopher L. Culp and Robert J. Mackay, "Regulating Derivatives: The Current System and Proposed Changes," *Regulation* 4 (1994), and Culp and Mackay, "Managing Derivatives Risk," op. cit.

6

THE QUEST FOR LEGAL CERTAINTY

What Derivatives Are Subject to the Commodity Exchange Act?

Mark D. Young, *Kirkland & Ellis*

No one disputes the central role derivatives transactions now play in our financial world. Derivatives have become the financial instruments of choice for businesses that seek to hedge or manage price risks or "take a view of the market" (the current euphemism for speculation). Through derivatives, corporations, pension funds, banks, mutual funds, and many other institutions manage or assume price risks relating to future movements in interest rates or currencies as well as the price of stocks (individually or marketwide), agricultural commodities, precious metals, and petroleum products. Efforts to measure the current size of the derivatives markets often break down into a numbers game that obfuscates the real point: Derivatives markets are big, real big, and are now as integral to the financial markets as stocks and bonds.

Like stocks and bonds, derivatives come in different styles and shapes, ranging from traditional exchange-traded futures or options and plain vanilla interest rate swaps to countless esoteric specially constructed instruments created by clever financial engineers. Unlike stocks and bonds, which we know are subject to the federal securities laws, derivatives (other than traditional exchange-traded instruments) have been plagued by fears of what is commonly referred to as legal uncertainty.

That uncertainty stems from the perceived absence of clear lines of federal statutory jurisdiction (or clear legal exclusions from any jurisdiction) over the new forms of derivatives that have emerged in the past decade.

Those that buy or sell derivatives preach the perils of legal uncertainty for good reason. No market could survive if the losing party to every transaction could void the transaction after the losses had been incurred. (It would be like the manager of a losing baseball team declaring every game his team lost to be a rain-out after the ninth inning.) Yet, on a number of occasions in recent years, the losing parties in certain derivatives transactions have gone to court to try to void the transactions as illegal. In some instances, those efforts have even been successful.[1]

The Commodity Exchange Act offers fertile (or at least frequently tilled) ground for claims that certain derivative transactions are illegal and unenforceable. Under the CEA, any futures contract, unless exempted, must be traded on an exchange (called a designated contract market) approved by the Commodity Futures Trading Commission, (7 USC §§ 6(a) and 6(c)), and any options contract must be traded in accordance with CFTC rules that require options, unless exempted, to be traded on a CFTC-approved exchange (7 USC § 6c(b); 17 CFR §§ 32.4 and 33.3 (a)). Based upon those CEA provisions, any derivatives transaction that is found to be a futures or options contract and is traded over-the-counter rather than on a CFTC-approved exchange could be voided as illegal by the losing party.

That threat of unenforceablity is the crux of legal certainty fears under the CEA. By and large, therefore, the issue of legal certainty turns on whether a derivatives transaction is a futures or options contract subject to the CEA.

The CEA defines neither *futures contract* nor *options contract.* Thus far, legal uncertainty concerns have focused on futures, not options.[2] This chapter also will concentrate largely on the legal uncertainty that now exists in the OTC derivatives markets due to the absence of established uniformly recognized legal principles for determining what a futures contract is. That issue and the uncertainty it has spawned has even spilled over into efforts by the CFTC to exempt swaps and other instruments from the CEA to promote legal certainty. And, finally, the courts and the CFTC have been wrestling unsuccessfully for two decades with a related issue and source of legal uncertainty: what instruments are excluded from the CEA under a provision enacted in 1974 called the Treasury Amendment.

SUMMARY

Although the CEA was designed to regulate futures contracts, the statute does not define *futures*. Agency and judicial attempts to supply both that definition and a working definition of forward contracts—the statutory flip-side of futures—have promoted great market confusion. One court, the U.S. Court of Appeals for the Ninth Circuit, became so bewildered by the current state of the law that it found the same set of precious metals transactions to be both futures contracts subject to extensive regulation under the CEA and forward contracts that are excluded generally from CEA regulation.[3] In 1992, Congress criticized that judicial decision in the Conference Report that accompanied the Futures Trading Practices Act of 1992. Congressional criticism, however, is no substitute for plain and simple statutory language outlining the rules of the game for all market participants.

One would think that the CFTC itself would be clamoring for that kind of legal certainty. That has not been the case. In 1992, former CFTC Chairman Wendy Gramm told Congress that the statute should not define a futures contract because *any* definition, including one the agency itself would draft, would be both too broad and too narrow. When called upon to enforce the law, former Chairman Gramm conceded the agency must prove the elements of a futures contract in enforcement actions. But, the CFTC told Congress, identifying those elements in the statute was impossible and unwise.

It would be odd, to say the least, if, for example, the Chairman of the Food and Drug Administration said that the term *drug* could not and should not be defined by law, or if the Chairman of the Federal Deposit Insurance Corporation said that the term *deposit* could not and should not be defined by law.[4] Should the term *futures contract* be any different? If the statute or the agency charged with administering it cannot define what the statute is supposed to cover, expecting market participants to comply with the statute and expecting agency officials to enforce the statute comes close to encouraging a form of legal anarchy that is wholly unsuitable for modern markets where legal certainty is critical to effective market performance.[5] Congress should revisit and resolve the question of what transactions are subject to the CEA and what transactions are excluded from the CEA. That issue is addressed in the section "The Futures/Forward Conundrum."

Second, in 1992 Congress granted the CFTC exemptive authority that allows the agency to excuse any transaction that is a futures contract from virtually any regulatory provision of the CEA or CFTC rules, including the exchange-trading requirement. Through that exemptive power, Congress hoped the CFTC could eliminate the legal certainty concerns for swaps and other OTC derivatives. Within four months of enactment, the CFTC used its exemptive powers to exempt a class of swaps transactions from all CEA provisions except the fraud and manipulation provisions. The CFTC's central purpose in adopting that exemption was to make certain that a disgruntled participant in an unprofitable swaps transaction would not rely on the CEA to claim the transaction was an illegal OTC futures contract and hence unenforceable. Unfortunately, one day swap market participants may find that the CFTC's well-meaning effort was not successful because the CFTC exemptive formula could promote exactly the same market confusion and uncertainty that prompted the exemption in the first place. Although the agency has toyed with the idea of reconsidering the swaps exemption, to date it seems unwilling to do so. Congress may therefore have to fix that problem. The second part of this chapter, "The CFTC's Swaps Exemption Perpetuates Legal Uncertainty," addresses that issue.

Third, in 1974 the CEA was amended to add a provision called the Treasury Amendment, which totally excludes certain "transactions in foreign currency and government securities" from the CEA. The scope of the Treasury Amendment's exclusion has been the greatest source of appellate litigation conflict under the CEA over the past two decades. During that period, the CFTC, other federal agencies, state regulators, exchanges, brokerage firms, banks, money managers, and the courts have been split on what transactions are excluded under the Treasury Amendment. A recent court of appeals decision explicitly tees up the issue for possible Supreme Court review. Nevertheless, the Court may decline to grant review. Even if it decides to decide what it thinks Congress intended in 1974, a fresh congressional look at the Treasury Amendment in the context of today's markets may be the best way to resolve the Treasury Amendment debate. "Reconsidering the Treasury Amendment," the third part of this chapter, addresses that issue.

THE FUTURES/FORWARD CONUNDRUM

Defining what a futures contract is would seem to be the logical place to start figuring out what derivatives are to be regulated under the CEA. Once that issue is resolved, deciding what kind of regulation is appropriate and what public interests, if any, require government protection becomes easier.[6]

The problem is that the CEA does not define the term *futures contract*. Instead the statute in various places describes futures as "contracts of sale of [a] commodity for future delivery" (CEA § 4(a)). Two of the three components in this seminal statutory phrase are defined by statute. "The term 'contract of sale' includes sales, agreements of sale, and agreements to sell" (CEA§ 1a(6)). "The term 'commodity' means wheat, cotton, rice, corn, oats, barley, rye, flaxseed, grain sorghums, mill feeds, butter, eggs, Solanum tuberosum (Irish potatoes), wool, wool tops, fats and oils (including lard, tallow, cottonseed oil, peanut oil, soybean oil and all other fats and oils), cottonseed meal, cottonseed, peanuts, soybeans, soybean meal, livestock, livestock products, and frozen concentrated orange juice, and all other goods and articles, except onions…and all services, rights, and interests in which contracts for future delivery are presently or in the future dealt in" (CEA § 1a (3)).[7] Both definitions are quite broad and do not circumscribe in any way the definitive futures contract phrase, "contracts of sale of a commodity for future delivery."

The third component is a nondefinition—the statute does not say what *future delivery* is; it tells us what *future delivery* is not. "The term 'future delivery' does not include any sale of any cash commodity for deferred shipment or delivery" (CEA § 1a (11)). Enacted in 1922, this "nonfuture delivery" provision is often called the *forward contract exclusion*. Any instrument that is "not for future delivery" is not a futures contract and therefore need not comply with the futures regulatory scheme. Some provisions of the CEA still apply to those nonfutures or forward transactions (antimanipulation and reporting primarily; see CEA §§ 4i, 6(c), 6(d),and 9(a)(2)), but generally forward contracts are outside the purview of the CEA.

Pre-1990: The Futures versus Forward Distinction

Prior to 1990, the courts and the CFTC had adopted consistent legal definitions of a futures contract and a forward contract under the CEA.

Both futures and forwards involve contractual promises to buy or sell something at some specified price and future date. But futures and forwards are very different. Futures contracts are entered into to transfer or assume price risks; parties to futures contracts typically offset or cancel out their contractual obligations before maturity, rather than making or taking delivery of the underlying commodity. Forward contracts are entered into by parties who actually want to transfer ownership of something for a price; that is, forwards are contracts where, on the maturity date, the buyer acquires something and the seller sells something (*CFTC* v. *Noble Metals International, Inc.*, 2 Comm. Fut. L. Rep. para. 26, 506 (9th. Cir. Sept. 26, 1995)), which decided that actual delivery was required for forward contracts; transfer of title was not an acceptable substitute for actual delivery.

Two elements therefore are critical to distinguishing futures from forwards: the intent of the parties (which is often based on subjective evidence buttressed by after-the-fact analysis of the parties' actual behavior) and the standardized or fungible nature of the contract itself (objective evidence). Both distinguishing elements help to resolve the central question of whether the parties intended to trade or offset these contracts or whether the parties intended to perform their contractual obligations through delivery or cash-settlement at the specified maturity date.[8]

The CFTC and the courts espoused this legal distinction for many years up to 1990. Then the CFTC, faced with a thorny interpretive problem, decided that both forwards and futures could be transactions where offset routinely occurs. At that point, the CEA lost its statutory moorings and since then no one has been sure what transactions are futures and what are forward contracts.

CFTC Pronouncements Defining Futures—Traditional Approach
In July 1989, the CFTC stated the "necessary elements" of a futures contract:

> Futures contracts are contracts for the purchase or sale of a commodity for delivery in the future at a price that is established when the contract is initiated, with both parties to the transaction obligated to fulfill the contract at the specified price. In addition, futures contracts are undertaken principally to assume or shift price risk without transferring the underlying commodity. As a result, futures contracts providing for delivery may be satisfied either by delivery or offset." [54 Fed. Reg. 30694, 30695 (July 21, 1989) (CFTC Swaps Policy Statement)]

In addition to those "necessary elements," the CFTC recognized that other elements are common to those futures that are traded on an exchange: standardized commodity units, margin requirements related to price movements, clearing guarantees, open and competitive trading in centralized markets and price dissemination. The CFTC emphasized that these additional elements facilitate trading of futures on exchanges but "[t]he presence or absence of these additional elements...is not dispositive of whether a transaction is a futures contract."

Through that legal formulation, the CFTC correctly observed that, as a matter of law, a transaction that has the above-described "necessary elements" of a futures contract will be found to be a futures contract, even if that transaction does not occur on an exchange (including a CFTC-approved exchange called a designated contract market). As the CFTC explained, "the requirement [in CEA § 4(a)] that a futures contract be executed on a designated contract market is what makes the contract legal, not what makes it a futures contract" 54 Fed. Reg. at 30695 n.8.

That last CFTC explanation holds the key to the conundrum of the futures definitional issue. If the CFTC had said that futures are instruments traded only on exchanges, much of the legal certainty issue would be resolved.[9] The CFTC has rejected that approach, correctly. Limiting the futures definition in that manner would lead to the following unacceptable consequences.

1. Bucket shop operators could operate "Ponzi schemes" to defraud the public through illicit futures trading *without violating the CEA in any way;* and

2. Even legitimate dealers would be free to operate professional markets in over-the-counter futures *without any of the costs* embodied in the many federal financial integrity, market integrity and sales practice safeguards exchange markets must bear, thereby *giving the dealers a vast competitive edge over the exchange markets.* (It would be like telling the Democrats they don't need to bother complying with the Federal Election Commission's regulations, since those rules only apply to Republicans (or vice versa).[10]

Treating only exchange-traded instruments as futures subject to the CEA, therefore, could have spawned rampant sales practice abuses and a most unlevel competitive playing field. The CFTC avoided those consequences by adopting the view embraced by many courts that any transaction, whether on-exchange or off-exchange, must be viewed "as a whole with a critical eye toward its underlying purpose" (54 Fed. Reg. at 30694 quoting from *CFTC* v. *Co Petro Marketing Group, Inc.*, 680 F.2d 573, 581 (9th Cir. 1982)). Rather than saying that all exchange-traded instruments are futures and all OTC derivatives are not, the CFTC proclaimed that the futures determination "entails a review of the overall effect of the transaction as well as a determination as to 'what the parties intended'" (54 Fed. Reg. at 30694).

The Co Petro Decision   The CFTC's July 1989 analytical approach to deciding what is a futures contract followed the principles set forth by the U.S. Court of Appeals for the Ninth Circuit in the 1982 *Co Petro* case. That decision provided the best legal guideposts for determining what is a futures contract. Co Petro involved a CFTC complaint that the defendants were selling illegal off-exchange futures contracts. The central issue was whether the transactions Co Petro marketed were futures.

In resolving that issue, the Ninth Circuit reasoned that exchange-traded futures should be considered to be the core of the futures contract definition. According to the court, exchange-traded futures show that standardization and fungibility are critical concepts in determining whether a transaction is a futures contract. Exchange-traded futures contracts are standardized as to all economic terms except price, because

> [t]he fungible nature of these contracts facilitates offsetting transactions by which purchasers or sellers can liquidate their positions by forming opposite contracts. The price differential between the opposite contracts then determines the investor's profit or loss [*Co Petro*, 680 F.2d, 579–580].

The defendants in *Co Petro* argued that their contracts were not futures because they were not as standardized or fungible as the contracts traded on exchanges. In short, Co Petro contended that its contracts could not be futures contracts since they were different from the futures traded on exchanges—the core of what is a futures contract.

In rejecting that contention, the Ninth Circuit confirmed that futures are not just those core instrument traded on exchanges. Instead, futures may be traded on-exchange or off-exchange. For the *Co Petro* court, the concepts of standardization, fungibility, and offset were the keys to making the futures determination. Even though the Co Petro contracts were not "as rigidly standardized" as exchange-traded contracts, Co Petro's contracts could still be futures.

More important, however, than the degree to which Co Petro's Agency Agreements conform to the precise features for standardized futures contracts is the rationale for standardization in futures trading. Standardized form contracts facilitate the formation of offsetting or liquidating transactions. The ability to form offsetting contracts is essential, since investors rarely take delivery against the contracts [*Co Petro*, 680 F.2d at 580].

Co Petro's contracts contemplated an investor's position that would be offset either by entering into a matching or offsetting transaction with Co Petro or by allowing the customer to cancel the contract and pay liquidated damages. Thus, the Ninth Circuit found Co Petro's contracts to be futures since they were sufficiently standardized and fungible to facilitate offsetting transactions—although not to the same degree as exchange-traded contracts.

Co Petro's Forward Contract Ruling   Not surprisingly, the Ninth Circuit in *Co Petro* also set down principles for analyzing whether a contract was a forward contract. After reviewing the text, legislative history, and context of the forward contract or "not for future delivery" exclusion, the Ninth Circuit identified two distinguishing features of forwards— delivery and commercial purpose. "Most important, both parties to the [forward] contracts deal in and contemplate future delivery of the actual grain." "[A] cash forward contract is one in which the parties contemplate physical transfer of the actual commodity." *Co Petro*, 680 F.2d, 578). In addition, the Ninth Circuit concluded that the forward exclusion should be unavailable to transactions that were entered into for pure speculation, where the commodities underlying the transaction did not have inherent value to the businesses of the respective parties. (For the Ninth Circuit, the farmer-grain elevator-miller relationship was considered to be the paradigm of forward contracting). Thus, the *Co Petro* court held that the forward contract exclusion was "unavailable to contracts...sold merely for speculative purposes and which are not predicated upon the expectation that delivery of the actual commodity by the seller to the original contracting buyer will occur in the future" (*Co Petro*, 680 F.2d, 579).

Synthesizing Co Petro   After *Co Petro*, the law was clear that forward contracts were entered into by commercial parties for nonspeculative purposes when the parties contemplated that actual delivery of the commodity would occur at maturity of the contract. In contrast, the parties to futures contracts intended to speculate or hedge price risks by entering into standardized, fungible contracts they expected to offset prior to maturity. Forwards were instruments for transferring commercial goods. Futures were trading instruments. The CFTC itself adopted these distinctions for many years.[11]

1990 and Beyond—Transnor, Brent Oil, and the End of Legal Certainty

The CFTC blurred the established futures/forward distinction in 1990 in order to accommodate a multilateral international trading network in Brent Oil contracts. The result of that change has been unprecedented confusion.

Transnor

This odyssey started on April 18, 1990, when U.S. District Court Judge William C. Conner decided *Transnor (Bermuda) Ltd.* v. *BP North American Petroleum*, 738 F. Supp. 1472 (S.D.N.Y. 1990). Transnor was a small business that had purchased two 15-day Brent crude oil contracts in December 1985 at a price of $ 24.50 per barrel for delivery in March 1986. By the end of March 1986, the price of Brent crude oil dropped to $13.80, resulting in a substantial loss for Transnor. Transnor claimed that certain oil companies that traded in the Brent oil market had manipulated the price down, thereby causing its loss. Transnor sued those companies under U.S. antitrust law and for manipulation in violation of the Commodity Exchange Act.[12]

The oil companies responded that Brent oil contracts are forward contracts, not futures, and therefore are excluded from the CEA.[13] Applying both the Ninth Circuit's decision in *Co Petro* and a number of CFTC precedents, Judge Conner rejected the oil companies' defense finding that Brent oil contracts were futures, not forwards. Judge Conner found that 95 percent of the Brent oil contracts were traded for speculative or hedging purposes rather than to take delivery of the oil (*Transnor*, 738 F. Supp., 1476). In the absence of evidence of an intent to take delivery under a Brent contract, Judge Conner reasoned that those contracts were futures. In so doing, Judge Conner observed that

> the high degree of standardization of terms such as quantity, grade, delivery terms, currency of payment and unit of measure, which facilitate offset, bookout and other clearing techniques available on the Brent market,

further evidence the investment purpose of Brent trading [*Transnor*, 738 F. Supp., 1492].

The oil companies also argued that the *Co Petro* "delivery versus offset" analysis should not be applied to Brent contracts because, in *Co Petro*, the customers had a contractual right to offset while the parties to Brent contracts do not. Judge Conner was not convinced. He ruled that as long as the parties had "tacitly expected" to end the contracts "by means other than delivery" the fact that delivery could occur under the contracts did not make them forwards:

> [W]here there is no 'right' of offset, the 'opportunity' to offset and a tacit expectation and common practice of offsetting suffices to deem the transaction a futures contract [*Transnor*, 738 F. Supp., 1492].

The CFTC's Brent Oil Interpretation

Following the *Transnor* decision (the case was eventually settled before an appeal could be filed), the oil companies and others urged the CFTC to issue an interpretation overturning the decision. Those companies had a legitimate fear: if all Brent oil contracts were off-exchange futures then all Brent contracts could theoretically be voided by the parties as illegal contracts under CEA § 4(a). Anyone who lost money on a Brent oil contract, therefore, could refuse to pay claiming the contract to be illegal and unenforceable. Today if that same threat existed the CFTC could exercise its exemptive powers under CEA § 4(c) and protect the market. In 1990, however, the CFTC had not been granted those exemptive powers.

On September 25, 1990, the CFTC issued an interpretation of the forward contract exclusion that adopted the view that Brent oil contracts were forwards, not futures. Without disagreeing with Judge Conner's factual conclusion that 95 percent of Brent oil contracts do not result in delivery of the oil, the CFTC fashioned a new concept of a forward contract. In essence, the CFTC concluded that forward contracts now could be regularly offset prior to delivery just like futures.

The CFTC's interpretation starts by accepting that the "underlying postulate" of the forward contract exclusion

> is that the Act's regulatory scheme for futures trading simply should not apply to private commercial merchandising transactions which create enforceable obligations to deliver but in which delivery is deferred for reasons of commercial convenience or necessity ["Statutory Interpretation

Concerning Forward Transactions," [1990–1992 Transfer Binder] Comm.Fut.L.Rep. (CCH), para. 24, 925 at 37, 367 (Sept. 25, 1990) (Forward Interp.).

The commission next acknowledged that its traditional emphasis on delivery as "the feature distinguishing" forwards from futures was rooted in the statute's legislative history. Then the CFTC repeated that forwards generally are entered into by businesses for commercial purposes.[14]

Having set out this traditional legal background, the CFTC proceeded to rewrite it. If the parties to the contract faced an actual delivery obligation under the contract that created "substantial economic risk" to the parties, but the parties offset those future contract obligations regularly prior to maturity of the contract, the commission said it would consider that contract to be a forward contract. The commission purported to limit this ruling by emphasizing that (1) all parties to these contracts must have the capacity to bear the economic risks of the transactions; (2) the contracts cannot be discharged through "exchange-style offset" (a phrase the CFTC did not define); and (3) the offsetting transactions that extinguish a party's delivery obligations must be "separate, individually negotiated, new agreements," rather than a contractual right of offset provided in the original agreement (Forward Interp., 37,368).

In capsule form, the CFTC's interpretation said that Brent contracts constituted forward contracts where 95 percent of the transactions were offset prior to maturity because (1) those contracts were not traded on an exchange and (2) they did not provide a contractual right of offset.[15] That conclusion conflicted with the prior holdings of the agency and the courts that:

1. Offset distinguished futures from forwards.
2. Where a contract was traded (on exchange or OTC) was irrelevant for purposes of the futures definition.
3. The parties' reasonable expectation of the ability to offset a transaction, rather than a contractual right of offset, was sufficient for purposes of classifying a transaction as a futures contract.

Bybee, Tauber and MG—What Is the Law?
Within a year of the CFTC's Brent oil interpretation, the courts began to offer proof that the CEA had been turned into an unsolvable riddle.

A bankruptcy trustee sought to set aside multimillion-dollar precious metals transactions involving a wholesaler, the bankrupt dealer, and public customers. The trustee claimed the transactions were illegal and unenforceable off-exchange futures contracts. By voiding these futures transactions, the trustee hoped to get the wholesaler to contribute millions to the bankruptcy and thereby begin to redress the customers' financial injuries.

The Ninth Circuit applied *Co Petro* and the CFTC's new Brent interpretation to these transactions (*In re Bybee*, 945 F.2d 309 (9th Cir. 1991)). The Ninth Circuit first concluded that the contracts were futures under *Co Petro* since A-Mark, the wholesaler, "implicitly represented that it would provide for offsetting contracts, even though the contracts it sold were not entirely standardized," which was "enough to satisfy the standardization requirement" for futures (*Bybee*, 945 F.2d, at 313). The Ninth Circuit also rejected the argument that the contract could not be futures because they were not traded in the same manner as exchange-traded contracts.

The Ninth Circuit then considered whether the contracts were forwards by canvassing the many CFTC statements on this issue culminating in the 1990 Brent interpretation. As the court understood it, the CFTC now said that in modern, more sophisticated forwards the parties "often agree to 'bookout,' or offset, the contractual delivery obligations" (*Bybee*, 945 F.2d, 314). Giving deference to the CFTC's view, the Ninth Circuit concluded that the very same contracts it had first found to be futures were also forwards because "both A-Mark [the wholesaler] and Bybee [the dealer] had the legal obligation to make or take delivery upon demand of the other (*Bybee*, 945 F.2d, 315).

The Ninth Circuit's result directly conflicts with the statute's terms. No instrument can be both a contract "for future delivery" and a contract "not for future delivery." The 1992 Conference Committee Report emphasized that point (p. 72). More important than the result, however, the *Bybee* court's confusion about the role of offset and delivery in the futures/forward dichotomy provides compelling evidence that no one can be certain what the CEA now covers. After all, the Ninth Circuit said that contracts with offset and real delivery obligations are forwards. That legal principle would make exchange-traded futures—which have both characteristics—forward contracts, which are generally excused from the CEA.[16]

The Ninth Circuit Bybee decision is not an isolated case of judicial confusion. In *Salomon Forex, Inc.* v. *Tauber* (8 F.3d 966 (4th Cir. 1993) *cert. denied*, 114 S.Ct. 1540 (1994), decided under the Treasury Amendment) the U.S. Court of Appeals for the Fourth Circuit made the following similarly chaotic observations. Having accurately summarized the traditional futures/forward distinctions of offset versus delivery (*Tauber*, 8 F.3d, 970), the Fourth Circuit cited the CFTC's Brent interpretation to conclude: "[I]n practice, cash forwards are often offset by other transactions in a manner similar to the way futures are traded" (*Tauber*, 8 F.3d, 975). Thus, now two courts of appeals believe that futures contracts and forward contracts are both regularly offsettable, a conclusion that hopelessly blurs the futures/forward line and leads to considerable legal uncertainty.

MG Refining & Marketing, Inc   Recent events suggest that this confusion can have important consequences. In July 1995, the CFTC imposed a $2.25 million fine on a petroleum company for engaging in unlawful off-exchange futures contracts (*In re MG Refining & Marketing, Inc. and MG Futures, Inc.*, CFTC No. 95–14, 1995 WL 447455 (July 27, 1995)). While the facts are somewhat sketchy, in that case MG Refining, an international trading company, entered into a series of petroleum contracts with independent gasoline station operators and others in the petroleum distribution chain. Those contracts allowed MG Refining's counterparties to take delivery of the petroleum after 45 days or to store that petroleum with MG Refining for a period of years. Another option for MG Refining's counterparties was to liquidate the buy contract when a particular price was reached so that the counterparties' profit (and MG Refining's loss) on the contracts could not exceed a certain amount.

The CFTC found these contracts to be futures primarily because the parties expected offset. Physical delivery could occur, but the actual experience of the parties and the standardized nature of the contracts showed that the contracts were not entered into as supply contracts. They were designed to assume or shift the risk of possible future price changes. In a sense, therefore, in *MG Refining* the CFTC could be viewed to be returning full circle to the pre-1990 days when futures were offsettable and forwards were not.[17]

The *MG Refining* decision has sparked a firestorm of complaints about legal uncertainty under the CEA. According to the *Economist*, "derivatives lawyers reckon that the CFTC's definition of what constitutes an illegal futures contract applies equally to OTC ones, creating legal uncertainty over the status of OTC contracts."[18] *The Wall Street Journal* also editorialized that the CFTC's *MG Refining* decision invoked "language vague enough to jeopardize swaps."[19] Nobel Prize winning economist Merton Miller warned: "The CFTC's extremely broad definition of 'all the essential elements' of futures inevitably calls into question the legality of numerous financial transactions."[20]

How Can This Confusion Be Remedied?

Leaving the questions of what is a futures contract and what is a forward contract to the CFTC and the courts has not resulted in the kind of legal certainty that market participants need. Virtually all regulatory statutes define the scope of those statutes by defining the things to be regulated (and excused from regulation). Congress should follow that pattern in amending the CEA to provide a definition of what transactions the CEA *covers* and what it *excludes*. The definitions' actual scope is less important than providing the markets, the courts, and the CFTC with ascertainable and workable legal benchmarks to apply. The current law leaves the development of those benchmarks to an *ad hoc* lawyer-intensive process that makes our markets more costly and less innovation-friendly, while inhibiting the development of a rational regulatory system of federal oversight. The CFTC's current approach of "we know it when we see it" reduces compliance with the CEA to a game of after-the-fact legal "gotcha," which serves no legitimate interest.

In the past, those opposing some form of legal certainty in this area have claimed that any definition of futures contract would be so broad that the definition would operate to outlaw a whole range of off-exchange transactions as a result of the exchange-trading requirement in CEA § 4(a). Today that argument should be given little weight. Futures no longer must be traded on a CFTC-approved exchange. Congress has now given the CFTC exemptive powers to tailor an appropriate exemptive-regulatory scheme to any futures contract (CEA § 4(c)). In effect, the CFTC has the power to permit any form of professional market in over-the-counter futures trading under whatever regulation (or lack thereof) it sees fit "consistent with the public interest" (CEA § 4(c)(1)). Giving the CFTC that flexibility was a wise first step in the process of modernizing the CEA. Writing the CEA so the markets know what is covered and what is not should be the next legislative steps in that process.

THE CFTC'S SWAPS EXEMPTION PERPETUATES LEGAL UNCERTAINTY

Everyone agrees that no one should be able to renege on an arm's length swaps transaction by claiming, after-the-fact, that the swap was an off-exchange and hence an illegal futures contract under the CEA. No market could operate effectively in the face of that kind of legal uncertainty.

After the *Transnor* decision in 1990 and even after the CFTC's subsequent Brent Oil interpretation, swaps dealers and market users feared that many swaps could be vulnerable to a legal challenge on the ground that they were illegal OTC futures contracts. In 1992, Congress responded to those concerns by adopting CEA § 4(c), 7 USC § 6(c), to authorize the CFTC to exempt swaps traded among professionals and institutions from the statutory exchange-trading requirement for futures contracts (CEA § 4(a)) and virtually all other CEA provisions. As we have seen, the exemption from the exchange-trading requirement was crucial because the prohibition against nonexchange futures trading is what would have been cited in a lawsuit as the basis for claiming that a swap was an illegal futures contract under the CEA and therefore unenforceable. In short, the exchange-trading requirement for futures is what would have made a swap illegal if the swap was found to be a futures contract.

Congress made its desire to foster legal certainty explicit in 1992. The Conference Report states that "the Conferees recognize the need to create legal certainty for a number of existing categories of instruments which trade today outside of the forum of a designated contract market" (H.R. Rep. No. 978, 102d Cong., 2d Sess. 80 (1992)). That report goes on to identify "swaps" as one of the "areas where significant concerns of legal uncertainty have arisen" (H.R. Rep. No. 978, 81).

Again, the reason for these "significant concerns" was that many feared that courts could find certain "plain vanilla" swaps to be futures contracts under the CEA. Thus, to remove any concerns about legal certainty, the CFTC could have adopted an exemption that said:

> Any swap transaction between eligible swap participants [the CFTC's term for the professional and institutional participants in the swaps market] which is, or may be found to be, a futures contract is exempt from the

prohibition against trading futures contracts other than on a designated contract market under section 4(a) of the Commodity Exchange Act.

That kind of an exemption would have removed any swap that was, or was found to be, a futures contract from the very threat of illegality and unenforceability that Congress identified as "significant." The commission also could have, and likely would have, added to that core exemption further exemptive relief from Commission regulations generally as it saw fit consistent with the "public interest" (CEA § 4(c)).

The swaps exemption the CFTC adopted does not take that kind of direct approach. Instead, in 1993 the commission adopted Part 35 of its regulations, which exempts from virtually all CEA provisions—including the exchange-trading requirement in CEA § 4(a)—only those swap transactions that are traded (1) among eligible swap participants, (2) without the benefit of a mutualized risk clearing system, and (3) not on an exchange (CFTC Rule 35.2, 17 CFR 35.2). The commission added one further significant limitation on this exemption. No exempt swap

> may be part of a fungible class of agreements that are standardized as to their material economic terms. [CFTC Rule 35.2 (b)].

Thus, any standardized or fungible swap transactions are *not eligible* for the swaps exemption the CFTC has adopted.[21]

The standardized/fungibility limitation in the CFTC's swaps exemption defeats the congressional purpose of legal certainty. Consider the following two points:

1. *Before* the CFTC adopted its swaps exemption in January 1993, any swaps transaction found to be standardized and fungible would have been found

   a. to be a futures contract (under *Co Petro, Transnor, MG* and certain other precedents)

   and that futures contract would be illegal unless traded on a contract market under CEA § 4(a).

2. *After* the CFTC adopted its swaps exemption in January 1993, any swaps transaction found to be standardized and fungible would have been found

   a. not to qualify for the swaps exemption under CFTC Rule 35.2 (b) and

   b. to be a futures contract (under *Co Petro, Transnor, MG* and certain other precedents)

   and that futures contract would be illegal unless traded on a contract market under CEA § 4(a).

While the post-swaps exemption analysis technically involves one more analytical step, it really is the same analysis. Both before and after the CFTC's swaps exemption, if a swap was or is found to be standardized and fungible, it would be an illegal futures contract.

Given that logic, the CFTC's swaps exemption, far from achieving legal certainty, has instead cloned the very same legal uncertainty that caused Congress to enact the CFTC's exemptive powers. In effect, the CFTC's swaps exemption says: "Those swaps that are not futures are exempt from the CEA. Those swaps that are futures are not exempt." In either case, the swaps exemption turns on whether the swaps in question are futures under the CEA, the same legal issue that Congress said in 1992 gave rise to "substantial concerns" about legal certainty.

Swaps dealers undoubtedly would resist this analysis. They want to preserve the existing legal fiction that the CFTC's Part 35 exemption provides for absolute legal certainty.[22] The more they cite that conclusion, the more entrenched that conclusion becomes in the media, lore, and public consciousness of this issue. But that kind of "wishful group think" will not deter an aggressive lawyer for a disgruntled swaps customer from some day seizing this argument and throwing, at best, a huge legal scare into the U.S. swaps industry. Rather than keeping their fingers crossed to prevent that day from ever arriving, Congress and the commission would be better served by taking action now to address this problem and finally provide legal certainty to the swaps markets and its thousands of participants.

RECONSIDERING THE TREASURY AMENDMENT

The Treasury Amendment debate compounds the jurisdictional uncertainty for derivatives under the CEA. Just recently, the U.S. Court of Appeals for the Second Circuit issued a decision reconfirming its view that the Treasury Amendment does not exclude options (and logically futures as well) from the CEA. In so doing, the Second Circuit acknowledged that its ruling squarely conflicted with that of the Fourth Circuit in the *Tauber* case. Other courts have taken equally divided interpretive routes under the amendment, as have various federal agencies and market participants. Congress should address these divergent views and resolve the Treasury Amendment debate once and for all.

The Treasury Amendment

In 1974 Congress amended the CEA to expand the definition of *commodity* to include, among other things foreign currency and government securities. Congress broadened the *commodity* definition to make certain that trading in futures contracts on currencies and government securities would be subject to the CEA (S. Rep. No. 1131, 93d Cong., 2d Sess. 19 (1974)).

At the same time, Congress enacted a provision that excluded from the CEA jurisdiction over certain transactions in foreign currency, government securities, and other enumerated instruments. This proviso, commonly known as the Treasury Amendment, states:

> Nothing in this Act shall be deemed to govern or in any way be applicable to transactions in foreign currency, security warrants, security rights, resales of installment loan contracts, repurchase options, government securities, or mortgages and mortgage purchase commitments, unless such transactions involve the sale thereof for future delivery conducted on a board of trade. [7 U.S.C. § 2(ii)].

Congress enacted the Treasury Amendment at the behest of the Department of the Treasury, which in a letter to the Chairman of the Senate Committee on Agriculture and Forestry had expressed concern with the 1974 legislation as it then stood:

> The Department feels strongly that foreign currency futures trading, other than on organized exchanges, should not be regulated by the new agency. Virtually all futures trading in the United States is carried out through an informal network of banks and dealers. This dealer market, which consists primarily of the large banks, has proved highly efficient in serving the needs of international business in hedging the risks that stem from foreign exchange rate movements. The participants in this market are sophisticated and informed institutions, unlike the participants on *organized* exchanges, which, in some cases, include individuals and small traders who may need to be protected by some form of government regulation. [S. Rep. No. 1131, 93d Cong., 2d Sess. 49–50 (1974)] (emphasis in original).

The committee noted its belief that this "informal network" is "more properly supervised by the bank regulatory agencies and that, therefore, regulation under this legislation is unnecessary."

In the somewhat understated words of the CFTC, the two decades since the passage of the Treasury Amendment have been marked by a "prevalence of litigation over the scope of the Amendment and [a] lack of unanimity in the courts over its precise contours."[23] The courts' struggle to interpret the amendment has not been facilitated by the sharp disagreements among the CFTC, the SEC, the Treasury, and state government officials over its meaning (see *Salomon Forex, Inc.* v. *Tauber*, 8 F.3d 966, 974 (4th Cir. 1993)).

Problems of Interpretation: Two Unresolved Questions

Determining the scope of the Treasury Amendment exclusion has been a formidable task. The principal interpretative questions are (1) what are "transactions in foreign currency and government securities," which are excluded from the CEA by the Amendment; and (2) what transactions "involve" those otherwise excluded transactions and are "conducted on a board of trade," thus earning reinclusion within the CEA under the Amendment's "unless" clause. Somewhat more attention has been focused on the first of these two questions, but neither has been resolved in a satisfactory or consistent manner.

"Transactions in"   Today, over 20 years since the enactment of the Treasury Amendment, no clear judicial answer exists to the central question of whether futures and options qualify as "transactions in." The answer is enormously important. If futures and options do qualify, the Treasury Amendment excuses them from CFTC regulation unless the "board of trade" standard is met. If not, the CFTC has jurisdiction over all trading in the vast, complex, and traditionally unregulated market for over-the-counter foreign currency futures and options.[24]

The Court of Appeals for the Fourth Circuit relied largely on the text and structure of the amendment to hold that currency futures and options are indeed transactions "in" foreign currency. The court reasoned that "the general clause 'transactions in foreign currency' must include a larger class than those removed from it by the 'unless' clause in order to give the latter clause meaning," and since the "unless" clause refers explicitly to futures, the general clause must therefore also include futures (*Tauber*, 8 F.3d, 975). Otherwise, the "unless" clause—the exception to the exclusion—would reinclude in the CEA transactions that were not excluded in the first place (See also *Chicago Board of Trade*, 677 F.2d, 1178–79, Cudahy, J., dissenting, which says that if GNMA options are not "transactions in" government securities, the "unless" clause is "both superfluous and contradictory").

In contrast, the Court of Appeals for the Second Circuit has emphasized that options on currency are not actual purchases or sales of currency; as a result, a currency option "does not become a 'transaction in' that currency unless and until the option is exercised" (*CFTC* v. *American Board of Trade, Inc.,* 803 F.2d 1242, 1248 (2d Cir. 1986, known as *ABT*)). At that point, the option becomes a transaction in the currency itself and presumably falls within the amendment's exclusion.

The Second Circuit has recently followed the "clear precedent" of *ABT*, even though its interpretation now "conflicts with that of the Fourth Circuit in" the *Tauber* case (*CFTC* v. *Dunn*, 2 Comm. Fut. L. Rep., para. 26,429 at 42,879–80 (2d Cir. June 23, 1995)). The Seventh Circuit came to the same conclusion as the Second Circuit with respect to options on Government National Mortgage Association certificates, holding that "[o]nly when the option holder exercises the option is there a transaction in a government security" (*CBOT*, 677 F.2d, 1154). The district court in *Sterling Capital* also held that options on foreign currency failed the "transactions in" test *CFTC and State of Georgia* v. *Sterling Capital Co.,* 2 Comm.Fut.L.Rep. (CCH), para. 21,169, at 24,784 (N.D. Ga. 1981)).

"Board of Trade"   The construction of "conducted on a board of trade" has produced similarly confused and confusing results. At one extreme, *board of trade* as a statutory term of art has the same meaning as it does in ordinary conversation; many take it to mean only formally organized exchanges, leaving all other entities free from CFTC regulation. At the other extreme, *board of trade* is defined broadly by statute to include any buyer or seller of the currency or government security at issue; the "unless" clause exception thus could swallow whole the Treasury Amendment's exclusion. The first interpretation seems plausible at first blush, but the statute precludes *board of trade* from being treated as a synonym for *exchange*:

> any exchange or association, whether incorporated or unincorporated, of persons who are engaged in the business of buying or selling any commodity or receiving the same for sale on consignment [7 USC § 1a(1)].

If *board of trade* is read literally to include every unincorporated, informal association of two or more persons who trade in commodities, "the very purpose of the [Treasury Amendment] exemption might be rendered meaningless by the subsequent 'unless' clause" (*CFTC* v.

Frankwell Bullion Ltd., No. C–94–2166 DLJ, 1994 WL 449071 (N.D. Cal. Aug. 12, 1994), *3).

These are unattractive alternatives from any perspective. The first goes a long way toward gutting the entire statute and regulatory scheme. After all, what is the point of setting up a regulatory structure for futures and options if that structure can be avoided by the simple expedient of trading in a dealer market off-exchange?[25] The second severely limits the scope of the Treasury Amendment.

Most courts have attempted to navigate a middle course. Through most of its opinion, the *Tauber* court equated *board of trade* strictly with formally organized exchanges. (See 8 F.3d at 976—"*all off-exchange* transactions" are excluded [emphasis added]). But the court signaled its willingness to temper its construction of *board of trade* in an appropriate case by observing that unlike the case before it, a case involving "mass marketing to small investors…would appear to require trading through an exchange, and our holding in no way implies that such marketing is exempt from the CEA."

In just such a case, where a company called Standard Forex was marketing currency futures to the general public, the court held that the company was a *board of trade.* (*CFTC* v. *Standard Forex, Inc.,* (1992–94 Transfer Binder) Comm.Fut.L.Rep. (CCH), para. 26,063, 41,446 (EDNY 1993)). Rather than limiting *board of trade* to its ordinary definition, the court held that "a formal structure for unsophisticated investors who need the assistance of such a formal organization in order to carry out their trading" fell within the "unless" clause.

This judicial rewrite of the *board of trade* definition, and, consequently, the Treasury Amendment, would be problematic to apply in modern markets. For example, under the *Standard Forex* ruling, the Chicago Board of Trade could cease to be an exchange and be liberated from CEA regulation if it merely barred "unsophisticated investors" from trading. Since over 95 percent of the trades at the Board of Trade are entered into for professionals and institutions, the trade-off suggested by the *Standard Forex* decision might be quite appealing.

Whatever its practical problems, the court in *Standard Forex* departed both from the literal statutory definition and from the ordinary meaning of *board of trade* to fashion its own definition to respond to the case before it. Similarly, the *Tauber* court's attempt to navigate between the competing interpretive poles was a creative effort that lacked the benefit of statutory guideposts. There is simply no language whatsoever in the Treasury Amendment or the definition of *board of trade* that supports the proposition that "mass marketing to small investors...require[s] trading through an exchange" (8 F.3d, 978).*

Why the Law Is Such a Mess

As the facts in *Standard Forex* amply demonstrate, it is entirely possible to market futures to the public without using an exchange. The *Tauber* court therefore must have meant that the statute requires exchange trading *only* for futures that are offered to the general public. But that isn't what the statute says. The CEA provides that, in the absence of a CFTC exemption, all futures, regardless of who trades them, must be traded on a CFTC-designated contract market. The recent *MG* precedent confirms that reading of the CEA (see note 17). The distinctions that courts and the CFTC have wanted to draw between sophisticated and general-public customers do not correspond to any language in the Treasury Amendment. As a result, the provisions that are in the statute—*transactions in* and *board of trade*—have been forced to bear the weight of these unrelated concerns, and it is now perfectly clear that certain courts and the CFTC will continue to deviate from the words of the statute.

The CFTC's 1985 "statutory interpretation" of the Treasury Amendment offers the best illustration of the inconsistency between the statute's terms and the policy result the agency favors. In that 1985 interpretation, the CFTC did not even try to couch its interpretation in the terms of the statute, an analytical approach the CFTC confessed to in its *Tauber* amicus briefs nearly a decade later. Instead, the agency simply declared that "any marketing to the general public of futures transactions in foreign currencies conducted outside the facilities of a contract market is strictly outside the scope of the Amendment" ("CFTC Statutory

---

*Thus far, the statutory phrase within the board of trade definition "persons who are engaged in the business of buying and selling any commodity" has escaped serious judicial consideration and analysis. 7 USC § 1a(1). That phrase suggests, however, that only persons in the business of trading futures could form a board of trade; two or more members of the public generally or two or more avocational speculators would not form a board of trade if trading futures. But an entity making a market in futures or acting as a broker-dealer in futures would surely come within the literal meaning of the "engaged in the business" test. Cf. 15 USC § 78c(a)(5) (Securities Exchange Act defines "dealer" to be "any person engaged in the business of buying and selling securities for his own account").

Interpretation and Request for Comments Regarding Trading in Foreign Currencies for Future Delivery," 50 Fed. Reg. 42983, 42985 (Oct. 23, 1985)). The commission's failure to attempt to justify this declaration by reference to the amendment is understandable since the amendment does not offer any satisfactory route to that conclusion.

Others have supported the CFTC's view that the Treasury Amendment should not exclude from the CEA the marketing of currency futures and government securities futures to the general public outside of licensed contract markets. The Treasury, Federal Reserve, and industry associations all appear to have agreed, at one time or another, that such conduct should violate the law.[26] Even that otherwise common thread—hostility to over-the-counter retailing of currency futures and options to the public—has now been broken. A federal district court decision has concluded that the Treasury Amendment prevents the CFTC from prosecuting wrongdoing in connection with off-exchange currency futures marketed to the general public.

In *CFTC* v. *Frankwell Bullion* (2 Comm. Fut. L Rep., para. 26, 484 (N.D. Cal. 1995)), the district court rejected the CFTC's argument that the Treasury Amendment does not exclude from the CEA retailing of currency futures to the general public. That district court decision concluded that the "plain meaning" of the Treasury Amendment is "that off-exchange foreign currency futures are exempted from the Act" (*Frankwell Bullion*, para. 26,484 at 43,148). The CFTC's view that OTC futures retailed to the public remain subject to the CEA "conflicts with the plain language of the Act...The Treasury Amendment makes no distinction based on the identity or character of the participants."

That plain meaning approach to the statute finds support (in one sense) in other decisions under the Treasury Amendment—including decisions that directly conflict in terms of the result reached in *Frankwell Bullion*—where courts have exhibited a good degree of intolerance of the "decide what is exempted by the identity of the parties" approach. For example, when the Second Circuit held that options on foreign currency were not "transactions in" currency, the case involved a self-proclaimed board of trade, and the court emphasized that the defendant had been selling the options to the general public (*ABT*, 803 F.2d, 1248–49). But the court did not limit its "transactions in" holding to transactions involving the general public, so *ABT* may fairly be read to hold that currency options are not within the scope of the Treasury Amendment irrespective of the identity of the counterparties and the circumstances of the case, a point the recent *Dunn* case makes emphatically.

Conversely, although the *Tauber* court did claim to "hold only that individually negotiated foreign currency option and futures transactions between sophisticated, large-scale foreign currency traders fall within the Treasury Amendment's exclusion from CEA coverage" (8 F.3d, at 978), the bulk of the opinion reads as if it were announcing a much broader holding more in line with *Frankwell Bullion*. Statements such as "[w]hat the statute commands...is the exemption of all trading off organized exchanges" (ibid., 977), place *Tauber* in disagreement with the CFTC's views and would allow OTC clones of popular exchange-traded currency and government security contracts to escape CEA regulation whether marketed to the public or professional traders.

The important point here is not who is right and who is wrong. When "plain meaning" is authoritatively invoked by courts reaching diametrically opposite conclusions, the waters in this area of the law have become hopelessly muddied, making it even more difficult for market participants to predict how the law will treat their conduct. The recent judicial decisions, in particular the Second Circuit's *Dunn* decision, have caused even the best law firms to reconsider their prior views of the Treasury Amendment's scope. As one firm bluntly acknowledged to its clients after the *Dunn* case, "it is not prudent to rely upon the Treasury Amendment to effect OTC foreign currency options transactions."[27]

The law under the Treasury Amendment is a mess. Even the CFTC has acknowledged that the law is far from clear (*CFTC Report,* at 155–56). The CFTC does not rely on and is not constrained by the statute, and has declared as much. Courts know this, and yet are not free to disregard inconvenient statutory terms so blithely and candidly. Market participants also know that they cannot order their activities in reliance on the law, because the law is in such a state of disorder as to make predictability and certainty impossible.

Why It Is Important to Clean Up This Mess

If all of this were merely an analytical or doctrinal problem it would properly be the concern of legal academics rather than Congress. But one must consider what is at stake. One study reported the average daily turnover in foreign currency forwards in 26 countries was approximately $100 billion in April 1995.[28] Uncertainty as to what transactions are permitted, how they may be structured, and who may be involved would undermine the efficiency of this vast and critically important market. Trading in government securities is of obvious importance to the federal government and worldwide interest rate markets. Conflicting court decisions that impose different rules for different regions of our country would disfavor certain participants for no good reason. The uncertainty and additional costs such a regime would impose could cause market participants to do business outside the United States altogether. When, after 20 years, a statute has not only failed to resolve confusion and settle an area of the law, but on the contrary has itself contributed to that confusion, the conclusion is inescapable: The statute needs to be fixed. The massive dollar amounts and broad ramifications of the trading affected by the Treasury Amendment make that prescription all the more urgent.

Possible Repair Strategies: A Statutory Change

Two readily apparent strategies for dealing with these problems involve working within the two principal statutory terms: *transactions in* and *board of trade*. Is it possible to interpret either or both statutory terms in a way that is consistent with their accepted meanings and the CEA's statutory framework as a whole? Not likely. In the CFTC's view, the Treasury Amendment excludes futures and options if traded off-"board of trade" and among only sophisticated financial institutions. That position promotes legal uncertainty, conflicts with the statute's terms, and undermines the CEA as a whole.

As we have shown (see note 3 above) given the broad statutory definition, ascertaining what is or is not a board of trade would be no easy task. Even if the meaning of *board of trade* is limited to *exchanges*, that term itself has sparked legal disputes. In *Board of Trade of the City of Chicago* v. *SEC* , (883 F.2d 525 (7th Cir. 1989)), the court divided 2 to 1 on whether an electronic trading system was an exchange. Moreover, with all due respect to *Standard Forex* and *Tauber*, it simply makes no sense to say that whether an entity is a board of trade depends on whether the market's participants are sophisticated. After all if *board of trade* refers only to those entities where public customers trade, would the Chicago Board of Trade cease being a *board of trade* if it excluded all public customers? What would be the result if an entity transacts over 95 percent of its business with sophisticated counterparties and less than 5 percent with public customers, as the Board of Trade does today? If the identity of the customer determines the classification of the trading forum, such an entity would seem to be a *board of trade* with respect to the 5 percent but not for the 95 percent. But it makes no sense to hold that a particular seller or market-maker is a board of trade only some of the time.

Manipulating the "transactions in" requirement is an even worse way to achieve the CFTC's interpretive goal. It is practically a nonsequitur to assert that a given transaction that is "in" foreign currency when engaged in by a bank somehow becomes not "in" foreign currency when engaged in by an individual. The term *transactions in* refers to the characteristics of the transaction, and cannot reasonably be made to turn on the identity of the parties to the transaction.

Even if the CFTC's view would clarify matters and could be squared with the statute, it is bad public policy and contradicts agency positions in other contexts. No basis exists for saying that only transactions on organized self-regulatory exchanges (if that is what *board of trade* means) need regulation. Those self-policing bodies could be excused from regulation, not singled out for it by definition. Similarly, the CFTC's *MG* decision contradicts the position that, in the agency's view, the CEA should apply to only on-exchange transactions involving general public participants. While a strong case can be made for a streamlined CFTC regulatory presence for all professional trading markets—whether on-exchange or off-exchange— the CFTC's reluctance to embrace the exchanges' more than three-year-old Rolling Spot and ProMarket petitions suggests the agency has not found that case to be compelling. Thus, the agency itself apparently has decided that regulation is warranted for transactions among institutions and businesses (see 60 Fed. Reg. 51323 (CFTC Oct. 2, 1995), which adopts Part 36 rules for regulating exchanges that allow only professional and institutional trading).

An alternative to the CFTC's approach, espoused by certain state regulators, is to read the Treasury Amendment only to avoid duplicative regulation by the CFTC of banks and other institutions that were already regulated by the Comptroller of the Currency and the Federal Reserve (see Senate Rep. No. 1131, pp. 49–51). But the text of the Treasury Amendment failed to distinguish between these entities and the many that are not regulated but engage in the same futures and options transactions as those that are. Thus the fit between the current statute and this goal is imperfect at best. *Tauber* presents one concrete example of this incongruity; the dealer, as a subsidiary of an investment bank rather than a commercial bank, was not subject to any regulation whatever (Br. Am. Cur. of Chicago Board of Trade and Chicago Mercantile Exchange, *Tauber* v. *Salomon Forex, Inc.,* No. 93–1314 (U.S.), pp. 13–15). Accordingly, if the states' reading of the amendment had been applied, the result of that litigation would have been altogether different.

Another approach would construe the Treasury Amendment to completely exclude from the CEA only currency and government security spot and forward transactions. Holding that all futures and options are subject to the CEA has the virtue of simplicity; it avoids the morass into which we are plunged if we must decide which futures and options, marketed by which dealers, to which customers, are excluded from the CEA solely on the basis of the ill-fitting and unilluminating statutory terms *transactions in* and *board of trade.*

On this view, the "unless" clause is not meaningless (contrary to the opinion of the *Tauber* court), because it provides that futures and options that result in actual delivery and thus become "transactions in" foreign currency are also subject to the CEA. The Second and Seventh Circuits have held that an option is ordinarily not a transaction "in" the underlying commodity but becomes such an excluded transaction "in" when it is exercised (See *ABT*, 803 F.2d, 1248; *CBOT*, 677 F.2d, 1154). Therefore, without the "unless" clause's reinclusion of futures and options that result in actual delivery, such transactions would be excluded from the CEA.[29]

By distinguishing all spots and forwards, on the one hand, from all futures and options on the other, this approach would foster certainty and predictability to the extent that market participants could correctly predict which label the CFTC or a court would attach to a particular transaction. This interpretation would also require Congress to define *futures* and *forwards*, however, a distinction current law has rendered amorphous, at best. Without that corresponding statutory reform, even this interpretation of the Treasury Amendment would compound the existing confusion in the market.

A Possible Solution: Repeal the Treasury Amendment and Leave the Issue to the CFTC

In light of the problems inherent in all of these strategies, the best solution may be to repeal the Treasury Amendment and leave these issues to the CFTC. After more than 20 years of the amendment, the law is in disarray and does not provide market participants with the predictability they need. Perhaps a statutory solution to this Gordian knot is simply impracticable. The CFTC itself has acknowledged that the statute's terms cannot be relied upon. Since the policies that some argue animate the amendment are not reflected in its text, the amendment is an extremely poor vehicle for furthering them and should be scrapped. Moreover, Congress now has given the CFTC exactly the tools it needs to tailor an appropriate exemption for professional markets in foreign currency and government securities (CEA § 4(c)). Congress should simply repeal the Treasury Amendment and let the CFTC issue a detailed exemption from regulation for those professional markets under terms and conditions the Commission finds are consistent with the "public interest" (CEA § 4(c)).

CONCLUSION

Before Congress decides how to regulate an activity, Congress must first decide what activity it wants to be covered by that regulation. The three issues discussed in this chapter all address this basic jurisdictional question: What activity should be covered under the CEA? Once Congress answers that question, modernizing the CEA to fit the realities of that activity should not be overly difficult. In contrast, trying to fashion a regulatory regime without first focusing on what is to be covered by regulation would be an unsound and unduly complicated approach.

Maintaining the CEA's status quo breeds intolerable legal uncertainty among market participants, lawyers, and government officials, including courts, charged with applying and enforcing the law. That uncertainty plagues not only financial markets, but as the CFTC's recent *MG* decision confirms, all commodity markets. Indeed, as OTC agricultural derivatives begin to catch up with interest rate and currency derivatives, the consequences of legal uncertainty will be visited upon those emerging and important markets as well.

To end that legal uncertainty, Congress should begin the process of reestablishing what activity should be covered by and excluded from the CEA in clear and reliable terms. The statutory dividing line for futures versus forwards was enacted in 1922. After more than 70 years of market innovation and financial engineering, reconsidering and shoring up that basic design seems to be very much in order to promote legal certainty.

ENDNOTES

1. See General Accounting Office, *Financial Derivatives: Actions Needed to Protect the Financial System* 64–65 (May 1994) (in the United Kingdom, a court invalidated certain over-the-counter swaps as illegal resulting in losses of $178 million to over 75 derivatives dealers). See also Group of Thirty, Global Derivatives Study Group, *Derivatives: Practices and Principles*, 52 (1993).

2. Perhaps the absence of legal uncertainty relating to options stems from the consistent legal definitions of options that the CFTC and the courts have employed. See *Commodity Futures Trading Commission v. U.S. Metals Depository Co.*, 468 F. Supp. 1149 (S.D.N.Y. 1979). The CFTC also historically had greater flexibility to address legal certainty concerns relating to options than it did for futures since Congress essentially gave the CFTC carte blanche to develop and adjust a regulatory scheme for options, including exemptions from that scheme, 7 USC § 6c(b). The CFTC used those powers to allow certain over-the-counter options called *trade options*, 17 CFR § 32.4. In contrast, until CEA § 4(c) was enacted in 1992, the CFTC was locked into the provisions of the CEA—including the exchange-trading requirement—and had no authority to grant exemptions from those statutory requirements.

3. The CEA's regulatory scheme for futures, in addition to the exchange trading requirement, includes registration of professionals, financial integrity safeguards, position limits and reporting, maintenance of books and records, mandatory disclosures, and other sale practices as well as proscriptions against fraud, manipulation, and various trading practices. See 7 USC §1, et seq. The CFTC has the power to enforce these regulatory requirements through administrative proceedings or injunctive actions filed in federal court. Not all transactions in commodities are subject to the CEA's regulatory scheme; the CEA's comprehensive regulation does not cover either the actual purchase or sale of a commodity for delivery today, called a cash or spot transaction, or the actual purchase or sale of a commodity for delivery at some future date, called a forward contract.

4. Section 321(g)(1) of the Federal Food, Drug, and Cosmetic Act defines the term *drug*, 21 USC § 321(g)(1), and Section 1813(l) of the Federal Deposit Insurance Act defines the term *deposit*, 12 USC § 1813(l).

5. That "we'll-make-it-up-as-we-go-along" approach may also be unconstitutional. "Even a regulation which governs purely economic or commercial activities, if its violation can engender penalties, must be so framed as to provide a constitutionally adequate warning to those whose

activities are governed." *Diebold, Inc.* v. *Marshall,* 585 F.2d 1327, 1335 (6th Cir. 1978).

6. Prior efforts to define a futures contract have been hamstrung by fears expressed by some derivative market participants that certain instruments they trade could be identified as futures. In part, that fear stemmed from the absence of CFTC authority to exempt any futures contracts from the contract market designation requirement in CEA §4(a). Congress has now taken care of that problem in CEA §4(c).The term *futures contract* is used to describe those transactions the CEA is designed to cover. No mystical significance attaches to *futures contract*, however. The transactions subject to the CEA could just as easily be labeled *derivatives, trading instruments*, or *hedging/speculation contracts*. The name employed isn't important; setting forth clear legal guidelines describing what Congress intends to be covered by the CEA is the crucial point.

7. The statute says that onion futures may not be traded "on or subject to the rules of any board of trade in the United States" (7 USC §13–1). Congress apparently believed that onion prices were too susceptible to manipulation to trade under the CEA. But Congress seems to have allowed off-exchange trading in onion futures to escape the CEA provision. No reason exists why onion futures should be tradeable outside the CEA in an unregulated over-the-counter market, but prohibited from being traded on a CFTC-approved exchange.

8. The concept of actual delivery on the maturity date of a contract is self-evident. Offset is not quite so clear. But understanding the offset process is vital to understanding the traditional legal approach to defining a futures contract. Through offsetting transactions someone who promises to buy something at a specified price and future date may liquidate that promise by, in effect, entering into a subsequent mirror-image transaction at a different price. For example, let's say on August 1 Party A agrees with Party B to buy 100 ounces of gold at $400 per ounce (or $40,000) for delivery on October 1. One month later, after gold prices have soared to $500, Party A decides to offset that original transaction and take the profit rather than wait until October 1 and run the risk that gold prices would decline. If the contract was sufficiently standardized and a willing counterparty could be found, Party A would enter into an offsetting transaction with, for purposes of simplicity, Party B to sell 100 ounces of gold at $500 per ounce on September 1. On the August 1 transaction, Party A would have to pay $40,000 for the gold. On the September 1 transaction, Party A would receive $50,000 for the gold. Taken together, the two offsetting transactions result in a

$10,000 profit for Party A. (They also result in a $10,000 loss for Party B.) Whether Party A enters into the transactions one month, one day, or one minute apart, the standardized offsetting transactions would generally be considered to be futures.

9. The uncertainty would not be completely resolved since the issue what is an "exchange" or to use the broader CEA term, what is a "board of trade," is not free from doubt. See CEA § 1a(1). See also *Board of Trade of the City of Chicago* v. *Securities and Exchange Comm'n*, 883 F.2d 525, 534–35 (7th Cir. 1989)(court "could not find a single case...discussing which attributes (if any) are necessary, and which are sufficient, for sorting a trading apparatus into the 'exchange' bin"); *Commodity Futures Trading Comm'n* v. *Standard Forex*, [1992– 1994 Transfer Binder] Comm. Fut. L. Rep. (CCH) para. 26,063 at 41,453 (E.D.N.Y. Aug. 9, 1993)(the "definition of the term 'board of trade' includes both formally organized exchanges and informal associations of persons engaged in the business of buying and selling commodities"); CFTC Interpretative Letter 77–11 [1977–1980 Transfer Binder] Com. Fut. L. Rep. (CCH) para. 20,466 at 21,908 (Aug. 17, 1977)(CFTC's Office of the General Counsel describes types of entities and activities that might be within the definition of "board of trade").

10. A strong argument can be made that professional trading markets—those operated both by dealers and exchanges—need no direct federal regulatory presence. A compelling argument also can be made for regulating only dealer markets that do not have built-in self-regulatory mechanisms, rather than exchanges that have tested and effective self-regulatory programs. But no argument can be made to regulate only exchange products and allow dealer markets immunity from federal regulation.

11. See, e.g., *In re Stovall*, (1977–1980 Transfer Binder) Comm. Fut. L. Rep. (CCH), para. 20, 941 (CFTC Dec. 6, 1979); "Characteristics Distinguishing Cash and Forward Contracts and 'Trade' Options," *Federal Register* 50, 39656 (Sept. 30, 1985); "Regulation of Hybrid and Related Instruments," *Federal Register* 52, 47022 (Dec. 11, 1987); "Policy Statement Concerning Swap Transactions," *Federal Register* 54, 30694 (July 21, 1989).

12. Transnor did not claim that the Brent oil contracts that gave rise to its losses were illegal and hence unenforceable off-exchange futures contracts. Brent oil contracts are not traded on an exchange; they are offered through a multilateral network of oil companies and trading houses in what could be described as a "phone and fax" market.

13. This defense was a bit strange since, as we have seen, while forward contracts are not generally subject to the CEA's regulatory scheme,

forwards *are* subject to the CEA's prohibition against the manipulation of any commodity price in itnerstate commerce (CEA §6(c) and 9(a)(2)).

14. The CFTC offered some clarity on the issue of who is a commercial. In short, anyone who bought or sold oil in connection with the conduct of a line of business would be a commercial (Forward Interp. at 37368). That broad concept would seem to include Wall Street refiners, investment banks that engage in proprietary trading in oil, as well as collective investment vehicles that speculate in the future value of oil.

15. The CFTC skirted the issues of what is an exchange or what is a board of trade under the CEA, thereby exacerbating the legal uncertainty its interpretation spawned.

16. The Ninth Circuit remedied (or exacerbated, depending on your viewpoint) this legal confusion, in part, in its recent decision in *Noble Metals*. In that case, the Ninth Circuit held that even where the contract specified that "the transaction could not be liquidated by offset" and that "delivery and transfer of title in return for payment are the essence" of the transaction, the contract would be found to be a futures contract where the evidence showed that there was "no legitimate expectation that...[the parties] would take actual delivery of the metal they bought" (*Noble Metals,* 43,281 and 43,285).

17. Another aspect of the *MG Refining* settlement bears comment. Many observers have argued that the CEA was not designed to apply to transactions between two commercial counterparties; that is, unless the public participated in trading the contract, the CEA should not apply. (That conclusion certainly underlies many precedents under the Treasury Amendment.) The *MG* settlement contradicts that view by finding the CEA to be applicable to commercial-to-commercial transactions without any public participation.

18. "The CFTC's Uncertain Future," the *Economist* (Oct. 28, 1995), pp. 93–94.

19. "Swaps in Danger," *The Wall Street Journal* (Aug. 17, 1995), p. A10.

20. M. Miller and C. Culp, "Rein In the CFTC," *The Wall Street Journal* (Aug.17, 1995), p. A10.

21. Some observers mistakenly believe that Congress told the CFTC to exempt only nonstandardized, nonfungible swaps. The statute belies that assertion. CEA §4(c)(5)(B) states that the CFTC
    may—(B) promptly...exercise the exemptive authority granted under [CEA §4(c)(1)]...with respect to classes of swap agreements that are standardized as to their material economic terms, to the extent that such agreements may be regarded as subject to the provisions of the Act.

(Emphasis added.) This provision does not direct the CFTC to do anything; it is advisory—the CFTC "may" take action. Furthermore, CEA §4(c)(5)(B) does not say that the CFTC should adopt the standardized/fungible criterion in any exemption it may ultimately adopt. To the contrary, the statute expressly gives the CFTC the flexibility to adopt any exemptive criterion or any other "terms or conditions" the agency determines to be consistent with the public interest (CEA §4(c)(5)).

22. The General Accounting Office has observed that the CFTC's swaps exemption "does not completely eliminate the risk that a swap contract could be found to violate [the] CEA" (GAO, "Financial Derivatives: Actions Needed to Protect the Financial System," 65 (May 1994). GAO also correctly recognized that CEA §4(c) precludes the CFTC's exemption from extending to swaps whose payments are based on the price of securities and stock indexes. For those equity swaps, the CFTC relies on a 1989 policy statement that provides the commission's policy view that swaps meeting certain criteria not need to comply with the CEA. Of course, if that policy statement was adequate for legal certainty purposes, Congress would not have needed to adopt CEA §4(c) in the first place.

23. *OTC Derivative Markets and Their Regulation*, Report of the CFTC, Oct. 1993, p. 156.

24. Any government securities futures contracts traded OTC also would be unregulated unless the CEA applies to them. Options on government securities, however, are securities subject to the federal securities laws. Options on currency traded on securities exchanges also are securities.

25. The first extreme view also raises the same unacceptable policy outcomes as defining futures to be limited to only transactions traded on an exchange. Widespread sales practice abuses and unfair competition for exchanges could be sparked by simply allowing off-exchange futures to be traded without any regulation. See supra at 12.

26. *See* CFTC Statutory Interpretation; comment letter from the Assistant Secretary, Department of the Treasury, to the Chairman of the CFTC (May 5, 1986); comment letter from the General Counsel, Board of Governors of the Federal Reserve System, to the General Counsel of the CFTC (March 5, 1986); Brief Am. Cur. of the Foreign Exchange Committee and N.Y. Clearing House Ass'n, *CFTC* v. *Dunn and Delta Consultants, Inc.*, No. 94–6197 (2d Cir.), 7.

27. *Swaps Monitor*, July 10, 1995, p. 2.

28. BIS, "Central Bank Survey of Foreign Exchange Market Activity in April 1995: Preliminary Global Findings" at 2, Table 1 (October 24,

1995); *cf.* BIS, "Central Bank Survey of Foreign Exchange Market Activity in April 1992" at 19, Table 1–A (March 1993).

29. The "unless" clause's scope is, of course, limited to transactions "conducted on a board of trade."

7

THE CASE FOR FEDERAL ANTIFRAUD AUTHORITY IN THE OTC DERIVATIVES MARKETS

Robert F. Klein, *Division of Enforcement*
of the Commodity Futures Trading Commission[1]

The last few years have brought a spate of highly publicized losses and resulting litigation stemming from off-exchange derivative transactions.[2] Banks, brokerage firms, and accounting firms have been accused of wrongdoing in offering derivatives products, auditing derivatives portfolios, or advising clients to enter into derivatives transactions. The defendants—and the larger community of derivatives dealers—have with some degree of justification characterized the litigation as the result of opportunistic counterparties exploiting legal uncertainties in an effort to nullify transactions that turned out to be unprofitable. Yet the facts as suggested by legal filings and press coverage raise troubling questions even if we discount the severity of wrongdoing for the hyperbole associated with litigation.

The events behind the publicized losses raise concerns about whether information and valuations provided by dealers adequately reflected the type and magnitude of risk involved, whether derivative dealers should have adopted and enforced stronger internal controls and procedures, whether counterparties to derivatives transactions possessed sufficient resources and experience to understand the transactions at issue, and whether state laws restricting or prohibiting municipalities from investing in "speculative" investments impose duties on derivatives dealers or only on the municipal officers making investment decisions.

Aside from controversy about what really was said and done, and legal debates about who is accountable for wrongdoing, much of the inquiry and dispute surrounding the litigation has centered on the issues of whether off-exchange derivative transactions are subject to a federal antifraud prohibition and, if so, under which statute or regulatory scheme.[3] The derivatives industry has argued strenuously that their business is limited to sophisticated people and entities capable of evaluating risks and protecting themselves, and that the industry can police itself for any abuse. Federal regulators—most notably the Commodity Futures Trading Commission (CFTC) and the Securities Exchange Commission (SEC)—have countered that application of antifraud provisions in federal law is necessary to protect customers who may be unsophisticated even if well-heeled, and to augment other protection against systemic risk.[4]

A review of the complaints and final orders in the litigation reveals a patchwork of statutes and other legal obligations that arguably apply to derivatives transactions. Without a clear governing antifraud provision, the off-exchange derivatives industry faces continued uncertainty about the legal standards it operates under, along with a lack of consistency and predictability greater than what is normally the case in litigation. At the same time, both regulators and counterparties face nagging questions about the efficacy of existing customer protection and the degree to which litigation risk might threaten exchanges of payments on obligations among brokers and dealers.

CASES AND THE PROBLEMS THEY DESCRIBE

The facts in derivatives-related cases brought by regulators and the facts alleged in various private lawsuits give some sense of the conduct that has prompted allegations of fraud and efforts to apply various statutes that prohibit fraud. The facts, alleged or documented, also provide the context for a discussion of why a more general antifraud statute or rule would be appropriate. What follows is not an exhaustive survey of the litigation, but a summary of several of the most highly publicized actions.

Bankers Trust

Perhaps the most notable litigation has resulted from the dealings of BT Securities Corporation, an affiliate of Bankers Trust. On December

22, 1994, both the CFTC and SEC filed and simultaneously settled administrative actions against BT Securities Corporation. These coordinated actions followed closely on the heels of a Federal Reserve written agreement with Bankers Trust that addressed the bank's business practices regarding the offer and sale of off-exchange derivatives transactions.[5]

The CFTC's complaint against BT Securities was based on alleged violations of one antifraud provision of the Commodity Exchange Act in connection with privately negotiated OTC derivatives sold by BT Securities to Gibson Greetings, a Cincinnati-based manufacturer of greeting cards and related products. More specifically, the commission alleged that BT Securities, based on fraudulent misrepresentation and omissions while acting as a commodity trading advisor (CTA) in connection with derivatives transactions with Gibson, violated section 4o(1)(A) of the Commodity Exchange Act. [6]

As described in the CFTC's complaint and order,[7] between November 1991 and March 1994, representatives of BT Securities and Gibson entered into approximately 29 derivatives transactions. These transactions, many of which included leverage factors that caused Gibson's losses to increase dramatically as a result of relatively small changes in interest rates, became increasingly complex, risky, and interrelated over time.[8] Generically speaking, the transactions were, or were variations on, what the financial services business refers to as swaps, caps, floors, or collars. The parties referred to them by names such as the ratio swap, the periodic floor, the spread lock 1 and 2, the Treasury-linked swap, the knock-out call option, the LIBOR-linked payout, the time swap, and the wedding band 3 and 6.[9] BT Securities also sold to Gibson three plain vanilla interest rate swap agreements.

All of the derivatives BT Securities sold to Gibson were customized and did not trade in any market. As a result, Gibson could not use any available market prices to determine the current value of the transactions. Instead, Bankers Trust estimated the value of these products by using sophisticated computer models.[10] These values, in turn, were reflected in the financial statements of BT Securities' parent company. As set forth in the CFTC's complaint and order, however, Gibson itself did not have the expertise or the computer models needed to value the derivatives it purchased from BT Securities; rather, it used information concerning value supplied by BT Securities to evaluate certain transactions and prepare its financial statements.[11]

The CFTC's allegations that BT Securities engaged in fraud were based on the fact that the values of the derivatives transactions that BT Securities provided to Gibson materially differed from those generated by BT Securities' own internal computer models. In particular, between October 1992 and March 1994, BT Securities' sales representatives misled Gibson about the value of the company's derivatives positions by providing values that significantly understated the actual amount of Gibson's losses.[12]

Conversations tape-recorded by an internal BT Securities taping system and other evidence described in the CFTC's complaint and order confirm that on a number of occasions BT Securities representatives materially misrepresented or omitted material information concerning the existence and magnitude of Gibson's losses in its derivatives transactions with BT Securities.[13] For example, in a February 23, 1994, conversation, a BT Securities managing director discussed the "differential" between what BT Securities' own computer model was showing as the value of Gibson's position and the valuations that BT Securities had given to Gibson:

> I think that we should use this [a downward market price movement] as an opportunity. We should just call [the Gibson contact], and maybe chip away at the differential a little more. I mean we told him 8.1 million when the real number was 14. So now if the real number is 16, we'll tell him that it is 11. You know, just slowly chip away at that differential between what it really is and what we're telling him.[14]

Later that day, the same BT Securities employee was recorded saying:

> [I]f the market hadn't changed at all, or was just kind of dottering around within a couple of ticks, then you know, there's nothing that we can really say. He is going to keep thinking that it is around 8.1 [million], when it is really 14 [million]...[15]

Given BT Securities' material misrepresentations and omissions, Gibson remained unaware of the extent of its losses from the transactions and continued to enter into deals with BT Securities.[16] In addition, Gibson used the values provided by BT Securities representatives in its own financial statements, causing Gibson to make material understatements of its unrealized losses on derivatives transactions in its 1992 and 1993 financial statements.[17]

As noted previously, the CFTC based its jurisdiction over BT Securities' conduct on Section 4o(1)(A) of the Commodity Exchange Act,[18] which prohibits a CTA from employing "any device, scheme or artifice to defraud" a client or prospective client. The CFTC's allegation that BT Securities acted as a CTA in its dealings with Gibson was supported by the evidence that BT Securities' managing director for the Gibson account had informed his supervisor that, "from the very beginning" Gibson had "really put [itself] in [BT Securities'] hands like 96%."[19] Through this and similar statements, the CFTC alleged, BT Securities had acknowledged the existence of an advisory relationship between itself and Gibson sufficient for it to have become a CTA with respect to its derivatives dealings with Gibson.

Although the SEC's complaint addressed different transactions, like the CFTC its specific allegations of fraud were based on evidence that the values of derivatives transactions that BT Securities provided to Gibson deviated sharply from the values generated by BT Securities' own internal computer models. The SEC based its jurisdiction on a finding that certain of the transactions between Gibson and BT were options on securities, or options on government securities, and therefore specifically included in the statutory definition of *securities*, and thus within SEC jurisdiction.[20] Given the misleading and inaccurate values BT Securities allegedly provided in connection with those transactions, the SEC alleged that BT Securities had violated various antifraud provisions of the securities laws.

Under its December 22, 1994, settlement with the CFTC and the SEC, BT Securities, while neither admitting nor denying the allegations of the SEC and the CFTC, agreed to an order finding that it had violated the antifraud provision of the Commodity Exchange Act relating to CTAs by making material misrepresentations and omissions in connection with the offer and sale of certain swaps transactions to Gibson. BT Securities at that time also consented to the issuance of a separate, parallel order finding that it had violated certain reporting and antifraud provisions of the securities laws. To settle both the CFTC's and the SEC's actions, BT Securities agreed to pay an aggregate civil monetary penalty of $10 million to the United States Treasury. BT Securities also agreed to cease and desist from the violations described above, to employ an independent consultant to review and make recommendations on the company's OTC derivatives activities, and, if necessary as a result of that review, to modify its derivatives marketing.[21]

Bankers Trust's earlier (December 4, 1994) written agreement with the Federal Reserve Bank of New York also focuses on allegedly inaccurate pricing and valuation. In that agreement, Bankers Trust New York Corporation, Bankers Trust Company, and BT Securities Corporation agreed to (among other things) conduct their business in a manner that assures the "reasonable transparency" of pricing and valuation to customers. To meet that goal, the companies agreed to develop written policies and procedures on pricing and valuation that address the following:

+ Provision of "indicative" and "firm" quotes.
+ Provision of daily indicative quotes to customers with "highly market sensitive" leveraged derivative transactions (LDTs) and monthly indicative quotes for all other LDTs.
+ The methodology to be used in making valuation adjustments.
+ The analytical basis for the valuation adjustment methodology to be used.
+ Documentation and review of customer quotes as related to LDT values in companies' books and all valuation adjustment decisions.[22]

In addition to the actions by federal government agencies, BT Securities and Bankers Trust have been the targets of private lawsuits. Gibson filed its own action against BT Securities in September 1994 in the federal District Court for the Southern District of Ohio. Gibson's complaint was based on common law theories of fraudulent misrepresentation and breach of fiduciary duty as well as claims under the Commodity Exchange Act. The complaint initially sought about $23 million and actual damages and $50 million in punitive damages. In November 1994, Bankers Trust and Gibson agreed to an out-of-court settlement under which Gibson would receive about $14 million from Bankers Trust.

Procter & Gamble Company, which similarly suffered multimillion dollar losses in transactions with BT Securities, also filed a lawsuit in federal court in Ohio against BT Securities and its parent, Bankers Trust. Procter & Gamble asserted misrepresentations and failures to disclose similar to those at issue in the actions stemming from the Gibson transactions. Procter & Gamble mounted its suit on a slew of legal theories, including violations of securities laws, the Commodity Exchange Act, and common law fraud, and sought punitive damages.

Significantly, on February 24, 1996, BT Securities moved to dismiss the Commodity Exchange Act, federal securities law, Ohio securities law, and Ohio deceptive trade practices law claims in the complaint.

The motion to dismiss argues that the portions of Proctor & Gamble's suit grounded in federal and state statutes are invalid as a matter of law. The motion is a compendium of the legal arguments for why no comprehensive federal statute applies to dealings in off-exchange derivatives. Among other things, the Bankers Trust motion asserts that the transactions involved were neither securities nor options on securities, and therefore not subject to antifraud provisions of the Securities Act of 1933 or the Securities Exchange Act of 1934. Similarly, Bankers Trust argues that the contracts were neither commodity futures contracts nor commodity options, and therefore not subject to the Commodity Exchange Act. In addition, Bankers Trust asserts that, even if the contracts were covered by the Commodity Exchange Act, the basic antifraud provision of the Act (section 4b) does not apply. According to the motion, that provision prohibits only fraud by a person acting "for or on behalf" of another person, and Bankers Trust and Procter & Gamble were engaged in arm's-length transactions, rather than Bankers Trust acting "for or on behalf of" Procter & Gamble.[23]

Other Litigation

Bankers Trust has not been alone in facing derivatives-related lawsuits. These suits often relate to alleged failures to disclose and involve contentions that the derivatives were not suitable for the investors involved, that the counterparties lacked sufficient knowledge and expertise to engage in various derivatives transactions, and that state laws restricting or prohibiting municipalities or pension funds from investing in certain speculative transactions impose duties on derivatives dealers, not just to the state or other officials making investment decisions.

Piper Jaffray Companies (Piper), a Minneapolis-based regional investment firm with approximately 450,000 client accounts, was charged in roughly a dozen lawsuits and arbitration claims with misrepresenting and failing to disclose the risks associated with off-exchange derivatives. The lawsuits filed arose as a result of losses in certain mutual funds managed by one of Piper's divisions, Piper Capital Management (Piper Capital), particularly the Institutional Government Income Portfolio. That fund incurred significant losses when the market for its derivative investments fell. Worth Bruntjen, the Piper Capital manager in charge of the fund, invested heavily in hybrids of mortgage-backed securities whose value would increase if interest rates fell, but decline if interest rates rose. Consecutive interest rate hikes by the Federal Reserve Board in 1994 resulted in big losses for fund.[24] The fund peaked at almost $800 million in late 1993 and dropped to $625 million by September 1994. Net asset value fell from $11.59 per share to less than $8 per share during the same approximate time period. After injecting $10 million into the failing fund, Piper closed it to new investors in June 1994.

Following the losses, fund investors brought a class action suit against Piper in May 1994, alleging that Piper had misrepresented the fund as conservative and misstated the duration for derivatives investments. Piper denied any misrepresentation. The action focused on investors who bought shares in the fund between July 1, 1991, and May 9, 1994. According to shareholders' lawyers, losses for that period equaled $118 million plus $21 million in lost interest. Shareholders alleged that the losses occurred as a result of Bruntjen's risky investment strategy for the fund, including the collateralized mortgage obligations (CMOs). In February 1995, Piper agreed to settle the suit by paying $70 million to compensate investors for losses.

Piper also faced separate actions by the University of Minnesota and the Minnesota Orchestra. The University filed a lawsuit against Piper after incurring losses of approximately $13 million. The Minnesota Orchestra filed an NASD arbitration claim after its portfolio, independently managed by Piper Capital, lost $5 million.

Litigation in the wake of huge and notorious losses suffered by Orange County's investment fund[25] also focused heavily on the adequacy of risk disclosures. The California Schools Excess Liability Fund's suit against County Treasurer Robert Citron, Merrill Lynch, and broker Michael Stamerson, for example, alleged that the defendants failed to disclose the true nature of risks to the fund participants, failed to properly advise participants that funds were so highly leveraged that it would dramatically increase the already substantial risk of investing in derivatives, and, as early as May 1994, knew but did not disclose the extreme volatility of the instruments held by the fund. In addition, the suitability of derivatives instruments to particular investors has been another big issue in lawsuits against Merrill Lynch relating to Orange County's investment pool.

In December 1994, after Orange County's $7.5 billion investment pool sustained losses of approximately $1.69 billion, the county filed for protection under Chapter 9 of the federal Bankruptcy Code. Orange County was the largest investor in the fund (holding 37 percent of the portfolio), followed by Orange County Transportation Authority (15 percent), and 37 school districts (holding 13 percent, collectively). The investment instruments in the fund were "inverse floaters," a type of debt-based derivative that moves inversely to the direction of interest rates.[26] Believing that interest rates would continue to decline, Orange County's former County Treasurer, Robert Citron, invested heavily in these securities with money borrowed by pledging other securities as collateral. When interest rates increased, the value of the county's fund dropped and loans were called in on the fund. Citron thereafter resigned and the county declared bankruptcy.

While Citron sought to portray himself as an unsophisticated investor encouraged to take risks by his advisors, Merrill Lynch asserted that Citron was an experienced investor who fully understood the risks he was taking with Orange County's investment pool. In fact, documents released by Merrill Lynch to a California Senate committee investigating Orange County's bankruptcy reportedly reveal that Citron understood the risks of the derivatives securities he was buying from Merrill Lynch and other dealers. According to press reports, the documents also show that Merrill Lynch repeatedly advised Citron (with no success) to pursue a different, safer investment strategy.

In January 1995, Orange County sued Merrill Lynch. The complaint in the action focuses on the firm's role in selling securities to the investment fund and on the firm's encouraging the county to incur debt through reverse repurchase agreements, which the county claims it could not enter into under California law. The complaint alleges that defendants failed to disclose the true nature of risks to pool participants; failed to properly advise participants that funds were so highly leveraged as to dramatically increase the already substantial risks of investing in derivatives; knew, as early as May 1994, of the extreme volatility of the derivative securities; and knew, as early as August 1993, that the treasurer's office was operating without adequate internal controls. The complaint also alleges that Merrill Lynch and Orange County engaged in a number of transactions designed to help Merrill Lynch meet certain financial statement ratios required by the SEC.

IS THERE A STATUTORY FRAMEWORK?

One of the difficulties faced in both bringing and defending litigation relating to off-exchange derivatives is figuring out what law applies.

Swaps and other off-exchange derivatives markets developed independent of securities and futures markets, and regulators have been reluctant to impose preexisting statutory schemes wholesale on OTC derivatives markets. Notwithstanding the actions against BT Securities, no fully litigated decision has found that swaps in particular fall within the jurisdiction of CFTC or SEC jurisdiction. The derivatives industry itself has persistently asserted that swaps and many types of structured arrangements are not securities, futures contracts, or commodity options, and therefore do not fall within the federal regulatory schemes that cover the securities and futures industries. Conventional wisdom has it that the off-exchange derivatives business exists, usually by choice and sometimes by happenstance, in a regulatory lacuna.

Yet it is becoming increasingly apparent that what seem to be regulatory gaps are sometimes regulatory overlaps. A CFTC report prepared in 1993 assumed that the markets for OTC derivatives products were subject to significant portions of futures, securities, and banking regulatory schemes.[27] And the CFTC and SEC were successful in obtaining consent orders from BT Securities that apply antifraud provisions from the statutes they administer. Although none of the private federal lawsuits has been fully litigated, dealers named as defendants have found that asserted application of banking requirements, the Commodity Exchange Act, several securities statutes, and state securities laws are at least not frivolous.

While some viewed the SEC's enforcement action against BT Securities as a surprising application of securities laws to swaps and similar off-exchange derivatives, the potential application of the Commodity Exchange Act has been debated since the late 1980s. Congress in 1992 granted the CFTC broad authority to exempt products that otherwise might be subject to regulation as futures contracts from the exchange trading and other requirements of the Commodity Exchange Act. Using that authority, the CFTC has exempted three types of instruments: (1) certain swap agreements,[28] (2) certain hybrid securities and bank deposits,[29] and (3) certain energy product contracts.[30] The CFTC also has exempted certain exchange-traded instruments from many provisions of the its regulatory scheme.[31]

These exemptions, however, contain important limitations. The swaps and energy exemptions, for example, have detailed eligibility requirements. "Eligible swaps participants," for example, include only banks, savings associations, credit unions, and other entities and corporations that meet specified net worth and asset requirements. Similarly, only commercial participants and governmental entities are eligible for the energy exemption. The swaps exemption also requires participants to evaluate the creditworthiness of any obligated party.

Most significantly, the CFTC has sought to maintain the applicability of its antifraud and antimanipulation standards to many types of off-exchange derivatives transactions and dealers. Under the CFTC's swap exemption, swap transactions remain subject to the basic prohibitions of fraud in the Commodity Exchange Act—to the extent that those provisions do apply as a matter of law. If swap dealers are futures brokers, operate commodity pools, or provide trading advice on contracts that fall within CFTC jurisdiction, various provisions of the Act and CFTC regulations continue to govern their conduct.

WHY AN ANTIFRAUD RULE?

If anything is clear when discussing off-exchange derivatives, it is that we are faced with an array of complex financial instruments that have resulted in headline-making losses, are scarcely understood by large segments of the public, and do not fit neatly under any state or federal statutory scheme. In this atmosphere, it is little wonder that regulatory agencies have been concerned about maintaining an ability to police financial markets or that the industry has been concerned about legislative or regulatory overreaction to press reports.

In any event, the unambiguous application of an antifraud rule to the market would serve several salutary goals. At the most basic level, it is difficult to gainsay the proposition that fraud should be prohibited, and that given the ambiguities about applying existing antifraud statutes, a separate antifraud rule for off-exchange derivatives would be appropriate. Although the market generally is confined to large institutions, size is not necessarily a protection from fraud and overreaching. This is particularly true in an off-exchange market for customized transactions, where no market prices or volume information is reported, and pricing information is not widely available. As suggested by the facts in the CFTC and SEC BT Securities actions, where parties to a transaction do not have equal access to information about pricing and current value, information disparities can lead to abuse. Also, anecdotal evidence suggests that as the OTC derivatives markets mature, participation is opening up to smaller businesses and even high net worth individuals. As this process continues, it will become less reasonable to expect market participants to possess the financial resources and acumen to protect themselves.

A federal interest also exists in policing this multitrillion-dollar market for fraud.[32] Fraudulent conduct can pose risks to payment flows, balance sheets, and transaction efficiency. Regulation of financial markets as it has evolved in the last half-century has sought to apply systemic protection to buffer the effects of isolated legal or financial problems. The market for off-exchange derivatives is linked to futures and securities markets and the banking industry through affiliations among participants and cross-market transactions and cash flows. If one derivatives dealer suffers a major financial loss or is unable to make a payment to other dealers or a clearinghouse because of legal action, the ripple effect on other firms could be severe. While wholesale regulation of the off-exchange derivatives segment of the business may be unwarranted at this time, basic guarantees of fair dealing in the market provide a floor for user protection and market stability.

A unified antifraud rule also would provide much greater consistency and predictability in legal disputes. Existing legal uncertainty simply adds to confusion about minimum standards of conduct and adds to the costs of disputes. Moreover, state governments have begun to consider, and in a few instances enact, state laws that impose significant burdens on the industry that would seem to far exceed any burden imposed by a federal antifraud statute. For example, in 1994 Texas adopted the Public Funds Investment Act.[33] The Act imposes substantial legal duties on dealers who engage in transactions with state and local government agencies in Texas. The prospect of complying with 50 sets of legal standards instead of a single federal standard only adds to existing legal uncertainty. Aside from the issue of legal certainty, if one goal is some level of effective government policing of fraud, it is legitimate to ask whether state governments truly have the resources and expertise to police fraud in large-scale, complex, and international financial markets.

It also seems inevitable that a general standard of what constitutes legitimate conduct or a breach of fiduciary duty in the off-exchange derivative markets will develop whether or not a unified antifraud rule is adopted. The significant problems users have encountered after investing in derivatives products have led a number of industry and self-regulatory groups to issue reports or standards in the hopes of improving market certainty and limiting the risks. Although these standards do not have the force of law and include careful disclaimers that they are not intended to increase or alter legal rights or obligations, they unavoidably create accepted standards of dealing that the conduct of both dealers and end-users will be judged against.

One such set of self-regulatory standards is the March 9, 1995, report of the Derivatives Policy Group (DPG), an advisory group of six securities firms formed to develop a voluntary oversight framework for derivatives activities of broker-dealers' unregistered affiliates.[34] The report suggests standards for management control, quantitative reporting to the CFTC and the SEC, estimation of risk in relation to capital, and relationships of professional intermediaries with nonprofessional counterparties.

DPG's standards require firms engaged in significant OTC derivatives activities to have comprehensive risk management control systems "commensurate with the scope, size and complexity of [such] activities...and the nature and extent of the risks they entail."[35] In particular, all OTC derivatives activities must be conducted pursuant to specific authorizing guidelines reviewed and adopted by a firm's governing body. Such authorizing guidelines must address the scope of authorized activity and any nonquantitative limits on the scope of authorized activities; quantitative guidelines for managing a firm's overall or constituent risk exposure, significant structural elements of a firm's risk management systems, and the nature and frequency of management reporting on risk; and procedures for reviewing the authorizing guidelines.

Under DPG's standards, participating firms engaged in OTC derivatives transactions on a principal basis as professional intermediaries with nonprofessional counterparties also have agreed to meet certain counterparty relationship guidelines. As well as setting guidelines for generic risk disclosures, counterparty relationships, marketing materials, transaction proposals and terms, and valuations, these standards require firms to set up internal policies and controls on the subject of counterparty relationships.

Among other requirements, intermediaries must exercise "good faith in the determination of valuations and quotations for OTC derivatives transactions." In addition, the standards prohibit intermediaries from preparing or communicating valuations or quotations to nonprofessional counterparties "with a view to misleading the counterparty." If a professional intermediary believes that a quotation or valuation being provided to a nonprofessional counterparty is unclear to the counterparty, the intermediary should take steps to clarify it.[36] If appropriate, the intermediary also should consider informing the counterparty that valuations may vary from firm or indicative price quotations and also may differ from valuations provided by other professional intermediaries.[37]

A July 27, 1994, paper issued by the technical committee of the International Organization of Securities Commissions (IOSCO) similarly addresses management control mechanisms for securities firms conducting OTC derivatives business. IOSCO's paper, the result of work by the CFTC, the SEC, and other regulatory authorities, was issued jointly with a similar paper by the Basel Committee on Banking Supervision. The coordinated release of these papers reflected the committees' common objective of promoting sound risk management controls for firms engaged in OTC derivatives business.

Like DPG's report, IOSCO's paper recommends specific risk management controls, including the following:

- An established framework for risk management policies, procedures, and controls.
- Market and credit risk management functions independent of a firm's trading function.
- In-house expertise and resources.
- Use of appropriate risk reduction techniques.
- Appropriate valuation and risk exposure measurement methodologies.
- Internal and external systems to ensure adequate information and reporting.
- Appropriate funding and liquidity policies.[38]

IOSCO's paper also addresses the role of regulators in deciding how to encourage firms to develop appropriate management control practices.[39]

Another example of self-regulatory standards is a report issued by the Futures Industry Association (FIA) Global Task Force on Financial Integrity. The report includes 60 recommendations for regulators, exchanges, clearinghouses, brokers, intermediaries, and customers.

Some of the major points in the FIA report directly involve customer protection standards. For example, the group suggested that brokers should establish and enforce policies and procedures to identify and protect customer property from risks of proprietary trading and that the board of directors or senior management of end users should make sure that they and other supervising managers understand proposed trading activities and establish general risk guidelines. The task force expects to issue final report in the future.

CONCLUSION

An enforceable prohibition of fraud is one of the fundamental protections that participants in any financial transaction should be able to rely on. There are, of course, common-law fraud prohibitions and various generally applicable state antifraud statutes that should apply to OTC derivatives transactions. But the adoption of a uniform standard will serve the goals of consistency and effective protection of market participants, and should do so without altering the overall legal rights of market participants.

ENDNOTES

1. The views expressed here are solely those of the author, and do not necessarily reflect the views of the Commodity Futures Trading Commission or its Division of Enforcement.

2. In general, the term *derivatives* refers to financial instruments with a return that is indexed to, or calculated by reference to, the price of a commodity or another financial instrument or an index of such prices. Basic types of derivative instruments include futures and options. Swap contracts and complex notes that are entered into in over-the-counter transactions (off-exchange) are also forms of derivatives. The value of these instruments can be based on currencies, interest rates, securities, physical commodities, or indexes representing the value of a group of such assets. The instruments can be used to hedge price exposure, manage cash flows, or speculate on price movements. See *OTC Derivative Markets and Their Regulation*, A Report of the Commodity Futures Trading Commission, October 1993, pp. 19–21.

3. See, e.g., "Motion of Defendants Bankers Trust Company and BT Securities Corporation to Dismiss the Procter and Gamble Company's Securities, Commodities, and Deceptive Trade Practice Claims," *Procter & Gamble Co.* v. *Bankers Trust Co.*, Case No. C–1–94–735 (D. Ohio February 24, 1996).

4. In this context, *systemic risk* refers to the risk that financial losses at one firm may spill over to other firms or clearing organizations as a result of the first firm's inability to perform on outstanding trades, contracts, or other commitments.

5. Both the CFTC and the SEC were careful to stipulate that their actions had limited precedential value. As stated in the CFTC's news release on the settlement, the agency's enforcement action against BT Securities was brought "to address and deter fraud." The action did not, the CFTC explained, "signal a determination by the Commission to apply new regulatory standards to these or any other swap transactions." The SEC's news release on the settlement similarly asserted that the SEC's action against BT Securities, "simply put," was a case involving fraud by a broker-dealer, "not a case about the suitability of any particular securities sold to Gibson." Nor, according to the SEC, did the case announce "any new regulatory regime with respect to derivatives."

6. 7 USC, §6o(1)(A).

7. See "Complaint Pursuant to Sections 6(c) and 6(d) of the Commodity Exchange Act and Opinion and Order Accepting Offer of Settlement, Making Findings and Imposing Remedial Sanctions," *In re BT*

Securities Corporation, CFTC Docket No. 95–3 (December 22, 1994) (*CFTC Complaint and Order*), para. 7.

8. Ibid.

9. Ibid. The CFTC complaint describes in some detail the complex pricing formulas of the transactions.

10. Ibid., para. 8.

11. Ibid.

12. Ibid., para. 11.

13. Ibid., paras.11–27.

14. Ibid., para. 12.

15. Ibid.

16. Ibid.

17. Ibid., para. 11.

18. 7 USC, §6o(1)(A).

19. Ibid., para 28, quoting transcript of tape-recorded statements by BT Securities' managing director for the Gibson account.

20. The SEC complaint covered two transactions: a so-called treasury linked swap, and a "knock-out call option." The former, while called a swap, was actually a cash-settled put option on the spread between a 30-year Treasury bond maturing November 15, 2022, and an average of yields of the most recently offered 2-year bonds. The latter transaction was a European-style, cash settled call option with a return based on the yield of a 30-year Treasury bond maturing February 15, 2023.

21. The SEC also filed and settled an administrative action against Gibson Greetings related to Gibson's financial reporting of gains and losses from its derivatives dealings with BT Securities. The SEC alleged that Gibson's derivatives were, for accounting purposes, "trading or speculation," and should have been marked to market, with changes in value recognized on the company's income statements. As a result of Gibson's failure to account for the transactions properly, its quarterly reports failed to disclose gains and losses. The SEC acknowledged that Gibson was misled by BT Securities as to the mark-to-market value of the derivatives for year-end 1992 and 1993, but alleged that Gibson had failed to obtain mark-to-market values as of the end of the quarters. Finally, the SEC alleged that Gibson's CFO and Treasurer failed to ensure that Gibson had proper accounting, disclosure, books and records, and internal controls, all of which had caused Gibson's violations.

22. *Federal Reserve Written Agreement,* 7.

23. While this book was in production, the district court granted the
Bankers Trust and BT Securities motion to dismiss. The court
concluded:

> [the] swap agreements are not securities as defined by the Securities
> Acts of 1933 and 1934 and the Ohio Blue Sky Laws; that these swap
> agreements are exempt from the Commodity Exchange Act; that
> there is no private right of action available to P&G under the
> antifraud provisions of that Act; and that the choice of law provision
> in the parties' agreement precludes claims under the Ohio Deceptive
> Trade Practices Act.

"Opinion and Order (1) Dismissing Securities, Commodities, and Ohio
Deceptive Trade Practices Claims; (2) Granting Summary Judgment on
Breach of Fiduciary Duty, Negligent Misrepresentation and Negligence
Claims; and (3) Setting Forth Duties and Obligations of the Parties,:"
The Procter & Gamble Co. v. *Bankers Trust Co.*, No. C-1-94-735 at 3
(May 8, 1996). In short, the lengthy opinion accepts virtually all of
Banker Trust's arguments about the application and interpretation of
federal securities laws and the Commodity Exchange Act to the
particular swap agreements at issue. As to the securities law issues,
however, the court cautioned that its holdings were limited to the
particular transactions that were the subject of the litigation, and
specifically did "not determine that all leveraged derivatives
transactions are not securities." Ibid., p. 22. The court also delined to
take a position on whether swaps are futures contracts for purposes of
the Commodity Exchange Act. Ibid., p. 26.

Finally, the court concluded that the remainder of Procter & Gamble's
claims would proceed to trial. Shortly after the court issued its order,
Procter & Gamble and Bankers Trust announced that they had reached a
settlement in the lawsuit.

24. Bruntjen reportedly expected a gradual rise in interest rates but did not
foresee a sharp upward spike in rates.

25. Orange County's $7.5 billion investment pool sustained losses of approx-
imately $1.69 billion. Believing interest rates would continue to decline,
Orange County's former Treasurer, Robert Citron, had invested heavily
in "inverse floaters," a type of debt-based security that moves inversely
to the direction of interest rates. When interest rates increased, the value
of the county's fund dropped and loans were called in on the fund.

26. Since 1991, the SEC has warned money-market mutual funds of the
risks of inverse floaters because of their leverage. Given the risks of
inverse floaters, the SEC since 1994 has instructed investment advisers
to develop a plan to dispose of inverse floaters from portfolios.

27. *OTC Derivatives Markets and Their Regulation,* 57–63.

28. 17 CRR Part 35 (Jan. 22, 1993).

29. 17 CFR Part 34 (Jan 22, 1993).

30. 58 Fed. Reg. 21293 (April 20, 1993).

31. See "Section 4(c) Contract Market Transactions," 60 Fed. Reg. 51323 (Oct. 2, 1995).

32. Estimates of market size vary. But even assuming large margins of error, the dollar value of transactions in swaps and similar products is enormous. The CFTC quoted estimates of roughly $10 trillion in outstanding notional principal for 1992. *OTC Derivative Markets and Their Regulation*, pp. 24–25 and Figure 15.

33. Tex Gov't. Code Ann. § 2256.

34. Participating firms are the six broker-dealers with the largest OTC derivatives affiliates: Goldman Sachs; Merrill Lynch; Salomon Brothers; Morgan Stanley; Lehman Brothers; and CS First Boston. As forth in DPG's report, the standards will apply only to affiliates of certain SEC-registered broker-dealers. Under DGP's standards, "OTC derivatives products" include interest rate, currency, equity, and commodity swaps, as well as OTC options and currency forwards.

35. Derivatives Policy Group. *A Framework for Voluntary Oversight of the OTC Derivatives Activities of Seurities Firm Affiliates to Promote Confidence and Stability in Financial Markets* (March 1995), p. 14.

36. Ibid.

37. Ibid.

38. Technical Committee of IOSCO, "Operational and Financial Risk Management Control Mechanisms for Over-the-Counter Derivatives Activities of Regulated Securities" (July 1994) (*IOSCO Paper*), 4–14.

39. See *IOSCO Paper*, Appendix B.

III

ASSET-BACKED SECURITIES

8

SECURITIZATION OF LOANS
Asset-Backed Securities and Structured Financing

Tamar Frankel, *Boston University School of Law*[1]

What is securitization? As the title of this chapter suggests, securitization has many names, and, as the following pages demonstrate, securitization has many descriptions—it is almost 20 years old, yet there is no agreement on a comprehensive definition for it.

Securitization is a new flexible form of intermediation—a channel through which savers transfer money to borrowers and receive the borrowers' obligations. Securitization enables us to convert illiquid loans into securities that are backed by these loans. That is why the securities are called *asset-backed securities*[2] and the process is called *securitization*. This new form of intermediation also offers a new form of financing. That is why, for those who focus on raising funds, the process is called *financing*. Securitization is a technique for separating and structuring the cash flow from the illiquid loans that are securitized. That is why the process is sometimes called *structured financing*.[3]

The disagreements about the definition of securitization stem mainly from four issues. First, because the process breaks traditional intermediation into many discrete activities, it can be described by one or more of these activities. Second, because it can involve many actors, each with his own motivation, securitization can be described by its utility to the actors. Third, it is hard to define securitization in terms of the traditional forms of intermediation or the financial system because securitization has changed these forms of intermediation and thereby the quality and structure of the whole financial system.[4] Fourth, securitization can take a number of forms, all resulting in the conversion of illiquid financial instruments into securities. Thus it is difficult to isolate its predominant features.

One commentator used the proverbial three blind men defining an elephant to describe the various definitions of securitization, including my own.[5] Taking heed, I discuss the process at length without attempting to provide a crisp definition.

Securitization has taken mainly two forms or processes. In one form a large loan is divided into small standardized parts that can be traded. This process is usually called *participation*. The second form is the most prevalent form of securitization. In this form an entity is created to receive illiquid loans (a pool), and this entity issues standardized obligations that can be traded. In this chapter we deal with the process of pooling.

POOLING

Pooling is used to securitize both numerous small loans and one or more large loans. I use the term *loans* broadly, to mean financial assets, including debts such as credit card receivables, and ownership claims, such as shares of stock or partnership agreements. The process consists of steps that break the functions of traditional institutional intermediaries into more discrete and specialized functions.[6] For example, while banks make loans, hold the loan instruments, and monitor the borrowers, securitization separates the functions of making loans and holding the loan instruments. The steps leading to securitization follow.

First, someone makes loans. Lenders, such as banks, thrifts, mortgage bankers, or manufacturers, make loans to borrowers and receive the borrowers' obligations to repay. Large borrowers, who can issue their securities to the markets, sometimes choose to securitize their own obligations instead, as a method of financing.

Second, lenders sell the loans either by securitizing the loans themselves or by selling loans wholesale to sponsors who securitize the loans.

Third, a legal entity (a pool) is created. The pool can be organized as a corporation, a limited partnership, a trust, or any other legal form.

The pool is usually a "single purpose entity," whose sole business is to passively hold the loans. The pool helps to:

- Create marketable, standardized securities in sufficient numbers and suitable denominations to market them to investors, even though these securities are backed by custom-made loans.

- Protect the assets it holds from third-party claims, including claims of the creditors of the seller of the loans if the seller becomes insolvent. The limited purpose of the pool reduces the costs of monitoring the safety of the pool's assets (the loans) and limits the risks of other businesses. Therefore, the limited purpose also lowers the cost of rating the pool's securities.

- Provide a pass-through tax treatment, usually in the form of a limited partnership or a trust or pursuant to special laws that allow such tax treatment.

In sum, the pool helps reduce investors' costs, and thereby the level of return that they demand. Indirectly, that benefits the borrowers.

Fourth, the loans are transferred to the pool.[7]

Fifth, someone services the loans in the pool's portfolio: collects the money from the borrowers, invests the money short term, as required, and distributes it to the investors on maturity dates. The servicer could be the originator of the loans, who retains the servicing business, or another entity who buys the servicing rights from the originator.[8]

Sixth, the pool issues its own securities to investors. The price that investors pay for the securities is then paid to the person who transferred the loans to the pool, minus expenses. As borrowers repay their loans, the money is distributed to the investors[9]

Seventh, the credit risk and other risks posed by the loans in the pool are directly or indirectly (fully or partially) underwritten by third parties such as the U.S. government, U.S. government corporations (e.g., FNMA), the originating lenders, banks, or insurance companies. The transferror of the loans can also provide some risk reduction to investors. These parties, alone or in combination, offer "credit enhancement" to the pools or to the investors in Pool securities directly.[10]

Eighth, broker-dealers develop secondary markets for pool securities. Thus investors obtain the liquidity that they value and for which they are willing to forgo some return.[11]

HIGHLIGHTS OF SECURITIZATION

Securitization as a Converter

The Main Feature of Securitization

I consider the most important element of securitization to be the combination of its first and final stages of the process, which results in the transformation of illiquid loans into securities.[12]

Securities and loans have much in common. Both are obligations to pay money, and both can be viewed as evidence of money claims and as financial assets. For the purpose of this discussion, we distinguish loans from securities by the costs of trading in them. Loans are less amenable to trading than are securities. The form, amounts, and terms of loans do not meet the conditions necessary to create efficient active markets in them.

Conditions for the Development of Markets

Markets are not likely to arise unless the traded instruments are standardized and available in sufficient numbers and denominations to attract trading investors. In addition, potential investors must have available to them relatively low-cost information about the issuers and borrowers.[13] Not all borrowers can or will provide such instruments and information, and not all savers or investors desire to accept such standardized market instruments.[14] Because loans lack the necessary attributes, markets in them rarely develop, and if they do, the markets are less efficient.[15]

The Two Traditional Channels of Intermediation

The difference between loans and securities affects the kind of channels (intermediaries) through which investors-savers' money flows to issuers-borrowers. Issuers sell, and investors buy and trade in, securities with the help of market intermediaries.[16] Underwriters distribute securities from issuers to investors and broker-dealers may participate in this distribution network and also maintain secondary markets in which investors trade among themselves.

When the conditions necessary for the creation of markets are absent, institutional intermediaries enter the picture and bridge the gap between the parties. Institutions usually raise money by issuing their own obligations on terms acceptable to savers, and they then use the proceeds to make loans on terms acceptable to borrowers.[17]

Some borrowers can raise funds both by issuing securities and by borrowing from institutions, and some investors can invest both by purchasing securities and lending to borrowers, directly or through institutions (e.g., hold bank deposits). But not all have the luxury of choice. Most small borrowers and investors cannot use the markets but must resort to institutional intermediaries.

For over 50 years, the financial system in this country consisted basically of two intermediation channels: the institutions and the securities markets. The channels were kept more or less separate, and banks functioned as the primary institutional lenders.[18] Since the early 1970s, however, the securities market channel has been widening considerably, and the separation between the two channels is being blurred.[19]

Paving the way to securitization was a movement to substitute securities for loans and increase the shares of market intermediation. Large borrowers chose to raise more funds by issuing securities (e.g., commercial paper or "junk bonds") and less by bank loans. Similarly, large investors chose to invest more funds in securities and less in bank deposits. By 1990, "nonfinancial companies had issued $130 billion in [commercial paper], a figure equivalent to 20 percent of the $642 billion in bank commercial and industrial (C&I) loans outstanding."[20] Small investors flocked to money market funds—a form of an investment company—and reduced their bank deposits.[21] These developments provided a warm receptive environment to securitization.

Securitization as a Tool for Liquidity

There is no doubt that securitization broadens the markets and brings their benefits and dangers to the parties and the economy. Arguably, in many respects, markets are more efficient than institutional intermediaries. This conclusion, even if iron-clad, only opens the door to a complicated debate and indeterminate conclusions. Imagine the beginning of this debate.

> *Banker:* Markets have a severe down-side effect of inducing instability and volatility.

> *Broker:* Institutions are not more stable than markets; institutions are as stable as the economy. As we found out when inflation was high, institutions cannot function long-term out of sync with the economy.

Banker: You assume that markets merely reflect the instability of the economic environment. In fact, markets contribute to instability through speculation.

Broker: Perhaps. Even so, markets provide liquidity to investors.

Banker: Institutions, such as banks, also provide liquidity to investors (by deposits, for example).

Broker: You then agree with me that, regardless of the effect on stability, liquidity is preferable to illiquidity. I argue that markets that provide liquidity directly to investors are preferable to institutions that provide liquidity but hold illiquid assets. For example, banks offer short-term deposits. If they lend the money long-term, they will fail if they experience a "run:" if withdrawals of deposits exceed new deposits. Therefore, these institutions require the support of insurance funds, like the FDIC, and that is costly. In addition, such institutions require substantial regulation, including regulation as to their investments and their obligations.[22] I prefer market actors to determine the type of securities that they will buy.

And so on.

Securitization as a New System of Intermediation

Securitization has emerged as a new intermediation system. It separates the traditional functions that institutions used to perform, and allows new actors to engage in selected functions. Securitization also combines institutional and market intermediation or converts one into the other to take advantage of both forms.[23]

Securitization as a Method of Selling Loans

Securitization can also be defined as an efficient way to sell loans. No doubt, this is an important feature of the process, historically and today.

Holders of loans, that is, other peoples' obligations, may desire to sell the loans for a number of reasons. Manufacturers who give credit to customers may wish to receive cash immediately to operate, and invest in, their businesses. Small manufacturers may raise funds more cheaply by selling the accounts receivables of their large customers with better credit ratings than their own. Depository institutions, such as banks, may also need to convert illiquid assets into cash to pay off short-term obligations.

In many cases institutions are motivated to sell their financial assets because of accounting and regulatory pressures. Most of the banks' liabilities are short term, such as demand deposits and savings accounts that depositors can withdraw on a short notice. The law and the regulators require, however, that a certain percentage of bank liabilities consist of capital, that is, long-term obligations and equity. Banks can raise capital in two ways. One is by selling stock or long-term bonds; the other is by reducing the assets and paying off some of the short-term liabilities. In both cases the capital as compared to the short-term liabilities will rise.

Before the 1970s, banks that needed to raise their capital were successful in issuing stock or long-term bonds, but in the 1970s capital became prohibitively expensive for the banks. They began to increase their capital by selling their assets, including illiquid loans. The need to sell illiquid loans created an incentive to securitize and convert the loans into liquid securities. Because investors value liquidity, they are willing to forgo a return. Therefore, securitizing the loans reduced the cost of capital for the sellers. Generally, pressures to securitize produced incentives to make the process more efficient for the sellers' net benefit.[24]

Securitization as a Mechanism for Unbundling Functions
Separating Lending from Other Functions
Securitization can also be described as a tool for separating the traditional functions of institutional intermediaries, such as banks, and allowing other actors to perform some of these functions. In the past, banks made loans, held them and serviced them to maturity or failure.

Securitization allows banks and other lenders to make loans and sell them rather than hold and service them. The process has opened the doors to nontraditional and unregulated lenders. Further, because making loans and securitizing the loans are separate activities, the promoters of the process need not be lenders. Wholesale markets for large and small loans have expanded dramatically, allowing promoters to buy and securitize loans made by others.

Many commentators believe that securitization has injured the banks. In the short-term, banks could sell their assets and raise their capital, but long-term banks shrank in size. They also increased the risk level of their assets by selling their best loans.[25] More importantly, securitization exposed banks to enormous competition for borrowers. The banks' position as the primary lenders in the country has been greatly weakened. Although banks may be proficient lenders, so are many of their competitors, such as the manufacturers, suppliers, or investment bankers, who provide financing to customers. Because banks bear regulatory and other costs that some of their lending competitors do not, with respect to lending they find themselves at a competitive disadvantage. In the securitization area banks also suffer legal barriers to full engagement in securitization.[26]

To these clouds, however, there are a number of silver linings. Securitization induced dramatic changes in the business and the culture of banks. If markets are going to be the more dominant intermediation channels in the future, then perhaps securitization will be credited with beneficial changes in the banks, well in advance of those in other countries. In addition, securitization offers banks fee income from various services, including ones in which banks were not actively engaged before. For example, when interest rates fell, mortgage loans that were sold could not be amended by an agreement between the borrowers and lenders, but had to be repaid and refinanced. When interest rates fell, the banks (and the lawyers) benefited from the surge in this refinancing. Thus, the question whether securitization has harmed the banks long term cannot yet be answered.

Other lenders, who entered or expanded the lending business, have gained. Arguably, borrowers also benefit because they have more available lenders. Through the markets, securitization allows for a more efficient transfer of funds from large savings institutions, such as insurance companies and pension funds, to small borrowers. It seems that more available funds caused interest rates to fall, although there is no reliable empirical data to support this argument. Borrowers, however, pay a price. The loan terms they get today are far more standardized than in the past because large buyers of loans impose their underwriting standards and terms, and lenders can sell standardized loans for securitization more easily. It is likely that custom-made loans are more expensive today than they were in the past. This change in availability and price is similar to a change that occurs when commodities are mass-produced instead of custom made.

Another disadvantage of securitization for borrowers is that they can no longer renegotiate the loan agreements with the lenders. Because the loans are sold, the servicers, which may be the original lenders, have no authority to amend the terms of the loans. If interest rates fall, and the borrowers wish to take advantage of these lower rates, they can only refinance their loans by prepaying the current loans and borrowing again on better terms. If refinancing is more costly than amending the existing loan agreements, the borrowers may not benefit as much as in the past.

Separating the Servicing Function

The separation of the intermediation functions also affects the servicing of loans. The right to service loans—to collect payments from the borrowers, invest the money short term, as required, and distribute it to the investors on maturity dates—does not pass automatically to the buyers of the loans. Securitization has helped "propertize" the right to service loans. This right is now viewed as a property of the original lender. In the past, lenders serviced the loans themselves. Now they can do so even after they have sold the loans, or they can sell the servicing rights to others. Although the sale of servicing rights may pose some risks to investors and borrowers, propertizing and creating markets for these servicing rights may benefit them as well as the originators of the loans. By making loans originators create a valuable product for which securitization has provided a market. In addition, this process allows some parties to specialize and offer economies of size, benefiting their clients and the system as a whole.

Securitization as a Tool for Flexible Creation of Securities

Some definitions of securitization emphasize the use of the process as a cost-effective financing method for large borrowers. This focus leads to the definition of securitization as "structured financing."[27] Large borrowers securitize their obligations even though they can issue their obligations in the form of securities directly to the markets. Yet instead of issuing their securities to the markets, some large borrowers transfer their own obligations to pools and the pools issue securities to the markets. Why would these large borrowers choose a seemingly roundabout way of reaching the markets through pools? A number of features make securitization attractive to investors. One of these features is the flexibility securitization offers in designing the securities.

Flexibility in Allocating Risk among Various Classes of Securities

Securitization allows large borrowers to issue obligations on certain terms acceptable to them and the pools that hold the obligations—to issue securities on terms that are more acceptable to investors.[28] The terms of the securities issued by the pool differ from the terms of the loans that the pool holds. That is so even if the pool issues one class of securities and each security holder receives a pro rata share of the cash flow from these assets. Even in this simple structure, what investors receive does not mirror exactly what the borrowers pay if the pool contains numerous small loans or numerous mortgages on different properties. In these scenarios, the pro rata share of each investor is more diversified.[29]

Usually pools issue more than one class of securities, and the risks and benefits from the cash flow of the assets that pools hold are divided among the classes. The beauty of this scheme is that the pools' securities can be designed in almost unlimited ways based on the expected cash flows from the pools' portfolios, and so long as the pools' total obligations are limited to whatever the cash flow their portfolios will bring, the pools cannot fail (except by embezzlement).

The terms of the securities that pools issue and the financial structure of the pools can be designed to meet market demand both of investors and of borrowers. At the same time, this structure allows pools to match their assets and liabilities. For example, mortgagors usually have the right to prepay their mortgage loans without penalty. That poses risks for investors, because the mortgagors usually will prepay when interest rates fall, and that is precisely the time when investors do not wish to have their investment repaid. Besides, some investors may desire a fixed, long-term investment and avoid the transaction costs of reinvesting the prepayments.

By manipulating the cash flows from the loan portfolios and by issuing different classes of securities that represent different parts of the cash flows, pools can issue securities that satisfy different investors: those who are willing to forgo returns in order to receive their investments on a fixed maturity date, and those who are interested in higher returns but value fixed maturities less. At the same time the securities that pools issue do not promise on the aggregate more than the anticipated cash flow from the pools' assets. In short, the pools' structures meet the desires of different groups of investors, including bankruptcy-proof status and credit enhancement that investors value, and at the same time create pools with matching liabilities and assets.

Since there is no free lunch, there is also a downside even to flexibility. The freedom to manipulate the cash flow is far greater than the freedom to design direct obligations of a particular borrower. Since there is no borrower with whom to negotiate, all that is necessary is a calculation of the stream of income from the assets in the pool. That allows for the creation of an enormous variety of instruments: complex, novel, and untested. Pool securities can truly be hard to understand and their terms can be very risky.

One example of such instruments is pool-issued securities called IOs (interest only) and POs (principal only) that were popular for a while. These securities represented the cash flow from mortgages that pools held, and promised all interest payments to the IO holders and all principal payments to the PO holders. These instruments were extremely sensitive to interest rates. Both types of securities were sold at a discount from face value, and the prices of both were calculated according to the anticipated prepayments of the mortgages. If mortgagors prepaid the mortgages faster than anticipated the POs would gain because they would receive their money earlier than anticipated, and IOs would lose their investments because no more interest payments would be due, ever. Conversely, if mortgagors prepaid their mortgages more slowly than anticipated, IOs would receive more payments than anticipated because interest payments would not terminate, but POs would lose because they would have to wait for their money longer than anticipated.

When interest rates fell sharply in 1993 and 1994, more mortgages were refinanced by prepaying existing mortgages and taking new ones (at lower rates). As the mortgage loans were prepaid, the PO holders received their principal payments faster than expected, and gained. The IO holders received no more payments, and lost. IOs were not "bad" but simply risky. They could bring high returns and high losses. Investors who understood how these instruments worked were not injured. Unfortunately, many investors, including some portfolio managers, did not understand the extent of the potential downside of these instruments. They were caught in the frenzy of gambling for high returns. They relied on their own predictions as to the movements of interest rates, and when the predictions turned out to be wrong, the losses they sustained were unexpectedly high. I believe that in time, with painful experiences, such instruments will be used cautiously and well. I count flexibility and the innovations it allows as good, but not without a price.

Flexibility in Designing the Risk Level of Pool Securities: Diversification and Credit Enhancement

Pooling enables sponsors to reduce the risks of investors in pool securities through diversification and credit enhancement, such as third-party guarantees and insurance policies. Credit enhancement can cover pool assets or securities. Credit enhancement provides investors with another alternative or additional debtor. Most credit enhancement reduces for investors the risk of default by the borrowers under the loan obligations the pools hold. Such credit enhancement increases the costs for the issuers-borrowers, but because it also reduces investors' risks, investors accept a lower return, which is to the issuers' advantage.

The originator of the loans sold to the pools can also provide credit enhancement, for example, by retaining some of the equity issued by the pool. This signals to investors that the originator is putting its money where its mouth is—that the originator of the loans is willing to lose its equity investment if the loans default. Usually the seller of the loans is interested in providing credit enhancement for the loans it sells. However, if the seller needs to reduce its assets, as banks and sometimes corporations do, accounting rules would not recognize the sale if the seller retained substantial risks posed by the sold loans.[30] Therefore, this avenue is not usually open to such sellers.

Many pool securities are also rated by rating agencies. Such rating reduces the investors' information and monitoring costs, for which investors are willing to forgo some returns, even though rating agencies offer no guarantees, and increase the costs of the issuer. Rating is now legally required of pools that would have fallen under the regulation of the Investment Company Act, but for Rule 3a–7.[31] Because pools cannot function under the constraints of the Act, the Securities and Exchange Commission enacted Rule 3a–7, exempting pools from the Act subject to certain conditions. Among these conditions the rule requires that the securities issued by a pool be rated.[32] Thus, flexibility in establishing the risk levels of the pool securities is sometimes constrained by law. By and large, however, there is substantial freedom for creating pool securities and their risk levels.

THE LEGAL ISSUES CONCERNING SECURITIZATION

The Interdisciplinary Aspect of Securitization Law

As the steps leading to securitization suggest, a lawyer who works in this area must be familiar with numerous branches of the law. The making of loans is governed by laws regulating the lenders and by commercial and consumer laws. The creation of pools is governed by the laws of their organization—corporate, partnership, or trust laws, for example. In addition, the Investment Company Act of 1940 and Rule

3a–7 must be examined to determine the applicability of the Act to the pools or their compliance with the rule.

The transfer of the loans to the pools involves commercial and bankruptcy laws and the margin rules under sections 7 and 8 of the Securities Exchange Act of 1934. The servicing aspects of loans involve contract law and mortgage laws, including rules of foreclosures.

The registration and distribution of the securities issued by pools are subject to the Securities Act of 1933 and the Securities Exchange Act of 1934. In addition, the laws regulating the particular actors— banks, thrifts, insurance companies, pension plans, underwriters and brokers—come into play.

Accounting rules are important to determine when the seller of the loans can take the loans off its books. Knowledge of how the rating agencies work is crucial in this area where almost without exception, the pools' securities are rated. And, of course, there is always tax law.

Legal Problems and Guides to Solutions

Because securitization starts with making loans—usually by institutional intermediaries—and ends with securities traded on the markets, the process raises issues of legal classification. Loans are governed by one set of rules, and securities by another set. Classification is a key to the rules governing the particular issues. Not surprisingly, one of the recurrent questions in this area is whether loans are securities, subject to the securities acts and their antifraud provisions. For example, is the contract between an underwriter-sponsor of structured financing and the borrower-issuer of obligations a security? Clearly, the obligations were destined to become securities. Yet if the contract is viewed as a mere sale of the obligation to the sponsor, should not the common law of fraud govern rather than the antifraud provisions of the securities acts? The issue has not been resolved. The answer may depend on (1) the facts of the particular case—whether the borrower merely sold his obligation to the sponsor or whether the borrower was involved in the securitization process—(2) whether borrowers-issuers and underwriters-sponsors are the parties the securities acts were designed to protect; (3) whether contracts between the borrowers-issuers and the underwriters-sponsors could affect the investing public; (4) whether the steps in the securitization process should be integrated or viewed and classified separately. The answer to this question can be guided by the policies on integration that the Securities and Exchange Commission has developed throughout the years.

Other classifications do not fit the process of securitization. For example, pools may fall within the definition of investment companies, subject to the Investment Company Act of 1940, but, since they are established for very different purposes, and must be structured very differently from the traditional mutual funds, pools cannot function under the regulation of the Investment Company Act of 1940. The Securities and Exchange Commission enacted a rule that provided relief from the Act subject to conditions for the protection of investors, thus designing a new regulatory system for the pools.[33]

Rather than trying to adjust the laws by looking for the "right" classification, we can adjust the laws through a critical inquiry into the financial environment on which they are based and the problems they address. If the environment and problems have changed by current technologies and market practices, the laws should respond accordingly. Such an approach may be more helpful than classification with respect to legal issues concerning the transfer of notes and other financial instruments to pools. The laws regulating these transfers do not fit modern transactions involving large numbers of instruments. For example, as protection against the borrowers' defenses vis a vis the original lenders, investors may desire that pools become the holder in due course of the borrowers' notes. The existing rules that require endorsement of the notes are impractical in the context of pools because they are too costly and burdensome. Some suggest, however, that the status of holder in due course has been overrated, and that the issue has become far less problematical than in the past. There is an ongoing process of adjusting the rules regarding the mass transfer of such notes, guided by today's reality rather than the realities of 18th-century England where these rules originated.[34]

Similar issues arise in connection with the borrowers' rights to set off their loans against the lenders' debts to them. Set-off rights were established long ago, and they may affect the efficiency of the securitization process. Here the investors' rights are pitted against the borrowers' rights, and the issue has not yet been resolved.[35]

The existing rules sometimes can prevent the markets from securitizing loans simply because the rules do not allow for the time or other conditions necessary to effectuate the process. For example, it can take up to three months to assemble a pool of loans. It may take even longer to receive the necessary ratings and clear a registration statement with the Securities and Exchange Commission. Both the sponsor and the sellers of the loans must enter into a binding agreement, but that agreement must be conditioned on the occurrence of other events. In a sense, the seller of the loans grants credit to the buyer of the loans with a view to future delivery. The margin rules under the Securities Exchange Act of 1934 would have restricted the contracts to a shorter period than the period usually necessary to close the transaction. The rules were amended accordingly to make securitization possible.[36]

Investors also face problems of tax law. Because pools are taxable entities, investors in pool securities would be taxed twice, once on the pool level and once on their personal level.[37] Congress has provided most financial intermediaries with a pass-through tax treatment so that investors would pay tax only once, when they receive income or capital gains on their investments. In 1986 Congress has passed the Tax Reform Act[38] to provide a pass-through tax treatment for mortgage-backed securities, and Congress now is considering a bill to award the same treatment to other asset-backed securities, under a similar structure.[39] Much has been done already to adjust the laws to the securitization process, but much work remains to be done.

WHERE IS SECURITIZATION HEADING?
The Reach of Securitization Today

Securitization has had a meteoric rise since the early 1970s. Through the pooling technique, the U.S. government propelled the securitization of mortgage loans into a huge secondary market in mortgage-backed securities. By 1990 $1.34 trillion of mortgage-backed securities were outstanding.[40] The process served as a model for securitizing other types of loans made by the government and the private sector. In a relatively short period, the amount of securitized loans has grown tremendously.

The variety of securitized loans has also increased. After residential mortgages came auto loans[41] and light truck loans, credit card and trade receivables, computer leases, health care receivables, and insurance premiums loans.[42] Loan-backed securities issued by the private sector amounted to almost $270 billion in 1986, up from $25 billion in 1980.[43] Note-issuance facilities, under which banks undertake to lend money to a borrower if its note issue cannot be placed, rose to $33 billion in 1986. In 1994 about $300 billion in interest-rate swaps were outstanding as were $680 billion of open positions in financial futures and options.[44] The amount of outstanding asset-backed securities (in addition to mortgage-backed securities) was estimated in 1990 at $107.5 billion.[45] There is also a limited market in securitized third-world loans, and attempts are being made to extend and deepen this market.[46] Markets in whole loans are also developing. In sum, the movement to securitize loans is sweeping the U.S. financial scene and is on its way to world markets.[47]

Can All Loans Be Securitized?

Although not all loans can be securitized today, it is likely that by the end of the decade most types of loans could be securitized. Some believe that by the year 2000 at least 80 percent of all new loans will be securitized.[48] Whether the loans, large or small, can be securitized by pooling, depends on a number of factors.

The first factor is information about the borrowers. The lower the information costs (to investors or guarantors of the pool assets or securities), the easier it will be to securitize the loans. As the saying on Wall Street goes, "if it's gradable, it's tradable." Since pools hold a large number of small loans, unless they are used for "structured financing" of large borrowers, information costs about pools' assets are relatively high. Therefore, the more standard and simple the terms of the loans are, the more predictable their cash flow and maturity are, the more easily they can be priced and securitized. This condition applies mainly to small loans. The terms of large loans whose cash flow is securitized can be quite complex, provided the cash flow is ascertainable.

The second factor is servicing costs. Costs depend on the number of loans in the pool and the frequency of the borrowers' payments and extent of their defaults.

The third factor is the level of credit risk, and the corresponding collateral and guarantees, attached to the securitized loans. The more risky the loans, the more costly it will be to securitize them, even if the loans are sold at a discount from their face value. That is in part because the laws regulating many purchasing institutions limit the risk level for their assets. However, risk can be reduced by guarantees and insurance and by diversification of the pools' portfolios.

Up to 1990, loans to medium-size commercial and industrial companies have not been securitized because they lacked many of the attributes described here. But a growing number of these loans are being securitized today. The prediction that these loans are next in line to be securitized seems to have materialized in 1995.[49] Entrepreneurs are seeking ways to standardize these loans for trade by gathering information, developing techniques, and using statistics and computerized modeling to rationally price these loans,[50] thus preparing for their securitization. Freddie Mac, a government corporation that securitizes mortgages, is currently providing lenders who participate in its programs with specific numerical cut-off points and a scoring system that reduces the costs of evaluating loan applications.[51] Wholesale markets in loans are also developing. Trade in large, whole commercial and industrial loans of large corporations, destined for securitization, has increased substantially.[52]

Interest in securitizing business loans to facilitate the flow of funds to small businesses, especially in the inner city, has increased since 1992 and continued in 1993. Arguably, to the extent that small business loans are not securitized, small businesses are "crowded out" from the financial market, as compared to the borrowers whose loans are securitized. In February 1993 Congressman Paul E. Kanjorski convened hearings titled "Secondary Market for Commercial Business Loans."[53] The testimony at the hearings reflected both the difficulties of securitizing such loans and the possibility of doing so.[54] Although the private sector is preparing to securitize small business loans, there may be a need for government action to put the structure in place.[55] To securitize, it may be necessary to develop a statistical model for such loans based on past experience. Private sector institutions can design such a model, based on their own experience, but they lack information about the experience of other institutions that consider the information proprietary. Most of this information, however, is available to the government. Similarly, the government can develop techniques to create the model more cheaply and to make it available to the private sector as a basis for further refinement in a competitive environment.

Some have suggested that a government agency be created, the Venture Enhancement and Loan Development Administration for Smaller Undercapitalized Enterprises (Velda Sue) to securitize small business loans. Others opted for the Small Business Administration.[56] Regardless of government initiative the private sector is likely to finally take over.

Perhaps the time will come when a small company, fitting a particular profile, could borrow by signing a round-figure note or another standard form. A rating agency will prepare the company's profile for a fee, which will be lower than the lenders' information costs today. Regulated professional appraisers would evaluate the collateral. The rating, appraisal, price, and terms of the loan could give sufficient information to the buyers about the risk level posed by the borrowers and a comparison with other similar loans. The originator might then sell such a loan to a pool or sell it directly in a secondary market for similar loans. Right now, however, this scenario is only a twinkle in someone's eyes.[57]

Is Securitization Here to Stay?

For a number of reasons I conclude that securitization is not a passing fad. First, securitization may be a better intermediation process than the traditional processes. It may be an innovation[58] that better utilizes markets, institutions, and new technologies, especially in an unstable economic environment. It may be a more rational financial intermediation system than the system of banks and thrifts.

Second, securitization is driven in part by technology. Technology will continue to develop and even a government cannot regulate it away. Further, as technology links financial markets globally, no one country can regulate its institutions except in cooperation with most other countries. Thus, even though the government had a substantial role in introducing securitization, it may find it hard to reverse the process because the benefits of the process continue to give incentives to securitize and to create markets.

Third, the institutional and market intermediaries continue to restructure internally, and there are indications that their transformation is taking hold. Money market banks trade in securities abroad, and market intermediaries and others have entered the lending and "near deposit" businesses. Large and regional banks are engaged in creating asset-backed securities. The higher the investment that institutions make in restructuring themselves and their businesses, the harder it will be to turn back the clock. It is true that structural changes resulting from economic pressures and catastrophic events, such as the Depression in the 1930s, are more lasting than changes introduced by law. But securitization was not imposed by law. It was offered as an option, and institutions chose it in light of their new environment. While the memories of the Depression contributed to the longevity of traditional banking and the thrifts, these memories are balanced today by the memories of inflation and deflation. People rely less on "bank money" and look for alternative financial assets.

I join others in concluding that securitization is here to stay, and that its impact is significant.[59] It is transforming our financial system, including the banks. It has broken old molds and has given more freedom to market actors to choose their future business niches.

Regulators have a crucial and difficult role to play in this process of change. They should allow the markets and the institutions to experiment, select their future businesses, and restructure. At the same time regulators should monitor closely the sensitive areas that historically have required regulation. After all, technology has changed much; human nature has changed little. Hopefully, when the dust settles we will find out which institutions do what best, and during the evolution of the banks and other intermediaries, what activities should be addressed by regulation. Securitization will help us discover the institutions into which the traditional banks have evolved, and the financial system of the future.

ENDNOTES

1. I am indebted to Michael E.S. Frankel for his insightful comments on this chapter, and to my assistant Elizabeth L. Hieck, Boston University School of Law L2, for her valuable and dedicated help in preparing this chapter. The chapter is adapted from Part I of my treatise, *Securitization: Structured Financing, Financial Asset Pools, and Assets-Backed Securities* (Little, Brown & Co., 1991), and from my paper, "Securitization Law: Are Banks At A Competitive Disadvantage," in *Structural Change In Banking* 309, eds. Michael Klausner and Lawrence J. White (Business One Irwin, 1993). I benefited from the comments on the paper by James P. Holdcroft, Jr., Ibid. p. 338, Martin E. Lowy Ibid. p. 348, and Jonathan R. Macey, Ibid. 353.

2. The word *asset* here denotes *financial asset*.

3. See Joseph C. Shenker and Anthony J. Colletta, "Asset Securitization: Evolution, Current Issues and New Frontiers," *Texas Law Review* 69 (1991), pp. 1369, 1373. In its report on investment company regulation, *Protecting Investors: A Half Century of Investment Company* p.1, the Division of Investment Management of the Securities and Exchange Commission used the term *structured finance*.

4. Banks have "securitized" loans for decades, (e.g., by dividing large loans and participating the portions among other banks), but securitization today differs greatly from the traditional bank securitization. Report by G. Alger, Moreland Commissioner, to H. Lehman, Governor of the State of New York, on the Management and Affairs of the Insurance Department (Oct. 5, 1934), pp. 9–10; Louis Perlstein, "What the 1920s Tell Us About Mortgage Backed Securities Today," *Probate & Property* Jan–Feb. 1987, pp. 19–21; Andrew Lance, "Balancing Private and Public Initiatives in the Mortgage-Backed Securities Market," *Real Property, Probate & Trust Journal* 18, pp. 426, 430; W.H. Knight, "Loan Participation Agreements: Catching Up With Contract Law," *Columbia Business Law Review* (1987), pp. 587, 592, n.21; Debrah L. Threedy, "Loan Participations— Sales or Loans? Or Is That the Question?, *Oregon Law Review* 68 (1989), pp. 649, 650.

5. See James P. Holdcroft, Jr., "Comment on Tamar Frankel, Securitization Law: Are Banks at a Competitive Disadvantage," in *Structural Change In Banking* 309, eds. Michael Klausner and Lawrence J. White (Business One Irwin, 1993).

6. The securitization process may be illustrated in Graph 1 as follows:

G R A P H   1

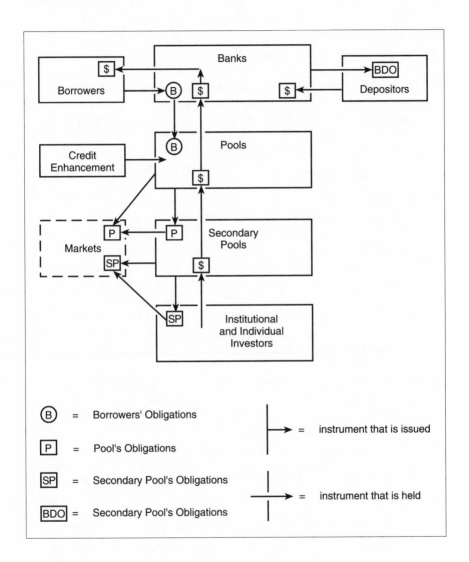

7. See the section "Legal Problems and Guides to Solutions" in this chapter discussing the legal problems involved in loan transfers.
8. See the section "Separating the Servicing Function" in this chapter discussing the market for servicing contracts.

9. See the section "Flexibility in Designing the Risk Level of Pool Securities: Diversification and Credit Enhancement" in this chapter discussing the financial structure of pools and the terms of asset-backed securities.

10. See the same section discussing credit enhancement.

11. See the section "Securitization as a Converter" in this chapter discussing conversion of illiquid loans to securities.

12. See T. Frankel, *Securitization* 1 (1991). For another definition see Joseph C. Shenker and Anthony J. Colletta, "Asset Securitization: Evolution, Current Issues and New Frontiers," *Texas Law Review* 69 (1991) pp. 1369, 1373. In its report on investment company regulation the Division of Investment Management of the Securities and Exchange Commission used the term *structured finance* instead of *securitization* and described the process as follows: "Structured finance is a financing technique in which financial assets, in many cases illiquid, are pooled and converted into capital market instruments." See *Protecting Investors: A Half Century of Investment Company Regulation* 1 (1992).

13. See J. Guttentag and R. Herring, *Financial Innovations to Stabilize Credit Flows to Developing Countries,* Brookings Discussion Papers (33, pp. 4–6, 1985) (unpublished); Paula C. Murray and Beverly L. Hadaway, "Mortgage-Backed Securities: An Investigation of Legal and Financial Issues, 11 Journal of Corporation Law" (1986) pp. 203, 204. Since there is no generic term for less tradable instruments evidencing money claims, and because most securitized debts arise from loans, I use the word *loans* interchangeably with *debts*.

14. A note of $122,426 issued by one mortgagor may be too small and custom-made to be efficiently traded in the market. For the same reasons, a saver's demand deposit (which is in fact the debt of the bank) cannot be traded efficiently in the market.

15. The parties to loans and securities are described by different words. These names highlight the different features of loans and securities. The parties to loans are called *borrowers-debtors* and *lenders-creditors*. The parties to securities transactions are called *issuers* and *investors*. Loans are named by the transaction and the relationship they create. Securities are named by the instruments that are traded.

16. Markets may be illustrated as follows (See Graph 2 on the next page):

17. Institutions include banks, thrifts, mortgage bankers, and consumer banks (banks), and insurance companies, pension funds, and investment companies (collectively, institutions). Institutions provide other services. Banks serve as a payment system and a tool for controlling the money supply; insurance companies pool and distribute risk; investment companies diversify investment portfolios and provide economies of

G R A P H   2

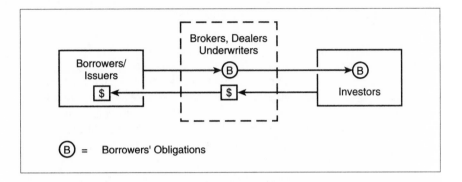

scale for small savers. Industrial and marketing enterprises act as institutions when they borrow and sell to customers on credit. The federal government and state governments also act as institutions—they borrow in the capital markets and lend the proceeds for particular purposes, for example, housing. Many counties, including Orange County in California, act as institutional intermediaries. Thus, traditional banks can be illustrated as follows (see Graph 3 below):

18. See John G. Gurley and Edward S. Shaw, *Financial Intermediaries and the Savings-Investment Process* (The Brookings Institution Reprint No.

G R A P H   3

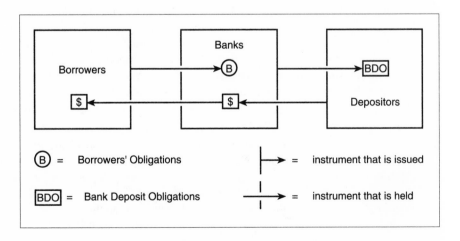

13, 1956). The share of nonbank institutions (insurance companies, investment companies, pension funds) in lending services has been slowly increasing since their appearance more than a hundred years ago. See Robert E. Litan, *What Should Banks Do?* (The Brookings Institution, 1986).

19. For example, an innovation that encouraged the movement from institutions to markets is "swaps." Like a do-it-yourself kit, the instrument enables one party to a loan agreement to change the terms of a loan for *it,* without a change for the other party, by contracting with a third party. The instrument enables borrowers to bypass institutions even when the borrowers' preferences do not match those of the lenders.

20. Robert E. Litan, *The Revolution in U.S. Finance,* (The Brookings Institution, 1991), p. 17.

21. For the composition of bank demand deposits and money market deposit accounts and their comparison to money market funds see Robert E. Litan, *The Revolution in U.S. Finance* (The Brookings Institution, 1991), pp. 9–10. In 1990 bank demand deposits held approximately $260 billion; bank money market deposit accounts held approximately $510 billion; money market funds held approximately $480 billion. See also Investment Co. Inst., News Release, ICI–89–45 (Dec. 28, 1989).

22. See Frankel, note 12, pp. 82–93.

23. See the section "Securitization as a Mechanism for Unbundling Functions" in this chapter.

24. Some banks facilitated securitization by using marketing personnel who were selling the banks' certificates of deposits, to sell loans as well. Through the tightening of the capital rules the government has played a crucial role in the development of securitization. See Frankel, note 12, pp. 224–225.

25. Because loans are carried on the banks' books not at market value but at par, unless downgraded, banks are loath to sell deteriorating loans at a discount and show losses on their balance sheets. Yet, banks later also sold their bad loans at par by adding credit enhancement to these loans.

26. The Glass-Steagall Act came close to closure this year, but did not quite make it to the president's desk.

27. See Joseph C. Shenker and Anthony J. Colletta, "Asset Securitization: Evolution, Current Issues and New Frontiers," *Texas Law Rev* 69, (1991) pp. 1369, 1373. In its report on investment company regulation, *Protecting Investors: A Half Century of Investment Company Regulation,* the staff of the Securities and Exchange Commission described used the term *structured financing* instead of securitization.

Structured financing mirrors the pooling process except that it is mostly used to securitize the obligations of a large borrower rather than the obligations of many small borrowers. In this case the borrower sells its own obligations to a pool, and the pool issues its securities to investors and pays the issuer the price it received for the securities, after deducting the costs.

28. Underwriters may prefer structured financing to direct underwriting in order to acquire the valuable right to service the loans. Servicing provides future fees or the present value of these fees in the form of the price for the servicing right.

29. Of course, if the assets in the pool are available in the form of securities and investors have sufficient funds, they can create their own diversified portfolios. Many investors, however, have neither. Note that the structure of pools, which is an aspect of securitization, is similar to that of any institutional intermediary. That is why, generally, the advantages of pool structure for a single or few large loans are the same as the advantages of pools to securitize numerous small loans.

30. The accounting rules applicable to banks, governed by the General Accounting Principles (GAP), are somewhat stricter than those applicable to other enterprises, governed by the General Accepted Accounting Principles (GAAP). See Frankel, note 12, pp. 224–241.

31. Other exclusions may be available, e.g. investment companies with less than 100 shareholders. See Investment Company Act § 3(c)(1), 15 USC § 80a–3(c)(1).

32. 17 CFR § 270.3a–7 (1995). Rating can be viewed as "outsourcing" government supervision to the private sector. Critics of the requirement to obtain rating point out that (1) the rule grants rating agencies a monopoly, (2) rating agencies are not regulated or accountable, (3) the agencies could be biased in favor of the issuer that pays them, and, somewhat in conflict with the prior criticism, (4) the agencies are bureaucratic and heavy-handed in their demands of issuers.

In answer it has been pointed out that notwithstanding the lack of regulation, and even though they are paid by the issuers, rating agencies are fairly strict in their demands of the issuers. That is because rating agencies have a very high stake in their reputation and in the public's confidence in them. These are the agencies' only valuable assets, and it takes a substantial investment and a long time to create them. The desire to protect these assets seems to be an effective regulator of the agencies' thoroughness, truthfulness, and reliability of their ratings.

33. See Rule 3a–7, 17 CFR § 270.3a–7 (1996); Frankel, note 12, p. 336.

34. See Edward L. Rubin, "Learning from Lord Mansfield: Toward A Transferability Law For Modern Commercial Practice," *Idaho Law Review* 31 (1995), p. 775.

35. See Frankel, note 12, pp. 385–414.

36. See Frankel, note 12, p. 60.

37. Double taxation can be avoided by organizing the pools as partnerships, limited partnerships, and some types of trusts.

38. Public Law No. 99–514, 671, SS 860A–860G, 1986 U.S. Code *Congressional and Administrative News* (100 Stat.) 2085, 2308–2318 (codified as amended at 26 USC SS 860A–860G) (1988); see also Frankel, note 12, p. 311.

39. Securitization Enhancement Act of 1995, H.R. 1967, 104th Cong., 1st Sess. (1995).

40. *Inside Mortgage Capital Markets*, Dec. 21, 1990, p. 2 (Financial World Publications, Wash. D.C.); Robert E. Litan, *The Revolution in U.S. Finance* 14 (The Brookings Institution, 1991). In 1986, the U.S. government began planning to securitize its loan portfolio (valued at more than $800 billion) starting with a $5 billion public offering in the late 1980s. See *Concurrent Resolution on the Budget for Fiscal Year 1988: Hearings Before the Senate Comm. on the Budget*, 100th Cong., 1st Sess. 93–275 (1987); *Loan Asset Sales: OMB Policies Will Result in Program Objectives Not Being Fully Achieved,* GAO/AFMD 86–79 (1986), reprinted in Staff Rep. House Comm. on Small Business, 100th Cong., 1st Sess., Government Loan Asset Sales 74–88 (Comm. Print 1988); Institutional Investors, *Bank Letter,* July 1, 1986. During 1987 and through July of 1988, the U.S. government sold $7.3 billion of loans for $4.7 billion, and planned to sell $6.5 billion of its loans in 1988 and $7.7 billion in 1989. "Government Loan Sales Are Recorded by GAO" *American Banker*, Oct. 12, 1988, p. 18. The program did not proceed because the government concluded that it was more profitable to continue to hold the loans and vigorously collect the amounts due.

41. Pamela S. Leven, "A Driving Business: Thrift Steers Its Way to Profits in Secondary Market," *American Banker*, Mar. 6, 1987, p. 22.

42. David Neustadt, *Hanover Tries New Approach to Securitization, American Banker*, Oct. 6, 1987, p. 2.

43. See Robert E. Litan, *The Revolution in U.S. Finance* 14–15. Securitized consumer loans have grown from $29 billion in January 1989 to more than $70 billion in November 1990—nearly 10 percent of all consumer installment credit.

44. Miller, *Commercial Loan Securitization—Review and Outlook, Loan Pricing Report* VI, no. 4, (Sept. 1991) p. 2. In the past three years, $9 billion worth of highly leveraged obligations have been securitized through collateralized loan obligations.

45. Dean Witter Reynolds Inc., *Asset-Backed Securities Reference Guide* (Jan. 1991), p. A–14. Cited in Joseph C. Shenker and Anthony J. Colletta, "Asset Securitization: Evolution, Current Issues and New Frontiers," *Texas Law Review* 69 (1991), pp. 1369, 1372.

46. Alfred J. Puchala, "Securitizing Third World Debt," *Columbia Business Law Review* (1989) p. 137; David W. Leebron, Jr. "First Things First: A Comment on Securitizing Third World Debt," *Columbia Business Law Review* (1989) p. 173; William W. Park, "Legal Policy Conflicts in International Banking," *Ohio State Law Journal* 50 (1989), pp. 1067, 1089, 1092.

47. "Thoughts from the Ministry," *Economist*, Sept. 24, 1988, p. 107; Mark Basch, "Mortgage Securities Get Slow Start in Europe, Catch On in Japan," *American Banker*, Mar. 3, 1987 p. 8. While securitized loans have not yet caught on in England, they are becoming very popular in Japan.; See "Annual Report: Structured Finance 1988 Review and 1989 Outlook," *Structured Finance*, March 1989 (discusses developments and projections in the U.S. markets).

48. *Changes in Our Financial System: Globalization of Capital Markets and Securitization of credit: Hearings Before the Senate Committee on Banking, Housing, and Urban Affairs,* 100th Cong., 1st Sess. (1988), p. 137 (statement of Lowell L. Bryan, McKinsey & Co.); Miller, "Commercial Loan Securitization—Review and Outlook," *Loan Pricing Report* VI, no. 4, (Sept. 1991) p. 2.

49. Lisabeth Weiner, "Securitization: What Will They Package Next?" *American Banker*, Jan. 7, 1987, p. 1, 14; Daniel B. Silver and Peter J. Axilrod, "Pushing Technology to Its Limits: Securitizing C&I Loans," *Bankers Magazine,* May-June 1989, pp. 16, 17; *Loan Pricing Report* 7, July-August 1990, pp. 19, 20; *Changes in Our Financial System: Globalization of Capital Markets and Securitization of Credit: Hearings Before the Senate Comm. on Banking, Housing, and Urban Affairs,* 100th Cong., 1st Sess. (1988), p. 137 (statement of Lowell L. Bryan, McKinsey & Co.); Miller, "Commercial Loan Securitization—Review and Outlook," *Loan Pricing Report* VI, no. 4 (Sept. 1991), p.2. This article describes the techniques for securitizing short-term commercial loans in 1991. These are joint programs established by banks. A separate entity makes direct loans to customers referred by participating banks. The banks provide credit enhancement to their customers. So long as the credit enhancements do not increase a bank's capital requirements, this technique helps banks reduce their capital requirements through sale of loans. Another form of securitization is by pooling loans, especially highly leveraged loans.

50. A current specialized publication provides information about these loans and their terms nationwide. See *Loan Pricing Reports*, published by Loan Pricing Corporation, 135 W. 50th Street, 10020.

51. Kenneth R. Harney, "Freddie Mac Puts its Weight Behind the Use of Credit Scoring," *Washington Post*, July 22, 1995 pp. E1, E19. The corporation has developed a scoring system for mortgage applicants that speeds the processing of applicants by using scores and eliminates some applicants with very low scores.

52. See *Problems in Mortgage Packaging: Hearing Before the Subcommittee on General Oversight and Investigation of the House Committee on Banking, Finance and Urban Affairs*, 99th Cong., 1st Sess. 89 (1985) (testimony of Lawrence D. Fink, Managing Director, First Boston Corp.).

53. Hearings Before the Subcommittee on Economic Growth and Credit Formation of the Committee on Banking, Finance and Urban Affairs, 103 Cong. 1st Sess., February 1993.

54. See Ibid., p. 89 (testimony of Thomas P. Hourican, Managing Director, Standard & Poor's).

55. See Hearings Before the Subcommittee on Economic Growth and Credit Formation of the Committee on Banking, Finance and Urban Affairs, 103 Cong. 1st Sess., February 1993 (testimony of Tamar Frankel, Boston University School of Law, pp. 52, 59). See also "Small-Business Securitization to Grow Willy-Nilly," *American Banker* (October 24, 1995) p. 18 (describing the problems of securitizing small business loans and the possible help the process could receive from the government).

56. See Anat Bird, "Small Firms Won't be Helped by Securitizing Lending," *American Banker*, July 8, 1993, p. 4; Robert Gruenfest, "An Adequate Mechanism Already Exists for Securitizing Business Loans," *American Banker*, (Mar, 31, 1993) p. 4; See also Christopher Noble, Bear Stearns, "Cargill in Venture, *American Banker*, (Aug. 2, 1993) p. 9; David Siegel, "Bankers Trust in Novel Securitization," *American Banker*, (March 19, 1993) p. 16; Karen Gullo, "Chemical to Securitize Commercial Realty Loans," *American Banker*, (Feb. 22, 1993), p. 1; Howard L. Siegel, Markets Emerging for Bank Loans, Whether They're Distressed or Triple A, *American Banker*, (July 14, 1993), p. 4.; Bradford T. Nordholm, "A Small Business Loan Market Forming With

or Without Banks," *American Banker*, (May 14, 1993) p. 4; Andrew Stone, "There's no Stopping Asset Securitization," *American Banker*, (Dec. 24, 1992), p. 4; and Claudia Cumming, "Small Business Loan Agency Might Fly Now," *American Banker*, (Feb. 3, 1993).

57. A similar development has occurred in the life insurance field. Whereas in the past each insured had to pass a medical examination, now many insureds are classified by a pool according to information provided in their application. It seems that this technique can be applied to commercial and industrial medium-sized borrowers.

58. As defined by Schumpeter, an innovation includes "a new form of organization" or "combines factors in a new way." Joseph A. Schumpeter, Business Cycles 87, 88 (1st ed. McGraw-Hill Book Co. 1939). Securitization fits this definition both because it introduces new processes of intermediation and because it produces new financial instruments. See also T. M. Podolski, Financial Innovation and the Money Supply (Basil Blackwell Ltd.); Herbert L. Baer and Christine Pavel, *Does Regulation Drive Innovation?*, Economic Perspectives, Mar/Apr. 1988, at 3; Tim S. Campbell, *Innovations in Financial Intermediation*, Business Horizons, Nov./Dec. 1989, at 70; Smith & Taggert, *Bond Market Innovations and Financial Intermediation,* Business Horizons, Nov./Dec. 1989, at 24, cited in Shenker and Colletta, "Asset Securitization: Evolution, Current Issues and New Frontiers," 69 *Texas Law Review* pp. 1369, 1370 n.2 (dealing with recent financial innovations including securitization).

59. See Robert E. Litan, *The Revolution in U.S. Finance* 36 (The Brookings Institution, 1991) (expressing a similar opinion).

IV

DEFINED CONTRIBUTION PENSION PLANS

9

THE REVOLUTION IN RETIREMENT SAVINGS

401(k) Plans and Investment Intermediaries

William A. Schmidt, *Paul, Hastings, Janofsky & Walker*

Privately sponsored retirement plans are changing, rapidly and fundamentally, with the dramatic shift from defined benefit plans to defined contribution plans. The implications of these changes for pension plan investment managers and advisers will be the most significant since privately sponsored retirement plans first became widespread in the 1940s. The rise of defined contribution plans presents new opportunities as well as risks, and managers will need to carefully evaluate the roles they can play.

Until well into the 1980s, the accepted model for individual retirement savings was the "three-legged stool"—Social Security, private pensions, and individual savings. The private pension was usually in the form of a defined benefit plan, providing for a formula benefit taking into account age, earnings, and years of service. Defined contribution, or individual account, plans were often seen as an adjunct to and a way of enhancing personal savings.

Although advance funding of defined benefit plans was not legally required until the enactment of the Employee Retirement Income Security Act (ERISA) in 1974, many defined benefit plans were funded in accordance with an advance actuarial cost method so that investment gains would reduce and investment losses would increase employer contributions to the plan. In other words, investment risk under these plans rested with employers. Consequently, employers had a keen economic interest in monitoring the investment performance of the plan and in taking prompt remedial steps where investment performance lagged behind.

In addition, employers had an economic interest in assuring that plan investments were managed efficiently and that economies of scale were realized wherever possible. This, in turn, led to the concentration of large amounts of pension assets in the hands of institutional money managers, particularly banks and insurance companies. These managers could then invest for the long term and could take advantage of the unique opportunities available to institutional investors, particularly in the private market and in alternative investments, such as real estate. Disputes about investments usually were resolved quietly, and litigation involving institutional investors was relatively rare.

Another historical feature of traditional defined benefit plans is that they were an important source of retirement income for all employees, from the mailroom to the executive suite. The primary body of law regulating these plans was the tax qualified plan provisions of the Internal Revenue Code, which focused on assuring that plans did not discriminate in favor of highly compensated employees. As a general matter, however, a plan was not considered discriminatory if the value of the benefits earned by highly compensated employees was the same, relative to the employee's compensation, as the smaller benefits earned by lower paid employees. Although limitations on the amount of compensation that could be taken into account in determining benefits were introduced in the 1970s, these limitations still allowed the bulk of executive retirement savings to be provided through a qualified plan. This across-the-board feature of defined benefit plans gave corporate management a personal stake in the soundness of the plan and its investment policies.

Defined benefit plans are still very much a part of the pension world. They are still the plans of choice for larger employers, and the enactment of the funding requirements of ERISA in 1974 has assured the accumulation of an exceptionally large pool of money that will need to be invested and reinvested well into the 21st century.

For the long term, however, the defined benefit retirement plan is a dinosaur. By its nature, a defined benefit plan is more expensive to administer than a defined contribution plan. In addition, both ERISA and the Internal Revenue Code impose extensive requirements that are applicable solely or principally to defined benefit plans. These requirements include extensive reporting obligations, joint and survivor annuity requirements, and, of course, advance funding requirements and contingent liability for underfunding in the event of plan termination. Moreover, defined benefit plans were designed to encourage long-term service, an incentive that has become less relevant in today's economy.

Virtually all of the growth in retirement plan savings since the mid-1980s has been in defined contribution plans, particularly the 401(k) plan. Rather than providing a formula benefit, defined contribution plans provide an individual account for each participant with benefits based solely on the amounts contributed to the account and earnings, gains, and losses that are attributable to the account. In other words, investment risk rests with the individual employee, and adverse investments will reduce the benefit that a participant would otherwise receive. In addition, 401(k) plans are funded in part from salary deferrals—amounts that would otherwise be payable to the employee in cash. As a result, many, if not most, 401(k) plan participants look at their accounts as their own money. Reflecting this attitude, virtually all 401(k) plans give participants some degree of control over their individual account investments.

The 401(k) plan is popular for a number of reasons. First, these plans are popular with employees. In a mobile society, they provide a portable benefit that can easily be transferred as a participant moves among employers. The benefit is also easy to understand: A participant's account balance looks much like personal savings and, under almost all 401(k) plans, participant loans are available and preretirement withdrawals may be made in hardship cases. All of these are popular features.

Second, 401(k) plans provide distinct benefits to employers. Because 401(k) plans are funded, in part, by salary deferrals, they can reduce the net out-of-pocket expense to the employer dramatically. In addition, 401(k) plans do not require the employer to make the kind of long-term funding commitment that defined benefit plans require. Once employers make their required contributions, their obligations are discharged. 401(k) plans are much easier and cheaper to administer than defined benefit plans, and these plans are not subject to the plan termination insurance program administered by the Pension Benefit Guaranty Corporation. Consequently, the employer can realize significant savings by using a defined contribution plan as its primary retirement vehicle.

Third, the 401(k) plan also has been popular with investment intermediaries, who have rushed to provide the services needed to support this rapidly growing market segment. Mutual funds, particularly, are well adapted as a way of giving plan participants significant control over the manner in which their retirement savings are invested while retaining the benefits of diversification and professional management. In addition, fund advisers can charge the same fees for plan investments in mutual funds as they do for individual investments; in other words, a retail price for a product that can be marketed wholesale. Also, a mutual fund's investment adviser is not subject to the fiduciary responsibility requirements of ERISA with respect to the management of mutual fund assets. This exemption is perceived as an advantage because even if the restrictions of the Investment Company Act are not less stringent than ERISA, they are at least more comprehensible. This shift has been advantageous to established mutual fund groups and relatively less so to banks and insurance companies, which historically have relied primarily on large defined benefit plans for their client base.

Despite sound reasons for the popularity of participant-directed 401(k) plans, the full implications of this sea change in retirement savings are far from clear. Several general trends can be identified, however, and we discuss them in the following sections.

Dispersion of Investment Decision Making

Perhaps the most obvious implication of the development of 401(k) plans is that certain investment decisions that were previously made by a select group of institutional investment managers (both in-house and outside) are now being made by a wide array of individuals with vastly differing degrees of investment sophistication and expertise. Because most 401(k) plans limit participant decision making to choices among pooled funds with differing investment objectives, however, this shift has been at a macro, rather than a micro, level. Decisions to invest in individual securities are still made by institutional managers, but individuals exercise considerable control over the choice of asset classes.

The most readily observable implication of the dispersion of investment decision making is that equities are underrepresented in most portfolios. Individual participants have demonstrated a clear preference for fixed income funds that provide a stated return on a fixed principal amount, rather than equities, which are seen as more volatile and even speculative. A number of commentators and pension professionals have been devoting considerable attention to devising participant education programs designed to overcome this aversion to equities and to correct the inefficient reliance on fixed income investments. These efforts have apparently met with some success, as evidenced by increasing pension plan representation in equity mutual funds.

Market Volatility

Even though institutional managers are likely to continue to manage most plan assets at the micro level, the behavior of individual plan participants will still have significant effects on market behavior. Individual plan participants are likely to be cautious investors, and they are likely to be easily spooked. They are not likely stewards of "patient money."

These aspects of participant behavior can have several consequences. First, it is not clear whether participants as a group fundamentally are comfortable with significant equity exposure, and participant behavior has not been tested by a significant bear market. Although participant education efforts generally try to emphasize the importance of investing for the long haul, short-term market downturns may well result in significant redemptions that will in turn fuel selloffs. Second, in view of plan participants' preference for "stable value" investments, even during periods of relatively low interest rates, participant-directed redemptions from equity mutual funds can be expected to accelerate when long-term interest rates rise as participants move to relatively more attractive stable value funds.

Litigiousness

Individual participants, particularly the members of the baby boom generation who are now approaching retirement, are not likely to be philosophic about market losses involving their retirement savings. This attitude will inevitably lead to a significant increase in litigation challenging the behavior of individual investment managers. This is particularly true in the context of ERISA. Although mutual funds investment advisers are not regarded as fiduciaries with respect to the management of mutual fund assets, many investment advisers or their affiliates serve as trustees to 401(k) plans and play important roles in helping plan sponsors select appropriate investment options and in participant education efforts. These activities can result in the advisers or affiliates being considered fiduciaries for ERISA purposes. Also, the managers of many collective investment funds, including bank collective trust funds and insurance company pooled separate accounts, are considered ERISA fiduciaries with respect to the management of those accounts, and of course employers who sponsor 401(k) plans almost always have significant fiduciary responsibilities under ERISA.

ERISA does have a provision (Section 404(c)) that supposedly insulates fiduciaries from liability for losses resulting from participant investment decisions. However, this protection does not extend to significant decisions that are usually made by the plan sponsor, including the selection of investment managers and administrative service providers. In addition, regulations issued by the U.S. Department of Labor make it clear that this protection does not extend to the individual investment decisions of investment managers. Finally, the Section 404(c) protections are only available if *all* of the requirements of the Department of Labor's regulations are satisfied. These requirements are comprehensive and complex, and the department has made it clear that the burden of demonstrating compliance with these requirements is with the person seeking to invoke the section 404(c) protections. Proving that all of these requirements have been met with respect to a particular transaction is likely to be a daunting task.

Where the Section 404(c) defense is not available, there are several aspects of ERISA that make an action for breach of fiduciary duty particularly burdensome for investment managers. One important point is that *any* plan participant can bring an action for breach of fiduciary duty on behalf of an employee benefit plan, and the courts have generally not required participants to demonstrate that plan officials have neglected to assert the plan's legitimate rights as a precondition to instituting a participant action.

Although any participant may initiate an action for breach of fiduciary duty, it does not necessarily follow that the participant bringing the action has authority to settle it. A participant bringing such an action does so as a representative of the plan, and any recovery is payable to the plan. Thus, settlement of these matters is difficult, if not impossible, without consideration of the position of the plan as a separate legal entity. Such consideration may very well require separate representation for the plan.

If settlement is unattractive, carrying defense of a participant's fiduciary breach claim to trial can also be perilous. A finding of a breach of fiduciary duty may require the fiduciary to restore losses not only to the plaintiff, but also to other similarly situated plan participants, and it can also subject the fiduciary to excise taxes and civil penalties. This can run into major financial exposure.

Pension Plans as a Source of Investment Capital

Defined benefit pension plans historically have been an important source of investment capital, not only for long-term corporate debt, but also for "nontraditional investments," especially venture capital and equity real estate. Defined benefit plans will continue to be around, of course, and—thanks to the funding requirements of ERISA—they will continue to constitute major pools of investment capital for some time to come. The *growth* of employee benefit plans is now almost exclusively in the defined contribution area, however. As a result, thoughtful real estate and venture capital managers are becoming aware that continued access to pension capital, particularly for purposes of exploring new market opportunities, will require development of vehicles for defined contribution plan investors. These vehicles will be vastly different from the real estate and venture capital limited partnerships that are familiar to institutional managers today, and issues of liquidity and volatility will have to be resolved before they can be made attractive as retail products for individuals investing through defined contribution plans.

CONCLUSION

The advent of the participant-directed defined contribution plan as the preferred form of retirement savings presents unprecedented opportunities for investment professionals. Taking advantage of these opportunities will require some adjustment in practice, however, and sensitivity to the behavior of individual investors. The managers who make these adjustments quickly and who are sensitive to the distinct risks of managing retirement savings for individuals will succeed. Those that fail to adjust their approach will face declining markets and, possibly, significant liabilities.

10

MUTUAL FUND INVESTMENTS IN PARTICIPANT-DIRECTED RETIREMENT PLANS
Required Disclosure versus Effective Communication

John M. Kimpel, *Fidelity Investments*

One of the most remarkable developments in the retirement plan area over the last decade has been the phenomenal growth of defined contribution plans. This growth has been characterized by three interrelated trends. First, much of this growth has been fueled by tax qualified salary reduction programs, including 401(k), 403(b), and 457 plans.[1] Under these types of programs, employees are able to set aside a portion of their pretax salary in a retirement savings vehicle whose income will accumulate on a tax-sheltered basis. Much of the decision-making authority is shifted from employers to employees under such an arrangement. The employee must decide whether to participate in the arrangement and how much to contribute to the plan. Furthermore, the risk and reward of investment performance thereupon flows to the employee rather than to the employer (as is the case with defined benefit plans). In other words, the amount available to an employee at retirement depends on the performance of the investment alternatives the employee has chosen.

According to the Employee Benefit Research Institute (EBRI), the participation rate in such salary reduction programs more than tripled between 1984 and 1991. As a consequence, EBRI reported that 37 percent of the civilian nonagricultural workforce (or 39 million workers) in 1993 worked for employers who sponsored a salary reduction plan, and these numbers continue to grow at a staggering rate.[2] Growth of 401(k) plans has been particularly dramatic. Virtually nonexistent before 1982, when the Internal Revenue Service (IRS) issued enabling regulations for a statute first enacted in 1978, there were over 210,000 plans with $475 billion by 1993.[3] By the year 2000, 401(k) assets are expected to exceed $1.2 trillion.[4]

Second is the trend toward participant-directed investments in defined contribution plans generally, and salary reduction plans in particular. To some extent, this trend results from the desire of employers to obtain the relief provided by compliance with § 404(c) of the Employee Retirement Income Security Act of 1974, as amended (ERISA). More importantly, however, participants have demanded control of their investments. It is their money after all, and it is they who suffer from poor performance. It is difficult from an employee relations standpoint to shift risk to employees without also shifting control to them as well. The Department of Labor (DOL) regulation issued under § 404(c) is perhaps best characterized as a reflection of this workplace reality in the regulatory arena.[5]

The third trend is the domination of mutual funds as the investment medium for the defined contribution market, particularly the 401(k) market.[6] This too should come as no surprise. Because employees view 401(k) contributions as their own money, because they have the risk regarding investment performance, and because they have investment control over their accounts, employees view these retirement savings programs in much the same way as they see their own IRAs, almost as if they were employer-sponsored "super IRAs." They want to be able to do the same things with their 401(k) accounts that they can do with their IRAs (have access to professional investment management and daily transaction capability, for example). Since mutual funds have dominated the IRA market for some time, it was natural for plan sponsors to look to mutual funds when the 401(k) market began to take off in the late 1980s.

The success of defined contribution plans depends on how well employees understand them and the role they play in assuring adequate retirement income. It is therefore imperative that plan sponsors effectively communicate essential plan and investment information and educate employees about their retirement needs and appropriate ways to meet them. However, plan sponsors, as well as the financial service firms that provide investment products, recordkeeping and employee communications services to such plans, are confronted by a labyrinth of laws and regulations that constrain such educational efforts.

Principal among these constraints are the requirements for, and the limitations on, such employee communications under the federal securities laws and ERISA. This paper will attempt to reconcile these two bodies of law focusing first on the federal securities law and then on ERISA. In each case, the paper will address both the current state of the law as well as existing initiatives that should help the law better respond to the issue of effective employee communications in the future.

PROSPECTUS DELIVERY REQUIREMENTS

In large part, the current federal securities laws flow from the great stock market crash that began in 1929 and devastated retail investors. To put the impact of the crash in perspective, the aggregate market value in September 1929 of all stocks listed on the New York Stock Exchange was $89 billion; by 1932, the aggregate value had plummeted to $15 billion,[7] having lost over 80 percent of its value. Over one-half of the securities sold between 1920 and 1933 were worthless by 1933.[8] One of the principal themes, therefore, of the Securities Act of 1933 (the '33 Act), the Securities Exchange Act of 1934 (the '34 Act), the Investment Company Act of 1940 (the '40 Act) and the Investment Advisers Act of 1940 (the Advisers Act) is the protection of retail investors through detailed reporting to the government by issuers of securities, both before initial offerings and on an ongoing basis, as well as full and accurate disclosure to investors before investment.

In particular, Section 5 of the '33 Act includes prospectus delivery requirements relating to an initial offering of securities.[9] Section 5 is of particular importance to mutual funds because mutual funds are deemed to be in continuous offering. As a result, the prospectus delivery rules of Section 5 continuously apply to a mutual fund, even one such as the Fidelity Magellan® Fund or the Vanguard Windsor Fund that are old enough and large enough to have become household names.

The prospectus delivery requirements under the '33 Act distinguish between an offer and a sale.[10] When an *offer* is made in writing (or via radio or TV), it must be made by means of a "statutory" prospectus that satisfies Section 10(a), or an "omitting" or "summary" prospectus that satisfies the requirements of Section 10(b).[11] In the case of a *sale*, it must be preceded or accompanied by a "statutory" prospectus meeting the requirements of Section 10(a).[12] Since Section 4 exempts from Section 5 transactions by any person other than an issuer, underwriter or dealer, the prospectus delivery requirements apply to the issuer of the mutual fund and *not* to the plan sponsor of a retirement plan under which the mutual fund is an option.

Furthermore, Section 3 of the '33 Act exempts from registration the offering of interests in a pension or profit-sharing plan (these interests are treated as a separate security under the federal securities laws). This exemption typically applies except in cases where the plan offers employees the opportunity to invest in the employer's own securities. Absent such an exemption, the prospectus delivery requirements would affect the offering of those interests in addition to the mutual funds in which the plans invest. Section 3 also exempts from regulation offering interests in bank commingled pools or insurance company separate accounts to plans. Banks and insurance companies are therefore generally unaffected by the prospectus delivery requirements.

Finally, Section 11 of the '33 Act provides for civil liability for material misstatements or omissions in a prospectus. Section 24 provides for criminal penalties for willful violations of the '33 Act.

Since this statutory framework preceded the development of participant-directed defined contribution plans by several decades, the '33 Act did not contemplate such plans and such plans do not fit neatly into this statutory framework. Plan sponsors, financial service firms, and the SEC have struggled over the past decade trying to pound the square peg of participant-directed plans into the round hole of the federal securities laws.

In recognition of the explosive growth of mutual funds over that same time period, the SEC used the 50th anniversary of the adoption of the '40 Act as incentive for an exhaustive reexamination of that and other federal securities laws relating to mutual funds. That effort culminated in the release on May 21, 1992, of the SEC Staff Report on Investment Company Regulation (the Investment Company Study). Among other things, the study recommended the adoption of legislation to amend the securities laws to require the delivery of prospectuses to plan participants who direct their investments among mutual funds. The Investment Company Study also endorsed rule changes to allow for a summary-type prospectus that could be of particular utility to the participant-directed defined contribution market.

By proposing the adoption of legislation that requires delivery of mutual fund prospectuses to participants, the Investment Company Study recognizes that this obligation does not clearly exist under current law. Moreover, the ability to do so may be limited as a practical matter. Obstacles that need to be taken into account include the following:

1. To *whom* should prospectuses be delivered? Must a fund deliver the prospectus for each investment option to all participants or could the fund provide prospectuses to just those participants who intend to invest in a particular fund or, alternatively, to a plan sponsor or other fiduciary in certain circumstances? What if the fund has no record of who the participants are, which will always be the case unless the fund or its affiliate is performing record-keeping services for the plan?

2. *When* must the prospectus be delivered—prior to an offer or purchase or upon confirmation of the sale? And if an offer is deemed to be made to participants, when is it made—only at the time of enrollment in the plan, or is it made on an ongoing basis each time contributions are actually made?

3. *What* form must the prospectus take? Must it be the same prospectus that is delivered to retail customers or can it be customized for a particular plan? The better question, perhaps, is *should* it be the same prospectus that is delivered to retail customers?

Current practice in the mutual fund industry reflects the uncertain status of the law. While practices vary in different factual contexts and sometimes from one fund group to another, the following generalization may be made: When fund groups have employee names and addresses, they are able to, and sometimes do, deliver statutory prospectuses, either in advance of purchase or upon confirmation of purchase. But when fund groups do not have employee names and addresses, they cannot and do not deliver statutory prospectuses. As is true with any generalization, however, this is not always the case. Some plan sponsors specifically direct the fund sponsor not to deliver fund prospectuses in advance of purchase or upon confirmation even when the fund sponsor has employee names and addresses. This is particularly true in the case of employers who use Form S-8 to register the offering of interests in the plan because the plan offers employer stock as the investment option, in which event the employer must deliver a prospectus for the plan to each participant. Such employers argue that a general distribution of mutual fund prospectuses in addition to the S-8 prospectus is counterproductive to effective communication. In such cases, the S-8 prospectus contains a summary description of each investment option and advises participants how to get mutual fund prospectuses if they desire more detail.

The overwhelming problem confronted by plan sponsors is simply that the statutory prospectus is not an effective communication vehicle for plan participants. In fact, many commentators argue that it is not an effective communications document for *any* investor. As SEC Chairman Arthur Levitt stated on "Wall Street Week," "my major priority is to try to get prospectuses and all of the materials we bring out to consumers to be in plain English, rather than the convoluted, garbled language that we have imposed…on investors."[13]

Since the issuance of the Investment Company Study, Congress has not taken up the call to introduce legislation modernizing the provisions of the '40 Act that bear upon the retirement market. But the SEC has initiated a number of rule-making projects in pursuit of this goal. Among them is the pilot project the SEC is currently conducting with eight mutual fund families to develop a simplified "profile" prospectus that would be considerably more user-friendly than the current form of statutory prospectus.

Furthermore, in April 1995, the SEC issued a no-action letter[14] to Fidelity Investments that goes a long way to resolving the prospectus delivery dilemma within the defined contribution context. In its ruling request, Fidelity proposed to supplement the information otherwise made available to plan participants by providing summaries of prospectuses (SPRs) of the Fidelity funds available under a particular plan. Each SPR would contain the following information:

1. Each fund's investment objectives, policies, and risks.
2. Each fund's expenses.
3. The historical performance of each fund.
4. Distribution practices.
5. Directions regarding how to obtain the statutory prospectus for each fund.

6. Directions regarding how eligible employees can enroll in their employer's plan and allocate contributions to one or more of the investment options described in the SPR.

Fidelity believed that such an SPR would qualify as an "omitting prospectus" under SEC Rule 482.[15] Because Rule 482(a)(5) prohibits such an omitting prospectus from being accompanied by a fund application and because Fidelity anticipated accompanying the SPR with a plan enrollment form, the specific issue presented for no-action relief was confirmation that such a plan enrollment form would not be deemed to be a fund application for purposes of Rule 482(a)(5).

In issuing its no-action relief, the SEC agreed with Fidelity's view that the plan enrollment form that accompanied the SPR would not be a fund application since it would be directed to the plan sponsor or trustee, and not to the issuer of the mutual fund shares. In doing so, the SEC effectively confirmed in this no-action letter its earlier position stated in the Investment Company Study that current law did not require the delivery of prospectuses to defined contribution plan participants.

This conclusion reflects the actual way in which participant-directed plans work. As required by ERISA, all monies contributed to a plan must be held in trust. The legal owner of the plan assets (and the investor in the mutual fund) therefore is the plan trustee. Although the plan participant directs the plan trustee (either directly or through the plan sponsor or other agent) how to invest those plan assets that are held in the plan for the account, the actual sale of mutual fund shares is made to the trustee, in whose name the shares are thereupon registered.

In light of this no-action letter, it now seems possible that investment companies and plan sponsors can work together to communicate essential details of the plan, including both necessary information about the investment options available under the plan and plan enrollment materials, as part of an effective communications campaign without necessarily delivering statutory prospectuses as part of such campaign.

ERISA

Like the federal securities laws, the Employee Retirement Income Security Act of 1974 (ERISA) was preceded by widespread abuse that led to devastating losses to average American citizens, in this case workers and pensioners. Among these abuses were many examples of fraud and malfeasance by plan fiduciaries who too often dealt with plan assets in their own self-interest. A principal thrust of ERISA, therefore, was to establish federal law fiduciary standards.

ERISA is similar in certain respects to the federal securities laws. As is the case with the federal securities laws, employee (as opposed to investor) protection is sought under ERISA by a combination of governmental reporting requirements and employee disclosure. Section 102 of ERISA sets forth detailed requirements that plan sponsors deliver a summary plan description to eligible employees after they become participants in the plan and periodically thereafter as plan amendments are made. The focus of such summary plan description (or SPD) is on the plan itself as opposed to investments made under the plan. In addition, § 102 of ERISA requires plan sponsors to distribute to participants each year a summary annual report (or SAR), which summarizes financial information concerning the plan. But the SAR provides nothing in the way of information about specific investments; it merely provides aggregate financial data. Finally, § 103 of ERISA allows a participant to request a statement of the value of their accounts under a plan. Although not required, most plan sponsors automatically distribute these participant statements at least once per year. As was also the case with federal securities laws, however, ERISA preceded the widespread development of participant-directed defined contribution plans, and its statutory framework assumes a pension would be dominated by defined benefit plans. For this reason ERISA does not mandate comprehensive investment disclosure to participants.

ERISA goes far beyond disclosure in establishing fiduciary responsibility rules for retirement plans. These rules impose strict standards on those who have discretionary authority over the plan, particularly those who have discretionary authority over the investment of plan assets. ERISA generally defines anyone who has discretionary authority over the plan or the investment of its assets as a *fiduciary*.[16] ERISA charges fiduciaries, in turn, to exercise their responsibilities for the "exclusive benefit" of plan participants and in accordance with the "prudent expert" rule.[17] Moreover, virtually any transaction between a fiduciary and the plan that could involve self-dealing or other conflict of interest is strictly prohibited,[18] absent a statutory exemption[19] or an administrative exemption granted by the Secretary of Labor.[20]

These ERISA rules are similar to the fiduciary responsibility rules imposed by the federal securities laws on mutual fund managers.[21]

Because of the fiduciary protections federal securities laws afford to mutual fund shareholders, ERISA exempts securities held in mutual funds from the definition of *plan assets*, thereby excluding mutual fund managers from the definition of *fiduciary*.[22] As a consequence, mutual fund managers are more concerned about the prospectus delivery requirements of the federal securities laws than about the ERISA fiduciary rules. Conversely, banks and insurance companies are more concerned about the ERISA fiduciary rules than about the prospectus delivery requirements of the federal securities laws.

In 1992, the DOL issued final regulations under § 404(c) of ERISA. These regulations set forth the conditions that plan fiduciaries must meet to be relieved of liability for the consequences of participants' control over their accounts. Among these conditions are three primary requirements. First, the plan must offer a broad range of investment alternatives, including at least three diversified "core" options that each have different risk and return characteristics.[23] Second, participants must be allowed to transfer among these options with a frequency commensurate with the investments' market volatility, but at least as often as quarterly in the case of the core options.[24] Third, participants must have access to sufficient information about each investment option so that they can make informed investment decisions.[25]

Specifically, the third condition requires that the plan provide the following information to participants before they invest in any of the available options:

1. An explanation that the plan is intended to constitute a 404(c) plan and that plan fiduciaries may therefore be relieved of liability for losses resulting from the participant's investment instructions. As a result, participants will know that they have control over their account and accordingly that they have the responsibility for the consequences of their investment decisions.

2. A description of each of the available investment alternatives, including their investment objectives, their risk/return characteristics, and the type and diversification of assets in which each of the investment vehicles invests.

3. An explanation of how participants can give investment instructions.

4. A description of transaction fees and expenses, such as sales commissions or redemption fees, that are charged to the participant's account.

5. Identification of the plan fiduciary or agent who will provide the participant additional information on request.

6. In the case of a plan offering employer securities as an option, a description of the procedures established to assure confidentiality regarding participants' instructions.

7. Immediately after investment in any investment vehicle that is registered under the '33 Act, a copy of the most recent prospectus for such a vehicle.[26]

Furthermore, the final regulations specify the type of information that must be provided to plan participants upon request. This information includes the following:

1. A description of the annual operating expenses of each investment vehicle, including the investment management and other fees, that are charged to the investment vehicle and thereby reduce its rate of return.

2. A list of assets included in the investment vehicle that are plan assets, and the value of each such asset (and, for GICs and similar investments, identification of the issuer of each contract, its maturity date and its interest rate).

3. Performance data for each investment vehicle, net of expenses, presented over reasonable periods of time calculated in a reasonable and consistent manner.

4. The participant's account balance as of the last valuation date (but no more frequently than quarterly).[27]

Most participant-directed defined contribution plans are trying to comply with §404(c). For example, *Institutional Investor* reported in its October 1993 issue that most 401(k) plans have increased the number of investment options available in the last three years and almost half plan to do so again in the near future. As a consequence, the survey reported, over 90 percent of 401(k) plans offer three or more investment options, and almost as many (85 percent) offer four or more options. In fact, the survey reported that over 60 percent offered more than five options. This compares to a 1990 survey by the magazine that reported that only slightly over 50 percent offered four or more options.

Finally, the survey reported that over 75 percent of plans indicated that they were complying with Section 404(c) regulations.

Although these informational requirements are seemingly straightforward, they do raise some issues. Among the issues that need to be scrutinized are the following:

1. *Necessary information.* Is literature available for participant distribution that describes the investment objectives, their risk/return characteristics, and the type and diversification of assets in which each of the investment options invests? These are the core informational requirements. In the case of mutual funds this requirement can be satisfied by the distribution of prospectuses and/or other readily available literature. But, as described above, practical obstacles inhibit prospectus delivery, particularly in cases where the plan offers unlimited investment changes or where the mutual fund sponsor is not also providing recordkeeping services to the plan.

2. *Investment Advice.* Does providing the necessary information constitute "investment advice" and thereby turn the information giver into an ERISA fiduciary? The regulations clearly state that providing the necessary information does not constitute or require the giving of investment advice to participants. Plan sponsors should therefore feel confident that they can satisfy 404(c) without giving investment advice for ERISA purposes.

3. *Timing.* Is the necessary information given to participants before investment directions are made? In addition to the prospectus delivery issue discussed above, a practical issue arises in the case of a plan's conversion from one investment provider to another. Traditionally, participants' accounts are "mapped" from the old investment vehicle to a new one having similar characteristics. Does 404(c) require a re-enrollment in such a case?

EDUCATION VERSUS ADVICE

Of these issues, the one that most troubles plan sponsors and financial service providers is the question of when investment information designed to be educational rises to the level of "investment advice" under ERISA. As Section 404(c) requires plan fiduciaries to provide investment information to avoid fiduciary liability—and as plan participants continue to demand even more by way of investment and education—plan sponsors and financial service providers have developed a variety of communications designed to better educate plan participants about investment allocation decisions. These include the following:

1. *General financial and investment information.* This includes such information as (a) the historic differences in rates of return between different asset classes based on standard market indexes, (b) the definition and impact of investment terms and principles such as diversification, compounded return, dollar-cost averaging, and tax-deferred investment, and (c) the importance of a participant's own time horizon for investments. Such information is provided in printed form or by oral presentation, video, or software media.

2. *Section 404(c) information.* This includes the specific information regarding plan investment options that the Section 404(c) regulation requires to be disclosed and made available to plan participants.

3. *Asset allocation information.* This type of information includes sample asset allocations for hypothetical individuals with different time horizons and risk profiles presented in the form of pie charts or case studies containing model portfolios. The model portfolios are typically expressed in terms of the three classic asset classes (i.e., equity, bond, and cash), although sometimes they refer to the specific investment options available in a plan. The model portfolios typically are based on well-established investment theories that demonstrate the positive effect that diversification among different asset classes has on the risk/return tradeoff over time.[28] These principles impact defined benefit investment decisions as well, with the result that the industrywide asset allocation of defined contribution assets is quite similar to that of defined benefit plans.[29] Moreover, these industrywide allocations, primarily by professional managers, are similar to the model portfolios typically described for "moderate" investors.[30]

4. *Self-scoring questionnaires, worksheets, software, and similar interactive tools.* These materials are based on the same asset allocation information described above, but are designed to provide participants with the means to assess their own asset allocation and savings strategies. Using these materials, participants can input their own financial and personal information to project retirement savings based on different investment strategies, portfolios, and economic assumptions. A participant can thereby see the interaction between various assumptions concerning contribution rates, time horizon, and rates of return and the consequences of varying any of these assumptions.

Under existing DOL interpretations, none of these types of educational materials should rise to the level of "investment advice." ERISA Section 3(21) defines a *fiduciary* to include a person who gives "investment advice for a fee or other compensation." The determination of what constitutes "investment advice" is made by reference to a regulation first issued by the DOL in 1975 and relied upon by the employee benefits community since then.[31] Under that regulation, a person is deemed to give investment advice for purposes of the definition of a *fiduciary* only if such person:

1. Renders advice as to the value of securities or other property, or makes recommendations as to the advisability of investing in securities or other property, *and*
2. Renders such advice:
   i. On a *regular* basis;
   ii. Pursuant to a *mutual* agreement that:
      a. Such advice will serve as a *primary* basis for investment decisions with respect to plan assets; *and*
      b. The person providing such advice will render *individualized* investment advice based on the particular needs of the plan.

Accordingly, four elements must *all* be present for educational information disseminated by a plan sponsor or financial services provider to a plan participant to constitute investment advice under ERISA. First, such advice must be given for a fee or other compensation. However, the provider of the types of information described above rarely charges an additional fee for such information.

Second, such advice must be provided on a "regular basis." But the types of information described above are not provided on anything approaching a regular basis. Rather, such information is provided only once on a widespread scale, typically when an employee enrolls in the plan (or the plan switches to a new investment provider) and thereafter only sporadically.

Third, such advice must be given pursuant to a mutual agreement between the party providing the advice and the plan participant that such advice will serve as a primary basis for the plan participant's investment decisions. But the types of information described above are certainly not given by plan sponsors or financial service providers with the intention that such information serve as the primary basis for participants' investment decision making. In fact, most of these informational materials specifically disclaim any such intention and urge plan participants to contact their own professionals if they want investment advice.

Fourth, such advice must be given pursuant to a mutual agreement that the provider of any such advice will individualize it based on the particular needs of the participant. Given the generic nature of the information described above, the providers of such information do not intend to individualize it and, as is the case above, will typically disclaim any such intention. While it could be argued that certain types of the information described above, such as the interactive software, might provide the necessary tools to allow participants themselves to individualize the information, such information is merely that: a generic tool that may allow participants to customize their own retirement strategy.

Early last year the DOL announced its intention to issue an Interpretative Bulletin to clarify that the types of educational materials currently being provided in the defined contribution marketplace do not constitute investment advice. As stated by Olene Berg, Assistant Secretary of Labor for Pension and Welfare Benefits,

> We don't want plan sponsors to be discouraged from providing information. Our overall policy goal is to find ways to make plan sponsors more comfortable about providing their employees information.[32]

The SEC has expressed its intention to join the DOL in this effort to assure the employee benefits community that participant education does not constitute investment advice. SEC Commissioner Steven Wallman recently said that ERISA and the Advisers Act:

> while very well intentioned, may have had this unintended consequence of discouraging the provision of investment education and advice to...plan participants.
>
> This is not the right or necessary result...At the moment, it is my hope that the SEC and the [DOL] will be able to issue an important release in this area.
>
> My hope and expectation is that the release will allow employers and investment advisers to provide meaningful investment information and

advice to tens of millions of Americans. If we can, the release will be a *joint release*—one that will provide attorneys and laypersons alike with a single uncontradictory source of information on protected activities.[33]

On December 8, 1995, the DOL issued an exposure draft of its long awaited Interpretative Bulletin.[34] The DOL released this draft, entitled "Interpretative Bulletin Relating to Participant Investment Education," in an effort "to encourage employers and others to give pension plan participants valuable investment education."[35] Public reaction to this exposure draft has been overwhelmingly positive since, as expected,it confirms current intrepretations of the scope of ERISA Section 3(21) and provides specific examples of educational materials that do not constitute investment advice, including all of the ones described above. At the same time the DOL released its exposure draft, the SEC made public a letter in which it expressed its view that employers who provide their employees with investment information of the type described in the exposure draft generally are not subject to registration or regulation under the '40 Act, because such employers are typically "not in the business" of providing investment advice to their employees.[36]

The issuance of the exposure draft and the release of the SEC letter go a long way to calming the fears of the pension community. As a result we should expect to see a substantial increase in participant education efforts by plan sponsors and financial service firms.

WHAT DO PLAN SPONSORS WANT?

Plan sponsors measure the success of participant-directed retirement programs by asking the following objective questions:

1. What is the participation rate? What percentage of eligible employees have elected to participate in the plan? The higher the percentage, the more likely it is that the plan will help attract and retain personnel.

2. What is the average contribution rate? Does it vary by job classification or salary range? The higher it is, and the more uniform it is among salary classes, the less pressure there will be on the employer to provide other programs for particular segments of the employer's workforce.

3. What is the average investment return? Higher investment returns inevitably lead to higher participation and

contribution rates. Moreover, higher investment returns lead to greater retirement income adequacy for participants. This in turn decreases employee demand for other, often more expensive, employer-provided retirement benefits.

The answers to these objective questions help answer a broader subjective question that ultimately should be asked of a benefit program: Do employees widely accept the program as an employee benefit? The ultimate purpose of any employee benefit program from an employer's perspective is, after all, to help attract and retain a capable workforce. The employer must effectively communicate a retirement benefit program if it is to be widely accepted. Regulatory disclosure is not enough and sometimes gets in the way. But efforts appear to be underway in Washington to support the educational initiative needed to promote further employee acceptance of defined contribution plans.

PLANNING FOR THE FUTURE

Given the current agenda at the SEC and the DOL, there is hope that we will soon see a regulatory framework that encourages, rather than discourages, effective employee communications. The recent SEC no-action letter concerning the SPR and the DOL regulations under ERISA Section 404(c) are both steps in the right direction. Taken together, they allow for effective employee communications that satisfy Section 404(c) without running afoul of SEC prospectus delivery requirements. The next steps should include the issuance by the DOL of its Interpretative Bulletin on the education versus investment advice issue in final form and ultimate approval by the SEC of the use of a profile prospectus in all markets including defined contribution plans. Once all those steps have been taken, plan sponsors and financial service firms should be able to improve the effectiveness of participant education efforts and enhance employee acceptance of defined contribution plans as a key employee benefit.

ENDNOTES

1. These different plans refer to the Internal Revenue Code (IRC) section under which they are authorized. While all of them enable employees to make pretax salary reduction contributions, the relevant IRC sections limit their adoption to different types of employers. 401(k) plans can be adopted by for-profit employers; 403(b) plans can be adopted by public schools and IRC § 501(c)(3) not-for-profit organizations; and 457 plans can be adopted by state and local governments.

2. Employee Benefit Research Institute, *EBRI Databook on Employee Benefits*, 3d ed. (1995).

3. Access Research, cited in "401(k) Plans: How Plan Sponsors See the Marketplace," *ICI Research Report* (Winter 1995) (Investment Company Institute).

4. Ibid.

5. Labor Regulation § 2510.404c–1.

6. According to the ICI, the percentage of 401(k) assets invested in mutual funds grew from 9 percent to 23 percent between 1986 and 1993. See "401(k) Plans: How Plan Sponsors See the Marketplace," op cit.

7. Louis Loss and Joel Selgman, *Securities Regulation*, vol. I (Boston: Little Brown and Company, 1989), p. 169.

8. Ibid.

9. The sale of publicly offered securities on the secondary market is governed by the '34 Act.

10. § 5(b)(1).

11. § 5(b)(1).

12. § 5(b)(2).

13. June 9, 1995.

14. Fidelity Institutional Retirement Services Company, Inc. (available April 5, 1995).

15. Rule 482 was promulgated by the SEC in 1979 to permit investment companies to publish advertisements using any information contained in a fund's statutory prospectus, including performance information.

16. ERISA § 3(21).

17. ERISA § 404.

18. ERISA § 406.

19. ERISA § 408(b).

20. ERISA § 408(a).

21. See, e.g., '40 Act Section 17, which prohibits transactions between the mutual fund and affiliated persons of its underwriter absent an exemption.

22. ERISA § 401(b)(1); ERISA § 3(21)(B).

23. Labor Regulation § 2510.404c–1(b)(1)(ii).

24. Labor Regulation § 2510.404c–1(b)(2)(i)(A).

25. Labor Regulation § 2510.404c–1(b)(2)(i)(B).

26. Labor Regulation § 2510.404c–1(b)(2)(i)(B)(1).

27. Labor Regulation § 2510.404c–1(b)(2)(i)(B)(2).

28. Among those who contributed to this body of knowledge are Nobel laureates Harry Markowitz and William Sharpe with their respective works regarding the efficient frontier and modern portfolio theory. The portfolios are also supported by historical performance data of different asset classes over time, including data originally generated by Roger Ibbotson and Rex Sinquefield (and updated annually by Ibbotson Associates).

29. Aggregate defined benefit assets were allocated in 1993 as follows: equity = 42 percent, bonds = 27 percent, cash = 10 percent, other = 21 percent; aggregate defined contribution assets were allocated in 1993 as follows: equity = 45 percent, bonds = 23 percent, cash = 13 percent, other = 19 percent. *EBRI Databook on Employee Benefits*, 3rd ed., 1995.

30. For example, Fidelity's model portfolio for moderate investors is: equity = 40 percent, bonds = 40 percent, cash = 20 percent.

31. Labor Regulation § 2510.3–21(c).

32. Quoted in *EBRI Notes* 16, no. 5 (Employee Benefit Research Institute, May 1995).

33. Keynote Luncheon Address, ICI Investment Company Directors Conference, Washington, D.C., September 22, 1995.

34. DOL Release USDL: 95–503.

35. Ibid.

36. Letter dated December 5, 1995 to Olena Berg from Jack W. Murphy, Associate Director (Chief Counsel) of the SEC's Division of Investment Management.

11

ELEMENTS OF THE REGULATORY LANDSCAPE APPLYING TO PENSION PLANS

Mark Greenstein, *Rosenman & Colin LLP*

This chapter provides a brief overview of some of the provisions of the Employee Retirement Income Security Act of 1974 (ERISA), which help safeguard the assets of employee benefit plans. It then discusses how the Department of Labor (the department) has addressed recent developments in the marketplace that affect how plans are designed and operated.

ERISA was enacted in response to abuse that had occurred.[1] Prior to ERISA, employers who sponsored plans were not required to separately account for and set aside the funds they promised their employees for their retirement.[2] As a result, if an employer went under, employees lost both their jobs and their retirement. ERISA addressed this problem by requiring that retirement plans that promise a fixed income for retirement (defined benefit plans) be prefunded under one of several different schedules. Further, a portion of the benefit under such plans is insured by a government agency, the Pension Benefit Guaranty Corporation (PBGC).

In contrast, no government guarantee underlies an employee's benefits in the other type of pension plan, individual account plans, which includes 401(k) plans. Such plans consist of individual accounts, one for each employee. The value of such an account wholly depends upon amounts that the sponsor and/or employee places in the account, and their investment experience. Both plans are generally operated on a tax-qualified basis. This provides substantial tax benefits to both the employer and the employee. Contributions an employer makes to such a plan are immediately deductible, earnings on amounts invested by the plan are generally not taxed, and employees are not taxed until they remove amounts from their accounts (if they do not place such amounts in another tax-favored vehicle such as another tax-qualified plan or an IRA).

In recent years, employers lost interest in defined benefit plans due to several factors. Recent legislation has increased the potential liability of a sponsor when it establishes a defined benefit plan.[3] Further, the cost of establishing and operating such a plan are significantly higher than those associated with defined contribution plans. The result has been a shift to defined contribution plans, which include 401(k) plans under which employees can have amounts deducted from their pay excluded from their taxable incomes. Because the amount in such a plan will, in large measure, depend upon investment experience, a great deal of recent focus has been on such investment experience.

Employers who sponsor defined contribution plans can invest the funds in such plans themselves, hire someone else to invest the funds, or permit employees to make their own investments. If, as is typical in 401(k) plans, an employer permits employees to make their own investments, the sponsoring employer will generally be relieved of responsibility for the results of the employees' decisions if the employer complies with regulations issued by the department under section 404(c) of ERISA.

These regulations require that an employee have a reasonable opportunity to control the investment return of his account. They also require that a plan offer at least three different diversified alternatives and the opportunity to transfer funds between the different alternatives, and that the plan provides certain information relating to the available investment alternatives.

The required information is largely a response to a comment on the proposed regulations filed by a division of the Securities and Exchange Commission (the SEC). The SEC commented that the regulation should include disclosure similar to that required under securities law for each investment alternative available under a plan. This disclosure should permit an investor to compare different vehicles with similar investment objectives (e.g., two equity funds). Unfortunately, because most plans provide very limited ability to choose between similar vehicles, this type of comparative information is not likely to be the most helpful to the employee.[4] Instead, the most valuable information for the employee relates to the anticipated difference in the performance between different types of vehicles (e.g., an equity fund and a bond fund) because it is this choice that is likely to make the greatest difference in the funds an employee has available for retirement.

INVESTMENT EDUCATION

Surveys indicate that many employees make choices that are dramatically different from those that a professional money manager would make. A large though falling percentage of the funds in such accounts is invested in vehicles such as money market funds or insurance company guaranteed investment contracts that are safe over the short term, but that have historically provided for inferior returns over the longer time horizon that is typically relevant for an employee's retirement funds (more than 10 years).

Sponsoring employers have stated that they would like to assist their employees in making more informed investment choices. However, such employers are concerned that if they assist participants in making investment decisions, they could incur liability under ERISA and lose the primary benefit they receive by complying with section 404(c) of ERISA. Sponsors would have potential liability if they provided "investment advice" within the meaning of 29 CFR 2510.3–21. The department has recently issued a proposed interpretative bulletin (the bulletin) that would provide safe harbors in order to encourage sponsors to provide this type of information.

The safe harbors provided by the bulletin are based, in part, upon the information provided being consistent with generally accepted investment theories (e.g., equities outperform bonds over the long term). Because a plan sponsor that provided such generally accepted information would be very unlikely to incur liability in connection with providing information even if the bulletin had never been released, the bulletin, if finalized, would not offer much additional protection as a practical matter. However, it will provide sponsors with added comfort, and it should result in more employers providing such information and therefore in more employees making more educated investment decisions.

Under the bulletin, an employer or others could provide several types of information without incurring potential liability by reason of providing investment advice. Such information includes:

1. Descriptions of the investment alternatives provided by a plan.
2. General investment information such as the historic differences in rates of return between different asset classes based on standard market indexes and estimates of future retirement income needs.
3. Information that provides employees with models of asset allocation portfolios of hypothetical individuals with different time horizons and risk portfolios. However, such models must be based on generally accepted investment theories.
4. Interactive materials based on the information described in number 3 that provide an employee with the means to estimate future retirement income needs and assess the impact of different asset allocations on retirement income.

The principles enunciated in the bulletin do not break ground in any meaningful fashion. However, because the bulletin should result in more sophisticated investment decisions by employees, the department should issue it, or similar guidance, in final form.

CORPORATE GOVERNANCE

The department has recently emphasized how investments made by plans relate to the governance of the companies in which they invest, as well as other effects of plan investments. In this regard, the department has issued two interpretative bulletins, one concerning proxy voting and the second on "economically targeted investments."

PROXY VOTING

Private (and public plans with similar objectives) own a large portion of the value of the publicly traded equities in the United States market. As a consequence, some analysts argue that plans, as a group, cannot easily sell underperforming securities into the market. Therefore, these people reason, in order to enhance performance, plans should be active shareholders that influence management to make decisions in their best interest. Because the department believed that plans had not been sufficiently active as shareholders, it issued an interpretative bulletin (IB 94–2) to encourage managers of pension funds to focus on proxy voting.

IB 94–2 emphasizes that the person designated to vote proxies is responsible under ERISA for that function. It also provides a road map for allocating fiduciary responsibility for voting proxies that enables sponsors to allocate responsibility to the same person who makes the decision to buy or sell securities or to a different person.

The bulletin encourages plans to act in concert to influence management. The department, under Secretary Reich, has stated that plans should consider whether companies are "high performance workplaces" that invest in their workers when determining whether to make or retain an investment in a company.

As reported in *The Wall Street Journal*, the trustees responsible for investing the public pension funds for the employees of California have pioneered this type of activist approach. Initially, the trustees focused on what they perceived as favorable corporate policies. Subsequently, they retained independent consultants to suggest how "underperforming companies" could increase their performance. The latter approach resulted in increased returns.

The experience of the California system indicates that encouraging plans to exercise oversight responsibility, if properly implemented, could result in enhanced returns for plans. California's experience further indicates that it is not productive to approach companies with a preconceived, "one size fits all" idea of how they could better run their businesses. However, like California's experienced activist shareholders, trustees can add value if they advocate an individually designed approach to improving the performance of a particular company.

ERISA requires that action or inaction with respect to shares owned by a plan must not disadvantage a plan as reflected by an economic criterion. Therefore, decisions about voting proxies, coordinating action with other shareholders, or retaining consultants must be based on an expectation that the expense of the action taken will be exceeded by the anticipated value added to the shares owned by the plan, over the period of time the trustees anticipate that the plan will own such shares. Accordingly, persons responsible for designing policies for voting proxies must take expenses into account.

This limitation may prevent plans from taking innovative approaches. A plan fiduciary who holds his position because of his position with the sponsor would be at risk in pursuing a new approach to voting proxies or acting in concert with other investors if he could not economically justify taking such an approach. The risk would be enhanced if he were to expend plan assets (including his time, if the plan compensates him for such time) developing unproven approaches or acting in concert with others. Therefore, it appears likely that innovations in this area are likely to be developed using the resources of other parties. Likely candidates are state governments and/or plan sponsors. Some maintain that private financial institutions are less likely innovators because they frequently have existing or potential commercial relationships with major corporations that could be jeopardized if they were viewed as pressuring existing management.

Plans could also, under limited circumstances, use cutting-edge approaches in voting proxies. For example, if a plan hires an investment manager with a positive track record for using innovations, it would probably be prudent for such a manager to pursue new approaches with that plan as well. Similarly, if a plan sponsor itself had a positive record for innovation, the sponsor could use innovative approaches to proxy voting for plans it manages, including the assets of the plan it sponsors. However, because such a sponsor could be viewed as using plan assets to establish a track record for an innovative approach, and thus to benefit itself by enhancing its own reputation in the field, the sponsor should be able to demonstrate that there were sufficient assets in the fund, not including the assets of the sponsored plan, to validate the new approach.

"ECONOMICALLY TARGETED INVESTMENTS"

ERISA requires that the assets of a plan must be used exclusively to benefit the employees of the sponsor (and their beneficiaries). The department has taken the position that this requirement does not preclude a plan fiduciary, including a sponsor acting as such, from taking account of other benefits a plan investment may bring, so long as the plan's ultimate choice of an investment alternative is at least equal to that of other investment alternatives available to the plan (see Advisory Opinion 85–36A, issued by the Department of Labor).

Prior to 1994, the department had issued a number of letters that took this position. In 1994, the department issued Interpretative Bulletin 94–1 (IB 94–1) The department stated that the purpose of IB 94–1 was to codify its previous statements and therefore provide an easy reference source to remove artificial barriers to "economically targeted investments" (ETIs). IB 94–1 explained that such investments are designed to confer economic benefits on others, apart from the return to the plan.

The department also contracted for an ETI clearinghouse, which would provide information to plans in order to facilitate investments in ETIs.

When Republicans took control of Congress later in 1994, they questioned whether IB 94–1 was merely a codification of the department's previous statements. They have sponsored legislation to revoke IB 94–1, and to remove any funds for the clearinghouse.

At this time, it is unclear what the result of such legislation will be. However, it has placed a spotlight on ETIs. Therefore, before making such an investment or taking a course of action that will result in such an investment, plan fiduciaries should be able to justify it on a purely economic basis. In other words, the fiduciaries should anticipate that return to the plan, taking account of all administrative costs, will be at least equal to alternate investments or courses of action otherwise available to the plan.

In this regard, the survival of the clearinghouse may affect how a plan fiduciary analyzes ETIs. Unlike typical investments, no standardized format exists to rate ETIs, so the initial cost in evaluating these investments is likely to be higher. The clearinghouse could eliminate this disadvantage if it provided reliable, unbiased, and easily understood information concerning ETIs. In the absence of the clearinghouse, someone—a sponsor, a union, or a plan—would have to do the analysis. A plan could pay for this added expense only under limited circumstances. The total anticipated return to the plan, which would have to include consideration of the expense of analyzing the ETIs, would have to be at least equal to alternate investments available to the plan. This requirement would, as a practical matter, require that ETIs return more than other investments in order to offset the additional cost associated with evaluating them.

BARRIERS TO PLAN INVESTMENT—CURRENT ISSUES

ERISA does not contain an approved list of plan investments. Similarly, ERISA does not restrict investment by plans, other than requiring that plans must have meaningful recourse in U.S. courts against those who mismanage plan assets. This requirement does not prevent investment by plans in foreign securities, under circumstances specified in a regulation issued by the department (see Labor Regulation 2550.404b–1).

However, the requirement that plan assets be invested exclusively for the benefit of the plan together with the prohibited transaction provisions of ERISA have caused practical difficulties. Two areas where such difficulties have arisen include the operation of mutual insurance company general accounts (general accounts) and transactions involving derivatives.

Mutual insurance companies are owned by their policyholders. Some of the policies provide for returns that vary, depending upon the performance of investments made by the insurance company. The Supreme Court recently held that when a plan owns such a policy, its assets include the assets of the general account of a mutual insurance company.

Parties that engaged in transactions with mutual insurance companies had assumed that the general accounts of mutual insurance companies did not contain plan assets in structuring such transactions. Therefore, these parties did not consider the prohibition transaction provisions of ERISA, which would have prohibited some of these transactions. The department recently issued a class exemption (Prohibited Transaction Exemption 95–60) that provides administrative relief for almost all prohibited transactions between general accounts and third parties.

However, this exemption did not solve the problem of insurance companies dealing with their own affiliates. It also did not solve problems concerning the requirement that plan assets must be invested exclusively for the benefit of the plan (and could not solve these problems because the department does not have the authority to provide such relief). Thus problems complying with the requirements of state law that are designed to protect all policyholders as well as the solvency of insurance companies remain. Relief for these problems will probably have to be provided by Congress. Such relief could, for example, provide for circumstances under which general accounts do not have to contain plan assets. Relief could require enhanced disclosure about what could or could not be done to affect the value of a plan's investment in a general account. This would emphasize that the plan fiduciary that makes the investment is responsible for considering the fact that the insurance company is not subject to ERISA when it makes decisions concerning the general account.

Similarly, the prohibited transaction provisions of ERISA may cause difficulties for plans investing in derivatives. For example, ERISA prohibits the purchase or sale between plans and "parties in interest" with respect to the plan including service providers to the plan. In the case of transactions where the identity of the counterparty is not known, such as securities transactions executed over an exchange, this provision is not applicable. However, because the identity of the counterparty is typically known in derivative transactions, purchases or sales of derivatives between a plan and a "party in interest" with respect to the plan would be prohibited. Further the guarantee of the performance of the counterparty that engages in a derivative transaction with a plan could also be prohibited. While relief for such purchases or sales or guarantees could be provided by existing class exemptions issued by the Department, the fiduciary that directs the transaction could not engage in the transaction with itself or any affiliate.

The rapid evolution of the financial markets as well as the shift to employee-directed investments will result in challenges to the existing regulatory scheme. Providing regulators with the ability to address the constantly changing innovations in the marketplace will resolve some of the problems that arise. However, the major issues may have to be addressed by legislation, as Congress has the most freedom to balance the many competing interests.

E N D N O T E S

1. ERISA is only applicable to nongovernmental pension and welfare benefit plans.

2. ERISA does not require that any plan be established, but requirements are imposed if a company establishes a plan.

3. The federal agency that insures such plan has been afforded substantial new rights and remedies that can interfere with an employer's ability to operate its business.

4. An employer who selects investment choices for a plan is responsible under ERISA for selecting and retaining each such vehicle. If a sponsoring employer limits employee choice to one or two funds in each category (e.g., equity) information necessary for comparing similar vehicles is most important to the sponsor, who is responsible for selecting such funds, not the employee.

V

BANKS, INSURANCE COMPANIES, AND MUTUAL FUNDS:

Activities in the Boardroom

12

BANKS, MONEY MANAGERS AND INSURANCE COMPANIES, AND CORPORATE GOVERNANCE

If Not Them, Who?

Nell Minow, *Lens, Inc.* [1]

Carl Ichan's 1988 proxy contest at Texaco was a tough call. Both sides made presentations to the then-new Council of Institutional Investors, each making a strong case. Some of the institutions voted for Ichan, some for Texaco management. But at least one voted for both—T. Rowe Price voted the shares of one of its funds for management, and the shares of another for Ichan. They explained that this was consistent with the funds' announced strategies. They voted the short-term fund proxies for Ichan, and the long-term fund proxies were voted for management.

We are all familiar with, and even comfortable with, the notion that these same two funds might have contrary approaches to buying and selling stock. A short-term fund might be selling Texaco while a long-term fund managed by the same firm was buying it. But I submit that the justification for these opposite transactions does not apply to the case of proxy voting and other share ownership rights. While in some macro sense selling a stock with one hand and buying it with the other may be a zero sum transaction, from the perspective of the funds' investors, both funds (and their investors) are left with value, indeed, with the value they intended to acquire. But in the case of proxy voting, contrary votes cancel each other out in a way that benefits no one.

It is important to emphasize that I am categorizing shareholder activism, from strategic use of proxy voting to more affirmative initiatives, as an investment strategy. In other words, I mean that the exercise of ownership rights is as much a financial decision as the decision to buy, sell, or hold. In the institutional investor context, that means it is also as much a fiduciary decision, and as subject to the requirements of care, skill, prudence, and diligence. Everything I am advocating here is based on the showings by empirical evidence that shareholder activism consistently adds value and is highly competitive as an investment strategy, and increasingly so as markets become increasingly institutionalized.

The first to recognize the economic benefits of shareholder activism were the public pension funds. With a history of activist positions on social issues (like South Africa), the crucial barrier of willingness to oppose management publicly had already been crossed. When the takeover era of the 1980's led to unprecedented abuses of shareholders by both raiders and management, the public pension funds were ready to object. It was Texaco's greenmail payment to the Bass brothers that led to the creation of the Council of Institutional Investors in 1985. Further abuses led to the first shareholder proposals on corporate governance issues filed by institutional investors.

Until then, shareholder proposals had been the exclusive province of legendary corporate gadflies like the Gilbert brothers, Evelyn Y. Davis, and Wilma Soss. Soss inspired the delightful play (later a movie) "The Solid Gold Cadillac," still remarkably relevant to current corporate governance issues. This small group, cheered on by a few, ridiculed by more, and dreaded by corporate management, really created the field of shareholder activism. In 1932, the late Lewis Gilbert attended the annual meeting of New York City's Consolidated Gas Co. Gilbert was unhappy with the Chairman's refusal to recognize shareholder questions from the floor. He and his brother John Gilbert began buying stock (their investment policy was "never sell") and attending meetings. Their actions led to the SEC adopting rule 14a–8 in 1942, giving shareholders the right to have their proposals included in the company's proxy statements. The early gadflies began submitting shareholder resolutions on corporate governance topics like executive compensation, cumulative voting, and the location of the annual meeting.

Their approach was noted with approval by public interest advocates in the 1960s, and the range of topics for shareholder proposals expanded beyond the governance realm into social activism. Public pension funds, union pension funds, and church groups sponsored shareholder resolutions on social policy issues such as investment in South Africa or the sale of infant formula. The vote of less than 3 percent for Ralph Nader's 1970 "Campaign GM" shareholder proposals was hailed as a victory of unprecedented levels for a shareholder initiative. These groups have continued to submit social policy proposals, which have received votes of up to 20 percent. Some of these proposals have become something of a hybrid, combining elements of social policy and corporate governance. These include proposals regarding tobacco, defense manufacturing, environmental issues, South Africa, and Northern Ireland. Many of the resolutions sponsored on these subjects are sponsored by members of the Interfaith Center on Corporate Responsibility, an organization that promotes corporate social accountability. Typically, social proposals achieve a 7 to 10 percent vote from shareholders.

As institutional investors began to use governance resolutions to fight disenfranchising antitakeover devices installed by corporate management to protect themselves from changes in control, the levels of support grew. A little more than 20 years after Campaign GM, shareholder resolutions routinely get votes ranging from 20 to 40 percent, and occasionally even get majority support. In 1987, the first corporate governance resolutions from institutional investors (mostly relating to poison pills) were submitted at 34 companies, with votes in favor ranging from approximately 20 to 30 percent. A year later, two of these resolutions got majority votes, one concerning a poison pill, one prohibiting payment of greenmail. Both were at companies where proxy contests for control provided a good deal of visibility (and engendered a good deal of shareholder support).

The more significant development that year, though, was the Avon letter, issued by the DOL on February 23 (and formalized and expanded as Interpretive Bulletin 94–2 in 1994). It was the first ruling by the agency with jurisdiction over the ERISA funds that the right to vote proxies was a "plan asset." Money managers across the country began to establish procedures and policies for voting proxies.

In each succeeding year, the number of and level of support for governance-related shareholder resolutions increased, in large part due to the controversy over CEO pay, the adoption of confidential voting procedures, and the revision of SEC rules so that it was much easier and less expensive for shareholders to communicate with each other. The empirical research demonstrating the reliable extraordinary returns from shareholder activism[2] also gave more credibility to shareholder activism as an investment strategy, and a very competitive one.

MUTUAL FUNDS, INSURANCE COMPANIES, AND BANKS

Within the category of institutional investors, mutual funds, insurance companies, and banks have tended to be the least involved. None (with the exception of TIAA-CREF, technically an insurance company as discussed below) have ever sponsored a shareholder resolution. The limited information and commercial conflicts of interest have resulted in little and inconsistent interest in the value of shareholder monitoring.

Banks

Banks make up one large category of institutional investor, as trustees for everyone from pension plans to private estates. Trust administration is dominated by the complexities of federal income, gift, and estate taxes. Like other institutions, trusts have different classes of beneficiaries who have different kinds of interests.

In most instances, trusts are irrevocable, and, unless there is fraud, which is almost impossible to discover or prove, the bank can expect to continue to serve and collect fees as trustee, regardless of its investment performance. The security of the trust business may well be the reason for banks' traditionally poor investment performance. After all, in quite literal terms, they—unlike the beneficiaries—have nothing to lose. The trust contains "other people's money."

Banks generally get the most profitable, and certainly the most interesting, portion of their business from prominent local corporations. The smaller the community in which the bank is located, the more completely its tone is apt to be dominated by the locally based businesses. Banks, especially trust departments, do not encourage innovation, especially positions that are contrary to corporate management's recommendations on proxies.

R.P. Scherer

A rare lawsuit exposed the conflicts of interest that can occur when banks are trustees. In the late 1980s, Karla Scherer watched her husband, as CEO, ruin the R.P. Scherer Corporation, the company her father founded. As a major shareholder and board member, Ms. Scherer soon realized that the inefficiently run company was more valuable to shareholders if it was sold. However, the board repeatedly refused to consider this option, forcing her to take the matter to shareholders in the form of a proxy fight for board seats. She filed a lawsuit, challenging the way her trust shares were being voted. Scherer recalls that the most devastating blow to the ultimately successful campaign to force a sale was when she had to deal with her own trustees:

> Manufacturers National Bank, the trustee of two trusts created by my father for my brother and me, indicated it would vote all 470,400 shares for management, in direct opposition to our wishes. Remember, the bank's chairman sat on our board and collected director's fees as well as more than half a million dollars in interest on loans to Scherer. During the trial, the then-head of the bank's trust department admitted under oath that he did not know what the "prudent man" rule was. He also stated that he had arrived at his decision to vote the stock for management in less than 10 minutes, without conferring with us and after affording management an opportunity to plead its case over lunch in a private dining room at the Detroit Club.

The court initially ordered the appointment of an independent voting trustee, but the ruling was reversed.

Citicorp

The officer of Citicorp responsible for voting proxies determined that a proxy proposal made by Boeing management in 1987 was contrary to the interests of the shareholders, so she voted against it. She was summoned to the office of the chief executive officer to be reminded that Boeing was an important customer of the bank.

Insurance Companies

Insurance is the only major industry that has successfully avoided any significant federal regulation, although "special accounts" and subsidiary manager investments are subject to ERISA, SEC, and other federal rules. Life and casualty insurance companies prefer to deal with state legislatures, with whom they have historically had a close relationship.

State law has until most recent times severely circumscribed the extent to which insurers are allowed to invest their own funds in equities. Even today, only 14 percent of insurance fund assets are invested in common stocks. The current limit on stock is 20 percent of a life insurer's assets, or one-half of its surplus. But insurers still may not take influential blocks: life insurers may not put more than 2 percent of the insurance company's assets into the stock of any single issuer, and property and casualty insurers may not control a noninsurance company.[3]

Insurance companies, perhaps more than any other class of institutional investor, have a symbiosis with the companies in which they invest. First, they are usually holders of debt securities of any company in which they have an equity investment; debt instruments are very compatible with their needs because they have a reliable, set payout. Second, they typically have—or would like to have—a commercial relationship with the company by providing insurance or a product to meet the company's pension obligations. Third, like most other institutional shareholders, they are under no obligation to report to their customers on their proxy voting (but the companies whose proxies they vote— and with whom they do business—do know how they vote). Finally, like all other shareholders, the collective choice problem makes any form of activism uneconomic. Therefore, it is not surprising that the insurance industry consistently votes with management, regardless of the impact on share value. For example, one Midwestern insurance company wrote that its policy "is to support management positions on normal corporate policy and matters falling within the conduct of a company's ordinary business operations."[4]

TIAA-CREF

The Teachers Insurance and Annuity Association–College Retirement Equities Fund is in a category of its own, a pension fund and insurance company that is neither quite public nor quite private. The $125 billion fund manages pension money for 1.5 million teachers and other employees of tax-exempt organizations. It has $52 billion in equity securities. Its size and its unique position have given it unusual freedom from commercial or political restrictions on involvement with corporate governance. It is therefore not surprising that it has often been first, if not most visible, with shareholder initiatives. Its proposal to put International Paper's poison pill to a shareholder vote was the first such proposal by an institutional investor to be voted on. And it pioneered the "preferred placement" initiatives, asking companies not to offer preferred equities to "white squires" without shareholder approval.

In 1993, TIAA-CREF announced a broader program and released a detailed list of their corporate governance policies, saying that

"TIAA-CREF acknowledges a responsibility to be an advocate for improved corporate governance and performance discipline."[5] The policies provided the basis on which TIAA-CREF said it intended to pursue all of their portfolio companies. "The significant is not the three of four laggards you catch—it's that you get the herd to run," said Chairman John Biggs. "We need to scare all the animals."[6]

TIAA-CREF's policy statement focused on the board of directors. The policy statement encouraged boards with a majority of outside, independent directors, and said that key board committees should be made up exclusively of independents. Moreover, TIAA-CREF did not believe that directors who have other business dealings with the corporation (as a legal representative for instance) should be considered independent.[7] Biggs said that the fund would be willing to withhold votes for directors "where companies don't have an effective, independent board challenging the CEO."[8] They went even farther in 1995, when TIAA-CREF was importantly involved in the departure of the CEO and Chairman of W.R. Grace.

The 1993 policy statement also gave considerable space to a discussion of executive compensation issues—specifically, determining what constitutes "excessive" compensation, evaluating the soundness of policies and criteria for setting compensation, and deciding what constitutes adequate disclosure. There is some irony in the fact that CREF's own 1993 proxy statement, issued to its plan participant/shareholders, included a shareholder resolution concerning the executive compensation at CREF itself, complaining about the CEO's salary of over $1 million a year.

Mutual Funds

Mutual funds are trusts according to the terms of the Investment Company Act of 1940, which governs them. Otherwise, they bear little resemblance to the other institutional investors because of one important difference: they are designed for total liquidity. The "one-night stands" of institutional investment, they are designed for investors who come in and out on a daily basis, or at least those who want the flexibility to do so.

The investors are entitled to take their money out at any time, at whatever the price is that day. The investment manager has no control over what she will have to pay out or when she will be forced to liquidate a holding. So she views her investments as collateral; they are simply there to make good on the promise to shareholders to redeem their shares at any time. This is not the kind of relationship to encourage a long-term attitude toward any particular company the fund happens to invest in, and if there is a tender offer at any premium over the trading price, mutual fund investment managers have to grab it.

In the face of the real need to attract new money and to retain the investors she has in a world of perpetual and precise competition, the mutual fund manager cannot concern herself with the long term, because her investors may all show up today, and she must be prepared to stand and deliver.

Perhaps the most important limitation on the involvement of mutual funds in monitoring corporate managers is that they do not get paid for it. Their compensation is transaction-based. They get paid for buying and selling, but they do not get paid for voting proxies, and even their expenses are not paid for anything more, as discussed by Fidelity General Counsel Robert C. Pozen in his article, "Institutional Investors: The Reluctant Activists."

Yet, reluctant or not, they have had no alternative but to become more active in some cases. Fidelity is, at this writing, generally perceived as having enough of a stake to determine the outcome of the dispute at Chrysler between management and Kirk Kirkorian. While a small group of public pension funds and church groups file shareholder resolutions and issue press releases, some of the mutual funds have been stealth activists. A rare public glimpse of their power came in newspaper stories reporting that a group of Wall Street money managers insisted that American Express CEO James Robinson be removed, reversing the board's reversal of Robinson's resignation. Even then, howevever, the press was unable to determine exactly which money managers were present. Fund managers like Gamco and LCL have been willing to take an active and visible role, and their experience (and returns) may set an example that others will be willing to follow.

TRADING VERSUS MONITORING

Each institutional investor must make decisions about asset allocation. As Charles D. Ellis, one-time President of the Institute of Chartered Financial Analysts, noted: "Investment management, as traditionally practiced, is based on a single basic belief: Professional investment managers *can* beat the market. That premise appears to be false, particularly for the very large institutions that manage most of the assets of most trusts, pension funds, and endowments, because their institutions have effectively become the market."

William Fouse, chairman of Mellon Capital Management, says that pension fund management is "like monkeys trading bananas in trees." As he observed in an interview with *Forbes* writer Dyan Machan, "The money managers end up with a lot of the bananas." The efforts by pension fund fiduciaries to find active money managers who can beat the market over time have been unsuccessful. Most pension funds give their money to whichever manager did well the previous year, and given the statistical "regression to the mean," the odds are that manager will not do as well in the future.

An alternative strategy is *indexing*, in which a fund buys every stock in a given index, such as the S&P 500. The holdings are held, not traded, so the fund neither beats the market nor underperforms it—but replicates it. Forbes described an index strategy in simple terms: "Don't Just Do Something, Sit There."

Decisions are often based on recommendations by consultants. But consultants rarely recommend indexing. "[I]t would put them out of business if everyone did it. Pension funds pay consultants for objective advice on which funds to hire, but the same consultants charge managers fees for measuring the managers' performance...There are plenty of stories about managers who are recommended by the consultants on the grounds that the managers pay the consultants the biggest fees."[9]

A rare contrarian exception is the General Mills pension fund, which has dared to "break entirely out of the cycle...Instead of firing the stock picker who happens to be performing below the mean in a given year, General Mills gives him more money, taking from highest ranked performer. "As a result, General Mills has produced one of the best long-term records with 17 percent annualized equity return over the 15 years ending in 1992. It is therefore not surprising that a study of 135 funds with $700 billion in assets, concluded that "There was no positive correlation between performance and money spent on staff, managers, and other high-priced advice to get it."[10]

Every investor, whether individual or institutional, hopes to be the exception and beat the averages. This is reminiscent of the line about the poker game, "If we all play well, we can all make money." This hope, rather than any statistical evidence, accounts in part for the change in the way shareholders see themselves today: no longer as an owner but as a speculator.

Of course another of the incentives for a minimal sense of ownership by money managers is short-term self-interest. Active trading produces immediate transaction costs. Monitoring involves the commitment of resources for gains that are not immediately quantifiable, with the possible exception of shareholders who are large enough and aggressive enough to underwrite contests for control. In the longer term, this has involved a high price for the business system as a whole.

Transferability has had consequences for corporations as well. It means that the interests of shareholder and managers are based on incompatible premises. The investor will want to sell at the first sign that the stock may have reached its trading peak, whereas the manager wants stable, long-term investors. The American corporate system was initially based on the permanence of investor capital. But while the capital may have remained in place, the owners kept changing. Unintentionally, the growth of the institutional investors may have served to reintroduce stability in stock ownership. But that could not happen until the institutional investors were shocked into activism by the abuses of the takeover era.

An essential part of the theoretical underpinning for the market was the notion that shareholders should sell to each other, and as often as possible, to keep the markets "efficient." During the takeover era, it became clear that, though the system was designed to promote transferability above all, there was one kind of transfer that the system would not tolerate: the transfer of power from one group to another. Despite a strong theoretical commitment to "the market for corporate control," as soon as the means to create a genuine market were developed, corporations, lawyers, legislators, and even judges, worked quickly to obliterate it.

The shareholder has the exclusive control of the stock itself. But as a condition of the shareholder's limited liability, the shareholder gives up the right to control use of the corporation's property by others. That right is delegated to the management of the corporation. Indeed, it is one of the benefits of the corporate organization to the investor; he can entrust his money to people who have expertise and time that he does not. But it is also one of the drawbacks. Thus, it is this separation between ownership and control that has been the focus of the struggles over corporate governance.

Professor Melvin Aron Eisenberg writes of the "limits of shareholder consent,"noting that "under current law and practice, shareholder consent to rules proposed by top managers in publicly held corporations may be either nominal, tainted by a conflict of interest, coerced, or impoverished." In Eisenberg's view, shareholder consent is "nominal" when (as permitted under proxy rules) the shareholder does not vote at all and management votes on his behalf, or shares held by the broker or broker's depository are voted with no direction from the beneficial owner. Shareholder consent is "tainted" by a conflict of interest when an institutional investor votes in favor of a management proposal it would otherwise oppose, due to commercial ties to the company management (see below).

Shareholder consent is "coerced" when, for example, management ties an action that is attractive to shareholders, like a special dividend, to passage of a provision that may be contrary to their interests. For instance, in 1989, shareholders of Ramada Inc. were asked to approve a package of antitakeover measures, bundled with a generous cash payment. And shareholder consent is "impoverished" when "for example, shareholders may vote for a rule proposed by management even though they would prefer a different rule, because the proposed rule is better than the rule it replaces and management's control over the agenda effectively limits the shareholders' choice to the existing rule or the proposed rule." This is a reflection of management's vastly superior access to the proxy, both procedurally (in terms of resources) and substantively (in terms of appropriate subject matter). Eisenberg has described shareholders as "disenfranchised."

The disenfranchisement of the modern shareholder has been developing for over a century, but it took the events of the last decade to bring it to public attention. In the 1980s, the takeover era itself was a symptom of the problems created by the failure to link ownership and control. As I describe below in more detail, the abuses of shareholders by both managers and raiders made it clear that there was not enough accountability to shareholders, and that this lack of accountability was detrimental to the competitiveness and vitality of American companies. But, as noted above, the fact that the disconnect was inadvertent was irrelevant to one important fact—it was convenient, even ideal, for those it most benefited. When efforts to reconnect ownership and control began in the mid-1980s, shareholders found that the very problem of their inability to act made it all but impossible to regain their ability to hold corporate management accountable, especially when corporate management had no interest in changing a system that was working very well from their perspective.

As a result, Harvard Professor Michael Jensen predicted in *The End of the Public Corporation* that the "ownerless" modern venture without the discipline of accountability would inevitably be unable to compete. He saw the leveraged buyouts that had reconnected management and ownership at the end of the 1980s as the model for the future.

Shareholders are often referred to as the "owners" of the corporation, but the corporation's "legal personality" raises questions about whether it can be "owned" in any meaningful and effective way. There will always be agency costs in any corporate structure in which someone other than management owns equity. Public companies will continue to have managers with agendas different from their owners'; the governance challenge is to require that the resolution of conflicts be an open process between entities that are informed, motivated, and empowered.

The regulatory framework governing the issuance and trading of public securities and the functioning of exchanges was almost entirely set up by two landmark statutes of the New Deal era. Congress passed the 1933 Securities Act and 1934 Securities and Exchange Act after exhaustive debate and in response to overwhelming evidence of mismanagement, deception, and outright fraud during the stock market boom of the late 1920s. In the Public Utility Holding Company Act of 1935 and the Investment Company Act of 1940, multiple classes of common stock with differing voting characteristics were flatly prohibited for the affected companies. Rather than attempt to remedy specific mistakes or abuses with industrial companies, lawmakers attempted a far more difficult task; they tried to set up a process of corporate accountability—an impartial set of rules preserving the widest possible latitude for shareholders to protect their financial interests. In searching for a reliable and familiar model, they turned to America's own traditions of political accountability.

Shareholders were seen as voters, boards of directors as elected representatives, proxy solicitations as election campaigns, corporate charters and by-laws as constitutions and amendments. Just as political democracy acted to guarantee the legitimacy of governmental or public power, the theory went, so corporate democracy would control—and therefore legitimate—the otherwise uncontrollable growth of power in the hands of private individuals. Underpinning that corporate democracy, as the universal franchise underpinned its political counterpart, was the principle of one share, one vote.

It is not difficult, in this context, to establish a standard for the prudent exercise of ownership rights for pension fiduciaries. Their commitment to the long term makes them good, if not perfect, corporate citizens. It is much more difficult to argue that effective monitoring is cost-effective for investors whose profit is principally derived from buying and selling in the short term. Robert Monks and I refer to these investors as the "one-night-stands." For institutions whose commitment is to liquidity, rather than long-term security, the prospect of buying low and selling high is so beguiling that a lucrative industry of "active money management" has flourished. This is, notwithstanding the reality that from a macro perspective institutional investors are the market and, therefore, cannot hope to beat its performance. Yet they still focus on trading, rather than monitoring, as a way to increase value.

For the effect of this difference, compare the T. Rowe Price votes at Texaco to the 1993 announcement of the proxy voting policies of the Campbell's Soup pension fund.

Campbell Soup Company
In July of 1993, Campbell Soup Company's $1 billion pension fund became the first major ERISA plan to make a commitment to "investing" in shareholder activism. Until that point, institutional shareholder activism had been largely the province of public pension funds. Proud of its own corporate governance structure and record, Campbell's pension fund announced that it would direct the firms managing their pension fund's equity investments to vote their proxies against companies that elect more than three inside directors or reprice stock options after falling stock prices leave them with little value. Campbell also said it would direct its money managers to vote their proxies to emphasize linking executive pay to performance.

But Campbell is an exception. Despite undeniable evidence of the value of share ownership rights, many institutional investors continue to ignore them. The two primary obstacles are collective choice problems and conflicts of interest.

Collective Choice

The incentives driving shareholder actions can be compared to the famous logical problem called "the prisoner's dilemma." Two co-conspirators are captured and placed in separate cells by the police. They are each told that if neither confesses, there will not be enough evidence , and both will go free. If one confesses, only that prisoner will get a reduced sentence. If both confess, both go to jail for a reduced term. Each must sit, unable to communicate with the other, and decide what to do. The dilemma is that an action that may benefit the individual making the choice (whether silence or confession) may have adverse consequences for the group (prison), whereas an action that benefits the group (silence) may have adverse consequences for the individual (prison, if the other confesses). This is also referred to as the problem of "collective choice" and the "free rider" problem. Any shareholder who wants to exercise ownership rights to influence a company must undertake all of the expenses, for only a pro rata share of the gains, if there are any. This problem has also produced one of this field's better oxymorons, by giving rise to the term for shareholders who deem it uneconomic to become involved in governance: "rational ignorance."

Conflicts of Interest

Money managers have commercial relationships with corporations. They also vote proxies on behalf of the beneficial holders. The beneficial holders do not know how the votes are cast on their behalf. In almost all cases, the companies who are or might be doing business with the money managers do know how their votes are cast. Thus, the money managers have every incentive to vote with management, even when it may not be in the interests of the beneficial holders. The results of this conflict of interest have been discussed in detail (see, for example, *Conflicts of Interest in the Proxy Voting System*, by James E. Heard and Howard D. Sherman).

Collective choice problems and conflicts of interest are the two classic justifications for government intervention. The Department of Labor (DOL), responding to just these two obstacles to effective exercise of ownership rights by institutional shareholders, has issued a series of letters, enforcement surveys, and, most recently, a formal interpretive bulletin, determining that exercise of share ownership rights is a fiduciary obligation. The department did not proscribe any particular action, and did not even require written proxy policies. It merely said that these decisions must be done prudently, based on thoughtful and reasonable analysis. The impact on the ERISA community has been dramatic. A similar ruling by the SEC seems at least equally justified and equally likely to produce meaningful results. My own recommendation would be to go further than the DOL and require disclosure of proxy policies (or even of the existence of proxy policies). And both the DOL and the SEC should make it clear that the costs of active monitoring may be paid for by the beneficiaries. Furthermore, the new law limiting shareholder lawsuits requires the involvement of institutional investors to prevent control of litigation by the "Delaware regulars" whose abuse of the system aided no one's interests but their own. The DOL and the SEC should consider issuing guidelines requiring institutional investors under their jurisdiction to evaluate involvement in these lawsuits with the same cost-benefit calculus they apply to trading decisions. The government needs to be involved to remove the restrictions to effective monitoring; the institutions will do the rest.

Ultimately, all institutional investors, including mutual fund managers, should consider share ownership rights a valuable asset that can and should be exercised to preserve and enhance value:

- They should do it because it makes money, as shown by empirical evidence.
- They should do it because they are required to, as a fiduciary, whether the SEC says so explicitly or not.
- They should do it because they need to, to be competitive, as investors become more aware of the benefits of effective exercise of share ownership rights.
- They should do it because if they don't, someone else will, and they won't like the results. The problem with being a free rider is that you can't control the direction of the ride.

The paradoxical result of passive investing is active owning. Says James Dowling, chairman of Burson-Marsteller, the public relations firm that in 1995 established a corporate governance practice to advise CEOs and boards on how to operate in the changed environment: "The public funds have so much money that they find it's harder to find new companies to invest in than to try to turn around poorly performing ones." Says Jennifer Morales, executive director of the Houston Firemen's Relief Retirement Fund: "We don't want to sell. If a company can be improved, why should we be the ones to leave?"[9]

ENDNOTES

1. A portion of this chapter is adapted from Robert A.G. Monks and Nell Minow, *Watching the Watchers: Corporate Governance for the 21st Century* (Cambridge, MA: Blackwell, 1995).

2. See, for example, Stephen L. Nesbitt, "Long-Term Rewards from Corporate Governance" (January 5, 1994); Stephen L. Nesbitt, "The 'CalPERS Effect:' A Corporate Governance Update" (July 19, 1995); and Tim C. Opler and Jonathan Sokobin, "Does Coordinated Institutional Activism Work? An Analysis of the Activities of the Council of Institutional Investors," (August 1995).

3. Mark J. Roe, "Legal Restraints on Ownership and Control of Public Companies," paper presented at the Conference on the Structure and Governance of Enterprise, Harvard Business School, March 29–31, p. 8.

4. James E. Heard and Howard D. Sherman, "Conflicts of Interest in the Proxy Voting System" (Washington, DC: Investor Responsibility Research Center, 1987), p.22.

5. TIAA-CREF, *Policy Statement on Corporate Governance* (New York: September 17, 1993).

6. Leslie Scism, "Teacher's Pension Plan to Give Firms Tough Exams," *The Wall Street Journal*, October 6, 1993, p. C1.

7. TIAA-CREF, *Policy Statement on Corporate Governance* (New York: September 17, 1993).

8. Leslie Scism, "Teacher's Pension Plan to Give Firms Tough Exams," *The Wall Street Journal*, October 6, 1993, p. C1.

9. Dyan Machan, "Monkey Business," *Forbes*, Oct. 25, 1993, p. 190.

10. Ibid., pp. 188, 190.

11. Thomas A. Stewart, "The King Is Dead," *Fortune*, January 11, 1993, p. 36.

PART

VI

MUTUAL FUNDS

13

THE REGULATION OF DISCLOSURE IN THE COMPUTERIZED AGE

Michael J. Downer, *Senior Vice President–Fund Business Management Group and Secretary–Capital Research and Management Company*[1]

"He who does not look ahead remains behind. "
—*Spanish proverb*

Imagine obtaining financial planning advice and handling your weekly banking and investment chores all with a few mouse clicks from a personal computer during the time it takes to drink a single cup of coffee. This financial future, for some, is now. Developments in technology are creating dramatic new opportunities for financial services firms that could further blur the traditional distinctions between the banking, insurance, and mutual fund businesses. The growing use of computer networks and other types of new electronic media[2] for personal finance raises a number of issues. In this chapter we will look at historical perspectives, various alternatives to current mutual fund disclosure practices, and some of the challenges technological advances may present.

NEW ELECTRONIC MEDIA

"The future isn't what it used to be."
—*Yogi Berra*

Innovations such as the personal computer, cellular telephone, compact disc player, CD-ROM, commercial cable television, on-line services, and commercial fax machines—each introduced during the past 20 years— have profoundly altered the way we live. These technologies—all novelties when introduced—have become ubiquitous and essential to daily life.[3] More than 200 million personal computers (PCs) are installed around the world (more than half are in the U.S.). In 1994, more PCs were purchased for homes than televisions. Commercial on-line services have also been growing at a lightning pace.[4] Subscriptions to U.S. on-line services have grown to 15 million in 1995 from 9 million in 1994. By comparison, it took more than 100 years for *The Wall Street Journal* to build its current base of less than 2 million subscribers.

In fact, because electronic media-related technology, and in particular the Internet,[5] is progressing so quickly, it is hard to pick up any news or legal publication these days without being confronted by stories about some aspect of the information highway[6] and cyberspace.[7] In spring 1995, *Time* magazine devoted an *entire* special issue to cyberspace. *Internet* has become a widely recognized term today, although most people had never heard of it a mere two years ago. The Internet's graphic- and commerce-oriented World Wide Web (the Web)[8] is attracting the most attention. Virtually every national news organization also publishes electronically through the Internet or an on-line service or both. These developments have led many people to believe that the Internet will not only become a primary source for investment information and disclosure but also a major vehicle for marketing mutual funds as well.[9]

When thinking about applications for new technology and their implications, it is always helpful to consider past predictions about how a certain technology would develop. One of my first experiences in kindergarten (which still seems like yesterday even though Ike was president at the time) was seeing a film about the future. The film told us that conventional phones would soon be replaced with phones that would also provide images of callers, and that robots would make most household chores obsolete. It is true that telephones and robots are now used in ways few could have predicted decades ago, but most people still do not see each other when talking on the phone and few homes are robot-equipped.

The future was clearly not obvious to those who made that movie. Likewise, those who believe that they know how the Internet and other new technologies will shape the future are probably in for a rude awakening. However, they are in good company. For example, in 1940, the jet engine looked very impractical to a committee of the National Academy of Sciences because it would have to weigh 15 times more than an internal combustion engine to deliver the same horsepower. In 1949, IBM believed that it would receive no more than 15 orders for its computer. (Of course, the fact that a single computer needed more than 18,000 vacuum tubes to function might have had something to do with this prediction.) Like many technologies, electricity and lasers did not find major uses for decades after their discovery because they did not replace something else that already existed.[10] George Orwell, in his classic book *1984*, suggested that the development of electronic media would permit a Big Brother police state to control the flow of information; however, the opposite turned out to be true. Electronic information is harder to control than just about any form of communication. Consequently, the more frequently information is transmitted in digital form, the more difficult it will become to regulate. Accordingly, regardless of whether you believe that the Internet and other computer networks will remain merely sophisticated communication systems or will eventually develop into centers of information and commerce used by the masses, replacing paper documents and the neighborhood mall, one thing is clear: new electronic media hold tremendous promise unimaginable just a few short years ago. This has led some of the largest fund marketers and advertisers to start thinking about ways they can reach their existing and prospective customers through the Internet and other new electronic media. The relentless stream of new and better technology of this type *without a doubt* will change investing habits especially as the computer literate youngsters of today become the investors of tomorrow; it is not as clear, however, over what time period and in what form this change will occur.[11]

While the use of personal computers and computer networks is growing tremendously in percentage terms, it is important to remember that not everyone is "wired." According to recent surveys, only a half to perhaps less than a third of U.S. households have computers.[12] The three largest on-line services, America Online, CompuServe, and Prodigy, for all their explosive growth, have a little more than 10 million subscribers combined. It is estimated that fewer than 40 million people worldwide have access to the Internet. Consequently, in spite of today's hyperbole, a relatively small number of individuals obtain information, let alone conduct business, through the Internet today.

Perhaps it will take some additional technological development for *most* individuals to conduct business electronically, such as the development of an interactive television system that would obviate the need to use personal computers for many functions. If such a system gets off the ground, it could have far wider appeal and probably would not involve passwords and boot-ups. Moreover, since the typical mutual fund shareholder today is a man in his 60s who tends not to care about technology-driven services, it may be a while until the Internet as a financial tool really catches on.[13] In fact, many businesses that are now jumping on the Internet bandwagon probably will wind up losing large amounts of money while new technologies continue to evolve.

THE DIFFERENCE ELECTRONIC MEDIA CAN MAKE

"In the future, everything will be digital."
—*William Gates*

Three major interrelated developments[14] have already begun to alter radically how mutual funds communicate.

The first is *interactivity*. The proliferation of personal computers now permits tremendous interaction with an amazingly broad array of information through computer networks such as the Internet and on-line services.[15] In addition, future disclosure documents may be able to talk back and answer questions. Electronic filters called *agents* may be used to create custom disclosure-type documents containing only information deemed to be important by the reader, not regulators or fund sponsors.[16]

The second is *digitization*. While it probably will be some time before clothing will be available in virtual form or individuals can be beamed through space as depicted in *Star Trek*, information and entertainment are increasingly becoming digitized. Hard copy of such materials will ultimately no longer be physically transported from place to place. Rather, most information will move instantly in digitized form weightlessly across the street or across the globe. For example, in the not too distant future, people will be able to purchase music by downloading it to their computer rather than going to a music store.

The third—and most significant—is *multimedia*.[17] The ability to integrate sound, graphics, video, and text together into a single document will have a profound impact on the future of mutual fund disclosure. As computers become more powerful, they will revolutionize the way disclosure is presented. Investors have complained for years about the "legalese" in prospectuses but simplification efforts have been at best imperfect solutions to a larger problem. Such simplified documents potentially can remove a level of detail that is important to some investors. Offering different levels of detail in the prospectus and statement of additional information, for example, does not solve the problem because the two documents cannot easily be read together. Traditional hard copy prospectuses, usually little more than black and white text that is generally complex and often poorly written, lend themselves to *linear* types of organization. Sentences, paragraphs, pages, and chapters follow one another in an order determined not only by the author but also by the physical structure of the document. Electronic multimedia, however, is more flexible. It emphasizes visual presentation, it deals with color inexpensively, and it allows more opportunities for multidimensional communication. With digital information, the physical limitations of paper disappear. Using hyper-links readers can move more freely between different levels of detail.[18] Digital information can be reordered, sentences expanded, and words given instant definitions. As multimedia is refined and incorporates concepts such as virtual reality,[19] these new ways of presenting information could truly gain mass appeal.

CURRENT REGULATORY ENVIRONMENT

"If you wait for tomorrow, tomorrow comes. If you don't wait for tomorrow, tomorrow comes."
—*Old West African Saying*

The Securities and Exchange Commission (SEC or commission) has recognized for some time the potential of electronic disclosure. Indeed, Commissioner Steven Wallman has said that "over time, electronic delivery is going to be the investor's choice of first resort."[20] In the last several years, the SEC staff has fostered the use of electronic delivery systems by converting to electronic filings via the "electronic data gathering, analysis and retrieval system" (known as EDGAR),[21] starting a Web site to make disclosure materials available to the public and, recently, making it clear that the "use of electronic media should be at least an equal alternative to the use of paper-based media."[22]

In February 1995, the SEC staff for the first time interpreted the term *prospectus* to include an electronically encoded prospectus. In an interpretive no-action letter to the law firm of Brown & Wood, the commission required a number of conditions to be met for the delivery of an electronic prospectus to be considered valid. The *Brown & Wood* letter paved the way for mutual funds to deliver prospectuses on-line, but left a number of unresolved questions, such as whether annual reports and proxies could also be delivered through electronic media. Because prospectuses could be delivered electronically, materials that are not required to be given to investors, such as supplemental sales literature and applications for funds, could now also be delivered electronically, subject, of course, to National Association of Securities Dealers (NASD) and state requirements for hard copy sales materials. Recognizing the growing use of electronic media for sales materials, the NASD (which regulates fund sales materials) has not surprisingly decided that rules governing advertisements and sales literature apply equally to electronic messages.[23]

In October 1995, the SEC superseded and significantly expanded the *Brown & Wood* letter by issuing an interpretive release clarifying that the securities laws permit companies to transmit prospectuses as well as other corporate information such as proxies and annual reports to investors through electronic media. The SEC said that "the extent to which required disclosure is made, as opposed to the medium for providing it, should be most important to the analysis of whether sufficient disclosure has occurred under the securities laws."[4]

Two factors must be taken into account in determining whether a disclosure document has been effectively delivered under the SEC's interpretation of the securities laws: notice and access. Investors must receive adequate and timely notice that a document is available to them. If an electronic document is delivered in a CD-ROM or by E-mail, that communication itself should constitute sufficient notice. However, things become trickier when a document is delivered through a computer network such as a Web site or on-line service. In such a case, funds should consider the extent to which the electronic communication provides notice and, if necessary, should provide a separate, similar notice on paper. When investors receive documents through the mail, they are generally provided with access to the required disclosure. Investors who receive information through electronic means should have comparable access. For example, if a document is delivered through a computer network, recipients should have access to it for as long as the delivery requirement applies. Funds delivering documents electronically should make it easy for intended recipients to get to the information provided. For example, readers should not have to wade through a series of ever-changing and confusing menus.

Since the ultimate responsibility for delivering disclosure documents to investors is with the issuer or other legally responsible party, issuers and others should have reason to believe that any electronic means selected for delivery will, in fact, result in the delivery. Examples of how delivery requirements may be satisfied include:

1. Obtaining an informed consent from an investor whereby the investor chooses to receive certain information through a specific electronic medium, together with sufficient notice and access.

2. Obtaining evidence that the investor actually received the information.

3. Faxing the information.

4. Establishing that an investor used a hyper-link embedded into a document to obtain required disclosure.

If an investor's consent to receive electronic documents is revoked, issuers must be prepared to deliver paper versions of documents.

Even as the SEC was helping mutual funds merge into traffic on the information highway, it was busy launching a Web site of its own in order to make SEC filings and other reports available to investors quickly. In April 1996, the SEC opened an electronic mailbox to encourage the public to send in comments about electronic prospectuses and other Internet related issues.[25] When the SEC Web site opened, SEC Chairman Arthur Levitt said it was all part of his goal of promoting the Internet as a way to reach investors faster and for securities issuers to cut down on paperwork.[26]

In May 1996, the SEC issued another interpretive release regarding the use of electronic media as a complement to its October 1995 intrepretive release. The May 1996 release makes it clear that broker-dealers, transfer agents, and investment advisers may use "electronic media as an alternative to paper-based media" (subject to the same kinds of notice, access and evidence of delivery considerations outlined in the October 1995 release), to satisfy their delivery obligations under the securities laws. The release goes on to state that electronic communications *from* broker-dealers' customers and investment advisers' clients can also satisfy certain requirements under the securities laws regarding written customer consent and client acknowledgment. Significantly, this May interpretative release paves the way for the broad use of electronic confirmation statements.

In May 1996, the SEC also adopted some technical changes to its rules and forms that are premised on the delivery of paper documents in light of the October 1995 release regarding the use of electronic media and the availability of electronic filings on the SEC's Web site. For example, if a mutual fund intends to disseminate its prospectus electronically and is an electronic filer, it must now include a statement on the cover of its prospectus that the SEC "maintains a Web site (http://www.sec.gov) that contains the Statement of Additional Information, material incorporated by reference, and other information regarding registrants that file electronically with the Commission." This requirement demonstrates the growing importance of the Web. Perhaps, one day the Web will largely eliminate the need to deliver individual prospectuses to investors.[27]

Clearly, there are no remaining federal legal impediments to conducting fund business through various electronic media. Not surprisingly, virtually every major fund company is either currently making information available electronically or actively studying its options in this area. A number of fund groups employ the Internet or commercial on-line services to get their messages to investors.[28] For example, both the Fidelity and Vanguard fund groups offer information through America Online. The Vanguard service offers a four-step course in portfolio diversification. Investors can also receive prospectuses (specifically tailored for electronic viewing), obtain account information, or share ideas with other investors through message boards. The Fidelity service offers investors an asset allocation worksheet and permits them to review fund performance and other data, order prospectuses, or retrieve a copy of Fidelity Online Xpress, which can be used to place orders for stocks, options, and mutual funds. In many cases, information about fund groups is available from third parties through the Internet without the direct cooperation of the funds involved.

In light of these developments, as methods for obtaining signatures electronically gain acceptance and conducting monetary transactions through the information highway becomes more secure, it may become common for many investor transactions, including fund purchases, to be done directly "off the screen."[29]

Given the potential benefits of disseminating investment information through electronic means, lawmakers and regulators should continue to do everything possible to promote the development of electronic media as an alternative for paper-based delivery. One further step that could be taken in that direction would be to aggressively update the EDGAR system to accommodate graphics and Web compatible text. Options regarding privatizing EDGAR should be seriously considered to aid its development.[30]

REGULATORY QUESTIONS AND ISSUES

"To err is human, but to really screw up requires a computer."
—*1990s Saying*

The expanded use of various electronic media, however, also has a dark side. It will become more difficult to protect investors because swindlers can now reach millions of potential victims quickly and inexpensively. This highlights the need to educate the public not only about investments and risk, but also about other considerations when investing, including what they should expect from a reputable fund manager. While the industry and regulators may be diligent in crafting appropriate positions and rules, those interested only in bilking investors can simply ignore them. In addition, electronic disclosure documents are susceptible to computer viruses and cyber-vandalism. Moreover, electronic sales materials are very easy to duplicate, even though they may be copyrighted. Accordingly, fund sponsors and regulators will need to monitor electronic media carefully. Finally, security concerns loom large in thinking about the Internet and commerce. Electronic thievery is bound to occur more often as more financial business is done on-line.[31]

The SEC, as well as other regulators and law enforcement authorities, understands the potential for on-line mischief. Bill McLucas, the SEC enforcement chief, has issued public warnings that the commission has the means to catch individuals who are determined to defraud investors. He said the SEC reviews certain on-line services and scans communications to identify potential fraud.[32] In addition, the commission staff is on the lookout for Internet users acting as unregistered broker-dealers and pushing phony securities. To date, however, the SEC has gone after only a handful of investment scams promoted through the Internet.

Do-it-yourself software also presents risks. The mutual fund adviser feature of Quicken's financial planning CD-ROM software is a good example of what is currently available. This program asks the user a number of questions and then presents her with an asset allocation mix consisting of several specific fund options. The program also illustrates risk concepts using video (unfortunately, by using a gambling analogy). *While interactive asset allocation programs can provide investors with investment analysis, they are not substitutes for human wisdom and judgment.* When a fund company provides such a program to potential investors, it raises questions as to whether the sponsor should be subject to the same types of suitability requirements as registered representatives.

With each passing day, state and national borders become less meaningful. When information enters the Internet, it is potentially available on a global basis.[33] Internet information promoting the sale of a fund registered in the United States (and not qualified for sale outside the United States) that is seen and acted upon by an investor in another country could potentially subject the fund and its distributor to liability if the fund accepts the investment.[34] The Internet also makes it easier for advisers based outside the United States to offer unregistered investments to U.S. investors.

The on-line gambling phenomenon illustrates the challenge that regulators face. Computer-savvy entrepreneurs are offering everything from card games and slot machines to horse racing and sports betting on the Web. Users gamble with real money, which is automatically withdrawn from an account they set up, usually by credit card. In the United States, gambling on the Internet is illegal. But it is not hard for casinos to get around the laws. On-line gambling providers keep their computer headquarters and gamblers' bank accounts outside of U.S. boundaries. Location makes no difference in cyberspace; it is just as easy to dial up a computer in Los Angeles as it is to connect to one in London. While casino operators may be beyond the reach of U.S. law, individual gamblers could face charges for violating gambling laws.[35] U.S. investors purchasing non–U.S. funds over the Internet would not be prosecuted; however, they would be running the risk of being fleeced.

Finally, the states have begun to consider the impact of the Internet on their securities laws. In December 1995, the "Offers on the Internet" and "Investment Companies" Committees of the North American Securities Administration Association, Inc. (the national voice of the 50 state securities agencies responsible for the protection of investors) issued a comment letter regarding the SEC's October 1995 interpretive release that was generally favorable. However, it emphasized additional procedures to provide evidence of delivery and better record keeping by issuers. In addition, Pennsylvania and at least nine other states have adopted rules which exempt from registration certain Internet offers of securities not intended for residents of those states.[36] Hopefully, the states will do nothing to impede the use of electronic media.

CONCLUSION

"I never think of the future. It comes soon enough."
—*Albert Einstein*

The electronic technological developments of today are like a tsunami—unpredictable, overwhelming, and unstoppable. From a legal and policy standpoint, we should be open to future developments so that investors can fully utilize the advantages of new technological advances. It would be a shame if the legal structure prevented investors from obtaining information in new and better ways. After all, perhaps the day will come when investors will prefer to obtain investment information from robots or through video phones instead of computers.

ENDNOTES

1. Capital Research manages the fourth largest group of mutual funds in terms of assets in the United States.

2. The term *electronic media* includes such items as videotapes, faxes, CD-ROMs, E-mail, etc. The term *E-mail* stands for *electronically transmitted message*. The term *CD-ROM* is short for *compact disc-read only memory*. One CD-ROM can hold the same amount of information as 700 floppy disks.

3. See Les Freed and Frank Derfler, *Building the Information Superhighway*, (Emeryville, California: Ziff-Davis Press, 1994) for a description of these technologies and how they and others are being combined.

4. See *AP Online* "U.S. Ready for Telecom Advance," (October 2, 1995). See also *Fortune*, "Why Every Red Blooded American Owns A...Personal Computer" (May 29, 1995) p. 86. Users of on-line services increased by more than 64 percent in 1995 to about 15 million according to the *Electronic Information Report*.

5. The Internet is nearly 40 million computers all connected and communicating with each other. Some observers consider it to be the most important branch of the developing "information highway." *See* Laurence Canter and Martha Siegel, *How to Make a FORTUNE on the Information Superhighway*, (New York: Harper Collins Publishers, Inc., 1994) for a description of the Internet and its use as a marketing tool. In describing the Internet *Time* magazine said, "It's as if some grim fallout shelter had burst open and a full-scale Mardi Gras parade had come tumbling out." "Special Issue: Welcome to Cyberspace," *Time*, 145, No. 12 (Spring 1995) pp. 10–11.

6. The term *information highway* refers to anything in the infrastructure that permits you to convey or transmit information. Whatever is available—cable, wire, wireless, or even the postal service—is part of the information highway. However, as used herein *information highway* refers to its electronic media. See "The Information Tidal Wave Issues and Challenges," *The Journal of the American Corporate Counsel Association—ACCA Docket*, 13, No. 1 (January/February 1995), p. 10.

7. The term *cyberspace* generally refers to "electronic networks...where many kinds of data and stimuli can be instantaneously communicated around the globe." It also refers to a "new order, a new vision, a new set of possibilities, interactions, and relationships, all of which we acknowledge are linked to new and powerful means for relating to information." See M. Ethan Katsh, *Law in a Digital World* (New York/ Oxford: Oxford University Press, 1995). *Cyberspace* was first used by

William Gibson in a science fiction novel entitled *Neuromancer* (New York: Berkeley Publishing Group), which was published in 1984.

8. The Web is a system for organizing information on the Internet, using hyper-links (see note 18 below). Most Americans are aware of the Internet (91 percent) and a smaller fraction are aware of the Web (8 percent). Leslie Miller, "Cyberspace Scares many PC Novices," See *USA Today*, (October 16, 1995) p. 1D.

9. See "Harnessing the Internet," *Fund Action* 6, No. 28 (July 10, 1995), p. 1.

10. See "Lack of Imagination Can Stifle Progress," *USA Today: The World of Science* 123, No. 2601 (June 1995), p. 16.

11. In fact, despite the clear potential of the Web as a new publishing and entertainment medium, too many questions are still unanswered about how to make it a marketplace. A year ago, companies putting up Web sites were saying that people would soon buy information and entertainment directly over the Internet. That strategy was a failure because people will not yet pay for much of anything over the Internet. Accordingly, firms have shifted to a new business model. Advertising will underwrite the costs of putting content on-line. See Denise Caruso, "A Study by A.C. Nielsen Seeks to Separate Buyers From Browsers on the Internet," the *New York Times* (August 21, 1995) at "Computers and Technology" on America Online.

12. See SEC Release No. 33–7233 (October 6, 1995), footnote 4.

13. See Tim Cavanaugh, "Investors Shrug Off High-Tech Services," *Securities Industry Daily* VII, No. 147 (July 31, 1995), p. 1.

14. See "The Information Tidal Wave Issues and Challenges," *The Journal of the American Corporate Counsel Association—ACCA Docket* 13, No. 1 (January/February 1995) pp. 10–24.

15. See "Mutual Funds Home Page" which is but one guide to mutual fund resources on the Internet. (The Internet address is http://www.ultranet.com/.)

16. The "Mercury Center Newshound," available through the *San Jose Mercury News* Web site, is a good example of this type of software. It automatically searches the stories in the *San Jose Mercury News* as well as hundreds of stories not published in the paper, every hour on the hour throughout the day, using the words and phrases supplied by the person requesting the search. Articles matching the profile are sent directly to a designated Internet address.

17. More powerful computers have allowed programmers the luxury of devoting time to the user interface, rather than just content. This

development has made multimedia possible. *See* Nicholas Negroponte, *being digital*, (New York: Alfred A. Knopf 1995), for a discussion of this trend and for insights into possible future digital developments.

18. Hyper-links (or hyper-text) link one electronic document to another. By clicking on a word or phrase that appears in a different color on the screen, a user can go directly to another document relating to that word or phrase.

19. A new technology called Virtual Reality Modeling Language or *vermel* allows data to be stored and sent through the Internet in a graphical, three-dimensional format. Users look through vermelized data as if they were walking down a street or rummaging through a file. *See* Hal Plotkin, "What's Next for Web Designers? How About the Third Dimension," *Securities Industry Daily* VII, No. 147 (July 31, 1995), pp. 1 and 14. See also "3-D Computing," *Business Week*, (September 4, 1995), cover story.

20. See "SEC Readies Electronic Disclosure Approval," *Institutional Investor*, XXI, No. 33 (August 21, 1995), p. 2.

21. All U.S. public companies are now required to file electronically through EDGAR.

22. See *Brown & Wood*, SEC No-Action Letter, (available February 17, 1995) and SEC Release Nos. 33–7233 (October 6, 1995) and 33–7288 (May 9, 1996).

23. See *NASD Special Notice to Members*, No. 95–80 (September 26, 1995) and "Ask The Analyst About Electronic Communications," *NASD Regulatory and Compliance Alert* (April 1996).

24. Note that the SEC, in June of 1995, solicited public comment on whether the current overall regulatory framework should be reassessed because of the increasing availability of disclosure through electronic media. This question now seems moot. *See* Section II.B to SEC Release No. 33–7183 (June 27, 1995).

25. The address to the SEC Web site is http://www.sec.gov. The address to the SEC electronic mailbox is e-prospectus@sec.gov.

26. See "SEC To Allow Investors, Firms To Use The Net," *The Los Angeles Times* (October 6, 1995), Business, Part D, p. 3.

27. See SEC Release No. 33–7289 (May 10, 1996).

28. See Paul Noglows, "Mutual Funds Set Up Shop on the Web," *Inter@ctive Week* (July 10, 1995), p. 52.

29. Note that it *is* currently possible to conduct mutual fund and stock transactions on-line. For example, an on-line discount brokerage service, PC Financial Network (PCFN) has recently been launched by

America Online. Through PCFN, you can trade stocks, options and over 500 mutual funds 24 hours a day. One development that may help electronic business transactions to proliferate is "E-cash." This is virtual money that moves largely outside the established network of banks, checks, and paper currency overseen by the Federal Reserve that can be earmarked for specific purposes like purchasing mutual funds only. See "The Future of Money," *Business Week* (June 12, 1995), cover story.

30. Representative Dan Frisa (R–NY) released a report on March 1, 1996 that describes a number of options for privatizing EDGAR. See *The Bureau of National Affairs, Inc. Securities Law Daily* (March 6, 1996). See "Company to Offer Free Access to SEC EDGAR Filings on Internet," *The Bureau of National Affairs, Inc. Securities and Law Report* 27, No. 34 (August 25, 1995), p. 1398.

31. From June to October of 1994, a Russian national tapped into Citibank's central computer at 111 Wall Street and made 40 transfers from the accounts of several Citibank customers amounting to $10 million into accounts opened by accomplices at banks in California and in Israel. See "Citibank Fraud Case Raises Computer Security Questions" *The New York Times* (August 19, 1995) at Computers and Technology on America Online. To counteract the possibility of computer fraud in situations such as the cracking of the security code in Netscape, a popular program for using the Internet, software firms are writing more elaborate encryptions for security purposes. See Eric Hubler, "CyberWallet Offered as Secure Way To Conduct Share Trading On-Line," *Securities Industry Daily* VII, No. 190 (September 29, 1995), pp. 1 and 16.

32. See Susan Antila, "Has Cyberspace Got a Deal for You!" the *New York Times* (March 19, 1995), Section 3, Column 1, p. 5. In addition, the Secret Service, the federal agency that, among other things, investigates credit card fraud, monitors commercial computer on-line services like Prodigy and America Online, as well as smaller, private computer bulletin boards, for illegal activities. See "Secret Service Goes On Line and After Hackers," the *New York Times* (September 12, 1995) at "Computers and Technology" on America Online.

33. In one of the first cases dealing with boundaries in the boundary-less medium of cyberspace, a district court in Ohio held that CompuServe could not obtain personal jurisdiction over a subscriber in Texas. *CompuServe* v. *Patterson*, Case No. C2–94–91 (S. D. Ohio, Aug. 11, 1994). See Gerard Daley and Patric Verrone, "On Guard Online," *Los Angeles Lawyer* 18, No. 4 (June 1995), p. 31.

34. Similarly, where there is an offer to sell funds over the Internet, the message can be received in every state, possibly putting these transactions within the scope of each state's securities regulations. It is unclear whether an entity soliciting transactions on a computer network is required to register as a broker-dealer in the states from which investors respond. Four states have issued cease and desist orders against computer activity relating to securities. See Melanie Fein, "Regulating Cyberspace: What Does It Mean to Banking?" *The Magazine of Bank Management* (September 1995).

35. See Dave McCombs, "The Net's Big Deal; Who's Betting that Gambling is the 'Killer App' the Web's Waiting For?," *The Daily Yomiuri* (October 13, 1995), p. 17 and Jim Simon, "Cyberbingo Sends Officials Scrambling for Their Law Books," *The Seattle Times* (October 8, 1995), Sunday final edition, p. C1.

36. See, for example, *In Re: Offers Effected Through The Internet That Do Not Result In Sales In Pennsylvania* (August 30, 1995).

14

MONEY MARKET FUND INVESTMENTS IN DERIVATIVES

Martin E. Lybecker, *Ropes & Gray*

THE CREATION OF VARIABLE RATE DEMAND NOTES

Variable rate demand notes were first introduced in the early 1980s as a response to the overwhelming demand from tax-exempt money market funds[1] for portfolio instruments tailored to the requirements of the Investment Company Act of 1940 (the 1940 Act).[2] Rule 2a–7 under the 1940 Act[3] provides a comprehensive regulatory scheme for managing investment portfolios of taxable and tax-exempt money market funds, and it is notable for the degree to which it dictates how a portfolio must be structured. Specifically, for taxable[4] money market funds Rule 2a–7 requires that:

- All instruments must be denominated in U.S. dollars.
- All instruments must present minimal credit risks.
- 95 percent of a money market fund's assets must be invested in first tier securities (i.e., rated in the highest category for short-term debt obligations), and no more than 5 percent of a money market fund's total assets may be invested in securities of any one issuer (except U.S. government securities).

- Of the 5 percent of a money market fund's assets that may be invested in second tier securities, no more than 1 percent may be invested in securities of any one issuer.
- Securities that are downgraded must, in many circumstances, be sold.
- No security (other than a U.S. government security) may have a remaining maturity greater than 397 days.
- The dollar-weighted average portfolio maturity of a money market fund cannot exceed 90 days.
- Special rules for calculating the "maturity" of certain U.S. government securities and variable rate demand notes (until the actual maturity, until the next interest rate adjustment, or until the next demand date) must be followed.

Most variable rate notes have a demand feature—upon seven days' notice or as of a specified date, for example. Including a demand feature in variable rate notes was necessary to allow a debt instrument with an intermediate- to long-term maturity to behave in the marketplace as if it were actually a short-term note. Moreover, the interest rate to be paid on the variable rate demand notes had to be adjusted regularly (or by reference to specified events occurring in the marketplace) so that the principal value of the intermediate- to long-term note could reasonably be expected to have a market value that approximated its par value at least at every interest rate reset date or event. In the December 1993 release proposing to amend Rule 2a–7,[5] the SEC took the position that the investment company adviser must be able to determine that the principal value of the instrument will have a market value that approximates its par value under all conceivable interest rate environments that might obtain through its final maturity, and each and every time the interest rate is reset.[6] Without the demand feature and the reasonably prompt interest rate readjustment characteristics, variable rate demand notes would not be able to sustain good mark-to-market values during periods of rapidly rising or falling interest rates.[7]

Wall Street investment bankers found municipalities were very eager to issue this kind of variable rate demand note because they provided cities and counties an assured source of funding at short-term rates for a much longer period of time. Investment company advisers were very eager to purchase this kind of variable rate demand note because they were overwhelmed with orders to buy shares of tax-exempt money market funds and needed "product" for their investment portfolios. In other words, wealthy investors seeking a stable net asset value per share vehicle with a tax-free return were willing to accept short-term interest rates to obtain the other features of a tax-exempt money market fund. The net effect was a wealth transfer of sizeable proportions from purchasers of shares of tax-exempt money market funds to the taxpayers in the nation's many municipalities. As a result, a substantial portion of the schedule of investments for a tax-exempt money market fund now consists of variable rate demand notes.

THE CREATION OF "STRUCTURED" NOTES

Several years ago Wall Street investment bankers started selling what are now referred to as "structured" notes issued by U.S. government-sponsored entities in the mortgage business, like the Federal Home Loan Banks, Freddie Mac, Fannie Mae, and Sallie Mae. Also called government "floaters," these taxable debt instruments generally have intermediate- to long-term maturities and interest rate formulas that are very complex. Among the features of these formulas are these:

- The interest rate to be computed from the formula may be capped in the amount it can change in terms of an absolute amount, an amount per quarter, or an annual amount.
- The interest rate may be indexed to one or more factors (the prime rate, LIBOR, the Cost of Funds Index of the Twelfth District Federal Home Loan Bank, and the like) that may lead or lag the 90-day Treasury bill rate by a significant period of time.
- The interest rate may reset relatively infrequently (every six months instead of every month or every three months).

These securities could also be loosely described as "derivatives" in that these interest rate formulas are intended to reflect interest rate movements outside the short-term debt market. To that extent, it might also be said that "structured" notes have certain features of "derivatives," such as leverage, embedded within them somewhat invisible to the eye. At all events, instruments with complex interest rate formulas should be difficult instruments to value on a daily basis, especially by pricing services used to pricing straight debt instruments with relatively simple matrixes.

THE 1994 CRUNCH

With the Federal Reserve Board actively pushing Federal Funds rates upwards during the first half of 1994, it became common knowledge by May and June of that year that many taxable money market funds were experiencing serious liquidity and pricing problems as a result of holding these types of "structured" notes. Because the issuers of the structured notes were all U.S. government-sponsored entities, the question was not credit quality, as had often been true of money market fund crises in the past. Instead, it was a question of temporary loss of principal value in the structured notes until the interest rate formulas could digest the steady, heavy, upward changes in the Federal Funds rates mandated by the Federal Reserve Board. Ultimately, a number of investment company advisers chose to make substantial cash infusions to protect the per-share mark-to-market value of their money market fund's investment portfolio, and to continue to use the amortized cost method of accounting and stable net asset value per share of $1.[8]

Just before the fourth of July, 1994, the SEC staff sent a letter to the Investment Company Institute stating that these types of government floaters were inappropriate investments for money market funds, thereby drying up entirely whatever remaining liquidity there was in the market.[9] By midsummer 1994, the federal bank regulatory agencies were issuing guidelines to their respective bank constituencies alerting them to the danger of investing any of the bank's own assets in structured notes.[10] In September 1994, the Community Bankers U.S. Government Money Market Fund announced that it was liquidating in kind its portfolio of structured notes at a value of 94 cents on the dollar.[11] This was the long-awaited situation where a money market fund "broke the dollar." That decision by the Board of Directors of the Community Bankers U.S. Government Money Market Fund has sparked lawsuits from its shareholders (largely community banks) and, reportedly, an SEC investigation.[12] It did not escape notice that this very fund had been the top performing of all U.S. government money market funds for the 12 months ending August, 1994![13] Additional periodic announcements regarding losses on structured notes in collective investment funds, common trust funds, and securities lending pools also occurred in the last quarter of 1994.[14]

Finally, no discussion of structured notes would be complete without reference to Orange County, California, and its notorious investment pools in which structured notes were a large part of the holdings. After

Orange County filed for bankruptcy in December 1994,[15] many taxable and tax-exempt money market funds were caught holding debt instruments issued by Orange County itself or by participants in the Orange County investment pools.[16] This is not the place to review the entire Orange County story, but this was the first time a number of money market funds were under serious financial pressure and there was little question that the investment company advisers involved had not made poor credit decisions in making those investments. Put another way, it was highly unlikely that the affected money market funds had a viable cause of action against their investment company advisers for gross negligence in buying inappropriate securities for their funds when the Treasurer of Orange County pleaded guilty to six separate fraud allegations, including disseminating false and misleading information to investors in Orange County securities.[17]

LEGAL ASPECTS OF CASH INFUSIONS

If it becomes necessary to infuse cash into a money market fund that has already or is about to incur capital losses, a series of business questions with legal overtones should be considered. First, any principal transaction between a registered investment company and any affiliated person thereof (which includes the investment company's investment adviser) and its principal underwriter is prohibited by Section 17(a) of the 1940 Act.[18] Section 17(d) of the 1940 Act goes on to prohibit joint transactions between the investment company and its affiliated persons (or principal underwriter).[19] In this situation, there are two possible ways of handling the debt instruments that are causing the problem: sell them at their market price into the market and have the money market fund take the capital loss directly; or sell them at their amortized cost (principal plus accrued interest) to the investment company adviser and let the investment company adviser suffer any capital losses that may occur. For a number of reasons, it is not unusual for the investment company adviser to buy the troubled securities at their amortized cost, which has the practical effect of making the money market fund whole again, so the investment company adviser can then take the interest rate risk or residual credit risk embedded in the debt instruments until each such security finally matures. Even though the money market fund's sale of a debt instrument to the investment company adviser may be prohibited by Section 17(a) of the 1940 Act, the money market fund has not been disadvantaged in any way—it is now "whole"

—and it is hard to imagine why a plaintiff would want to sue where there are no damages. Nonetheless, many investment company advisers still want to receive some level of assurance from the SEC staff that they will not recommend that any enforcement action be taken against the investment company adviser for possibly violating Section 17(a), and the SEC staff has been willing to give oral no-action assurances in those circumstances where the money market fund has been made absolutely whole.[20]

The Orange County situation has apparently spawned less routine arrangements, including where the money market fund receives a temporary "put" from the investment company adviser that allows the money market fund to exercise the put and sell the offending security to the investment company adviser at its amortized cost at the end of or over a specified period of time. The SEC staff has given some level of no-action comfort to investment company advisers taking this route, subject to the conditions that the put be rearranged as soon as practicable with a first-tier issuer (bank or insurance company) and that the temporary put be collateralized with first-tier securities if the investment company adviser is not itself a first-tier credit.[21] Absent the unusual circumstances surrounding the Orange County situation, it is unlikely that these more exotic arrangements would have been tolerated by the SEC staff.

If the 1940 Act issues have been resolved, the second question is who is going to infuse the cash. Assume for this purpose that a bank is the investment company's adviser, and recognize that banks are subject to their own stringent conflict of interest rules in Sections 23A and 23B of the Federal Reserve Act.[22] For purposes of Sections 23A and 23B, the money market fund will be an affiliate of the bank and any operating subsidiaries that it may have.[23] Because the troubled debt instrument is likely to be either of low quality or not the type of security that the bank's treasurer will want in the bank's own investment portfolio, it will usually not be possible for the bank (or any of its operating subsidiaries) to satisfy the arms-length and other tests in Section 23A and Section 23B.[24] Therefore, the troubled debt instrument will usually be purchased at its amortized cost by the bank holding company or one of its nonbank affiliates, which are not subject to the restrictions in Section 23A and 23B. The troubled debt instrument will, of course, have to be written down immediately to its actual market value, causing the bank holding company to take an immediate capital loss. If the situation is not too desperate, it may be possible for the money market fund to "sell" the troubled debt instruments over a period of time and realize the losses in different fiscal quarters.

ACCOUNTING AND FEDERAL INCOME TAX ASPECTS OF CASH INFUSIONS

Finally, according to recent SEC staff pronouncements cash infusion transactions must be disclosed in a footnote to the next semiannual or annual report prepared by the money market fund.[25] This disclosure will be required whether the money market fund took the capital loss on the sale of the security and the cash infusion should not be characterized as a Section 17(a) transaction, or whether the investment company adviser purchased the security from the money market fund at its amortized cost in a transaction arguably subject to Section 17(a). Depending on all the circumstances, prospectus disclosure may also be warranted. The accounting treatment of the cash infusion transaction needs to be squared with the federal income tax treatment of the cash infusion so that, for both purposes, the cash infusion is characterized as a capital transaction and not as "bad" income to the money market fund.[26] For all of the obvious reasons, this means that the money market fund's independent public accountants need to be closely involved in the situation, virtually from the beginning.

CONCLUSION

Money market funds have proven to be flexible, exceedingly safe vehicles for cash management and investment for large portions of the American public—individuals and corporations. The wisdom of the comprehensive regulatory scheme embodied in Rule 2a–7 has been tested repeatedly and seems fully justified. It would seem that one lesson to be learned from this costly experience with derivatives is that new investment instruments must be recognized as such and evaluated carefully. In this particular instance, even casual stress testing on how the structured notes would behave in different interest rate environments should have exposed their high sensitivity to rapidly rising interest rates. A related point is that the rules and regulations applicable to SEC-regulated investment vehicles are often exported by reference into other, non-SEC regulated areas such as common trust funds, collective investment funds, and private investment companies (like securities lending pools). While it is important to stay on top of market developments, it is equally important for investment company advisers like banks to understand how other regulatory schemes treat certain instruments or require certain behavior: investment management clients tend to show little appreciation for legalistic regulatory boundaries or related niceties, and can be expected to take the position that the rights and remedies that they have become accustomed to in the SEC's 1940 Act arena be respected in the way bank trust departments manage their affairs, too.

ENDNOTES

1. A money market fund is an investment company that invests in very short-term debt instruments whose principal values will not fluctuate much in response to interest rate movements in the market so that the mark-to-market net asset value per share of the fund will be $1 under virtually all expectable circumstances. A "tax-exempt" money market fund is a money market fund that distributes income exempt from regular federal income taxation.

2. 15 USC §80a–1 et seq.

3. 17 CFR §270.2a–7 (1995). Rule 2a–7 was initially adopted in 1983 as a codification of the numerous "amortized cost" method of accounting exemptive orders issued to various money market funds in the early 1980s. See SEC Investment Company Act Release Nos. 13380 (July 11, 1983)(adoption), 14606 (July 9, 1985)(amended), 14983 (March 12, 1986)(amended), 18005 (Feb. 20, 1991)(amended), 18177 (May 31, 1991)(amended). The SEC has announced more proposed changes to Rule 2a–7, but they have not yet been adopted. SEC Investment Company Act Release No. 19959 (Dec. 17, 1993).

4. Tax-exempt money market funds are not subject to the diversification requirements in Rule 2a–7(c)(4).

5. SEC Investment Company Act Release No. 19959 (Dec. 17, 1993).

6. Ibid., pp. 61–65. The proposed changes to Rule 2a–7 would also require that funds maintain written records of this determination.

7. In that release, the SEC specifically criticized "inverse floaters," "capped floaters," "CMT floaters," leveraged floaters, and other instruments linked to an interest rate that significantly lags prevailing short-term rates for containing risks to principal value of those instruments that are inappropriate for a money market fund to assume. Ibid., p. 64. The SEC Division of Investment Management had previously expressed concerns on a number of occasions about money market funds holding certain types of "derivatives." Letter dated December 6, 1991, from Marianne K. Smythe, Director, SEC Division of Investment Management to Matthew P. Fink, President, Investment Company Institute (inverse floaters); Letter dated July 24, 1992, from Office of Chief Counsel, SEC Division of Investment Management to Morgan Keegan & Co. (SBA floaters); Investment Company Institute Memorandum dated November 6, 1992, re: Morgan Keegan letter; Investment Company Institute Memorandum dated January 15, 1993, re: Sallie Mae floaters; SEC Division of Investment Management "Dear Registrant" Letter dated February 22, 1993; Investment Company Institute Memorandum dated June 17, 1993,

re: SEC Letter of June 16th regarding Capped Floating and Variable Rate Instruments; Letter dated June 25, 1993, from Robert E. Plaze, Assistant Director, SEC Division of Investment Management to Amy Lancelotta, Associate Counsel, Investment Company Institute (capped floating and variable rate instruments).

8. "A History of Stepping Up To The Plate," *Fund Action* (September 12, 1994), p.9.

9. Letter dated June 30, 1994, from Barry P. Barbash, Director, SEC Division of Investment Management, to Paul Schott Stevens, General Counsel, Investment Company Institute.

10. "Regulators Warn National Banks Away from Investments in Risk-Laden Notes," *BNA Banking Report* 63 (Aug. 1, 1994), pp. 150–151; "Fed Joins Other Banking Regulators in Issuing Structured Notes Guidance," *BNA Banking Report* 63 (Aug. 22, 1994), p. 229; "FDIC Directs Examiners to Heighten Scrutiny of Risk-Laden Structured Notes," *BNA Banking Report* 63 (Sept. 12, 1994), p. 311.

11. "Investors Face First Money Market Fund Loss," *New York Times*, Sept. 28, 1994, p. D1; "Losses on Derivatives Lead Money Fund to Liquidate," *Washington Post*, Sept. 28, 1994, p. F1; "Derivatives Force First Closure of Money Fund," *The Wall Street Journal*, Sept. 28, 1994, at C1.

12. See, "SEC Probes Insider Trading at Money Fund," *The Wall Street Journal*, Oct. 24, 1994, p. C1.

13. "Investors Face First Money Market Fund Loss," *New York Times*, Sept. 28, 1994, p. D1.

14. Mellon Bank Corporation took a $130 million after-tax charge on a loss of $210 million in the fourth quarter of 1994 due to structured notes held in a securities lending pool maintained by The Boston Company, a newly acquired subsidiary. "Mellon Takes $130 Million Loss on Investments," *New York Times*, Nov. 29, 1994, p. D4; "Mellon Will Take a Charge," *Boston Globe*, Nov. 29, 1994, p. 45; "Two Boston Co. Executives Fired," *Boston Globe*, Nov. 30, 1994, p. 51. "Shareholder Sues Mellon Over 'Risky' Investments," *Boston Herald*, Dec. 2, 1994, p. 517. Harris Trust & Savings Bank of Chicago had previously posted a $33 million after-tax charge because of structured notes held for fiduciary accounts.

15. "Orange County, Mired in Investment Mess, Files for Bankruptcy," *The Wall Street Journal*, Dec. 7, 1994, p. A1; "Orange County Files for Bankruptcy," *Washington Post*, Dec. 7, 1994, p. F1; "Big County Could Seek Protection," *New York Times*, Dec. 7, 1994, p. D1.

16. From a Rule 2a–7 perspective, Orange County was initially just a very serious credit downgrade experience, followed by increasingly dicey

questions during spring 1995 about how to properly calculate the money market fund's average weighted portfolio maturity when an existing security's maturity was extended, how to treat a delay in payment after a maturity date has been passed, and how to treat a default when the issuer on its own motion extends the maturity of the existing instrument an additional 11 months or more.

17. "Citron Pleads Guilty to Fraud," *Washington Post,* April 28, 1995, p. F8; "Orange County Ex-Treasurer Pleads Guilty," *The Wall Street Journal,* April 28, 1995, p. A3. In January 1996, the SEC filed civil anti-fraud initiative actions and related administrative actions against the Treasurer and Assistant Treasurer of Orange County, and against Orange County itself and five members of its Board of Supervisors. "Orange County Settlement Sends a Signal from SEC," *New York Times,* Jan. 25, 1996, p. D4; "SEC Accuses Orange County of Fraud," *The Wall Street Journal*, Jan. 25, 1996, p. B5; "SEC, Orange County Settle Case," *Washington Post,* Jan. 25, 1996, p. D10. The SEC also issued an extremely significant report setting forth its views of the omissions and misstatements contained in the various 1994 Official Statements. SEC Securities Exchange Net Retrace No. 36761 (Jan. 24, 1996).

18. 17 USC §80a–17(a).

19. 17 USC §80a–17(d). Section 17(d) is not self-operative; Rule 17d–1 thereunder requires that exemptive applications be filed with respect to all joint transactions that are not excluded by the other provisions of the rule. 17 CFR §270.17d–1 (1995).

20. An undated five-page memorandum prepared in or about June 1994 by the SEC Division of Investment Management to respond to Freedom of Information Act requests lists 14 different money market funds that had sought and obtained no-action positions. See also, letter dated August 4, 1994, from Heidi Stam, Assistant Chief Counsel, SEC Division of Investment Management to Kirkpatrick & Lockhart (Paine Webber Managed Investments Trust: Paine Webber Short-Term U.S. Government Income Fund) (kitchen sink structured notes).

21. Letter dated June 23, 1995, from Robert E. Plaze, Assistant Director, Office of Disclosure and Investment Adviser Regulation, SEC Division of Investment Management to David B. Mathis, Chairman of the Board, Kemper Corporation, re: Kemper Money Market Funds. In this instance, Kemper Corporation and an affiliate entered into a "put" agreement to protect the Orange County-related securities owned by four of Kemper's money market funds. In January and February 1995, the "put" agreement was replaced with a letter of credit involving Bank of New York and a Kemper affiliate in the amount of $205 million to guarantee

the principal and accrued interest in the Orange County–related securities. Bank of New York had first tier ratings on its short-term debt obligations. The Letter of Credit was amended again in June 1995 in anticipation of the July 10, 1995, extension of the maturity on the remaining Orange County security held by the Kemper money market funds. In each instance, the SEC Division of Investment Management took a no-enforcement position with respect to Sections 17(a), 17(d), and Section 12(d)(3) of the 1940 Act, declining to express any legal conclusions on the issues presented.

22. 12 USC §§371c, 371c–1. Sections 23A and 23B of the Federal Reserve Act function in a manner comparable to Section 17(a) of the 1940 Act in that conflict of interest transactions are prohibited, except that Sections 23A and 23B permit conflict of interest transactions to go forward if they meet certain self-administered tests for fairness, while Section 17(b) of the 1940 Act requires each such transaction to be the subject of a discrete application seeking an exemptive order from the SEC.

23. Section 23A(b)(D)(ii) defines an affiliate to include "any investment company with respect to which a member bank or any affiliate thereof is an investment adviser as defined in section 2(a)(20) of the [1940 Act]." The investment adviser bank would be an investment adviser as defined in Section 2(a)(20) of the 1940 Act. Section 23B(d)(1) cross-references the definition of affiliate in Section 23A.

24. Section 23A(a)(1) allows a "covered transaction" only if "(A) the aggregate amount of covered transactions of the member bank and its subsidiaries will not exceed 10 per centum of the capital stock and surplus of the member bank; and (B) in the case of all affiliates, the aggregate amount of covered transactions of the member bank and its subsidiaries will not exceed 20 per centum of the capital stock and surplus of the member bank." The test in Section 23B(a)(1) is whether the proposed transaction "(A) is on terms and under circumstances, including credit standards, that are substantially the same, or at least as favorable to such bank or its subsidiary, as those prevailing at the time for comparable transactions with or involving other nonaffiliated companies, or (B) in the absence of comparable transactions, on terms and under circumstances, including credit standards, that in good faith would be offered to, or would apply to, nonaffiliated companies."

25. Investment Company Institute Memorandum dated September 23, 1994, re: Accounting Treatment of Capital Contributions by and the Sale of Securities to an Affiliate at a Price in Excess of Fair Market Value; Investment Company Institute Memorandum dated February 7, 1995,

re: SEC Staff Issues 1995 Generic Comment Letter and Supplemental Generic Comment Letter to Investment Company CFOs.

26. Under Subchapter M of the Internal Revenue Code [26 USC §851 et seq.], a regulated investment company must earn at least 90 percent of its income from dividends, interest, or capital gains from the sale of securities (as defined in the 1940 Act). 26 USC §851(b)(2). All other income is colloquially referred to as "bad" income. A companion question is whether any payment made by an investment company adviser is deductible as an ordinary and necessary business expense under §162 of the Internal Revenue Code, 26. U.S.C. §162. *See* Fritts and Mangefrida, *Deductibility of Investment Advisers' 'Bail Out' Payments*, 2, The Investment Lawyer (July, 1995), p.1.

15

DERIVATIVES AND RISK

Challenges Facing the Investment
Management Industry*

Michael E. S. Frankel, *Skadden, Arps, Slate, Meagher & Flom***

$\mathbf{A}$s the next century approaches, one of the primary challenges facing financial institutions, regulators, and businesses will be innovation in financial instruments. The pace of innovation in financial instruments has increased as dramatically as in technology. In the past two decades alone we have seen the birth and tremendous growth of financial derivatives, the explosion of mutual funds and other managed money, and the integration and increasing interdependance of international markets. As we look forward, a primary concern must be how the financial markets, their users and their regulators will deal with the increasing pace of innovation and development without stifling it. As with technology, increased complexity in financial instruments brings both opportunity and difficulty. The challenges posed by derivative instruments to investment management are excellent analogues for this problem.

*The author gratefully acknowledges the assistance and advice of Cliff Kirsch, Susan
    Woodward, Merton Miller, Geoffrey Miller, William Landes, and Tamar Frankel.
    Any valuable thoughts are likely attributable to them, while any errors are my own.
**The views expressed in this chapter are solely those of the author and do not necessarily
    represent the views of Skadden, Arps, Slate, Meagher & Flom.

We are now in the midst of the second wave of controversy over derivatives in a decade. The use of these financial instruments grew exponentially during the 1980s, though a recent Securities and Exchange Commission (SEC) survey suggests that they remain relatively unknown to the general public even today. In the wake of the 1987 crash, many regulators and legislators and some in the financial industry laid the blame on the burgeoning derivatives market, particularly options and program trading, and there were calls for new regulation of these instruments. In the past year, the debate has been reignited by a series of large trading losses on derivatives by corporate users, investment banks, and investment funds.

In particular, questions have been raised about the use of derivatives by mutual funds and money market funds (hereinafter *funds*). Both Congress and the Securities and Exchange Commission have been developing new regulation or supervision of derivatives investments by funds. These proposals and their underlying concerns can be divided into four main categories: risk and complexity, disclosure, fund board duties, leverage, and valuation. The risky or volatile and complex nature of derivatives has created concern for various types of investors, including fund shareholders in particular. There is also concern about the level, accuracy, and clarity of disclosure to fund shareholders concerning derivatives investments and the risks incurred by such investments. These two issues in turn drive questions about the duties of a fund's board of directors regarding derivatives investments. Another concern is that investments in derivatives are a form of leverage for funds. Finally, the difficulty of day-to-day market valuation of derivatives creates serious concerns for funds that issue redeemable securities. Such funds redeem their shares at net asset value. If the valuation is too high the remaining shareholders lose; if it is too low the redeeming shareholders lose.

This chapter will begin by discussing the characteristics of derivatives that have raised concerns in the context of funds. The chapter will specifically examine the risk and complexity of derivatives and examine methodologies for measuring the risk of derivatives' positions within an overall fund portfolio. In particular, the chapter will examine the portfolio-level risk measurement methodologies many large financial institutions and exchanges employ, and their applicability to funds. The chapter will discuss the use of risk measurement methodologies both for internal risk management in funds, and for purposes of fulfilling disclosure obligations. The chapter will provide an analysis of the strengths and weaknesses of different methodologies in this context. The chapter also will discuss the relevance of these issues to the duties of fund boards, and it will touch upon concerns about valuation of derivatives positions and the question of whether such positions create leverage.

RISK AND COMPLEXITY OF DERIVATIVES

Over the past decade most of the criticisms leveled at derivatives have related to their risk and complexity. The most recent set of Congressional hearings on derivatives trading by mutual funds placed similar emphasis on the risk of these assets.[1]

Derivative instruments are generally more volatile, or risky, than other financial instruments. One way of looking at the issue is by dissecting a standard security instrument. We might view a share of stock A as having two components: a foundation value that is unlikely to change in the short term (equivalent to a Treasury bond or blue chip corporate debt), and an additional "value at risk" that is likely to fluctuate. An investment in a share of stock gives the investor both pieces, whereas a derivative allows the investor only to purchase the "value at risk," leaving aside the foundation value that is unlikely to change.

The fluctuation pattern of a derivative instrument is similar to the underlying asset, but it is amplified since it is not buffered by the investment in the foundation value. It is simply a more volatile version of an investment in the underlying asset.

This characteristic allows derivatives to function as a hedging tool by isolating the volatile segment of an asset's value and allowing the investor to offset the direction of risk in her asset portfolio with a position in the corresponding derivative. Further, the leverage afforded by derivatives allows a proportionally smaller derivative position to hedge a larger asset position. For example, in order to hedge a portfolio of 100 shares of stock B (current price $100), an investor would simply have to purchase 100 put options (an instrument giving the holder the option to sell a share of stock) with a much lower price of perhaps $1 per put. Thus, for approximately $100 the investor has effectively hedged her $10,000 position in stock A. In effect, the investor has purchased shares of "antistock A" stock since the price of a put will move in the opposite direction from the underlying asset. Further, the investor has only purchased the volatile segment of "antistock A" and none of the foundation value. Thus, the leverage provided by derivatives has allowed her to hedge her portfolio without having to purchase an equal amount of "antistock A."

For this hedging investor, the only risk created by the derivatives position is the potential loss in value of the derivatives. Since in a properly hedged portfolio, this will be offset exactly by gains in the value of the underlying asset, the investor has actually eliminated risk by creating offsetting risk patterns in her assets and derivatives positions.

The potential, or perceived, problem arises when an investor uses derivatives as an investment tool rather than a hedging tool. If an investor buys derivatives without holding the offsetting underlying asset, the investor is effectively able to leverage her capital, as if she were trading on margin to create a high volatility investment. For example, suppose we posit two investors with $10,000 each, operating in a world of two time periods. Investor A purchases 100 shares of stock A at $100 per share. Investor B purchases 10,000 call options at $100 on stock A at $1 per option. Each investor has taken positions that are driven by the same underlying asset, but they will have radically different volatilities. A $1 increase in the price of stock A will give investor A a 1 percent return and investor B a 100 percent return. By contrast, a $1 decline in the price of stock A will give investor A a 1 percent loss, and investor B a 100 percent loss. By investing in derivatives, investor B has achieved the same level of volatility and risk as if she had purchased shares of stock A on 99 percent margin, and thus has achieved and been exposed to a high level of volatility.

However, it is important to note the difference between risk and purely downside risk. Risk, or volatility, simply refers to the range of price fluctuation and not the direction. Presumably, in an efficient market, every risk of loss incurred will be compensated with corresponding risk or chance of gain. While derivative instruments tend to gain attention for large trading losses, there are symmetrical trading gains from investment in these instruments. For instance, although Orange County, California, recently suffered large losses through derivatives trading, these same instruments were a source of unusually high returns for many years.

Further, while derivatives can be high-risk financial instruments, they are not unique in their risk. Funds regularly invest and have always invested in a variety of similarly risky nonderivative investments. The list of such investments is long and includes high-risk equity, like the stock of start-up firms, some foreign debt and equity, and junk-bonds.

Perhaps more importantly, the risk level associated with derivatives cannot be meaningfully assessed in a vacuum. Rather, derivatives' risk must be viewed in the context of the overall portfolio. Derivatives are often used to hedge other portfolio risk and thus serve to reduce rather than increase risk. Furthermore, since investors own a slice of the entire portfolio of the fund, meaningful measures of risk must be at the portfolio level. Thus, if highly risky derivatives positions are either hedged against offsetting positions in underlying assets or pooled with very low-risk investments, the net portfolio risk will be significantly lower than the derivatives portion.

This suggests that the level of risk of particular investments like derivatives is not the relevant inquiry for fund investors. Rather, the issue is the net risk of the portfolio. In the context of investor protection, then, the question is whether the net risk of the portfolio matches the risk level that the fund purports to offer to investors. In fact, the Investment Company Act (the Act) specifically bars funds from deviating from their investment policies as set forth in their registration statement unless authorized by a vote of the majority of outstanding shares.[2]

Similarly, if we presume that the board of the fund, on its own, or through its investment advisors, has an effective understanding of derivative instruments, or at least understands the limits of the board's own understanding, then the complexity of these instruments should not be a concern. Specific statutory language, as well as a rich common law foundation, create a duty for the board of directors to maintain just such a knowledge (discussed below). Fund investors do not need to understand, and are unlikely to even be aware of, the details and intricacies of all of the investments underlying the fund. Indeed, one of the primary purposes of funds is to offer investors the expertise of the fund manager and monitoring by the fund's board of directors.

The risk of derivatives investments does raise concerns about disclosure to investors, to the extent that such investments might conceal an increased level of portfolio risk. While one might argue that this is not a derivatives-specific issue, but rather a general question of the accuracy of overall fund disclosure, the recent focus has been driven specifically by risks created by derivatives trading.

Congressional discussion of this issue has been surprisingly restrained. Members of the House Committee on Banking, Finance and

Urban Affairs appear to recognize that there is a place in mutual fund portfolios for such investments.[3] Instead, the committee has emphasized on the importance of effective disclosure, suggesting that recent fund losses from derivatives trading have come as a shock to investors who thought they were holding "safe" investments.[4]

In discussing disclosure of risk, it is important to note the difference between the information provided to investors and their perceptions. The regulations that govern mutual funds deal with their actual disclosures to investors through prospectuses and other required documentation. The adequacy, accuracy, and clarity of such disclosure will be discussed below. However, under current law, inaccurate investor perceptions do not, in and of themselves, create liability for funds. While investors must certainly be protected from false statements by funds, irrational or uninformed false impressions despite technically accurate disclosure do not create any liability for funds or fund managers. In other words, in regulating funds, the law presumes that accurate prospectuses prevent investors from being misled and that funds should not be punished for their shareholders' naiveté. Thus, Congressional efforts are justified only to the extent that they are aimed at enhancing factual disclosure by funds, rather than creating liability based on investor perceptions (a more detailed discussion of such concrete disclosure will follow).

It is also important to note that the Investment Company Act does regulate changes in investment policy by mutual funds. While a fund may choose to invest in derivatives, any change in fundamental investment policy must be approved by a vote of the majority of its outstanding voting shareholders.[5] This approval requirement applies to any significant deviation from a policy recited in the funds' registration statement. Thus, if the fund's registration statement claimed that it would not invest in derivatives or would only use them to hedge, the fund would need a shareholder vote to approve derivatives speculation. However, if the registration statement is silent on derivatives, the fund appears to be free to use these instruments as it wills. Any major shift in net fund risk would come into conflict with stated policy in the registration statement, thus requiring a shareholder vote. However, an increased use of derivatives within a similar risk level portfolio would presumably not trigger the requirement.

Additionally, SEC rules already put in place another powerful barrier to the perceived dangers of derivative risk in the form of a hard limit on their investments in illiquid assets to 15 percent of net assets (10 percent in the case of money market funds).[6] Many derivatives, particularly those purchased in the over-the-counter (OTC) market, fall within this limitation.[7] In fact, the SEC has recently raised the possibility, in response to concerns about the risks of derivative instruments, of lowering the limit on illiquid investments to 10 percent for all funds.[8] Of course, the "percent of net assets" limitation is not particularly effective because it applies to notions of market value of present value, whereas derivatives can be constructed to have little market value but still be a substantial source of either insurance or risk in a portfolio. Far out of the money options, for instance, can have little market value and still provide a powerful hedge against huge market moves.

Finally, there is the issue of complexity. Derivatives are probably the most complex type of widely utilized financial instrument in today's market. The fact that they have only been widely utilized in the past two decades only serves to enhance their complexity to users.[9] The complexity of these instruments is also amplified by the vast number of variations offered through exchanges and the OTC market.[10] Finally, and most importantly, the products themselves are highly complex and intricate. Most modern derivatives' trading operations are maintained by traders with tremendous academic and technical expertise.[11] These so-called rocket scientists have developed more complex derivatives at a high velocity.

Their efforts have been supported by a similarly rapid development of computer technology in the past two decades.[12] The nexus of a recently developed financial instrument, radically enhanced computing capabilities, and a frenetic financial market produced rapid development of complex derivatives in the 1980s. The complexity of these new instruments coupled with the speed of their introduction has likely made it particularly difficult for market participants to handle the use and risks of these products. However, note that this is at least partially a temporary condition. To the extent that the rapid nature of derivatives development is a factor, the passage of time should allow participants to develop an understanding of them.

Some analysts argue that the very complexity of some derivative instruments makes them dangerous to fund shareholders since fund managers themselves may fail to understand, or perhaps even be misled, about the risks and values of these instruments. The answer to this concern is twofold.

As with any complex instrument, there is a certain *caveat emptor* argument for any investor, and particularly for the presumably more sophisticated fund managers. Derivatives are no different from any number of complex investments or investment strategies, and fund managers have a duty to inform themselves and to recognize the limits of their understanding of such instruments (discussed in greater detail below). Secondly, misleading statements about any investment by a broker or investment advisor are already punishable under the securities laws. Thus, the complexity of derivatives presents no clear justification for additional regulation.

There is one more nagging but potentially very important issue: tax treatment. Under the so-called short-short rule, a fund that derives more than 30 percent of its income from short-term investments is in danger of losing its special tax status as a pass-through entity. Although this regulation is not explicitly targeted at derivatives, the rhetoric that accompanies such a rule suggests that it was designed, at least in part, to limit the extent to which a fund can invest in short-term and thus (as the argument goes) speculative high-risk assets. The argument for retaining the rule, as applied in recent years to derivatives, is certainly driven by such an intent. Thus, one might argue that the short-short rule is driven by the same perception of derivatives as dangerous high-risk assets discussed above. This argument suggests that the rationale presented in this chapter might also be the basis for an argument against the retention of the short-short rule. In more general terms, rules in the form of limits on asset maturity, percentage of net asset value, or timing the realization of income to limit risk are all likely to be ineffective in addressing derivatives. Derivatives are sufficiently elastic that they can be shaped and reshaped to circumvent any risk-controlling rule not explicitly based on risk. If the present rules are kept in their current forms, derivatives will likely enfeeble them.

Although the risk characteristics of derivatives certainly present new challenges to funds in terms of risk management and disclosure, such challenges can be overemphasized. However, although current regulations are in place to limit a fund's level of investment in derivatives and to control sharp changes in investment policy, there is no current mechanism for funds, investors, or regulators to measure fund risk. The introduction of derivatives exacerbates this problem since their risk characteristics are certainly more variable and difficult to discern. Thus, the direct and immediate need is for a measure of fund portfolio risk that captures the risk of derivatives positions. I will expand on this issue in detail below.

RISK MEASUREMENT METHODOLOGIES
Introduction

Although all financial instruments have an inherent level of risk, the relative public ignorance concerning derivatives and their high level of volatility has sparked particular concern about risk management and measurement. The Securities and Exchange Commission (SEC) has recently emphasized disclosure enhancement in its efforts to address these "risky trading instruments."[13] The centerpiece of an SEC report on derivatives trading by funds is a proposal to create a simple numerical measure of riskiness for mutual funds.[14] However, the SEC has not, as yet, proposed any particular such measure.

Since fund investors are concerned and affected by the entire fund portfolio, emphasis should be placed on measuring overall portfolio risk rather than simply the risk of derivatives holdings. An easy to understand, yet accurate overall portfolio risk measure would be best suited to addressing the needs of investors, and thus the concerns of the SEC. The challenge then is to develop a risk methodology that effectively incorporates the risks of derivatives positions and other instruments into a simple yet accurate measure.

One might define risk as the likelihood and magnitude of changes in value triggered by changes in a variety of parameters. At the outset, the difficulty is in defining the parameters. For some derivatives, the "underlying asset" may provide a good predictor of changes in valuation. Thus the risk of the derivative could be defined as some fraction or multiple of the risk of the underlying asset. Other derivatives may have multiple underlying variables such as interest rates, currency rates, and various equity indexes. Of course, each of these variables is, in turn, driven by a myriad of additional variables. A variety of methodologies can measure or quantify risk for financial instruments and whole portfolios.

Despite the array of variants, nearly all risk measurement methods are driven by an examination of historical volatility (or standard deviation) of a portfolio's value or returns.[15] In general terms, models can be further defined as either fund-based or portfolio-based. Fund-based models look at the historical data for the firm or fund itself, whereas portfolio-based models look at the historical data for the particular instruments that currently form the portfolio. In a portfolio-based analysis further information can be gleaned from the correlation between different securities' historical prices. This correlation data allows for offsetting volatility characteristics among different securities in a portfolio. Thus, two inversely correlated securities would yield a portfolio with a lower volatility than that of either individual security, since a downward price move in one security would be offset by an upward price move in the other.

I will now discuss fund-based and portfolio-based risk measures, as well as some related alternatives. I will then discuss the merits of these various methods in the context of funds' and regulators' efforts to balance accuracy, complexity, reliability, and accessibility of results to investors.

Firm/Fund-Based Risk Measures

Since publication of projections of hypothetical returns is in violation of the SEC Statement of Policy on Sales Literature,[16] past performance data is the most powerful advertising tool available to funds.[17] Nonmoney-market funds that use performance figures in advertisements and sales literature are actually required to quote uniformly calculated 1-year, 5-year, and 10-year average total returns.[18] Proponents of a mandatory risk measure argue that such performance data only presents the upside of the equation and should be paired with corresponding historical risk data.[19]

The obvious starting point for risk measurement is with basic historical data. In its simplest form, a risk measure could simply be an expansion of the average historical returns data that funds currently provide. By breaking out returns into a series of daily, weekly, or monthly data points, the investor could get information on the volatility of returns. Such information could be presented as data or as a graphical chart of returns over time (see Chart 1).

There are several benefits to this simple approach. Funds already have all the returns data and could easily integrate it into prospectuses. The data is straightforward and not easily subject to manipulation. Finally, periodic returns data matches perfectly with the average returns information currently provided; it is in fact simply an unbundling of the average returns number. However, historical returns data is hard to interpret and even harder to compare. A set of data points or even a graph

CHART 1

Five-Year Monthly Returns

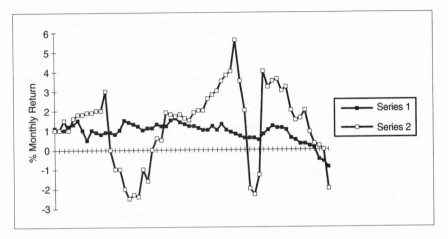

of returns fluctuations will not give the reader a precise measure of volatility with which to compare different funds. As for average returns, risk information is primarily valuable as a tool for comparing different investment vehicles, and most often for comparing different funds.

This leads to the next level of historical fund-based risk measure: basic standard deviation. Standard deviation is a measure of the average deviation from the mean for a distribution of historical returns. It is a simple statistical measure for how widely returns vary, both positively and negatively, over time. As such it is attractive since it is easy to calculate and relatively easy to understand. Standard deviation is also a fairly accurate reflection of what most people think of as risk; the level of change or variance in returns over time.

The predictive value of all these fund-based historical risk measures is based on the assumption that the future will mirror the past in all respects. Not only do they presume, as all historical measures do, that external variables like the market and the economy will continue as before, they also presume that internal variables like the composition of the fund portfolio and the strategy and even identity of the fund manager and advisor will remain the same in the future. Therein lies a primary weakness of fund-based measures. It is unclear how great a weakness these presumptions represent. At least one study done at the SEC suggests that historical standard deviation provides an 86 percent level of accuracy in predicting future standard deviation for some sample groups.[20] However, for other types of funds (with changing investment strategies, portfolio compositions, or fund managers or advisors) or other periods of reporting (periods of high market volatility or dramatic change) historical standard deviation may be far less accurate. More importantly, it is often exactly these types of funds or periods of reporting that are of greatest concern to investors who are trying to measure risk. Similarly, fund-based measures are least effective with new or young funds with little historical data. It is precisely these funds for which investors are most in need of risk measurement.

Portfolio-Based Risk Measures

Portfolio-based historical risk measures address these concerns about changes in portfolio composition and lack of historical fund data by focusing not on the history of the fund, but on the history of the instruments that currently make up the portfolio. In recent years the use of portfolio-based risk measurement and management has dramatically increased.

Standard deviation and related concepts can be employed on a portfolio basis by examining the volatility of the instruments in a fund portfolio, rather than the volatility of the fund itself. This allows the measure to reflect the risk of the current composition of assets. Thus, the standard deviation of the portfolio would be a weighted average of the standard deviations of the individual assets.

However, such a measure does not embody the offsetting effects of different instruments. Many organizations using portfolio-level risk measurement have taken it a step further by factoring in the offsetting effects that different instruments can have on one another. Two primary examples of such portfolio-level risk measures are the Chicago Mercantile Exchange's Standard Portfolio Analysis of Risk (SPAN) and the "value-at-risk" (VAR) methodology.

Futures Exchanges

The Chicago Mercantile Exchange (CME), the Options Clearing Corporation, and other major futures exchanges use a standard deviation or volatility basis for their portfolio-level risk measurements to set margin levels for customers. However, they also allow for offsetting effects of different instruments (hedging).

The CME's SPAN margining system begins by examining historical volatility for all the instruments traded on the exchange. The CME chooses to establish the risk level at 95 percent. This means that an instrument is presumed to have a risk level equal to the 95th percentile of fluctuation or volatility within the range of historical observations chosen. Thus in a set of 100 observations, an instrument will be given a volatility of the 95th most volatile observation.

SPAN then adds a second step of examining historical correlations between different instruments in a given portfolio and reducing risk to the extent that combinations of instruments have offsetting historical volatility.

The data derived from SPAN becomes the starting point for determining margins for exchange customers. The CME Clearing Division additionally considers qualitative variables like the climate of the market and of the particular instruments' market, as well as the concerns of their regulators. The final margin level is a combination of these quantitative and qualitative measures of risk.

Value at Risk

A variation on the portfolio approach of the CME is the value-at-risk (VAR) methodology. In general terms, VAR involves estimating the volatility of a portfolio by combining historical volatility data for each instrument in the portfolio with correlation data between each instrument to discount for any offsetting risk characteristics, just as the SPAN methodology does.

This methodology has recently gained attention. Large financial institutions have already begun to implement VAR methodology. In August 1994 Citicorp became the first financial dealer to publicize its "earnings at risk," a "probability-weighted measure of how much the bank stands to lose on a given day from its trading operations."[21] Several other major U.S. banks including J.P. Morgan, Chase Manhattan, Bankers Trust, and Chemical Bank also use VAR.[22] This methodology was developed to monitor the risk and value of a portfolio, including derivatives holdings.[23] In general terms, the methodology measures "how much money a firm could potentially lose by holding a position for a specific period"[24] by taking into account various aspects of market risk including currency, interest rates, and stock indexes fluctuations.[25] The Financial Accounting Standards Board (FASB) has recommended that companies using derivatives as a hedging device use VAR-type methods to assess the risk of such positions. The FASB is considering additional proposals for risk measurement as well.[26] The SEC plans to implement detailed rules in mid-1996 that would require companies to disclose the risk of their derivatives holdings.[27] The rules will require companies to provide information including VAR calculations in their annual report's management discussion and analysis section.[28] The Basel Committee on Banking Supervision also has proposed that banks use VAR to measure the risks of their holdings.[29]

Application to Funds

Although the methodologies just discussed are not completely developed or standardized,[30] they do offer an attractive way to measure the risk inherent in derivatives products and other new financial instruments in a firm's portfolio.

Given the sophistication of the firms and exchanges that have adopted these portfolio-level methodologies, it is at first glance attractive for the SEC and/or funds to follow their lead. In fact, in the general context of derivative investments by corporate customers, the SEC Chief Accountant is pressing derivatives users to adopt the VAR methodology.[31] Further, the efforts of these organizations in developing, and perhaps even beginning to standardize VAR method would help the SEC implement it more quickly. Finally, the very financial institutions that serve the funds are among those adopting the method. Thus, rather than trying to develop a different risk measure, piggybacking on the efforts of the largest banks, securities firms, and financial exchanges would provide a faster, easier, and more cost-effective way of quickly establishing a risk measure for mutual funds. It may be that although a VAR method doesn't yield a single "magic risk measure," it could provide a discrete set of correlations between commonly understood variables and the risk of the funds portfolio.

However, there are significant concerns about the accuracy of portfolio-level methodologies on one hand, and their clarity or "usability" on the other. In this section, I will discuss the advantages and weaknesses of several methodologies, including VAR, as risk measures for funds, regulators, and investors.

Under the VAR and SPAN methodologies the historical volatility of each security in a portfolio is used to create a bell curve of likely price movements for each security. The data is weighted so that older data has less impact. The risk of the security is defined as two standard deviations, or the size of the loss at the 95th percentile of probability on this bell curve of possible gains and losses. Thus, the risk level derived from this method represents the size of the loss, which will be exceeded in only 2.5 percent of the cases (since the normal distribution is symmetrical, the 5 percent that falls outside the model will be half downside and half upside). (See Chart 2.) The risk for a portfolio is generated from the standard deviations of each security and the correlations among the securities. What emerges is a single risk measure for the *entire* portfolio. The VAR and SPAN methodologies are most commonly used to measure daily earnings at risk for a 24-hour period, thus providing firms with a picture of potential portfolio losses for themselves and their customers for the following business day.

Both the VAR and SPAN methodologies require a data set of historical volatility and correlations, and a supporting software package. Though the collection and maintenance of these data sets may be expensive, the basic calculation methodology is not particularly complex. However, it produces somewhat abstract data, which requires some sophistication to interpret effectively. As a result, it has only been utilized by the most sophisticated financial institutions. The proprietary data sets and methodologies that have been developed by these institutions

CHART 2

Normal Distribution of Probability of Returns

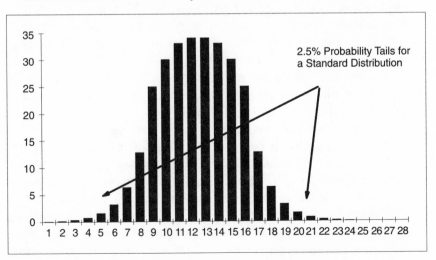

have been kept confidential.[32] Historically, the large banks and financial institutions kept such systems and data highly confidential. However, in the fall of 1994, J.P. Morgan introduced RiskMetrics, a software product based on its own proprietary VAR methodology and corresponding access to data. Low cost or publicly available software and data sets allow any firm with basic computer systems to do VAR measurements.[33] J.P. Morgan estimates that 10 to 15 banks and corporations are already using its product.[34] More than 16,500 downloads of Risk-Metrics data have been recorded in the first five months since its launch.[35] Similarly, the CME has provided volatility and correlation data on its products as well as the basic SPAN software. However it is important to note that even with these two significant data sources, there is still a wide range of financial instruments, particularly OTC instruments, for which data is not publicly available.

Perhaps most importantly, VAR and SPAN are touted for their ability to measure risk for derivatives. A firm can directly measure risk for derivatives without option features in the same fashion as for the instruments underlying the derivatives. Nonoption derivatives include instruments such as futures, swaps, and forward rate agreements (FRAs). For option-type derivatives, data for direct risk measurement may not be available for the VAR software, but nonoption derivatives data can be used in concert with other approaches to generate market scenarios and stress tests and to estimate their effects upon the value of positions.

Strengths and Weaknesses of Portfolio-Based Measures

Before embracing the portfolio-level methodologies as a universal standard, it is important to recognize the significant limits and pitfalls of these approaches.

Like the firm/fund-based methods, portfolio-based methods are, in part, based on the presumption that the future will mirror the past. The methods are driven by historical volatility and correlation data. The underlying assumption is that an instrument's future volatility will be much like its volatility in the past, or at least that changes in instrument volatility are slow and steady and thus show a predictable data pattern. Similarly, the methods presume that correlations between instruments are either static or change at a steady and predictable rate.

A similar problem underlies the use by some portfolio methods, including SPAN and VAR, of a 95 percent probability standard. In one sense the use of a 95 percent confidence level is conceptually deceiving.

What the models say is that on average, based on historical data, losses will not exceed a particular level on 39 out of every 40 trading days (and gains will not exceed a particular level on 39 out of 40 trading days). The difficulty is that the aberrant events that make up the 2.5 percent margin are extreme and highly disruptive. This confidence margin approach arguably underestimates the importance of these aberrant events. While a defender of the method might point out that aberrant losses are balanced by similar aberrant gains, this is not a sufficient justification. If potential gains offset concerns about potential losses, risk management would be largely unnecessary. The development of VAR and SPAN is concerned precisely with downside risk, even when offset by upside potential. It is important to note that the accuracy limitations of the methodology are not a result of inaccurate correlation or volatility data, but rather the limited ability of the model to predict changes in external variables. In effect, the model is weakest when dealing with aberrant changes in familiar variables[36] or changes in unfamiliar variables that effect market prices.[37]

Additionally, both the historical reliance and the use of the confidence margin are driven by a long-term perspective. Since both are based on a statistical approach to prediction, their predictive power lies in a long-term average. Both historical averages and the use of a confidence level smooth away aberrant events. Thus, a VAR or SPAN calculation for a longer period of months or years is likely to be far more accurate but far broader. In the extreme we can predict with 100 percent certainty over an infinite range of possibilities. The difficulty is that VAR is generally used for very short 24-hour periods.

Beyond any questions of accuracy, there is a major problem with deciphering the results of a VAR or SPAN calculation. The very power of the approach—its simplicity (providing a single risk measure for an entire complex portfolio)—is also its flaw. To the uninformed, VAR and SPAN can lead to both over- and underestimation of risk. If the risk level is understood as a likely or possible decrease in value, rather than a form of worst-case scenario, then the user will vastly overestimate risk. By contrast, if the risk level is misinterpreted as an absolute maximum decrease, the investor is underestimating potential losses by completely discounting the 2.5 percent tail of the loss distribution. Thus, if the user does not have a clear understanding of the measure as an historical estimate of losses that are no more likely than 2.5 percent, there is a danger of misinterpretation. Further, the actual data these methods communicate is not intuitively comfortable. Thus in their raw form, the data produced by both SPAN and VAR are inappropriate as a guide of risk for fund investors and the general population.

Simplification of Data

One alternative to SPAN and VAR, which has not yet been explored at a commercial level, is a portfolio-level standard deviation measure over a monthly or yearly period. Such a measure might be more meaningful to individual investors. Even more meaningful would be a further simplification of the risk measure to some artificial scale that, while not meaningful for doing a detailed breakdown and analysis of the portfolio, would be an excellent comparative tool between different funds or portfolios. Like the basic ratings used by organizations such as Standard & Poor's (Aaa, Bbb, AAA, etc.), a simple risk scale would achieve the primary goal of providing investors with a tool for comparing different funds' risk, as the average 5- and 10-year returns data did for comparing fund returns. Presumably, the small population of highly sophisticated individual investors could do a more sophisticated analysis by using the raw returns data of the fund.

Alternatives

Stress Tests, Scenarios, Beta

There have been some recent efforts to develop forward-looking models of risk.[38] Rather than using historical volatility to predict future volatility, these models try to infer future volatility from implied volatility derived from current options prices. The presumption is that current options prices reflect market predictions of volatility in the underlying instrument. Thus, by using data from options, the model is effectively driven by market predictions of future volatility rather than simply by the historical volatility of the asset. These models purport to provide more effective "forward-looking" estimation of volatility on a daily basis.[39]

However, there are several significant limitations to the immediate application of such models to the evaluation of fund portfolios. First, the models are still the subject of academic debate and development. Thus, they are more properly the focus of academicians and advanced finance experts who can recognize and deal with the potential weaknesses of the models. Funds, by contrast, should be concerned with methods and models that are well tested and established. Mutual fund management is not the proper testing ground for cutting-edge finance theory. Secondly, these forward-looking models appear to depend upon an active options market, which provides the predictive power of the model. Many of the assets in which funds invest do not have directly corresponding options markets from which to draw implied volatility data.

Thus, while forward-looking predictive volatility models are a potentially valuable development, these methods are not currently ripe for use by funds, particularly for disclosure purposes.

Another alternative risk measure is the use of scenario and stress tests. These forms of "what-if" examination measure potential risk from particular changes in underlying variables such as interest rates, currency rates, or equity indexes. Utilizing historical data such as that presented by SPAN or VAR, one can develop a what-if scenario for a particular change in a particular variable. The advantage of this methodology is that it produces precise and discrete results. If the assets examined are directly driven by the variable chosen, the results should be exact. For instance a particular change in the S&P 500 will produce a precisely measurable change in the corresponding stock index future. In fact, the use of the beta measure is in fact specifically this kind of stress test. Beta measures the sensitivity of an instrument or portfolio to changes in the overall market.[40] Even if the assets examined are not directly driven by the variable, correlation and volatility data should provide a fairly accurate assessment of price movement resulting from a change in the chosen variable. Using this methodology a fund can answer specific what-if questions with significant accuracy. For example, a fund could present estimates of how the fund value would be immediately affected by a 1 percent shift in interest rates, or a 100-point drop in the Dow Jones Industrial Average, or (particularly for international funds) a 10-yen change in the value of the dollar vis à vis the Japanese currency. In practice, a fund might offer a matrix of VAR measures for particular movements in a discrete set of variables. This data would provide the investor with some measure of the sensitivity of the portfolio to the more common underlying variables and more likely changes in those variables. The disadvantage of this method is that it leaves to the investor the more complex, and uncertain, job of predicting likely changes in the economy and primary variables.

Man-Made Alternatives

Perhaps the most user-friendly risk measurements are the ratings developed and marketed by private sector firms like Standard & Poor's and

Morningstar. These measures are usually a combination of a quantitative risk measurement like VAR or SPAN, coupled with qualitative analysis by industry specialists. This information is then fashioned into an easily understood and readily comparable range of ratings. Such a rating system for funds would provide sufficient accuracy for the purposes of individual investors, in a form they could easily utilize in making investment decisions.

The difficulty is that no firm currently provides a combination of universal coverage and universal accessibility. Since these firms must be able to generate revenues, they either charge the funds that are rated or the customers purchasing the ratings. Thus, while S&P provides its ratings to the public for free, many funds are not willing to pay to be rated. And while Morningstar could achieve full coverage of all funds, the price they charge to customers is significant enough to dissuade the majority of individual investors from subscribing. At present no firm is willing, or perhaps even capable, of providing free ratings for the entire universe of funds.

Short of an SEC mandate for funds to hire a particular rating agency or a full subsidy of that agency's costs, we are unlikely to see such universal coverage and availability of fund risk ratings in the foreseeable future.

PRIMARY USES FOR RISK MEASUREMENT METHODOLOGIES
Disclosure

Even under a strong free market approach that presumes investors are rational actors who should be able to protect themselves, their ability to do so is only as good as the information that drives their decisions. A primary source of information for investors is the fund's own disclosures. This is particularly true for small investors who use mutual funds and have less access than large institutional investors to other sources of accurate information and analysis. Thus, to the extent that derivatives present any new concerns in terms of risk, complexity, or valuation, corresponding concerns emerge over disclosure of these factors. A strong argument has been made that despite these characteristics, funds should not be prevented from investing in derivatives, but it is equally evident that derivatives investments may change the character of the fund's portfolio in ways that should be communicated to investors if they are to make optimal investment decisions. Balanced against this need to inform investors are the direct costs of disclosure and the need of funds to protect their proprietary trading strategies. Note that both of these costs will be reflected in the bottom line for investors (through higher management fees and possibly lower returns). Thus, investors will bear both the costs and benefits of disclosure.

Funds are currently required to file a standard registration statement[41] and give each investor a prospectus.[42] Although most funds have a "derivatives portion" in their prospectuses, the level of disclosure and how well the derivatives' positions are explained vary widely.[43] Derivatives disclosure is often either incomplete and limited or "unduly lengthy and technical."[44] The level and clarity of this disclosure has been criticized—some argue that it "has left retail investors clueless about how their funds use these instruments."[45] In one recent article, funds were called upon to "spell out the types of derivatives used, the amount of money invested in them and how they might behave under pressure."[46]

In early 1995, the SEC addressed the issue by calling on funds to "modify their disclosure to enhance investor understanding of the risks associated with derivative instruments" and heightened their scrutiny of derivatives disclosure in prospectuses.[47] In April 1995, the SEC issued a concept release that specifically requested comments on "improving descriptions of risk by mutual funds and other investment companies."[48] In particular the SEC sought comments and suggestions on "how to improve the descriptions of risk provided to investors by mutual funds and other management investment companies."[49]

Although the relatively new expansion of investments into derivatives certainly merits greater disclosure, rushing to disclosure has its own danger. As discussed in the risk section above, any particular investment must be viewed in the context of the overall fund portfolio. Thus extensive disclosure of the risks of particular derivatives positions may actually give investors an exaggerated impression of fund risks.

Emphasis should be placed, instead, on accurate disclosure of net fund risk, which accurately reflects the contribution of derivatives holdings to the entire portfolio. In this vein, the notion of a quantitative risk measure for fund portfolios is attractive, but should be viewed with caution. Such a simple measure would be a boon to the individual investor, but it raises the spectre of blindsiding the investor if it is incomplete or inaccurate. Investors will depend upon any such measure to the exclusion of other research into a funds's historical volatility and return. The danger of not monitoring any of the possible variables is demonstrated by the Orange County fiasco, where managers apparently did not give enough attention to the interest rate variable, or at least to its potential downside effect on the portfolio.[50]

However, it is important to note that any increased disclosure creates costs, as well as value, for fund investors. The costs of developing any risk measure, and of implementing and maintaining any disclosure regime, will be borne by the fund. Such costs will then be reflected in the profitability of the fund, and will ultimately be borne by the fund investors. Thus when defining the appropriate level of disclosure, we must balance the value to the investor of such information against the costs of producing and disseminating it.

This factor supports the use of the VAR and SPAN methodology, which would allow funds to piggyback on the efforts of financial institutions and exchanges rather than trying to create, implement, and support a new "soup to nuts" risk management measure.

However, use of portfolio-level measures in disclosure to investors has significant pitfalls. As discussed above, the VAR and SPAN methodologies provide a measurement of likely losses with 95 percent probability in a given 24-hour period, based on historical averages. The first question is the relevance of this day-to-day data. Although the investor receives a figure that purports to represent likely losses during a discrete period, be it a day, a week, or a month, she is actually getting an historical average. Further, rather than getting a figure representing likely losses, she is getting a measure of likely losses within two standard deviations on the normal distribution of historical losses. Thus, investors will not easily interpret this measure, which may mislead many of the less analytical. The data from these methodologies will not be accessible or useful to many fund investors, and may even create false impressions of risk in some. This is too high a price to pay for the simplicity and low cost of adopting this measure.

There are, however, two clear alternatives that would provide meaningful risk data to investors. In the short term, scenario analyses for particularly common variables would be a valuable tool to communicate risk to investors. By providing investors with a measure of the sensitivity of the fund portfolio to particularly meaningful variables, such as interest rates, major stock indexes, and currency rates, the fund will enable investors to measure risk in terms they understand and consider important. Such scenario analyses could be done fairly cheaply by utilizing the data used for VAR calculations, and any number of commercially available risk management software packages. However, unless the scenarios are defined uniformly, investors will not be able to easily compare different funds.

A second and more long-term method of providing risk information to investors would be the adoption of some uniform risk scale or rating standard to serve as a benchmark for comparison. Such a standard would best be imposed by, or under the auspices of the SEC, to insure uniformity and impartiality. Such a measure could make use of the VAR methodology to produce ratings. Such ratings would have no objective meaning to investors, but they would be extremely meaningful as a method of comparison, a scale, between different funds. Since most investors presumably make an initial choice to invest in funds and then pursue a comparative analysis of alternative funds, such a relative risk measure will be a valuable tool for them. It will allow investors to combine currently available data on fund returns with a relative measure of fund risk.

This scale or rating system would eliminate the problem of misunderstanding and misinterpretation of the VAR/SPAN data. Instead it would provide investors with a ruler they can use to judge fund risk levels. Much like the current ratings system for corporate debt, which has no objective meaning (Aaa versus BBB for instance), such a system would nonetheless provide investors with valuable data. The SEC could choose to develop such a rating measure internally or enlist the involvement of traditional rating agencies, some of whom have already begun to rate the risk of funds on their own.[51] Since the fall of 1994, the SEC has noted the need for the development of a quantitative risk measure for funds. However, it is less clear that the SEC is willing to take responsibility for the development and maintenance of such a measure.[52]

Until the SEC or the private market of data providers undertake such an effort, funds would be well advised to begin providing basic scenario data to their investors in a simple and clear form. However, they should be wary of distributing VAR data in its raw form, for fear of misinterpretation by investors.

Internal Risk Management

It is important to note that many of the weaknesses of the VAR/SPAN methods (discussed above) are absent when we discuss their internal use by a fund board or advisor. Presumably, a fund board, with the assistance of its advisor, should be able to effectively interpret the data. Thus, current methodologies are a powerful and appropriate tool for internal risk management by funds. Such methodologies can help a fund and its board to understand the risk level of its portfolio, and thus to maintain a risk level commensurate with its disclosures and commitments to shareholders.

OTHER ISSUES RAISED BY FUND DERIVATIVES TRADING
Duties of Directors and Management

The discussion of disclosure presumes that the board of a fund possesses accurate information, which it can then disclose to shareholders in some form. This presumption is based on the duties imposed on the board and advisors by both common law and statute.

Directors have a common law duty to be informed about the business of their fund, and a continuing obligation to keep informed about the activities of the fund.[53] Further, directors have a duty to exercise ordinary care, and thus they cannot avoid liability for failure to exercise care due to lack of knowledge.[54] The Investment Company Act also creates specific duties for fund directors, including the duty to examine all the information necessary to evaluate the terms of investment advisory contracts and make other decisions vested in them by the Act and by rules promulgated under the Act.[55] Similarly, investment advisors have the duty, under the Act, to only recommend securities to funds after proper research and investigation, and only recommend securities that are suitable to the fund.[56]

Thus, fund directors and investment advisors already have duties to remain informed about fund investments. None of these duties are specific to particular instruments, and therefore they can be applied easily to derivatives. It is important for directors and investment advisors to note that while their abstract duties have not changed, the introduction of derivatives into a fund's portfolio does create new demands on them. As is true for any new and complex financial instrument, derivatives have a learning curve. As these instruments are incorporated into funds' trading strategies, directors and investment advisors must ensure that they understand their characteristics and risks. In particular, the development of new methods of measurement may effectively create new duties upon boards and advisors. Analogizing to the famous decision in *T.J. Hooper*,[57] we might argue that fund boards and advisors have an affirmative duty to make use of any measurement "technology" that has become readily available. Further, under the *T.J. Hooper* logic, such a duty is driven by a court-defined level of prudence, so it would be no defense to argue that other funds have not yet adopted the VAR methodology. Thus, particularly for internal risk management, a failure to make use of portfolio-level methods might constitute a violation of fiduciary duties under common law and statute.

However, fund boards must balance this duty to make use of readily available tools with the need to provide investors with comprehensible data. Effective disclosure (as discussed above) is a matter of quality as well as quantity. Simply throwing the proverbial kitchen sink into disclosure documents will not be sufficient to effectively inform investors. Thus, a fund that inundates its shareholders with data they cannot digest will likely incur the displeasure of the SEC, which has recently emphasized "understandability" of disclosure.

Leverage

Like risk, leverage is often raised as a problem or danger of derivative instruments. However, the proposition that all derivatives are a form of leverage as contemplated by the Investment Company Act has a fundamental fallacy. Some analysts argue that derivatives act like investments in the underlying asset, except that they are made on margin. Thus, investments in derivatives are the equivalent of increasing leverage, effectively a form of debt. In a recent memorandum on policy initiatives related to mutual funds' use of derivatives, SEC Chairman Levitt pointed to the leverage potentially "made available to mutual funds through the use of certain derivative instruments."[58] Levitt pointed to both direct leverage created by investments that create obligations, and the "economic equivalent of leverage" created by other derivatives through increased price sensitivity to market fluctuations. His expansion of the definition of leverage in the latter phrase is not merited by the terms of the Investment Company Act or by the economic characteristics that are generally attributed to leverage. *Leverage* is most commonly defined as incurring debt or obligation in an investment.[59] Further, the language of the Investment Company Act suggests a similar definition. Section 18(f) of the Act specifically prohibits open-end funds from issuing any "senior security" other than limited bank borrowing.[60] *Senior security* is defined broadly under Section 18(g) as "any bond, debenture, note, or similar obligation or instrument constituting a security and *evidencing indebtedness*"(emphasis added).[61] The SEC expanded on this limitation vis à vis derivatives in the late 1970s, requiring funds to "cover" any obligation created by derivatives by establishing segregated accounts consisting of cash or other high-grade liquid assets, or by holding the underlying instrument or other offsetting instrument.[62] The SEC has justifiably viewed this section as applying to any transaction that may cause a fund to have future payment obligations or risk of loss exceeding its initial investments.[63] Such a definition of leverage encompasses writing derivative instruments (thus creating potential obligation to the purchaser) and selling short. However, it does not encompass the purchase of a wide range of other derivative instruments where the maximum exposure is the loss of the purchase price.

The broader "economic equivalent" definition of leverage focuses on the increased volatility created by leverage. However, since the language of Section 18(g) focuses on whether an instrument creates a future obligation, increased volatility should not alone qualify an instrument as a senior security. A definition of leverage that is driven by volatility also does not seem intuitively useful. Since nearly any investment has an increased price sensitivity to market fluctuations when compared to the most safe investments such as government debt, gold, or even cash, this definition of leverage could include any and all financial instruments.

The analogy of derivatives to a purchase on margin is similarly misplaced. There is a great difference between the purchase of the underlying asset on margin and a purchase of the derivative. When investors purchase an asset on margin, they are generally required to put up at least enough margin to cover the portion of the asset value that is at short-term risk. Effectively, the asset is dissected into "foundation value," which is unlikely to dissipate in the short term, and "risky value," which is likely to fluctuate in the short term. Another way to look at this dissection is that every investment is a combination of a low to no-risk investment like Treasury instruments and a high-risk investment in the form of the risky value. Thus, in effect the underlying asset risk profile can be simulated by holding both a derivative instrument and a low-risk asset like a government security that simulates the foundation value of the asset.

By holding a form of a lien on the securities, the broker is assured of being able to recover the foundation value and thus only seeks cash margin to cover the risky value. By contrast, a purchase of derivatives is effectively a dissection of the asset before purchase. In effect, the investor is purchasing only the risky value. While this certainly results in a more risky investment, no debt and no potential liability for any value beyond the cost of the instrument are incurred. By contrast, a purchaser on margin is still theoretically liable for any decrease in value beyond her margin. If the foundation value is depleted, the investor is liable to the broker. Thus, the only definition of leverage that would encompass derivatives would theoretically also encompass all investments since an investment, by definition, has greater risk than cash.

Only the definition of leverage as an investment that creates a future obligation above and beyond the purchase price is both intuitively useful and suggested by the language of the Act. A definition that encompasses any high volatility, high-risk asset goes beyond the meaning of the Act and is too broad to be of practical value. With this definition of direct leverage, there is no need for additional limitations on fund investments. Perhaps the commission does need to reexamine its statements on some derivative instruments. The senior security prohibition already eliminates concern about funds incurring future obligations, and the question of instrument risk is best dealt with directly and broadly across all instruments, since derivatives are not alone in presenting this concern.

Valuation

Valuation of assets is a particularly important issue for funds, for both logistical and statutory reasons. Since some derivative instruments are difficult to accurately value on a regular basis, derivative investments can create valuation problems for funds.

Open-end funds are in the business of offering a liquid or redeemable asset.[64] This is one of their main selling points.[65] Thus, open-end funds can be liquidated at will by shareholders.[66] While closed-end funds don't have the problem of valuation for redemption, they must also be able to value their assets in order to price any shares they sell.[67] Thus day-to-day or periodic valuation of fund assets is a logistical requirement of fund operation. Just as importantly, the public has grown to expect regular and accurate valuation of fund assets. The importance of such valuation to the public is demonstrated by the attention focused on the recent failure of Fidelity funds to accurately report fund valuation.[68] The failure to report updated valuation of the funds was a major embarrassment for Fidelity, as well as a possible violation of section 22(c) of the Act and the SEC and NASD rules thereunder, and it received significant coverage and criticism.

In addition to any logistical concerns, there is also an explicit statutory requirement for regular valuation of fund assets. The Act requires any fund issuing redeemable securities to sell, redeem, or repurchase them at a price based on their current net asset value.[69] In particular, funds are required to price their redeemable securities no less frequently than once daily.[70] Exchange-traded derivatives are easily priced since they are traded on liquid markets. Similarly, it may be possible to price some very standard OTC derivative instruments daily. However, most OTC derivatives are written to meet the particular needs of the investor, and they have no liquid market to regularly price them. If market quotations are not available, the board of directors of a fund may in good faith determine the value of a security.[71] Thus, fund managers have the discretion to price illiquid securities using mathematical models.

Valuation models are the subject of debate and regulatory concern.[72] Arguments are made that these mark-to-model methodologies produce widely different results and are not particularly reliable.[73] However, the active and successful trading operations in complex derivatives by a variety of large institutions suggest that at least some of the models are effective and accurate.

Such theoretical pricing models fall into three major categories.[74] Deterministic models use a defined set of factors to determine exact value. Such models will only be available for derivatives in a few cases. Stochastic valuation models are based on probabilities rather than concrete cause and effect relationships. The most famous models, Black-Scholes and the Binomial model, are commonly driven by historical data. Moreover, proprietary stochastic models vary from firm to firm as each player tries to gain an edge through slight modifications. Thus, there are no industry standards for such models. Finally, delivery valuation models try to measure the value of all deliveries. For example, one might measure the difference between the value of the stock and the exercise price at a future point, weighted by the probability of the stock achieving that price.

Although there is still no accepted standard model, the financial technology to price derivatives appears to exist or to be on the horizon. This is particularly important for the more complex derivatives since these instruments have most eluded uniformity in the financial community. Models used for more common derivatives already seem to be fairly uniform. It is also important to note that models for pricing derivatives are highly sophisticated by comparison to pricing methods for some other illiquid assets. Both regulators and representatives of the financial community have advocated the development of a standard valuation model, and efforts have begun to develop such a standard.[75] Most recently, the U.S. Internal Revenue Service asked Los Alamos National Laboratory to develop and implement computer models for valuing complex derivative transactions.[76] However, at present, a standard pricing methodology has not yet been developed, and at least in the short term, the cost of maintaining in-house models or adapting the basic models to a fund's particular investments may not be cost effective for some funds.[77]

Though valuation tools are available to fund managers, there are no industry standards. This lack suggests that while funds may effectively be able to manage a derivatives portfolio, shareholders have no uniform valuation method to judge these holdings. While awaiting the development and completion of a standard, the optimal solution may be found in more basic disclosure. By requiring funds to disclose their pricing methodology and, more importantly, to adopt and use a particular methodology consistently, shareholders will have some guide to the value of each fund's derivatives holdings. Sophisticated shareholders may actually evaluate the fund's methodology. And even unsophisticated investors will be able to judge fund derivative performance through historical data from the fund's pricing model. Though there may be some variance between model valuation and "real" value, if we assume that the error is consistent, historical data from the same model will give investors a clear indication of the success, failure, and volatility of the fund's derivatives investments.

Finally, an argument may be made that the VAR methodology can provide risk measures that may be applied to valuation. The argument is based on the presumption that high-risk investments like derivatives should be discounted in a funds portfolio valuation. However, inasmuch as volatility creates both an upside and a downside, high-risk instruments do not have an inherently lower value. The risks associated with these assets are already reflected in their market price. Further discounting their value would be the equivalent of double counting the associated risk.

Thus, I would argue that derivatives do not present significant additional concerns for funds in terms of leverage or valuation. Derivatives, other than those written by the fund, do not create leverage as commonly defined, and the valuation problems created by derivatives are no greater than those for other uncertain or illiquid instruments.

INVESTOR PROTECTION POLICY

One issue that underlies the entire debate over risk, disclosure, and derivatives is the question of how much investor protection is appropriate in the first place.

In seeking to regulate the market for derivative financial products, the government is presumably seeking to protect parties who are affected, directly or indirectly, by these transactions. Individuals are often the recipients of paternalistic[78] government protection efforts, and the regulation of financial products is often driven by consumer protection goals. However, in the case at hand, the vast majority of end-customers of derivatives products are not individuals, but rather sophisticated institutions and corporations. Nonetheless, recent major losses in derivatives trading by such sophisticated institutions have raised arguments that they need some paternalistic protection (these losses have, in fact, raised questions about just how sophisticated these institutions really are). In particular, the question here is whether the risk or complexity of derivatives justifies regulation in order to protect these consumers.

Free market proponents argue that social utility will be maximized when participants have access to all possible instruments, and that these free market participants are the best decision makers for investment strategies. Further, we can make a *caveat emptor* argument vis à vis investors: Investors are responsible for monitoring the firms, and in an efficient market they will effectively punish any firm that misuses assets.[79] However, both of these arguments rest on the presumption that the market and information flow are perfectly, or at least highly, efficient. To the extent that they are not, there is a role for regulation. Similarly, these arguments presume that we are only concerned with the net result, regardless of who wins and who loses. In point of fact, our system attaches great importance to protecting even a minority of individuals. Thus, while there is strength to the free market argument, it does not extinguish the case for government regulation of derivatives and the market in general.

The case for regulation is particularly strong for instruments like derivatives, which can dramatically change the risk of a portfolio with a very small proportion of total investment. To the extent that investors are not aware of a fund's investment in derivatives, the efficient market arguments may fail, leaving a need for government intervention.

The complexity of derivatives presents a similar argument for regulation to that driven by their high-risk characteristics; namely, that customers need to be protected against instruments they do not fully understand. This argument is strongest for funds where many customers are individual investors who are not likely to have a sophisticated understanding of financial instruments, but far weaker for institutional customers who invest in derivatives.[80]

Thus, while a strong free market argument and a *caveat emptor* argument may be made against government regulation of derivative investments by institutional investors, these arguments weaken significantly for funds. Although funds are managed by professionals, they are an investment vehicle for small individual investors. The need of such investors for government protection is far stronger and the free market argument far weaker.

CONCLUSIONS

Derivative instruments are powerful hedging and investment tools for funds. It is clear that in the coming decade nearly all funds will maintain some derivative positions, whether for purposes of hedging or speculation. It is equally clear that derivatives create new concerns and problems for both funds and regulators. However, it is important to note that some concerns about derivatives are either overstated or lack foundation. With the exception of short positions and some particular instruments, derivatives do not, in a fundamental sense, create additional leverage to a fund. Similarly, the problems of valuation are no greater for derivatives than for any number of other assets, and they are particularly small for the most highly liquid exchange-traded derivatives.

However, concerns about monitoring, managing, and measuring the risk in a fund portfolio are certainly magnified by the addition of derivatives positions. Thus, it is important that the SEC and fund managers incorporate effective risk measurement into internal risk management and disclosure by funds. However, in doing so they cannot rush to embrace new methodologies or measures without examining the balance between accuracy and clarity. Across the range of risk measurement methods there is a clear trade-off between the accuracy of the data and the ease with which it can be digested by individual investors. Opponents of increased disclosure would argue that the level of abstraction necessary to make such data comprehensible removes any value in disclosure. They would argue that the "assistance" provided to investors through such simplification simply replaces the investors' chosen intermediary in the investment decision-making process (the fund) with another party that the investor did not choose (a particular risk measurement model). Thus, they would argue that the job of measuring risk and matching portfolio volatility to the needs of the investor is properly the job of the fund in which the investor has chosen to invest.

A significant counterargument is that while funds are primarily responsible for providing investors with the kind of portfolio they bargained for, current mechanisms for ensuring fund performance of this duty are ineffective. Thus, by providing investors with an unbiased assessment of fund risk, we enable the investors themselves to monitor whether funds are providing the type of investment they bargained for.

To the extent that the costs of such disclosure are de minimus, and the methodology used is established and accepted, funds should have no quarrel with the inclusion of risk disclosure. Further, if such disclosure only leads to shifts in assets between different funds, the industry as a whole should be neutral, or even supportive of such an effort, since it may increase confidence in fund investments.

The most extreme argument, that derivatives and other highly complex instruments should only be utilized by experts and quarantined from individual investors entirely, is shortsighted and ineffective. As financial markets develop, new instruments are constantly entering the stream of commerce. Blocking individual investors from choosing them would both stymie their development and hamstring individual investors' efforts. More importantly, as institutional investment management (through funds, annuities and other institutional products) becomes the norm for individual investors, the line between individual investors and institutional investors will be blurred. In a fundamental sense, few large institutional investors are not backed directly or indirectly by individual investor assets. Highly complex investments like derivatives are a part of the financial market that will have an impact on individual investors, and for which they must be given some preparation and information.

The portfolio-level methodologies offer some significant value but in their present form they may not be "ripe" for use as direct disclosure to fund shareholders. Rather, they should be used in the short term for funds' internal risk management, and they should drive the effort by the SEC to develop a more comprehensible risk scale or standard. The SEC apparently intends to leave such development to the private market, but much could be gained if the SEC instead would assume more leadership in the development and universal implementation of a standard. Similarly, it is important that funds pursue the emerging risk measurement methodologies aggressively, both as a method of marketing their products, and as a defense against potential liability. In the short term, funds should introduce more basic risk disclosure in the form of sensitivity to primary economic variables like interest rates and major equity indexes. In the long term the investment management industry must recognize that disclosure of such variables as portfolio risk is not only inevitable, but in their interest. To the extent that such disclosure gives investors greater comfort in their ability to compare different funds through a standard scale or measure, it will increase the total pool of funds made available for investment management. The division of this increasing pie is properly a matter for free competition between different fund managers. Further, a failure to pursue these issues in the industry will press the hand of the SEC to unilaterally enforce a measure that may or may not be the optimal solution. Thus, the investment management industry would be best served by accepting the principle of some risk disclosure and concentrating on the choice of its measure, method, and implementation.

ENDNOTES

1. Testimony of Congressman Richard E. Neal, House Committee on Banking, Finance and Urban Affairs, October 5, 1994 (Federal Document Clearing House).

2. Investment Company Act of 1940, 15 USC §80a–13(a)(3) (1994).

3. Testimony of Congressman Richard E. Neal, House Committee on Banking, Finance and Urban Affairs, October 5, 1994 (Federal Document Clearing House).

4. Testimony of Congressman Richard E. Neal House, Committee on Banking, Finance and Urban Affairs, October 5, 1994 (Federal Document Clearing House); Testimony of Congressman Jack Fields, House Energy and Commerce Committee, Subcommittee on Telecommunications and Finance, September 27, 1994 (Federal Document Clearing House).

5. Investment Company Act of 1940, 15 USC §80a–13(a) (1994).

6. See Investment Company Act Release No. 5847 (Oct. 21, 1969); Investment Company Act Release No. 18612 (Mar. 12, 1992), 57 FR 9828 (Mar. 20, 1992); Letter from Marianne K. Smythe, Director, Division of Investment Management, Securities and Exchange Commission, to Matthew P. Fink, President, Investment Company Institute (Dec. 9, 1992).

7. "An illiquid asset is any asset that may not be sold or disposed of in the ordinary course of business within seven days at approximately the value at which the mutual fund has valued the investment." Testimony of Arthur Levitt, Chairman, Securities and Exchange Commission, Committee on Banking, Housing and Urban Affairs, January 5, 1995 (Federal Document Clearing House Congressional testimony), citing Guidelines for Form NIA, Guide 4.

8. Brett D. Fromson, "SEC Offers Plan to Police Derivatives," *The Wall Street Journal*, Sept. 27, 1994, p. C1.

9. The first exchange-traded financial futures (interest rate contracts) were introduced by the Chicago Mercantile Exchange (CME) in 1972. Exchange-traded stock index futures first were introduced in 1982, again by the CME. Exchange-based financial futures trading in Europe began in 1982 at the London International Financial Futures Exchange (LIFFE). M. Desmond Fitzgerald, Financial Futures (London: Euromoney Publications, 1983), p. ix.

10. The Comptroller of the Currency has found that more than 1,200 financial derivative products are currently being offered. Albert R. Karr, "Bank Regulator Signals Move on Derivatives", *The Wall Street Journal*, Apr. 21,

1994, p. A3. The range of derivative instruments includes swaps, options, inverse floaters, caps, floors, collars, swaptions, embedded options, synthetic indexing, synthetic stocks, barrier options, best-of-two options, down-and-out options, ceilings, deferred stop or deferred start options, lateral options, look back options, performance options, and exploding options, among others. Elayne Sheridan, "FCMs Capitalize on OTC Business," *Futures Industry*, Nov./Dec. 1993, pp. 26, 29.

11. "Financial innovation is being produced almost exclusively by mathematical Ph.D.'s or individuals with science and quantitative backgrounds." Adam R. Waldman, "OTC Derivatives and Systemic Risk: Innovative Finance or the Dance Into the Abyss?" *American University Law Review* 43 (1994), pp. 1023, 1025 n.2. The former head of derivatives trading at Morgan Stanley was, in fact, an astrophysicist. Saul Hansell, "Inside Morgan Stanley's Black Box," *Institutional Investor* May 1989, pp. 204, 205.

12. See Waldman, "OTC Derivatives and Systemic Risk," p. 1025 n. 3, citing Martin French, "The Comeback of the Number-Crunchers," *Euromoney*, Oct. 1988, pp. 69, 71 (describing how the increase in computer capabilities has fueled financial quantitative analysis); William Glasgall and Bill Javetski, "Swap Fever: Big Money, Big Risks," *Business Week*, June 1, 1992, pp. 102, 102 (noting that Sun Microsystems' workstations are now integral to the world of financial engineering); John W. Verity, "Street Smarts: The Supercomputer Becomes a Stock Strategist," *Business Week*, June 1, 1987, p. 84.

13. Brett D. Fromson, "SEC Offers Plan to Police Derivatives," *Washington Post*, September 27, 1994, p. C1.

14. Ibid.

15. Some more sophisticated models make use of proprietary predictions of future volatility rather than, or in concert with, historical data.

16. Statement Director, Division of Corporate Regulation (1968), CCH [1967–1969 Trans. Binder] Fed. Sec. L. Rep. para. 77,625.

17. Tamar Frankel, 3 *Regulation of Money Managers* (Boston: Little, Brown & Company, 1980), Chapter XXV, §13.6, p. 567.

18. 17 CFR §230.482, proposed, IC–15315, adopted, IC–16245 (1987), CCH [1987–1988 Trans. Binder] Fed. Sec. L. Rep. para. 84,217; see also Investment Co. Inst., Corres. (1988), CCH [1987–1988 Trans. Binder] Fed. Sec. L. Rep. para. 78,690 (calculation of yield and total return).

19. The partial fallacy of this argument is that neither "risk" nor "return" are particularly negative or positive data sets. Negative returns are bad,

whereas low risk is good. Although the presentation of returns alone is
an incomplete picture since it does not show the volatility with which
those returns are delivered, it is not necessarily a pro-fund data set.
Returns data can over- or underestimate the performance of a fund.

20. Professor Susan Woodward, Address at ALI-ABA Investment
    Management Regulation course of study (October 12, 1995).

21. Barbara Donnelly Granito and Steven Lipin, "Alarmed, World's Central
    Banks Call for Full Exposure of All Risk," *The Wall Street Journal*,
    Sept. 29, 1994, p. C1.

22. Charles Seeger, Business World: How to Prevent Future Nick Leesons,
    The Wall Street Journal, Aug. 8, 1995, p. PA13.

23. Michael R. Sesit, "Derivatives Dealers Show Progress in Managing Risks,
    a Survey Shows," *The Wall Street Journal Europe*, Dec. 6, 1994, p. 14.

24. *Ibid.*

25. For a concise description of the "value at risk" methodology, see
    "Measuring Value-at Risk," *Derivatives Week*, Sept. 26, 1994, p. 6.

26. *Ibid.*

27. Lee Berton, "SEC's Long Delayed Plan on Derivatives," *The Wall Street
    Journal*, Nov. 27, 1995, p. A2).

28. *Ibid.*

29. Becky Gaylord, "Central Bankers Set Global Plan to Cover Risks,"
    The Wall Street Journal, April 13, 1995.

30. Many derivative products, particularly those traded over the counter,
    may not be regularly marked to market, thus making it difficult to
    evaluate their value or risk at particular points in time. Even for those
    derivatives that are marked to market, one critic has noted an additional
    weakness in the methodology, as used by some firms, in the one-day
    time horizon for measuring risk. "Despite daily marking to market, for
    some products it may be unrealistic to assume large positions can be
    promptly liquidated without substantial adverse market impact."
    "Mullins Critiques G-30s Work," *American Banker Washington Watch,*
    Aug. 2, 1993, 1993 WL 2772853 (quoting from a speech given by
    Federal Reserve Vice Chairman David Mullins on July 28, 1993 at a
    conference sponsored by the International Swaps and Derivatives
    Association).

31. "Schuetze Pushes Firms to Mull Overall Risks," *The Credit Union
    Accountant* 4, Nov. 14, 1994, p. 5.

32. Clive Davidson, "Thanks to JP Morgan Anyone Can Calculate Their
    Market Exposure," *The Guardian*, March 9, 1995, p. 4.

33. RiskMetrics is now publicly distributed and JP Morgan makes the data to support it available through various sources including the internet. Under a recently announced expanded coverage JP Morgan will soon distribute 900 volatility figures for financial instruments daily, and more than 200,000 market correlations. The product covers many of the most heavily traded markets and is being expanded regularly.

34. Peter Heap, "JP Morgan Gives an Answer to Problem of Measuring Risk," *The Bond Buyer*, March 21, 1995, p. 8.

35. "JP Morgan Expands RiskMetrics by Adding Commodities and More Market Enhancements," *Business Wire*, March 15, 1995 (citing Jacques Longerstaey, head of Market Risk Research at JP Morgan).

36. The precipitous drop of the Mexican peso in the winter of 1995, triggered by an intense change in Mexican government policy, is an example of such an aberrant change.

37. One excellent example would be a radical political event such as the assassination of a U.S. president.

38. Campbell R. Harvey and Robert E. Whaley, "Market volatility prediction and the efficiency of the S&P 100 index option market," *Journal of Financial Economics* 31 (1992), p. 43.

39. Ibid., p. 71.

40. Thus a portfolio with Beta = 1 can be expected to move proportionally in lock-step with the market (1 percent up in the market = 1 percent up in the portfolio).

41. Funds are required to fulfill the registration requirements of the Securities Act of 1933, 15 USC §77aa (1994). Investment Company Act of 1940, 15 USC §80a–24(a) (1994).

42. Similarly, the prospectus requirements are identical to those in section 10(a) of the Securities Act of 1933, 15 USC §77j(a) (1994). Investment Company Act of 1940, 15 USC §80A–2(a)(31) (1994) (definition of *prospectus*).

43. Abby Schultz, "Quarterly Mutual Funds Review: Spotting Derivatives in a Portfolio Can Prove to Be a Tough Chore," *The Wall Street Journal*, July 7, 1994, p. R11.

44. Testimony of Arthur Levitt, Securities and Exchange Commission, Senate Committee on Banking, Housing and Urban Affairs, Jan. 5, 1995 (Federal Document Clearing House Congressional Testimony).

45. Brett D. Fromson, "SEC to Require More Reporting by Mutual Funds," *Washington Post*, June 24, 1994, p. F1.

46. Stan Hinden, "When Funds Sound Too Good to Be True," *Washington Post*, Sept. 4, 1994, p. H3.

47. Letter from Carolyn B. Lewis, Assistant Director, Division of
    Investment Management, Securities and Exchange Commission, to
    Investment Company Registrants (Feb. 25, 1994); Testimony of Arthur
    Levitt, Securities and Exchange Commission, Senate Committee on
    Banking, Housing and Urban Affairs, Jan. 5, 1994 (Federal Document
    Clearing House Congressional Testimony).

48. Improving Descriptions of Risk by Mutual Funds and Other Investment
    Companies, Exchange Act Release No. 33–7153; 34–35546 (March 29,
    1995).

49. Ibid.

50. Depending on your source, the Orange County managers were either
    painfully ignorant of the risks, or actually embraced them by
    maximizing their exposure.

51. For example, Morningstar currently offers a publication that includes
    proprietary risk measures for mutual funds, though the basis and
    structure of these measures is not publicly disclosed.

52. In a speech before the National Press Club in the fall of 1994, SEC
    Chairman Arthur Levitt said that he favored a risk rating scale for
    mutual funds, but that such a measure would not be a matter for the
    SEC to tackle. "Levitt Encourages One-Page Summaries of Mutual
    Fund Prospectus," *BNA Banking Report* 63, no. 14 (October 24, 1994),
    p. 591.

53. Charles R. O'Kelley, Fr. and Robert B. Thompson, *Corporations and
    Other Business Associations* (Boston: Little, Brown & Company, 1992),
    p. 249.

54. Ibid.

55. Investment Company Act of 1940, 15 USC §80a–15(c) (1994).

56. T. Frankel, 2 *Regulation of Money Managers* (Boston: Little, Brown &
    Company, 1978), p. 670.

57. In this decision by Judge Learned Hand, owners of tugboats were held
    liable for sunk barges on the theory of negligence, for failing to install
    radios that were readily available, despite the fact that the tugboat
    owners conformed to the standard of care in the industry. *The T.J.
    Hooper*, 60 F.2d 737 (2d Cir 1932).

58. Testimony by Arthur Levitt, Chairman Securities and Exchange
    Commission, September 27, 1994, Subcommittee on Telecommunica-
    tions and Finance, Committee on Energy and Commerce (Federal
    Document Clearing House Congressional Testimony).

59. "Borrowing is said to create financial leverage or gearing. Financial
    leverage does not affect the risk or expected return on the firm's

assets..." Richard A. Brealey and Stewart C. Myers, *Principles of Corporate Finance*, 4th ed. (New York: McGraw Hill, 1991), p. 190. Marcia Stigum defines *debt leverage* as "the amplification in the return earned on equity funds when an investment is financed partly with borrowed money." Marcia Stigum, *The Money Market* (Homewood: Dow Jones-Irwin 1983), p. 696.

60. Investment Company Act of 1940, 15 USC §80a–18(f) (1994).

61. 15 USC §80a–18(g) (1988) (emphasis added).

62. Testimony of Arthur Levitt, Chairman Securities and Exchange Commission, Committee on Banking, Housing and Urban Affairs, January 5, 1995 (Federal Document Clearing House Congressional Testimony), citing Investment Company Act Release No. 10666 (Apr. 18, 1979), 44 FR 25128 (Apr. 27, 1994).

63. Eric D. Roiter, "Investment Companies' Use of OTC Derivatives: Does the Existing Regulatory Regime Work?," *Stanford Journal of Law, Business & Finance* 1 (1995), pp. 270, 280.

64. The Act defines an open-end investment company as "a management company which is offering for sale or has outstanding any redeemable security of which it is the issuer." Investment Company Act of 1940, 15 USC §80a–5(a)(1) (1994).

65. A *redeemable security* is defined as "any security, other than short-term paper, under the terms of which the holder, upon its presentation to the issuer or to a person designated by the issuer, is entitled (whether absolutely or only out of surplus) to receive approximately his proportionate share of the issuer's current net assets, or the cash equivalent thereof." Investment Company Act of 1940, 15 USC §80a–2(a)(32) (1994).

66. While technically a fund can simply give the shareholder a proportional share of the assets of the fund, in practice, for all but the largest shareholders, a fund will choose to give the shareholder the cash equivalent.

67. 15 USC §80a–2(a)(41)(B); 17 CFR §270.22c–1.

68. In June of 1994 Fidelity experienced a computer failure that made it impossible to produce valuation of their funds. Instead, a fund manager decided to report the funds' value as unchanged. Since the funds' actual value, along with the market, had dropped during the week, this had the effect of leading newspapers to report an inaccurately high valuation of the fund. Floyd Norris, "Incorrect Prices Turn Fidelity's Face Red," *New York Times*, June 22, 1994, Sec. D, p. 1.

69. 17 CFR §270.22c–1(a) (1994).

70. 17 CFR §270.22c–1(b) (1994).

71. Investment Company Act of 1940, 15 USC §80a–2(a)(41)B(B) (1994). There are some limitations on the board's authority to determine the value of a security for majority–owned and other controlled companies.

72. Richard Y. Roberts, "The Constantly Evolving Nature of Federal Securities Law: An Introduction to the Symposium," *Alabama Law Review* 45 (1994), pp. 729, 739.

73. One derivatives consultant argues that it is not uncommon to find a variance of up to 60 percent between different pricing models for complex derivatives, and up to 10 percent even for plain vanilla derivatives. Terence P. Pare, "Learning to Live with Derivatives," *Fortune*, July 25, 1994, p. 106.

74. Testimony of Peter Vinella, Senior Consultant, Smith Barney, House Telecommunications and Finance Subcommittee, June 30, 1994 (Federal Document Clearing House Congressional Testimony).

75. Testimony of Dr. Camilo C. Gomez, Los Alamos National Laboratory, House Subcommittee on Telecommunications and Finance, July 13, 1994 (Federal Document Clearing House Congressional Testimony).

76. "US Tax Agency Seeks Model to Value Derivatives," Reuters Newswire, Bonds Capital Market, Dec. 15, 1994.

77. Joanne Morrison, "Mastering Pricing Tools for Derivatives Can Be Arduous for Firms," *The Bond Buyer*, Nov. 9, 1994, p. 7.

78. This term does not connote any value judgment; it is simply a description of protection given to parties that are perceived as unable to help themselves or even unaware of the danger.

79. There is a significant debate over whether there is effective shareholder control or discipline of management, and whether institutional shareholders have changed this balance of control. See, for example, Roberta Romano, "Public Pension Fund Activism in Corporate Governance Reconsidered," *Columbia Law Review* 93 (1993), p. 795; Bernard S. Balck, "Shareholder Passivity Reexamined," *Michigan Law Review* 89 (1990), p. 520, 575–91; and John C. Coffee, Jr., "Liquidity Versus Control: The Institutional Investor as Corporate Monitor," *Columbia Law Review* 91 (1991) pp.1277, 1336. This paper will assume that shareholders (individual or institutional) have some significantly effective level of control over long-term corporate behavior and thus can punish bad management investments. If this is not the case, the need for supervision goes beyond derivatives to all investments.

80. One might argue that losses in derivatives are not a sign of ignorance on the part of these customers, but simply an example of the powerful downside to such risky investments. While they are not as well reported, there are many cases of firms that make a healthy profit in derivatives trading. It is this potential for above-market returns that has lured these firms to the high-risk game of derivatives. This interpretation of events is bolstered by the character of the players. It seems unlikely that professional managers and investment officers would fail to understand these instruments, and further that they would seek to invest in instruments that they did not understand. A more likely explanation is that they actively chose to invest in instruments that offered the opportunity for above-market returns. Finally, even if we do believe that these institutions are baffled by the complexity of these instruments, there is a powerful *caveat emptor* argument to be made. While these institutions may not understand these particular products, they cannot claim to be unfamiliar with the securities market in general (since such an admission would be paramount to negligence for most financial officers). Thus, they should be sophisticated enough to measure their own knowledge and recognize the dangers of investing in such complex products.

VII

FUNDS FOR THE RICH; FUNDS FOR FOREIGN INVESTORS

16

HEDGE FUNDS IN THE 1990s
Private Risk Taking, Public Consequences?

Susan C. Ervin[1], *Chief Counsel and Deputy Director of the Division of Trading and Markets, Commodity Futures Trading Commission*

Hedge funds have become a controversial phenomenon in the financial marketplace—a potent combination of market power, aggressive trading strategies, and intense reclusiveness. They have come to serve as a lightning rod for fears concerning the dangers of derivatives, capturing the imagination of the financial press, and "conjur[ing] up an image of wealth, risk, a mysterious, highly talented trader, a giant moving the market."[2] More than merely "mutual funds for the rich," hedge funds are aggressively traded pools of capital that elude definition, strive to avoid regulation, and appear to hold vast sway in the marketplace. They have become the objects of Wall Street's envy, Washington's cautious scrutiny, and an admixture of suspicion and admiration on the part of the public generally. Indeed, hedge funds recently received the ultimate in dubious honors—the spotlight of congressional hearings convened to consider their potential risks to the banking system and the financial structure at large.

The recent dramatic expansion of the hedge fund market reflects a confluence of several forces in this century's last decade: rapid expansion of the high net worth sector of the American population, the core clientele of hedge funds; intense investor interest in innovative investment vehicles promising to provide returns above fixed income yields; participation in the hedge fund arena by multiple high-profile money managers with spectacular track records; and the proliferation of a host of new investment alternatives, including an endlessly varied menu of derivative products and an increasingly global array of markets. It is as if the "masters of the universe," the financial star warriors of the 1980s, had turned to billion-dollar money management for the well heeled even as the "financial innovation spiral"[3] generates new forms of structuring and transferring risk for their consumption on a virtually continuous basis. The star hedge fund managers evoke Henry Kaufman's image of the "ultimate evolution of the risk-taking financial entrepreneur," "the portfolio manager who can go long or short in any market in any currency, and on a leveraged or an unleveraged basis—and who often can do this in a tax-advantaged off-shore vehicle, with minimal, if any, official supervision."[4]

Hedge funds have risen to prominence in an environment in which the risk propensities of individual products and of the system as a whole have been etched in the public mind through the public drama of market crashes, bankruptcies of municipalities and 200-year-old banks, and other disasters befalling presumably sophisticated market players. The vulnerability of this financial environment to rapid transmission of risk through an increasingly linked marketplace is not merely a matter of anecdote and press hyperbole. Recognizing the impact of wholesale growth in the volume and complexity of derivative instruments, coupled with quantum leaps in technology and telecommunications, federal financial overseers have recognized that "the rate at which shocks spread throughout the financial system" has markedly increased.[5]

In this context of interconnectedness and interdependence, hedge funds have been accused of playing a key role in transmitting instability. To some, they exemplify the phenomenon of " 'hot money,' a multi-trillion-dollar pool of capital that races around the world's stock, bond, and currency markets in search of higher returns each day."[6] The "growing presence in the markets of an expanding group of " 'high-octane' portfolio managers who are free to roam throughout the financial sphere…with primarily a very near-term focus and no particular loyalty to any national marketplace" has been targeted as a cause of vulnerability in the financial markets.[7]

Their critics argue that hedge funds are "rogue elephants: over-leveraged, undersupervised, and disruptive to the markets."[8] If the spirit of the times demands a scapegoat for every major market disturbance, hedge funds have come to provide a large and colorful target. Thus, "[w]hen the bond market collapses in a molten heap, when currencies and stocks and even commodities tumble, the Big Three [renowned hedge fund managers George Soros, Michael Steinhardt, and Julian Robertson, Jr.]—and hedge funds generally—get the blame."[9]

Distilling fact from hyperbole in the context of hedge funds is a critical challenge for policymakers. The absence of systematic data about hedge funds permits myths to take root and flourish. Further, the charges that have been leveled against hedge funds relate in many cases to broad market movements whose causes and dynamics are difficult to reconstruct and verify. At the same time, hedge funds raise central issues of public policy for the 1990s and beyond because they exemplify a powerful trend sweeping the financial markets: the proliferation of risk-concentrating products and structures operating largely outside of, but with important links to, established, regulated markets. Massive concentrations of assets, aggressively traded, largely without investment restrictions or governmental oversight, have suggested to legislators, regulators, and financial commentators the elusive, yet essential, concept of "systemic risk"—the possibility that the painstakingly private investment activity of hedge funds may in fact have public consequences. The following discussion examines the phenomenon of hedge funds from a public policy perspective, considering their current marketplace and regulatory status, their perceived dangers, and the public policy concerns they pose for financial regulators as the new millennium approaches.

EXPLOSIVE GROWTH, VOLATILITY, AND PUBLIC SCRUTINY— AN INDUSTRY IN TRANSITION

The term *hedge fund* is said to have originated in the 1960s to refer to new types of speculative investment vehicles using sophisticated hedging and arbitrage techniques in the corporate equities market.[10] These funds employed the investment strategy of contemporaneously buying and selling related equity securities and were considered to be "hedged" because they held stocks that would gain if the market went up while also maintaining short positions that would gain if stock prices decreased.[11] The activities of such funds expanded during the 1970s and 1980s and now encompass cash, futures, and options markets, including transactions in foreign currencies, government securities, and commodities, as well as merger and acquisition activities. Hedge fund trading has moved increasingly beyond U.S. stocks to strategies based on global stock market, currency, and interest rate movements—speculations on the overall direction of the markets rather than movements of individual stocks.[12] In short, "[a]bout any investment anywhere is fair game, limited only by the managers' knowledge about the instruments available and their trading strategy."[13]

The term *hedge fund* is notable more for its inclusiveness than its descriptive accuracy. Lacking an enforced structure or investment profile, hedge funds range freely through the whole gamut of the global securities, futures, and derivatives markets. In fact, hedging is neither the purpose nor the normal practice of hedge funds, which are more aptly characterized as speculative trading vehicles that take positions designed not to offset risks created by existing investments but to assume calculated risks in pursuit of above-average gains. A hedge fund publication, *MAR Hedge*, which began reporting on the hedge fund industry in 1994, has identified nine categories of hedge funds: arbitrage (between securities), emerging markets, market-neutral, opportunistic (directional), short-selling, small-cap, special situations (bankrupt or near-bankrupt companies), value (securities priced below net asset value), and yield-curve arbitrage.[14]

Following a period of quiet expansion during the 1980s, the hedge fund industry has in recent years become notable for extensive use of leverage and large global speculations, with the leading hedge funds becoming huge market players. Growing from approximately 100 funds in 1987,[15] the hedge fund market now is estimated at, variously, from 800 to 1,000 funds with aggregate capital of between $75 to $100 billion, to 3,000 funds with assets exceeding $160 billion.[16] Assets under management of hedge funds reportedly doubled between the end of 1991 and 1994.[17] Intense investor interest, coupled with regulatory constraints, has placed managers with the best track records "in the invidious position of having to turn away investors and maintain waiting lists."[18] The Soros group of funds reportedly has over $10 billion of capital and the Tiger group over $6 billion, amounts comparable to those of some large U.S. commercial and investment banks.[19]

The rapid growth of the hedge fund market coincides with a period of significant expansion of the upper tier of American wealth, the number of Americans with more than $1 million having tripled during the last decade alone.[20] At the same time, low short-term interest rates have

led investors to seek higher returns from riskier investments, and the
low cost of borrowed funds has facilitated hedge funds' leveraging their
assets, geometrically increasing potential earnings and losses.[21] Private
investor interest in "nontraditional investing" is at an all-time high, the
business of money management for the wealthy has become a growth
industry, and hedge funds have become among the fastest-growing
segments of Wall Street.[22]

The hedge fund explosion also has been fueled by an inflow of
new fund managers, lured by the favorable compensation structures
available to hedge fund managers. Hedge fund managers typically receive
a management fee of 1 percent of fund assets and an incentive fee of
20 percent of the fund's trading profits.[23] The hedge fund business
attracts entrepreneurs because of ease of entry and hefty rewards for
high performance.[24] The top hedge fund managers are among the most
successful investors in the world, known both for vast self-confidence
and tolerance for risk.[25]

However, the hedge fund phenomenon is larger than the well-pub-
licized exploits of George Soros, Michael Steinhardt, Paul Tudor Jones,
and other big league fund managers assiduously tracked in the financial press. Bankers commonly distinguish between two types of hedge
funds, those organized by investment entrepreneurs with individualized
trading philosophies, such as Soros Fund Management, Tiger Management Corporation, Steinhardt Management Company, and other high-
profile fund managers, and a second category consisting of funds advised
by the proprietary trading desks of investment banks and international
commercial banks. Further, hedge funds resemble other institutional
trading vehicles such as pension funds, mutual funds, and proprietary
trading accounts of banks and broker-dealers in that they also represent
massive pools of discretionary capital that may be used for assuming
risk positions.[26]

Despite the diversity of their investment activities, hedge funds typically have several operational characteristics in common. Generally,
hedge funds (1) are organized as investment partnerships that are exempt
from most, if not all, forms of regulation; (2) seek high rates of return
by investing or trading in an extremely wide variety of financial instruments; (3) may take short as well as long positions; (4) use leverage;
and (5) compensate their managers based upon the financial performance of the fund. Hedge funds are sold to wealthy investors, in minimum
investments typically ranging from $250,000 to $5 million. Participation

in some funds is further restricted to professional traders or persons with specialized knowledge of particular markets regardless of their wealth. They typically borrow heavily from banks and broker-dealer firms.[27]

CURRENT REGULATORY STATUS

The distinctive regulatory status of hedge funds is perhaps best illustrated by comparing hedge funds to mutual funds, a more conventional vehicle for collective investment. Hedge funds are designed to evoke a minimum of regulation and scrutiny; mutual funds operate under a regulatory structure that has been called "the most intrusive financial legislation known to man or beast."[28] Hedge funds are designed to engage in speculative trading and to exercise maximum investment latitude without internal constraints or the regulatory restrictions upon permissible assets, leverage, and concentration of assets that apply to mutual funds. By contrast, mutual fund regulation is fundamentally designed to discourage speculation, imposing restrictions upon the use of leverage, issuance of senior securities, transactions with affiliates, governance of the fund, and other matters.

Avoidance of regulatory restrictions, especially those applicable to mutual funds, is thus a key determinant of the design and operation of hedge funds. Fund managers are able to achieve this end by organizing and operating their funds offshore and closing investment to U.S. investors, a course chosen by George Soros, among others, or by operating within existing exemptions from regulation available under U.S. law. In the United States, hedge funds can avail themselves of exemptions from regulation under the securities laws, but if they engage to any substantial extent in futures transactions, they will fall within the regulatory purview of the Commodity Futures Trading Commission.

Securities Regulation

Hedge funds generally are organized as investment partnerships and interests in them constitute securities. However, hedge fund interests typically are offered privately and only to wealthy investors constituting "accredited investors," a category including individuals with a minimum of $1 million in net worth or an annual income in excess of $200,000, as well as a variety of corporate and institutional entities. As a result, hedge funds qualify for the Securities and Exchange

Commission's safe harbor from registration under the Securities Act of 1933 and are not required to file offering documents with the Securities and Exchange Commission (SEC) or to provide investors with such documents. However, the antifraud prohibitions of the securities laws remain applicable to the offer and sale of interests in such funds.[29]

In addition, the operation of hedge funds would be subject to the Investment Company Act of 1940, which regulates U.S. mutual funds, but for the availability of the "private investment company" exception. This exception, Section 3(c)(1) of the Investment Company Act, provides an exclusion from the definition of *investment company* for any issuer whose outstanding securities are owned by fewer than 100 persons[30] and which is not making, and does not propose to make, a public offering of such securities. Thus, hedge funds typically are organized as private limited partnerships, admit no more than 99 participants, and generally restrict their investors to multimillionaires or at least investors with sufficient financial wherewithal to qualify as accredited investors under the federal securities laws.

The SEC receives limited information regarding the activities of large market participants, including some hedge funds, through reports required to be filed when 5 percent or more of a class of security issued by a publicly traded company is acquired and reports filed by managers exercising investment discretion over accounts having $100 million in equity securities.

Futures Regulation

Notwithstanding the availability of these regulatory carve-outs from securities regulation, many U.S. hedge funds do not altogether escape regulation. Hedge fund managers routinely use futures contracts and commodity options, as do operators of other collective investment vehicles such as mutual funds and pension funds, to manage the risks of their stock portfolios or other investments, to effect changes in investment strategies or portfolio mix, to synthetically replicate bonds or other interests, to modify portfolio durations, and for myriad other reasons.[31] These activities bring into play the regulatory mandate of the Commodity Futures Trading Commission (CFTC), the federal regulatory agency responsible for overseeing the nation's futures and commodity options markets. The CFTC administers a regulatory framework that parallels, in many ways, that of the SEC for the securities industry, including regulatory requirements applicable to futures exchanges, brokers, and professionals who offer advisory services concerning futures (commodity trading advisors) or who operate funds that trade in futures (commodity pool operators).

If hedge funds are significant traders in the futures markets, they become subject to the CFTC's large trader reporting system, under which futures traders with positions that exceed specified reporting levels must provide certain information to the CFTC. The large trader reporting system is a key market surveillance tool, designed to enable prompt identification of the substantial traders in each futures market, the size of their positions, and in specific cases, their trading intentions. This reporting system collects large trader positions in all futures contracts and aggregates related accounts. Hedge funds trading in U.S. futures markets are also subject to speculative position limit rules, which are designed to prevent market distortions.[32]

Hedge funds that trade in the futures markets and have a sufficient U.S. nexus (if the location of the pool operator or pool participants is in the United States, for example) also become subject to the CFTC's regulatory framework for commodity pools, the futures equivalent of the mutual fund. Commodity pools essentially are collective investment vehicles that trade in the futures markets as one of their investment activities. The so-called macro hedge funds—those that take broad, leveraged bets on the global bond, currency, and stock markets—are said to be "profligate users" of futures contracts and thus are subject to regulation as commodity pools under CFTC requirements.[33]

Regulation as a commodity pool requires the operator of the fund to register with the CFTC, provide a disclosure document to prospective investors containing specified information, provide pool participants with periodic account statements and certified annual reports for the pool, and maintain books and records subject to inspection by regulators. All activities of the pool are subject to the CFTC's antifraud rules. There is no general exception to regulation under the CFTC's regulatory structure (the Commodity Exchange Act) for privately offered funds that is comparable to the safe harbors available under the securities laws. Consequently, absent the applicability of some other type of exemption, hedge funds engaging in more than *de minimis* futures transactions are required to operate in accordance with CFTC requirements. However, hedge funds subject to CFTC regulation may qualify for exemptions from providing specified disclosures and reports to investors based upon the financial qualifications of their investors, which are measured by higher standards than the SEC's accredited investor requirements, or the small extent of their futures as compared to their securities activities.[34]

THE PERILS OF SUCCESS: PUBLIC POLICY CONCERNS PRESENTED BY HEDGE FUNDS

In April 1994, Congressional hearings on "Risks that Hedge Funds Pose to the Banking System" spotlighted public concerns that hedge funds had grown from quietly successful private investment vehicles into aggressive market giants. Then House Banking Committee Chairman Henry B. Gonzalez targeted hedge funds as among "the largest purchasers of derivative products from banks," holding "massive financial clout," and engaged in speculative activity that "has a tremendous effect on the stability of our financial markets."[35] At the same time, SEC Chairman Arthur Levitt acknowledged that "the trading activity of a handful of very large, aggressive hedge funds has become a matter of legitimate national inquiry and importance."[36]

Like the proliferation of new derivative products, hedge funds evoke concerns that risk is being created in new forms that are not fully understood or controlled by their designers, their users, or the established financial oversight structures. Also, like derivative products generally, hedge funds came to prominence long after the principal regulatory frameworks were enacted into law, and they were designed to operate largely outside of those frameworks. However, hedge funds may create more complex risk profiles than individual derivative transactions because they are structures that concentrate risk by aggregating wealth, leveraging it, and deploying it in strategies devised by some of the markets' most sophisticated money managers, often involving a wide range of derivative transactions. Consequently, hedge funds may present, in magnified form, fundamental questions presented by the expanding derivatives marketplace, including, for example:

- Whether they create significant dangers to the financial system or to their customers.
- How other market participants can protect themselves against the risks created by these investment vehicles.
- What actions, if any, regulators should take to safeguard against systemic risks and other potential public harms created by such investment vehicles.

Size, Leverage, and Freedom from Restrictions: Concentrated Market Power

A core concern about hedge funds is that their concentrated economic power may be a source of systemic risk. This concern stems from key characteristics of large modern hedge funds such as their substantial size, extensive use of leverage, and virtual freedom from trading or investment restrictions. In effect, hedge funds concentrate the assets of multiple investors but can trade in the manner of a single speculative trader. Further, the sizeable aggregate assets of hedge funds may effectively be multiplied by extensive leverage and the alleged "herd" effect of multiple hedge funds acting in parallel. Consequently, regulators express concern that "a handful of hedge funds," acting alone or in concert with other large funds, may be capable of trading in volumes "sufficiently large to significantly or disproportionately influence market movements."[37] This concern may exist most strongly in the context of markets that may not have sufficient liquidity to accommodate simultaneous efforts by hedge funds, banks, and other large market participants to modify their exposures.[38]

In recent years, the largest U.S. hedge funds have repeatedly been accused of moving the markets. The Report of the Presidential Task Force on Market Mechanisms (Brady Report) on the 1987 market crash included hedge funds among the "aggressive trading-oriented institutions" whose active selling in mid-October 1987 stimulated reactive selloffs by portfolio insurers and mutual funds.[39] A 1992 joint study of the Treasury securities markets by the Department of the Treasury, SEC, and Federal Reserve Board recognized that hedge funds had recently begun "to play a major role" in the government securities market, "apparently hav[ing] the capability to assume large positions in Treasury securities because of their size, capacity for leverage and willingness to take substantial risks with their capital."[40] Subsequent complaints filed against two hedge fund managers by the SEC and the Department of Justice claiming, respectively, manipulation of and conspiracy to restrain competition in the markets for two-year Treasury notes in 1991 (later settled by consent judgments), underscored the potential for the conduct of large hedge funds to create public concerns.[41] George Soros was widely reported to have successfully speculated against the British pound in 1992, gaining a $1 billion profit for his funds. In August 1993, European central bank clients blamed hedge funds for attacking the

French and Belgian currencies and forcing them out of their narrow bands within the European exchange rate mechanism. Selling by large hedge funds was partly blamed for declines in global bond markets in early 1994.[42]

Regulators have repeatedly recognized that hedge funds, due to their capacity for leverage, are able to take trading positions "disproportionate to their capital base."[43] Hedge funds reportedly are leveraged at "anywhere from 2x to 20x, which is similar to that of the futures trading industry and significantly higher than mutual funds, pension funds and trusts."[44] Although fund managers may be adept at controlling their market risk, "the sheer size" of their positions raised concerns about "systemic risk that these funds may introduce into the financial markets."[45]

In 1994 congressional testimony, federal regulators acknowledged that the substantial market importance of hedge funds warranted caution but stressed that hedge funds are neither the largest market participants nor the source of unique risks. Although some large hedge fund groups such as the Soros group of funds have capital comparable to or exceeding that of large U.S. commercial and investment banks, a relatively small number of hedge funds, perhaps a dozen, are said to have net asset values greater than $1 billion. The great majority of hedge funds are said to be quite small, with the average fund managing about $20 million and even the largest hedge funds characterized as "small relative to the broader markets in which they operate."[46]

Hedge funds are also small relative to traditional mutual funds and other institutional investors. The estimated $160 billion in hedge fund assets is dwarfed by the more than $3 trillion in total net assets of the regulated mutual fund industry and the more than $6 trillion in assets under the management of other institutional investors, such as banks serving as trustees, pension plans, and insurance companies. Thus, Federal Reserve Governor John P. LaWare testified before the House Banking Committee in 1994 that hedge funds can be beneficial by "add[ing] depth and liquidity to financial markets and can be stabilizing influences" and that "[it] would be wrong to single out hedge funds as being responsible for moving global prices of financial assets or as being a major source of risk in financial markets."[47]

Nonetheless, there is considerable debate about the role of hedge funds in trend-following behavior, that is, buying in response to a price rise or selling in response to a price decline, which in extreme cases may be associated with market dislocations. A herd effect allegedly results from hedge funds acting in concert or at least in parallel, resulting in large-scale asset shifts when hedge funds take or liquidate positions. However, at least one prominent hedge fund operator, George Soros, contends that hedge funds are less likely than other traders, including institutional investors generally and mutual funds in particular, to engage in trend-following behavior. Unlike mutual funds and other institutional investors whose performance is measured relative to their "peer group," hedge funds, at least those whose managers are rewarded on absolute performance, act "more like a sophisticated private investor than an institution handling other people's money." Soros thus sees in hedge funds "a healthy antidote to the trend-following behavior of institutional investors."[48]

The proposition that hedge funds do not behave in the same way is also supported by evidence that some funds specialize in specific markets while others trade in a wide variety of markets; funds also vary in their time horizons, degrees of leverage, and risk-reward profiles. Evidence of wide ranges in trading results for multiple hedge funds during the same time period reflects substantial disparities in trading positions and/or behavior by funds.[49]

But while hedge funds may not themselves be trend followers, they may engender trend following in others because, despite their desire for secrecy, others in the market watch and emulate them. For example, George Soros, reportedly known on Wall Street as "a man who moves markets," is followed by other traders who are "on the lookout for...his 'footprints,' signs that he is taking a new position in a stock or currency."[50] When such signs appear, "the news is quickly flashed across the wires, sometimes moving entire markets."[51] Henry Kaufman views the "high-octane portfolio manager" as "a potential incubator of the next round of financial excess" not because of deliberate machinations by large funds but because these high-profile managers naturally evoke imitators. When large portfolio managers enter the market to build substantial positions, "others inevitably follow, since it is practically impossible to disguise these substantial positions completely."[52]

Others suggest that the herd effect of hedge funds is felt only when there is already a market move. In "trendless times when their strategies are quite diverse," hedge funds have little impact on the markets, but once a trend has been set, by the markets themselves or by government policies, "directional funds act more as a herd" and their highly leveraged positions give them the power to make the markets "oversteer."[53]

Concerns have also been raised about the impact of hedge fund sales of securities and other assets to meet margin calls in a declining market. Selling by large hedge funds and other large traders was blamed, for example, for contributing to the rapid declines of global bond prices in early 1994 because such funds reportedly liquidated European, Japanese, and U.S. government bonds to cover losses created when U.S. bond prices fell.[54] The "dynamic hedging" activity of hedge funds in connection with derivatives positions is also cited as a potential source of systemic concern. Dynamic hedging essentially reinforces a market shift, such that in the event of a market move against the issuer of a derivative instrument, for example, the issuer must trade in the same direction as the market, "thereby amplify[ing] the initial price disturbance."[55] If unusually large volumes of dynamic hedging occur in the same direction, price movements may become discontinuous, potentially leading to financial dislocations. Conversely, if those who wish to engage in dynamic hedging cannot execute their orders, they may suffer "catastrophic losses."[56]

Commentators have thus identified a variety of potential market risks perceived to be associated with the size and leverage of hedge funds, ranging from concerted exercises of market power to spillover effects from efforts to minimize or cover losses. However, these perceived dangers have not been shown to differ from those common to other forms of institutional investment activity. Moreover, most allegations of hedge fund responsibility for specific market disturbances have not been demonstrated to be valid or have been called into serious question. Assertions about the market power of hedge funds thus represent hypotheses forming a basis for further factual inquiry rather than proven explanations of events.

Moreover, even as their success has brought hedge funds into the public eye, market forces may be inhibiting their further growth and even causing retrenchment by some of the largest funds. In 1994 and 1995, large hedge fund operators were said to be "trimming their bets." Hedge fund activity reportedly declined in 1994 due to a recognition that the size of the largest hedge funds might be impeding their performance and to market results that compared unfavorably with those of conventional mutual funds. In 1995, George Soros, Paul Tudor Jones, and other large fund operators reportedly found that the size of their funds made the markets more difficult to navigate. Soros, for example, observed that their size had reduced his funds' ability to rebound from profitless periods and in July 1995 advised investors in his largest fund, the Quantum Fund, that the fund's "macro" investments would be significantly limited.[57] Other fund managers encountering similar problems have returned funds to investors. The Caxton Corporation, for example, returned over $1 billion to investors, linking its size to a decline in performance.[58]

Competition from mutual funds in 1995 also spurred hedge fund retreats. The higher fee structure of hedge funds (typically 1 percent or 2 percent in management fees plus 20 percent of profits) would render hedge funds a less attractive investment than mutual funds, assuming the same level of market returns. Hedge funds are supposed to outperform the market by taking advantage of their ability to make both bullish and bearish bets. However, with the stock market up by over 30 percent in 1995, bearish positions have not recently been profitable, and hedge fund returns that would normally be attractive may not be sufficient to keep investors from withdrawing. The hedge fund "give backs" of 1995, following a sharp decline in hedge fund assets in 1994, are estimated to have caused the industry to begin 1996 about one-fourth smaller than in 1993.[59]

In the longer run, however, many believe that hedge funds are likely to reach new heights, perhaps helped by inflows of funds from new sources such as pension funds. Consequently, the market power of hedge funds is likely to remain a matter of concern. At least to date, the perceived market impacts of hedge funds have not been shown to differ in quality or degree from those common to other forms of institutional investment activity. However, in the absence of information from which to accurately measure and catalog hedge fund activity or its attendant risks, the relative size of hedge funds as compared to other market players, many of whom operate under more stringent regulatory restrictions, may not provide an adequate gauge of the risks of hedge funds. Development of fuller data about hedge fund activity thus appears essential before expert judgments can be made about the potential dangers of hedge funds.

Risks to Lenders and Counterparties

In addition to their feared or assumed influence upon markets, hedge funds raise concerns because of the potential for spillover impacts of a hedge fund failure or default on obligations to lenders or other counterparties. In an increasingly interdependent financial environment, as illustrated by the disastrous experiences of Metallgesellschaft, Barings Bank PLC, Daiwa Bank, and others, Federal Reserve Board Chairman Alan Greenspan, echoed by other market observers, has stressed that "massive internal breakdowns could occur that spill over to other institutions."[60]

The potentially high-risk profiles of hedge funds, compounded of high-volume derivatives transactions and other leveraged transactions resulting in exposures that may dwarf their capital, may create significant credit risks for their lenders and other counterparties. Market participants recognize the difficulty of making credit evaluations of derivative transactions, especially in relation to transactions with "new types of organizations, such as leveraged funds for which conventional credit ratings are inapplicable."[61] However, notwithstanding their often suspect creditworthiness, many hedge funds have become such important derivatives customers that dealers reportedly are loath to forgo their business.[62]

Skepticism concerning the ability of hedge funds to control the risks that they assume reflects a larger debate about the effectiveness of risk controls in the financial markets generally, particularly those that users of derivative instruments employ. Studies confirm what the press reports of successive derivatives calamities suggest anecdotally: Many derivatives users have not fully mastered the risk management challenges presented by derivatives.[63] Even in relatively established marketplaces such as the exchange-traded futures markets, the arena in which Barings Bank's primary losses occurred, rogue traders and other forms of "outlier" behavior will test, and occasionally undermine, the efficacy of firms' management controls.

Pointed questions thus have been directed to the adequacy of the risk management systems of hedge funds to manage the risks of their derivatives activities and the potential vulnerability of lenders and other parties transacting with hedge funds. A recent study of derivatives usage by 143 investment management companies in the United States, United Kingdom, Ireland, and France indicates that a high proportion of such funds have not adopted basic risk management policies. For example, nearly two-thirds of the respondents who were derivatives users did not have a supervisory board or risk management committee responsible for setting limits on derivatives usage; three-fourths of the respondents did not employ a risk management team that was separate from the trading function.[64] This study attributes the 1994 collapse of three hedge funds operated by David Askin in part to imprudent reliance on the portfolio manager to set derivatives usage limits. This latitude enabled Askin to build the funds' mortgage-backed portfolio to unacceptable levels, leading to massive losses, liquidation of the funds, and repercussions in the mortgage-backed securities market generally.[65]

The Askin debacle also illustrates risks created for counterparties by aggressively leveraged hedge fund trading. Although the sequence of events remains subject to debate, according to the SEC's account, Askin's three hedge funds reportedly had investor capital in excess of $450 million but had borrowed $2.50 for every dollar invested. The values of the funds' holdings declined in early 1994, resulting in liquidation of fund holdings in order to meet margin calls. The rapid sell-off resulted in losses by brokers who auctioned off the funds' assets but were unable to recover the full value of their outstanding loans to the funds. However, the SEC reported that the losses suffered by broker-dealers were "not significant in relation to firm or industry capital."[66]

Risks to lenders generated by hedge fund borrowing were a central focus of the House Banking Committee's 1994 hedge fund hearings, as bank lending to "these highly leveraged and largely unregulated investment funds raises a number of serious safety and soundness questions about hedge funds and their use of derivatives."[67] Banking regulators testifying at the 1994 hearings acknowledged that comprehensive data on banks' activities with hedge funds were not available, but they believed that only a relatively small group of banks was involved with hedge funds. The bank regulators also stressed the importance of banks' risk management controls, noting, for example, that national banks lending to hedge funds secure a large portion of such funds' credit exposure by requiring collateral, including in excess of 100 percent collateral in appropriate cases.[68] The regulators also identified various aspects of banks' management of their relationships with hedge funds that were being addressed through the supervisory process. Federal Reserve Governor LaWare stressed that banks should "increase personnel with expertise in dealing with hedge funds, strengthen internal controls, and improve senior management review capability," as well as evaluate the potential for concentrated exposures.[69] However, the Federal Reserve Board did not advocate increased disclosure or reporting by banks in this area, commenting that "[a]ctual exposures currently appear in only a few banks and are not substantial."[70] Similarly, the Comptroller of the Currency reported that national banks did not appear to be exposed to significant risks as a result of their dealings with hedge funds. Eight national banks and nine national banking companies had been found to have some form of exposure to hedge funds, but those exposures were relatively small and appeared to be adequately controlled.[71]

The Comptroller also observed that six national banks acting as derivatives dealers and some major state banks engage in activities that present comparable risks to those of hedge funds, namely proprietary trading of cash and derivatives instruments to establish risk positions for the bank. This proprietary trading of banks and brokerages is said to dwarf the trading activity of even the largest hedge funds.[72]

Hedge funds must manage the risks arising from their derivatives transactions and hedge fund lenders must manage the analogous risks of their exposure to hedge funds. The growing emphasis upon internal controls in response to the substantial derivatives losses attributable to basic failures of risk management at a succession of large, well-known firms is thus highly relevant to hedge funds. At the same time, a wellspring of regulatory and private sector efforts has dramatically increased the available guidance concerning desirable internal controls and risk management practices. These efforts reflect increasing recognition that an efficacious structure for assuring sound internal controls requires primary efforts at the individual firm level, subject to oversight and standard setting by self-regulators and regulators. As summarized by former CFTC Chairman Mary L. Schapiro, the regulatory structure in this context should be a pyramid: "management at the broad base, then the self-regulator, and finally the regulator providing oversight, performance standards and prophylactic requirements on the top." However, "[n]o regulator or regulatory regime can totally compensate for failure of internal controls at the firm level."[73] Consequently, increasingly integrated efforts by regulators and regulated market participants to fortify the internal controls of market users can be expected, and these efforts are likely to have at least indirect effects upon hedge funds.

Customer Protection: The Sophisticated Investor Model

The relevance of customer protection concerns to hedge funds is a matter of considerable dispute. Generally, hedge funds are designed to fit within regulatory niches that appear to reflect a relatively weak public interest in customer protection in the contexts to which they apply. The 1992 Treasury securities study, for example, stressed that the regulatory issues relevant to hedge funds "involve not so much the protection of the investors who invest in them, typically high net worth individuals or institutions, but the potential of these funds, due to their size, active market presence, and use of leverage, to cause market disruptions."[74]

Although the presumed sophistication of hedge fund investors may reduce the importance of customer protection concerns, recent experience suggests two countervailing factors. First, the substantial derivatives losses of an apparently unanticipated nature that large corporations and governmental entities have incurred in the last several years suggests that presumptions of sophistication based upon size or net worth may not be uniformly apposite. Second, the complexity and lack of transparency of especially exotic investment vehicles may challenge the acumen even of those who would clearly satisfy standards of "sophistication" suitable for more conventional investments.

Consequently, in the view of some observers, the primary danger created by hedge funds may be "the risk of loss to the unwary investor."[75] Vast investment discretion coupled with a predilection for highly leveraged trading creates the potential for precipitous loss as well as spectacular gain—and hedge funds have experienced both extremes in recent years. The rapid expansion of the hedge fund market during a recent period of widely publicized high returns may have exacerbated the dangers for investors by engendering a small but rising number of hedge funds operated by persons with little investment experience.[76]

In addition, hedge funds operating outside the scope of CFTC disclosure requirements may avoid extensive disclosure of their positions even to their own investors, challenging the investor's ability to protect himself. In the worst case, the question whether hedge fund investors have the same appetite for risk as the fund's managers may be answered only after the fund has suffered substantial losses. However, if a hedge fund is subject to CFTC regulation as a commodity pool, the fund manager generally must provide a specified disclosure document to prospective and current investors and apprise investors of any material changes in the matters so disclosed. Further, a recent position statement of the American Institute of Certified Public Accountants (AICPA) has been designed to reduce the disclosure gap generally for hedge funds and other private investment companies. A May 1995 AICPA statement requires that hedge funds provide investors with certain basic data in financial reports, including a condensed schedule of investments that categorizes investments in percentage terms by type (e.g., preferred stocks, options written or short sales), geographic region, and industry, and separately identifies material investments (more than 5 percent of net assets) in any one issuer.[77]

The securities regulatory frameworks applicable to hedge funds do not, however, suggest a strong interest in assuring customer protection in such contexts. The key difference between hedge funds—the largely unregulated "mutual funds for the rich"—and the mutual funds extensively regulated as such under the Investment Company Act is that hedge funds do not publicly offer their interests and they limit the number of their investors to fewer than 100 to qualify for the "private" investment company exclusion from regulation under the Investment Company Act. This exclusion reflects Congress's belief that no significant public interest warrants federal oversight of certain privately held investment companies. It also represents "a pragmatic approach to conserving the limited resources" of the SEC, "since regulating a vast number of private investment pools would prove extremely burdensome and probably unfeasible."[78] The legislative history indicates that the 100-investor limitation "represents an outer limit of an investor base likely to be composed of persons with personal, familial, or similar ties."[79] Even though such small investment pools could include investors of modest means and little sophistication, the SEC has commented that "in any case, federal oversight of these pools under the Investment Company Act would be impractical."[80] To the extent that small vehicles, even if not comprised of truly sophisticated or even financially accredited investors, are exempted from mutual fund regulation, this dispensation does not appear to be based upon a determination that customer protection concerns are irrelevant in this context, but rather on the view that such funds are too small to warrant extensive regulatory intervention.

The other important regulatory "safe harbor," under which hedge funds avoid registration of their securities, requires that the securities be privately offered to investors meeting the relatively low levels of financial accreditation set forth in SEC Regulation D, for example, individual net worth of $1 million or annual income of $200,000. This accreditation standard is unlikely to limit participation to the sophisticated, although it may identify investors who can afford professional investment advice.

Given the relatively weak accreditation benchmarks that hedge fund investors must meet for the fund to avail itself of the safe harbor from securities registration, CFTC regulation is likely to provide a greater degree of customer protection. CFTC regulation has no private offering exemption comparable to that provided under the securities laws. Under CFTC requirements, no matter how financially accredited or sophisticated the fund's investors, the fund manager must be registered. Registration of the fund manager entails satisfaction of fitness screening and proficiency test requirements. In addition, the fund manager must provide specified written disclosures concerning such matters as the risks of investment in the fund, the fund manager's business background and performance history, and the fund's trading strategies and investment objectives. These requirements apply unless the fund is offered only to persons who are both accredited investors and satisfy a portfolio requirement of owning $2 million in securities or other investments or maintaining a futures account with at least $200,000 in exchange-specified minimum margin deposits. These portfolio standards are designed to measure actual investment sophistication as well as wherewithal to withstand investment risks.

If these CFTC requirements do not apply, the prospective hedge fund customer may be most effectively protected by the high minimum investment thresholds (generally from $250,000 to $5 million) or other participant restrictions established by the funds themselves. Hedge funds place a premium upon the investor's knowledgeable election of an investment that entails significant risk and provides relatively few protections for the unsophisticated. For example, hedge funds differ from mutual funds in that hedge fund investments tend to be "locked in" for a substantial period—under most hedge fund partnership agreements, investors may redeem their interests only at the end of a quarter and often are locked in for as much as one to three years.[81]

Pending legislation initially introduced as H.R. 1495, The Investment Company Act Amendments of 1995, would create an additional exception from Investment Company Act regulation premised largely upon the use of high financial thresholds for participation to assure investor sophistication.[82] The proposed new exception from regulation under the Investment Company Act would apply to investment pools whose shareholders are all highly sophisticated, qualified purchasers, defined as any natural person who owns at least $10 million in securities or any person, including an institutional investor, who owns and manages on a discretionary basis at least $100 million in securities. This proposed statutory provision would permit an unlimited number of such qualified purchasers, addressing complaints concerning the restrictiveness of the current 100-investor limitation upon exempt private investment companies. The proposed qualified purchaser provision "would recognize that financially sophisticated investors are in a position to appreciate the risks associated with investment pools that do not have the Investment Company Act's protections" and "generally can evaluate on their own behalf matters such as the level of a fund's management fees, governance provisions, transactions with affiliates, investment risk, leverage, and redemption rights."[83]

An Information Vacuum

If secrecy is not the raison d'etre of hedge funds, it is certainly one of their signature features. Despite the continued fascination of the press and the active scrutiny of federal regulators, systematic information about hedge funds remains lacking. Without the benefit of government-mandated reporting duties for hedge funds, regulators, other than the CFTC in some circumstances, have limited authority to obtain information about hedge fund activities. As a result, no comprehensive data are available concerning the number of hedge funds, their assets under management, types of transactions, degrees of leverage, rates of return, or positions in particular securities, apart from large positions in futures contracts and corporate equities.

This information void deprives regulators of the ability to measure the true risks of hedge funds or to identify specific sources of concern. The regulators' 1992 joint report on the Treasury securities market acknowledged that regulators had scant information "that might help them assess the market impact of a failure of a hedge fund or that would warn of an impending failure."[84] The shortage of information about hedge funds, coupled with growing concerns about their potential market power, has resulted in regulators' recognition of a "compelling need" for further information about hedge funds.[85]

Spurred by market developments and legislative interest, regulators have made ad hoc efforts to obtain information concerning hedge fund activities and have identified information access as a key oversight issue. Further, as the hedge fund industry becomes larger and more competitive, market forces are operating to reduce the information void concerning hedge fund activities. A collateral business in providing information and advice about hedge funds has developed, including private databases and publications developed by nongovernmental entities such as newsletters and managers of "funds of funds." For example, Managed Account Reports of New York, a futures fund periodical, now publishes *MAR Hedge*, a publication tracking over 600 hedge funds.

To the extent that hedge funds are large participants in regulated markets or are operated by banks or regulated brokers, they leave a trail of information that regulators can assemble to piece together a picture of at least some of their activities. For example, the CFTC's large trader reporting system provides important surveillance data concerning regulated futures markets, and this information can be supplemented on an ad hoc basis by special calls for information about the reporting trader's other activities. However, reporting requirements such as these, which are internal to regulated markets, do not routinely provide information concerning over-the-counter derivatives transactions and other exposures that do not arise on such markets. Consequently, to the extent that entities such as hedge funds are large futures traders, their futures transactions will become transparent to regulators and data concerning their other activities will become accessible on a case-by-case basis. Information concerning the activities of hedge funds that are not operating in CFTC-regulated markets is likely to be far less accessible. Of course, if all relevant financial regulators pooled the information available to them concerning hedge fund activity in the various markets under their oversight, a more comprehensive picture of both specific individual hedge funds and hedge fund activity in general would be provided.

CONCLUSION: DEFINING THE REGULATORY BALANCE

This is a period of reassessment of the regulatory approach to hedge funds as well as to many other aspects of financial services regulation affected by the sweeping financial innovations of the last two decades. The prototypical large hedge fund differs in perceived impact and range of portfolio investments from the private investment companies of the past, which lived in relative obscurity within the confines of various regulatory exemptions. However, if the modern hedge fund is an unintended consequence of existing regulatory provisions, that does not necessarily signal that those provisions are inappropriate but, rather, recommends reexamination of the regulatory framework to assure that it has the flexibility to be applied to new circumstances.

To date, federal regulators have maintained an agnostic or even unqualifiedly negative attitude concerning the desirability of additional regulation of hedge funds. They have recognized a compelling need for additional information concerning the activities of hedge funds, stressed the importance of effective risk management controls on the part of their regulatees in transacting business with such funds, and pursued a course of careful monitoring pending the availability of more comprehensive factual data. As we approach the year 2000, however, there appears to be growing interest in reconsidering the basic financial regulatory structure in light of the complex marketplace changes that have occurred since that structure was put in place. From this perspective, hedge funds may be seen as exemplars of a new species of investment activity for which a correspondingly new approach to regulatory oversight and risk management may eventually be formulated. However, the case for such a fundamental shift has not yet been made. The regulators' current prudential approach toward hedge funds appropriately recognizes both that a better factual record is needed on which to base a systematic reassessment of the public policy issues hedge funds present and that hedge funds are close analogues of other widespread but less controversial forms of investment activity. Key topics for the future may include the following.

INFORMATION DEVELOPMENT:
FROM RISK PARADIGM TO RISK ASSESSMENT

Systemic risk issues have been raised concerning hedge funds based upon their sizeable asset base and its potential amplification by extensive leverage and parallel or trend-following behavior. Risk scenarios involving large hedge funds typically rely upon broadbrush characterizations of hedge fund behavior that reflect press hyperbole, extrapolation from the alleged activities of certain high-profile fund managers, and an absence of solid data. The core concerns voiced repeatedly about hedge funds relate principally to a prototypical large hedge fund that employs a high degree of leverage, takes large-scale speculative positions, and engages extensively in derivatives transactions. Although the alleged involvement of such funds in various market "events" has generally not been substantiated, such funds may represent the extreme form of risk characteristics present in various gradations across the spectrum of hedge funds and other types of investment vehicles. The large hedge fund prototype thus may be useful in identifying relevant risk factors, in effect providing a risk paradigm or model to test against marketplace realities to determine the nature of the risks that exist and their actual size and frequency.

The process of distilling concerns about perceived systemic risks into analytically and factually supportable conclusions is formidable and not unique to hedge funds. The combination of systemic risk concerns coupled with an acknowledged lack of factual data on which to precisely define and quantify the risks resembles the current regulatory posture toward systemic risk in the OTC derivatives markets. Experts have recognized the need for regulators to obtain systematic information concerning derivatives in order to address systemic risk issues. Drawing upon public policy approaches from other disciplines, two aspects of such an undertaking have been highlighted, *hazard identification*, which involves determining "whether a risk agent can cause harm under plausible circumstances," and *risk assessment,* estimating "the severity and likelihood of harm from exposure to a risk agent."[86] In the derivatives context, the absence of any centralized reporting mechanism makes hazard identification difficult, and lack of detailed information about the volume of and participants in such activity hampers assessment of the severity and probability of harm.

Hedge funds appear to present a variant of these difficulties for regulators endeavoring to gauge their potentially systemic risks. In fact, hedge funds will in many cases be derivatives users and thus will subsume the analytical dilemmas posed by derivatives in portfolios that include derivatives as well as other types of transactions. As in the case of OTC derivatives, there is no centralized reporting mechanism and thus no comprehensive source of data from which to derive an inventory of hedge funds, a survey of the types of hedge funds, or insights into individual hedge fund portfolios.

Information is the lifeblood of sound decision making. Although market developments during the past two years appear to have produced a quieter, perhaps smaller, hedge fund market, the cause of information access remains compelling. In the absence of information, rumor and myth flourish, and the proclivity of the press and market participants to demonize hedge funds has been amply demonstrated. As in the case of OTC derivatives, coordinated consideration by federal financial regulators of the availability of hedge fund information and of methods for increasing the data available is needed. Regulators currently have available data from certain individual markets, such as the futures markets, and information drawn from bank supervisory activities. Development of a mechanism to share and, if possible, integrate the information available to produce composite profiles of hedge fund activity across markets appears desirable. Alternatively, regulators may wish to consider developing a voluntary information-gathering effort in cooperation with the industry to obtain basic data about market composition, profiles of large hedge funds, and the factual support needed to test various risk scenarios, assess the extent of large fund exposures, and determine the need for formal mechanisms to obtain data on a routine basis.

DEFINING THE PUBLIC INTEREST IN HEDGE FUNDS

Until their recently exponential growth, hedge funds evoked little attention from either a customer protection or systemic risk perspective. They were assumed not to present significant public policy issues because the financial accreditation of their investors obviated customer protection concerns and the limited number of their investors, due to the constraints of the private investment company exclusion, deflected systemic concerns.

However, the 1994 hedge fund hearings highlighted concerns relating to the market impact and potential systemic risk consequences of hedge funds. Although no mandate for additional regulation was recognized, these hearings underscored the potential market effects of hedge funds and spillover impacts upon lenders to hedge funds. Notwithstanding these systemic concerns, however, proposed legislation that would create the potential for larger unregulated hedge funds than under current law is pending before Congress and proceeding with apparently widespread support. The public policy perspective on hedge funds thus reflects potentially inconsistent objectives.

To a great extent, hedge funds have developed within the boundaries of regulatory safe harbors or exemptions from the securities laws that reflected a relatively low level of public concern with these vehicles. This relative lack of concern was due to the accredited investor status of their participants, the relatively small size of the vehicle, and the absence of a public securities offering. Hedge funds may be viewed as exemplars of the growing dominance of the institutional investor (including large commercial firms as well as wealthy individuals), "[o]ne of the most striking developments in financial markets during the latter half of this century."[87] As institutional investors have become more significant in the marketplace, they have demanded reductions in regulatory burdens, contending that they have the knowledge and where-withal to protect themselves. Regulators have adopted this rationale to a substantial extent, creating two-tier regulatory structures in many con-texts—a streamlined regulatory framework for the sophisticated, insti-tutional investor and a more extensive framework applicable to the retail marketplace.[88] Hedge funds, as private offerings to accredited investors, are able to avail themselves of the SEC's Regulation D safe harbor from registration, one of the benchmark codifications of a two-tier market-place. Hedge funds also rely upon the private investment company exclusion from regulation under the Investment Company Act of 1940, an exclusion that apparently was designed to facilitate unregulated col-lective activity by family members and other affiliated persons.

The two-tiered regulatory approach that reduces regulatory pro-tections applicable to institutional investors appears to be growing in strength, in part due to the persuasive force of the argument that regu-lation should be tailored to reflect the self-protective capacity of insti-tutional investors and in part due to the increasingly evident need to conserve government resources. As noted previously, the private invest-ment company exception from investment company regulation recog-nizes both the impracticability and relative lack of importance of policing investment vehicles comprised of a small number of investors, many of whom may have preexisting family or social relationships.

Pending legislation permitting hedge funds comprised of an unlim-ited number of highly accredited investors illustrates the force of the sophisticated investor regulatory approach. In permitting unlimited num-bers of well-heeled investors to pool funds in a relatively unregulated investment vehicle, the new proposed exemption would depart from the rationale of the existing private investment company exclusion for small investment funds that are deemed of insufficient size or public involve-ment to warrant federal regulation. Because the legislative proposal would permit an unlimited number of qualifying investors and thus potentially larger hedge funds, it suggests that systemic risk concerns remain diffuse and relatively weak as compared to the interest of sophis-ticated investors in innovative investment vehicles.

These developments suggest that the public interest in collective investment vehicles such as hedge funds has not been consistently artic-ulated over time, in part due to the difficulty of defining and quantifying systemic risks. Increased interest in the hedge fund structure will likely test the boundaries of the public policies in this area. Refinement of the public concerns relevant to hedge funds is needed to assure consistency of regulatory approach.

REGULATORY NICHES AND
MULTIPURPOSE INVESTMENT VEHICLES

The current regulatory framework applicable to hedge funds consists of provisions developed largely in the context of simpler investment vehicles, which were generally assumed to operate within a single regulated market, or at least primarily within a single regulated market. For example, commodity pool regulation originated at a time when futures transactions were likely to have been the dominant investment of commodity pools, and private investment companies excluded from Investment Company Act regulation could be assumed to consist mainly of securities investment vehicles. Such generalizations may well be inaccurate in the current marketplace. Although regulation has tended to be introduced to address specific categories of investment activity, hedge funds (and some other forms of collective investment vehicles) are highly fluid in content and potentially encompass investments that span the regulatory spectrum.

Further, product innovations permit funds to assume risk profiles that may not correlate with the regulatory framework that applies. For example, a hedge fund may assume a risk profile comparable to that of a commodity pool by engaging in OTC securities transactions or unregulated derivatives transactions rather than futures or commodity option transactions. Such a vehicle may thus avoid regulation under a regulatory framework specifically designed for regulation of collective investment vehicles engaging in highly leveraged transactions (the CFTC regulatory framework for futures and commodity option transactions). Although such a fund would be subject to the accredited investor requirements and other criteria for exemption under the SEC's safe harbor from securities registration, that safe harbor was designed as a general exemption for privately placed securities and is not specifically geared towards highly leveraged, speculative investment vehicles. Conversely, some funds that engage significantly in futures and are thus regulated as commodity pools under the CFTC's regulatory framework contend that their futures transactions represent hedging or risk management transactions that are ancillary to securities transactions and actually reduce the risks to investors; they claim to be primarily securities investment vehicles that should be regulated only under the securities laws.

In short, the freedom and fluidity of the hedge fund structure permit types of trading activities that differ, perhaps materially, from those contemplated when the relevant regulatory structures were established. These circumstances suggest that the current regulatory approach should be revisited to assure that it provides a coherent approach to hedge funds based upon the risks they present and the public interests relevant to such vehicles. This process entails development of a more systematic information base, as suggested above, to identify and measure the risks presented, as well as reconsideration and refinement of the public interest concerns relevant to hedge funds. Given the financial accreditation standards applicable to hedge fund investors, this analysis would perhaps most profitably focus on the potential market impacts and systemic risks of hedge funds and other collective investment vehicles, in light of their risk profiles.

ENDNOTES

1. The views expressed herein are solely those of the author and do not necessarily reflect those of the Commodity Futures Trading Commission or its staff.

2. M. Burns, "10 Common Misconceptions About Hedge Funds," *Futures Industry,* July–August 1994, p. 16.

3. D. Warsh, "Financial Regulation, Now That We Aren't In Kansas Anymore," *Boston Globe*, Oct. 17, 1995, p. 39.

4. Henry Kaufman, "New Financial Threats to the Economic Expansion," First Boston Global Banking Conference, New York City, April 25, 1994 p. 10.

5. Hedge Fund Hearings, "Risks that Hedge Funds Pose to the Banking System: Hearing Before the House Committee on Banking, Finance and Urban Affairs, 103d Cong., 2d Sess., 70, 79, April 13, 1994 (prepared testimony of Eugene Ludwig, Comptroller of the Currency).

6. J. Berry and C. Chandler, "Fast Currency Trades Feed Fears of a Crisis," *Washington Post*, Apr. 17, 1995, p. A1.

7. Kaufman, "New Financial Threats," pp. 2–3.

8. G. Weiss, "Fall Guys?" *Business Week*, April 25, 1994, p. 117.

9. Ibid.

10. Department of the Treasury, Securities and Exchange Commission, Board of Governors of the Federal Reserve System, *Joint Report on the Government Securities Market* (January 1992), pp. B–64ff.

11. S. Hansell, "A Primer on Hedge Funds: Hush-Hush and for the Rich," *New York Times*, April 12, 1994, p. D-15.

12. Ibid.

13. D. Jobman, "Hedge Funds: Today's Financial Wizardry," *Futures Industry,* July-August 1994, pp. 11, 13.

14. "So, What Are Hedge Funds?," *Euromoney*, April 1994, p. 29.

15. Hansell, "A Primer on Hedge Funds."

16. "The Investment Company Act Amendments of 1995," Hearing Before the Subcommittee on Telecommunications and Finance of the House Committee on Commerce, 104th Cong., 1st Sess. 68–69, prepared testimony of Marianne K. Smythe.

17. R. Bennett and D. Shirreff, "Let's Bash the Hedge Funds," *Euromoney*, April 21, 1994, p. 31.

18. "The Investment Company Act Amendments of 1995," p. 70. Consequently, according to Smythe, "[e]nterprises that are in need of

capital, and whose attributes are familiar to sophisticated fund managers, may be deprived of capital because the managers must limit participation in their pools to 100 or fewer investors."

19. P. Truell, "Some Big Funds, Like Soros's, Have Difficulty Despite Trend," *New York Times*, July 27, 1995, p. D2; See Hedge Fund Hearings, (prepared statement of John P. LaWare, Member, Board of Governors of the Federal Reserve System) p. 86.

20. M. M. Cardona, "Tuning in on the Wealthy," *Pensions & Investments*, Nov. 13, 1995, p. 47, (citing research report indicating that 3.3 million U.S. households have over $500,000 in discretionary assets, of which 1.2 million have $1 million or more and 90,000 have $5 million or more).

21. Hansell, "A Primer on Hedge Funds."

22. N. Jacob, "Portfolio Management and Non-Traditional Investing," *Trusts & Estates*, June 1995, p. 14; Cardona, "Tuning in on the Wealthy"; Hansell, "A Primer on Hedge Funds."

23. Hansell, "A Primer on Hedge Funds."

24. Ibid.

25. Ibid.

26. Hedge Fund Hearings, LaWare statement, pp. 85–87; Hedge Fund Hearings, Ludwig statement, p. 72.

27. Hedge Fund Hearings, LaWare statement, pp. 84–88; Hansell, "A Primer on Hedge Funds."

28. "Why Can't a Commodity Fund Be More Like a Mutual Fund?" *Futures Industry Magazine*, July/August 1993, p. 12 (quoting David Sawyier, of the law firm of Sidley & Austin).

29. See generally *Joint Report on the Government Securities Market*; Ralph Janvey, "Hedge Funds," *Review of Securities & Commodities Regulation* p. 91 (June 8, 1988); Thomas P. Lemke and Gerald T. Lins, "Private Investment Companies Under Section 3(c)(1) of the Investment Company Act of 1940," *Business Lawyer* 44 (February 1989), pp. 401–406.

30. This 100-person limitation has been construed to permit artificial entities, including other partnerships, to be counted as only one person. Thus, hedge funds may have far more than 100 indirect investors, investing through collective investment vehicles which would be deemed only one "person" for purposes of applying the private investment company exclusion. See Lemke and Lins, "Private Investment Companies," p. 407.

31. Application of the Commodity Futures Trading Commission's regulatory framework to hedge funds is extensively addressed in

the agency's testimony at the 1994 hedge fund hearing held by the House Banking Committee. See Hedge Fund Hearings pp. 144 ff., (prepared statement of Barbara Pedersen Holum, Acting Chairman, Commodity Futures Trading Commission).

32. In addition, apart from routine reporting, special calls for information may be made in urgent or special situations. Information about cash market transactions of the trader may also be obtained. See Hedge Fund Hearings, Holum statement, pp. 166–167.

33. Weiss, "Fall Guys?"

34. See Hedge Fund Hearings, Holum statement, pp. 158-164.

35. Hedge Fund Hearings, p. 311, (floor statement of Henry B. Gonzalez, Chairman, House Committee on Banking, Finance and Urban Affairs, March 24, 1994).

36. Hedge Fund Hearings, p. 111. (prepared testimony of Arthur Levitt, Chairman, U.S. Securities and Exchange Commission, April 13, 1994).

37. Hedge Fund Hearings, Levitt testimony, p. 114.

38. Hedge Fund Hearings, Ludwig testimony, p. 79; Hedge Fund Hearings, Levitt testimony, p. 115.

39. *Report of the Presidential Task Force on Market Mechanisms* (Jan. 1988), p. 15.

40. *Joint Report on the Government Securities Market*, p. B–64.

41. *United States* v. *Steinhardt Management Co. and Caxton Corp.*, 94 Civ. 9044 (S.D.N.Y. 1994); *SEC* v. *Steinhardt Management Company,* 94 Civ. 9040 (S.D.N.Y. 1994).

42. Hedge Fund Hearings, Levitt testimony, p. 115; Bennett and Shirreff, "Let's Bash the Hedge Funds," pp. 26, 30.

43. *Joint Report on the Government Securities Market*, p. B–70; Hedge Fund Hearings, Levitt testimony, p. 114.

44. Hedge Fund Hearings, p. 282 (prepared testimony of Ezra Zask).

45. *Joint Report on the Government Securities Market*, p. B–70.

46. Hedge Fund Hearings, LaWare statement, pp. 87, 100; R. Waters and P. Gawith, "Why Steinhardt's Loud Roar Will Be Heard No More," *Financial Times*, Oct. 13, 1995, p. 15.

47. Hedge Fund Hearings, LaWare statement, pp. 86–87, 100.

48. Hedge Fund Hearings, pp. 216–219 (prepared statement of George Soros). Soros comments, *inter alia*, that "[l]opsided trend-following behavior is necessary to produce a violent market crash, but it is not sufficient to bring it about."

49. Hedge Fund Hearings, LaWare statement, p. 96 (citing voluntarily supplied data for 94 hedge funds during the first two months of 1994, which reflected returns ranging from $+20$ percent to -17 percent.)

50. J. Palmer, "Market Mover," *Barron's*, Nov. 6, 1995, pp. 33, 34.

51. Ibid.

52. Kaufman, "New Financial Threats," p. 11. Further, as many hedge fund transactions are in derivatives, when the giant portfolio managers make losing bets, the resulting losses "may lead to what used to be called a domino effect" due to the relationships among participants.

53. R. Bennett and D. Shirreff, "Let's Bash the Hedge Funds," *Euromoney*, April 1994, p. 28.

54. Hedge Fund Hearings, Levitt testimony, p. 115.

55. Hedge Fund Hearings, Soros testimony, p. 217.

56. Ibid.

57. P. Truell, "Some Big Funds Like Soros's Have Difficulty Despite Trend," *New York Times*, July 27, 1995, Sec. D, p.37.

58. Ibid.

59. Laura Jereski, "Many Hedge Funds Are Saying 'Uncle'," *The Wall Street Journal*, November 17, 1995, p. C23.

60. John R. Wilke, "Daiwa Scandal Spurs a Review of Banking Bill," *The Wall Street Journal*, December 5, 1995, p. A4 (referring to Daiwa and Barings PLC losses).

61. Kaufman, "New Financial Threats," p. 12.

62. See R. Bennett and D. Shirreff, "Let's Bash the Hedge Funds," *Euromoney*, April 1994, pp. 27, 32.

63. James C. Allen, "Global Firms' Financial Execs Say They Lack the Right Tools to Measure Derivatives Risk," *American Banker*, Dec. 5, 1995, p. 32 (citing survey indicating that nearly two-thirds of the 80 financial executives of multinational companies that responded said that they had neither the understanding, the expertise, or the systems to make value-at-risk measurements).

64. Ernst & Young, LLP, *Derivatives Usage by Investment Funds* (1995) pp. 1, 10.

65. Ernst & Young, LLP, *Derivatives Usage by Investment Funds*, pp. 12–14.

66. Hedge Fund Hearings, Levitt testimony, pp. 116–17.

67. Hedge Fund Hearing, p. 311 (floor statement of Henry B. Gonzalez, Chairman, House Committee on Banking, Finance and Urban Affairs "Banks, Derivatives and Hedge Funds," March 24, 1994).

68. Hedge Fund Hearings, Ludwig testimony, p. 76.

69. Hedge Fund Hearings, LaWare statement, pp. 93–94.

70. Ibid., p. 94.

71. Hedge Fund Hearings, Ludwig testimony, p. 71.

72. Hedge Fund Hearings, Ludwig testimony, p. 72; See Weiss, "Fall Guys?", p. 119, noting that the "only genuine difference between hedge funds and the proprietary trading operations of the big institutions is that hedge funds are much smaller."

73. Remarks of Mary L. Schapiro, chairman, Commodity Futures Trading Commission, 18th Annual Commodity Law Institute and 4th Annual Financial Services Law Institute Conference, Chicago, Illinois, October 19, 1995, p. 5 (citing Barings, Metallgesellschaft, Daiwa, Kidder Peabody and Merrill Lynch incidents involving losses attributable to failures of internal controls). With respect to recently published guidance on internal controls and risk management, *see, e.g.,* "Operational and Financial Risk Management Control Mechanisms for Over-the-Counter Derivatives Activities of Regulated Securities Firms" (Technical Committee of the International Organization of Securities Commissions, July 1994).

74. *Joint Report on the Government Securities Market*, pp. B-68–69.

75. Weiss, "Fall Guys?," p. 121.

76. Ibid.

77. Statement of Position 95-2, "Financial Reporting by Nonpublic Investment Partnerships," American Institute of Certified Public Accountants, May 19, 1995, applies to financial statements of exempt partnerships (with certain exceptions) prepared in accordance with generally accepted accounting principles.

78. Lemke and Lins, "Private Investment Companies," pp. 401, 402.

79. Division of Investment Management, United States Securities and Exchange Commission, *Protecting Investors: A Half Century of Investment Company Regulation* (May 1992), p. 106.

80. Ibid.

81. Weiss, "Fall Guys?," p. 118.

82. As of this writing, the proposal for an expanded private investment company exception had been incorporated in a substitute bill, the proposed Securities Amendments of 1996, which on May 15, 1996 was reported out by the House Commerce Committee and was expected to reach the House floor in July. Comparable Senate legislation is expected.

83. "The Investment Company Act Amendments of 1995," pp. 15–16 (statement of Barry Barbash, Director, SEC Division of Investment Management).

84. *Joint Report on the Government Securities Market*, p. 70.

85. Hedge Fund Hearings, Levitt testimony, p. 112.

86. This discussion relies upon the risk assessment analysis in Henry T.C. Hu, "Misunderstood Derivatives: The Causes of Informational Failure and the Promise of Regulatory Incrementalism," *Yale Law Journal* 102, no. 1457 (April 1993), pp. 1502–05.

87. Jerry W. Markham, "Protecting the Institutional Investor—Jungle Predator or Shorn Lamb?" *Yale Journal on Regulation* 12, pp. 345, 346 (1995).

88. Ibid., pp. 353–58.

17

OFFSHORE INVESTMENT FUNDS

Robert W. Helm, *Dechert Price & Rhoads**

As the domestic financial services marketplace has grown and matured, particularly since the 1980s, many U.S. financial services firms have determined to seek new markets for investment products by looking internationally. To achieve success in non–U.S. markets, investment firms must develop and offer a wider range of investment products that are particularly attractive to non–U.S. resident investors. These products include investment funds, real estate funds, bank deposit products, managed or private accounts, and currency or commodity trading vehicles. Any of these products may be created with global management and distribution in mind; in other words, they may be organized under the laws of one jurisdiction, managed from another, and offered within still another national market, a regional market such as the European Union (the EU), or a global market. Whatever their particular form, these products allow U.S. firms and their clients to access regional or global markets and increase the variety of investment opportunities available to investors worldwide.

---

*Sonya Tsiros and Douglas Dick contributed to this chapter. Copyright Dechert Price
   & Rhoads.

The ability of investment firms to offer many of these global investment products depends on the existence of offshore financial centers. The term *offshore financial center* generally refers to a type of jurisdiction that seeks out business from nonresident financial organizations by offering flexible financial regulation, financial secrecy laws, and an advantageous tax regime, with limited or no taxes imposed on certain domestically organized investment vehicles or on nonresident investors in such vehicles. Because of these latter attributes, the popular image of the offshore financial center is that of a "no questions asked" domicile used by investors seeking to hide illicitly obtained assets or avoid taxes. Although some offshore financial centers are used for such purposes, offshore centers also serve important and legitimate functions in the global capital formation process. The regulatory flexibility and tax advantages offered by the centers have enabled investment firms to create a variety of financial products and to distribute these products to global markets, without regard to the national origin of the investor.

A leading offshore financial product is the offshore fund. As more firms have begun to exploit the advantages of offshore financial centers, the offshore fund industry has grown at a tremendous pace, as the experience of two of Europe's largest offshore centers, Luxembourg and Dublin, demonstrates. In mid-1995, the assets of offshore funds domiciled in Luxembourg exceeded $341.6 billion,[1] compared with $156 billion in assets in 1992,[2] and only $21.5 billion in 1985.[3] Similarly, between 1993 and 1994 Dublin experienced a 50 percent rate of growth in asset volume and in the number of new fund management operations,[4] and by mid-1995 assets under management at Dublin's International Financial Services Centre were estimated at $22.4 billion.[5]

This chapter is intended as an introduction to the issues involved in the organization, offering, and management of offshore funds, principally from the perspective of a U.S.-based investment management firm. The second section of this chapter addresses the rationale for the development of offshore investment vehicles and describes some of the more common types of funds. The third section addresses U.S. regulatory considerations that affect a U.S. firm's involvement in the offshore fund sector and that may affect its ability to compete effectively in the offshore marketplace. The fourth section discusses organizational issues involved in establishing offshore funds, including the selection of an appropriate domicile and the appropriate structure for the fund itself.

Finally, the fifth section concludes with a discussion of some of the issues currently facing this rapidly growing sector.

WHY GO OFFSHORE?

Offshore funds and related investment products have traditionally been viewed principally as tax-avoidance or asset-protection devices. Many offshore fund jurisdictions have special laws governing the preservation of professional secrecy (sometimes referred to as *banking secrecy*) that prevent professionals in that jurisdiction from providing information about a client or the client's financial condition to third parties without the client's consent.[6] Such laws can make it easier to carry on money laundering activities, for example, by not requiring the reporting of large cash deposits to government authorities, as is obligatory in the United States.[7]

In recent years, international conventions and enhanced international enforcement efforts have placed increasing pressure on jurisdictions that purport to practice a pure form of professional secrecy, with the "legitimate" offshore jurisdictions becoming more vigilant in their efforts to detect and prevent money laundering activity from taking place within their borders.[8] Typical of many of the present initiatives to combat money laundering is the placement of increased responsibilities on financial institutions to establish preventative measures to identify suspicious transactions.[9] In addition, many of these international initiatives are aimed at strengthening enforcement mechanisms to combat money laundering, most notably by calling for the forfeiture of all proceeds of criminal activity.[10] These efforts notwithstanding, the use of offshore centers for the purpose of sheltering income from tax authorities remains an important function of at least a segment of the offshore fund industry. The need to protect "flight capital" from expropriation or hyperinflation is another important function.

There are also "legitimate" reasons for an investment manager to create offshore products. These reasons often relate to burdensome regulations in the country of origin, which may restrict the ability of an investment manager to pursue a particular investment strategy or to structure an offshore product in a particular way. In the case of U.S. investment managers, a number of regulatory and tax considerations may make an offshore product particularly attractive when compared to a U.S.-registered product:

- Fiduciary-based restrictions on U.S. funds that require equal treatment of shareholders, which may preclude, for example, charging differential advisory fees to shareholders of the same fund.
- Tax restrictions applicable to U.S. mutual funds, such as portfolio diversification requirements and limitations on short-term trading, that impede the manager's ability to manage a portfolio in a preferred manner.
- Unfavorable tax treatment of non–U.S. investors in U.S. mutual funds, including, in particular, the imposition of withholding tax on income dividends paid by a U.S.–regulated investment company to non–U.S. investors.
- Inflexibility or procedural delays arising under U.S. domestic corporate law, securities laws, or regulations that make it more difficult to change the nature, structure, or operations of a fund or product, particularly in a timely fashion and at acceptable cost.
- The burden of complying with substantive provisions of the U.S. Investment Company Act of 1940 (the 1940 Act), which imposes certain investment restrictions, capital structure requirements, governance provisions, and restrictions on affiliated transactions, or of the U.S. Investment Advisers Act of 1940 (the Advisers Act), which, among other things, restricts the levying of performance-based fees.
- The burden of complying with the federal commodities laws.
- The overall compliance burden and related cost resulting from U.S. regulation.

By using an offshore fund or other offshore investment product, a U.S.-based investment manager can minimize the burden of compliance with these laws and regulations, thus making the investment product more attractive to investors domiciled outside the United States. Offshore funds may offer a cost-effective means of pooling both offshore and onshore capital, which may then be managed on a commingled basis. Investment managers also may use offshore vehicles to access markets where access would otherwise be limited, or to achieve certain tax planning objectives. Pursuit of these goals leads U.S. investment management firms and other sponsors of investment products to use offshore financial vehicles in a number of ways outlined below.

Pass-Through Vehicles

The pass-through vehicle is a product developed for situations in which local investment restrictions or potentially negative consequences arising under existing tax treaties would make it less advantageous for an investment fund to invest in a particular country. The pass-through or intermediary vehicle is organized in a jurisdiction that offers treaty benefits with the country in which investments will be made. The investment fund then invests in the pass-through vehicle rather than making investments directly. Although the concept of a pass-through is fairly simple, these vehicles must be structured carefully so that they are not disallowed as mere shams. Hence pass-throughs are generally used only in rare circumstances. Registered investment companies seeking special treatment or other relief to invest in particular foreign markets have obtained regulatory approval to use such investment vehicles.[11]

Special Purpose Funds

Certain U.S. laws and regulations impose substantive or operational restrictions on the investments that funds may make. As a result, some special purpose funds, such as U.S.-source commodities or managed futures funds, use offshore jurisdictions for certain types of activities. These activities include currency and precious metals trading, real estate investment, and the operation of hedge funds. If any such fund has U.S.-based shareholders and is primarily engaged in the business of investing in securities, it generally must be structured so as to qualify as a private investment company under the 1940 Act. In general, a private investment company is a company that is not making, and has no present intention of making, a public offering in the United States and that has, moreover, no more than 100 beneficial owners of its shares who are U.S. residents.[12]

Offshore Funds as Institutional Vehicles

U.S. managers also use offshore funds to create investment products that they will market to both domestic and foreign institutional investors. One particular advantage to using an offshore fund in such circumstances is that a fund domiciled outside the United States can avoid the potential adverse consequences of U.S. tax withholding rules that may otherwise deter foreign investors. Alternatively, a fund manager may wish to select a domicile that has the potential to offer tax benefits under existing tax treaties, or to offer performance fee arrangements that would not be possible under U.S. law (although a U.S.-registered adviser to such a vehicle may still be subject to those restrictions under U.S. law). Moreover, many of the disadvantages of offshore centers, such as a lack of regulatory oversight, may not be of great concern to sophisticated institutional investors, as long as they are assured of adequate protections through custodial and other contractual arrangements.

Retail-Oriented Offshore Funds

Significant activity in recent years has occurred in the development of retail-oriented offshore fund products. Many of these are organized to mirror domestically offered products but in a non-U.S. resident marketplace. Other funds may be designed specifically for a particular market.

Because they are aimed at the retail market, distribution of these funds is a critical issue. A fund promoter may rely on its own international distribution capabilities (such as the private banking group of a large bank or the client base of an international securities brokerage firm) or on a network of multiple independent dealer arrangements. Distribution arrangements for these funds therefore are frequently global in scope, while asset management services are typically provided by specialists working out of one or more of the leading financial centers.

In light of the pressures placed on fund promoters, who must compete both for "shelf space" for their products with the most desirable dealers and for investor assets, retail products are often structured flexibly to offer a wide range of investor and dealer options and services that can be changed easily to reflect market developments. Offshore fund structures such as master-feeder arrangements,[13] multiple classes of shares[14] and multiple investment portfolios were developed for this purpose. The choice of domicile for a retail-oriented fund also may be influenced more heavily than in the institutional market by the reputation of the fund's domicile. At least some global investors, may have a natural preference for a fund with the perceived imprimatur of a "legitimate" jurisdiction, such as Dublin or Luxembourg, over a fund domiciled in a jurisdiction more readily associated with piracy, money laundering, or other unsavory activity.

Offshore Structured Finance Vehicles

Offshore funds and companies also may be used in connection with specially tailored financial transactions, such as those involving the issuance of structured bonds or notes. The bonds or notes may be issued by a securities firm, bank, or finance company and may be collateralized by investments in an underlying vehicle that itself has the characteristics of an investment fund. This structure permits the transformation of the income derived from the underlying asset pool into the form a particular class of investors desires. This result may also be achieved by the arrangement of swap agreements (or contracts for differences) by the issuer. Depending on the particular structure used for the transaction, securities issued by an offshore structured vehicle may be placed privately in the United States without requiring the underlying vehicle to register under the 1940 Act.[15]

Structured financial transactions are typically created to meet the particular financing demands of a securities firm's or bank's large institutional clients. Because they are often heavily market- and time-sensitive, these types of transactions may be drawn to jurisdictions such as the Cayman Islands, Bermuda, Jersey, or Guernsey, where it is possible to create funds and companies rapidly, with less regulatory oversight.[16] If the underlying vehicle will invest in certain types of securities, however, the choice of jurisdiction may be dictated by whether tax treaty benefits are available.

Private Trust and Banking Business

U.S. investment firms have traditionally not been as active in the offshore private banking and trust business as investment firms in other countries (such as the United Kingdom). In part, this is because the U.S. Internal Revenue Service (the IRS) is an efficient enforcer of U.S. tax laws, which, in general, require U.S. taxpayers to be taxed currently on earnings from offshore activities. More recently, U.S. investment firms, securities firms, and banks have been more active in the offshore area, but almost exclusively on behalf of *bona fide* nonresident alien clients. As noted below, proposed legislation would further limit the ability of U.S. nationals or certain foreign settlors to avoid U.S. tax by using offshore trusts.[17]

REGULATORY CONSIDERATIONS AFFECTING U.S. SPONSORS OF OFFSHORE FUNDS

Any involvement by a U.S. sponsor, distributor, or investment adviser with an offshore fund raises potential issues under U.S. securities, tax, and commodities laws. Depending on the level and degree of U.S. contacts by the fund, these considerations can affect the structure, investment management process, or distribution arrangements of an offshore fund. A brief overview of some of these key issues follows.

Investment Company Act of 1940

Section 7(d) of the 1940 Act prohibits any investment company organized outside the United States from using the U.S. mails or facilities of interstate commerce in connection with a public offering of its securities, except pursuant to a Securities and Exchange Commission (SEC) order. Such an order must be based on a finding that "it is both legally and practically feasible effectively to enforce the provisions of [the 1940 Act] against such company."

The 1940 Act offers no statutory definition of *public offering*. However, the SEC staff has historically read the public offering language in Section 7(d) to have the same meaning as in the Securities Act of 1933 (the 1933 Act) and in Section 3(c)(1) of the 1940 Act, the "private investment company" exception from the statute's definition of *investment company*.[18] Section 3(c)(1) of the 1940 Act provides that an issuer will not be considered to be an investment company

> whose outstanding securities (other than short-term paper) are beneficially owned by not more than one hundred persons and which is not making and does not presently propose to make a public offering of its securities.

Under this staff interpretation of Section 7(d), which was endorsed by the SEC in 1990,[19] an unregistered foreign fund making a public offering of its shares outside the United States may make a private offering of its securities to U.S. residents without registering under the 1940 Act provided it has, at the end of the day, no more than 100 beneficial holders of its shares who are U.S. residents (not counting any holders of short-term paper).[20]

In a recent no-action letter, the SEC staff has indicated that it may be possible for an offshore fund organized in series form (an "umbrella" fund under local law) to apply the 100-person resident beneficial owner test of Section 3(c)(1) to each separate series of shares of the fund rather than to the investment fund as a whole. In this particular case, the fund was organized in Ireland as a unit trust, with each separate series of shares constituting a separate trust. The fund was able to represent to the SEC staff that, under Irish law, each series is a separate legal trust, and that only the assets of that trust may be applied to discharge claims of that trust and cannot be applied to discharge claims of other trusts.[21] In a more recent no-action letter, the SEC staff took the position that a non-U.S.-registered Canadian investment company need not count toward the 100-U.S. shareholder limit Canadian shareholders who become resident in the United States, provided the only new share purchases made by such persons are made through dividend reinvestment.[22]

The SEC staff has also granted no-action relief to a number of U.S. sponsors of offshore funds with respect to the conduct of administrative and distribution support activities for offshore funds in or from the United States. U.S.-based sponsors of offshore funds have sought assurances that they would be able to engage in a wide range of activities in or from the United States without the funds being deemed to be engaged in a public offering in the United States. In these letters funds have generally represented that the principal administrative offices of the fund would be offshore and that all prospective purchasers of shares of the funds would be required to represent at the time of subscription that they were not "U.S. persons" and that they had not been solicited to purchase shares while physically present in the United States.[23] Today, most large U.S. brokerage firms and banks offer offshore funds to their nonresident alien clients in transactions that are carefully designed to avoid U.S. registration requirements.

The 1940 Act, and the tax considerations discussed below generally combine to limit the degree of permissible U.S. contact by an offshore fund. Offshore funds with U.S. sponsors or advisers generally attempt to keep as much of their activity offshore as possible, including fund administration and distribution efforts. Moreover, an unregistered offshore fund generally regulates share ownership and restricts the transfer of shares to non–U.S. persons so as to avoid potential registration issues under the 1940 Act. Consequently, such funds may be less concerned about potential extraterritorial applicability of the 1933 Act to their offerings conducted abroad than other issuers that may have U.S. underwriters or other more significant U.S. contacts. Regulation S under the 1933 Act,[24] which sets forth certain safe harbor rules for securities offerings to foreign investors (and specifically is not available to investment companies "registered or required to be registered" under the 1940 Act) may nevertheless provide some guidance to help a fund sponsor determine that the fund's distribution activities are truly being conducted in "offshore transactions" as defined in the regulation.[25]

Investment Advisers Act of 1940

An offshore fund client of a U.S.-registered investment adviser, like all clients of the adviser, is entitled to a wide range of protections under the Advisers Act. The Advisers Act imposes significant fiduciary obligations and disclosure requirements on all registered advisers, and further subjects registrants to compliance with rules governing the custody of client assets, adviser advertising and the presentation of past performance information, and the imposition of performance-based fees. Under limited and special circumstances, it may be possible for a U.S.-based adviser to charge a performance-based fee to a non–U.S. client, such as an offshore fund, that does not comply with applicable U.S. regulation when the law of the jurisdiction in which the client is based permits such a fee.[26]

Commodities Law Issues

The U.S. commodities laws govern a wide range of activities involving both U.S. and foreign futures markets when use of the "means and instrumentalities" of interstate commerce create a U.S. nexus. U.S. promoters of or advisers to offshore funds that use commodity futures need to consider, in particular, the potential applicability to their activities of commodities law rules regulating commodity pool operators (CPOs) and commodity trading advisers (CTAs).

Assuming an offshore fund uses financial futures contracts only for bona fide hedging or other incidental purposes, the Commodity Futures Trading Commission (the CFTC) or its staff may be willing to exempt an offshore fund and its adviser or sponsor from CPO or CTA registration or regulation. In a series of interpretative letters, the CFTC staff has not required such entities to register, or has granted exemptions from certain regulatory requirements, where the offshore fund was organized and operated under the laws of a jurisdiction other than that of the United States, would not hold shareholder or board meetings within the United States, would have no U.S. persons as shareholders, and would not contain capital raised directly or indirectly from sources within the United States.[27] Similarly, the CFTC staff has granted exemptions from registration as a CTA to advisers of offshore funds so long as the funds' activities take place outside the United States, the funds' clients are located outside the United States, and the advisers do not hold themselves out as CTAs to any offshore fund or to its prospective investors.[28]

Tax Issues

An offshore fund will want to avoid carrying on a "U.S. trade or business" so as to avoid the potential imposition of U.S. corporate income tax on its earnings and profits. Under an IRS safe harbor, an offshore fund with a U.S.-based investment adviser generally can avoid being deemed to be carrying on a U.S. trade or business provided the fund maintains its principal office offshore by carrying out all or a substantial portion of certain administrative and distribution-related functions offshore (the so-called IRS Ten Commandments).[29] An offshore fund with a non–U.S. adviser could, at least in theory, have more extensive U.S. contacts than the Ten Commandments would permit for a fund with a U.S. adviser and still escape potential liability for U.S. corporate income tax.

ERISA Issues

The U.S. Employee Retirement Income Security Act of 1974 (ERISA) is a comprehensive statute that governs the operation and administration of U.S. private pension and welfare benefit plans. These plans are attractive potential shareholders for non–U.S. funds because, as tax-exempt entities, they avoid many of the tax problems faced by U.S. shareholders in non–U.S. funds. However, investment by a U.S. pension plan in a non–U.S. fund may raise certain issues both for the plan and the fund. In particular, if employee benefit plan investors (not limited to U.S. plans) hold 25 percent or more of the shares of a fund, the fund's assets, in addition to shares of the fund, will be regarded as plan assets for purposes of applying various ERISA reporting, fiduciary, and custody requirements. Moreover, designating fund assets as ERISA plan assets may make the fund's promoter and directors "fiduciaries with respect to the plan" as ERISA defines that concept, and hence it may invest them with certain responsibilities and potential liabilities. These responsibilities and potential liabilities—particularly responsibilities applicable to prohibited transactions with affiliates—may be more extensive than those existing under the law of the fund's domicile. In order to avoid being considered an ERISA fiduciary, offshore funds may seek to limit ownership of any class of equity securities of the fund by benefit plans (both U.S. and non–U.S.) to less than 25 percent at all times. The fund subscription process may require certain representations or include reporting mechanisms to monitor and enforce this limitation.

Broker-Dealer and Banking Law Issues

It is likely that any offer or sale of shares of a foreign investment fund in the United States or to U.S. residents would have to be made through a U.S. registered broker-dealer or through an entity that is exempt from registration as such.[30] The SEC has adopted a territorial approach to broker-dealer regulation that provides, in essence, that an entity or person conducting activities relating to the offer, sale, or inducement to purchase or sell any security within the United States must register with the SEC as a broker-dealer, even if the clients of the broker-dealer are U.S. persons resident abroad. In a related rule, the SEC extends the benefits of this territorial approach to foreign broker-dealers who do not solicit U.S. customers and, under specified conditions, it generally exempts from U.S. registration such entities even if U.S. persons transact business with them.[31]

Provisions of the Banking Act of 1933 (the Glass-Steagall Act) generally limit the extent to which U.S. banks may engage in securities activities in the United States, limiting them principally to buying and selling securities on the order and for the account of their customers. Moreover, these provisions do not permit U.S. banking organizations to act as principal underwriters for a mutual fund. The International Banking Act of 1978 applies these restrictions to the U.S.-based activities of foreign banks. The non–U.S. activities of U.S. or foreign banks are not subject to these limitations. A U.S.-based banking institution may, however, provide investment advisory services to an offshore fund, and may, consistent with the tax considerations discussed above (the Ten Commandments) also provide custody and administrative services to an offshore fund. These restrictions on bank involvement in certain aspects of the distribution of offshore funds distinguish the United States from many other jurisdictions where banks play a significant role in sponsoring and distributing offshore funds.[32]

ORGANIZING FUNDS OFFSHORE

A World of Offshore Financial Centers

A number of offshore fund jurisdictions exist, and many of them fiercely compete against one another for business. Geographically, the leading jurisdictions are grouped in two areas: Europe and the Caribbean. Although they have yet to achieve the prominence of the European and Caribbean centers, centers located in the Indian Ocean area, such as Mauritius, the Seychelles, and Malaysia, are expected to play an increasing role in the offshore financial services sector due to their proximity to growing Asian markets.[33]

Competition among the leading offshore centers is, to a large degree, based on the regulatory and legal structures (or lack thereof) they provide to their clients. Each fund jurisdiction has a unique profile regarding the degree of local regulation, the necessity of minimal contacts with the jurisdiction (e.g. resident directors), the requirement to retain local fund administrators, minimum capital requirements, and status and reputation in the financial community. "Legitimate" jurisdictions tend to require more local contacts, including the presence of significant local administration. Such contacts are beneficial from the standpoint of establishing that the fund does not carry on a "U.S. trade or business" for U.S. tax purposes.[34] "Legitimate" jurisdictions also tend to be stricter when it comes to enforcing compliance with international conventions dealing with money laundering.[35] Toronto's growth as an offshore fund administrative center is attributable not only to its geographical and cultural proximity to the United States and its money centers, but also to Canada's status as a respected member of the international community.[36] Dublin and Luxembourg benefit from similar status.

Of the European centers, Luxembourg is by far the leading center for offshore mutual funds in terms of asset value. A number of administrative and back office operations for U.S.-based financial institutions (not limited to fund management, and including insurance and banking) have been attracted to Dublin's International Financial Services Centre because of its relatively low labor costs, high quality of the local workforce, and status of English as the principal working language. Other major European centers include the traditional offshore territories of the British Isles, Guernsey, Jersey, and the Isle of Man. More recently, offshore centers in Gibraltar, Madeira, Malta, and Cyprus have begun to emerge.

The growth of the European domestic offshore fund business has been greatly aided by the Directive on Undertakings for Collective Investment in Transferable Securities (UCITS), which the Council of the (then) European Community adopted in 1988.[37] Funds organized in any EU member state in accordance with the UCITS directive may obtain approval to offer their shares in other EU member states by complying with a notice requirement. Such funds must, however, also comply with local distribution rules (including advertising rules) and tax rules, and they generally must appoint a local paying agent. These additional requirements can constitute significant barriers to entry in some EU national markets, where local institutions dominate fund distribution and are unwilling to offer competing fund products to their customers.

Although most UCITS funds are sold principally in the country of the fund sponsor,[38] a discernable recent trend is toward the development of pan–European products. Accession of new member states to the EU (notably Austria, Norway, and Sweden) may hasten the development of funds sold in multiple jurisdictions.

Because of the access they potentially grant to EU countries, offshore UCITS funds have become a favorite vehicle for U.S. investment management firms to establish and market mutual funds to the European markets. Fidelity Investments, Federated Investors, Prudential Securities, Smith Barney, and Merrill Lynch are among the more prominent U.S. firms that have established footholds in Europe through the use of offshore funds organized in UCITS form.[39]

Another major geographic concentration of offshore financial centers is the Caribbean. Principal centers include the Cayman Islands, the British Virgin Islands, the Bahamas, Bermuda, the Netherlands Antilles, and the Turks and Caicos Islands. Due to their location, the Caribbean offshore financial centers tend to focus on investment products designed for sale in Latin America and on non–U.S. funds investing in the United States. Such centers also may attract institutional offshore business from the United States that values a jurisdiction with a common time zone with New York and Boston. Many of the Caribbean jurisdictions are renowned for their secrecy laws and minimal regulations, and consequently they have somewhat murkier reputations than their European counterparts.[40]

Offshore funds are not the only investment funds that are offered and sold on a cross-border basis. A number of countries, including Germany, the U.K., Japan, and Hong Kong[41] have domestic statutes that, at least in theory, permit the approval of nondomestic funds for local offer and sale. Some U.S. firms have had success selling U.S. funds in those jurisdictions on a registered, public basis. Despite the complications imposed by tax laws and other competitive considerations, there is a fair amount of cross-border fund activity in the world today.

Factors Influencing the Selection of an Offshore Fund Jurisdiction

Investment managers must consider numerous factors in selecting a jurisdiction in which to organize an offshore fund. Usually more than one jurisdiction meets most or all of the business objectives of the fund promoter. In the final analysis, business and practical considerations, including existing relationships with service providers who have established fund administrative operations in these domiciles, may be more significant than details of local regulation.

The selection of an offshore fund jurisdiction often follows the design phase of product development. In this phase, the promoter determines the basic objectives and purpose for establishing the fund, including an analysis of investment management, administration, and distribution. Depending on the particular investment policies and objectives to be pursued for the fund, some jurisdictions may be more attractive than others because they may permit more flexibility in the design of fund investment policies and restrictions. Some jurisdictions may further restrict specific investment activities or strategies, such as investment techniques involving derivative instruments, whereas other jurisdictions have no such rules.

Distribution considerations may be as important as investment policy considerations when establishing an offshore fund. A fund sponsor must consider the practical considerations affecting distribution, particularly for an open-end fund, which sells and redeems shares daily. In particular, the jurisdiction's time zone should be practicable for the markets that the fund is trying to reach. This has been a factor in developing the Caribbean islands as a leading location for funds sold in Latin America, and Luxembourg for funds sold in continental Europe. It is also important to know the local rules on distribution and advertising, and how they will they affect marketing efforts, if at all.[42]

The corporate structure of a fund is often dictated by the needs of the intended shareholders and the marketing strategy of the fund sponsor. An obvious consideration in choosing a jurisdiction is whether the local law permits the desired form of corporate organization for the fund. For example, it may be desirable to organize a fund as a limited partnership or in some other specialized form, such as the master/feeder structure.[43] In addition, for some fund structures, such as funds with multiple investment portfolios, flexibility of a jurisdiction's corporate law is an important consideration. One indication of such flexibility is the ability to organize a fund that requires minimal shareholder approvals for changes in corporate structure or in a fund's foundation documents. Other indications of corporate law flexibility are the absence of annual meeting requirements, the ability of a board to amend the fund's constituent documents at will, and the absence of taxes imposed on the issuance and redemption of shares.

If the sponsor is interested in maximum distribution flexibility, it will be necessary to establish that, under local law, funds can issue shares of multiple investment portfolios (series), preferably with the ability to add new series without shareholder approval. Moreover, a fund should be able to issue separate classes of shares with respect to a single series, and to serve as the "master" fund for a master/feeder fund arrangement.[44]

If it is possible or likely that a U.S.-registered fund will be purchasing shares in an offshore fund, it may be useful if the local fund can issue securities that will not be voting securities as the 1940 Act defines that term. This may help address issues arising under the "fund of funds" provisions of the 1940 Act, which can restrict the investment by registered investment companies in other investment companies.[45]

The establishment of offshore vehicles, especially those targeted at the retail market, requires elaborate coordination of service providers based in a number of different jurisdictions. Selecting the right combination of service providers can make a project a complete success, whereas a poor selection can produce delays and frustration for all. As some services may be required to be performed in the intended jurisdiction, it is important to inquire into the quality and cost of local service providers, such as lawyers, accountants, and fund administrators. The quality of local infrastructure, including telecommunications, courier services, and postal service will also affect the level of service provided. A sponsor may prefer a jurisdiction in which it has existing relationships because contacts can be used to negotiate fees and to establish data networks. Finally, the sponsor should determine the degree of local administration and control of the fund required in the intended jurisdiction, and whether the sponsor will be able to subcontract out some or most of these functions, either to itself or to its regular service providers.[46]

Fiscal considerations are often paramount in determining whether a particular investment strategy is viable. The most obvious source of tax liability for a fund is the taxes levied on the fund or its shareholders by the fund's jurisdiction of incorporation. In addition, a sponsor should also examine the tax laws of the country in which potential shareholders live and of the country or countries in which the fund may invest. If there are tax treaties between the proposed jurisdiction and the countries in which the fund will invest, the treaty benefits will affect the fund's liability for withholding and other taxes and thereby affect the potential yield to investors. A sponsor should also evaluate the local taxes levied on the adviser/sponsor's activities, on the fund's activities, or on use of local service providers (such as value added taxes or VAT).

Finally, selecting an offshore fund jurisdiction involves intangible factors. Intangibles range from the integrity, strength, and reputation of the local regulatory authority (indeed whether there is in fact any local regulation or control), to the work ethic and quality of the local work force, to the issue of who else does business in the jurisdiction and whether the sponsor feels comfortable being associated with them.

Structuring Offshore Funds and Integrating Offshore Funds with Domestic Products

Offshore funds may be structured in a variety of ways depending on the manager's evaluation of the marketing prospects for the fund and on whether projected asset size is sufficient to sustain a stand-alone product. If a stand-alone product is not feasible, a master/feeder structure can be used to gather assets from a number of sources, both onshore and offshore. Alternatively, a multiple share class arrangement can offer a variety of distribution options to investors with differing investment needs. In this section we discuss the principal structures used for offshore fund products and how these structures permit integration with onshore products.

"Mirror" Offshore Funds

An adviser with an extensive existing family of funds has numerous approaches to structuring offshore funds. One is to create funds that "mirror" domestic products in most respects, possibly including fees and expenses. A variation on this theme would be to use the same investment philosophy and guidelines for the offshore fund to take advantage of a positive U.S. track record, but to vary fees to address differences in investor sensitivity and market demand. Yet another approach would be to create an investment product designed specifically for a particular national market, regardless of whether the adviser offered a comparable U.S. product. In seeking to identify potential economies of scale and to permit necessary flexibility in designing distribution options, the adviser may also consider the relative merits of classes of shares or master/feeder arrangements.

Integration and Coinvestment Issues   One issue that may arise under the U.S. securities laws with respect to a U.S.-registered fund and its offshore mirror fund is the possibility that the funds' offerings could be integrated and treated as a single offering for purposes of compliance with the securities laws. It is unlikely, however, that funds will be integrated if the U.S. fund is registered and fully regulated and the non-U.S. fund is offered exclusively to non–U.S. investors, or if the two offerings are otherwise distinct or addressed to separate, defined categories of investors.[47]

Coinvestment or bunching orders to purchase securities for both an offshore and U.S.-registered fund generally should not implicate the 1940 Act's prohibition of joint transactions,[48] except in cases that have a potential for overreaching or unfair treatment, as with investments in privately negotiated illiquid investment opportunities[49] or with funds where the manager is a substantial investor or participates on a different or more favorable basis, such as receiving an incentive fee.

Use of the Adviser's Performance Record   A new offshore fund may, depending on rules applicable in its jurisdiction of organization, wish to use the performance record of its adviser (including the records of other funds managed by the adviser) in connection with promoting the offer of its shares. If the adviser to the fund is a U.S.-registered entity (or if a foreign adviser has used the U.S. "jurisdictional means" in connection with its advisory activities), the adviser will need to determine whether and to what extent any presentation of its past performance record in this context complies with the antifraud provisions of the Advisers Act and with a series of SEC no-action letters governing the content of adviser advertising.[50]

Multiple Classes of Shares

Offshore funds have historically offered classes of shares: dividend-paying or income shares, and dividend capitalization or roll-up shares. Offshore funds also may feature share classes with net asset values calculated in terms of different currencies. Multiclass arrangements featuring different distribution structures have become more common in the offshore fund arena as U.S. firms, principally, have created products offshore that combine various attributes of domestically offered products. In these arrangements, a fund may offer two or more classes of shares to different classes of investors. Each class may have a different sales load and distribution fee structure. The fund may provide certain administrative services only to particular classes, with only those classes bearing the expense of such services.

In most offshore jurisdictions, no special relief is needed to offer multiple classes of shares and no special conditions apply to a multiclass arrangement. However, offshore jurisdictions may insist that differences in treatment of shareholders be justified and reasonable, and that services that benefit all shareholders (such as custody and advisory services) not be subject to differential fee rates. Offshore jurisdictions may also require that all classes of shares be offered through a common prospectus.

U.S. funds that plan to issue multiple classes of shares generally obtain a private letter ruling from the IRS stating that the fund's adoption of a multiple class structure will not cause its dividend distributions to be considered preferential dividends for federal income tax purposes. No such ruling is required in the typical offshore jurisdiction. Because of issues under the U.S. federal securities and tax laws, the use of a multiple class distribution structure with one class of shares offered in the United States and another class of shares offered outside the United States is probably not a viable alternative.

Master/Feeder Structure

Multiple tier, or "master/feeder" structures, are being used increasingly in both domestic and offshore contexts. Master/feeder arrangements have long existed outside of the United States, and they are conditionally exempted from the "fund of funds" restrictions in the 1940 Act.[51] In a typical master/feeder structure, individual feeder funds are organized to gather assets from different sources, which are then invested on a commingled basis in a single master fund. The feeder funds' investment objectives are the same as those of the master fund, but the feeder funds achieve their objectives by investing solely in the master fund. Shares of the feeder funds may be offered to investors in different national markets. Asset management, fund accounting, and custody functions are performed at the master fund level. Distribution, shareholder servicing, and transfer agency functions are accounted for at the feeder fund level and can be tailored to the needs of investors in the various markets.

Some jurisdictions, like the United States, may regulate or prohibit master/feeder arrangements, or funds of funds, by limiting the ability of a registered investment fund to invest in shares of other investment funds, particularly open-end funds. It is common, however, for jurisdictions to make exceptions for "special situation" funds (i.e., funds established to invest in a particular country) or where a fund is only a pass-through vehicle used for purposes of satisfying local laws or for obtaining tax treaty benefits.

The UCITS directive imposes similar restrictions on investments by a UCITS fund in shares of other open-end funds. However, a fund organized in non-UCITS form or in a jurisdiction without fund of funds restrictions may serve as a feeder fund for a UCITS fund. There are no restrictions on UCITS funds functioning as the master fund for a master/feeder arrangement. Proposed amendments to the UCITS directive would permit master/feeder arrangements involving UCITS funds as both master and feeder funds.[52]

The 1940 Act permits the creation of U.S.-registered master/feeder funds and further permits a U.S.-registered master fund to have unregistered offshore feeders. Because of U.S. tax considerations, a U.S.-registered master fund with offshore feeders must structure certain management and distribution functions offshore so as to avoid being deemed to be engaged in a "U.S. trade or business" for U.S. tax purposes. Because of the attractiveness inherent in the ability to manage both onshore and offshore assets on a commingled basis, some U.S. investment managers have organized funds using the onshore/offshore master/feeder structure. Other managers have used wholly offshore master/feeder arrangements to permit "private labeling" of offshore feeder funds or to permit greater flexibility in designing pricing structures for different offshore distribution channels.

THE FUTURE OF OFFSHORE PRODUCTS

The marketplace for offshore investment products has expanded rapidly in a relatively short period of time, much faster than the ability of any one national system or interlocking system of international cooperation to regulate it. The absence of burdensome regulation is one of the key factors that has encouraged investment-related business to go offshore. The investment opportunities offered by a more flexible regulatory climate may be particularly attractive to certain types of investors. On the other hand, most investors appreciate the need for some form of guarantee that their assets will be invested prudently and safely and will not be subject to expropriation or even theft.[53] Certain offshore jurisdictions and their regulators have earned a reputation for prudence and investor protection, at least with respect to activities that take place within their borders. Other jurisdictions have somewhat less positive reputations as regulators. In any case, an offshore jurisdiction is likely to be powerless to regulate the activities of funds organized within its borders that take place abroad.

Against this background of relative regulatory uncertainty, investors, sponsors, and other participants in the offshore fund arena are often left to rely principally on the reputation of their counterparties as a substitute for the formal guarantees that would be available if the parties were engaged in a commercial transaction in a jurisdiction with a significant regulatory structure and enforcement mechanism. The principal weakness of this approach is that parties may assume that certain guarantees and protections that would be applicable to their relationship with, for example, a service provider in that entity's country of origin, will apply similarly to transactions with that entity, or with an affiliate of that entity, that occur offshore. Unfortunately, this is not always the case, and it may well be naive to expect that a firm's desire to maintain its international reputation intact will cause it to act, in an offshore setting, in a manner not required under the local law governing the transaction.[54]

Sponsors of offshore products that are subject to significant regulation in their country of origin also face risks when investors begin to expect that products offered offshore are fully comparable to those offered domestically. Offshore investors may expect, reasonably or not, that the sponsor of an offshore fund will treat all of its customers, globally, in an equal fashion, without concern for whether there are formal legal requirements that it do so.[55] On the other hand, a firm also may recognize that its reputation as a highly respected and highly regulated institution has, at least in part, been responsible for whatever success it may have achieved in distributing investment products in foreign or offshore markets. The offshore customer's expectations of comparable treatment therefore may be wholly reasonable, if not overtly encouraged by the firm in the promotion of its offshore product line.

An area of significant concern for all participants in the offshore fund and investment business is the problem of preventing the use of offshore investment products for money laundering purposes. As noted above, domestic legislation, international conventions, and less formal efforts at cooperation have established minimum standards for institutional inquiry as to the source of funds and identity of potential customers of offshore firms and funds. However, these limited efforts are not sufficient to stem the vast tide of money laundering activity that occurs globally through a variety of financial media. Increasing focus on initiatives against money laundering may encourage the "legitimate" offshore fund business to further concentrate itself in a smaller number of better-regulated jurisdictions, while the less-regulated jurisdictions may come under increasing pressure to tighten controls over domestic institutions and to abandon their *laissez faire* approach to regulation.

Finally, the offshore fund industry perpetually faces issues of fiscal accountability and transparency and must adjust to the uneasy place occupied by offshore financial transactions in any national system of taxation. The potential use of offshore products as tax avoidance mechanisms by individual investors cloaked by laws on banking secrecy remains a difficult issue for national policy makers. It seems clear that, in general, U.S. tax policy is not offended if U.S. corporate taxpayers provide services to offshore funds. On the other hand, U.S. tax policy is offended if offshore funds or vehicles are used to avoid U.S. taxes.

Proposed legislation would further restrict the ability of some U.S. tax-payers to use offshore vehicles for tax avoidance purposes.[56]

Moreover, offshore funds always face the risk that national revenue authorities may disallow certain tax benefits or structures that in their view offend national tax policy. While an offshore fund will generally obtain assurances about its fiscal status in its domicile, the tax treatment of the fund as an investor in a particular country, or of its shareholders wherever they may be domiciled, is rarely completely free from doubt. International tax advisers can offer only carefully qualified opinions on these issues.

From time to time, there is talk within the EU about the need to modify tax policies that encourage or permit the use of offshore centers, including centers located within the EU itself. To date, these initiatives have not been successful, possibly reflecting the economic and commercial reality that leading EU financial institutions maintain offices in tax havens, not limited to Dublin and Luxembourg, and earn taxable revenue from offshore financial business. Offshore financial centers also produce employment opportunities for local residents or, in the case of Luxembourg in particular, for individuals from all over the EU. Similar economic realities permit the existence of a vibrant offshore financial culture in the Caribbean only miles off the coast of the United States, in countries that otherwise depend on U.S. assistance and that could likely be discouraged from any activity that the U.S. Government seriously wished to prohibit.[57]

As governments grapple with these difficult issues, it is hoped that what results is not the end of the offshore investment products marketplace. Offshore funds and related investment products provide continual sources of innovation and challenge to existing regulatory systems and patterns of thought. Offshore funds offered multiple classes of shares for the same investment portfolio long before any U.S. fund ever sought permission from the SEC to do so. The same is true of the master/feeder structure. Innovations in the development of offshore investment products continue to this day. A vibrant, active offshore marketplace for investment products remains important for national markets as an incubator of new fund structures and ideas and as a perpetual challenge to the complacency of national regulatory systems.

ENDNOTES

1. "Funds Continue to Grow," *Investors Chronicle*, May 26, 1995.

2. Phillip Crawford, "Luxembourg, in Many Languages, Claims Right to the Offshore Fund Industry Throne," 1 *Int'l Fund Investment* no. 2 (Autumn 1992) p.19; see also Baie Netzer, "Dublin's Race Against Time," 3 *Int'l Fund Investment* no. 4 (Winter 1994–1995), p.39.

3. Institut Monétaire Luxembourgeois, 1995.

4. Part of the growth in the number of offshore funds located in Dublin is attributable to a limited-time offer of a 10 percent corporate tax rate through the year 2005 to investment management companies established in Dublin prior to the end of 1994. The deadline to take advantage of the tax incentive was recently extended to December 31, 2000.

5. John Murray Brown, "Survey of Ireland," *Financial Times,* May 26, 1995.

6. Worldwide, nearly 40 countries are considered secrecy and tax havens, including Luxembourg, the Cayman Islands, Gibraltar, and the Bahamas. Geoffrey Smith, "Competition in the European Financial Services Industry: The Free Movement of Capital versus the Regulation of Money Laundering," *University of Pennsylvania Journal of International Business Law* (1992) pp.101, 125.

7. Under the Bank Secrecy Act of 1970, 12 U.S.C. §§1730d, 1829b, 1951-1959 (1995), financial institutions in the United States are required to report cash deposits of over $10,000. However, even this reporting is an imperfect method of detecting money laundering, as it does not apply to electronic transfers. An estimated one-tenth of 1 percent of such transfers involve laundered funds. In total, estimates are that over $300 billion is laundered through financial institutions worldwide each year. Margaret Jacobs, "Software May Dry Up Money Laundering," *The Wall Street Journal*, Sept. 13, 1993, p. B2. The primary enforcement mechanism for initiatives against money laundering in the United States is the Money Laundering Control Act of 1986, 18 U.S.C. § 1956 et seq. (1995). This Act makes it a crime for someone who knows that property involved in a financial transaction represents the proceeds of some form of unlawful activity to conduct or attempt to conduct a financial transaction that involves the proceeds of a specified unlawful activity with the intent to: (1) promote the carrying on of a specified unlawful activity; (2) conceal or disguise the nature, location, source, ownership, or control of the proceeds of the specified unlawful activity; or (3) avoid a transaction reporting requirement under federal or state law. Section 1956(f) of the Act establishes extraterritorial jurisdiction if prohibited conduct is committed by a U.S. citizen or, in

the case of a non-U.S. citizen, the conduct occurs in part in the United States and the transaction or series of related transactions involves funds or monetary instruments of a value exceeding $10,000. For the U.K. counterpart to the U.S. Act, see the Criminal Justice Act 1988 (making it a criminal offense to facilitate the retention or control of proceeds of criminal conduct or to use the proceeds of criminal conduct, to acquire property by way of investment, or to conceal or disguise proceeds from criminal conduct, or convert or transfer such proceeds from the jurisdiction); the Criminal Justice Act 1990 (making it a criminal offense if a person who knows or has reasonable grounds to suspect that property is derived from drug dealing conceals, disguises, transfers, converts, or removes property from the jurisdiction of the courts for the purpose of assisting any person to avoid prosecution for a drug trafficking offense).

8. In 1991, the European Community adopted the Directive on the Prevention of the Use of the Financial System for the Purpose of Money Laundering, 1991 O.J. (L166) 77, 10.6.1991, which to date has been implemented by most EU member states. Other international efforts to combat money laundering include the United Nations Convention Against Illicit Traffic in Narcotic Drugs and Psychotropic Substances, signed in Vienna, Austria, on December 20, 1988, 28 ILM 493 (1989), the Council of Europe Convention on Laundering, Search, Seizure and Confiscation of the Proceeds of Crime, Nov. 8, 1990, 30 ILM 148, 150 (1991), and the adoption in 1992 by the General Assembly of the Organization of American States of Model Regulations Concerning Laundering Offences Connected to Illicit Drug Trafficking and Related Offences, CICAD/INF.58/92. In addition, a number of countries participate in the Basle Committee's Financial Action Task Force on Money Laundering, created in 1989 by the G7 countries to assess the results of cooperation already taken and to prevent utilization of the banking system and financial institutions for the purpose of money laundering and to consider additional preventative efforts in the field. Participants in the Basle Committee's Task Force on International Money Laundering include all of the EU member states plus the United States, Canada, Hong Kong, Japan, New Zealand, Australia, Ireland, Singapore, and Switzerland.

9. See Directive of the Council of the European Communities on the Prevention of the Use of the Financial System for the Purpose of Money Laundering, 1991 O.J. (L166) 77, 10.6.1991, Art. 5 ("Member States shall ensure that credit and financial institutions examine with special attention any transaction which they regard as particularly likely, by its nature, to be related to money laundering").

10. See Model Regulations Concerning Laundering Offenses Connected to Illicit Drug Trafficking and Related Offenses, May 23, 1992, CICAD/INF.58/92, Art. 4 ("the court or competent authority shall issue...without prior notification or hearing, a freezing or seizure order...to preserve the availability of property, proceeds or instrumentalities connected to illicit traffic"), Art. 5 ("When a person is convicted of an illicit traffic...the court shall order that the property, proceeds or instrumentalities connected to such an offence be forfeited and disposed of in accordance with the law"). See also The Convention on Laundering, Search, Seizure and Confiscation of the Proceeds of Crime, Nov. 8, 1990, 30 ILM 148, 150 (1991) (the purpose of the Convention is to facilitate international cooperation as regards investigative assistance, search, seizure, and confiscation of the proceeds from all types of criminality, especially serious crimes; the Convention specifically requires signatories to establish as an offense international money laundering).

11. Section 12(d)(1)(A) of the 1940 Act makes it unlawful, in part, for any registered investment company to purchase or otherwise acquire any security issued by any other "investment company," if, as a result of such transaction, certain ownership percentage limitations would be exceeded. Pass-through vehicles may qualify as investment companies under the 1940 Act. In a letter to *The Spain Fund, Inc.* (pub. avail. Mar. 28, 1988), the staff of the Securities and Exchange Commission (the staff) permitted a U.S.-registered investment company to create a Netherlands Antilles partnership of which the fund would be the sole general partner in order to take advantage of the tax treaty between the Netherlands and Spain. The fund represented that it would liquidate the partnership if anyone other than the fund or a subsidiary of the fund acquired any interest in the partnership. In addition, the fund represented that the fund's investment adviser would manage the partnership's assets at no additional charge to the fund, the partnership would not charge a sales load to the fund, and there would be no significant duplicative custodian fees or other costs as a result of the fund's investment through the partnership. Similar no-action assurance was given in a letter to *The Thai Fund, Inc.* (pub. avail. Nov. 30, 1987), where a U.S.-registered investment company sought assurances allowing the creation of an investment vehicle under Thai law to allow the investment company to purchase Thai securities.

12. See *Peavey Commodity Futures Fund* (pub. avail. June 2, 1983); *Currency Fund* (pub. avail. Sept. 25, 1986); *Commodities Corporation* (pub. avail. June 7, 1991).

13. See text at notes 51–52.

14. See text at note 51.

15. Rule 3a-7 under the 1940 Act provides an exemption from the registration requirements of the 1940 Act for certain structured finance vehicles. Structured finance vehicles eligible to rely on Rule 3a–7 must issue only high-quality debt and fixed-income securities, must utilize the services of a qualified trustee, and must deposit periodically the cash flows from the vehicle's assets into a segregated account maintained by the trustee to satisfy the vehicle's obligations to its security holders. In *ESI SA* (pub. avail. May 8, 1995), a Luxembourg limited liability company requested no-action assurance in connection with a proposal to conduct a private placement of debt securities to investors within the United States. Each series of the proposed debt was to be issued by or on behalf of an EU member state and secured by the rights of ESI under an interest rate and currency exchange swap agreement. ESI had previously issued securities offshore in transactions that would have complied with Rule 3a–7 except for two provisions. Accordingly, to issue securities in the United States, ESI employed a U.S. bank to act as trustee in compliance with paragraph (a)(4)(i) of the rule, and to deposit cash flows derived from the vehicle's assets into a segregated account maintained by the trustee in compliance with paragraph (a)(4)(iii) of the rule. Based on these undertakings, the staff assured ESI that it would not recommend enforcement action if ESI did not register as an investment company under the 1940 Act.

16. Establishing an offshore fund can take anywhere from several days in many island jurisdictions to three to five months in other jurisdictions. Jersey recently established a two-hour service for company formations, which has led to a marked increase in the number of companies incorporated there. Peter S.W. Henwood, Eurotrust International Group SA, "The Offshore Industry: Towards the 21st Century" 13 (1995).

17. See Rod Smith, "U.S. Opens Fire on Offshore Trusts," *International Money Marketing*, Sept. 22, 1995, p. A1.

18. In *Touche, Remnant & Co.* (pub. avail. Aug. 27, 1984), a foreign investment company operating abroad sought to use the U.S. jurisdictional means to make a private offering in the United States consistent with Rule 506 under the Securities Act of 1933 without violating the registration requirement under Section 7(d) of the 1940 Act. Reading Section 7(d) together with Section 3(c)(1) of the 1940 Act, the SEC staff stated that a foreign investment company making an offering in the United States would be subject to the registration requirements of the 1940 Act if, upon completion of the offering, more than 100 persons resident in the U.S. would be beneficial owners of its securities, even if the company is in full compliance with the Rule 506 registration exemption for private offerings.

19. See Securities Act Rel. No. 6862 (Apr. 23, 1990).

20. *Alpha Finance Corporation* (pub. avail. July 27, 1990) (for purposes of compliance with Section 7(d) of the 1940 Act, short-term notes issued by a foreign investment company in the United States are not considered in determining whether the company is in compliance with the 100 U.S. securityholder limit).

21. *Coutts Global Fund* (pub. avail. Dec. 7, 1994).

22. See *Investment Funds Institute of Canada* (pub. avail. March 4, 1996).

23. *Shearson International Dollar Reserves* (pub. avail. July 15, 1981); *Merrill Lynch & Co. Inc.* (pub. avail. May 12, 1986); *Prudential-Bache Securities Inc.* (pub. avail. May 20, 1987); *Walsh, Greenwood & Co.* (pub. avail. Sept. 30, 1987); *G.T. Global Financial Services, Inc., et al.* (pub. avail. Aug. 2, 1988); *Huntington World Investors Funds Limited* (pub. avail. Sept. 18, 1989). See also *Fiduciary Trust Global Fund* (pub. avail. Aug. 2, 1995) (in which an open-end Irish unit trust received assurance from the staff that certain discretionary accounts held for the benefit or account of non–U.S. persons by dealers or other fiduciaries organized or resident in the United States would be excluded from the definition of *U.S. person* for purposes of determining compliance with Section 7(d) of the 1940 Act).

24. Securities Act of 1933, Rules 901–904.

25. Under Regulation S certain offers or sales of securities that are deemed to occur outside of the United States are not subject to the securities registration requirements of the 1933 Act. Securities Act of 1933, Rule 903. To qualify under Regulation S, the offer or sale of securities must be made in an "offshore transaction." Under Regulation S, the "offshore transaction" requirement is met if (1) the offer is not made to a person in the United States; and (2) at the time the buy order is originated, the buyer is outside the United States, or the seller reasonably believes the buyer is outside the United States; or the transaction is executed through a physical trading floor of an established securities exchange outside the United States; or the transaction is executed through a designated offshore securities market and the seller does not know that the transaction has been prearranged with a buyer in the United States. However, offers and sales of securities specifically targeted at identifiable groups of U.S. citizens abroad (i.e., members of the U.S. armed forces) will fail the definition of "offshore transaction." Securities Act of 1933, Rule 902(i).

26. *Nikko Securities Trust & Management Co., Ltd.* (pub. avail. May 17, 1985) (a no-action assurance was given to a U.S.-registered investment adviser who charged performance fees in the management of investment trusts in Japan not in compliance with Section 205(1) of the Advisers Act, where such performance fees were specified in the trust deed and approved by the Japanese Minister of Finance); *Rosenberg Institutional Equity Management* (pub. avail. Mar. 14, 1990) (a performance-based fee charged by U.S.-registered investment adviser for the management of an offshore fund with no known U.S. shareholders was permitted on condition of compliance with Rule 205–3 under the Advisers Act); but *see Reavis & McGrath* (pub. avail. Oct. 29, 1986) (SEC declined to agree that Rule 205-3(d) under the Advisers Act regarding requirements for exemption from the Section 205(1) performance fee prohibition should not have to be satisfied by a U.S.-registered investment adviser who advises offshore funds with non-U.S. investors).

27. CFTC Interpretative Letter No. 90–6, Comm. Fut. L. Rep. (CCH) para. 24,825 (Apr. 25, 1990). See also CFTC Interpretative Letter No. 92–3, Comm. Fut. L. Rep. (CCH) para. 25,221 (Jan. 29, 1992); CFTC Interpretative Letter No. 93–52, Comm. Fut. L. Rep. (CCH) para. 25,756 (Apr. 27, 1993).

28. See CFTC Interpretative Letter No. 76–21, Comm. Fut. L. Rep. (CCH) para. 20,222 (Aug. 15, 1976); CFTC Interpretative Letter No. 88–5, Comm. Fut. L. Rep. (CCH) para. 24,166 (Feb. 2, 1988); CFTC Interpretative Letter No. 88–6, Comm. Fut. L. Rep. para. 24,167 (Jan. 28, 1988); CFTC Interpretative Letter No. 91–7, Comm. Fut. L. Rep. (CCH) para. 25,079 (June 28, 1991).

29. See Treas. Reg. §1.864-2(c).

30. U.S. banks are generally exempt from U.S. broker-dealer registration requirements. See Securities Exchange Act of 1934, § 3(a)(4),(5) (exempting banks from the definition of broker and dealer). U.S. branches and agencies of foreign banks may be eligible for this exemption if they engage in a substantial deposit-taking or fiduciary business in the United States and are regulated under federal or state law. Eligibility for this exemption depends on the facts of a particular case.

31. Securities Exchange Act of 1934, Rule 15a-6.

32. Currently, much activity in the U.S. Congress is directed at reform of the Glass-Steagall Act and related banking regulation. These initiatives may greatly expand the ability of federally insured financial institutions to affiliate with full service securities firms and investment companies, and they may increase the powers of bank holding companies to become

involved in securities activities. See The Financial Services
Competitiveness Act of 1995 (H.R. 1062); The Depositary Institution
Affiliation Act of 1995 (S. 337). Although the ultimate outcome of
banking reform is uncertain at this point, it is likely that significant
changes in U.S. banking laws will be forthcoming in the near future.

33. See Philip Moore, "Tales From Ireland and The Indian Ocean,"
Financial Times, February 1995. Due to India's high rate of taxation on
capital gains, as of December 1994, 37 Indian funds had been registered
in Mauritius, with more expected to follow. In addition, Mauritian
authorities are hoping to market their advantages to funds targeting
South Africa should South Africa introduce a capital gains tax. As of
November 1994, Malaysia's offshore center had attracted 367 offshore
companies, although only one of those companies was a fund manager.

34. See Treas. Reg. §1.864-2(c).

35. See notes 9–11 above.

36. Toronto's increasing prominence in the fund management industry has
been identified as a competitive threat to established fund management
centers as far away as Hong Kong. In addition to Toronto's
geographical proximity to New York and Canada's international
reputation, Toronto's rental and labor costs represent a significant
competitive edge over established offshore locations such as Hong Kong
and Luxembourg. Duncan Hughes, "Ill Winds Blow for Fund
Management," *South China Morning Post,* Oct. 18, 1994.

37. Directive 85/611/EEC, O.J. (L375), 31.12.1985, at 3, as amended by
Directive 88/20/EEC, O.J. (L100), 19.4.1988 at 31 and by Directive
95/26/EC, O.J. (L168), 18.7.1995 at 7.

38. Norma Cohen, "EU Collective Investment Scheme Law a Failure,"
Financial Times, Oct. 28, 1994. This article notes that just over one-
third of funds organized under the UCITS Directive are marketed across
European borders.

39. Judy Rehak, "U.S. Fund Industry's Marketing Drive Takes Off:
Investors See the Light (Refreshments)," *Int'l Fund Investment* 4, no. 1
(Spring 1995), p. 51.

40. Ingo Walter, *The Secret Money Market* (1990) pp. 188–9.

41. In Germany, the Federal Supervisory Agency for Banking in Berlin
regulates the distribution of foreign mutual fund shares pursuant
to the Law on the Distribution of Foreign Investment Certificates
and on Taxation of Proceeds from Foreign Investment Certificates
of 1969, as amended, known as the Foreign Investment Law (the
Auslandsinvestmentgesetz). In Japan, the relevant law is the Securities

Investment Trust Law of 1951. In Hong Kong, the relevant authority is the Hong Kong Code on Unit Trusts and Mutual Funds. Pursuant to the U.K. Financial Services Act 1986 (the Act), recognition is available to three classes of collective investment schemes. First, pursuant to Section 86 of the Act, a fund scheme that has been constituted and received regulatory approval in an EU member state (other than the United Kingdom) that has implemented the directive need only give the U.K. Securities and Investments Board (the SIB) two months' notice of the fund's intention to market its shares to persons in the United Kingdom. Second, Section 87 provides for recognition in the United Kingdom of fund schemes authorized under the laws of a "designated country" (other than an EU member state). Third, Section 88 of the Act permits U.K. recognition of investment funds not eligible for treatment under Sections 86 and 87 to make an individual application for recognition to the SIB. Thereafter, the SIB is required to determine whether the scheme (1) affords adequate protection to prospective fund participants, and (2) essentially meets the same standards for organization and operation as set forth in the regulatory requirements governing U.K. unit trusts.

42. As noted above, UCITS funds are subject to local distribution rules for each state in which they are distributed.

43. See text at notes 51–52.

44. As discussed below, UCITS funds are currently restricted from serving as feeder funds under a master/feeder arrangement.

45. See note 12 above.

46. Many jurisdictions, including Bermuda, Dublin, and Luxembourg, require local custodians and managers. Others, such as the Cayman Islands and the Netherlands Antilles, have minimal requirements in this regard.

47. See *Shoreline Fund, L.P.* (pub. avail. Apr. 11, 1994) (securities issuance of U.S limited partnership offering interests through private placement under Rule 506 of the Securities Act of 1933, and Cayman Islands mirror fund offering shares to tax-exempt institutional investors in the United States under Rule 506 were not integrated for purposes of determining compliance with the 1940 Act because the respective securities were intended for two distinct groups of investors, and therefore were materially different).

48. Section 17(d) of the 1940 Act and the rules promulgated thereunder limit the ability of investment company affiliates to enter into joint transactions with affiliated investment companies.

49. See Investment Company Act Rel. Nos. 18857 (July 21, 1992) (notice of exemption from Section 17(d) of the 1940 Act and Rule 17d–1 thereunder), and 18899 (Aug. 18, 1992) (order).

50. *Growth Stock Outlook Trust* (pub. avail. Apr. 15, 1986) (closed-end company may include in its prospectus and advertisements during its first year of operations information about the performance of private clients' accounts managed by its investment adviser, provided the figures are computed under certain conditions and the advertisements disclose the fact that the figures are based on the management of private accounts); *Clover Capital Management, Inc.* (pub. avail. Oct. 28, 1986) (investment advisers may advertise model performance figures where the adviser recommended the same securities to all advisory clients, provided extensive safeguards are undertaken to prevent fraudulent, deceptive, or manipulative advertising)*; Investment Company Institute* (pub. avail. Aug. 24, 1987) (adviser performance figures may be presented without reflecting custodian fees, but they should reflect deduction of advisory fees).

51. Investment Company Act of 1940, § 12(d)(1)(E).

52. Amended Proposal dated July 20, 1994, O.J. (242), 30.8.1994 at 5.

53. See, e.g., *IIT* v. *Cornfeld*, 619 F.2d 909 (2nd Cir. 1980) (complaint by a Luxembourg trust against a U.S. oil and gas entrepreneur claiming over $70 million in compensatory and punitive damages related to a series of fraudulent securities transactions); *Bersch* v. *Drexel Firestone, Inc.,* 519 F.2d 974 (2nd Cir. 1975) (claim for $110 million brought against a Canadian corporation by U.S. and foreign investors alleging antifraud violations); *Securities and Exchange Commission* v. *Vesco et al.,* 542 F. Supp. 1270 (S.D.N.Y. 1981) (1972 complaint against the chief executive of International Controls Corp., Robert Vesco, in which the SEC charged that Vesco had diverted assets of the company and several offshore funds managed by company subsidiaries to offshore banking entities he controlled. The SEC estimated that Vesco and his accomplices stole fund assets in excess of $224 million).

54. The jurisdiction of United States courts over international transactions may be effectively limited by choice of law contract provisions. See *Rayapratama* v. *Bankers Trust Co.,* 1995 U.S. Dist. LEXIS 11961 (S.D.N.Y. 1995) (choice of law provisions in swap agreement construed broadly to bar private claims under U.S. RICO and Commodities laws where parties agreed to be governed by English law).

55. U.S. laws may be found to govern offshore transactions even where the parties involved are not U.S. persons or U.S. entities, if there are sufficient U.S. contacts in the transaction or an expectation of the non-U.S. parties that U.S. law should govern. See *Psimenos* v. *E.F. Hutton & Company, Inc.*, 722 F.2d 1041 (2d Cir. 1983) (jurisdiction under the Commodity Exchange Act extends to transactions executed on U.S. markets even though both broker and customer were foreign). See also *Tamari* v. *Bache & Co., S.A.L.*, 730 F.2d 1103 (7th Cir. 1984), *cert. denied*, 105 S. Ct. 221, 469 U.S. 871, 83 L.E.2d 151 (1984) (United States federal court found to have jurisdiction over an action brought under the Commodity Exchange Act between a Lebanese citizen and Lebanese corporation based on the effect and significance of conduct in the United States).

56. See the Foreign Trust Tax Compliance Act of 1995 (H.R. 2356). This act targets tax avoidance through the use of foreign trusts by U.S. taxpayers by creating comprehensive reporting requirements for the creation and operation of foreign trusts, and by mandating serious civil penalties based on a percentage of trust assets for noncompliance with the reporting requirements. In addition, the Act establishes certain measures designed to prevent foreign settlors planning to become resident in the United States from sheltering assets and income in foreign trusts prior to their U.S. residency.

57. See "Wishful Thinking: A World View of Insurance Solvency Regulation," A Report by the Subcommittee on Oversight and Investigations of the Committee on Energy and Commerce, U.S. House of Representatives, 103d Congress, 2d Session (October 1994).

VIII
RETHINKING THE REGULATORY FRAMEWORK

18

SHOULD FUNDS AND INVESTMENT ADVISERS ESTABLISH A SELF-REGULATORY ORGANIZATION?

Tamar Frankel, *Boston University School of Law*[1]

Never before has the investment management industry constituted the significant segment of the financial system it does today. In the past 20 years we have witnessed an explosion in the number and assets of investment companies, which we will call funds.[2] In 1970, 361 funds held assets of approximately $48 billion. Currently, approximately 6,000 funds manage assets of about $3 trillion.[3] The number of investment advisers to such funds and to individuals and the assets under their management has also grown. In October 1980 approximately 4,500 advisers, including financial planners, were registered with the Securities and Exchange Commission (SEC).[4] In 1989 there were approximately 15,000 such advisers,[5] and in 1995 more than 21,000.[6]

The growth of the industry has raised the costs of the Securities and Exchange Commission, which has been regulating the industry since 1940. Arguably, the cost of examining large funds and small funds should be the same. But the investment management industry has not only grown in size but also has become far more innovative, presenting a rich variety of funds and products, some highly complex. In addition, investment management is now offered not only by the traditional investment advisers and funds but also by insurance companies and banks. These new players pose special problems that call for adjustments to the Investment Company Act, which regulates funds, and to their own brand of regulations. Today, preventive measures, such as examinations of industry members, seem more important than ever to protect investors, and pressure is growing to increase the frequency and depth of these examinations.[7] All this requires more regulators and examiners than before. And that presents a problem. An efficient expert examination system is costly and would result in expanding the staff of the Securities and Exchange Commission at a time when Congress is pressing to reduce government budget and personnel.

It is not surprising that one of the recent proposals to resolve the problem was to establish one or more self-regulatory organizations (SROs) for the investment management industry.[8] Such a proposal is not new. From time to time, and as recently as 1993, proposals surface to establish SROs for investment advisers. The 1993 proposals, unlike their predecessors,[9] would have applied not only to advisers but also to funds.[10] Like former proposals, they would have required members of the investment management industry to regulate themselves under the watchful eye of the Securities and Exchange Commission. The models of such SROs are the National Association of Securities Dealers, Inc. (NASD) and the securities exchanges, such as the New York Stock Exchange, both of which are SROs for broker-dealers.[11] However, the 1993 proposals met the same fate as all proposals before them—though they came close to enactment, they were not passed.

THE PROS AND CONS OF SROS

The pros and cons of SROs for the securities industry have been analyzed and debated for years.[12] No wonder—there are so many convincing arguments on both sides:

   ◆ SROs reduce government regulatory costs,[13] but this gain is offset by the cost of adding another regulatory body (the SRO) and the cost of government supervision of the SRO.

   ◆ SROs' personnel, familiar with industry practices, could regulate more efficiently than government employees. Some argue, however, that these private sector regulators pose the same problems as any bureaucracy. In addition, their own interests could conflict with the objectives of the laws they are required to enforce. As an example critics suggest that SROs (e.g., the securities exchanges) have slowed the development of a national market system, which has been mandated by Congress, in order to keep their business and customers. A national market system makes it harder for the exchanges to keep their customers, because it makes it easier for customers to trade elsewhere.[14]

◆ For the securities industry, SROs are more flexible and arguably cheaper regulators than the government. More importantly, SROs insulate the members of the industry from direct, often undesirable, government intrusion. But other commenters argue that not all members of the industry are protected by the SROs. SROs can develop a "private club mentality" and put the interests of "club members" above the interest of the industry as a whole.[15]

◆ SROs provide "public goods." They enable the industry as a whole to meet its social responsibilities: They oversee the marketplace, educate the public and the industry regarding the marketplace, and inculcate industry members with ethical standards.[16] SROs represent a "more direct and rational way" of dealing with the "bad apples" of the securities industry[17] and protect the more reputable and successful members (the "deep pockers") from costly litigation.

However, it is not clear to what extent an SRO, such as the NASD, protects the investors' interest. In July 1995, the SEC was considering filing a disciplinary action against the NASD for failing, mistakenly or even intentionally, to prevent dealers from conspiring to keep their profit margins artificially high in the over-the-counter markets.[18] This saga is not yet over, but the NASD is vigorously defending itself against these charges at great costs.[19] It seems that the NASD is weaker in protecting investors than the SEC.

◆ Allowing a degree of self-regulation "promotes a dynamic public interest, constantly evolving from project to project."[20] Through SROs investors participate in the regulatory process and interact with market experts more than they do in the government rule-making process.[21] However, self-regulation downplays the distinction between the interests of the state and those of the individuals participating in the market.

◆ The flexibility of self-regulation can help American markets maintain their competitive advantage as modern technology advances and more markets develop around the world. In contrast to SROs, government can weaken the competitive position of American markets in the global markets because older, unnecessary rules on the books do not fit the newer developing markets. Also SROs can keep up with technology and developments in the world economy more quickly and efficiently than government regulators.[22] And, of course, there are some necessary actions that government cannot take.[23] In short, SROs can help American securities markets maintain their leadership in the world of finance.

Yet the SEC has shown that it can respond to technological innovations quite quickly.[24] More importantly, it is doubtful whether our society should allow its markets to lower their ethical or legal standards whenever competitors around the world do so. It is not clear that such lower standards will help our markets' long-term competitive position. One of the greatest strengths of the American securities markets is precisely their high ethical standards, which investors all over the world value greatly. Competition does not involve only prices and technology; it also involves reliability and trust in the system.

Notwithstanding all these arguments for and against SROs, there is a broad-based consensus that the stock exchanges and the NASD have been highly successful in achieving the goals of divergent groups and the public interest.[25]

Where do these arguments lead us with respect to SROs for the investment management industry? I believe that, on balance, it may be appropriate to establish SROs for advisers who serve individuals and small groups, but it is inappropriate to establish an SRO for funds and fund advisers. Such an SRO would require a fundamental change of the federal Investment Company Act of 1940 that currently regulates the industry, and that would be a serious and costly mistake. There are other ways to strengthen the regulation of funds and their advisers without increasing substantially the costs to the government.

THE INDUSTRY'S RESISTANCE TO ESTABLISHING SROS

Notwithstanding the success of SROs in the broker-dealer industry, and the pressures to establish SROs for members of the investment management industry, SROs have not materialized either for funds and their advisers or for advisers serving individuals. To be sure, advisers have organized trade associations, such as the Investment Counsel Association of America,[26] and Investment Company Institute (ICI), the trade organization for funds and their advisers. But the ICI does not traditionally regulate its members, with some exceptions. For example, the ICI has behaved like an SRO when personal investing by portfolio managers raised questions of conflicts of interest.[27] In that case the ICI promptly consulted with an independent outside committee and recommended to its member funds that they include certain provisions in their Codes of Ethics and limit personal investing by their portfolio managers. Many member funds have voluntarily implemented the ICI's recommendations.[28] In this case the ICI assumed the position of an SRO to contain undesirable practices by portfolio managers that threatened public trust in members of the industry. Yet, generally, the industry and its trade organizations have resisted proposals to establish or act as SROs. The question is, why?

SUCCESSFUL SROS

Thousands of SROs have been flourishing in this country for quite some time. Successful SROs include professional, trade, and manufacturing organizations. An analysis of why the members of these SROs voluntarily join and submit to self-regulation and why these SROs work efficiently can help predict whether advisers would establish SROs voluntarily and how effective these SROs would be.

SROs benefit their members. The organizations protect the members' reputation for quality and reliability of services and products by requiring members to acquire and maintain expertise, and establishing ethical standards.[29] Because reputation reduces the consumers' costs of ascertaining the quality of what they buy from any member, consumers will pay higher prices for reputable goods and services, and that benefits all members. Similarly, when the financial strength of industry members is crucial to the group's reputation, SROs may organize a guaranty fund to support members in temporary financial distress and regulate the members to ensure their prudential operations.

Also, qualification requirements benefit SRO members by limiting entry to the practice and by reducing competition among the members.[30] Moreover, SROs benefit specialized professionals, for example, oral surgeons and orthodontists, by referral systems among themselves. In addition, since the practice of most professions and trades requires expertise, members prefer to be governed by their peers, rather than by nonpracticing government bureaucrats, and to avoid greater burdens of direct government regulation.[31] Often SROs offer members services, such as continuous education and information at discounts. SROs of traders help establish orderly dealings among the members by creating networks, fairs, or exchanges, and providing effective and inexpensive processes for resolving disputes among the members themselves and between members and customers.[32] Thus banks have organized bank check clearinghouses and regulate banks' trading on swap exchanges.[33] Securities broker-dealers created exchanges voluntarily decades before the Securities Exchange Act of 1934 recognized their existence.

The NASD is interesting because it provides member broker-dealers with many of these benefits, even though it was organized under an authorizing statute.[34] The NASD is similar to both professional and trading SROs—its members must satisfy educational requirements and pass examinations, and they can hardly conduct business without dealing with each other.

It is not clear that investment advisers, including fund advisers, would benefit from SRO regulation as much. First, it is relatively easy to comply with the Advisers Act of 1940, which regulates advisers. The Act does not require advisers to meet any educational or financial qualification.[35] Past attempts to impose such requirements have failed mainly because advisers offer diverse services, with various degrees of discretion and control over investment decisions and customers' funds.[36] Therefore, they pose different dangers to clients and different regulatory problems. Large groups of advisers do not lend themselves to standardized qualifications or uniform rules.[37] Second, and more importantly, unlike broker-dealers, advisers do not deal with each other in connection with their business. They conduct no joint ventures and manage customers' portfolios independently of each other. Danger to reputation alone does not seem to offer sufficient incentives for advisers to submit to regulation by competitors. Third, advisers seem to thrive on competition, which SROs would restrict.[38] Fourth, advisers compete by distinct management techniques, talented portfolio managers, and differentiating fee structures. Sometimes, they compete by offering lower fees and expenses. Scrutiny of advisers' books and records by an SRO may reveal confidential information that would hurt their competitive advantage. Thus, there are few reasons for advisers to organize and submit to an SRO. Although fund advisers constitute a more homogeneous group, they share all the other characteristics of advisers. These characteristics do not seem to provide sufficient incentives for them to organize and submit to SROs.

THE SRO AS A REGULATORY SCHEME FOR THE FUND INDUSTRY

Funds are institutional intermediaries that pool investor-advisees' money and offer efficient and expert management on a fully discretionary basis. The federal Investment Company Act of 1940 that regulates funds resembles the regulation of banks, pension funds, and insurance companies. This type of regulation differs from the regulation of market intermediaries such as brokers, dealers, underwriters, and market makers because investors in funds are exposed to higher risks of loss from mismanagement of their money. In addition, investors' controls over the funds' managements are far weaker than their controls over their broker-dealers.[39]

The Investment Company Act provides a strict and detailed regulatory scheme for funds and their advisers,[40] broader than the regulation of broker-dealers.[41] The Act creates a special governance structure for funds. It requires that the funds' board of directors consist of a minimum percentage of disinterested directors[42] with special powers and duties to serve as "watchdogs," to supervise the funds' operations for the protection of investors. In particular, a majority of these directors must approve the terms of the contracts between the funds and their advisers and underwriters.[43] Addressing the risk of self-dealing and mismanagement by fund affiliates, the Act prohibits or severely restricts such self-dealing transactions,[44] makes embezzlement of fund assets a federal offense,[45] and requires special safekeeping arrangements for funds' assets.[46] The Act imposes a fiduciary duty on fund managers with respect to their fees,[47] requires that the fees be approved by the majority of the disinterested directors or by the fund shareholders,[48] and expressly grants the shareholders the right to sue on behalf of their funds to recover excessive fees.[49] The courts have recognized fund shareholders' rights to sue for a number of violations of the Act, even though these rights are not expressly provided for in the Act.

The enforcement of the Investment Company Act and its adjustment to the changing environment is vested in the SEC, the courts, internal governance (directors and shareholders) and external private sector actors, such as accountants. In contrast, the regulation of broker-dealers presents a different picture. Broker-dealers are not regulated through internal governance, and their relationships to customers are governed mainly by common law, strengthened by the rules of the NASD and the SEC.[50]

The proposed SRO for funds would substitute a weaker enforcement regime by an SRO for a stronger regime by the SEC.[51] That is in contrast to the NASD, which substitutes a stronger and less costly investor protection regime for the common-law regime.

If an industry is flourishing under a particular regulatory system, *which the fund industry is,*[52] there should be a presumption in favor of maintaining the regulatory status quo, and no fundamental changes should be introduced without a serious investigation into alternatives. The existing regulation of funds does not seem "broke," and so need not be "fixed."[53] The fund industry's success is based upon broad investor confidence, and this confidence is more crucial today than ever before. The growth of funds has increased their visibility and public scrutiny concerning, for example, the compensation of fund advisers, the behavior of the funds' independent directors, the performance of particular fund managers, and—above all—funds' commitment to investors' interests before their own. Investors may withdraw their money not only if securities prices fall, and not only if they suspect dishonesty and manipulation by fund management, but also if they believe they are unfairly treated, and that their fiduciaries take advantage of them. Such withdrawals can have a domino effect on funds of the same type, on funds managed by the same adviser, and on the secondary markets in the securities in which these funds have invested.[54]

Further, funds are the only large segment of the financial system that is not supported by government guarantees: They have no equivalent to the Securities Investor Protection Corporation that covers customers of broker-dealers who become insolvent, or the Federal Deposit Insurance Corporation that covers the depositors of banks that fail, or the Pension Board Guaranty Corporation that supports the participants in pension plans. The fund industry's success in maintaining the public's confidence and its scandal-free reputation are due largely to its strict compliance with the Investment Company Act and to the SEC's diligent enforcement of the act—the only form of government support the industry and the investors receive.

Additionally, the risks and consequences of losing public confidence may be greater today than they have been in the past. During the past 20 years, the SEC has allowed advisers and sponsors of funds greater flexibility in structuring funds and advisory fees. Overall, this greater flexibility has helped the industry's growth and innovation, but it also has permitted greater complexity, which has made monitoring by the market and government more difficult and costly. Finally, public perception about fund management and public confidence in funds can be affected by the new entrants, such as banks, into the fund business. In their core business operations, these institutions are usually subject to quite different, and in many respects more lax, conflict of interest regulation than that imposed by the Investment Company Act. New entrants unfamiliar with the 1940 Act may make mistakes and innocently confuse the public. For example, when banks first introduced money market *funds,* which are not insured by the FDIC, these funds were not clearly distinguished from money market *accounts,* which are insured by the FDIC, and a substantial number of investors assumed that the money market funds offered by the banks were insured by the FDIC. Such mistakes and confusing facts, when publicized, could erode the public trust in the funds involved.[55]

Thus, while the federal Act has served the industry and the public well, funds are more vulnerable today to loss of public confidence than ever before. This may be the time to signal the markets that the *government* stands ready to strengthen the funds' regulation, as it has done in the past so successfully, rather than to introduce *self-regulation*—a different, untested scheme of regulation that signals reduced regulatory supervision.

OTHER OPTIONS TO REDRESS POSSIBLE PROBLEMS IN THE FUND INDUSTRY

If the current regulation of funds is deficient, solutions other than an SRO could be far more advantageous to investors, the industry, and the SEC. It seems that the main drive for creating an SRO for funds and their advisers is the need to examine them closely and more often to protect investors, and the limited government resources to fund the cost of such examinations. However, creating an SRO is not the only way to expand supervision of funds for the protection of public investors without increasing the cost to the government. Alternatives to SROs should be explored.

First, SEC examinations may be revised to provide more efficient and focused government inspections;[56] new technology could be introduced, similar to the SEC's controls of the securities exchanges.[57] The SEC could work with the regulators of new entrants into the industry, such as the bank regulators, and utilize their examiners to reduce the SEC's needs for examiners and to avoid duplication. In fact, the SEC has taken all these measures recently. A new Office of Compliance Inspections and Examinations has been established at the SEC, and the examiners in this office have begun to conduct joint inspections with bank examiners. Another avenue is to encourage the development of a new private sector professional, the compliance auditor. Such auditors should be expert in evaluating legal risks and internal controls in funds. The experts can be certified public accountants, compliance officers with a number of years' experience, lawyers, and other qualified people. The law could require that the compliance auditors certify funds and their advisers periodically.[58] Alternatively, funds and advisers may choose to seek such certification, and if they receive it, the SEC examiners would space their examinations at longer intervals. In fact, we detect the emergence of this new profession of compliance auditors. Compliance professionals are already organized in a National Society of Compliance Professionals, which produces a publication: *NSCP Currents*.[59] Their examinations and reporting may support the SEC's prevention and enforcement efforts while the states may be called upon to regulate small advisers.[60]

The ICI can also play a role in preventive compliance. It has been working with the SEC to improve fund regulations. The SEC need not delegate its authority to regulate the industry; the industry could still create, change, and enforce its own rules, subject to the SEC's oversight. The successful result of the ICI's recent contribution to the creation of industrywide ethical standards regarding personal investing by portfolio managers demonstrates that the fund industry can be induced to introduce and implement self-limiting changes, and that it is able and willing to regulate itself when a need arises to strengthen the public trust in the industry.[61]

It is interesting that a majority of the funds failed to implement another suggestion of the ICI, that the funds disclose more fully the personal investing of their portfolio managers.[62] Funds gave different explanations for this failure. Some said that they were waiting for the SEC to provide them with disclosure instructions; others promised to add disclosure in the future.[63] It may well be that funds found it costly to improve their methods of disclosure—more costly than to implement other suggestions, which consisted mostly of substantive and procedural limitations on personal investing by portfolio managers. This story suggests that SEC regulation may still be essential to protecting the public interest when the SEC finds that a particular regulation is necessary even though it would impose costs on the industry.

Cooperation with the ICI can help the SEC reduce its enforcement costs and improve its regulation of funds. The SEC can decide on an issue-by-issue basis whether to press the ICI to recommend a rule to the membership or to take action on its own. We can expect the ICI to influence the funds as a trade association rather than a full-fledged SRO, if a new regulation could benefit funds more than it could cost them, especially if the SEC applies some pressure on the ICI to act. But if a new regulation would serve the public interest at the expense of funds' interests, the SEC might have to act on its own.[64] In addition, the costs of SEC examinations of funds could be charged to the funds that are examined or to the members of the industry as a whole (through a collective fund to which they all contribute by certain measures). These alternatives and others should be thoroughly studied before introducing a drastic and fundamental change in the regulation of the fund industry.

CONCLUSION

The idea of an SRO for funds and their advisers is innovative; in theory it may work even better than the SEC direct regulation. But regulatory innovations can become the bane of financial institutions. Such regulatory changes are risky because we cannot predict all their direct effects, let alone side effects.[65] An ineffective SRO of funds could injure a successful segment of the financial system that provides satisfactory services to millions of Americans.

SROs for advisers that serve individuals or small groups may be advantageous for investors and the industry and at the same time reduce the costs of government regulation. However, legislation must be enacted to provide added incentives to advisers, including financial planners, to organize effective SROs; for example, to impose minimum educational and financial qualifications on advisers. These SROs can help maintain high quality advisory services and integrity of advisers at lower government costs. In addition, for small advisers, whose activities are more local than those of funds, the states are the most natural and effective regulators.

In short, a fundamental change in the regulatory system of funds should be approached with the utmost caution; such a change should be introduced if, and only if, after serious study, less drastic alternatives are not feasible.

E N D N O T E S

1. Professor of Law, Boston University School of Law. A shorter version of this chapter was published as an article entitled "The Pros and Cons of a Self-Regulatory Organization for Advisers and Mutual Funds," 1 *The Investment Lawyer*, 6, p. 3 (September 1994). I am indebted to my research assistants William Hecker, Esq. and David Van Why, Boston University School of Law 2L, for their thorough research and dedicated help.

2. The main types of investment companies include open-end investment companies that have managed portfolios and issue redeemable securities; closed-end companies that have managed portfolios but whose shares are not redeemable; unit investment trusts that offer redeemable shares in fixed portfolios (and no management); and face amount certificate companies that offer annuity-like arrangements. Face amount companies are not currently prominent. In this chapter we use the term "funds" for all these types of investment companies.

3. Testimony of Barry P. Barbash, Director, Division of Investment Management, United States Securities and Exchange Commission, Concerning H.R. 14959, the Investment Company Act Amendments of 1995, Before the Subcommittee on Telecommunications and Finance, Committee on Commerce, United States House of Representatives (Oct. 31, 1995) available in *LEXIS*, Legis library, Cngtst file [hereinafter Barbash Testimony].

4. Curtis C. Verschoor, William J. Goldberg, and Phyllis J. Bernstein, "Financial Adviser Regulation Alert," *Journal of Accountancy*, Sept. 1990, pp. 59, 64.

5. Ibid.

6. "Levitt Tries His Hand at Regulatory Relief," *Bank Mutual Fund Report*, Oct. 30, 1995, at 1, available in *LEXIS*, News library, Curnws file.

7. Concern about the scarcity of government examinations of investment advisers and funds is not new. See Concept of Utilizing Private Entities in Investment Company Examinations and Imposing Examination Fees, SEC Release No. IC-13044, 48 Fed. Reg. 8485, 8486 (proposed Feb. 23, 1983) (hereinafter 1983 Proposal) (proposing the establishment of an SRO to increase the number of and frequency of examinations of investment advisers); Robert McGough, John R. Emshwiller & Sara Calian, "Mutual Muddle: Deliberate Mispricing at Fidelity Highlights Lax Controls on Quotes," *The Wall Street Journal*, June 23, 1994, pp. A1, A6 (expressing concern about inaccurate pricing of Funds shares and calling for examinations to monitor the problem).

8. Oversight Hearing on the Mutual Fund Industry: Hearings Before the Subcomm. on Securities of the Senate Committee on Banking, Housing, and Urban Affairs, 103d Cong., 1st Sess. 8-9, 11 (1993) [hereinafter 1993 Hearings] (statement of Arthur J. Levitt, Chairman, SEC) (stating the realities of SEC budgetary and staffing constraints in the face of a growing Fund market); ibid., p. 22 (implying that funding is one of the reasons for advocating the establishment of an SRO).

9. Investment Adviser Self-Regulation Act, H.R. 3054, 101st Cong., 1st Sess. (1989), available in *LEXIS*, Legis library, BTX101 file (hereinafter 1989 Proposal). The 1989 Proposal explicitly excludes "advisory activities of a registered [fund adviser] undertaken pursuant to a written contract to an investment company registered or being registered under the Investment Company Act of 1940." 1989 Proposal, sec. 3, §203A(b)(10). In the 1983 Proposal, note 7, p. 8487, the staff stated: "Although the creation of one or more self-regulatory organizations for investment companies that have similarly broad functions is a matter which may merit consideration in the future, the development of a system for investment companies involving self-regulatory organizations empowered under the Investment Company Act to set business practice standards and discipline members would, even assuming that support for this type of self-regulatory system existed, present complex issues that could take significantly longer to resolve than those raised by the proposal discussed herein."

10. 1993 Hearings, note 8, p. 12 ("[I]n general, an SRO has proven to be one of the most effective ways of monitoring a growing complex of financial services in our society, and it's a way that I am seriously considering with respect to investment companies and even considering more seriously with respect to investment advisers"). The House bill, Investment Adviser Regulatory Enhancement and Disclosure Act of 1993 (H.R. 578) which passed the House in May 4, 1993: (i) authorized the SEC to collect registration fees from advisers, to suspend advisers' registration for failure to pay fees, and to use the fees to defray specific costs of regulating advisers; (ii) authorized the SEC to designate SROs to examine, to discipline for non-compliance, and to collect examination fees from members and affiliates (except affiliates primarily engaged in investment advisory activities, and thrifts); (iii) directed the SEC to arrange for inspecting advisers and to survey and report to Congress on advisers that failed to register, to establish a toll-free number for inquiries concerning advisers, and to promulgate investor protection rules, setting bonds for certain advisers to cover larceny and embezzlement; (iv) disqualified certain persons (convicted of felonies, etc.) from acting as advisers; (v) prohibited advisers from conducting

certain transactions, including giving unsuitable advice and disclosing confidential client information; and (vi) required advisers to disclose certain information to clients, including referral fee arrangements. See *Bill Tracking Report*, H.R. 578, 103d Cong., 1st Sess., available in *LEXIS*, Legis library, BLT103 file.

The Senate bill, Investment Adviser Oversight Act of 1993 (S. 423), which passed the Senate on Nov. 20, 1993, was more limited. It amended the Investment Advisers Act of 1940 (hereinafter Advisers Act) authorizing the SEC to (i) establish registration fees and filing fees for other applications and papers that advisers must file. The fees were to cover efforts to register all persons to whom the Act's registration requirement applies, and to regulate advisers; (ii) suspend advisers' registration on failure to pay the fees and to reinstate upon payment; (iii) require registered advisers to be bonded against larceny and embezzlement, with certain limits; (iv) require the SEC to study the impact of such bonding on the competitive position of small advisers and those outside urban areas. See *Bill Tracking Report*, S. 423, 103d Cong. 1st Sess., available in *LEXIS*, Legis library, BLT103 file; "*Congress To Address SEC Self-Funding, Investment Advisers, Financial Fraud*," *1994 Daily Report for Executives* (Bureau of National Affairs) (Jan. 14, 1994), available in *LEXIS*, Exec library, Drexec file (document d89) (Senator Gramm opposed the legislation as an additional "tax" on advisers on an item which the SEC does not consider a priority). The major differences in the bills involved disclosure and suitability requirements. In the meantime, the SEC has proposed a rule imposing on advisers a suitability requirement under §206(4) of the Investment Advisers Act. See Suitability of Investment Advice Provided by Investment Advisers, SEC Release No. IA-1406, 59 *Federal Register* 13, p. 464 (to be codified at 17 C.F.R. §275.206(4)-5) (proposed March 16, 1994).

11. 1989 Proposal, note 9 (SEC approved a plan for establishing an SRO for registered advisers, except broker-dealers, banks, certified public accountants, and advisers who only advise Funds. The SRO would set qualifications and business practice standards and, most importantly, conduct examinations of the members. Membership would be mandatory. The NASD could be one possible SRO for advisers' inspection and registration. Other SROs could also be organized); 1983 Proposal, note 4; see also 1 Tamar Frankel, *The Regulation of Money Managers* §10, pp. 37-38 (1978); *id.* at 13-14 (Supp. 1995).

12. Sam S. Miller, "Self-Regulation of the Securities Markets: A Critical Examination," *Washington and Lee Law Review* 42 pp. 853, 854-56 (1985) and authorities cited therein.

13. "SEC Reconsidering Adviser SRO, Urges Passage of Pending House Bill," Securities. Regulation and Law Report 22 p. 1060 (Bureau of National Affairs) (July 20, 1990) (quoting Commissioner Schapiro who testified before the House Energy & Commerce Telecommunications and Finance Subcommittee that with respect to advisers, "direct regulation [by the SEC] is clearly preferable and far more cost effective").

14. See Miller, note 12, p. 879.

15. Philip Mathias, "Regulator Hits 'Private Club Mentality'," *Financial Post* Mar. 4, 1995, p. 48 (Larry Waite, Director of Enforcement for the Ontario Securities Commission, noted the practice of awarding of bonuses to investigators and other questionable practices).

16. Miller, note 12, pp. 855-856.

17. 141 *Congressional Record* S1085 (daily ed. Jan. 18, 1995) (arguing for a self-disciplinary organization similar to SROs for accountants to protect them from excessive litigation under the Dominici-Dodd Private Securities Litigation Reform Act of 1995).

18. Jeffrey Taylor and Molly Baker, "SEC Weighs Filing Disciplinary Case Against NASD on Alleged Dealer Abuses," *The Wall Street Journal*, July 10, 1995, p. A4; see also Barnet D. Wolf, "NASDAQ Working Hard to Erase Negative Report of Academics," *Columbus Dispatch*, July 9, 1995, p. 1F (discussing accusations made by professors at Ohio State and Vanderbilt universities of price fixing in the over-the-counter market).

19. See William Power, "Nasdaq Faces Huge Legal Costs in Probes," *The Wall Street Journal*, July 19, 1995, p. C1.

20. See Eric Bregman and Arthur Jacobson, "Environmental Performance Review: Self-Regulation in Environmental Law", *Cardozo Law Review* 16 (1994), pp. 465, 467.

21. Ibid. pp. 469-70 (describing how self-regulation may enhance the political participation of ordinary citizens).

22. Consider the following argument expressed in the "Testimony of John F. Sandner Chairman of the Board of Directors Chicago Mercantile Exchange Before the Comm. on Agriculture, Nutrition, and Forestry United States Senate," *Federal News Service Washington Package*, Jan. 26, 1995, 1995 WL 6624022, pp. *31, 33

   "The hard truth is: we cannot expect to remain globally competitive for the balance of this century and into the 21st, unless we move now to rethink and reshape our country's scheme for regulating financial services. In a nutshell, America cannot continue to regulate a space-age industry with horse-and-buggy rules . . ."

   "The laws now on the books are vestiges of a very different era: business was retail-oriented; there was little or no international competition; and futures and securities were clearly delineated. Now it's all blurred: products, services, market participants and the marketplaces themselves. Meantime, regulation has been piled upon regulation, nearly always in reaction to some 'problem that had to be fixed.'"

23. Joanne Morrison, *Regulators Should Aid Dealers in Suitability Effort, Lawyers Say*, BOND BUYER, May 18, 1995, at 3 (comment made by Joanne Medero: "There are some things the government cannot do").

24. Barbash Testimony, note 3 ("interpretive guidance and proposed rules designed to assist funds and other issuers in using electronic media to provide investors with information required under the securities laws") (citing Use of Electronic Media for Delivery Purposes, SEC Releases No. 33-7233, 33-7234, 60 Fed. Reg. 53,458, 53,468 (1995)).

25. 1993 Hearings, note 8, p. 12 (statement of Arthur J. Levitt, Chairman, SEC) ("[I]n general, an SRO has proven to be one of the most effective ways of monitoring a growing complex of financial services in our society...")

26. The Association was established in 1937, and worked with Congress in drafting the 1940 Act. See Testimony of Douglas M. Loudon, President, on behalf of the Investment Counsel Association of America (ICAA), Hearing on H.R. 2131 "Capital Markets Deregulation and Liberalization Act of 1995" Submitted to the Subcommittee on Telecommunications and Finance Committee on Commerce, U.S. House of Representatives (Dec. 5, 1995), available in *LEXIS*, Legis library, Cngtst file. The Association received in the 1940 Act protection of the title "investment counsel" for its members, whose main business is to render investment advice. See Investment Advisers Act of 1940, §208(c), 15 U.S.C. §80b-8(c) (1994).

Similarlly, the Institute of Certified Financial Planners imposes a Code of Ethical Conduct on its members and enforces the Code by suspending and rescinding membership. See, e.g., Jim Lawless, *Investor's Memo*, Gannett News Service, Feb. 1, 1995, available in *LEXIS*, News library, GNS file.

27. Investment Company Institute, Report to the Division of Investment Management U.S. Securities & Exchange Commission, Implementation of the Institute's Recommendations on Personal Investing (1995), summarized in "Mutual Funds Have Implemented Institute's Recommendations on Personal Investing, ICI Survey Finds," *PR Newswire*, Apr. 21, 1995, available in *LEXIS*, News library, Prnews file.

28. Ibid.

29. For example, the SRO for the accounting profession has recently instituted a program in which member firms would examine and review each others' practices and internal controls. See Lee Berton, "Accountants Vote Required Program of Self-Regulation," *The Wall Street Journal*, Jan. 14, 1988, p. 12.

30. See Silver v. N.Y. Stock Exch., 373 U.S. 341, 347-49 (1963) (describing the potential anti-competitive effects of self-regulation by the N.Y.S.E.); Marianne K. Smythe, "Government Supervised Self-Regulation in the Securities Industry and the Antitrust Laws: Suggestions for an Accommodation," *North Carolina Law Review* 62, pp. 475, 476 (1984) (arguing that SROs may be more interested in preserving the market dominance of certain industry members than in the public interest).

31. See Miller, note 12, pp. 855-56.

32. See, e.g., Lisa Bernstein, "Opting Out of the Legal System: Extralegal Contractual Relations in the Diamond Industry," *Journal of Legal Studies* 21, pp. 115, 124 (1992) (describing the dispute resolution methods of the New York Diamond Dealers Club).

33. See, e.g., David G. Oedel, "Private Interbank Discipline," Harvard Journal of Law and Public Policy 16 (1993), pp. 327, 353-56, 381-85.

34. Securities and Exchange Act of 1934, §15A, 15 U.S.C. §78-3 (1994).

35. With few exceptions, all advisers must register under the Advisers Act. Funds must register under §§7 and 8 of the Investment Company Act of 1940. 15 U.S.C. §§80a-8, -9 (1994). The Fund registration does not impose educational or financial qualification requirements on Fund advisers or the board members of the Funds. The Advisers Act requires no qualifications of advisers, but only that advisers provide clients with a brochure describing their education and experience. See Investment Advisers Act of 1940, §203, 15 U.S.C. §80b-3 (1994); 17 CFR. §275.203 (1995); 2 Frankel, note 111, p. 98 (1978). In addition, all advisers are subject to restrictions on their fee structure, Investment Advisers Act of 1940, 15 U.S.C. §80b-5 (1994), and are exposed to liabilities under the common law, the anti-fraud provisions of the Advisers Act, Investment Advisers Act of 1940, §206, 15 U.S.C. §80b-6 (1994), and the anti-fraud provisions of the Securities Exchange Act of 1934, see, e.g., Rule 10b-5, 17 CFR. §270.10b-5 (1995), under which individual clients can claim directly, and Fund shareholders can sue Fund advisers derivatively.

36. The industry is not homogeneous. There are advisers to individuals and advisers to institutions. Advisers to individuals offer many various personal services with various degrees of discretion. Advisory services become institutional when (i) the service is fully discretionary and

(ii) non-personal, and (iii) advisees' money is pooled with the money of others, and (iv) advisees acquire undivided interests in the pool. Not surprisingly, this definition resembles that of a "security."

Institutional advisers include pension funds, insurance companies, banks and similar institutions although they are not all governed by the Advisers Act.

Personal and institutional advice can be given separately, or in conjunction with other services, such as brokerage and investment banking. Personal advice can be offered with financial planning, and can combine with advice the sale of securities, insurance, and other investments. Advisers differ in the amount of assets under their management from over $60 billion to a few thousand dollars. Therefore, advisers have, as a group, relatively little common interests.

37. Note, *Financial Planning:* "Is it Time For a Self-Regulatory Organization?" Brooklyn Law Review 53 (1987), pp. 143, 184-85. (Commissioner Cox's argument that financial planners lack common interests, required for a successful SRO).

38. See "Cox Says Commission Should Reject Federal Licensing of Financial Planners," *Securities Regulation and Law Report* 16, p. 1726 (Bureau of National Affairs) (Nov. 2, 1984).

39. In 1940, Congress determined that disclosure alone is not a sufficiently effective regulatory tool for investment companies. 1 Frankel, *supra* note 11, p. 31 n. 97 (1978); see Investment Company Act of 1940, §1(b), 15 U.S.C. §80a-1(b) (1994) (describing the problems addressed by the Act).

40. 1 Frankel, note 11 (1978), pp. 89-92.

41. To adjust this detailed regulatory scheme to unintended results and unforeseen new situations, the federal statute grants the SEC broad exemptive powers.

42. Investment Company Act of 1940, §§2(a)(19), 10, 15 U.S.C. §§80a-2(a)(19), 10 (1994).

43. Ibid. at §15, 15 U.S.C. §80a-15 (1994).

44. Ibid. at §§17(a), (d), (e), 15 U.S.C. §80a-17(a), (d), (e) (1994); see 2 Frankel, note 11, ch. 13 (1978).

45. Investment Company Act of 1940, §37, 15 U.S.C. §80a-36 (1994).

46. Ibid. at §17(f), 15 U.S.C. §80a-17(f) (1994).

47. Ibid. at §36(b), 15 U.S.C. §80a-35(b) (1994).

48. Ibid. at §15, 15 U.S.C. §80a-15 (1994).

49. Ibid. at §36(b), 15 U.S.C. §80a-35(b) (1994).

50. See generally 6 Louis Loss and Joel Seligman, *Securities Regulation* 2787-816 (3d ed. 1990).

51. Miller, note 12, pp. 855-56 (regulators and self-regulators seek different objectives. "[T]he government aims at substituting a regulatory scheme as efficacious as that which it would provide directly." The self-regulators have something else in mind, such as cheaper and more flexible regulation and insulation from government involvement). This does not mean that the Investment Company Institute (ICI), the trade association of Funds, should not play a role in the regulation of its members. The SEC would greatly benefit from the ICI comments on various regulatory issues and from surveys of its members. It is in the interests of the ICI membership to supply such information and have an impact on its regulation. In fact, this model is close to the type of relationship that currently exists between the ICI and the SEC.

52. 1993 Hearings, note 8, p. 2 (opening statement by Senator Christopher J. Dodd) ("[T]his industry has been an extraordinary success story."); Ibid., pp. 70-71 (statement of James S. Riepe, Managing Director, T. Rowe Price Associates, Inc.) (asserting that funds regulation is stringent but does not prevent innovation; the funds "are the success story of the financial services industry because…[they] have garnered investor confidence.").

53. Bank Sales of Mutual Funds: Hearings Before the Subcomm. on Financial Institutions Regulation and Deposit Insurance of the House Comm. on Banking, Finance and Urban Affairs, 103d Cong., 2d Sess. 360 (1994) (statement of Matthew P. Fink, President, Investment Company Institute) (attributing a "vital role" to the "strict regulatory scheme to which mutual funds are subject"); 1993 Hearings, *supra* note 8, at 94 (statement of Matthew P. Fink, President, Investment Company Institute) (stating that "The Institute believes that the regulatory scheme to which mutual funds are subject is working well").

54. Arguably, Funds can act to reduce sales pressure during a downtrend of market prices. 1993 Hearings, note 8, p. 92 (statement of Matthew Fink, President, Investment Company Institute).

55. See Karen Talley and Debra Cope, "SEC Survey: Many People Don't Grasp Fund Risks," *American Banker*, Nov. 12, 1993, pp. 1, 13.

56. 1993 Hearings, note 8, pp. 7, 11-12 (statement of Arthur J. Levitt, Chairman, SEC) (the Funds are "willing to consider . . . internal audits, enforcing compliance structures at each of the funds, and a variety of other things as part of a package that may diminish the need for an SRO"); Ibid. P. 35 (statement of Matthew P. Fink, President, Investment Company Institute) (strongly supporting "congressional efforts to provide the SEC with greater resources to oversee the industry in the years ahead" and use fees that are paid by Funds to regulate mutual funds); see Sheldon Yett, "Fund Industry Fears SRO Creation," 25 *Wall Street Letter* 46, p. 1 (Inst. Investor, Inc.) (Nov. 22, 1993), available in *LEXIS*, News library, Iinews file) (the industry "is quietly promoting as a more palatable initiative than the creation of an SRO . . . an enhanced role for investment company compliance officers . . . [and] the ICI has proposed expanding their rile [sic] to include internal audit responsibilities").

57. It may well be that the recent problem regarding mispricing of Fund shares could be addressed by the use of available technology.

58. See McGough, Emshwiller & Calian, note 7, p. A1 (suggesting need for timely evaluations of current price of portfolios).

59. The Society is located in 24 Millerton Rd, Lakeville, CT 06039 (860) 435-0843 and seems to be quite active. See NSCP Currents Special Edition/Oct. 1995, at 8 (announcing the meeting of the organization in Washington D.C. hosting Congressman Dan Frisa).

60. "Securities, Roberts Says Industry Should Act to Ban Fund Managers' Personal Trading," *1994 Daily Report for Executives* (Bureau of National Affairs) (March 7, 1994), available in *LEXIS*, Exec library, Drexec file (document 40) (Commissioner Roberts, who supports the establishment of SROs for investment advisers, also recommended such state involvement).

61. "Mutual Funds Have Implemented Institute's Recommendations on Personal Investing, ICI Survey Finds," *PR Newswire*, Apr. 21, 1995, available in *LEXIS*, News library, Prnews file (showing that "an overwhelming majority of fund groups have voluntarily implemented Institute recommendations to adopt measures—beyond those required by law—to address potential conflicts of interest arising by personal investment by fund managers and other investment company personnel").

62. Investment Company Institute, note 27.

63. Ibid.

64. Taylor and Baker, note 18, suggest that SROs can not be expected to sacrifice their own interests without serious prodding. Hence, the failure of ICI members to provide for additional disclosure on personal investing, Ibid., and the NASD's alleged failure to limit price fixing.

65. Interestingly, serious questions have been raised recently about the adequacy of the provisions of rule 17j-1 under the Investment Company Act, 17 C.F.R. §270.17j-1 (1995). The rule requires Funds to establish codes of ethics and regulate their employees and managers, mainly

regarding activities such as insider trading, appropriations of Funds'
investment opportunities, and trading on the effects of the Funds' own
purchases and sales. Recent concerns about Fund managers' trading for
their own accounts raises serious questions about the adequacy of these
codes of ethics. James M. Gomez & Jonathan Weber, "End Near in ICN
Battle; But Issues Raised in the Squabble Will Persist," *Los Angeles
Times*, Jan. 31, 1994, p. D1, col. 2; Geoffrey Smith, "Mutual Funds:
The Rules on Insider Trading, Please," *Business Week*, Jan. 31, 1994,
p. 60; "Mutual Fund Panel to Study Questionable Practices," *The Reuter
Business Report* (Reuters Ltd.) (Feb. 16, 1994), available in *LEXIS*,
news library, Arnws file (the industry formed an advisory panel to
consider more stringent codes of ethics); "Levitt Says Staff Reviewing
Trading by Fund Managers for Own Accounts," *Banking Report News*
62 (Bureau of National Affairs) p. 339 (Feb. 21, 1994) (announcing that
the Commission's staff is reviewing Fund mamagers' trading for their
own accounts). The SEC has proposed an amendment to rule 17j-1
designed to tighten the provisions of the codes of ethics with respect to
personal trading of Fund portfolio managers. See IC-21341, 60 *Federal
Register* 47,844 (Sep. 8, 1995).

19

MULTIPLE REGULATORS
Where Are We? How Did We Get Here?

Joel Seligman, *The University of Arizona Law School*

The history of financial regulation in the United States has been characterized by overlapping jurisdictions among federal or federal and state regulatory agencies. In some instances Congress has adopted a concurrent jurisdiction approach; in others, it provided an exemption from the relevant federal law; in still others, it has vested one of two relevant agencies with exclusive jurisdiction. During much of the recent past, the practical issue has been how well do agencies with overlapping jurisdictions harmonize their efforts to avoid unnecessary conflicts and efficiently regulate. The results have been mixed and have evolved considerably over time.

Let me illustrate this history with three illustrations that involve the SEC, the federal agency I study. In part, I intend to use history to illustrate that simple sloganistic solutions to problems of financial regulation often appear less attractive after a careful study of the relevant historical and empirical contexts.

AN EXAMPLE OF CONCURRENT REGULATION:
STATE SECURITIES REGULATION

In 1911, the failure of lax state corporation statutes to prevent securities fraud gave rise to the first significant legislative response when Kansas enacted the first well-known state securities law, popularly known as a "blue-sky" law because it was intended to check stock swindlers so barefaced they "would sell building lots in the blue sky."

This Kansas type of statute is today popularly known as *merit regulation* because it vests an administrator with the ability to block the marketing of a security when he or she finds it to be "unfair, unjust, inequitable, or oppressive." After the United States Supreme Court held the Kansas-type blue sky law to be constitutional in 1917, the blue sky movement swept the country. By 1933, every state except Nevada had adopted a securities law.

Rarely have statutes enacted with such fanfare and general support subsequently been so universally deprecated. In the brutal glare that followed the stock market crash from 1929 to 1932, it was apparent to virtually all commentators and congressional witnesses on the subject that the blue sky laws never really had a chance to succeed. As early as 1915, for example, the Investment Bankers Association reported to its members that they could "ignore" all blue sky laws by making offerings across state lines through the mails.

After Congress enacted federal securities laws, primarily in 1933 and 1934, the intriguing historical question is, why did the blue sky laws endure? There appear to be three general reasons.

First, political sentiment favored retention of a state role. SEC legislation specifically preserved the blue sky laws. Far from preempting the field when interstate commerce is involved, Congress affirmatively yielded to local regulation by inserting a number of intrastate exemptions even when the mails or facilities of interstate commerce are used and jurisdiction falls to the state securities commissions.

Second, the state statutes have generally been rewritten to reduce compliance burdens at the state level when a securities issuance is registered at the federal level. Today, over 40 state jurisdictions authorize registration by coordination. Most of these jurisdictions follow the coordination procedure specified in Section 303 of the Uniform Securities Act of 1956 and limit this procedure to issuers that have filed a registration statement employing the Securities Act of 1933. In essence, the coordination procedure requires filing copies of the registration state-ment filed with the SEC at the state level. If specified conditions are met, the registration statement automatically becomes effective at the state level at the moment the federal registration statement becomes effective.

Third, at least some states have performed a significant enforce-ment role with respect to fraud in local securities offerings. But the results vary significantly from state to state. In many jurisdictions, par-simonious state budgets have meant understaffing of state securities law programs.

Today the most significant augmentative aspect of the state blue sky laws may well be in providing broader private relief in many instances than do the federal securities laws.

A residual tension between federal and state securities law has endured. While the mandatory disclosure system of the federal secu-rities laws purports only to require full and complete disclosure of mate-rial information, virtually all state jurisdictions specify standards for the denial, suspension, or revocation of securities registration. In a minority of 18 jurisdictions, traditional "merit" regulations remain in force. A significant additional number of jurisdictions employ a mod-ified form of merit regulation, adopting the language of Uniform Secu-rities Act § 306(a)(2)(F), which permits merit regulation only when "the offering has been or would be made with unreasonable amounts of underwriters' and sellers' discounts, commissions, or other compen-sation or promoters' profits or participations, or unreasonable amounts of kinds of options..."

In recent years, the leading policy debate concerning state secu-rities regulation has centered on the wisdom of merit standards.

Proponents of merit regulation argue that by giving state securi-ties administrators power to halt "nonmeritorious" issues, investors are better protected from fraud or overreaching than they would be under a pure disclosure form of regulation like the Securities Act of 1933. Even if we assume that the case for merit regulation can be persuasively artic-ulated in a national context, this debate takes on a different character when state law merit standards are applied to domestic or foreign issuers that can sell securities abroad. If enforcement of merit standards tended to encourage securities issuances to be distributed solely abroad, it would be neither to the advantage of United States issuers nor investors.

To some extent, most states have reduced the conflict between their merit standards and actual or potential international offerings by adopting a marketplace exemption from merit review for securities listed on the New York and American stock exchanges. Some states also exempt securities traded in the over-the-counter market through the computerized NASDAQ National Market System list.

The practical problem given an increasingly international economy is more fully to perfect a system of state securities regulation that will not impede registration within the United States. Potentially this might mean a system of partial preemption by the Securities Act of 1933 for registered offerings. Under such a system, the states would be prohibited from imposing disclosure and other standards more demanding than those enforced under the Securities Act of 1933. In effect, merit regulation for issues registered under the federal Securities Act would be prohibited.

Such partial preemption would have little, or no impact, on those states that today do not employ merit regulation and on those states where merit regulation is effectively reserved for offerings exempt from the 1933 Securities Act, for example, by dint of the marketplace exemption. Under this approach merit regulation might continue to exist in those states that wished to employ it for offerings exempt from the Securities Act of 1933.

More significantly, all states could continue to require registration by coordination (that is, simultaneously with SEC registration) and could continue to play a role in securities law enforcement. But the filing requirements at the state level would essentially be limited to a filing of documents required by the Securities Act of 1933 for registered offerings.

Besides simplifying the often quite burdensome task of "blue skying" a securities issuance in up to 50 states as well as the District of Columbia, Puerto Rico, and Guam, partial preemption along these lines would end concerns of domestic and foreign issuers about the possibility of being able to satisfy federal, but not state registration requirements, or the possibility that state registration requirements might significantly delay or add to the costs of an issuance.

Inevitably, the application of merit standards to issuers capable of selling securities abroad has and will continue to shrink. This is not a consequence of an academic or purely domestic debate about the wisdom of merit standards. It is, instead, a consequence of the increasingly international context of securities sales. The emergence of a global securities market ultimately should result in the United States federal level becoming the sole level of concern for issuers capable of selling abroad.

A concurrent system that operated well enough when securities sales were generally domestic runs the risk of becoming self-defeating when securities issuers have the option of selling in foreign securities markets.

A PARTIAL EXEMPTION EXAMPLE: THE MUNICIPAL SECURITIES EXEMPTION FROM THE SECURITIES ACT OF 1933

If the tendency in the boundary between federal and state securities law is generally in favor of a further diminution of the state role, matters are notably different with respect to the scope of the Securities Act of 1933. This is the Act that requires issuers to file a registration statement when distributing securities to the public.

During the past decades, the frequency with which corporate issuers have had to provide a detailed description of their firms and their businesses in a registration statement has significantly declined, primarily as a result of the greater use of truncated, transaction-oriented disclosure requirements and increased use of the private placement exemption. The significance of the mandatory disclosure system under the 1933 Act, in effect, has shrunk as a consequence of the combined effect of the efficient market hypothesis (which suggested that disclosure under the 1933 Act is unnecessary if the same disclosure is made to the market under the periodic requirements of the Securities Exchange Act), the rise of foreign capital markets (which created a practical alternative to the domestic sale of securities), and the increased demand for securities by institutions (which effectively broadened the private placement market.)

At the same time, it seems clear that in the foreseeable future there may well be further significant expansion of the SEC's role in one of its largest areas of exemption, municipal securities regulation.

In contemporary finance, the term *municipal securities* broadly refers to securities issued by states, their political subdivisions such as cities, towns, or counties, or their instrumentalities such as school districts or port authorities.

In 1933 the "SEC Staff Report on the Municipal Securities Market" stated:

> The municipal securities market comprises approximately 50,000 state and local issuers with an outstanding principal amount of securities in excess of $1.2 trillion...Approximately 2,600 municipal securities dealers, banks, and brokers actively trade in municipal securities.

Later the Commission added:

> In 1993, a record level of over $335 billion in municipal securities was
> sold, representing over 17,000 issues. This record financing was heavily
> influenced by refundings. Nevertheless, the level of long term new money
> financings, representing 49% of financings for the year, reflected con-
> tinued growth. In 1993, there were $142 billion of new money long term
> financings, compared to $81 billion in 1988, a 75 percent increase.

Section 3(a)(2) of the 1933 Act exempts virtually all municipal securities from SEC registration, but not antifraud, requirements. The near
default of New York City securities in 1974–1975, the subsequent default
by the Washington Public Power Supply System (WPPSS) after expend-
ing $2.25 billion to construct two nuclear power plants, and more recent
events in Orange County have revived the debate whether issuers, particularly of industrial revenue or conduit bonds, should be subject to a
mandatory disclosure system comparable to that for corporate issuers.

As the full commission explained after the 1988 staff report on
WPPSS:

> [T]he most disturbing aspect of the Supply System problems is that they
> arose after the New York City Report, after the subsequent voluntary
> improvements in municipal disclosure, and after most of the additional
> regulatory actions discussed [elsewhere in the report]. Events such as
> the Supply System default inevitably focus attention on the adequacy of
> the current regulation of the municipal securities markets.

The commission found that the New York City and WPPSS instances
were not isolated. "In the period from 1972 to 1983, there were eleven
defaults involving general obligation instruments, 25 defaults involving non-conduit revenue bonds, and at least 82 private purpose (conduit)
bond defaults...Moreover, the Bond Investors Association indicates that,
from 1983 to the first quarter of 1988, over 300 municipal issuers
defaulted on their obligations." In all, the municipal debt default rate
of approximately 0.7 percent was nearly equal to the corporate debt
default rate of 1.1 percent.

The SEC and Congress have moved incrementally, but steadily, in
the period after the New York City bond crisis and WPPSS, to expand
federal securities regulation.

First, in 1975, Congress enacted Section 15B of the Securities
Exchange Act to establish jurisdiction over municipal securities dealers subject to the Municipal Securities Rulemaking Board (MSRB).

Second, in 1990, the commission approved the MSRB's rule proposal to require the mandatory filing of offering statements by municipal issuers.

Third, the Commission adopted Rule 15c2–12, which makes it unlawful for any broker, dealer, or municipal securities dealer to act as underwriter in a primary municipal securities offering with an aggregate offering price of $1 million or more unless:

1. Before bidding for or buying the securities it obtained and reviewed an official statement that was complete except for certain transaction-related data.

2. It forwarded copies of the official statement to any potential customer on request.

3. It obtained final copies of the official statement within seven business days after any final agreement to buy or sell the municipal securities.

4. It forwarded copies of the final official statement to any potential customer from the time the final official statement became available until the earlier of 90 days from the end of the underwriting period, or the time when the official statement was available to any person from a nationally recognized municipal securities information repository, but in no case less than 25 days after the end of the underwriting period.

Along with the rule, the commission published interpretative commentary emphasizing the obligation of a municipal underwriter to have a reasonable basis for recommending any municipal securities, and its responsibility in fulfilling that obligation to review in a professional manner that accuracy of offering statements with which it is associated. These are similar to the "due diligence" requirements applicable to corporate issuers under Section 11 of the 1933 Securities Act.

Fourth, in 1993, after a spate of allegations of illegal payoffs and influence peddling during the last Congress, Congressmen Dingell and Markey requested an SEC statement of whether the "Tower Amendment" in Sections 15Bd(1)–(2) of the 1934 Act (which prohibits disclosure documents under the 1933 Act from being filed *before* a municipal issuance) should be repealed in whole or in part. A few Republican lawmakers have echoed that concern in this Congress.

Underlying this evolution toward greater federal securities regulation has been a notable change in investors of municipal securities. As a 1993 SEC staff report explained:

> The profile of the typical investor in municipal securities also has changed dramatically over this century. Historically, investors in municipal bonds were institutions and wealthy individuals wishing to take advantage of the tax-exempt status of fairly low-risk municipal securities. The interest received by holders of most municipal securities was exempt from federal income taxation, and in some cases, from state and local income taxation, and thus was very attractive to taxpayers in higher tax brackets. With the changing income tax rates, persons of more moderate means increasingly have invested in municipal securities. Today, households are the largest holders of municipal debt, followed by municipal bond mutual funds, property and casualty insurers, commercial banks, and money market funds.

In essence, just as a growth in individual investor interest in corporate securities may have been the key dynamic in prompting and sustaining interest in a mandatory disclosure system, similar interest in tax-exempt municipal securities appears to have fueled a more recent enthusiasm for greater federal mandatory municipal securities regulation.

AN EXCLUSIVE JURISDICTION EXAMPLE: CFTC REGULATION OF STOCK INDEX FUTURES

Building in part on the premise that "the markets of stocks, stock index futures, and stock options—are in fact one market," the Brady Report, in its most controversial proposal after the October 1987 stock market crash, urged "that one agency must have the authority to coordinate a few but critical intermarket regulatory issues, monitor intermarket activities and mediate intermarket concerns." In making this proposal, the Brady Report distinguished intramarket (within one market) regulatory issues, which it believed should be left to the SEC and CFTC, from intermarket (across markets) issues. "The few important intermarket issues which need to be harmonized by a single body include clearing and credit mechanisms, margin requirements, circuit breaker mechanisms such as price limits and trading halts, and information systems for monitoring intermarket activities." After a brief canvass of the possible alternatives, the report concluded: "we are...aware that the weight of the evidence suggests that the Federal Reserve is well qualified to fill the role of the intermarket agency."

In these terms, the Brady Report intermarket agency proposal proved short-lived. Less than one month after its publication, Federal Reserve Board Chairman Alan Greenspan "seriously [questioned] this recommendation:"

> To be effective, an oversight authority must have considerable expertise in the markets subject to regulation, something that the CFTC and SEC have developed over time. Moreover, were the Federal Reserve to be given a dominant role in securities market regulation there could be a presumption by many that the federal safety net applicable to depository institutions was being extended to these markets and the Federal Reserve stood ready to jump in whenever a securities firm or clearing corporation was in difficulty.

In May 1988, the authors of the Brady Report, in effect, withdrew their proposal for a single intermarket regulatory authority.

Beyond the Federal Reserve Board's lack of enthusiasm, there was a more fundamental reason for rejecting the one intermarket regulatory proposal, as initially formulated. The proposal was overgeneral. In effect, it attempted to name one agency to manage what are three quite distinct tasks:

1. The liquidity of the banking system in making credit available to stock brokers, futures commission merchants, and relevant clearing corporations.

2. Stock market, stock option, and stock index futures coordination issues including circuit breaker mechanisms, information systems, market surveillance, and enforcement, as well as contingency planning for market emergencies.

3. Harmonized margin requirements across marketplaces.

The first task was already vested in the Federal Reserve Board. Before the U.S. equity markets opened on October 20, 1987, the Federal Reserve Board stated that it would provide needed liquidity to the financial system, and this statement helped restore investor confidence and was an appropriate use of the Fed's powers.

Similarly the third task, harmonizing margin (or broker loan) requirements across marketplaces, proved legislatively remediable. In 1992 the Federal Reserve Board was empowered to set margins on stock index futures. Early in 1993 the Fed delegated authority to the CFTC to establish and change margin levels in stock index futures contracts and options.

In contrast, the issue of whether the CFTC's jurisdiction over stock index futures should be transferred to the SEC occasioned one of the most significant legislative defeats in the SEC's history.

This jurisdiction conflict dates back to the Commodity Futures Trading Commission Act of 1974, which amended the Commodity Exchange Act by expanding its coverage beyond agricultural commodities and transferring its administration from the Department of Agriculture to the then newly created Commodity Futures Trading Commission (CFTC). In the process, Congress defined *commodity* to mean a couple of dozen agricultural items, "and all other goods and articles" (except onions),

> and all services, rights, and interests in which contracts for future delivery are presently or in the future dealt in: *Provided*, That the [Commodity Futures Trading] Commission shall have exclusive jurisdiction with respect to accounts, agreements (including any transaction which is of the character of, or is commonly known to the trade as, an "option," "privilege," "indemnity," "bid," "offer," "put," "call," "advance guaranty," or "decline guaranty"), and transactions involving contracts of sale of a commodity for future delivery, traded or executed on a contract market designated pursuant to section 7 of this title or any other board of trade, exchange, or market...*And provided further*, That, except as hereinabove provided, nothing contained in this section shall (i) supersede or limit the jurisdiction at any time conferred on the Securities and Exchange Commission or other regulatory authorities under the laws of the United States or of any State, or (ii) restrict the Securities and Exchange Commission and such other authorities in accordance with such laws...Nothing in this chapter shall be deemed to govern or in any way be applicable to transactions in foreign currency, security warrants, security rights, resales of installment loan contracts, repurchase options, government securities, or mortgages and mortgage purchase commitments, unless such transactions involve the sale thereof for future delivery conducted on a board of trade.

The SEC, in 1974, distracted by its efforts to deal with unfixing brokerage commission rates and other stock market structural issues then pending before Congress, contented itself with recommending the language in the statute after the phrase "And provided further." Neither Congress nor the SEC exhibited great awareness of the implications of granting a new agency "exclusive" jurisdiction over financial futures based on securities subject to SEC jurisdiction.

That issue soon was raised before Congress. In 1978, while the CFTC was undergoing a reauthorization proceeding, the SEC attempted to secure jurisdiction from the CFTC over certain futures, options, and leverage contracts. Both the House Agriculture and the Senate Agriculture, Nutrition, and Forestry Committees rejected the SEC's attempt, emphasizing a preference that jurisdiction over all futures trading should remain in a single agency. This was perhaps an inevitable consequence of vesting Congressional oversight of the SEC and the CFTC in separate committees in both the House and the Senate.

Congress did enact Section 2(a)(8)(B)(i) of the Commodity Exchange Act requiring the CFTC to

> maintain communication with the Department of the Treasury, the Board of Governors of the Federal Reserve System, and the Securities and Exchange Commission for the purposes of keeping such agencies fully informed of [CFTC] activities that relate to the responsibilities of those agencies, for the purpose of seeking the views of those agencies on such activities that relate to the responsibilities of those agencies, for the purpose of seeking the views of those agencies on such activities, and for considering the relationships between the volume and nature of investment and trading in contracts of sale of a commodity for future delivery and in securities and financial instruments under the jurisdiction of such agencies.

In early 1981, the SEC approved proposed rule changes by the Chicago Board Options Exchange (CBOE) designed to accommodate trading in options on Government National Mortgage Association or GNMA securities. On petition of the Chicago Board of Trade (CBOT), which had traded GNMA *futures* since 1975, the Seventh Circuit in a split decision reversed. The majority not only held that the SEC was without jurisdiction because of the CFTC statute—the two commissions could not by agreement "reapportion their jurisdiction in the face of a clear, contrary statutory mandate"—but also gratuitously went on to say that GNMA options were not even "securities" despite the "right to...purchase" language of the securities laws' definition.

Against this background, the chairmen of the SEC and CFTC entered into an agreement to clarify the respective jurisdiction responsibilities of the two agencies, pending the enactment of clarifying amendments to the securities and commodities laws.

The agreement left untouched the CFTC's exclusive jurisdiction over commodity futures trading on boards of trade in *futures contracts* (or options on futures contracts) on securities issued or guaranteed by the United States government or other SEC-exempted securities (except municipals).

On the other hand, the agreement recognized the SEC as the sole federal regulator of the securities *options* markets (apart from options on futures contracts). And, in recognition of the SEC's unique responsibilities over the markets for corporate and municipal securities, the two agencies specified certain criteria to govern approval by the CFTC of futures trading in a *group* or *index* of such securities, in addition to affording the SEC an opportunity for an oral hearing before the CFTC (together with judicial review) in order to present the bases for any objection.

As part of the Futures Trading Act of 1982, Congress enacted the SEC-CFTC accord into law, with the significant refinement that after December 9, 1982, any futures contract on a group or index of securities (or options on such contract) could be vetoed by the SEC if the SEC found that the contract (1) could not be settled in cash, (2) was readily susceptible to manipulation, or (3) was not reflective of the market (or a substantial segment of the market) for all publicly traded equity or debt securities. The Seventh Circuit decision concerning CBOE options in GNMA securities, in effect, was legislatively overruled by the 1982 legislation.

In late 1983, the SEC took the position with the CFTC that four stock index futures contracts proposed by the CME did not satisfy the statutory criteria of the new Act. In particular, the SEC felt that the contracts were susceptible to manipulation and did not represent a "substantial segment" of the market. This and other incidents led to a second accord between the two commissions, with the publication of guidelines for designation as a contract market for futures contracts (or options on such contracts) involving a nondiversified industry index of domestic equity securities.

Through the time of the October 1987 crash, the controversy between the SEC and the CFTC had largely been a legalistic one occasioned by the one-sidedness of the exclusive (rather than concurrent) jurisdiction formula in the Commodities Futures Trading Commission Act. This formula had its major impact on the question of which agency would regulate new financial instruments.

The October 1987 crash raised far more profound questions about the extent to which trading in financial futures could have an impact on stock market trading. The October 1987 break, in particular, revealed problems caused by the popularity of portfolio insurance. Because these programs were typically meant to insure against market declines by selling futures, they tended to add to sales pressure in the stock market when the price of the stock index futures was being driven down. There was an irony here. Futures stock indexes were preferred then generally to stock transactions because of the greater liquidity of the futures markets. But sales pressure in the stock index futures market rapidly led to dramatic price declines in the futures markets, which in turn led to sales pressure in the stock market because of index arbitrage and direct portfolio insurance *stock* sales. The Brady report found, "By reasonable estimates, the formulas used by portfolio insurers dictated the sale of $20 to $30 billion of equities over this short time span [October 19–23, 1987]. Under such pressures, prices must fall dramatically. Transaction systems, such as DOT, or market stabilizing mechanisms, such as the NYSE specialists, are bound to be crushed by such selling pressure, however they are designed or capitalized." Overall, the SEC staff reported that at least 39 million shares of institutional selling on October 19 was attributable to portfolio insurance strategies (some of which call for the reduction of stock positions through stock sales either in lieu of futures transactions or as a supplement to futures transactions, when this alternative appeared more efficient).

From the SEC's point of view, coordinating a response to the October 1987 market crash with the CFTC offered significant problems. This was not just an idiosyncratic belief. Even the CFTC complained in its final report on the October 1987 market break that "interindustry coordination could have been better" on October 19 and 20 in deciding whether to halt trading in individual stocks and whether to close the entire NYSE at midday on October 20 as rumored. These coordination problems were aggravated by what were then stark differences in the regulatory approaches at the two agencies. The CFTC was then perceived as taking more of a "free-market" approach whereas the SEC was seen as more "regulatory" in nature. As a matter of agency culture, the CFTC was more prepared to believe that the relevant self-regulatory organizations (the commodities and stock markets) could solve problems without government oversight.

On the other hand, there was also a respectable case for nonconsolidation, which turned on the advantages of rivalry between two agencies with similar, but largely nonduplicative, jurisdictions. It may well be that the inevitable differences in policy or practice at the two agencies stimulate a healthy process of cross-pollination—ideas employed in the securities field should be considered in the futures industry, and vice versa. It may be the case that if the SEC were the sole regulator, it might develop a tendency to be less sensitive to developments in futures trading than if the CFTC retained its jurisdiction. The SEC has a proud and distinguished history, which might make it more likely to assume that what it currently requires in the securities field is "correct," and what has been developed elsewhere is inferior.

This point should not be overstated. SEC approval of standardized options trading in the early 1970s displayed a sophisticated flair for assimilating ideas both from the securities and the futures fields. It is also possible that the CFTC, as the younger and smaller agency, might act more defensively and be less willing to consider innovations in the securities field than the SEC would be to consider innovations in futures trading. Nonetheless, just as potential competition may affect markets, there is the possibility that agency rivalry may improve regulation.

At any rate, the rationale for not transferring jurisdiction in 1978— that all futures trading should be administered by a single agency—is unpersuasive by itself. Just as the CFTC has regulatory jurisdiction over futures contracts traded on the floors of the CBOE (an options exchange) or the NYSE (a stock exchange), the SEC could have regulatory jurisdiction over a stock index futures contract on the floor of the CME. The SEC recognized in its July 1988 proposal that if stock index futures jurisdiction was transferred, this would impose certain costs both on the futures exchanges (required to register both with the SEC and the CFTC) and on the futures traders. This is a minor consideration that should be weighed in the balance against consolidation. But it is remediable through transfer legislation or SEC regulation that could seek to minimize the additional burden on futures exchanges and traders.

Against this backdrop in July 1988, the SEC, by a three-to-two vote, proposed amendment of the federal securities laws and the Commodity Exchange Act to transfer to the SEC the CFTC's jurisdiction over stock index futures and options on stock index futures.

Given separate congressional oversight committees of the SEC and CFTC, any reasoned review of the SEC's proposal was unlikely. The most likely way to have a mature consideration of the advantages and disadvantages of consolidation would have been to create a single committee in each house of Congress with oversight responsibility over all stocks, stock options, and stock futures (or, perhaps all futures). Unless and until this occurred, any consideration was likely to be influenced as much by the protective instincts of the oversight committees as by the protective instincts of the agencies themselves.

SEC Chairman David Ruder appeared to concede that SEC absorption of the CFTC's jurisdiction over financial futures was not likely to occur in October 1988 when he stated:

> Although I believe that the best arrangement for regulating the linked market between securities, options, and derivative index futures is to have the Securities and Exchange Commission serve as a single regulator, I foresee instead a growing willingness by the SEC and the CFTC to act cooperatively in improving an increasingly connected securities and futures market.

Ruder's successor as Chairman, Richard Breeden, revived the SEC's effort to assume jurisdiction over financial futures. In 1990 the Bush Administration formally proposed legislation to give the SEC jurisdiction over "any and all stock index products." With the CFTC and oversight committees in Congress adamantly opposed, this proposal ultimately failed in its original and various compromise forms.

CONCLUSION

Ultimately, the resolution of the boundaries of federal financial regulation involves a complex interplay of contextual and political factors. What is clear is that no single dynamic alone should be decisive in all applications.

While political enthusiasm, at the moment, is at an apogee for revolutionizing the structure of financial regulation, if history is any guide, this enthusiasm may wane as legislators begin to wrestle with the complexities of the relevant regulatory problems.

20

THE EMERGING PARALLEL BANKING SYSTEM

Jane D'Arista, *Boston University School of Law, the Economic Policy Institute*
Tom Schlesinger, *Southern Finance Project*

Mutual funds' rapid growth rates and expanded role in financial intermediation have contributed to dramatic changes U.S. financial markets. Among other things, the mutual fund boom gave rise to an unregulated parallel banking system that has captured growing market shares at the expense of regulated depository institutions.

Unprecedented mutual fund growth and the parallel banking system's emergence symbolize a fundamental reshaping of the U.S. financial services industry. This restructuring process challenges many of the assumptions undergirding the current framework for financial regulation and supervision. Financial restructuring also affects the adequacy and cost of existing protections for financial industry consumers. And it raises fundamental questions about the financial system's responsiveness to monetary policy and the needs of the real economy.

THE GROWTH OF MUTUAL FUNDS

Over the past two decades, American savings have been institutionalized at an extraordinary pace, diminishing the role of banks as a repository for savings. Between 1978 and 1995, savings in the form of insured pension reserves, private pension plans, and state and local government retirement funds grew eightfold to $5.04 trillion while mutual fund assets multiplied 42 times over to $2.7 trillion. During this period, the share of total U.S. financial sector assets held by mutual funds and pension funds rose from 20 percent to 42 percent while banks' and thrifts' share fell from 57 percent to 32 percent.[1]

In large measure this transformation testifies to the success of public policy initiatives designed to increase the flow of private savings into retirement accounts. An assortment of provisions in the tax code and the Employee Retirement and Income Security Act (ERISA) have explicitly supported the steady expansion of pension assets. And in recent years, the combination of government incentives and retirement fund growth has helped fuel a mutual fund boom. Between 1984 and 1994, pension fund holdings more than doubled as a percentage of mutual fund assets, driven by the surge in defined contribution pension plans. During this period, mutual funds nearly tripled as a portion of total Individual Retirement Account (IRA) assets. By the end of 1994, mutual funds held one-third of the $917 billion in IRA assets. In the aggregate, retirement assets (IRAs, Keogh plans, and pension funds exclusive of variable annuities) accounted for nearly one-quarter of mutual fund assets at year-end 1994.[2]

Retirement savers' move to mutual funds reflects the long-term nature of their investment objectives as well as a broadening appetite for higher-yield instruments. While the inflationary experience of the 1970s stoked this appetite, it also instilled a countervailing aversion to longer-term financial assets. The historically high real interest rates and stagnant earned incomes of the 1980s and 1990s intensified demand for high-return, short-term assets. As a result, banks lost their competitive advantage in attracting short-term savings and former depositors poured cash into money market mutual funds (MMMFs). The number of shareholder accounts in MMMFs almost doubled in the decade ending in 1994 (from 13.8 million to 25.3 million accounts) and the number of funds rose from 421 to 963 over the same period.[3]

As more and more savings flowed into pension plans and mutual funds, the primacy of depository institutions as portfolio lenders necessarily declined. Spurred by stricter capital standards, heightened competition for funding, the lure of fee income, and growing capital market demand for securitized credits, depository institutions steadily expanded the volume of loans they originated and sold in relation to the volume they held in portfolio to maturity. At the same time, banks' role as the primary providers of short- and medium-term business credit fell precipitously. In 1950, banks accounted for 91 percent of short-term credit market debt owed by nonfinancial corporate business. By 1995, that share had fallen to 47 percent as an emergent parallel banking system skillfully exploited cost and regulatory advantages to expand its presence in U.S. loan markets.[4]

THE EMERGENCE OF A PARALLEL BANKING SYSTEM

Banks' declining role in short-term business lending mirrors the growth of the unregulated commercial paper market. Commercial paper issues are noncollateralized corporate IOUs that are not defined as a security and are issued only in large denominations for purchase by institutional investors. Thus, the disclosure provisions of the Securities Act of 1933 do not apply to the opaque market in which commercial paper is bought and sold. Indeed, like a growing number of nonpublic financial markets, the commercial paper market offers no surveillance of trading practices and no systematic, routinely accessible information on prices or the volume of issuance and trading. While it provides an important source of unintermediated short-term credit for all large nonfinancial corporations with good credit ratings, the commercial paper market primarily fills the funding needs of finance companies. They account for over half of total outstanding issues of commercial paper, using the market to fund their own growing share of business lending.[5]

The introduction of MMMFs in the 1970s greatly increased demand for commercial paper and lowered its cost. MMMFs provided a cheaper and more plentiful source of funding for finance companies, enabling them to reduce, then eliminate, their reliance on bank loans to fund their operations. Linked by the commercial paper market, MMMFs and finance companies became two symbiotic halves of an evolving entity that moved from the fringes of the financial industry to a position that paralleled the banking system. Each half of this new entity deals with the public directly through only one side of the combined balance sheet.

MMMFs compete with banks for funds and, like banks, issue their liabilities directly to households, businesses, and other financial and nonfinancial institutions. Unlike banks, MMMFs do not lend directly to households, businesses, and other public and private institutions.

Instead, they invest in short-term, tradable instruments such as commercial paper, bank certificates of deposit, and government obligations.

Conversely, finance companies do not compete with banks or MMMFs in attracting funds from the public. Larger finance companies raise over half their funds in the commercial paper market and the rest in short- and medium-term bond markets. Bank credit accounted for only 3 percent of the aggregate liabilities of finance companies in 1995, and only the smallest firms continue to rely on bank borrowing as their primary source for funding.[6]

Measured by aggregate assets and liabilities, the three components of the parallel banking system remain considerably smaller than depository institutions. For example, in 1995, commercial banking assets totaled $4.5 trillion compared with $745 billion in assets for MMMFs, $824 billion in assets for finance companies, and $678 billion of outstanding commercial paper. Nevertheless, the parallel banking system has grown at an exceptional pace that far surpasses the expansion in commercial bank assets. Between 1980 and 1995, MMMF and finance company assets increased by 876 percent and 302 percent, respectively, while outstanding commercial paper issues rose by 457 percent. Moreover, the assets of the largest finance companies—General Motors Acceptance Corporation, General Electric Capital Corporation, and Ford Motor Company's combined finance operations—placed these companies on a par with the largest U.S. depository institutions prior to the wave of big-bank mergers in 1995.[7]

Business credit markets provide a more telling indication of the parallel banking system's success in competing with commercial banks. At year-end 1995, finance companies' total assets equaled less than one-fifth of commercial banks' assets. However, their outstanding business loans amounted to more than half of outstanding business loans held by banks.[8]

REGULATORY INEQUALITIES BETWEEN THE TWO SYSTEMS

The expansion of the parallel banking system is rooted in regulatory inequalities. In competing with banks for funds, MMMFs enjoy a stark advantage in their freedom from reserve requirements. Banks hold a monopoly on interest-free, third-party transferable demand deposits and can attract substantial amounts of low-cost funding. However, reserve requirements "sterilize" $10 of every $100 of demand deposits so that only $90 can be invested in interest earning assets. Since MMMFs invest all their funds in interest-earning assets, they earn a higher return on total assets than do banks and can offer savers a higher yield on the liabilities they issue.

MMMFs benefit from a host of additional cost advantages that helped them grow at the expense of banks. Because mutual fund customers receive no direct insurance protection, MMMFs pay no deposit insurance premiums. Since they do not make individual loans, money funds pay less than banks to develop information about the assets in which they invest. And, unlike banks, MMMFs neither maintain branch offices and automated teller machines nor provide low-fee services to less affluent customers.

By expanding a source of lower-cost funds, these MMMF advantages confer a significant benefit on finance companies too. But finance companies also enjoy their own unique cost and competitive advantages. Finance companies make the same kinds of loans—to many of the same customers—as banks. Nevertheless, they are not subject to soundness regulations such as capital or liquidity requirements, limits on loans to single or related borrowers, or limits on loans to parents or affiliates. They are also free of restrictions on affiliations with commercial enterprises and are not bound by community investment standards imposed by the Community Reinvestment Act. The instruments through which they obtain the majority of their funding (commercial paper) are unregulated. As a result, finance companies enjoy major advantages over banks in terms of their cost of funds, pricing of loans, and opportunities for growth and profitability.

While reaping the rewards of low regulatory costs, the parallel banking system also benefits from a panoply of direct and indirect public supports that compound its competitive advantages. Ironically, banks have nurtured the growth of their unregulated rivals by issuing billions of dollars of guarantees to back up finance companies' commercial paper. At year-end 1991, for example, fully 90 percent of the paper issued by the 15 largest finance companies was backed by bank credit lines.[9] While these bank guarantees seemingly substitute for public support, they actually create a pipeline through which commercial paper issuers gain indirect access to lender-of-last-resort protection from the Federal Reserve System. Moreover, a little-noted provision of the 1991 FDIC Improvement Act expanded direct lender-of-last-resort coverage for the entire financial industry by relaxing the

Federal Reserve Act's collateral and institutional eligibility requirements for borrowers seeking emergency liquidity from the Fed's discount window.

In addition to taking a free ride on the public's promise of liquidity,
the parallel banking system ranks as a major beneficiary of tax expenditures, public credit guarantees, and publicly sponsored secondary markets. A few examples suggest the breadth and depth of public supports.
Finance companies and mortgage banks originate more than four-fifths
of all FHA- and VA-insured mortgage loans, then sell the bulk of those
credits on a government-promoted secondary market dominated by Fannie Mae and Freddie Mac. Ever since 1983, a single finance company—
The Money Store—has ranked as the leading user of U.S. Small Business
Administration credit guarantees.

Mutual funds receive a bounty of tax benefits. Due to their size
and tax-favored status, retirement plans—a leading source of new investment in mutual funds—account for the single largest federal tax expen-
diture. According to the congressional Joint Committee on Taxation,
tax expenditures on pension plans, IRAs, and Keogh plans will exceed
$450 billion between fiscal year 1995 and fiscal year 1999. Moreover,
affluent investors have flocked to tax-free money market funds. Between
1980 and 1994, tax-exempt money market funds became the fastest-
growing type of mutual fund as their assets multiplied more than
55 times over. Due to the staggering growth in MMMFs' tax-exempt
assets—as well as the concurrent but more modest rise in municipal bond
fund assets—the federal government will forgo approximately $9.9 bil-
lion in tax revenues from mutual funds and their investors during the
second half of the 1990s.[10]

THE EMERGING PUBLIC POLICY ISSUES

The parallel banking system's success in exploiting regulatory imbalances and public supports highlights the need for a new approach to
financial regulation. Many public policymakers and market participants
agree that restoring rational, fair competition within the financial industry requires reshaping the regulatory framework to focus on functions
and products rather than institutional classifications. Federal Reserve
chairman Alan Greenspan, among others, has pointed to the additional
need for an umbrella supervisor to coordinate any system of function-
based regulation.[11]

In our view, functional regulation and umbrella supervision are necessary but insufficient elements of effective reform. The missing ingredient is comprehensive, even application of regulatory costs and protections. Our proposed Financial Industry Licensing Act—described in detail in other published work—would apply comprehensive safety and soundness requirements to all entities that engage in the core businesses of finance, including finance companies and other firms that currently are not regulated for soundness. The act calls for prudential standards to be administered through a program of functional supervision, renewable chartering, and more systematic self-regulation.[12]

As important as competitive equality is in a market economy, the emergence of a parallel banking system—and the broader financial restructuring it symbolizes—raises a number of other public policy questions that also require attention. The following sections briefly explore three additional issues critical to modernizing public oversight and support of the financial system.

PROBLEMS IN IMPLEMENTING MONETARY POLICY

During the past two decades, an assortment of deregulatory initiatives has helped deplete the inventory of tools that central banks once used to implement monetary policy. The casualty list includes limits on interest rates, restrictions on permissible types of lending, and quantitative limits on the volume of new loans. Perhaps most importantly, the Federal Reserve acquiesced to pressure to reduce or selectively eliminate reserve requirements on depository institutions.

These changes in reserve requirements loosened the ties between the central bank's policy initiatives and the resulting expansion or contraction of aggregate financial system assets that transmit the intended policy objective to the real economy. The Fed's incremental decisions to prune reserve requirements provided a drawn-out, defensive response to the welter of competitive inequalities that spawned extraordinary growth in the Eurocurrency markets, enhanced the position of offshore banks in domestic loan markets, and supported the development of a parallel banking system in the United States.

In 1990, for example, the Fed attempted to redress reserve requirement imbalances that had helped foreign banks boost their position in U.S. loan markets. Twelve years earlier, the Fed had imposed reserve requirements on loans made to U.S. customers by U.S. banks' foreign offices. But it failed to persuade other countries of the need to extend reserve requirements to all offshore operations. Foreign institutions boosted their U.S. lending from non-U.S. offices. As a result, their share of total bank loans to U.S. commercial and industrial borrowers jumped from 18 percent in 1983 to 45 percent at year-end 1991.[13]

When the damage became apparent, the Fed removed both the reserve requirement on U.S. banks' Eurocurrency loans to domestic borrowers and reserve requirements on all nonpersonal time deposits, thereby eliminating one of the more important cost advantages benefiting the Eurodollar market. Subsequently (in April 1992), the Fed reduced reserve requirements on transaction accounts from 12 to 10 percent of deposits, an action that only fractionally shaved the cost advantage for mutual funds and other nonbanks competing with depository institutions.

These initiatives contrasted sharply with an earlier central bank effort to enhance monetary control. In 1980, the Fed implemented a credit restraint program in response to a presidential directive issued under the Credit Control Act. The program extended beyond the banking system, the usual boundary of the Fed's scope of action, to include a special deposit requirement of 15 percent on all extensions of consumer credit through credit cards, check-credit overdraft plans, unsecured personal loans, and many types of secured loans (excluding those issued to finance purchase of the collateral). This deposit requirement applied to all consumer lenders, not just depository institutions, and extended to money market mutual funds as well. In addition, the Federal Reserve brought all finance companies, as well as depository institutions, under a voluntary credit restraint agreement designed to limit the growth of credit to industrial and commercial borrowers.[14]

The Federal Reserve's 1980 program briefly illuminated the role of the unregulated parallel banking system. But no further action was taken after the credit restraint program ended. The implications of a growing parallel system were ignored. Meanwhile, the Fed's reductions in bank reserve requirements began to reshape the channel through which open market operations affect credit market conditions.

Long a primary tool of monetary management in the United States, open market operations increasingly have replaced alternative policy instruments (notably a routine use of the discount window to provide liquidity) in other industrial countries.[15] Indeed, many proponents of deregulation advocate eliminating reserve requirements altogether on the grounds that open market operations provide a sufficient policy mechanism. However, this argument ignores the primary purpose of open market operations, which is to change the supply of bank reserves and thus change the price and volume of bank lending.[16]

In the past, open market operations constituted a highly effective monetary policy tool because a binding link existed between the changes they produced in the Federal Reserve's balance sheet and changes in money supply and bank lending. By altering the volume of government obligations on its books, the Fed could alter the volume of bank reserves, thereby directly affecting the supply of money and the availability of credit. However, that link weakened with the diminution of banks' traditional role as the primary portfolio lenders in U.S. credit markets. As a result, central bank influence over the volume of total credit has eroded. Simultaneously, the widespread use of credit cards and checks written on mutual fund accounts has undermined the Fed's most important function: controlling the money supply.

Although they target the banking sector, open market operations necessarily affect a broader spectrum of institutions and markets through their impact on interest rates—a second channel of influence that has grown increasingly dominant with the decline in banks' lending function and the increase in nonbank financial firms' market share. This channel relies on Federal Reserve purchases and sales of Treasury bills to change the amount of T-bills available for private investment and, thus, to change their price.

When the Fed increases or reduces its holdings of T-bills, it produces a mirror-image change in the holdings of these assets by both bank and nonbank financial sectors. Raising or lowering private financial institutions' holdings of T-bills reduces or increases their demand for tradable, private money market instruments that are close substitutes for government obligations and, thus, changes the price of these assets as well. Changes in the demand for these substitutes—and in their price—influence borrowers' willingness to issue new instruments.

This second channel of influence preserves the ability of open market operations to affect the prices of financial assets. However, this channel is limited. By influencing asset prices it can only shape the *demand* for credit. By contrast, central bank control over the volume of bank reserves—the primary channel of open market operations—directly affects the *supply* of money and credit.

As the share of total credit supply directly amenable to central bank influence shrinks—and as the Fed increasingly relies on open market operations to influence credit demand indirectly by adjusting short-term interest rates—transmission of monetary policy initiatives sputters. With its influence over the supply of money and credit weakened, the central bank must produce larger shifts in the price (or interest rate) of T-bills to alter credit demand. In other words, the Fed must hammer asset markets with larger, more abrupt interest rate changes to achieve its policy goals. As a result, open market operations have become a source of instability as well as a weaker policy tool. The consequences of this destabilizing dynamic include growing volatility in the prices of financial assets, and mounting household debt burdens.[17]

Reviving the role of reserve requirements is essential to restoring monetary policy's ability to combat these signs of economic and financial instability. But, as the Eurodollar phenomenon made clear, monetary authorities cannot effectively influence the supply of money and credit if one sector that offers a given product or service is subject to restrictions while another sector, offering the same product or service, is not. The market inevitably shifts to the unregulated provider as the pricing advantage emerges. To regain its ebbing effectiveness, the Federal Reserve will have to revive its 1980s campaign to obtain agreements among other central banks to extend reserve requirements or comparable monetary policy tools to the Euromarkets. It will have to take a series of parallel steps in the domestic market as well.

Ideally, reserve requirements should be reinstated on banks' time deposits and on all short-term liabilities comparable to time deposits issued by nonbanks. Specifically, reserve requirements should cover all the liabilities of money market mutual funds, the commercial paper and other short-term borrowing of finance companies, and that portion of the liabilities of equity and bond mutual funds that are withdrawn by check or by other means within a period of less than a year. If the Federal Reserve continues to move in the opposite direction and acquiesce to pressure for further deregulation, continued financial instability and unrestrained credit growth may only lend support to those who argue that the monetary authority itself be eliminated to permit the free play of market forces.

SUSTAINABLE SAFETY NETS

The shift of aggregate savings toward mutual funds, defined contribution pension plans, and variable annuities has sharply increased households' exposure to portfolio, market, and interest rate risk. This shift also has contributed to growing financial market volatility.

According to a 1993 study by Birinyi Associates, mutual funds have become the leading source of intraday volatility in equity markets. Fixated on daily performance, mutual fund managers turn over equities at higher rates than do pension fund managers whose performance is evaluated on a quarterly basis.[18] This hyperactivity mirrors the flighty behavior of mutual fund investors themselves. Pointing to a steady, three-decade-long rise in mutual fund redemption rates, Vanguard Group chairman John Bogle terms the image of patient mutual fund owners a "myth."[19]

Rising redemption rates and growing market volatility have fueled concern about potential runs on mutual funds. Liquidations of equity funds in response to rising interest rates or other market events could "set in motion a self-reinforcing downward spiral in equity prices as falling share prices encourage yet more liquidations of funds."[20] Expanding retirement plan investments in mutual funds may moderate the possibility of runs since automatic payroll deductions and comparatively long time horizons make retirement investors less likely to bolt in the face of short-term market disruptions. However, the relatively "sticky" money invested by retirement plans and annuities still accounts for less than one-third of mutual fund assets. Meanwhile, unwary new money is still cascading into mutual funds.

In crafting tax, monetary, regulatory, and retirement income policies that encouraged the growth in mutual funds and defined contribution plans, government officials implicitly assumed a growing sophistication on the part of investors. Yet many signs point in the opposite direction. A survey by the Securities and Exchange Commission found that two-thirds of all investors in bank-managed mutual fund shares believed their funds were federally insured. Released in November 1993, the survey found that nearly half the mutual fund investors who purchased shares through brokers also thought their funds were federally guaranteed.[21]

Two years later, federal regulators announced that banks were still doing a poor job of disclosing the uninsured status of nondeposit investment products, despite the introduction of new disclosure guidelines. After the Dow Jones industrial average dropped more than 300 points in the spring of 1994, Investors Arbitration Services Inc. logged 1,600 inquiries in a single week—eight times the normal volume of calls—

from mutual fund investors asking how to recover losses from their banks. "Unsophisticated, first-time investors who bought mutual funds through their banks are the biggest single category of small investors now contacting IAS," the company asserted.[22]

In fact, average Americans—even financially literate ones—have good reason to be bewildered by the public safety net for savings and investment products. That net includes the deposit insurance funds for banks and thrifts, state guaranty associations for insurers, the Securities Investor Protection Corporation for securities firms, and the Pension Benefit Guaranty Corporation for defined benefit pension plans. But these various public guaranty programs provide different (and, in some cases, uncertain) degrees of protection to customers while extending only partial or indirect coverage to some sectors. In some instances— notably unallocated annuities such as guaranteed investment contracts (GICs)—investors holding identical contracts may receive radically different levels of guaranty coverage. [23]

GICs account for a large portion of defined contribution pension plan assets and investment managers exercise enormous influence over those holdings in their role as evaluators, purchasers, and poolers of GICs. The 1991 collapse of Mutual Benefit Life Insurance Company (MBL)— the largest insurance insolvency in U.S. history—spotlighted the issue of GIC guaranty coverage. At the time it failed, Mutual Benefit had outstanding at least $4 billion in GICs. Investment firms managing those contracts played a prominent role in MBL customers' successful efforts to negotiate maximum recoveries from state insurance regulators and guaranty funds.

In the years following MBL's collapse, several states initiated, clarified, or expanded guaranty fund coverage of GICs and other unallocated annuities. As a result, instruments originally designed for sale to sophisticated institutional investors now place an increasing burden on the taxpayers who bankroll guaranty funds in most states.[24] Twenty-three states now promise limited guaranty coverage for unallocated annuities ranging up to $7.5 million. Between 1991 and 1993, guaranty fund payments for unallocated annuities *alone* eclipsed the sum of all guaranty fund payments for life insurance, health insurance, and annuity contracts in triennial periods during the mid-1980s.

Whenever it validates the "guarantee" in "guaranteed investment contract," the insurance industry's safety net implicitly underpins fees charged by GIC managers as well as a major portion of defined contribution pension plan investments. By fail-proofing elements of their portfolios, the guaranty fund system offers money managers the reputational equivalent of an FDIC window sticker. Conceptually, these indirect benefits even extend to mutual fund families that take their name from prominent investment managment firms.

For example, when the $30 billion Confederation Life Insurance Company failed in August 1994, regulators discovered that virtually all U.S. GIC managers had Confederation contracts in their portfolios. Fidelity Investments, the name synonymous with the U.S. mutual fund industry, led the pack with $400 million of the Canadian company's GICs.[25] When insurance guaranty funds cover those Fidelity-managed GICs, they compound the general confusion a first-time mutual fund investor faces when navigating his or her savings toward a safe harbor. What's insured and what isn't? How can you tell the difference?

At first glance, the growth of institutionalized savings and nonbank lenders—and the concomitant decline in on-balance-sheet banking and insured deposit-taking—appears to have lightened the burden on America's financial safety net. But the growth of public guarantees for GICs suggests a diametrically different trend. So does the growing pipeline to public liquidity that bank guarantees provide nonbank intermediaries. So does FDICIA's formal expansion of lender-of-last-resort coverage to all segments of the financial industry. And so does the protection afforded mutual fund investors by the U.S. government's "creatively ambiguous" use of standby liquidity during Mexico's 1994 peso crisis.

Indeed, all these developments strongly suggest that the nation's financial safety net has not only become more inconsistent but also overburdened. In effect, a host of factors including public policy incentives, stagnant incomes, and a long bull market, have pushed household assets away from instruments covered by a universally understood, carefully standardized savings insurance system and into instruments covered by a perplexing patchwork system that is being improvised as crises erupt and imperil Americans' savings.

This unsustainable condition clearly demands a more even, equitable, and affordable distribution of public guarantees. The answer is to stop insuring institutions altogether. Instead, individual savers should receive guarantees directly—up to a specified amount—on the basis of their Social Security numbers. The guarantee should apply to all funds, so long as they are invested in institutions subject to federal soundness regulation. All transaction balances held in the form of noninterest-bearing demand deposits in federally regulated depository institutions should receive 100 percent coverage.[26] And comprehensive safety and soundness reforms should be instituted to alleviate mounting pressures on the public sector's lender of last resort.

CREDIT FLOWS AND COST OF CAPITAL

In changing the way capital is allocated, the process of financial restruc-turing bears profound implications for different groups of borrowers as well as the real economy's overall health. By exacerbating market volatil-ity—and by weakening the central bank's ameliorative powers—the new financial order burdens all users of capital and credit with what amounts to an instability premium. This premium pushes up the required rate of return on all financial assets, raises the cost of capital for non-financial corporations, and pressures them to pare back investment.[27]

At the same time, market restructuring exposes nonfinancial com-panies to the growing potential for concentration and anticompetitive practices in the financial sector. Indeed some characteristics of the reshaped financial system conjure up memories of the subject matter dissected by the famous Pujo, Armstrong, Pecora, and Patman hearings of eras past. Episodes ranging from the takeover of Kaiser Steel Cor-poration to the merger of Chase Manhattan Bank and Chemical Bank-ing Corporation demonstrate the enormous power mutual fund companies now exercise over the direction and fate of individual companies. In 1995, according to CDA Spectrum Research Services, a single mutual fund company, Fidelity, held more than 8 percent of the equity in more than 250 publicly traded companies.[28]

Fidelity also accounts for an estimated 10 percent of daily trading on the New York Stock Exchange. Moreover, the company's officers have publicly celebrated new institutional linkages that challenge some bedrock precepts of financial law and regulation. "Ten years ago, there was a lot more worry on the part of a bank, a broker or an insurance company as to whether Fidelity was competition," the president of Fidelity Investment Advisor Group told an industry trade group in 1994. "They are now increasingly comfortable with the fact that you can be my competitor, you can be my supplier and you can be my customer."[29]

The American financial system's cornerstone principles of eco-nomic neutrality and robust competition are being tested in equally potent (if more circumspect) fashion by the growth of captive finance companies operated by nonfinancial corporations. These firms—notably the Big Three carmakers' finance companies—exercise considerably more market power than do independent finance companies, banks, securities firms, or insurance companies. As long as regulatory guidelines mandate a standard of economic neutrality for other financial sectors but not them, the captive companies represent a growing potential for anticompetitive practices such as self-dealing or tying. If an an expanding share of credit decisions is channeled through in-house intermediaries aiming to promote parent and affiliate products and services, lending judgments may be distorted at the firm level and, eventually, throughout the broader marketplace.[30]

In some areas of the real economy, financial restructuring poses a more basic problem of access. Regardless of their creditworthiness—and despite their critical contributions to innovation and job creation—new, young, small, and middle-market businesses face chronic barriers to obtaining capital and credit. Leery of higher transaction costs, lenders often shun smaller, less standardized deals in favor of larger, more familiar ones. The absence of liquidity also hampers smaller enterprises' search for long-term debt or equity. Comparable obstacles confront mortgage borrowers in poor, moderate-income, and minority communities.[31]

In many cases, the borrowing needs of these households and businesses can only be answered by a patient, labor-intensive, judgment-centered, and relatively illiquid lending process. Yet the fastest growing outlets for household savings—pension funds and mutual funds—have no direct lending capacity. Indeed, institutional savings generally bypass vast areas of the entrepreneurial economy, save for some targeted and venture capital investments by pension plans and small capitalization mutual funds that finance modest-sized companies with ready access to capital markets. Mutual funds "have grown into the gorilla" of the junk bond market and have amassed King Kong-sized holdings in emerging-market debt and equity issues.[32] But as far as prosaic investments in domestic smaller business is concerned, mutual funds remain smaller than a flea.

A similar story obtains on the other side of the parallel system. Sensitive to the liquidity needs of their funding sources, nonbank lenders seldom originate nonstandard credits, negotiate flexible terms, or structure the unique deals critical to small business development. At the same time, the permissive culture of unregulated lending has proved eminently hospitable to redlining and other abusive practices. An analysis in *The Wall Street Journal* of the nation's 100 most active mortgage lenders identified 50 nonbank financial firms among the 63 institutions that "most assiduously avoided black areas" in 1992. "We have underserved our cities," the chief executive of PNC Mortgage Corporation conceded to the Journal. "I should kick myself in the butt for it."[33] Some finance companies have underserved economically vulnerable borrowers in more aggressive fashion by engaging in loan churning, deceptive advertising, insurance packing, coercive collection tactics, and unfair arbitration procedures.[34]

Nonpredatory portfolio lending to many businesses and households remains a market primarily served by banks. However, as commercial banking diminishes relative to other segments of the financial industry, consolidation is rapidly thinning the ranks of small institutions that have been the most active and most patient small business lenders. At the same time, larger banks have resorted to more nonbanking activities and jettisoned offices that once served as the focal point of asset-origination in hard-pressed communities. As a result, federal and state community reinvestment laws cover a numerically shrinking industry that is cutting back traditional lending and deposit-taking activities. Business and household borrowers who depend on community-based capital markets increasingly find themselves stranded in an ocean of global finance.[35]

The troubling side effects of financial restructuring demand a new, evenly applied system of limits on concentration and prohibitions against conflicts of interest and self-dealing. They also demand wholesale reform of community reinvestment standards. In this vein, we recommend the establishment of a National Reinvestment Fund.[36] Financed with investments by all private nonbank financial institutions—including mutual funds and finance companies—and administered by the 12 Federal Reserve Banks, the fund would undertake a twofold mission: It would help capitalize the growth of community development financial institutions (CDFIs). And it would provide credit enhancements, financial guarantees, and policy coordination for federal loan guarantee programs. Key features of the National Reinvestment Fund would expand the central bank's leverage, enhance its accountability, and renew the Reserve Banks' regional development mission.

By supporting the growth of CDFIs, the fund would boost reinvestment in sectors served poorly by conventional capital markets and enable one of the emerging strengths of the existing financial system—CDFIs' success in local intermediation—to remedy one of its emerging weaknesses—the diminution of patient, labor-intensive direct lending. By rationalizing federal credit programs and paring taxpayers' exposure to them, the fund would strengthen a major component of reinvestment policy.

Like the safety net and supervisory reforms described in this chapter, the National Reinvestment Fund would modernize financial regulation by leveling the playing field upward. This framework for reform should encourage ongoing evolution, innovation, and experimentation throughout the parallel banking system as well as the broader financial economy. It will also minimize the regulatory distortions that have made credit markets less responsive to monetary policy and less capable of promoting sustainable growth.

ENDNOTES

1. Board of Governors of the Federal Reserve System, *Flow of Funds Accounts*, various issues.

2. Investment Company Institute, *Mutual Fund Fact Book 1995*, Washington, DC, 1995. Ellen E. Schultz, "Tidal Wave of Retirement Cash Anchors Mutual Funds," *The Wall Street Journal*, September 27, 1995.

3. Investment Company Institute, *Mutual Fund Fact Book*.

4. Board of Governors of the Federal Reserve System, *Flow of Funds Accounts*;. George G. Kaufman and Larry R. Mote, "Is Banking a Declining Industry? A Historical Perspective," *Economic Perspectives*, Federal Reserve Bank of Chicago, May/June 1994.

5. Board of Governors of the Federal Reserve System, *Flow of Funds Accounts*.

6. Ibid.

7. Ibid.

8. Ibid. Board of Governors of the Federal Reserve System, *Federal Reserve Bulletin*, March 1996, Table 1.26.

9. Jane D'Arista and Tom Schlesinger, "The Parallel Banking System," Economic Policy Institute, Washington, 1993.

10. Southern Finance Project, "Reinvestment Reform In An Age of Financial Change," Philomont, VA, 1995.

11. Alan Greenspan, Testimony before the Committee on Banking and Financial Services, U.S. House of Representatives, February 28, 1995.

12. Jane D'Arista and Tom Schlesinger, "The Parallel Banking System;" Jane D'Arista and Tom Schlesinger, "Financial Markets: Restructuring and the U.S. Regulatory Framework" in *Reclaiming Prosperity: A Blueprint for Progressive Economic Reform* (Armonk, NY: M.E. Sharpe, 1996).

13. Robert N. McCauley and Rama Seth, "Foreign Bank Credit to U.S. Corporations: The Implications of Offshore Loans," *Quarterly Review*, Federal Reserve Bank of New York, Spring 1992.

14. Martin H. Wolfson, *Financial Crises: Understanding the Postwar U.S. Experience* (Armonk, NY: M.E. Sharpe, 1986).

15. Bank for International Settlements, 62nd Annual Report, Basle, Switzerland, June 1992.

16. For a detailed description of how monetary policy is implemented, see Board of Governors of the Federal Reserve System, *The Federal Reserve System: Purposes and Functions* (Washington, DC 1994).

17. After soaring throughout the 1980s, household debt accumulation tapered off between 1990 and 1992. However, as median real wages

continued to stagnate, aggregate debt-to-income ratios rose to new, record highs in 1994 and 1995. During the first half of 1995, outstanding consumer credit topped $1 trillion for the first time ever. Southern Finance Project, "Another Day Older and Deeper In Debt," Monograph, Philomont, VA, January 1996; Glenn Canner, Arthur B. Kennickell, Charles Luckett, "Household Sector Borrowing and the Burden of Debt," *Federal Reserve Bulletin*, April 1995.

18. Joel Chernoff, "Mutual Funds Biggest Culprit In Volatility of Stocks*,"* *Pensions & Investments*, June 28, 1993.

19. Robert McGough, "Mutual Funds' Growth Spurt Leaves Some Fearful of Slide," *The Wall Street Journal*, May 26, 1993.

20. David Hale, "The Economic Consequences of America's Mutual Fund Boom*,"* *The International Economy*, March/April 1994.

21. Christi Harlan, "Most Holders of Money-Market Funds Have Wrong Ideas On Bank Insurance," *The Wall Street Journal*, November 11, 1993. Similar findings emerged from a January 1994 poll commissioned by state securities regulators and the American Association of Retired Persons. Princeton Survey Research Associates, "Bank Investment Products Survey," conducted for the American Association of Retired Persons and the North American Society of Securities Administrators, January 1994.

22. Market Trends Inc., "Survey of Nondeposit Investment Sales at FDIC-Insured Institutions," May 5, 1996. "Small Investors Ask Help On Fund Losses," *Banking Week*, April 18, 1994; Charles Gasparino, "Who Says Mutual Fund Investors Don't Panic*?"* *The Wall Street Journal*, March 4, 1996; Diana B. Henriques chronicles investors' long-term withdrawal from mutual funds during the 1970s in *Fidelity World: The Secret Life and Public Power of the Mutual Fund Giant* (New York: Scribner, 1995).

23. The description of guaranty fund coverages of unallocated annuities is based upon Southern Finance Project and the Public Policy Institute of the American Association of Retired Persons, "Working Without a Net: Legal, Legislative and Regulatory Developments Affecting Pension Annuity Protection," American Association of Retired Persons, Washington, DC: July 1994.

24. Ibid. According to the National Association of Insurance Commissioners, 41 states permit insurers to recoup all or some of their guaranty fund assessments by taking offsets against their premium taxes. In the remaining nine states, insurers are allowed to fund their assessments by raising premiums on consumers.

25. Telephone interviews with Janet Jason, Hueler Companies, and Victor Gallo, Primco Capital Management, October 1994; Robert McGough,

"Canada Insurer's Collapse Sparks Move To Deal With Affected GICs In the U.S.," *The Wall Street Journal*, August 23, 1994; "Fidelity Holds GICs Issued By Failed Canadian Insurer," *The Wall Street Journal*, August 25, 1994; Brian Cox, "Fidelity Sued Over Confed GIC Investment Advice," *National Underwriter*, November 21, 1994.

26. Jane D'Arista, "Briefing Paper: No More Bank Bailouts: A Proposal for Deposit Insurance Reform," Economic Policy Institute, Washington, 1991.

27. Paul Kupiec, "Stock Market Volatility In OECD Countries: Recent Trends, Consequences For the Real Economy and Proposals For Reform," OECD Working Paper, Autumn 1991; Sean Becketti and Gordon Sellon, "Has Financial Market Volatility Increased?" in *Financial Market Volatility and the Economy* Federal Reserve Bank of Kansas City, (Kansas City, MO, 1990); "A View From the Fed," *National Times*, December/January 1995; Willem Thorbecke, "The Distributional Effects of Disinflationary Monetary Policy," Jerome Levy Economics Institute Working Paper, July 1995.

28. Diana B. Henriques, *Fidelity's World: The Secret Life and Public Power of the Mutual Fund Giant*; Jeffrey M. Laderman, "Ask Chase If He's a 'Passive' Investor," *Business Week*, October 23, 1995. Alyssa A. Lappen, "Fidelity Grapples With Giantism," *Institutional Investor*, September 1995.

29. "Market Snapshot," *National Underwriter*, May 30, 1994.

30. Jane D'Arista and Tom Schlesinger,"The Parallel Banking System."

31. Southern Finance Project, "Reinvestment Reform."

32. Laura Jereski, "Risks in Junk Bonds Rise as Mutual Funds Play a Growing Role," *The Wall Street Journal*, October 1, 1993.

33. Ralph T. King, Jr., "Some Mortgage Firms Neglect Black Areas More Than Banks Do," *The Wall Street Journal*, August 9, 1994. Using a larger sample—four years of loan reports from 2000 lenders—and a broader range of performance measures, a study by the National Community Reinvestment Coalition turned up results similar to the Journal's analysis. Of the 52 firms identified by the NCRC study as neglecting poor, moderate-income, and minority borrowers between 1990 and 1993, 34 were nonbank lenders. National Community Reinvestment Coalition, "America's Worst Lenders: A Comprehensive Analysis of Mortgage Lending In the Nation's Top 20 Cities," monograph, Washington, January 1995.

34. Southern Finance Project, "Reinvestment Reform."

35. Ibid.

36. Ibid.

CHAPTER

21

FUNCTIONAL REGULATION

Martha L. Cochran, *Arnold & Porter*
David F. Freeman, Jr., *Arnold & Porter*

As we approach the year 2000, financial services companies through-out the world are developing strategies to compete in the markets of the next century. Trillions of consumer and capital formation dollars are at stake.

It, therefore, confounds policy makers in this country that U.S. financial institutions continue to operate under a regulatory structure that derives from laws a half-century or more old, a series of piecemeal actions by regulators that have sought to accommodate an evolving marketplace, and a patchwork of judicial decisions emanating from legal challenges to those actions. Efforts to rationalize the statutory frame-work repeatedly have fallen victim to warfare between competing seg-ments of the financial services industry, turf fights among regulators, and jurisdictional battles among committees of Congress.

For many years, the central issue in the public policy debate has been the "powers" question, specifically, what powers should be autho-rized for banking organizations? The answers provided by the Glass-Steagall Act of 1933 and other laws enacted between 1863 (the National Bank Act) and 1956 (the Bank Holding Company Act) in certain respects are out of date with the financial world of the 1990s. Securities firms, insurance companies, and other financial services companies have expanded their products and services to place them firmly in the business of banking, just as banks now are in the securities and insurance businesses.

For example, securities firms and their affiliates can, and do, offer virtually every product or service offered by banks, and then some. Securities firms or their affiliates can provide transaction accounts, credit cards, travelers checks, bank certificates of deposit, and brokered deposits. They can provide loans of all types, including commercial, consumer, small business, and mortgage loans; they also can arrange and participate in commercial loan syndicates, letters of credit, and bridge financing. Securities firms can offer fiduciary accounts and investment advice, and they can own and operate savings associations, credit card banks, trust companies, and industrial loan companies.

Securities firms also may engage in activities from which banks are excluded. They may engage in securities underwriting and dealing activities without revenue limits, organize and distribute mutual funds, engage in a full range of commodities transactions, and engage in merchant banking. Securities firms that engage in these activities may be part of large financial services companies that include insurance companies and commercial companies as well.

As securities firms and other nonbank financial services firms have engaged in a broader range of banklike activities, bank regulators have acted to preserve the banking franchise by interpreting the words of old statutes to authorize an expanded portfolio of powers for banking organizations. Specifically, banks may affiliate (under a holding company structure) with broker-dealers that derive less than 10 percent of their gross revenues from underwriting and dealing in securities other than U.S. government securities and general obligation municipal securities, and these securities affiliates may underwrite and deal in debt and equity securities. Banks themselves may engage or have affiliates or subsidiaries that engage in private placement activities, dealing in municipal securities, dealing in U.S. government securities, securities underwriting and dealing offshore, offshore insurance agency activities, and offshore and certain other limited insurance activities other than property and casualty underwriting.

Banks or their affiliates or subsidiaries also may serve as an investment adviser; serve as an investment adviser, administrator, custodian, and transfer agent/registrar to mutual funds and act as retail broker in sales of mutual funds (but not as a distributor or principal underwriter to mutual funds); serve as a sponsor, general partner, investment adviser, administrator, and custodian to closed-end investment companies; serve as an investment adviser to variable annuities and act as retail sales agent for fixed and variable annuities; serve as a sponsor, general partner, investment adviser, administrator, and custodian to private investment funds; act as a futures commission merchant, commodity trading adviser, and commodity pool operator; and operate insurance agencies (where permitted by state law and in towns of 5,000 or fewer persons, and in certain other situations).

In many respects, these developments have addressed the "powers" question. As stated above, securities firms and other financial services companies clearly are in the business of banking, and the business of banking now involves securities and other financial services activities. But the debate, obviously, does not end there. These powers are exercised unevenly, incompletely, and under different regulatory schemes; thus, industry complaints about a "level playing field" have been a continuing refrain. Securities firms complain that banks and their securities salespersons can engage in many securities activities without complying with the registration, qualification, and other requirements applicable to nonbank securities firms. Banks complain that securities firms and insurance companies operate under fewer regulatory restraints (Community Reinvestment Act, Truth in Lending, Truth in Savings) than banks, despite the fact that these firms compete directly with the deposit-taking and lending activities of banks and thrifts and have been able to dramatically erode the banking industry's share of commercial and industrial loans.

The happenstance nature of this evolution and convergence of players in the financial services industry—which has been based largely upon whether courts affirm or reject regulators' interpretations of laws adopted many decades ago—has prodded Congress to one attempt after another to reassert its prerogatives. Thus, on numerous occasions since the early 1980s, Congress has attempted to pass legislation to "modernize" the statutes governing financial institutions. In each attempt, it was inevitable that Congress would, for the most part, put forth proposals that largely ratified decisions already made by the marketplace and by regulators. Nonetheless, the importance of *Congress*, and not the regulators, making the decision has been a major impetus for the legislative efforts. (Of course, while it is understandable that Congress would want to act for the purpose of reasserting its prerogatives in these areas, it also has not been lost on members of Congress that considering legislation of great importance to competing industries with vast political fundraising capabilities has certain other benefits.)

As Congress attempted to address these issues in the early 1980s, a regulatory concept, the concept of *functional regulation,* was put forward as a way to address existing and proposed new securities powers for banks. In brief, the theory of functional regulation derives from the old Washington principle that substance is never as important as form, and that it does not matter so much *what* is done as *who* has the jurisdiction to decide it. Like the three most important considerations in real estate (location, location, and location), the Washington political environment also has three most important considerations: jurisdiction, jurisdiction, and jurisdiction. Jurisdictional concerns often are a driving force behind the actions of regulatory agencies and committees of Congress.

FUNCTIONAL REGULATION VERSUS ENTITY REGULATION

Functional regulation, according to Treasury Secretary Robert Rubin, "refers to a regulatory process in which a given financial activity is regulated by the same regulator regardless of who conducts the activity. The purpose is to bring greater order and efficiency to the regulatory process."[1]

The proponents of functional regulation, most prominently the securities industry and the Securities and Exchange Commission (SEC), see its benefits as the centralization of authority in one agency to interpret and apply laws governing a particular function, in order to create a consistent system of regulation without loopholes for some participants or inconsistent interpretation and enforcement of laws. Proponents also view functional regulation as necessary to create a level playing field for fair competition among industry segments and to provide more consistent standards for protection of investors. They believe that only an agency devoted solely to administration of the securities laws can adequately examine for and enforce compliance with those laws, and that subjecting a company to dual supervision of its securities activities by both the SEC and a banking regulator would impose an unnecessary burden on the company and result in potentially inconsistent requirements.

The particular words used to describe the concept of functional regulation appear to have been suggested first by former SEC Chairman John Shad in 1982 testimony in support of a Reagan White House/Regan Treasury proposal to expand the securities powers of banking organizations. The proposal would have permitted banks to conduct a wide range of securities activities in separate subsidiaries, which would be regulated by the SEC as broker-dealers. Chairman Shad testified,

> [T]he functional approach to regulation has many advantages. First, it allocates to each regulatory agency jurisdiction over those economic functions it knows best. The principal concern of the bank regulators is assuring the safety and soundness of the banking system. Their statutory mandate gives priority to the protection of banks and their depositors over protection of investors. Thus their expertise in the protection of investors is not as great as that of the SEC. It is sensible, therefore, to charge the SEC with regulating securities activities and the banking agencies with regulating banking activities.
>
> Allocating regulatory jurisdiction by function also permits the application of a consistent regulatory philosophy. A major thrust of the securities laws is full disclosure. By contrast, bank regulators are concerned about the need for public confidence in banks, and therefore tend more toward confidentially....
>
> A third advantage of a functionally based system of regulation is that it minimizes regulatory conflict, duplication, and overlap. A regulatory system based in some respects on regulation by industry segment and in others on functional regulation creates confusion. Jurisdictional lines based on industry categories inevitably become blurred as the industries evolve and economic conditions change.
>
> Finally, functional regulation has the distinct advantage that it establishes the conditions for equal treatment of competitors.[2]

The SEC has continued to urge the functional regulation approach. In 1995 Congressional hearings, Chairman Arthur Levitt testified:

> Under existing law, banks and securities firms that offer the same range of securities services are regulated differently, based on who they are rather than on what they do. As a result, investors who buy securities from banks receive a different standard of protection than do investors who purchase securities from broker-dealers. The Commission believes that this distinction ill-serves investors; for more than a decade we have urged Congress to adopt a system of functional regulation for all participants in the securities markets in order to close the existing gaps in investor protection.[3]

The champions of "entity regulation," most prominently the federal banking agencies [the Office of the Comptroller of the Currency (OCC), the Board of Governors of the Federal Reserve System (Federal Reserve), the Federal Deposit Insurance Corporation (FDIC) and the Office of Thrift Supervision (OTS)], see the benefits of entity regulation as the establishment of one regulator to examine and regulate all functions conducted by an entity so that (1) all facets of its business are considered as they may impact the safe and sound operation of the whole entity, and (2) the entity is not subjected to multiple federal regulators and examiners, each with a different mission and set of requirements and expectations, which may be in direct conflict with one another. Proponents of entity regulation may note that one of the lessons being drawn from the collapse of Barings is that the best way to assure that material weaknesses in various functions will not be overlooked is to have a single government agency supervise and examine *all* of an entity's activities.

The merits of an entity regulation approach were articulated by Comptroller of the Currency Eugene Ludwig in 1994 Congressional testimony:

> A single regulator is in a better position to evaluate risk across product lines, to assess the adequacy of bank capital and operational systems to support all of the activities of the bank, to take integrated supervisory and enforcement actions that address problems affecting several different product lines, and to identify and deal with emerging supervisory issues. This strength of the institutional approach is particularly appealing in an era when supervisors more and more are finding that many risk factors, market risk, interest rate risk, legal risk, and so on, exist across product lines and are interconnected.
>
> Integrated supervision also avoids imposing unnecessary layers of regulation on financial institutions. Because all product lines potentially affect the bank's condition, bank examiners and SEC staff in a functional system of regulation would have to examine the same records and interrupt the work of the same bank personnel as they went about their supervisory responsibilities. This would create opportunities for conflicting priorities and conflicting instructions from different regulators. There would also be a danger of enterprising bank managers exploiting the fault lines that duplicative supervision creates by playing one supervisor against the other. While cooperation between functional regulators can mitigate these problems somewhat, only making a single agency responsible for integrated supervision of the bank as a whole will avoid these problems altogether.[4]

With legislative proposals to remove barriers to full competition (in the form of antiaffiliation provisions in federal banking statutes and state insurance laws) and to consolidate various industry segments, the debate over functional regulation intensified in the 1990s. The legal debate has been largely about whether to continue certain bank exclusions contained in the federal securities statutes from the definitions of *broker* and *dealer* and *investment adviser*, which exempt banks from registration, examination, and regulation under the SEC rules that govern broker-dealers and investment advisers. As a statutory drafting matter, the exclusions could be eliminated either by amending these definitions in the federal securities statutes to remove or limit the exclusions, or by amending the federal banking statutes to require these activities to be conducted in a registered securities subsidiary or affiliate of the bank.

While the discussion of functional regulation is usually framed in terms of administrative efficiency and creating a level playing field, the jurisdictional (or "turf") considerations of the relevant agencies and committees of Congress have been apparent. The three branches of the financial services industry that currently are regulated at the federal level—banking, securities, and commodity futures—correspond in jurisdiction to three different committees in the House of Representatives and two in the Senate and to the federal banking agencies (OCC, Federal Reserve, FDIC, and OTS), the SEC, and the Commodity Futures Trading Commission (CFTC). Each of these committees and federal regulators is fully aware that a movement toward more functional regulation on the one hand, or entity regulation on the other, affects its jurisdiction and power base, as does any change in the federal and state laws that currently balkanize the financial services industry into different industries for regulatory purposes. The fourth segment of the financial services industry—insurance—is largely unregulated at the federal level, with that function left to the states by the McCarran-Ferguson Act (although federal banking regulators have authorized such activities for banking organizations, and legislation proposed in Congress would attempt to allocate state versus federal responsibilities in this area). Any potential change in the status quo that would award *de facto* jurisdiction over the insurance industry to one regulator or Congressional committee would attract great interest from the others.

The fact is that an industry disadvantaged by a particular proposal usually can find an ally in the regulator whose jurisdiction may be affected. And, in a controversy between regulators over which regulator should have jurisdiction over a particular function or entity, a regulatory agency usually can find a friend in the chairman or other members of the committee that has jurisdiction over the particular agency. This process of taking sides has resulted in legislative stalemate, despite repeated attempts over the past 15 years to pass financial modernization legislation.

FUNCTIONAL REGULATION IN PRACTICE

Functional regulation comes in at least two variations. The more modest form would subject all companies engaging in the same activity to exactly the same rules, but not necessarily to the administrative and enforcement jurisdiction of the same federal agency. The more complete form of functional regulation would subject all companies conducting the same activity to the same rules *and* to the same federal agency, which would examine for compliance with those rules and enforce them.

Regulatory agencies with jurisdiction over financial services institutions have four basic authorities:

1. The authority to establish rules and issue legal interpretations.
2. The authority to license or to approve or disapprove applications by regulated entities.
3. The supervisory authority to require reports from regulated entities and to inspect or examine their operations.
4. The authority to bring enforcement actions against a regulated entity.

Under the more complete formulation of functional regulation, all of these four powers would be in a single functional regulator. Under the more modest form of functional regulation, the functional regulator handles only the first of these four items.

The common view is that securities firms, insurance firms, and commodities futures firms are subject to functional regulation (but not entity regulation), whereas banking firms are subject to entity regulation (but not functional regulation). In fact, however, each of these subgroups of the financial services industry is now subject both to functional regulation and to entity regulation.

REGULATORY JURISDICTION OF FEDERAL BANKING AGENCIES

Virtually all U.S. banking firms of any size are organized with a holding company that owns one or more subsidiary banks. The holding company is permitted to own certain other types of nonbank financial services subsidiaries. Depending on the particular holding company, these may include securities broker-dealers, investment advisers, trust companies, insurance agencies, commodity trading advisers, futures commission merchants, savings and loan associations, industrial loan companies, mortgage and other lenders, and certain other financial services entities. A bank may in turn have its own subsidiaries that conduct many of these same functions. The jurisdiction of the federal banking agencies is largely (but not entirely) determined by the type of entity involved.

Federal Reserve Jurisdiction

The Federal Reserve has jurisdiction (but not exclusive jurisdiction) over bank holding companies and their nonbank subsidiaries under the Bank Holding Company Act (the BHC Act, 12 USC §§ 1841 et seq.). The Federal Reserve shares regulatory and examination authority over nonbank subsidiaries of bank holding companies, such as subsidiary broker-dealers, investment advisers, insurance agencies, commodity trading advisers, and futures commission merchants. Jurisdiction over these entities is shared with the SEC, state securities or insurance commissioners, or the CFTC, as appropriate based upon the type of activity the subsidiary conducts.

Under the BHC Act, the Federal Reserve has:

1. Rulemaking authority over the operations of bank holding companies generally and authority to establish the kinds of activities a bank holding company may conduct, what kinds of nonbank subsidiaries it can acquire, and the way those activities must be conducted by bank holding companies and their nonbank subsidiaries.

2. Authority to approve or disapprove on a case-by-case basis applications or "notices" filed by bank holding companies to acquire new companies or conduct new activities.

3. Authority to examine and require reports from bank holding companies and their nonbank subsidiaries.

4. Authority to bring administrative enforcement actions against bank holding companies and their nonbank subsidiaries.

The Federal Reserve also has authority to approve or disapprove acquisitions of banks by bank holding companies (except acquisitions effected by merging the acquired bank with an existing bank subsidiary of the holding company). The BHC Act does not regulate the activities of banks or give the Federal Reserve ongoing jurisdiction over bank subsidiaries of bank holding companies.

The Federal Reserve also has broad authority, pursuant to the Federal Reserve Act (12 USC §§ 221 et seq.), over state-chartered banks that are members of the Federal Reserve System (and subsidiaries of such banks). The Federal Reserve shares this authority with the state banking commissioner who charters and establishes the powers of state banks. The Federal Reserve shares regulatory and examination authority over nonbank subsidiaries of state member banks (such as subsidiary broker-dealers, investment advisers, insurance agencies, commodity trading advisers, and futures commission merchants) with the SEC, state securities or insurance commissioners, or the CFTC, as appropriate based upon the type of activity the subsidiary conducts.

Pursuant to the Federal Reserve Act, the Federal Reserve has:

1. Rulemaking authority over the operations of state member banks and their subsidiaries.
2. Authority to approve or disapprove on a case-by-case basis various types of applications by state member banks.
3. Authority to examine and require reports from state member banks and their subsidiaries and affiliates.
4. Authority to bring administrative enforcement actions against state member banks and their subsidiaries or affiliated persons for unsafe or unsound operations or violations of any law (not just federal banking laws) or breach of conditions that were imposed in writing in an approval order or other regulatory action.

The Federal Reserve also has a certain degree of functional jurisdiction over entities for which it is not the primary federal regulator. It regulates the offshore activities of national banks and the U.S. activities of foreign banks, and it interprets the Federal Reserve Act and Glass-Steagall Act (which apply to national and state member banks). The Federal Reserve's rules and interpretations of certain provisions (such as Sections 23A and 23B of the Federal Reserve Act regarding affiliate transactions) are applicable to all banks. The Federal Reserve also sets the margin rules for all borrowers and lenders of securities-related credit (including banks, broker-dealers, and other borrowers and lenders).

OCC Jurisdiction

The OCC has entity jurisdiction over national banks and their subsidiaries. The OCC charters national banks and does not share supervisory jurisdiction over national banks with state banking, securities, or insurance regulators. State authorities are not permitted to examine national banks (12 USC § 484). The OCC shares regulatory and examination authority over nonbank subsidiaries of national banks, such as subsidiary broker-dealers, investment advisers, insurance agencies, commodity trading advisers, and commodity pool operators with the SEC, state securities, or insurance commissioners, or the CFTC as appropriate based upon the type of activity the subsidiary conducts.

The powers of national banks and the activities that they may conduct are established by federal law under the National Bank Act (12 USC §§ 21 et seq.). The National Bank Act, in certain cases, looks to local state laws to define those powers, such as branching authority, trust powers, permissible interest rates, and retention of assets owned after conversion of a state bank into a national bank.

The OCC's authority over national banks and their subsidiaries includes:

1. Rulemaking authority over the operations of national banks and their subsidiaries, including interpreting the National Bank Act to establish what kinds of activities a national bank or its subsidiaries may conduct.

2. Authority to approve or disapprove on a case-by-case basis various types of applications by national banks.

3. Authority to examine and require reports from national banks and their subsidiaries and affiliates.

4. Authority to bring administrative enforcement actions against national banks and their subsidiaries or affiliated persons for unsafe or unsound operations or violations of any law (not just federal banking laws) or breach of

conditions that were imposed in writing in an approval order or other regulatory action.

The OCC also has a certain degree of functional jurisdiction over one type of entity for which it is not the primary federal regulator. The OCC regulates common trust funds under authority of the Internal Revenue Code (26 USC § 584). All common trust funds (a type of pooled investment vehicle operated by banks for collective investment of their trust accounts) must comply with OCC regulations in order to obtain favorable tax treatment, and with local trust law, regardless of whether maintained by a state or national bank.

FDIC Jurisdiction

The FDIC has entity jurisdiction over state banks whose deposits it insures, if the banks are not members of the Federal Reserve System (state nonmember banks). The FDIC shares this authority with the state banking regulator who charters and establishes the powers of state banks. The FDIC also has authority to approve or disapprove deposit insurance applications (by any bank), and to interpret the Federal Deposit Insurance Act (FDI Act).

The FDIC shares regulatory and examination authority over nonbank subsidiaries of state nonmember banks, such as subsidiary broker-dealers, investment advisers, insurance agencies, commodity trading advisers, and futures commission merchants, with the SEC, state securities or insurance commissioners, or the CFTC, as appropriate based upon the type of activity the subsidiary conducts.

The FDIC's jurisdiction over insured state nonmember banks includes:

1. Rulemaking authority over the operations of the banks and their subsidiaries, including interpreting the FDI Act to establish what kinds of activities, permitted by state law, may be conducted by a state bank or its subsidiaries.

2. Authority to approve or disapprove on a case-by-case basis various types of applications by state nonmember banks.

3. Authority to examine and require reports from state nonmember banks and their subsidiaries and affiliates.

4. Authority to bring administrative enforcement actions against state nonmember banks and their subsidiaries or affiliated persons for unsafe or unsound operations or violations of any

law (not just federal banking laws) or breach of conditions that were imposed in writing in an approval order or other regulatory action.

The FDIC also has a certain degree of functional jurisdiction over all FDIC-insured institutions. It must approve or disapprove new deposit insurance applications, and its rules and interpretations of certain provisions of the FDI Act, such as the registration of "deposit brokers" and regulation of "brokered deposits" rules, are applicable to banks and nonbank deposit brokers alike.

OTS Jurisdiction

The OTS has authority over state and federal savings and loan associations, their subsidiaries and affiliates. The OTS charters federal savings associations, the powers of which are established by federal law under the Home Owners Loan Act (HOLA), 12 USC §§ 1461 et seq.). OTS approval is required to acquire a savings association, and a holding company that owns a savings association is subject to OTS jurisdiction under Section 10 of HOLA.

The OTS's jurisdiction over savings associations includes:

1. Rulemaking authority over the operations of the savings associations and their subsidiaries, including interpreting the HOLA to establish what kinds of activities may be conducted by a savings association or its subsidiaries.

2. Authority to approve or disapprove on a case-by-case basis various types of applications by savings associations.

3. Authority to examine and require reports from savings associations and their subsidiaries and affiliates.

4. Authority to bring administrative enforcement actions against savings associations and their subsidiaries or affiliated persons for unsafe or unsound operations or violations of any law (not just federal banking laws) or breach of conditions that were imposed in writing in an approval order or other regulatory action.

Notably, a "unitary" savings and loan holding company that owns a single savings association is not subject to federal restrictions on the lines of business in which the nonthrift affiliates may engage, if the savings association subsidiary meets the qualified thrift lender test.

The SEC takes the position that savings associations are not banks for purposes of the federal securities laws and are not within the exclusions from coverage under the federal securities laws governing broker-dealers and investment advisers. Thus, savings associations that wish to engage in brokerage or investment advisory activities do so through an SEC-registered entity.

REGULATORY JURISDICTION OVER SECURITIES ACTIVITIES AND SECURITIES FIRMS

SEC Jurisdiction

The SEC has jurisdiction to administer and enforce the federal securities laws with respect to all persons, including banks. This is functional regulation of a sort.

The SEC also has jurisdiction to require the registration of certain types of entities active in the securities business (securities exchanges and the NASD, broker-dealers, investment advisers, and investment companies), and to examine those entities, adopt special rules governing their operations and bring administrative actions to enforce compliance with the federal securities laws. This SEC jurisdiction is defined for most participants in the securities industry in terms of the function conducted by the company, rather than the type of charter it holds, although the bank exclusions create exemptions from broker-dealer and investment adviser registration and regulation based upon an entity having a bank or trust company charter.

Notably, in contrast to the federal banking agencies, the SEC does not regulate or supervise the holding company or other affiliates of a securities firm (although it does obtain certain information from securities firms concerning affiliates that may pose risks to the broker-dealer), nor does it approve or disapprove acquisitions by securities firms or their holding companies. The SEC's regulation and supervision is confined to the particular entity conducting the particular function (such as being a broker-dealer) that triggers the registration requirement under the federal securities laws.

For certain entities in the securities industry that may be banks (government securities dealers, municipal securities dealers, transfer agents, and clearing agencies), the SEC shares its regulatory and supervisory role with state and federal banking regulators, the Municipal Securities Rulemaking Board (for municipal securities activities), and the Treasury Department (for government securities activities).

The SEC shares regulatory jurisdiction with state securities commissioners over broker-dealers, investment advisers, and investment companies (although Congress is considering limiting state jurisdiction in this area), and it shares jurisdiction with state insurance commissioners over broker-dealers that are registered as insurance agencies and over companies that issue variable insurance products (variable annuities and variable life insurance).

The SEC has delegated most aspects of broker-dealer regulation and supervision to the NASD and the national securities exchanges, although rule makings and enforcement actions are subject to SEC review, and the SEC is involved in the most significant enforcement matters. The SEC itself administers the Investment Company Act of 1940 (the 1940 Act), with the exception of sales literature review, which is conducted by the NASD for the most part. The SEC also directly administers the Investment Advisers Act.

The Bank Exemptions

Much of the call for functional regulation by the SEC is directed at certain definitional exclusions for banks contained in the federal securities statutes. Despite these bank exemptions, and contrary to popular notions, the SEC has regulatory jurisdiction over the securities activities of bank holding companies and their subsidiaries, as discussed below.

Mutual Funds and Other Investment Companies

The area of bank securities activity that has in recent years attracted by far the most public attention—management of mutual funds and other investment companies—is an area subject to comprehensive SEC supervision and regulation, even when conducted by a bank. Curiously, this comprehensive SEC oversight is more an example of entity regulation than functional regulation. The SEC examines and comprehensively regulates mutual funds and other investment companies registered under the 1940 Act. This SEC authority is so pervasive that, with the support of the SEC and the Investment Company

Institute (and with little opposition from the states) Congress currently is considering broad-scale preemption of state regulation of investment companies.

Investment companies advised by banks are subject to the same laws and rules and the same degree of SEC supervision and examination as all other investment companies. Banks are not excluded from the definition of *investment adviser* in the 1940 Act. As a result, the activities of a bank as investment adviser to an investment company are subject to precisely the same 1940 Act requirements as any other investment adviser. The SEC is permitted to and does examine books and records in the custody of banks regarding the operation of the investment companies banks advise.

Two specialized types of pooled investment vehicles operated by banks, common trust funds and collective investment funds, do enjoy exemptions from registration and regulation under the 1940 Act. Common trust funds are pooled investment funds maintained by trust departments of banks for the investment of their fiduciary accounts. They are subject to detailed and stringent regulation under 12 CFR § 9.18 and state trust law. Collective investment funds are pooled investment funds maintained by banks for the investment of pension and employee benefit plan assets. They are subject to detailed and stringent regulation under the Employee Retirement Income Security Act (ERISA) and 12 CFR § 9.18 (when operated by national banks) and state law (when operated by state banks).

Broker and Dealer Activity

Banks (a term defined in the securities laws to include trust companies but not savings associations) are excluded from the definitions of *broker* and *dealer* in the Securities Exchange Act of 1934 (the 1934 Act). The securities laws of most states include a similar provision. As a result, banks may conduct brokerage activities without registration with the SEC as broker-dealers and without becoming members of the NASD. Nonbank subsidiaries and affiliates of banks, however, do not fit within the exclusion and, in order to conduct broker or dealer activities, are required to register with the SEC and the states and become members of the NASD just like any other broker-dealer.

The exclusion from the definitions of *broker* and *dealer* is less significant than may at first appear. Banks are precluded by the Glass-Steagall Act and FDIC regulations from engaging directly in the most significant types of securities dealer activities, such as underwriting and making markets in corporate securities. The major exceptions are dealing in U.S. government securities and general obligation municipal securities. Municipal securities and U.S. government securities dealer activities are not within the scope of the 1934 Act *dealer* definition, but are instead regulated under Sections 15B and 15C of the Securities Exchange Act of 1934. Banks are *not* excluded from the definitions of *municipal securities dealer* or *government securities dealer* and are regulated under the 1934 act, as are other government securities dealers and municipal securities dealers.

Banks are permitted under the Glass-Steagall Act and FDIC regulations to engage directly in securities brokerage activity. Most retail brokerage activity conducted on bank premises, however, is in fact conducted by registered broker-dealers and therefore subject to SEC and NASD regulation and supervision. The General Accounting Office determined in a September 1995 report that 88 percent of the retail brokerage activity conducted in banks is conducted by registered broker-dealers, and that the 12 percent conducted directly by banks consists solely of discount brokerage, in other words, accepting orders from customers to buy or sell a security, without recommendations or advice to the customer. Some banks establish subsidiaries or bank holding company affiliates to conduct brokerage activities; others contract with third-party brokers to set up shop on the bank's premises. Relatively few banks engage in direct retail sales of securities (by the GAO's count, only 287 out of 11,100 U.S. banks).

Those few banks that do engage directly in retail brokerage activities are subject to regulation and supervision by their respective federal banking regulator. The federal banking agencies have adopted confirmation rules patterned upon SEC Rule 10b–10 (which governs confirmations of registered broker-dealers) and the "Interagency Guidelines For Retail Sales Of Nondeposit Investment Products," which is patterned in part upon SEC and NASD rules and interpretations governing retail brokers. Banks are subject to capital requirements that are stricter than those applicable to broker dealers. The federal banking agencies examine the retail brokerage function closely and require banks to comply with the Interagency Guidelines. In addition, certain of the antifraud provisions of the federal securities laws, such as SEC Rule 10b–5, apply to banks in their brokerage of securities, as do prospectus delivery requirements.

Investment Advisers Act

Banks and *bank holding companies* (but not nonbank subsidiaries of banks or bank holding companies) are also excluded from the definition of *investment adviser* in the Investment Advisers Act. The securities laws of almost all of the states include a similar exclusion. As a result, banks may conduct investment advisory activities without registration with the SEC as investment advisers. Given the almost total lack of SEC staff and resources to examine investment advisers adequately, other than those that advise mutual funds,[5] and the very close oversight of bank and trust company investment management activity by the state and federal banking agencies as a part of the trust function, this is one securities function that is far more comprehensively supervised by the federal banking agencies than by the SEC.

Issuance of Securities

Securities issued by "banks" are exempt from registration with the SEC, and are instead registered with the appropriate federal banking agencies. Although the securities are not registered with the SEC, sales of the securities are subject to the antifraud provisions of the federal securities laws and to disclosure rules adopted by the federal banking agencies that incorporate by reference SEC forms, rules and disclosure requirements for registration and public sale of securities.

Most banking organizations of any size, however, have a parent bank holding company. Those that do not have a holding company, more often than not are closely held rather than publicly sold or traded. Securities issued by bank holding companies are not subject to any special exemptions and must be registered with the SEC in precisely the same manner as securities issued by other companies.

JURISDICTION OVER COMMODITIES ACTIVITIES

The CFTC has exclusive jurisdiction over the commodities futures industry. The CFTC has delegated much of the supervision and regulation of the industry to the National Futures Association (NFA), the self-regulatory organization for the futures industry. State laws regarding the futures business are almost entirely preempted, so that the CFTC and NFA alone regulate and examine commodity trading advisers and commodity pool operators, futures commission merchants and introducing brokers, and boards of trade and their contract markets. Commodity trading advisers may also be investment advisers and, hence, must be registered with and regulated by the SEC and the states, in addition to the CFTC. Similarly, futures commission merchants may also be broker dealers and, hence, registered with and regulated by the SEC and the states as well as the CFTC.

The bank exemptions from the commodities laws, for fiduciary activities and "hybrid instruments" for example, are very narrow and do not allow banks to engage in commodities futures business in a significant way without registration with and regulation by the CFTC. Other exemptions from CFTC jurisdiction within which some banks conduct derivatives business—the swaps exclusion, the Treasury amendment exemption, the dealer option and trade option exemptions, and the forward contract exclusion—are not limited to banks; a variety of market participants rely on them without CFTC objection.

JURISDICTION OVER INSURANCE ACTIVITIES

Congress has left regulation of the insurance business largely to the state insurance commissioners pursuant to the McCarran-Ferguson Act (15 USC 1101 et seq.). State insurance statutes generally do not contain any bank exemptions or exclusions. Thus, banks and bank affiliates that conduct insurance agency activities and insurance underwriting activities (the insurance underwriting authority of banks and their affiliates is very narrow under federal law, and generally is limited to a few grandfathered entities, unitary savings and loan holding company affiliates, and credit life underwriting) are, as a matter of state law, required to register as insurance agencies or insurance companies, and are subject to examination and regulation by state insurance commissioners.

Insurance agency activities conducted within a department of a national bank, however, may not be subject to state regulation, pursuant to preemption of state laws under the National Bank Act and 12 USC § 484. Nonetheless, as a matter of actual practice, national banks frequently voluntarily register their insurance agency departments with the state insurance commissioner, or establish a subsidiary insurance agency that is registered with the state insurance commissioner, except where the state refuses to license the bank or bank subsidiary based upon state antiaffiliation laws that purport to prohibit banks from owning or operating insurance agencies.

Because state insurance statutes do not contain bank exemptions or exclusions from coverage, a debate over functional regulation of banks has not occurred in those industries. However, as a result of the U.S. Supreme Court's March 26 decision in *Barnett Bank of Marion County, N.A.* v. *Nelson,*[6] in which the Court held that the National Bank Act preempted a state law prohibiting banks and their affiliates from engaging in insurance agency activities, a similar functional regulation debate may emerge over the insurance agency activities of national banks. Thus, although the powers issue has been resolved, the question of who will regulate bank insurance activities may continue to be debated.

CONCLUSION

The evolution of financial services over the past two decades has brought about a substantial, but incomplete, convergence in the banking and nonbanking financial services industries. As discussed in this chapter, in some respects the powers issue has been resolved: Banks are engaged in a wide variety of securities, insurance, and other financial services activities, just as nonbank financial services organizations are engaged in activities traditionally considered banking (although the question of whether banks may affiliate with nonfinancial commercial and industrial companies remains at issue).

The debate over functional regulation is at root a debate over which federal agencies should be given jurisdiction over the various financial services functions of banking organizations. Functional regulation is already in place to a far larger degree than the debate currently reflects, however, because most banks that conduct securities dealer, retail securities brokerage, or insurance agency activities on any significant scale have chosen to do so through registered subsidiaries or affiliates (or, in the case of municipal securities and government securities dealer activities, through a licensed separately identifiable department), all of which are subject to uniform regulation under the securities, commodities, and insurance laws.

Still, the failure to fully resolve jurisdictional concerns among the federal agencies and Congressional committees in the larger debate over financial modernization has meant a continuation of the artificial structures banking organizations use to fit today's financial services activities within the statutory framework enacted many decades ago. Continued delays in developing a regulatory structure for U.S. financial institutions that enables them to compete in the markets of the year 2000 are inevitable.

As of this writing, legislation to address some of these issues was pending in Congress, but, as might be expected in Washington political deals, the cost of removing some restraints on banking organizations would be the imposition of others. For example, under one proposal, in return for full debt and equity underwriting authority, banking organizations would be required to "push out" into separate securities affiliates certain securities activities. In addition, a post *Barnett* proposal on bank insurance activities would make explicit state authority to regulate the manner in which national banks provide insurance, leaving future OCC rulemaking in doubt.

In addition to placing artificial restraints on the operations of financial services organizations, the current regulatory structure exacts a price by virtue of overlapping regulators, a price that would not necessarily be reduced through the application of greater functional regulation as between the banking and securities activities. Much of this duplication and overlap comes as a result of the inability of banking regulators—who have been strong proponents of entity regulation—to agree to a regulatory structure under which *bank* regulators would cede jurisdiction over certain institutions to *other bank* regulators. Proposals in the 103rd Congress to restructure the jurisdictional authority of the Federal Reserve, OCC, OTS, and FDIC in order to remove duplicative regulation fell victim to the internecine warfare among bank regulators, none of whom was interested in ceding territory. Perhaps it should not have been surprising that the financial modernization proposals in the 104th Congress provoked strong disagreement between the Federal Reserve (which supported increased securities powers by banks under a holding company structure—under the Federal Reserve's jurisdiction) and the Treasury and the OCC (which supported increased securities and other powers for national banks through a separate subsidiary of the bank—under the OCC's jurisdiction).

Thus, the concept of functional regulation, which was put forward in the early 1980s as a way to rationalize the regulation of expanded securities powers by banking organizations, has not led the way to agreement among regulators and Congressional committees on a structure for financial institutions entering the markets of the year 2000. As we approach the next century, financial institutions continue to look to piecemeal actions by regulators and the courts to determine the nature and scope of their activities.

ENDNOTES

1. *H.R. 1062, The Financial Services Competitiveness Act of 1995, Glass-Steagall Reform, and Related Issues (Revised H.R. 18) Part I: Hearings Before the House Committee on Banking and Financial Services,* 104th Cong., 1st Sess. 267 (1995) (statement of Robert E. Rubin, Secretary of the Treasury).

2. *Securities Activities of Depository Institutions: Hearings Before the Subcommittee on Securities of the Senate Committee on Banking, Housing and Urban Affairs,* 97th Cong., 2d Sess. 28 (1982) (statement of John S.R. Shad, Chairman, Securities and Exchange Commission).

3. *The Financial Services Competitiveness Act of 1995: Hearings Before the Subcommittee on Telecommunications and Finance and the Subcommittee on Commerce, Trade and Hazardous Materials of the House Committee on Commerce,* 104th Cong., 1st Sess. 15 (1995) (statement of Author Levitt, Chairman, Securities and Exchange Commission).

4. *Securities Regulatory Equality: Hearings Before the Subcommittee on Telecommunications and Finance of the House Committee on Energy and Commerce,* 104th Cong., 2d Sess. 82 (1994) (statement of Eugene V. Ludwig, Comptroller of the Currency).

5. See S. Rep. No. 177, 103d Cong., 1st Sess. 4 (1993); U.S. General Accounting Office, *Investment Advisors: Current Levels of Oversight Put Investors At Risk* (June 1990).

6. *Barnett Bank of Marion County, N.A.* v. *Nelson,* No. 94–1837 (U.S. Mar. 26, 1996).

22

STRATEGIES FOR REGULATING RISK IN FINANCIAL INTERMEDIARIES

General Approaches and Their Application to Regulation of Investment Companies

Howell E. Jackson, *Harvard Law School*

$\mathbf{A}$s we approach the 21st century, the regulation of financial intermediaries in the United States is in a state of turmoil. The lines between traditional categories of intermediaries have clouded. The Glass-Steagall Act notwithstanding, our banks regularly and aggressively compete in many areas that were once the exclusive preserve of securities firms. The spectacular growth of money market mutual funds has on the other hand pulled on the order of a trillion dollars out of demand deposits and savings accounts. Meanwhile insurance companies compete with securities firms and banks on numerous dimensions. Unending innovation in the development of financial products further blurs traditional categories. Every day, it seems, the financial press reports the introduction of a new derivative instrument designed to satisfy some hitherto unrecognized market need. As the result of these and other similar trends, it is no longer possible to say with confidence where the business of banking ends and the spheres of insurance, securities activities, and futures markets begin.

In the midst of this interindustry confusion, the legal structure of our system of financial regulation is increasingly challenged. Attorneys and their clients in the financial services industry, as well as regulators and courts throughout the country, spend countless hours trying to decipher which of our overlapping systems of legal rules govern the seemingly infinite variety of new financial products that our markets spawn. Does the sale of a variable annuity product fall within the business of banking? What about the underwriting of such a product? Can a variable annuity be a permissible banking product if it is also a security for purposes of the federal securities laws? Might it also be an insurance product subject to regulation by state authorities? Whether or not such an annuity is subject to state insurance regulation, might such a product also be subject to state securities regulation?

The doctrinal puzzle is intricate, and many of the chapters in this book analyze pieces of it with insight and acuity. Fidelity's John Kimpel, for example, considers the legal rules that apply when mutual funds (traditionally governed by Securities and Exchange Commission or SEC regulations) are sold into 401(k) pension accounts (traditionally regulated under the Employee Retirement Income Security Act or ERISA). Similarly, Mark Young's contribution on derivatives regulation explores the line between the regulation of futures markets under the Commodities Exchange Act and the over-the-counter market for swaps and associated products. Joel Seligman explores the peculiar contours of SEC jurisdiction in the area of derivatives and municipal securities. Cliff Kirsch's introductory essay addresses many of the same issues from a cross-industry perspective.

In this chapter, I approach these problems from another direction. Rather than focusing on how particular transactions are or should be treated under current law, I direct my attention at differences in risk-regulation strategies employed in various sectors of the financial services industry. As the analysis explains, risk regulation is a central goal of regulation in every financial sector, but the legal mechanisms used to control risk differ considerably from one area to another. Each sector of the financial services industry—securities markets, investment companies, depository institutions, and insurance firms—has a distinctive regulatory structure with its own approach to risk regulation. Many of the debates discussed in this volume are directly related to these distinctions. Industry participants seek the regulatory regime or product classification that best suits their interests and the needs of their customers. Regulatory authorities often have different views as to how different products or activities should be classified, sometimes to advance legitimate public policies; other times (it seems) primarily to preserve jurisdictional prerogatives.

This chapter is, for the most part, descriptive. I sketch the basic contours of four approaches to risk regulation: disclosure strategies, portfolio-shaping rules, dynamic regulation, and finally fiduciary rules and other more general standards of conduct. As part of this sketch, I explore how each of these strategies is, to some extent, employed in the regulation of investment companies in the United States. Finally, I describe two recent SEC initiatives to refine the regulation of risk in investment companies: one concerns investment company investments in derivatives and the second deals with risk disclosures to investment company investors. I then briefly consider which of the four regulatory strategies the SEC has used to deal with the problems these initiatives address.

The analysis presented in this chapter suggests, but does not pursue, a number of additional lines of inquiry. First, if we accept the claim that the current regulatory arsenal includes a wide array of tools for controling risks, we are necessarily confronted with the subsidiary question of whether our current deployment of these tools constitutes efficient and effective regulatory policy. As my discussion of investment company regulation illustrates, in many areas we employ redundant mechanisms of risk regulation. Perhaps overlapping controls are appropriate, but perhaps they are excessive in some contexts or incomplete in others. Still, as the business of the various sectors of the financial services industry becomes increasingly interwoven, it becomes more and more anomalous that our regulatory structures vary so pronouncedly from sector to sector, particularly as the products within each sector are tending to converge.

Another intriguing question suggested in the analysis concerns the unintended consequences of the current regulatory structure—a structure, in which different sectors of the financial services industry are subjected to different degrees of regulatory control with very different levels of regulatory burden. How much of the interindustry competition described elsewhere in this book is the product of incommensurate regulatory structures? How many recent innovations in financial products were designed not to meet emerging market requirements but to evade existing regulatory burdens? To be more concrete: To what extent does the migration of bank deposits into money market mutual funds over the past decade reflect an effort to avoid the high costs of bank regulation as opposed to a response to more efficient investment company operation?

Finally, and most deeply, might it be possible to reformulate our legal system so that financial products are subject to the same system of risk regulation (and thus the same level of regulatory burden) wherever in the financial services industry those products are offered? The vision of functional (as opposed to institutional) regulation has been the subject of government reports and academic inquiry for many years. (Martha Cochran and David Freeman's chapter provides an excellent overview of some of the problems of implementing functional regulation.) Would it be possible to maintain the integrity of regulation at the institutional level and simultaneously treat particular products equally across sectors? That, in my mind, is the greatest regulatory challenge of the new century. And, it is one that we should be preparing ourselves to address, even if we cannot answer it fully today.

WHY REGULATE RISK IN THE FINANCIAL SERVICES INDUSTRY?

Before considering various strategies for regulating risk in the context of the financial services industry, I begin my discussion with a few preliminary comments on the meaning of risk and the reasons why risk taking is the subject of so much concern in the regulation of financial institutions. But first, a word of justification for my focus on risk: In centering my analysis on risk regulation, I admittedly shortchange several other policy concerns behind certain aspects of financial services regulations. Antitrust considerations, for example, figure prominently in the federal Bank Holding Company Act and certain areas of federal securities laws. A variety of redistributive norms are at work in U.S. pension plan regulation as well as insurance law more generally. And, civil rights concerns undoubtedly motivate the Community Reinvestment Act as well as various fair lending rules that govern a variety of intermediaries. These other policy concerns are, I contend, peripheral and episodic in this field. Across sectors and over time, risk regulation stands as the dominant regulatory policy in this field, and it is this common policy that I address in this chapter.[1]

A Few Preliminary Comments on the Meaning of Risk

In the regulation of financial institutions, risk is a central and, in many respects, problematic concept. The public often understands risk to be a bad thing. And, indeed, if you look the word *risk* up in the dictionary, you find that the first definition given is "the possibility of suffering harm or loss; danger." As an illustration of usage, the American Heritage Dictionary offers: *"the usual risks of the desert: rattlesnakes, the heat, and lack of water."* As this example suggests, risk in common parlance is something we discover from the past misfortunes of others, something that we ourselves are advised to avoid, or at least prepare for, in the future.

For the economist, however, risk has a quite different meaning. Rather than a collective memory of past bad events, the economist's conception of risk entails a prediction about the future and, in particular, the variation in possible outcomes from a particular activity or course of action. Unlike the lay understanding of risk as danger, the economist sees risk has having both an upside and a downside. An economist thus speaks of Bill Gates's investment in Microsoft as having the same amount of *ex ante* risk as that associated with hundreds of other high-tech startups of the past few decades that have long since dissolved into bankruptcy.

Another important preliminary point to be made about the economist's perspective on risk is its presumed relationship to return. Various foundational theorems of finance postulate—and an extensive body of empirical and anecdotal evidence generally confirms—that as average rates of return on various categories of assets increase so does the risk (or variation in return) associated with those assets. Much of modern financial economics proceeds on the now-familiar assumption that there is a trade-off between risk and return. Implicit within this conception of risk is a policy preference that individuals generally should be given the freedom to make high-risk, high-return investments. For an economist, after all, higher levels of average return are associated with more productive and socially useful investments. Although most economists accept that certain individuals may prefer to place some or all of their assets in low-risk investments, many other people will have more tolerance for risk and will want to invest their resources in higher-risk, higher-return projects. On balance, the economist reasons, society will be better off if willing and informed investors are permitted to take on whatever degree of risk they choose.

In some areas of financial regulation—most notably our corporate disclosure rules established in the Securities Act of 1933 and the Securities Exchange Act of 1934—our legal rules generally reflect the economist's bias in favor of investor autonomy. Those laws principally serve to facilitate the disclosure of accurate and complete information about the financial condition and future prospects of public companies. The field of financial-institutions regulation, in contrast, is characterized by elaborate and overlapping systems of substantive rules designed to regulate risk taking by regulated entities. Many mechanisms operating at many levels limit the amount of risk financial institutions can assume and pass on to the general public.

Basic Justifications for Risk Regulation

There are many reasons for our extensive regulation of risk taking by financial institutions. Some concern the kinds of investors that place their funds in financial intermediaries and the limited capacity of these investors to protect themselves when dealing with a financial intermediary.

Protection of Public Investors
A Collective Solution to Transaction Costs that Impede Self-Help   A common explanation of risk-regulation in financial intermediaries proceeds on the assumption that public investors in financial intermediaries (that is, depositors, insurance policyholders, and mutual fund shareholders) want some degree of protection from risk taking in financial intermediaries. At a minimum, investors want to know the degree of risk associated with particular investments before they transfer their resources to an intermediary, and ideally they also want a sense of how those risks compare with the risks associated with other comparable investments. Equally important, once an investment is made, investors want assurances that the risk profile of their intermediary does not change in way that disadvantages the investor. Because their individual investments are small and the business of financial intermediation complex, public investors by themselves lack the expertise and incentives to demand appropriate information about the risk profile of financial intermediaries, to decipher that information, or to monitor subsequent behavior on the part of an intermediary. The government, according to this line of reasoning, has a critical role to play in regulating and supervising the riskiness of financial intermediaries. In this view, much of our regulatory structure can be understood as a collective "best guess" regarding the form and content of advance disclosure of institutional

risk taking that most investors would demand before making an investment, as well as a continuing set of restrictions on institutional risk taking. These restrictions reflect a trade-off between risk and return that most of the investing public would demand from financial intermediaries if the public had the time and expertise to police intermediaries directly.

Absolute Protection of Terms of Investment   A second justification for risk regulation in financial intermediaries proceeds from a desire to offer complete or near-complete safety for members of the public who invest in financial intermediaries. People who make deposits in banks or purchase insurance contracts, it is sometimes said, expect (or should expect) to have those investments honored according to their literal terms. In other words, it is assumed, these investors don't want or expect to accept any degree of variation in return on their investments.[2] Governmental regulation of intermediary operations ensures that the obligations of financial intermediaries are, in fact, honored according to their terms. Government insurance programs, such as those the FDIC operates for depository institutions, also achieve this goal for insured depositors.

Elimination of Externalities from the Failure of Intermediaries
Other justifications for risk regulation of financial intermediaries focus on possible externalities from risk taking in financial intermediaries. In other words, these justifications proceed on the assumption that public investors may willingly and knowingly place their funds in high-risk intermediaries (presumably in return for the expectation of higher returns). Regulatory justifications that arise out of concerns over externalities are not directly concerned with the losses that a failed intermediary might impose on individuals who have invested funds in that intermediary, but on the costs that the intermediary's failure might impose on other members of society.

The Imposition of Social Losses   The fiscal ramifications of financial intermediary failures are one sort of externality. The premise here is that the public fisc pays at least partially for intermediary failures, either through underfunded guarantee programs like the now-defunct Federal Savings and Loan Insurance Fund, or general welfare programs that have to support individuals who lose resources through intermediary mismanagement. To contain these public costs, the argument runs, the government must constrain risk taking in intermediaries.[3]

Systemic Costs of Intermediary Failures   Another form of externality is the systemic cost from financial failure, that is, the cost transmitted from failed institutions onto other participants in the economy. Irrational bank runs are perhaps the most common example of systemic costs, but there are other illustrations, including problems in clearing systems, disruption of capital underwriting, and unexpected contractions of the money supply. Because those injured by systemic costs have no easy way to prevent individual institutions from taking excessive risks and causing uncompensated losses to third parties, the government has another role in regulating financial institutions.

BASIC STRATEGIES FOR REGULATING RISK

For a combination of the foregoing reasons (and to serve various other public goals), the regulation of financial institutions consists of numerous and overlapping strategies designed to constrain the risks associated with financial intermediaries. For purposes of organization, we can divide these approaches to risk regulation into several general categories: disclosure strategies, portfolio-shaping rules, dynamic regulations, and fiduciary rules and other prudential standards of conduct. In this section, I describe each of these strategies briefly, and then discuss the extent to which the strategy is currently employed in the regulation of investment companies in the United States.

Disclosure Strategies

General Description
In many contexts, including some involving financial intermediaries, disclosure requirements are the strategy of choice for dealing with risk. Mandatory warning labels on products serve to inform consumers of the risks associated with various activities and products. Individuals willing to assume the risks are free to engage in activities regulated in this way, while those averse to the risks can protect themselves at the outset by avoiding the activities altogether or to some more limited degree. The great advantage of disclosure-based strategies is that they constitute a minimalist form of government intervention. Consumer knowledge is enhanced, while consumer preferences are left largely undisturbed.

The drawback of disclosure strategies is that they are inappropriate or ineffective in a variety of contexts. For example, where the disclosure involves information of a highly technical or scientific nature, many consumers will find it difficult to assess the disclosure efficiently and accurately. In dealing with medicines, housing codes, or airline safety records, for instance, few policy analysts would recommend risk regulation based entirely on disclosure. For similar reasons, disclosure is seldom considered a complete regulatory strategy for financial institutions.[4] (Indeed, many of the reasons for regulating risk in the context of financial intermediaries are based on the assumption that public investors can't or won't correctly process information about risk.) While disclosure requirements often supplement financial-institutions regulation (e.g., the Truth in Lending Act, the Truth in Savings Act, the Real Estate Procedures Settlement), most regulatory structures rely primarily on other forms of regulation, particularly when risk is the primary source of regulatory concern.

Disclosure under the 1940 Act

Disclosure is one of the principal means through which the Investment Company Act of 1940 or the 1940 Act addresses risk. Built as it was on the disclosure-based regimes of the Securities Act of 1933 and Securities Exchange Act of 1934, the 1940 Act relies on disclosure-based regulation more than any other comparable regulatory structure in the United States. Principal illustrations of the importance of disclosure under the 1940 Act can be found in:

- Section 8, which establishes the basic registration procedures for investment companies, including specific requirements that investment companies disclose investment policies and other matters of fundamental policy.
- Sections 20, 24, and 30, incorporating the basic prospectus, annual report, and proxy statement requirements of the federal securities laws, which the SEC has modified to a considerable degree over the past 55 years to reflect the specialized disclosure needs of investment companies. (See, e.g., Form N–1A, the basic registration form for open-end investment companies.)
- Regulation 482 et seq., which are good examples of the many SEC regulations that amplify the commission's basic disclosure rules to meet the specialized disclosure needs of investors in investment companies. Another recent illustration of this

regulatory approach can be found in the SEC staff's recent
acceptance of an Investment Company Institute proposal for
the development of "Mutual Fund Profiles" as a supplement
of, or posteffective amendment to, more traditional (and more
lengthy) disclosure materials. See the letter from Jack W.
Murphy, SEC Associate Director and Chief Counsel, to Paul
Schott Stevens, ICI General Counsel (July 31, 1995) 1995 SEC
No-Act, *LEXIS* 3102 (Aug. 4, 1995).

In addition to serving the important function of getting critical information to current and potential investors, these rules help investors
make meaningful comparison between the many different kinds of investment companies available to the public.

Given the central importance of disclosure in the regulation of investment companies under the 1940 Act, lawyers in the United States often
assume that there is something in the nature of pooled investments that
necessitates a disclosure-based regime of regulation. This assumption is
not well-founded. Within our own regulatory structure, many other financial products entail pooled investments. With common trust funds at
banks, defined-contribution pension plans, and various participating insurance policies, investing customers share pro rata returns from investment
pool investment returns. In none of these other contexts, however, does
disclosure regulation play as important a role as it does under the 1940
Act. Bank trust funds and defined-contribution pension plans are regulated primarily through fiduciary rules, whereas participating insurance
policies are governed for the most part by portfolio-shaping requirements.[5]

Portfolio-Shaping Rules

General Comments

A second category of risk regulation, which I term portfolio-shaping rules,
generally takes the form of specific requirements or prohibitions. As
opposed to disclosure-based regulations, which depend upon consumers
to absorb and respond rationally to information statements, portfolio-
shaping rules are generally the product of government intervention. A
classic example of a portfolio-shaping rule would be a rule prohibiting
financial institutions from investing in stock or engaging in other activities perceived to have a high degree of risk. Thus, the Glass-Steagall
Act, which prevents U.S. banks from engaging in a wide variety of

securities, is a good illustration of a portfolio-shaping rule. Other provisions of U.S. banking law that erect similar barriers to bank expansion into many kinds of insurance underwriting, as well as commercial activities more generally, have the same effect. Insurance companies face comparable restrictions on their investments.

In most areas of financial regulation, portfolio-shaping rules extend to the liability side of an institution's balance sheet. The form and content of insurance contracts (the principal liability of most insurance companies) are, for example, heavily regulated. The liabilities of depository institutions are also subject to portfolio-shaping rules. The collateralization of deposits is generally prohibited, and many deposits have reserve requirements. For banks as well as insurance companies, however, the most important portfolio-shaping rules are capital requirements, which specify the maximum leverage a depository institution or insurance company can undertake. Capital requirements reduce risk in two ways: They provide a buffer to losses for depositors and insurance policy holders, and they encourage institution owners and managers to monitor more carefully the activities of their institutions.

Other illustrations of portfolio-shaping regulation are diversification and affiliated-party rules. Both set fixed limits on the kinds of investments financial institutions can make. Diversification rules—known in the banking field as *loan-to-one-borrower limits*—govern the amount of investment institutions can make to individual borrowers or groups of affiliated borrowers. Affiliated party rules establish stricter guidelines for transactions between financial intermediaries and certain related parties. Like other forms of static regulation, diversification rules and affiliated-party transactions are prophylactic measures designed to prevent the kinds of investments thought to pose unacceptable degrees of risk.[6]

Though it is well beyond this scope of this chapter to explore in any comprehensive way the reasons why portfolio-shaping rules, as opposed to disclosure requirements, figure so prominently in the regulation of insurance companies and depository institutions, we can hazard a few tentative comments. First, public investments in banks and insurance companies are inherently multifaceted. Unlike stocks and bonds, insurance policies and deposits are not simply investment vehicles; they also involve a combination of investment product and ancillary financial service: payment services on the part of many bank deposits and risk spreading on the part of insurance policies. The multifaceted nature of the insurance and bank liabilities makes disclosure strategies more difficult to implement in these areas.[7] In addition to the inherent complexity of bank and insurance products, several other factors confound the use of disclosure strategies in these fields. Bank and insurance liabilities are often held by a wide range of small public investors, a distribution mechanism that compounds the informational and organizational problems that make it difficult for these investors to fend for themselves. Moreover the assets of these intermediaries, most notably depository institutions, are often illiquid and difficult to value, thus further undermining the effectiveness of disclosure-based regimes. Finally, at least historically, public concern over negative externalities has traditionally been greater for depository institutions and (to a somewhat lesser extent) insurance companies.[8] All of these factors favor a more interventionist governmental posture, reflected in portfolio-shaping rules.

Portfolio-Shaping Rules and the 1940 Act

To a certain degree, the economic function of investment companies limits the role of portfolio-shaping rules in the 1940 Act. Investment companies are, by definition, vehicles for pooling the resources of many individuals. As a general matter, the act does not limit the kinds of investments individuals can make through the investment company structure. Moreover, the function of investment companies is to allow investors to participate in the performance of the pool, not to insulate the investor for risks associated with the pool. Accordingly, the sort of activities restrictions and capital requirements that govern depository institutions and insurance companies does not fit easily in the investment company structure.

Rules Governing Investment Company Assets   What the 1940 Act does require is that the investment policies of the company be clearly explained in various disclosure documents, and then remain the same unless changes have advance approval of a majority of the company's shareholders (see section 13(a) of the 1940 Act). Section 13(a)'s restrictions on changes in investment policies are not, however, the only portfolio-shaping rules under the 1940 Act. Rather, the act includes a surprisingly large number of portfolio-shaping rules that serve to reduce certain kinds of risks. Some deal with assets held by investment companies:

  ◆ To ensure that mutual funds can offer timely redemption, the SEC has established minimum liquidity requirements, which generally limit mutual funds to investing no more than 15 percent of their assets in illiquid investments. See Revisions of Guidelines to Form N–1A, Release No. 33–6927; IC–18612, 1992 SEC *LEXIS* 1083 (Mar. 12, 1992).

- Section 17's rules, similar to those found in other areas of financial regulation, are prophylactic standards designed to prevent the sort of insider abuses that plagued the investment company industry in the 1920s and 1930s. (The 1940 Act also includes a number of related prophylactic standards that go beyond the balance sheets. For example, section 10(a) mandates that at least 40 percent of investment company directors be independent, and section 17(f) sets forth basic requirements for the use of independent custodians.)

- In order to qualify for pass-through taxation treatment under subchapter M of the Internal Revenue Code, U.S. investment companies must also comply with elaborate gross income, diversification, and distribution requirements. For an introduction to these rules, see James E. Hillman, Regulated Investment Companies (Boston: Little, Brown Tax Practice Series, 1995). For all practical purposes, these Internal Revenue Code rules dictate the operational policies of investment companies in the United States and strongly influence the shape of their balance sheets.

- In SEC Rule 2a–7, which governs all money market mutual funds, the SEC regulates with great precision the kinds of investments permissible in this subsector of the industry. In many respects, the money market mutual fund rules are more strict than analogous portfolio-shaping rules in the depository institution and insurance company fields. As a result of this rule, money market mutual funds are almost as safe as federally insured bank deposits.

Rules Governing Investment Company Liabilities   Many of the most important portfolio-shaping rules under the 1940 Act concern the liability side of the balance sheets.

- Section 18 rules on capital structure severely limit the amount of leverage investment companies can undertake; moreover subsection (i) requires that all management companies limit themselves to a single class of voting stock. More exotic capital structures, which can entail additional risks, are prohibited in most circumstances.

* Section 22's mandatory rules governing the redemption of securities fix the terms and the times for mutual funds to redeem shares from their investors. This section includes the complex and influential rules governing calculation of the net asset value of mutual fund shares. In addition, this provision, SEC regulations, and NASD rules establish a general rule of uniform pricing, designed to prevent shareholder losses from dilution and other forms of favoritism.

In sum, while it is accurate to say the 1940 Act relies extensively on disclosure strategies, we should also recognize that the Act includes a wide variety of portfolio-shaping rules. These rules strongly influence the structure and operations of investment companies in the United States.

Dynamic Regulatory Structures

General Comments

Over the past decade, the trend in the financial services sector has been away from static regulatory structures, such as mandatory portfolio-shaping rules, and towards more flexible regimes. Risk-based capital requirements, which vary the amount of capital depository institutions (and increasingly insurance companies) must maintain in order to comply with statutory leverage requirements, are the most prominent example of this trend. The goal of these risk-based capital requirements is to force riskier institutions to maintain larger capital reserves. Another illustration of dynamic regulations would be the capital-sensitive rules that Congress and federal regulatory agencies have adopted for depository institutions since the late 1980s. These rules permit well-capitalized depository institutions to engage in what are perceived to be more risky (or at least more controversial) activities, but they deny the same powers to marginally capitalized or inadequately capitalized institutions. The acceptance of brokered deposits, the conduct of nontraditional activities at state-chartered banks, the authority of banks to expand across state lines, even the amount of insurance premiums paid to the FDIC are all, in one way or another, contingent upon the adequacy of an institution's capital reserves. In a similar vein, innovations in supervisory techniques mandate increased oversight and diminished operational autonomy for institutions with inadequate levels of capital reserves. Comparable risk-based regulatory rules are also being developed in the field of insurance regulation.

Although there is not room here to explore in any detail the pros and cons of these dynamic regulatory structures, a brief discussion of their strengths and weaknesses is possible. The insight underlying all these rules is that the amount of regulatory oversight imposed on individual financial institutions should vary based on the level of risks individual institutions undertake.[9] Thus, well-capitalized institutions are less risky and therefore more capable of bearing the risks associated with nontraditional activities, whereas poorly capitalized institutions are prone to risk-taking and failure, and thus more deserving of regulatory oversight. Contrary to the one-size-fits all approach of traditional portfolio-shaping rules, dynamic regulation is custom built for each regulated entity.

On other side, the most common and important criticism of dynamic regulatory structures is that they all depend on very rough measures of risks. The risk-based capital requirements developed for banks and thrifts in this country divide all assets into four basic risk-weightings designed to reflect the credit risk of particular assets. The classifications are thus very crude—an unsecured line of credit for a start-up business often will receive the same weighting as investment grade commercial paper—and certain kinds of risk (such as interest rate risk) did not even figure into the original risk-based capital calculation. Risk-based calculations also make little effort to reflect the aggregate risks of an institution's portfolio; rather, the rules analyze balance sheets on an asset-by-asset basis, and then aggregate these individual risks to produce a final capital requirement.[10] Another problem with the current risk-based capital rules is that the dynamic structure of the rules constitutes at best an imprecise regulatory response to the risks that the rules are designed to address. So, for example, the FDIC risk-based insurance premiums charge high-risk institutions a few pennies more for every hundred dollars of insured deposits than low-risk institutions pay. There is little basis for this cost differential, nor is there a firm foundation for other regulatory prescriptions built into the new dynamic regulation structures. (For instance, there is little support for the risk-based capital requirement that commercial loans be supported by twice as much capital as residential mortgages.)

Dynamic Regulation and the 1940 Act

In a crude sense, the 1940 Act has always had elements of dynamic regulation. The regulation structure has from the start distinguished between open-end and closed-end companies, diversified and nondiversified companies, and management companies and unit-investment trusts. The 1940 Act sets different regulatory standards for all of these categories, responding in part to the different kinds of risk associated with different structures. Until quite recently, however, the 1940 Act rules governing various subcategories of investment companies (for instance, the important category of open-end management companies, that is, mutual funds) had very few, explicitly dynamic regulations.[11] More recently, however, the SEC has begun to experiment with more dynamic regulatory structures:

- One example of dynamic regulation under the 1940 Act has been the relatively strict set of regulatory rules imposed on money market mutual funds, as opposed to ordinary mutual funds. (See SEC Rule 2a–7 discussed above.) The premise of this distinction is that investors in money market mutual funds expect (and are entitled to enjoy) an almost risk-free investment.

- Other examples of dynamic risk-regulation under the 1940 Act are recent developments in performance reporting. Under rules adopted by the SEC several years ago, disclosures about the historic performance of mutual funds must be organized under several basic categories of fund type, and performance data must be given for individual funds. In essence, these new rules require that historic performance data be presented in a way that makes it easier for investors to compare an individual fund's performance to indexes that represent appropriate market averages. These requirements, which might best be described as a dynamic disclosure model, vary the content of SEC disclosure rules based on the investment (and risk) characteristics of mutual fund portfolios.

- Hybrid funds, with periodic redemption options, are another illustration of dynamic rules. The SEC has, on a limited number of occasions, allowed such funds to deviate from the daily redemption rules that govern most open-end investment companies.

Fiduciary Rules and other General Standards of Conduct

General Comments

A fourth strategy for constraining institutional risk is the imposition of various general standards of conduct to govern the conduct of managers and employees. In the area of banks and thrifts, managers are required to protect the safety and soundness of their institutions. Authorities police this general requirement by reviewing call reports and conducting periodic examinations. In a similar vein, fiduciary norms as well as the NASD's Code of Fair Conduct set general standards for the daily operations of broker-dealers in this country. Violations of these general standards can lead to supervisory action and, in the case of broker-dealers at least, civil litigation. In many contexts, prudential standards are written into regulatory approval procedures. So, for example, in ruling on a change-of-bank control application or a registration form for a new broker-dealer, the relevant regulatory authorities are required to consider such intangible factors as the quality of management or the business prospects of the applicant.

In contrast to static and dynamic regulatory structures, which usually establish express rules of conduct, fiduciary duties and other prudential rules set more open-ended standards designed to reach a wider range of conduct, some of which may not even be imaginable at the time the standard is promulgated. The fuzziness of open-ended standards is both a strength and a weakness. By relying on vague standards of conduct, governmental authority need not be concerned with developing detailed rules that reach every conceivable form of abuse. The vagueness of such standards, however, also creates problems for regulated entities and individuals who lack clear guidance as to the scope of legal requirements or prohibitions. These individuals thus may refrain from activities that regulatory authority never intended to impede. Vague standards are also suspectible to opportunistic enforcement, either by private parties through private suit or by unprincipled government officials through traditional enforcement procedures.

General Standards of Conduct and the 1940 Act

The 1940 Act makes extensive use of generalized standards of conduct and fiduciary rules. For example, the relationship between an investment company and its investment adviser is expressly fiduciary under section 36(b) of the 1940 Act. In addition, a basic element of the Act is the requirement that each investment company have a board with a substantial block of independent directors. The Act and its implementing regulations then impose a unique series of procedural requirements designed to force potentially problematic decisions into the hands of these independent directors, and occasionally back out to the fund shareholders themselves:

- Section 15(a) of the Act requires that an investment company's two most important service contracts—its advisory contract and its underwriting contract—be approved annually by the board of directors, if not the shareholders themselves.

- Section 15(f) of the Act establishes another set of procedural/fiduciary safeguards that come into play whenever an investment adviser attempts to sell or assign its advisory contract. Not only must the new advisory contract be approved by the company's shareholders, but for three years after the assignment at least 75 percent of the directors of the company must be independent, and the assignment itself must not impose an "unfair burden" on the company.

- Rule 12b–1, which establishes rules determining when investment company assets can be used to defray the cost of underwriting fund shares, also relies upon fiduciary oversight by mandating that these arrangements be approved by a majority of independent directors of the company and by setting up procedures to ensure that truly independent directors are appointed.

In all of these contexts, the premise is that fiduciary oversight (policed by the threat of civil suit or supervisory action) offers a more efficient and effective form of regulation in these areas than other alternatives, such as potentially inflexible portfolio-shaping rules and potentially ineffective disclosure strategies.

Prudential standards permeate many other areas of the 1940 Act. One important area is the SEC's broad exemptive and interpretive powers under the 1940 Act. Through provisions such as sections 6(c) and 17(b), the SEC has considerable latitude to grant relief from various requirements of the Act. In most areas, the Commission's exemptive powers are governed by open-ended legal standards, such as "fairness," "reasonableness," and "consistency with the statutory structure." The periodic examinations that investment companies undergo constitute yet another form of prudential oversight.

RECENT SEC INITIATIVES TO REFINE RISK REGULATION FOR INVESTMENT COMPANIES

To conclude this chapter, I offer a few tentative comments about two recent SEC initiatives to refine risk regulation under the 1940 Act. The first initiative is the SEC staff's response to recent losses from fund investments in derivatives and related nontraditional products (see the Memorandum of the SEC Division of Investment Management Concerning Mutual Funds and Derivative Instruments, 1993–1995 Transfer Binder, Mutual Funds Guide [CCH] para. 13,210 [Sept. 26, 1994]). The second initiative is the commission's recent concept release on improving descriptions of risk by mutual funds and other investment companies (see 60 Fed. Reg. 17,172 [Apr. 4, 1995]).

Derivatives in Mutual Fund Portfolios

The most notable aspect of the staff's reaction to recent derivative losses is the multifaceted nature of the response. The staff drew on almost every mechanism of risk regulation to combat problems that derivatives were perceived to present for the investment company industry.

- *Disclosure strategies:* Much of the staff's response focuses on improving the disclosure of risks from derivatives. In its memorandum to Chairman Levitt, the staff recommended more careful attention to fund names, more complete and comprehensible disclosure of derivative risks, and perhaps even new disclosure requirements to deal with risks associated with fund investments in derivatives.

- *Fiduciary standards:* Elsewhere, the staff and Chairman Levitt have emphasized the importance of fiduciary oversight to establish and monitor new management systems designed to control risks peculiar to derivatives. In a similar vein, the commission staff is considering improvements in record-keeping requirements to facilitate better board (and commission) oversight of fund investments in derivatives.

+ *Portfolio-shaping rules:* Finally, the staff has used portfolio-shaping rules to deal with the problems posed by derivatives. This response is clearest in the case of money market mutual funds, where the staff has made several pronouncements clarifying that certain adjustable rate securities are not permissible investments under Rule 2a–7. For other mutual funds, the commission staff has imposed less stringent limits on derivative investments, simply requiring that certain contracts be supported by appropriate "cover" so as not to create excessive economic leverage of the sort that could be considered to violate section 18's leverage limits.

Concept Release on Improving Risk Disclosures

The Division of Investment Management's concept release on improving the disclosure of mutual fund risk is also a revealing exercise in risk regulation. The release also reflects staff dissatisfaction with the 1940 Act's approach to certain kinds of risks:

+ The concept release is partially an outgrowth of the problems that funds have experienced with derivatives in the recent past. One of its goals is to develop more enlightening information about fund risks to supplement current disclosure rules that emphasize historic performance. In that sense, it is an extension of the 1940 Act's traditional reliance on disclosure strategies.

+ The concept release also reveals a weakness in the crude form of dynamic disclosure built into the current disclosure requirements for fund performance. As mentioned above, funds are now grouped into general performance categories. These categories (like the categories built into bank risk-based capital requirements) are quite crude and in certain respects misleading. What the commission is looking for are better and more refined measurements of risk upon which to develop a more useful system of dynamic disclosure. The length and complexity of the release demonstrate how difficult it is to develop better risk classifications—precisely the same problem that has bedeviled bank regulators in developing their new risk-based capital standards.

◆ Third, the measurements of risk that the staff has set out for public comment reflect a number of different conceptions of risk. Most of the measurements represent the economists' *ex ante* perspective of risk. Others, however, are more closely related to the lay understanding of risk as a worst case report of past fund performance. Preliminary industry reactions suggest that consumers may actually prefer risk disclosures that reflect lay (as opposed to technical) definitions of risk.

ENDNOTES

1. A recurring tension in the design of financial-institutions regulation is the extent to which other policies should be advanced at the expense of institutional safety and soundness (that is, risk regulation). For instance, in the banking field, liberalization of geographic constraints tend to increase market concentration (that is, threaten anticompetitive goals), but they are simultaneously thought to improve institutional stability (enhance risk regulation). In the insurance field, rate regulation suppresses price discrimination (thereby distributing wealth from lower-risk to higher-risk policyholders), but is often said to diminish insurance company solidity. Similarly, the Community Reinvestment Act sometimes is intended to enhance access to credit, but it also is criticized for achieving that goal at the expense of depository institution safety and soundness. Although the existence and the extent of these trade-offs are often contested, a common dimension in measuring alternative public policies for regulating financial intermediaries is the extent to which they compromise or complicate the fundamental policy of risk regulation.

2. This justification for risk regulation can be understood as simply an extension of the preceding point: Investors are assumed to want complete protection from failure and therefore government policies seek to effect that desire. However, this explanation usually has a paternalistic overlay, a notion that some financial assets, such as savings accounts, are so important that they should not be exposed to any risks. Elements of the paternalistic justification are, however, closely related to explanations of risk regulation that are based on concerns of the costs that society would assume (through welfare payments or otherwise) if public investors suffer losses on their core savings. These justifications are discussed below under "Elimination of Externalities from the Failure of Intermediaries."

3. A well-functioning public insurance system could theoretically force the internalization of these social costs. In practice, however, such insurance systems are hard to implement. Practical and political considerations limit the ability of public regulators to price insurance properly and to create efficient risk classifications.

4. As stated above, regulation of the securities markets is one area in which disclosure is the dominant regulatory form. This statement, however, concerns the SEC regulation of corporate issuers. Capital market participants, such as registered brokered-dealers, are subject to a variety of regulations that go well beyond pure disclosure. The NASD's suitability rules are one example, as are the SEC's net capital rules for

broker-dealers as well as the SEC's elaborate requirements governing the safekeeping of customer securities and the maintenance of Securities Investor Protection Corporation or SIPC insurance coverage. In addition, market regulation rules promulgated by the SEC and various self-regulatory organizations go well beyond simple disclosure rules.

5. Chapter 10 in this book—John Kimpel's analysis of disclosure documents in 401(k) plans—explores precisely this distinction. As mutual funds become an increasingly common investment vehicle for ERISA-regulated retirement plans, regulatory authorities must determine which disclosure-based SEC rules, ERISA-style standards, or combination of the two should govern these transactions. See also *John Hancock Mutual Life Insurance Co.* v. *Harris Trust & Savings Bank*, 114 S. Ct. 517 (1993) (exploring the division of regulatory authority when pension plan assets are placed with insurance companies).

6. In extreme cases, portfolio-shaping rules can extend beyond the legal boundaries of the financial institutions. In the United States, for example, our Bank Holding Company Act replicates for bank holding companies and affiliates many of the elements of risk regulation imposed on banks themselves (e.g., activities restrictions and capital requirements). For an extended discussion of the regulation of financial holding companies, see Howell E. Jackson, "The Expanding Obligations of Financial Holding Companies," *Harvard Law Review* 107 (1994), p. 507.

7. Indeed, disclosure-based strategies in the fields (for example, the Truth in Savings Act, the Expedited Funds Delivery Act, or rate information in insurance regulation) tend to focus on one aspect of the public's relationship with the intermediary, as opposed to the full-disclosure approach of SEC rules.

8. With the market break of 1987 and more recent concerns about the integrity of the OTC derivatives markets, however, concerns of systemic risk are increasingly being raised in the context of other kinds of financial arrangements. One consequence of these new concerns has been the introduction of stricter portfolio-shaping rules in areas that have traditionally relied on disclosure-based regulations. As discussed below, this trend is readily apparent in the regulation of money market mutual funds. A similar, albeit not yet resolved, discussion is going on in the regulation of OTC derivatives, discussed in Mark Young's chapter on The Quest for Legal Certainty: What Derivatives Are Subject to the Commodity Exchange Act? There the debate is whether OTC derivatives should be brought under the regulatory scrutiny of the Commodity Exchange Act, where mandatory clearing requirements protect investors from the risks of counter-party default. SEC-mandated

shortening of settlements periods is an illustration of mandatory terms being tightened in the capital markets.

9. Risk-based regulation can be explained either as an efficient mechanism for allocating regulatory resources to instituitions most likely to get in trouble, or as a market-mimicking device designed to force individual enterprises to internalize (through different levels of regulation) the costs associated with their business strategies.

10. In technical terms, what risk-based capital requirements generally fail to consider is the co-variance (or interrelation) between various risks.

11. I say *explicit* here, because the disclosure-based rules built into the 1940 Act are in some respects analogous to dynamic regulation. The actual information disclosed to investors (such as a fund's investment policies) varies from fund to fund. Indeed, oftentimes the premise of disclosure-based regulation is that investors will be capable of evaluating and acting upon differences in the content of disclosure. In addition, one might consider the SEC's broad exemptive powers to be a crude form of dynamic regulation under which the commission staff offers exemptive relief on a case-by-case basis.

INDEX